ENCYCLOPEDIA OF
AMERICAN
IMMIGRATION

Volume 2

James Ciment
Editor

 SHARPE REFERENCE

An imprint of M.E. Sharpe, INC.

SHARPE REFERENCE

Sharpe Reference is an imprint of *M.E. Sharpe,* INC.

M.E. Sharpe, INC.
80 Business Park Drive
Armonk, NY 10504

© 2001 by *M.E. Sharpe,* INC.

Library of Congress Cataloging-in-Publication Data

Encyclopedia of American Immigration / James Ciment, editor
p. cm.
Includes bibliographical references and index.
ISBN 0-7656-8028-9 (set; alk. paper)
1. United States—Emigration and immigration—Encyclopedias. 2. Immigrants—United States—Encyclopedias. I. Ciment, James.

JV6465.E53 2000
304.8′73′03—dc21

00-026560

Printed and bound in the United States of America

The paper used in this publication meets the minimum requirements of American National Standard for Information Sciences—Permanence of Paper for Printed Library Materials,
ANSI Z 39.48-1984.

BM (c)   10   9   8   7   6   5   4   3   2   1

CONTENTS

DEMOGRAPHICS

Introduction

Fertility
David Heer

Immigrants and the Census
Susan Wierzbicki

Return Migration
Stephen Sills

Settlement Patterns
Aonghas Mac Thòmais St.-Hilaire

INTRODUCTION

Section 3 of Part II of the *Encyclopedia of American Immigration* focuses on the demographics of immigration. The section includes entries on the U.S. Census, fertility, return immigration, and settlement patterns.

In his entry on fertility, David Heer begins with an exploration of how fertility is measured before moving on to an examination of the fertility data provided by the U.S. census and how it explains trends within the various immigrant communities. Next, Heer discusses various fertility theories and how they apply to the immigrant population.

In "Immigrants and the Census," Susan Wierzbicki opens by looking at the history of the census form and how it has recorded and continues to record information on immigrants. She also examines the many difficulties of collecting data on the immigrant population of the United States, as well as the trends revealed by that data.

Stephen Sills discusses return immigrants in his entry. First, he defines who qualifies as a return immigrant before examining why immigrants tend to go back to their homelands. There is also a discussion of the methods used to study return immigration and the impact return immigrants have on their homelands.

Finally, in the entry "Settlement Patterns," Aonghas Mac Thòmais St.-Hilaire discusses where and why immigrants settle. He begins with a brief history of settlement patterns among immigrants in the nineteenth and first half of the twentieth centuries. In his discussion of contemporary immigration patterns—largely since passage of the 1965 Immigration and Nationality Act—the author discusses how educational levels and professional backgrounds influence where immigrants settle. He concludes with a discussion on the settlement patterns of specific immigrant communities, including Asian, Latin American, Caribbean, and European peoples.

FERTILITY

Ideally, data on fertility should be derived from a combination of two sources. The first of these is a registration system that records the number of births according to various characteristics of the mother and father. The second is a census or sample survey that records relevant characteristics of persons at risk for giving birth. A fertility rate is obtained when birth registration data are used as a numerator and the number of persons at risk of giving birth is used as the denominator. Fertility rates represent the number of births per thousand persons at risk of giving birth. Most fertility rates are computed only for females. However, it is also possible to compute rates of siring births for males. With respect to females, the reproductive period is strictly limited to the period between menarche and menopause. Accordingly, fertility rates for females are confined to those for women ten to forty-nine years of age (or sometimes to women fifteen to forty-four years of age, since relatively few women give birth before age fifteen or after age forty-four).

MEASURES OF FERTILITY

The three most commonly used measures of fertility are the general fertility rate, age-specific birthrates, and the total fertility rate. The crude birthrate is not an accurate measure of fertility because its denominator includes the entire population and not just the population at risk of giving birth; it therefore is heavily biased by variation in the proportion of the total population below the age of fifteen or beyond the age of forty-four. The general fertility rate is the number of births per 1,000 women age fifteen to forty-four years of age. The denominator of the general fertility rate reflects most of the women exposed to the risk of bearing a child. However, a few women have babies at an earlier age and a few at a later age. Age-specific

birthrates can be computed for women of reproductive age. Sometimes, age-specific rates are computed for single years of age from age ten through age forty-nine. More commonly, they are computed for five-year age groups beginning with age group ten to fourteen and ending with age group forty-five to forty-nine. Age-specific birthrates are used to compute the total fertility rate. In a period total fertility rate the age-specific birthrates from age ten to age forty-nine for a particular year (or other short period) are summed. (If rates for five-year age groups are used, they must be summed and the resultant sum multiplied by five.) In a cohort total fertility rate, the age-specific birthrates for a particular birth cohort of women are summed over the forty-year period in which they are capable of bearing children. Cohort total fertility rates can be computed only for birth cohorts of women who have passed menopause. Thus they are computed only for women age fifty and over. An example of a cohort total fertility rate would be that for women born in 1940. All of these women completed their reproductive period by 1990.

As substitutes for the ideal measures of fertility in which the numerator of the rate is derived from a birth registration system, recourse is frequently made to measures of fertility derivable only from a census or sample survey. Many censuses and surveys include a question for women concerning the number of babies she has had. Another question frequently asked of women is whether they had a baby during the past year. The data on children ever born for women age forty-five to fifty-four or age forty-five and over provide a good approximation of cohort total fertility rates. The data on whether a baby has been born during the past year for women of particular ages provide not only a good approximation of age-specific fertility rates but also of the total fertility rate.

However, the data from a census or survey may have some biases when used as a substitute for data combining figures from a birth registration system as

Throughout American history, first-generation immigrants—like this Kurdish couple—have tended to have larger families, a phenomenon that often disappears by the time the American-born or -raised children start families of their own. *(Mel Rosenthal)*

the numerator and figures from a census or survey in the denominator. With respect to data on either children ever born or whether the woman had a live birth during the past year, survey data refer only to women alive and present in the United States at the time of the survey. Women who lived in the United States prior to the survey date but who have since died or emigrated from the United States are not included. Moreover, survey data on children ever born and whether a woman had a birth during the past year include data for women who immigrated to the United States at any time before the survey date. Consequently, with respect to foreign-born women, some or all of the babies who are reported in a survey may have been born outside the United States. Finally, a question asking women whether or not they had a birth during the past year does not fully reflect the number of babies born during the period, because a few women experience multiple births.

On the other hand, census and sample survey data on fertility have one advantage. Generally, birth certificates carry less information concerning the characteristics of the mother and father of the child than is obtainable from a census or sample survey. Furthermore, for reasons that have not been publicly explained, the National Center for Health Statistics has never published fertility rates for foreign-born women. Accordingly, all of the data concerning the fertility of foreign-born women in the United States must come from census or sample survey data. Nevertheless, the National Center for Health Statistics has published some data on the characteristics of foreign-born and native-born mothers giving birth in the United States. These data are mainly of importance in determining the life chances of any given baby dependent on maternal characteristics. Hence they will be described only after discussing the data available from census and sample surveys.

Data on the fertility of immigrant women in the United States by country of origin are found in decennial census data and in annual data from the Current Population Survey (CPS) conducted by the U.S. Bureau of the Census. The data originating from the decennial census come from a very large sample, approximately one-sixth of the total population of the United States.

Data from the CPS on fertility are usually published annually. The size of the CPS sample is very much less than that of the decennial census sample. Altogether the CPS sample consists of about fifty thousand interviewed households. However, the number of foreign-born households interviewed is only about one-tenth the size of the total number of interviewed households. Due to the relatively small sample size, the data on the fertility of immigrants obtained from the CPS are inferior, because of much higher sampling error, to those collected from the 1990 census. For years following the 2000 census, the Census Bureau plans to conduct the American Community Survey, projected to have a much larger sample size than the CPS. It is planned that the American Community Survey will have a question for females fifteen to fifty years of age concerning whether they gave birth to any children during the past twelve months.

FERTILITY DATA

What sorts of fertility data have been collected from the decennial census and the CPS? Perhaps the most important type of data are those on number of children ever born. These data were asked of all women in the 1990 decennial census and for all women age fifteen to forty-four years old in the CPS. Data for older women, age forty-five and over, essentially represent the total cumulative fertility of women who will not bear further children. However, such data by no means represent current levels of fertility but rather the fertility of past decades. The data for the women age fifteen to forty-four represent cumulative births for age groups in which the births to date, particularly for the younger of the age groups, may be substantially augmented by future births. Women thirty-five to forty-four years of age have already had most of the children they will ever have. Moreover, the fertility of these women more nearly represents the fertility of the more recent past in contrast to the data on children ever born for women age forty-five and over. As a result, the U.S. Bureau of the Census,

in its published reports for the 1990 Census of Population, focused on the number of children ever born per thousand women thirty-five to forty-four years of age; the data are shown in the third column of Table 1 (which also shows various other characteristics of each immigrant group by country of birth). Foreign-born women as a whole had a higher number of children ever born per thousand women (2,254) than did native-born women (1,927). Foreign-born women who entered the United States before 1980 had a slightly higher number of children ever born per thousand women than did immigrants who arrived in 1980 or later. It is evident from Table 1 that there is considerable variation in the figures depending on country of birth. The highest number of children ever born per thousand women thirty-five to forty-four years of age (3,289) was to women born in Mexico. Other countries of origin where the number of children ever born per thousand women was substantially higher than the figure for native-born women were El Salvador (2,673), Guatemala (2,567), Dominican Republic (2,513), Vietnam (2,451), and Haiti (2,421). The lowest number of children ever born (1,649) was to women born in Poland. Almost as low was the figure for women born in Japan (1,650). Two other nations with quite low figures were Taiwan (1,670) and the Soviet Union (1,690). Note that the figures for each of these four countries of origin are considerably lower than that for native-born women. On the other hand, the figure for Mexican-born women is more than 70 percent higher than the figure for native-born women. Moreover, it should be noted that the number of children ever born per thousand Mexican women age thirty-five to forty-four had a heavy impact on the number of children ever born for all foreign-born women. This is because in 1990 the proportion of all foreign-born persons in the United States who were born in Mexico was around 22 percent.

The data from the CPS provide the only data on fertility subsequent to the year 1990, and they are limited due to sampling error. As of now, the latest data on the fertility of foreign-born women are published from the CPS for June 1995.

Table 1 also provides data on the very large variation in children ever born by country of birth. There are high correlations between the number of children ever born in each country of birth and (1) the proportion of persons twenty-five years old and over who have a high school diploma or more (a negative relationship), (2) the percent of persons in poverty (a positive relationship), and (3) the percent of persons who do not speak English well (a positive relationship).

Table 1
Characteristics of the Native Population and Foreign-Born Population by Year of Arrival and by Country of Birth, 1990

Nativity and Country of Birth	Number of Persons (in thousands)	Children Ever Born per Thousand Women, 35 to 44 Years Old	Percent Who Do Not Speak English Well	Percent of Persons 25 Years and Older with High School Diploma or Higher	Percent of Persons in Poverty
Native-born	228,943	1,927	2.3	77.0	12.7
Foreign-born	19,767	2,254	47.0	58.8	18.2
Entered between					
1980 and 1990	8,664	2,200	59.9	59.4	26.2
Entered before					
1980	11,104	2,282	37.2	58.5	12.0
Mexico	4,298	3,289	70.7	24.3	29.7
Philippines	913	1,866	31.8	82.5	5.9
Canada	745	1,772	5.0	72.6	7.8
Cuba	737	1,765	60.1	54.1	14.7
Germany	712	1,816	13.1	75.9	7.7
United Kingdom	640	1,761	1.1	81.3	6.6
Italy	581	2,126	42.0	39.3	8.0
Korea	568	1,789	62.0	80.1	15.0
Vietnam	543	2,451	68.2	58.9	25.5
China	530	1,812	72.1	60.6	15.7
El Salvador	465	2,673	72.4	32.7	24.9
India	450	1,993	27.1	87.2	21.6
Poland	388	1,649	46.8	58.1	9.7
Dominican Republic	348	2,513	68.7	41.7	30.8
Jamaica	334	2,171	1.7	67.9	12.7
Soviet Union	334	1,690	52.1	64.0	25.0
Japan	290	1,650	56.2	86.4	12.6
Colombia	286	1,821	61.1	66.8	15.3
Taiwan	244	1,670	57.9	91.6	16.7
Guatemala	226	2,567	70.7	37.5	19.6
Haiti	225	2,421	55.3	57.6	21.7
Iran	211	1,821	38.8	86.7	15.3
Portugal	210	2,106	56.0	32.1	7.0

Source: Bureau of the Census, *1990 Census of Population, The Foreign-born Population in the United States, 1990* (Washington, DC: Government Printing Office, 1993): CP-3–1, pp. 257–320.

The data for June 1995 are shown in Table 2. These data concern the number of children ever born and the number of mothers giving birth during the past year per thousand women age fifteen to forty-four. From these data we can compare figures for all native-born women with those for all foreign-born women. Additionally, less complete data are available for foreign-born women by region of birth.

From Table 2, we see that the fertility of foreign-born women in 1994–95 was substantially higher than the fertility of the native-born. For all women fifteen to forty-four years of age, total mothers giving birth in the last year were 83.1 per thousand for foreign-born women as compared to only 58.9 per thousand for native-born women. For this same age group, mothers per thousand with first births were also higher for foreign-born women (27.4) than for native-born women (22.7). For this same age group

Table 2
Women 15 to 44 Years Old by Percent Childless, Number of Children Ever Born, and by Number of Births in the Last Year per Thousand Women by Age, Nativity, and Region of Birth, United States, June 1995 (Numbers in thousands)

Place of Birth	Number of Women	Percent Childless	Children Ever Born per 1,000 Women	Total Births in the Last Year per 1,000 Women	First Births in the Last Year per 1,000 Women
Women 15 to 44 Years Old					
All	60,225	41.8	1,243	61.4	23.2
Native-born	54,168	42.8	1,204	58.9	22.7
Foreign-born	6,056	33.1	1,585	83.1	27.4
Asia	976	41.2	1,292	59.1	N.A.
Mexico	1,996	23.7	2,038	108.3	N.A.
Other Latin America	1,536	33.8	1,502	75.5	N.A.
Europe (including former USSR)	654	37.4	1,263	62.1	N.A.
Northern America	145	50.4	1,111	64.9	N.A.
Women 15 to 29 Years Old					
All	27,742	65.7	596	81.2	38.1
Native-born	25,097	66.9	568	79.2	37.8
Foreign-born	2,644	54.5	860	100.6	41.3
Women 30 to 44 Years Old					
All	32,483	21.3	1,794	44.4	10.4
Native-born	29,071	21.9	1,753	41.5	9.6
Foreign-born	3,412	16.5	2,147	69.6	16.6

Sources: www.census.gov/population/socdemo/fertility/fert95/tabH6.txt and Bureau of the Census, *Current Population Reports*, Washington, DC: Bureau of the Census, ser. P-20–499 (October 1997).

the proportion childless (i.e., never having given birth) for foreign-born women (33.1 percent) was substantially lower than for native-born women (42.8 percent), and the number of children ever born per thousand foreign-born women (1,585) was substantially higher than for native-born women (1,204). Similar differences in fertility between native-born and foreign-born women were found for the younger women age fifteen to twenty-nine years and for the older women thirty to forty-four years of age.

The data by region of origin shown in Table 2 are very similar to the data from the 1990 census shown in Table 1. In particular, the high fertility of persons born in Mexico compared to native-born persons is manifest not only in the number of children ever born per thousand women (2,038 versus 1,204) but also in total mothers per thousand giving birth in the last year (108.3 versus 58.9).

FERTILITY THEORY

Several theories attempt to explain variations in fertility. All studies of fertility variation have shown a strong negative relationship between children ever born and the woman's educational attainment. Theorists of fertility variation explain this strong relationship as due to several factors. One relates to the fact that having and rearing children demands not only considerable expenditure of money but also of a woman's time in market labor. Since better-educated women on average can earn a higher wage in market labor than can poorly educated women, they face more potential loss in wages if they leave the labor market in order to rear children. A second factor relates to budget constraints—parents must choose between having more children and spending less money per child (particularly for a college education) or fewer children and spending more money per child. It is believed that better-educated mothers are less willing to sacrifice spending per child than less well-educated mothers. Fertility theorists also believe that a high level of educational attainment allows women to be more knowledgeable about different methods of birth control; thus they are more likely to use birth control to limit their fertility.

Fertility theorists also believe that women in poverty are less interested in high levels of spending per child than women who are better off. Therefore, we see the strong positive relationship shown in Table 1 between the percentage of a given immigrant group in poverty and the average number of children ever born. Finally, it is possible that the strong positive relationship shown in Table 1 between the proportion of an immigrant group that does not speak English well and the average number of children ever born may reflect the possibility that women who do not speak English well find it difficult to utilize family-planning services in which the service providers speak only English.

The data published by the National Center for Health Statistics concern the characteristics of births to native-born and foreign-born women. As mentioned earlier, these data are mainly of use in looking at the differential life chances of babies born to mothers of different characteristics. These data pertain to births in 1997 and are shown in Tables 3 and 4. Table 3 presents data on the characteristics of mothers for births classified by race and by whether the mother was born in the United States. Table 4 presents data on the characteristics of mothers for births classified by type of Hispanic origin and whether the mother was born in the United States. Both Table 3 and Table 4 present the proportion of mothers with four characteristics that most persons associate with unfavorable life chances for the child: (1) the proportion of births to mothers under age twenty, (2) the proportion of fourth and higher-order births, (3) the proportion of births to unmarried mothers, and (4) the proportion of births to mothers with less than twelve years of completed schooling.

Let us confine our attention to a comparison of the births occurring to non-Hispanic whites born in the United States (data shown in Table 4) and births to two groups of foreign-born mothers, those of Asian or Pacific Islander race (data shown in Table 3) and those of Mexican origin (data shown in Table 4). Comparing the foreign-born mothers of Asian or Pacific Islander race with native-born non-Hispanic whites, we see that the births to the first class of mothers have a lower proportion of unfavorable characteristics on

three of the four measures: percent of births to women under age twenty, percent of fourth and higher-order births and percent of births to unmarried mothers. Note in particular the much higher proportion of births to unmarried women among the native-born non-Hispanic whites (22.1 percent) as compared to the foreign-born mothers of Asian or Pacific Islander race (12.3 percent). On the other hand, when we compare the births of foreign-born persons of Mexican origin with those of native-born non-Hispanic whites, the first group uniformly displays less favorable characteristics than births to the second group. The difference is particularly great with respect to the proportion of births to mothers with less than twelve years of completed schooling; among births to native-born non-Hispanic whites it is only 13.1 percent, whereas among births to women born in Mexico it is 68.4 percent.

CONCLUSION

The fertility of immigrants influences the total contribution of international migration to population change, which measures not only the volume of net international migration in a given period but also the natural increase (excess of births over deaths) induced by that net migration during the same period. The U.S. Bureau of the Census has recently (1996) calculated the total contribution of projected future net immigration to future population change in the United States. In the latest series of population projections prepared by the bureau from a base year in 1994, the total contribution of net immigration to future population change in the United States can be calculated by comparing the Middle Series projection with that for the Zero Immigration Series. The bureau considers its Middle Series to be the projection most likely to occur, since its assumptions are considered more plausible than the assumptions of the other projections. The Zero Immigration Series has assumptions concerning future fertility and mortality that are identical to those of the Middle Series. However, unlike the Middle Series, which projects an annual net immigration of 820,000, the Zero Immigration Series assumes that there will be no net immigration during any year of the projection period. For the year 2050 the Middle Series projects that the total population of the United States will be 393,331,000. The Zero Immigration Series projects that the population of the United States in 2050 will be only 314,085,000. Thus the Middle Series projects a population increase from 1995 to 2050

Table 3
Total Number of Births and Percent of Births with Selected Characteristics by Race of Mother and Place of Birth of Mother, United States, 1997

| | | | Percent Distributions | | | | | | | |
| | | | Mothers Born in the U.S. | | | | Mothers Born Outside the U.S. | | | |
Race	Number of Births (in thousands)	Percent of Births to Foreign-Born Mothers	Births to Mothers Under Age 20	Fourth and Higher-Order Births	Births to Unmarried Mothers	Births to Mothers Completing Less than 12 Years of School	Births to Mothers Under Age 20	Fourth and Higher-Order Births	Births to Unmarried Mothers	Births to Mothers Completing Less than 12 Years of School
All births	3,881	19.3	13.7	9.8	33.3	17.9	8.4	13.0	28.1	40.0
White	3,073	17.6	11.5	8.6	24.8	15.5	9.8	14.2	30.5	49.2
Black	600	10.7	24.0	15.1	72.2	28.5	7.4	13.6	43.5	19.9
American Indian	39	3.4	21.2	19.7	59.7	33.0	8.8	12.5	30.2	26.5
Asian or Pacific Islander, total	170	84.4	15.2	8.2	33.6	12.9	3.3	8.0	12.3	14.2
Chinese	28	90.4	4.5	3.5	13.4	4.1	0.6	2.1	5.7	13.1
Japanese	9	56.0	4.5	4.4	16.1	3.4	0.5	3.8	5.4	1.4
Hawaiian	6	2.1	18.7	15.3	49.4	16.9	13.1	15.0	36.1	11.7
Filipino	32	82.3	17.4	7.8	40.7	12.8	3.4	6.9	14.9	6.1
Other	95	90.9	19.6	7.0	33.1	17.7	4.3	10.3	13.8	17.8

Source: National Center for Health Statistics, *National Vital Statistics Reports*, vol. 47, no. 18, "Births: Final Data for 1997," p. 38. Washington, DC: National Center for Health Statistics, 1997.

Table 4
Total Number of Births and Percent of Births with Selected Characteristics by Hispanic Origin of Mother and Place of Birth of Mother, United States, 1997

| | | | Percent Distributions | | | | | | | |
| | | | Mothers Born in the U.S. | | | | Mothers Born Outside the U.S. | | | |
Race	Number of Births (in thousands)	Percent of Births to Foreign-Born Mothers	Births to Mothers Under Age 20	Fourth and Higher-Order Births	Births to Unmarried Mothers	Births to Mothers Completing Less than 12 Years of School	Births to Mothers Under Age 20	Fourth and Higher-Order Births	Births to Unmarried Mothers	Births to Mothers Completing Less than 12 Years of School
All births	3,881	19.3	13.7	9.8	33.3	17.9	8.4	13.0	28.1	40.0
Hispanic, total	710	60.9	25.6	11.2	47.7	36.0	11.5	15.4	36.5	59.6
Mexican	499	60.8	26.7	11.7	46.2	37.9	11.9	16.8	34.2	68.4
Puerto Rican	55	36.7	24.3	11.1	61.6	36.6	18.7	15.1	55.5	37.8
Central and South American	97	91.0	22.4	4.6	44.5	22.2	9.3	11.8	41.5	41.3
Other and unknown Hispanic	45	25.7	23.4	10.6	46.8	31.0	9.3	12.1	33.1	27.6
Non-Hispanic, total	3,115	10.0	12.6	9.7	32.0	16.2	4.0	9.6	16.7	13.1
White	2,333	4.9	9.8	8.3	22.1	13.0	3.7	9.5	10.7	9.8
Black	581	9.3	23.9	15.1	72.2	28.5	6.7	14.0	41.2	17.3

Source: National Center for Health Statistics, *National Vital Statistics Reports*, vol. 47, no. 18, "Births: Final Data for 1997," p. 39. Washington, DC: National Center for Health Statistics, 1997.

of 131,111,000, whereas the Zero Immigration Series projects a population increase of only 52,085,000. The difference between the population increase projected for the Middle Series and that projected for the Zero Immigration Series is 79,026,000. This figure represents the total contribution of immigration to population change, which can also be decomposed into the net projected immigration of 45,100,000 persons and the natural increase induced by this net immigration (33,926,000). Thus, of the total population increase of 131,111,000 projected by the Middle Series, 52,085,000 (39.7 percent) can be attributed to the natural increase of the existing population in 1994, and 79,026,000 (60.3 percent) can be considered as the total contribution of immigration to population change. In turn, 45,100,000 (34.4 percent) of the population increase projected by the Middle Series will be due to net immigration itself, and 33,926,000 (25.9 percent) will be due to the natural

increase of the net immigration. Thus the natural increase of the net immigration is projected to be almost as important in explaining future population change as the net immigration itself.

David M. Heer

See also: Natural Disasters, Environmental Crises, and Overpopulation (Part II, Sec. 1); Children and Adolescent Immigrants, Family, Gender (Part II, Sec. 4).

BIBLIOGRAPHY

Bureau of the Census. *Current Population Reports*, ser. P-25, no. 1130, "Population Projections of the United States by Age, Sex, Race, and Hispanic Origin: 1995 to 2050." Washington, DC: Government Printing Office, 1996.

Heer, David M. *Society and Population*. 2d ed. Englewood Cliffs, NJ: Prentice-Hall, 1975: 74–79.

IMMIGRANTS AND THE CENSUS

Pursuant to Article 1, Section 2 of the U.S. Constitution, the national government counts the population every ten years through a regular census as a way of apportioning political power. Very early on, the country started asking about immigration status and through eighteen censuses has collected data on the size and demographic characteristics of the immigrant population. While the Immigration and Naturalization Service provides data on legal status and flows of immigrants, the Bureau of the Census provides the statistical portrait of who the immigrants are.

INTRODUCTION OF CENSUS QUESTIONS ON IMMIGRATION

The United States conducted its first census in 1790, and the number of census questions about immigration and nativity has risen and ebbed in rough correspondence to the great periods of immigration in American history (see Figure 1). Rudimentary census statistics on immigration date to the early nineteenth century. Thomas Jefferson first proposed a question on nativity for the 1800 census, and the 1820 and 1830 censuses contained a category for foreigners who had not been naturalized. More detailed data on place of birth were gathered beginning in 1850, when Congress overhauled the census and when immigration from northwestern Europe was rising. Information on nativity has been collected consistently over the decades and is basically comparable to the modern data, with one caveat. The definition of "foreign-born" was changed slightly in 1890 to exclude those born abroad if they had at least one parent who was an American citizen.

The nativity question was supplemented in 1870 with a question on parents' country of birth. That question remained on the census form through 1970.

But by 1980, when less than a tenth of the population had a foreign-born parent, the Census Bureau replaced the question on parents' birthplace with one about ancestry.

In 1890, four new immigration-related questions were added to the census. The first asked the number of years in the United States. That question was discontinued in 1930, then reappeared in 1970 as a question on when the person came to the United States to stay. The second and third questions covered naturalization status and whether the person had taken out naturalization papers. Those questions covered only adult males; not until 1930 did citizenship data became available for all immigrants. The last question covered ability to speak English.

In 1910, the census added questions on mother tongue as well as parents' mother tongue and any language other than English spoken at home. The instructions to enumerators listed forty-two other languages, from Albanian to Yiddish. However, from 1910 to 1940, data on mother tongue were tabulated only for whites (nonwhites comprised less than 2 percent of the foreign-born). In 1960, the wording of the question was changed to language spoken in the home before the person came to the United States. In 1980, the question was changed to whether the person spoke a language other than English at home, a concept distinct from mother tongue. Those who say they speak another language at home are also asked which language and how well they speak English ("very well," "well," "not well," "not at all").

After the United States greatly restricted immigration in the 1920s, the number of immigration-related census questions declined, too. The number of questions rose again once immigration levels began to climb in the 1960s. However, immigration-related questions are no longer asked of every household. Rather, they comprise a small section within the long

Undocumented immigrants often avoid any contact with government officials, including census workers like these in an immigrant neighborhood of Detroit. *(Jim West/Impact Visuals)*

form distributed randomly to one of about every six households.

As nonwhite groups emigrated to the United States, their presence was reflected in the census race question. Chinese were listed as a race starting in 1860 and Japanese in 1870. Other Asian "races" were added in 1910. "Mexican" was listed in 1930 as a possible answer to the "color or race" question, but the classification was dropped when many objected. The racial categories for Koreans and Hindus were dropped in 1950, but the Korean category returned in 1970. After the urging of Asian groups, the race question now lists six distinct Asian and three Pacific Island categories as well as write-in categories. A separate question on Hispanic self-identification was added to the 1970 census in the sample form that went to 5 percent of households; it was expanded to the whole census in 1980.

The long form from the 2000 census contained the following questions geared specifically to immigration:

- Does this person speak a language other than English at home?

- If yes . . . What is this language?
  How well does this person speak English?

- Where was this person born? (If outside the United States, give name of country)

- Is this person a citizen of the United States?

- If born outside the United States . . . when did this person come to live in the United States?

In addition, the long form asks where the person lived on April 1, 1995. While this question is geared to the entire population, it contains a space for filling in the name of a foreign country.

Historically, the Census Bureau has not only measured immigration but become enmeshed in the politics of immigration. For example, Francis A. Walker, superintendent of the Census Office in 1870 and 1880, also wrote widely. One of his essays decried the immigrants from southern and eastern Eu-

Figure 1
Number of U.S. Immigrants and Related Census Questions, 1820–2000

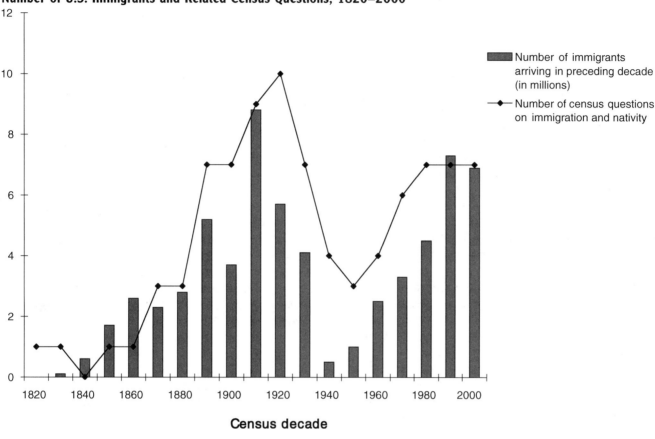

Source: INS immigration statistics through 1997.

rope as "beaten men from beaten races." A monograph produced by the Census Office in 1909 was used in Congress to justify the setting of immigration quotas in the 1920s at the 1890 level of the population; this effectively allowed in British immigrants at the expense of those from southern and eastern Europe.

For the 1980 and 1990 censuses, the Census Bureau had to defend against suits that would have compelled it to exclude undocumented immigrants in the population count used for apportionment. In these suits—*FAIR v. Klutznick* (1980) and *Ridge v. Verity* (1989)—plaintiffs argued that undocumented aliens increased representation in states where they lived in concentrations and diluted representation elsewhere, in violation of the "one man, one vote" decisions of the Supreme Court. A counterargument was that the apportionment covered the entire population. In *FAIR v. Klutznick,* the Supreme Court ruled that the plaintiffs lacked standing to bring the suit.

DIFFICULTIES OF COLLECTING ACCURATE CENSUS DATA ON IMMIGRANTS

The biggest obstacle to collecting good data on immigrants is the difficulty in counting them. Immigrants may be isolated and suspicious of the government; illegal immigrants may fear deportation despite laws ensuring the confidentiality of their responses. Many speak poor English and may be illiterate as well, so they have trouble with the forms. Because the census has been distributed by mail since 1960, it depends on good address lists. Yet postal lists may have trouble picking up immigrants, who may be especially likely to be living doubled up, in makeshift apartments, or in other hard-to-find places. Migrant farmworkers, many of them from Mexico, are particularly hard to track. While enumerators follow up nonresponses with personal visits, the population remains hard to find. As a result of all these difficulties, urban Hispanic renters, many of whom are immigrants, are estimated to have been undercounted by 6 to 9 percent in 1990; illegal immigrants may have been undercounted by 20 to 30 percent.

To overcome these difficulties, the Census Bureau has formed partnerships with many immigrant community organizations and churches to encourage responses to the census. In 2000, the Census Bureau offered forms in Spanish, Chinese, Vietnamese, Tagalog, and Korean and language guides in about forty-nine languages.

Another obstacle to collecting good data is the difficulty of measuring emigration from the United States by those originally born outside it. The Census Bureau has estimated the level of foreign-born emigration at 195,000 annually in the 1980s by subtracting actual counts of the foreign-born from an estimated population. But no one directly measures who leaves the country.

A truly complete portrait of the immigrant population requires more questions than the census can ask. Sensitive questions such as legal status no longer appear on the census form. Questions on religion are prohibited. Plus, in a time when circular migration is commonplace, immigrants may be unable to give an easy or accurate answer to the question of when they came to live in the United States. For example, more than a fourth of those who reported in 1990 that they had come to stay in the United States between 1985 and 1990 also reported that they also lived in the United States on April 1, 1985.

The ancestry question, asked since 1980, in particular has shown wide variation in answers. It suggests that many respondents, especially whites, may lack a deep attachment to any particular ethnic identity. Answers also appear to depend on where in the survey the question is asked and which ethnic groups are listed as examples. In 1980, English was the most commonly cited ancestry; in 1990, it was German. Ancestry and country of birth often do not match or match at the same level. For example, of two people from the same country, one might identify as Scandinavian and another as Norwegian. Someone born in Switzerland might claim one of several ancestries. First-generation immigrants were more likely to answer the question than the U.S.-born. A small minority, typically southern whites who are native-born and have low education, cites its ancestry as "American."

WHAT THE CENSUS DATA SHOW

For all the difficulties in measurement, the census data provide a wealth of information, at both the geographical and individual levels. In aggregate files based on geography, the census data can show to within blocks where particular kinds of immigrants have settled. The Public Use Microdata Samples from the census provide individual-level demographic, economic, and housing characteristics of immigrants. Between censuses, the Census Bureau collects sample data on the foreign-born every March in its Current Population Survey (CPS). Through these data, it is possible to determine the size of the immigrant population (26.4 million as of 1999, or 9.7 percent of the total population). It is also possible to determine the source of immigration (more than half from Latin America and another quarter from Asia), age structure (disproportionately of working age), sex ratio (more female than male), region of destination (predominantly the West and Northeast), and economic status (poverty rates in 1996 of 12.9 percent for the native population and 21.0 percent for the foreign-born). The CPS in particular provides data on means testing, pensions, and health insurance.

Susan Wierzbicki

See also: Legal and Illegal Immigration: A Statistical Overview (Part II, Sec. 2); Immigrant Politics II: Electoral Politics (Part II, Sec. 6).

BIBLIOGRAPHY

Ahmed, Bashir, and J. Gregory Robinson. "Estimates of Emigration of the Foreign-Born Population: 1980–1990." In *Technical Working Paper No. 9.* Washington, DC: Bureau of the Census, Population Division, 1994.

Anderson, Margo J. *The American Census: A Social History.* New Haven: Yale University Press, 1988.

Anderson, Margo J., ed. *Encyclopedia of the U.S. Census.* Washington, DC: Congressional Quarterly Press, 2000.

Anderson, Margo J., and Stephen E. Fienberg. *Who Counts? The Politics of Census-Taking in Contemporary America.* New York: Russell Sage Foundation, 1999.

Bureau of the Census. *Twenty Censuses Population and Housing Questions, 1790–1980.* Washington, DC, 1979.

Choldin, Harvey M. "Statistics and Politics: The 'Hispanic Issue' in the 1980 Census." *Demography* 23:3 (August 1986): 403–418.

Ellis, Mark, and Richard Wright. "When Immigrants Are Not Migrants: Counting Arrivals of the Foreign Born Using the U.S. Census." *International Migration Review* 32:1 (Spring 1998): 127–44.

Farley, Reynolds. "The New Census Question About Ancestry: What Did It Tell Us?" *Demography* 28:3 (August 1991): 411–29.

Gibson, Campbell J., and Emily Lennon. "Historical Census Statistics on the Foreign-born Population of the United States: 1850–1990." In *Working Paper No. 29*. Washington, DC: Bureau of the Census, 1999.

Government Accounting Office. *Immigration Statistics: Information Gaps, Quality Issues Limit Utility of Federal Data to Policymakers*. Washington, DC, 1998.

Petersen, William. "Politics and the Measurement of Ethnicity." In *The Politics of Numbers,* ed. William Alonso and Paul Starr. New York: Russell Sage Foundation, 1987.

Schmidley, A. Dianne, and Campbell Gibson. "Profile of the Foreign-Born Population in the United States: 1997." In *Current Population Reports,* series, pp. 23–195. Washington, DC: U.S. Census Bureau, 1999.

RETURN MIGRATION

While return migration has been acknowledged in the historical and sociological literature for more than a century, the systematic study of this phenomenon has been complicated by the lack of reliable data, as few nations' governmental organizations track the movements of individual migrants from home to destination and back. In his influential 1885 article "The Laws of Migration," E. G. Ravenstein recognized that there are countercurrents of migration flows, in which individuals move from receiving areas to traditional sending areas. Ravenstein also noted that at the time, data for estimating the number of these counterstream migrants who were former residents of the sending areas, and thus return migrants, were scarce. More than a century later, migration researchers still note that quantification of the return migration is problematic. As a result, recent studies have attempted to compile data from various governmental and nongovernmental sources to construct an image of the return migration process. Concentration has been on return as the ultimate phase of a lifelong migration cycle.

RETURN MIGRATION DEFINED

One of the difficulties in the study of return migration is defining exactly who is to be included among return migrants. Studies of return migration have incorporated such classifications as labor migrants who, as part of the migration cycle, have returned to live in the home country as a result of successfully earning enough money in the host country; individuals who have left the labor market and returned to retire in their native land; migrants who failed to obtain work and returned soon after arriving in the destination country; migrants who have returned to their home countries to take advantage of improved social, economic, or political conditions; and those who could not, for some cultural or personal reason, settle in the destination country and eventually returned home. Typically not included in these definitions are the related categories of circular or cyclical migration, such as short-term guest workers, and forced repatriations of refugees and other nonvoluntary migrants. Most important to the study of all types of return migration is the realization that the individual who relocates to a new country continues to maintain ties with the homeland and that these ties influence the possibility of return migration.

TYPOLOGY OF RETURN MIGRATION

Following the work of scholars Francesco Cerase, George Gmelch, and Russell King, a typology of return migration may be constructed from the empirical studies of historical return migrations. This typology distinguishes the temporary or permanent plans of the migrant, the reasons for return, and the duration of the stay in the destination country. The first classification of return migrants are "failed" migrants. Generally occurring in the first few months (but, according to some schemes, including returns up to five years after the migration), this return is due to inability to find work or to adjust to the social conditions of the host country. Sociologists George J. Borjas and Bernt Bratsberg point out that failed migrants often base their initial move on misinformation and are disillusioned upon finding out the truth. The second category of return migrants are the successful short-term migrants. These are the migrants whose original intention was to work toward a savings target or for a given period of time and then to return to their homelands. The distinction between this form of migration strategy and cyclical or circular migration is often based on the physical distance between the sending and receiving countries or on the relative cost and risks of the journey. Those temporary labor mi-

Figure 1
Typology of Return Migration

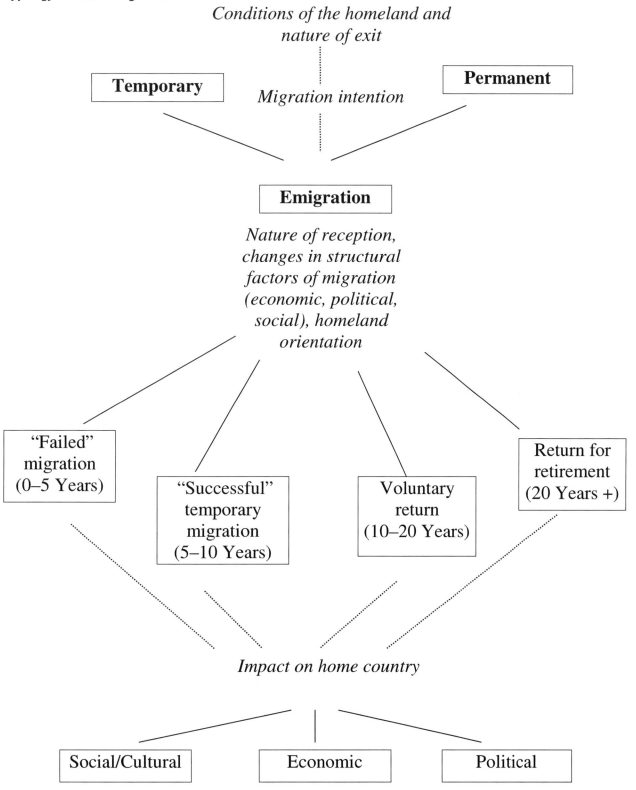

grants who live closer to the destination country will often engage in circulation, while those who live much farther will more likely work toward a savings target and then return. This classification may also include those who migrate for education or training purposes. The fourth category, voluntary return, includes long-term migrants whose goal may have been to settle in the destination country but who found that for various reasons (such as lack of further advancement opportunities in the receiving country, aging relatives in the homeland, changes in the economic or political circumstances of either country) return would be the best strategy for improving their lives. The final category corresponds to successful long-term or permanent migrants who, after leaving the labor market in the United States and other core nations, find that returning to their native countries will help to maximize their retirement savings. George J. Borjas and Bernt Bratsberg call this an "optimal life-cycle residential location sequence." This form of return is most likely to occur when migrants have maintained contact with relatives and friends in the homeland throughout their years abroad.

METHODS FOR STUDYING RETURN MIGRATION

A variety of approaches have been used in studies of historical and contemporary return migration. These techniques have included statistical analysis of data compiled from census and other governmental sources; referencing of official population registries; examination of passenger lists of transatlantic shipping companies; the study of biographies, letters, and diaries of migrants who returned to their homeland; and in-person interviews with returnees. Yet the most ambitious projects, and the most useful for providing information on the nature of return migration as a social process, have been those that assemble data on mass population movements and include the characteristics of individual returning migrants as well as those of settlers. This data has been useful in determining the overall rate of return for a migrant population, the demographic characteristics of returnees as compared to settlers, and the clarification of the structural variables that influence the propensity for migrants to return.

There are many examples of studies of historic periods of return migration. Historian Gunter Moltmann analyzed European return migration of the mid- to late nineteenth century by using the lists of passengers on ocean liners to calculate a return rate of 18.4 percent of settlers in this period. This analysis did not, however, tell us why those passengers returned or whether their original intention was to emigrate permanently, nor did it provide any socioeconomic data other than perhaps the class of their boarding ticket. Biographies and life histories of return migrants were used to personalize the migration narrative in several historical studies and have been helpful in establishing the concept of a migratory life cycle. Scholar Adam Walaszek (as cited in the work of Karen Schniedewind) studied post–World War I Polish return migration using letters and diaries, along with other personal documents. He was able to reveal the migrants' thoughts and feelings throughout the migration cycle and to describe their opinions and feelings about their culture of origin, the migration process, and difficulties of integration into American culture and reintegration into Polish society. This approach, however, was limited by the nature and availability of the writings. Moreover, these cases do not comprise a representative sample of all return migrants; thus it is difficult to infer patterns of return migration from these writings. Schniedewind used city directories, church registries, and U.S. naturalization records, as well as interviews with surviving relatives, to reconstruct the biographies of 610 German individuals who had migrated to the United States and returned during the early 1900s. In this way, she was able to supplement the incomplete statistics provided by state records with data that was more subjective and qualitative in nature, and thus gain some insight into individual motivations for migration and return.

Another common methodology for studying both historical and contemporary return migration has been economic analysis of monetary remittances made by migrants to family or friends in the homeland. The theory is that as long as migrants envision that they may return, they will continue to take part in the daily lives of those left in the homeland. Remittances can be quite significant to the economic health of the sending country. For example, in 1995 the International Monetary Fund estimated remittances from the United States to Mexico exceed $3.7 billion annually, while the overall international movement of remittances was approximately $70 billion. However, as scholar Russell King points out, remittance patterns used as a proxy for intent to return do not equate with actual return migrations. Moreover, the study of remittance patterns does not provide the researcher with much in the way of supporting socioeconomic or demographic data, as financial institutions do not collect such information during transactions.

Statistical analysis of large governmental data sets, such as Census Bureau and Immigration and Naturalization Service (INS) data, has frequently been used to determine patterns of return migration. Few countries specifically track the outward flow of individuals who previously emigrated to their countries or incoming expatriates who may have returned after years in the exterior, yet governmental data can be very useful in establishing rates of migration from a particular country, present visa status of immigrants, and years of residence before acquiring citizenship. Borjas and Bratsberg used a combination of census data and INS records to determine that return migration occurs as a result of a planned migration life cycle or as a result of misinformation on the employment opportunities in the destination country. They were also able to calculate an overall rate of outmigration from the United States (departure of previous immigrants, assuming return to the home country) of approximately 21.5 percent for all countries combined. By looking at home ownership and acquisition of citizenship status, sociologist Philip Yang demonstrated that these large data sets could be used to determine the overall homeland orientation of a cohort of migrants and their attitudes toward eventual return versus permanent settlement. He concluded that Chinese immigrants to the United States had among the highest rates of home ownership and naturalized citizenship and thus have the least potential for return migration.

Scandinavian countries have been the exception to the rule that government data is not easily applicable to the study of return migrants. Swedish governmental data, provided from a population registry rather than a census, has been useful in determining both the rate of return and the characteristics of the return migrants from the late 1800s until today. This information has been useful in documenting the effects of migration and return on the home country and was used to establish a pattern of migrants departing from rural, farming regions to return to urban, industrial centers. This pattern has also been noted in the return of Italian migrants in the 1950s and 1970s and in contemporary Mexican returns.

Although time-consuming and expensive, interviews and surveys yield specific information on the individual's motivations for return to home country, as well as providing socioeconomic and demographic information that can be used to analyze patterns of return migration. Scholar Francesco Cerase utilized this method in a study of southern Italians who came to the United States between 1900 and 1924. He calculated a return rate of 56 percent for this region, as many temporary migrants had the goal of simply earning enough money to be able to return and buy farms or small shops. He also argued that return migrants had a direct social effect on the home country, altering the attitude of subservience to the wealthy landholders. A contemporary project, the Mexican Migration Project (MMP), has surveyed more than seven thousand households in fifty-two communities in Mexico and more than five hundred households in the United States. Demographic and socioeconomic information has been collected along with number and duration of trips to the United States, legal status, wages earned, occupations, and use of funds upon return to Mexico. These data have indicated that the most important factors for determining return migration to Mexico are the migrant's age, marital status, and ownership of property in the homeland. Interestingly, in a 1997 analysis of the MMP data, sociologist Belinda Reyes found that 50 percent of all immigrants return to Mexico within two years, and 70 percent return within ten years; 40 percent of women who migrate to the United States stay in the country for more than fifteen years, while only 20 percent of men stay for this long.

MOTIVES FOR RETURN AND FACTORS THAT INFLUENCE RETURN

As many of these studies have shown, there are social, cultural, economic, and political motives for return that are related to the migrants' original intentions when migrating and to intervening factors that influence the propensity for return. Migrants' motives for return have included strong family ties in the home country, dissatisfaction with the social status or condition in the receiving country, obligation to relatives, feelings of loyalty or patriotism, perception of better opportunities in the homeland, and nostalgia. Intervening factors that influence return include marriage while in the destination country, having children in the host country, changes in the social or political conditions in either homeland or receiving context (such as recession or political opposition to migration), and incentives or inducements to return. There are also many variables that have been identified as indicators of potential return: the per-capita gross national product of the source country; the distance between source country and destination country; the form of government in the home country; inequality in the source country's income distribution; acquisition of citizenship in the host country; length of stay in the destination country; age at time of migration; number of family members who have also migrated; and ownership of property in the receiving country.

Migrants who left the home country to take advantage of better wages or more liberal social policies, or for political reasons, are more likely to return when the conditions have changed sufficiently in the homeland to induce return migration. Similarly, the conditions of reception in the country of immigration may change (i.e., economic downturn, a new political regime, social policies against immigration), causing the migrants to find more benefit to living in the home country. However, in most cases, return rates decrease as the duration of stay in the destination country lengthens, the number of relatives and other social contacts in the host country increases, and the migrant builds ties in the country of residence.

IMPACT OF RETURN MIGRANTS ON HOMELAND

The impact that return migrants have on the home country has been debated in the findings of the various studies. While in some analyses the returning migrant has been shown to alter the social structure of the homeland, introduce new cultural practice, and influence both the economic and political framework of the homeland, others have determined that the overall effects are negligible. For example, a returning migrant who left as an agricultural worker may return to become a shopkeeper or a landowner; the relative wealth earned abroad permitted a change in social class and community standing. While this change may be considerable for the individual, the effect of this social mobility on the greater society is only slight.

Many countries have begun to recognize the role that migrants can play in the further development of their nations. The emigrant's role in the economic life of the sending country has been well documented through the tracking and analysis of remittances. Yet a sending nation benefits not only from the remittances of emigrant workers, but also from the education, skills, and information acquired by its citizens abroad. Significant percentages of the most highly trained and educated do not return to their homeland. For example, over 68 percent of foreign students earning doctorates in the sciences and engineering fields had plans to stay and work in the United States after graduation. As a result, many countries have recently begun to actively pursue policies that would entice human capital back to the country of origin and cap-

italize on the expertise acquired abroad. Taiwan, for example, has begun to encourage the return of highly educated overseas talent. According to statistics from Taiwan's National Science Council and National Youth Commission, between 1990 and 1995 twenty-three thousand migrants with advanced degrees earned while abroad returned in part due to government incentives. These returned specialists, though nowhere near as many in number as the exodus of emigrants, often give up lucrative positions in top American firms to go back to their native country. Motivation for accepting pay cuts of up to 40 percent include responsibilities to aging parents, strong ties with relatives, and prospects for upward mobility in a growing economy.

In a similar effort, the Philippine government embarked on a project entitled Philippines 2000 (since renamed Philippines 2004). Among the many economic goals that would place the Philippines among the "Asian tigers" was the ambition to regain the more than 1 million current overseas workers by offering enough jobs within the domestic economy for the entire population. The Philippines is second only to Mexico in the export of labor, and plans such as this can be seen as a national call for the return of expatriates who may have valuable skills and experience learned in the exterior to contribute to the progress of a developing nation. Yet those who return usually do so not to improve their country of origin, but to improve their own lives. Some of the factors described in influencing the return of an estimated 15 percent of Hong Kong Chinese from Canada were "lack of servants, job shortages, high taxes, and separation from friends and relatives." Furthermore, it is notable that most of the Hong Kong Chinese who returned from Canada waited until they had obtained Canadian citizenship, thus introducing the concept of transnationalism and dual citizenship among returnees, a more and more common occurrence in the growing process of globalization.

Not all studies have shown that the impact of return migrants on the homeland is positive and beneficial for further development. Scholar George Gmelch argues that return migrants do not necessarily bring new skills and attitudes, do not fundamentally improve the economic condition of the homeland (most foreign earnings are spent on consumable goods rather than invested in land or other properties), and may influence continued chain migration based on false expectations. Sociologists Russell King, Alan Strachan, and Jill Mortimer further maintain that while return migrants may individually fare better than nonmigrants, the overall effect on the home country is negligible.

Stephen Sills

See also: American Emigration Abroad, Connections to Homeland, Transnationalism: Immigration from a Global Perspective (Part II, Sec. 2); Immigrant Politics III: The Home Country (Part II, Sec. 6); Impact on the Home Country Economy (Part II, Sec. 7).

BIBLIOGRAPHY

Abadan-Unat, Nermin. "The Socio-Economic Aspects of Return Migration in Turkey." *Migration: A European Journal of International Migration and Ethnic Relations* 3 (1988): 29–59.

Borjas, George J., and Bernt Bratsberg. "Who Leaves? The Outmigration of the Foreign-born." *The Review of Economics and Statistics* 78:1 (1996): 165–76.

Cerase, Francesco P. "Migration and Social Change: Expectations and Reality. A Study of Return Migration from the United States to Italy." *International Migration Review* 8:2 (1974): 245–64.

Cinel, Dino. *The National Integration of Italian Return Migration, 1820–1929.* New York: Cambridge University Press, 1991.

Couch, Stephen R., and Roy Bryce-Laporte, eds. *Quantitative Data and Immigration Research.* Washington, DC: Research Institute on Immigration and Ethnic Studies, Smithsonian Institution, 1979.

Gmelch, George. "Return Migration." *Annual Review of Anthropology* 9 (1980): 135–59.

———. *Double Passage: The Lives of Caribbean Migrants Abroad and Back Home.* Ann Arbor: University of Michigan Press, 1992.

Hernández Alvarez, José. *Return Migration to Puerto Rico.* Berkeley: Institute of International Studies, University of California, 1967.

Hoerder, Dirk. *Labor Migration in the Atlantic Economies: The European and North American Working Classes During the Period of Industrialization.* Westport, CT: Greenwood Press, 1985.

Johnston, R. J., Derek Gregory, and David Smith. *The Dictionary of Human Geography.* Cambridge, MA: Blackwell Reference, 1994.

Kayser, Bernard. *Cyclically Determined Homeward Flows of Migrant Workers.* Paris: Organisation for Economic Cooperation and Development, Manpower and Social Affairs Directorate, 1972.

King, Russell. "Return Migration and Regional Economic Development: An Overview." In *Return Migration and Regional Economic Problems,* ed. Russell King, pp. 1–37. Dover, NH: Croom Helm, 1986.

King, Russell, Alan Strachan, and Jill Mortimer. "Gastarbeiter Go Home: Return Migration and Economic Change in the Italian Mezzogiorno." In *Return Migration and Regional Economic Problems,* ed. Russell King, pp. 38–68. Dover, NH: Croom Helm, 1986.

Kiran, Frank, and Frank Harrigan. "Swedish-Finnish Return Migration, Extent, Timing, and Information Flows." *Demography* 23:3 (1986): 313–27.

Kulu, Hill, and Tiit Tammaru. "Ethnic Return Migration from the East and West: The Case of Estonia in the 1990s." *Europe-Asia Studies* 52:2 (2000): 349–69.

Lindstrom, David P. "Economic Opportunity in Mexico and Return Migration from the United States." *Demography* 33:3 (1996): 357–74.

Massey, Douglas S. "Understanding Mexican Migration to the United States of America." *Journal of Sociology* 92:6 (1987): 372–403.

Massey, Douglas, Rafael Alarcón, Jorge Durand, and Humberto González. *Return to Aztlan: The Social Process of International Migration from Western Mexico.* Berkeley: University of California Press, 1987.

Migration Dialogue. "Chinese Migration." *Migration News—Asia* 2:2 (February 1995). Online at http://migration.ucdavis.edu/Archive/feb_1995–18.html (accessed online December 26, 2000).

Migration Dialogue. "Hong Kong Emigrants Return from Canada." *Migration News—Asia* 2:2 (February 1995). Online at: http://migration.ucdavis.edu/Archive/feb_1995–21.html (accessed online December 26, 2000).

Migration Dialogue. "U.S. Taiwanese Return to Homeland." *Migration News—Asia* 2:4 (April 1995). Online at: http://migration.ucdavis.edu/mn/pastissues_mn.html (accessed online December 26, 2000).

Migration Dialogue. "China/Hong Kong." *Migration News—Asia* 5:10 (October 1998). Online at http://migration.ucdavis.edu//MN-Archive/oct_1998–16.html (accessed online December 26, 2000).

Migration Dialogue. "Remittances." University of California at Davis, 2000. Online at: http://migration.ucdavis.edu/Data/remit.on.www/remittances.html (accessed online December 26, 2000).

Moltmann, Gunter. "American-German Return Migration in the Nineteenth and Early Twentieth Centuries." *Central European History* 113:4 (1980): 378–92.

National Science Foundation. "Indicators 1998: Chapter 2—Higher Education in Science and Engineering." Online at http://www.nsf.gov/sbe/srs/seind98/access/c2/c2s4.htm (accessed online December 26, 2000).

Ong, Paul M., Lucie Cheng, and Leslie Evans. "Migration of Highly Educated Asians and Global Dynamics." *Asian and Pacific Migration Journal* 1:3–4 (1992): 543–67.

Parnwell, Mike. *Population Movements and the Third World.* New York: Routledge, 1993.

Ravenstein, E. G. "The Laws of Migration." *Journal of the Statistical Society of London* 48:2 (1885): 167–227.

Reyes, Belinda I. *Dynamics of Immigration: Return Migration to Western Mexico.* San Francisco: Public Policy Institutes of California, 1997.

Richmond, Anthony H. "Return Migration from Canada to Britain." *Population Studies* 22:2 (1968): 311–35.

Roberts, Bryan R. "Socially Expected Durations and the Economic Adjustment of Immigrants." In *The Economic Sociology of Immigration: Essays on Networks, Ethnicity, and Entrepreneurship,* ed. Alejandro Portes, 42–86. New York: Russell Sage Foundation, 1995.

Schniedewind, Karen. "Migrants Returning to Bremen: Social Structure and Motivations: 1850 to 1914." *Journal of American Ethnic History* 12:2 (1993): 35–55.

Skeldon, Ronald. *Population Mobility in Developing Countries: A Reinterpretation*. New York: Belhaven, 1990.

Stalker, Peter. *The Work of Strangers: A Survey of International Labour Migration*. Geneva: International Labour Organisation, 1994.

Stinner, William, Klaus de Albuquerque, and Roy Bryce-Laporte, eds. *Return Migration and Remittances: Developing a Caribbean Perspective*. Washington, DC: Research Institute on Immigration and Ethnic Studies, Smithsonian Institution, 1982.

Swinbanks, David. "Taiwan Welcoming Home Top Ph.D.s from U.S. Research Technology." *Management* 38:2 (1995): 3–4.

Van Gendt, Rien. *Return Migration and Reintegration Services*. Paris: Organisation for Economic Cooperation and Development, Manpower and Social Affairs Directorate, 1977.

Yang, Philip Q. "Sojourners or Settlers: Post-1965 Chinese Immigrants." *Journal of Asian American Studies* 2:1 (1999): 61–91.

SETTLEMENT PATTERNS

*T*he United States of America is a nation of immigrants. With the exception of the indigenous peoples whose ancestors predated Columbus's first sighting of the continent, all Americans have ancestral roots elsewhere. People emigrating, either voluntarily or by force, from Europe, Africa, Canada, Latin America, Asia, and the Caribbean profoundly affected the evolution of the American nation. Contemporary immigrants continue to exert a strong influence on the course of U.S. national development. Where immigrants originally settle and where they and their descendants later move to have significant repercussions for the cultural, political, and economic life of the country and its regions. The first immigrants, the English colonists who settled along the Atlantic coast of North America from Georgia to Maine, established the predominant social, cultural, and linguistic norms to which later immigrants would conform. Near the end of the seventeenth century, approximately 90 percent of all settlers were of English birth or descent. Early in American history, however, slaves from the various nations of the west coast of Africa, speaking different languages and following different religions and cultural practices, were forcibly brought over in order to meet the labor needs of the emerging plantations of the South. Attempts by plantation owners to lure and keep English indentured servants failed to supply the requisite labor to sustain and expand the southern plantation economy. Enslaved Africans filled the labor shortage, adding complexity to the racial, ethnic, cultural, and linguistic makeup of the American colonies, particularly in the South. In the North during the eighteenth century, German-speaking immigrants added further ethnic, cultural, and linguistic diversity to the colonies, especially in the mid-Atlantic region where they formed the majority in some communities.

The influx of enslaved Africans to the South and of German-speaking migrants to the mid-Atlantic region notwithstanding, most immigrants to the American colonies were English speakers from England or Scotland, settling throughout the North Atlantic seaboard. After 1776, however, and through most of the nineteenth century, the young American nation maintained an open-door immigration policy as national borders were expanded westward. During and after the 1830s, growing numbers of immigrants, especially German and Irish, came to the United States, transforming the previously predominantly Anglo-Saxon American society into a more multicultural melting pot. The Irish showed a marked preference for settlement in the large cities of the Northeast, with New York City and Boston taking up the lead. The Germans also settled in urban areas, but increasingly opted for life on the frontier. Scandinavian immigrants were similarly drawn to the availability of wide expanses of land west of the urbanized eastern seaboard, especially in the northern Midwest. The settlement patterns of immigrants to the United States before and through the first half of the nineteenth century shaped the ethnic and cultural landscape of the country. People of English and Scottish descent remain demographically powerful in New England and the South. Descendants of enslaved Africans have maintained a strong demographic, political, and cultural presence in the South. Pennsylvania and other areas of the mid-Atlantic states as well as much of the Midwest and the plains states remain heavily populated by people of German ancestry. Those of Scandinavian descent similarly figure strongly in many parts of the Midwest, particularly in Minnesota.

During the later part of the nineteenth century and the early part of the twentieth, immigration to the United States intensified, adding further layers of racial, ethnic, and cultural diversity to the country. Chinese and Japanese immigrants, attracted first to Hawaii because of the geographic proximity of the islands to their homelands and because of employment opportunities there, later settled along the Pacific coast, especially California during this period.

Immigrants from the same country often settle together in the same urban neighborhoods like Flushing, New York, as these multiple signs in Korean indicate. *(Hazel Hankin/Impact Visuals)*

However, nativist fears led to the cessation of Chinese immigration in 1882 and Japanese immigration in the 1920s. The Irish continued to flock to the large cities of the Northeast, drawn by the preexistence of Irish ethnic enclaves, and to other parts of the country. The Germans maintained their immigration flow, settling in both German ethnic enclaves of the Northeast and mid-Atlantic or in the western, German-populated hinterland. The Italians and Jews were drawn to the large cities of the Northeast, with New York City the most popular destination by far, and like the Irish and Germans, they established and settled in ethnic enclaves in inner-city neighborhoods. The early ethnic enclaves served to attract later immigrants in search of residence, work, and social support, thereby perpetuating established patterns of settlement. Geographic proximity served to encourage the settlement of Mexican and Canadian immigrants in the Southwest and New England, respectively, and these early immigrant enclaves in the region of initial settlement patterned later immigration. Patterns of settlement laid down during the second half of the nineteenth century and the first half of the twentieth explain in

large part the continued geographic concentration of Italian and Jewish Americans in New York City and in other northeastern cities, Mexican Americans in California, Texas, Arizona, and New Mexico, and Franco-Americans in New England. As a result of varying patterns of immigrant and migrant settlement, significant geographic differences in the ethnic makeup of each region of the United States endure, influencing contemporary American culture.

POST-1965 IMMIGRANTS

The settlement patterns of contemporary immigrants, like those of earlier immigrants, are changing the face of America. Unlike their predecessors, contemporary immigrants are predominantly non-European. However, like earlier immigrants, post-1965 immigrants continue to show a preference for settling in large urban centers. After the Civil War, cheap land in the Midwest and West became increasingly scarce, forcing later immigrants to cast their lots in the cities. This is especially true of current, post-1965 immigrants. In 1987, for example, less than 7 percent of all immigrants settled outside the urban conglomerations of the country. Like earlier immigration, post-1965 immigration is guided by social networks through which newcomers can call on ties of friendship, family, and nationality to secure housing and employment. These networks are typically embedded within urban ethnic enclaves. Since the 1960s, ethnic enclaves, serving as a point of social contact for a wide variety of immigrant populations, have come into existence in large cities throughout the United States, altering the social and cultural fabric of many American cities. While relatively few cities attracted the bulk of immigrants in the nineteenth and early twentieth centuries, namely New York City, Boston, Chicago, and Philadelphia, after the 1960s a larger number of cities on both coasts drew immigrants and witnessed the emergence of dynamic ethnic enclaves.

While the historical geographic concentrations of immigrants in the early twentieth century endured into the late twentieth century, since 1965, the settlement of immigrants of diverse national origins has tended to spread throughout the United States. In spite of the increased geographic dispersal of immigrants since 1965, however, most still tend to gravitate to New York City, Los Angeles, San Francisco, Chicago, Miami, Houston, San Diego, and Washington, D.C. Moreover, in 1987, more than 70 percent of all legal immigrants settled in only six states: California (26.8 percent), New York (19.0 percent), Florida (9.1 percent), Texas (7.0 percent), New Jersey (5.1 percent), and Illinois (4.3 percent). During the second half of the nineteenth century and first half of the twentieth, New York City was unquestionably the most attractive point of destination and place of settlement for immigrants—especially those from Europe, who made up more than 80 percent of all immigrants at the time. After 1965, New York City maintained its status as the most popular urban place of settlement for immigrants, although not to the same degree as during previous migratory flows. Los Angeles emerged as second in popularity following not far behind New York City. With the rapid influx of immigrants from Latin America and the Caribbean, Miami rose as the third most popular place of settlement, surpassing Chicago, which became fourth. Washington, D.C., grew to fifth place, followed closely by San Francisco. Boston continued to attract immigrants, but the city's share had fallen drastically since the earlier migratory waves. Houston, San Diego, and other cities not historically associated with the large-scale settlement of immigrants became intermediate points of

destination for growing numbers of immigrants after 1965.

A large portion of contemporary immigrants initially settle in inner-city neighborhoods of relatively large urban areas, perpetuating a pattern in force since the early nineteenth century. As earlier immigrants and their descendants left the core of many older American cities, recent immigrants moved in. In many cases, post-1965 immigrants have been instrumental in the urban renewal of many older, declining cities by creating small businesses, providing relatively low-wage labor, and sustaining the population base needed to boost local economic activity. Whether unskilled workers, professionals, or entrepreneurs, current immigrants settling in inner-city environments have enhanced the flow of investment, provided workers for factories and service industries, and revitalized declining urban neighborhoods. Los Angeles, New York, Miami, and San Francisco, contemporary poles of attraction for immigrants, have especially benefited from the establishment and growth of ethnic enclaves within city boundaries. Los Angeles and Miami owe the lion's share of their growth in the past decades to immigration. Moreover, New York City would have registered negative population growth during the past two decades if it were not for the continued influx of large numbers of immigrants. Philadelphia and Baltimore, cities that attracted significant numbers of immigrants during the late nineteenth and early twentieth centuries, saw their urban infrastructure decline as longtime residents left for the suburbs or other parts of the country. With relatively few contemporary immigrants settling in Philadelphia and Baltimore, the trend toward population decline will likely remain unchanged in the near future.

EDUCATIONAL LEVEL AND PROFESSIONAL BACKGROUND

Immigrants with high levels of education, professional training, and a command of the English language tend to settle in more widely dispersed patterns throughout the United States than poorly educated, low-skilled immigrants with limited English-speaking abilities, who tend to settle in existing ethnic enclaves in the larger American cities. U.S. immigration policy perpetuates the influx of both types of immigrants, encouraging the dispersed patterns of settlement among many immigrants who qualify for residency based on their academic and professional credentials and the more tightly knit patterns of settlement within urban ethnic enclaves among many immigrants who qualify for entrance into the country based on family ties. Moreover, illegal immigrants, who comprise a large percentage of total immigrants within some national origin groups, also tend to settle in urban ethnic enclaves, where they can often circumvent legal barriers to employment. Patterns of settlement differ by ethnic group in part because professionals form a higher proportion of particular national origin groups in the United States than others and in part because of historic patterns of settlement and the geographic propinquity of different regions of the United States to the countries sending immigrants. National origin groups composed primarily of working-class individuals tend to be clustered within specific neighborhoods in a few large cities relatively near their countries of origin. National origin groups composed disproportionately of highly educated and professional individuals tend to be represented in scattered urban, suburban, and even rural communities throughout the country, although these immigrants, too, show some preference for the building of geographically cohesive ethnic communities.

Urban entrepreneurs, another category of immigrants, display marked differences in patterns of settlement in contrast with poorly educated, low-skilled immigrants and professional immigrants with high academic credentials. Not necessarily dependent on a well-established ethnic enclave through which to find employment and lacking the skills and qualifications to secure employment in the U.S. professions, some immigrants go into business to support themselves and their families. These immigrants, like many professional immigrants, often live in dispersed communities. However, entrepreneurial immigrants do tend to settle and establish their businesses within the larger cities of the United States in an effort to tap into a large local market. Post-1965 immigrant entrepreneurs have often invested in inner-city neighborhoods with relatively little economic activity, thereby offsetting trends of economic decline in many larger American cities. These entrepreneurs have commonly carved out a niche for themselves as middleman merchants or lenders for the native-born working class. Other immigrant entrepreneurs, however, invest in ethnic enclaves with which they share a language and culture. Hiring from within the ethnic enclave, immigrant employers benefit from informal and reliable channels of communication through which they can evaluate the employability of a job seeker and build toward greater understanding and trust with employees. Hiring from within the ethnic enclave also protects immigrant entrepreneurs somewhat from the economic forces operating in the larger labor market.

Moreover, the decision by immigrant entrepreneurs to settle and invest in an ethnic enclave is often influenced by the attractiveness of opportunities to make money by providing services to co-ethnic members of the enclave community.

The relatively recent influx of refugees fleeing political persecution in their countries of origin and the phenomenon of chain migration (immigrants who are U.S. residents take advantage of the U.S. immigration family preferences policy to sponsor their immediate relatives who, once they themselves are established, in turn sponsor their immediate relatives) have increased the relative and absolute numbers of working-class immigrants who otherwise would not have qualified for legal entry into the country. The inflow of working-class immigrants, in addition to entrepreneurial immigrants, has fueled the growth of urban ethnic enclaves. For immigrants with low levels of education, few job skills, and limited proficiency in English who enter the United States either legally through immigration policy favoring family reunification or through some other legal or illegal means, an existing ethnic enclave typically offers social support, including housing and employment opportunities. These opportunities would otherwise be unavailable to the working-class immigrant given their unfamiliarity with local culture, their lack of domestically recognized educational credentials and job skills, and their inability to communicate effectively in English. Family and friends offer immediate assistance in the settlement process. Shared language, culture, and experiences in the country of origin tend to bind established immigrants and more recent immigrants together, allowing them to create a community of mutual support. This is particularly true and important if members of the immigrant group receive prejudicial, discriminatory, and hostile treatment from native-born Americans. The ethnic enclave provides recent immigrants employment and immediate ladders of socioeconomic mobility that are not readily attainable within the larger host society.

In sharp contrast with working-class immigrants who turn to family and friends within the ethnic enclave for their immediate livelihood, professionals—especially physicians, engineers, and scientists—tend to rely on their own skills and qualifications to gain employment in the United States. Professional immigrants, many of whom have pursued their studies in American universities, commonly enjoy recognition for their educational and occupational achievements by U.S. employers. Fluency in English also frees this population from reliance on the ethnic enclave in the process of cultural adaptation to life in the United States. Since 1965, approximately 25 percent of immigrants have been professionals and more than 40 percent have been white-collar workers. As professionals, these immigrants tend to settle where the jobs that match their skills are located. Engineers in high-tech industries, for example, typically settle in Silicon Valley, California, and in other booming high-tech corridors. Physicians and their immediate families often take up residence in urban, suburban, and rural communities throughout the United States. Foreign-born physicians commonly accept employment in poorer communities shunned by native-born medical professionals. Professional immigrants, in contrast to their working-class counterparts, have considerably more options in making settlement decisions. Moreover, relatively high levels of education and English-language proficiency facilitate the cultural and social adaptation of professional immigrants and their children in American society. Immersed in a social milieu dominated by American-born peers and frequently removed from the sustained influence of the ethnic enclave, children of professional immigrants are among the most culturally and linguistically assimilated of the second generation of contemporary U.S. immigrants.

ASIAN IMMIGRANTS

The settlement patterns of Asian immigrants in the United States are as diverse as the occupational backgrounds and national origins of this multicultural, multilingual continental group. Nevertheless, on the whole, Asian immigrants show a marked preference for the Pacific states, with California in the lead as the most popular place of settlement by far. According to the 1990 census, while Asians were found to represent only 2.9 percent of the total American population, in California nearly one in every ten residents was Asian or a Pacific Islander. New York City, Houston, Chicago, Washington, D.C., and other cities outside the West Coast, however, also attract considerable numbers of contemporary Asian immigrants. There are currently Asian immigrant populations established in all fifty states of the Union, reflecting a willingness of growing numbers of Asians to settle in regions not traditionally attractive to immigrants from Asia. The diffuse patterns of contemporary settlement notwithstanding, the great majority of Asian immigrants take up residence and find employment in the United States's larger urban areas. Asian immigrants with low levels of education and few marketable professional skills, in particular, tend to settle in large cities, where they find work in service industries and light

manufacturing. Professional Asian immigrants, following the demands and opportunities of the larger domestic job market, tend to settle in a more geographically scattered manner.

Between 1965 and 1990, the Chinese-American population grew from approximately 360,000 to 1,645,000, overtaking Japanese Americans as the single most populous Asian-American group. Between 1990 and 1995, more than 380,000 additional Chinese emigrated to the United States. Many of the post-1965 immigrants settled in the small historic Chinese ethnic enclaves established in the late nineteenth and early twentieth centuries, giving new life to the declining ethnic communities. Most of the immigrants from mainland China and Hong Kong came through the family reunification category adopted into 1965 U.S. immigration policy. Less than one-fifth of immigrants from mainland China and even fewer from Hong Kong came through the professional category of U.S. immigration policy. Among Taiwanese immigrants, however, nearly one-third entered the United States as professionals. Chinese immigrants with limited English-language skills tend to gravitate to established Chinatowns, where they frequently work in low-paying, unstable service-sector jobs. Among all Asian immigrant groups, the Chinese have the highest rate of individuals working in low-paying service-sector jobs, commonly within Chinese ethnic enclaves in San Francisco, New York, and Los Angeles. Professional and entrepreneurial Chinese immigrants have settled diffusely throughout the United States and have also formed new ethnic communities outside the historic Chinatowns. New Chinese communities in San Gabriel Valley and Monterey Park, California; Flushing and Brooklyn, New York; Houston, Bellaire, and Richardson, Texas; and Chamblee, Georgia, were primarily settled by relatively well-educated, bilingual, and professional Chinese immigrants.

Filipinos, the second-largest Asian immigrant group in the United States, have one of the highest proportions of professionals among all immigrant nationalities, easily exceeding the average of the American-born population as well. However, reflecting the strong family orientation of Filipino culture, by 1989, the proportion of Filipinos entering the United States through occupational categories fell to 8 percent, while the proportion coming through family categories increased to 88 percent. Between 1965 and 1990, the number of Filipino Americans grew phenomenally from 200,000 to over 1,400,000. Unlike most Chinese immigrants, Filipino immigrants, coming from a country in which English is an official language and is widely spoken as a second language, do not have to contend with initial linguistic barriers and, hence, are not as compelled to settle in ethnic enclaves for immediate support. Nevertheless, most contemporary Filipino immigrants continue to be concentrated in their areas of traditional settlement, Hawaii and the West Coast, especially California. In 1990, for example, California was home to 731,685 Filipinos, followed in the distance by Hawaii with 168,682 Filipinos. In San Francisco, in particular, Filipino-owned businesses have steadily increased since 1965, providing a boost to that city's economy. However, nowhere have Filipino immigrants created ethnic enclaves with the discernible cohesion of the Chinese and their Chinatowns. The Filipinos' English-speaking ability probably accounts for the relative absence of Filipino ethnic enclaves in the United States. Moreover, many of the Filipino physicians, surgeons, dentists, and nurses who emigrated to the United States since 1965 have settled in areas of relatively little historical Filipino settlement, particularly in large urban areas in the Midwest and Northeast, but also in cities in the South and Southwest. In addition to high levels of English-language proficiency, the high proportion of professionals among Filipino immigrants serves to further work against the establishment of cohesive Filipino ethnic enclaves.

Between 1965 and 1990, the number of Korean Americans increased from 45,000 to almost 800,000. Small Korean ethnic enclaves from earlier migratory flows provided many later Korean immigrants an initial base from which to prosper. A high proportion of Korean immigrants are college-educated and of middle-class backgrounds. However, poor English-language skills have prevented many of them from entering the U.S. professions. Partially in response to blocked ladders of upward mobility within the U.S. establishment, Korean entrepreneurial immigrants have created a thriving Korean business community in Los Angeles both in and outside the Koreatown ethnic enclave. In New York City and other northeastern cities, however, most Korean entrepreneurs are geographically dispersed, playing largely a role of middleman merchants to an American-born population. The main destination of Korean immigrants remains Los Angeles, where the Korean ethnic enclave continues to grow at a healthy pace. Smaller numbers of Korean immigrants have entered produce retailing and have created small businesses in New York, Chicago, and Washington, D.C. Through the decade of the 1980s, they were also the single largest immigrant group arriving in Philadelphia and Baltimore. According to the 1990 census, approximately half of all Koreans lived in Los Angeles and Orange counties of southern California (250,000) and in greater New York City (150,000). Chicago was the third most common place of settlement, with a population of 40,000 Korean immigrants. Los Angeles's Koreatown provides newcomers who speak no or very little English immediate opportunities for employment. Moreover, rotating credit associations operating within the different Korean immigrant communities of the United States provide entrepreneurial immigrants the funds with which to create their own businesses, thereby strengthening the institutional base of Koreatown and the presence of Korean-owned businesses outside the main ethnic enclave in Los Angeles.

Immigrants from India, like those from the Philippines, are mainly professionals and managers. Between 1965 and 1990, their numbers increased from 50,000 to 815,500. Of all Asian immigrant groups, the Indians are the most geographically dispersed in their settlement patterns in the United States. Many post-1965 South Asian immigrants are highly educated, professional, and financially secure. For all adults over the age of twenty-five, nearly 70 percent hold B.A. degrees, 34 percent M.A. degrees, 8 percent professional degrees, and nearly 9 percent doctoral degrees. Furthermore, over 46 percent of South Asian males hold managerial or professional jobs. Relatively high levels of educational and professional development and English-language skills account for much of the geographic dispersal in South Asian patterns of settlement. Highly educated and English-speaking South Asians take lucrative professional and managerial jobs throughout the United States. Like the Filipinos and in contrast with the Chinese and Koreans, the South Asians have yet to create discernible ethnic enclaves, which are precluded by patterns of settlement. In the 1990s, nevertheless, the major industrialized states—New York, Pennsylvania, New Jersey, Texas, Michigan, Illinois, Ohio, and California—accounted for 70 percent of the South Asian population living in the United States. Even within cities with large numbers of South Asian immigrants, however, most immigrants live in dispersed, scattered communities.

Vietnamese, Cambodians, and Laotians represent other significant groups of Asian immigrants in the United States. The bulk of Southeast Asian immigrants arrived as political refugees since 1975. The first wave of Southeast Asian immigration between 1975 and 1977 consisted primarily of well-educated, relatively Western-oriented middle-class urbanites who were better prepared for the transition to life in the United States than later, less-educated, and more rural waves of immigrants. By 1992, there were 1,223,699 Southeast Asian immigrants in the United States (Vietnamese, 69 percent; Laotians, 19 percent; Cambodians, 12 percent). The Southeast Asians are the largest refugee group to enter the country since the Second World War. Of all major Asian immigrant groups, the Southeast Asian refugees are the least equipped, in terms of education and job skills, for success in the United States. This is especially the case for the more rural Laotians and Cambodians. Many of the poorly educated refugees remain dependent on welfare. The U.S. government initially attempted to settle many of the Southeast Asian refugees in scattered communities throughout the country, including rural communities in which few foreign-born people lived. The aim of this policy was to encourage the assimilation of the Vietnamese, Laotians, and Cambodians by preventing their concentration in any one geographic location. However, many Southeast Asians, in search of the social support a community of co-ethnics could provide, soon relocated to California. In 1982 alone, 24,000 Southeast Asian refugees migrated to California from their states of initial settlement. By 1987, 40 percent of all Southeast Asians lived in California, followed distantly by Texas with only 7.5 percent of all Southeast Asians. Orange County, California, is now home to the largest Vietnamese ethnic enclave in the United States. Similarly, the majority of Cambodians and Laotians now reside in California as well. However, significant communities of Vietnamese, Cambodians, and Laotians continue to thrive in the Northeast, Midwest, Mid-Atlantic, and South.

LATIN AMERICAN IMMIGRANTS

As with immigration from Asia, immigration from Latin America increased rapidly after 1965. Although most Latin American immigrants speak the same language, they represent a wide array of nationalities, races, and educational and professional backgrounds, confounding attempts to make generalizations about them as a group. Furthermore, patterns of settlement differ by both the national origin and the level of educational and professional development of the Latin American immigrant. Many U.S. government authorities, including the Census Bureau, use the term "Hispanic" as a catchall for people from a Spanish-speaking country or with a Spanish-speaking family background. According to the 1990 U.S. census, 9 percent of the U.S. population classified themselves as Hispanic. However, among many Latin American immigrants, regional differences in patterns of settlement by national origin as well as divergent national experiences and national loyalties, typically encourage the maintenance of nationally based ethnic identities and prevent a shared panlinguistic, pancultural Hispanic identity—although among some urban youth and among some politicians and academics there is evidence of an emerging Hispanic identity. According to the 1990 U.S. census, self-classified Hispanics were heavily represented in the state populations of the Southwest—New Mexico (38.2 percent), California (25.8 percent), Texas (25.5 percent), Arizona (18.8 percent), Colorado (12.9 percent), and Nevada (10.4 percent)—the Northeast—New York (12.3 percent) and New Jersey (9.6 percent)—Florida (12.2 percent), and Illinois (7.9 percent). The concentration of Hispanics in relatively few states notwithstanding, Latin American immigrant communities, of various national origins, exist in every state of the Union.

Mexican immigrants represent by far the largest national-origin immigrant group of all contemporary immigrants in the United States. Historically, immigrants from Mexico settled primarily in the Southwest. Contemporary immigrants generally follow the patterns of settlement initiated by their early-twentieth-century predecessors, although post-1965 Mexican immigration is much more of an urban phenomenon than were earlier migratory flows. Due to geographic propinquity and historic patterns of settlement, the vast majority of Mexican immigrants settle in the Southwest of the United States, with some exceptions. In the early 1900s, for example, large numbers of Mexicans emigrated to Chicago, setting a pattern of migration and settlement that Mexican immigrants continue to follow to this day. Hence, Illinois, lying miles away from the Mexican border, is home to a large number of contemporary Mexican immigrants. Exceptions notwithstanding, more than 84 percent of an estimated 17 million people of Mexican descent live in the Southwest, in the states of California, Arizona, New Mexico, Colorado, and Texas. When the Mexican and Mexican-descended people of Illinois are added, this figure rises to 88 percent. Los Angeles has consistently remained the most common destination of Mexicans coming to the United States. Other southwestern cities as well as Chicago draw large numbers of Mexican immigrants. Most have relatively low levels of education and professional development, and many lack proficiency in English. In the urban areas of settlement, where there exist large co-national communities, Mexican immigrants of modest means typically find initial employment in low-paying, unstable service-sector jobs through co-national contacts.

With a population of more than 2.7 million, Puerto Ricans are the second-largest Hispanic group in the United States. Puerto Ricans, not immigrants in the formal sense, initially settled in New York City, with some communities in other northeastern cities and in New Jersey. In the 1970s, however, more Puerto Ricans moved to and took up residence in the north central, southern, and western regions of the United States. Nevertheless, most mainland Puerto Ricans continue to live in either New York City or in the contiguous areas of New Jersey and Connecticut. Relatively inexpensive flights between New York City and San Juan, Puerto Rico, explain much of the historic and contemporary preference Puerto Rican islanders have for migrating to New York City. Moreover, once an initial Puerto Rican community was established in New York, later migrants relied on networks of family and friends in the city to find housing and employment. Patterns of circular migration between New York and Puerto Rico entrenched the city's status as the preferred destination of Puerto Ricans coming to the mainland. Historically, Puerto Rican migrants have been predominantly working-class, with limited education and professional skills. The social networks of established urban ethnic communities in New York and other northeastern and midwestern cities have been essential to Puerto Rican adaptation and acculturation to life in the United States and explain continued patterns of settlement by many contemporary Puerto Rican migrants.

With a population greater than 1 million, Cubans and their descendants represent the third-largest Latin American national group in the United States. Even more than Mexicans and Puerto Ricans, Cubans coming to the United States show a marked preference for settlement in a particular geographic region. Like Southeast Asians, most Cubans emigrated to the United States as political refugees. U.S. authorities, attempting to ease the social and economic pressures of the rapid inflow of Cubans into southern Florida, initially settled the Cuban refugees throughout the country. However, during the following decades, Cubans originally settled in other parts of the United States steadily made their way to Miami, where they came to form a thriving ethnic enclave which later Cuban immigrants were able to join, finding housing, employment, and social support with relative ease. In 1965, 42 percent of all Cubans in the United States lived in Dade County; by 1980, it was 52 percent. Since the 1970s, the great majority of Cuban immigrants have settled in Miami. In 1987, for example, 77 percent of the 28,916 Cubans immigrating to the United States chose Miami as their final destination. The geographic propinquity of Miami to Cuba partially accounts for the initial attraction of this city to Cuban immigrants. A strong, economically dynamic Cuban enclave in the city accounts for most of Miami's current appeal to Cuban immigrants and Cuban

Americans living outside of southern Florida. The first wave of immigrants were middle- and upper-class Cubans with many professional and entrepreneurial skills. In Miami, originally hopeful of Castro's imminent downfall, the first wave of immigrants successfully applied their considerable talent to create a multitude of businesses, transforming the city, over the course of the following decades and with the help of later immigrants, into a Cuban-oriented metropolis.

Immigrants from other parts of Latin America have also arrived in large numbers to the United States since 1965, settling in distinct patterns in different parts of the country. Dominicans have replaced Puerto Ricans as the largest Spanish-speaking population in New York City. Approximately two-thirds of all Dominican immigrants to the United States, 714,543 in total by 1995, chose New York City as their point of destination and settlement. A small Dominican enclave established in the city after World War II provided the base from which the Dominican immigrant population later soared. Post-1965 immigrants from Central America, some of whom arrived as refugees, some as professionals, and many others through family reunification, have tended to gravitate to the large urban centers of the Northeast, the Pacific Coast, and the Gulf Coast states—particularly greater New York, Washington, D.C., Los Angeles, San Francisco, Houston, and New Orleans. Professional, relatively well-educated immigrants make up a larger proportion of newcomers from South America than from Central America and, hence, tend to settle more diffusely in the United States. This is particularly true of Argentinian immigrants. Nevertheless, Los Angeles and San Francisco on the West Coast, Chicago in the Midwest, and New York in the Northeast are common places of settlement among South American immigrants. Colombians, for example, the largest South American national group living in the United States, show a marked preference for New York City and Chicago, where economically diverse and established Colombian enclaves serve to attract continued inflows of Colombian immigrant settlers.

WEST INDIAN AND HAITIAN IMMIGRANTS

Of the English-speaking Caribbean territories, Jamaica has sent the largest number of immigrants to the United States, followed by Guyana and Trinidad. By 1995, a total of 544,963 Jamaicans, 178,309 Guyanese, and 139,698 Trinidadians had emigrated to the United

States Small West Indian enclaves in New York City, established after the Second World War, attracted the mass labor immigration of Jamaicans, Guyanese, Trinidadians, and other English-speaking Caribbean nationals after 1965. In addition to New York, Miami and Boston have been favored places of settlement for West Indian immigrants since 1965. Relatively affordable and frequent flights between these cities and the different territories of the West Indies have encouraged the immigration and settlement of Caribbean newcomers in these cities. In recent years, however, increasing numbers of West Indians have chosen California as their point of destination. Pre-1965 West Indian immigration was primarily of relatively well-educated and high-skilled immigrants, who took professional jobs in New York City and other large urban areas of the United States. Later West Indian immigrants, who in contrast with the pre-1965 immigrants were poorly educated and low-skilled, tended to follow their better-off predecessors, settling in areas where they could take advantage of the social support of an established, relatively affluent conational community.

By 1995, 334,366 Haitians had immigrated to the United States. Unlike their British West Indian counterparts, most Haitian newcomers to the United States speak English with limited proficiency. While English-speaking West Indian immigrants, particularly those with high levels of education and job skills, have adjusted relatively well to the culture of U.S. life and the U.S. workplace, French and, especially, Creole-speaking Haitians, many of whom emigrate to the country with poor education and few job skills, have faced the added obstacle of having to learn an unfamiliar language. Nevertheless, after the Second World War, a small Haitian immigrant enclave, composed primarily of well-educated and professional members of the Haitian middle and upper classes, came into existence in New York City. For these early Haitian immigrants, the transition to life in the United States occurred with relative ease. However, later Haitian immigrants, who fled the political repression and disastrous economic conditions of their homeland, tended to be less well equipped for immediate success in the United States. For these later immigrants, the initially small Haitian enclave in New York served as a point of attraction; as this enclave grew in dynamism and strength, further Haitian immigrants were attracted to New York, finding employment primarily in the low-paying service sector. Since the 1980s, a large Haitian immigrant community has also emerged in Miami, composed predominantly of poorly educated, low-skilled Haitian refugees from rural communities in their country of origin. Many of Miami's

Haitians have yet to attain legal status in the United States. Given the humble social origins and precarious legal status of many post-1965 Haitian immigrants, particularly in Miami, Haitian immigrant enclaves provide the social support essential to adaptation to life in the United States.

EUROPEAN IMMIGRANTS

During the first half of the twentieth century, immigrants from Europe settled primarily in the urban Northeast and the urban Great Lakes region. In the post-1965 period, Europeans represent a small proportion of the total number of immigrants settling in the United States; in the late 1950s and early 1960s, they accounted for half of all immigrants to the United States, but in the late 1980s, they amounted to less than 10 percent. In 1990, only 14 percent of all immigrants were from Europe. Nevertheless, with the collapse of the Soviet Union in 1991 and with political turmoil and ethnic strife in much of Eastern Europe beginning in the 1980s, new waves of European immigrants headed for the United States. Between 1990 and 1995, 302,603 immigrants from the former Soviet Union entered the United States. Approximately half of the post-Soviet, post-1990 immigrants settled in New York City. However, of the more than three hundred thousand post-1990 immigrants, approximately fifty thousand are ethnic Russians, two-thirds of whom are religious dissidents who settled in California, Oregon, and Washington. A large proportion of immigrants from the former Soviet Union in the 1990s are Jews. These immigrants predominantly opt for New York City as their place of initial settlement. The Brighton Beach area of Brooklyn has emerged as the single most visible enclave of contemporary Russian Jewish immigrants, supporting a vibrant Russian-language community life.

Immigrants from Poland represent the other relatively large contingent of Europeans coming to the United States after 1965. In the decade of the 1980s, 34,903 refugees and 28,966 immigrants from Poland legally entered the United States. At the same time, 374,622 Polish nationals entered the United States as vacationers. Many of these probably stayed on in the country illegally. For early Polish immigrants of the late nineteenth and early twentieth centuries, Chicago emerged as the leading center of settlement, followed by other industrial cities in the Midwest and the Northeast. The most recent Polish immigrants, arriving during the 1980s and 1990s, partially mirror the settlement patterns of previous waves of Polish immigrants. Approximately one-quarter of recent Polish immigrants have chosen to settle in greater Chicago, where they receive some social support from the established Polish ethnic community, with many of the remainder establishing themselves in other areas of traditional Polish immigration and settlement. However, unlike their turn-of-the-century predecessors, most recent Polish immigrants are relatively well-educated, high-skilled, and speak English, thereby freeing them up somewhat from reliance on established ethnic enclaves for their survival and transition to life in the United States.

Aonghas Mac Thòmais St.-Hilaire

See also: Chain Migration (Part II, Sec. 1); Immigrants and the Census (Part II, Sec. 3); Segmented Assimilation (Part II, Sec. 4); Housing (Part II, Sec. 7); Houston, Los Angeles, Mex-America, Miami, New Jersey and Suburban America, New York City, Rural America, San Francisco, Washington, D.C. (Part II, Sec. 12).

BIBLIOGRAPHY

Cruz, Jon. "Filipinos." In *A Nation of Peoples,* ed. Elliott Barkan, pp. 200–217. Westport, CT: Greenwood Press, 1999.

Daniels, Roger. "What is an American? Ethnicity, Race, the Constitution and the Immigrant in Early American History." In *The Immigration Reader: America in a Multidisciplinary Perspective,* ed., David Jacobson pp. 29–47. Malden, MA: Blackwell Publishers Ltd., 1998.

Gold, Steven. "Southeast Asians." In *A Nation of Peoples,* ed. Elliott Barkan, pp. 505–19. Westport, CT: Greenwood Press, 1999.

Grenier, Guillemo, and Lisandro Pérez. "Cubans." In *A Nation of Peoples,* ed. Elliott Barkan, pp. 138–55. Westport, CT: Greenwood Press, 1999.

Gutiérrez, David. "Mexicans." In *A Nation of Peoples,* ed. Elliott Barkan, pp. 372–90. Westport, CT: Greenwood Press, 1999.

Hing, Bill. "Asian Immigrants: Social Forces Unleashed after 1965." In *The Immigration Reader: America in a Multidisciplinary Perspec-*tive, ed. David Jacobson, pp. 144–82. Malden, MA: Blackwell Publishers Ltd., 1998.

Kasinitz, Philie, and Milton Vickerman. "West Indians/Caribbeans." In *A Nation of Peoples,* ed. Elliott Barkan, pp. 520–41. Westport, CT: Greenwood Press, 1999.

Kim, Illsoo. *New Urban Immigrants: The Korean Community in New York.* Princeton, NJ: Princeton University Press, 1981.

Kim, Kwang Chung. "Koreans." In *A Nation of Peoples,* ed. Elliott Barkan, pp. 354–71. Westport, CT: Greenwood Press, 1999.

La Brack, Bruce. "South Asians." In *A Nation of Peoples,* ed. Elliott Barkan, pp. 482–504. Westport, CT: Greenwood Press, 1999.

Massey, Douglas. "The Settlement Process among Mexican Immigrants to the United States." *American Sociological Review* 51 (1986): 670–84.

Muller, Thomas. *Immigrants and the American City.* New York: New York University Press, 1993.

Pacyga, Dominic. "Poles." In *A Nation of Peoples,* ed. Elliott Barkan, pp. 425–45. Westport, CT: Greenwood Press, 1999.

Portes, Alejandro, and Ruben Rumbaut. *Immigrant America.* Berkeley: University of California Press, 1990.

Radzilowski, Thaddeus, and John Radzilowski. "East Europeans." In *A Nation of Peoples,* ed. Elliott Barkan, pp. 174–99. Westport, CT: Greenwood Press. 1999.

Sassen-Koob, Saskia. "The New Labor Demand in Global Cities." In *Cities in Transformation,* ed. Michael Smith, pp. 139–71. Beverly Hills, CA: Sage, 1984.

Ueda, Reed. "The Changing Face of Post-1965 Immigration." In *The Immigration Reader: America in a Multidisciplinary Perspective,* ed. David Jacobson, pp. 72–91. Malden, MA: Blackwell Publishers Ltd., 1998.

———. *Postwar Immigrant America.* Boston: Bedford Books of St Martin's Press, 1994.

Whalen, Carmen. "Puerto Ricans." In *A Nation of Peoples,* ed. Elliott Barkan, pp. 446–63. Westport, CT: Greenwood Press, 1999.

Williams, William. "Immigration as a Pattern in American Culture." In *The Immigration Reader: America in a Multidisciplinary Perspective,* ed. David Jacobson, pp. 19–28. Malden, MA: Blackwell Publishers Ltd., 1998.

Yung, Judy. "Chinese." In *A Nation of Peoples,* ed. Elliott Barkan, pp. 119–37. Westport, CT: Greenwood Press, 1999.

Section 4

IMMIGRANT INCORPORATION AND ACCULTURATION

Introduction

Children and Adolescent Immigrants
Martin D. Smith

Elderly
Patricia Cedeño-Zamor

Ethnic Intermarriage
Tomás Jiménez

Family
Daniel James

Gay and Lesbian Immigration
Lionel Cantú

Gender
Teal Rothschild

Segmented Assimilation
Aonghas Mac Thòmais St.-Hilaire

INTRODUCTION

Section 4 of Part II of the *Encyclopedia of American Immigration* includes entries that deal with how immigrants are absorbed into American society and life. Once referred to as *assimilation,* the process is more properly defined as *incorporation,* since the latter word dispenses with the idea that immigrants give up their previous cultural identity as they become American. *Incorporation,* the term preferred by sociologists, implies that immigrants adopt certain aspects of American life, even as they retain elements of their native culture.

The entries in this section largely deal with various types of immigrants and how they adjust to American life. Section 4 contains entries on children and adolescent immigrants, elderly immigrants, and gay immigrants. In addition, there are entries on the immigrant family, ethnic intermarriage, immigration and gender, and finally segmented assimilation, the process whereby immigrants assimilate some aspects of American society while resisting others.

In "Children and Adolescent Immigrants," Martin D. Smith begins with a discussion on how the intergenerational incorporation of immigrants functions. He then goes on to provide a demographic and geographic portrait of young immigrants and where they live. Next, he talks about the impact of immigration on children and adolescents, and the ways they adjust to life in the United States.

In her entry on elderly immigrants, Patricia Cedeño-Zamor begins with a discussion of how Asian and Hispanic families take care of their elderly members and how that tradition is affected by immigration. The author also examines the various economic, social, and health problems faced by elderly immigrants.

In the entry on ethnic intermarriage, Tomás Jiménez explores the phenomenon of marriage between immigrants and native-born Americans and between immigrants from various ethnic backgrounds. The author begins with a discussion of terminology and how the U.S. Census deals with interethnic couples and their children before going on to look at social-group influence on these people. Next, there is a discussion of trends in ethnic intermarriage, both in the recent past and in the near future.

In his entry on the immigrant family, Daniel James explores the topic of relay—or chain—immigration, whereby immigrant families move to the United States either one by one or in groups, with a breadwinner usually preceding dependents. Next, the author goes on to discuss marriage and gender issues within the immigrant family before going into an examination of different types of immigrant families, and the different kinds of relations that exist among them. This is followed by detailed discussions of Asian and Hispanic immigrant families.

Next, Lionel Cantú examines the barely studied phenomenon of gay immigrants to the United States. He begins with a history of the subject—particularly in terms of the law—before exploring contemporary issues, including the fight for lesbian and gay immigration rights.

In her entry on immigration and gender, Teal Rothschild explores the context and cultural differences involved in the subject before moving on to look at the immigration patterns of men and women. Following a brief discussion of gender and the immigrant family, Rothschild explores the topic of immigrant women and work, as well as the role of immigrant women in volunteerism and political activism. A brief exploration of immigrant women's education is followed by a discussion of the transformations in gender that are due to immigration.

In his entry entitled "Segmented Assimilation," Aonghas Mac Thòmais St.-Hilaire begins with a discussion of the theories behind the subject before moving on to a discussion of the process in both historical and contemporary terms. Next, the author looks into the role of ethnicity in social mobility, a key element in the process of segmented assimilation, before discussing the topic of social capital in the process of cultural adaptation.

CHILDREN AND ADOLESCENT IMMIGRANTS

*H*istory has shown that the long-term incorporation of immigrant groups is heavily influenced by the progress achieved by the second generation, that is, the immediate descendants of immigrants. However, for much of the last century, immigration research in the United States centered predominantly on the experiences of adult immigrants. This is because the children of earlier European immigrants were observed to assimilate (that is, become Americanized) more easily than their parents, giving rise to the general acceptance of a succession model of long-term immigrant incorporation, where subsequent generations assimilate more comfortably than preceding ones. The salience of the succession model has had repercussions for the utility of important data sources, with large-scale social surveys still focusing primarily on the adult world. However, the situation is beginning to change, mainly in response to more recent waves of potentially problematic immigration. Mass immigration since 1965 has led to the early-twenty-first-century emergence of a predominantly nonwhite, non-English-speaking, and rapidly growing second generation whose adaptation is not expected to mirror the generally smooth pathways followed by the second generation of the earlier European immigrants.

INTERGENERATIONAL INCORPORATION OF IMMIGRANTS

Researchers generally agree that the life chances of the descendants of the earlier European immigrants were shaped largely by the social status of their parents, and that English-language acquisition, high educational attainment, social networking, and acculturation all acted as catalysts for upward social mobility and residential mobility (in this case, movement away from the decaying urban zones of transition to the more affluent suburbs). Resistance to cultural assimilation and spatial isolation (e.g., ethnic enclaves and ghettos) was considered to account for cases of immobility, if not downward mobility.

The scenarios forecast by scholars for today's second generation, by contrast, seem to contradict this model. The scenarios include (1) downward mobility despite having affluent origins, (2) immobility despite good progress made by first-generation immigrants from poor backgrounds, and (3) upward mobility despite spatial concentration, language maintenance, and cultural isolation. The principal worry among researchers is that some sectors of the new second generation (particularly the large Mexican sector) could form an underclass, mirroring the African-American underclass found in deteriorating inner cities. This type of variable assimilation is termed "segmented assimilation." Investigations into these "divided fates" have now commenced, and the main lines of inquiry focus on a series of external and internal factors, all operating in specific geographical and historical contexts. External factors include the recent restructuring of the U.S. labor market, which has seen the expansion of the higher and lower occupational classes and a contraction of the middle—the so-called hourglass economy—and the rise of racial discrimination. Internal factors, relating more to the psychosocial development of the young migrants, the nature and extent of their acculturation, and levels of family and community resources (social capital), also appear to shape patterns of adaptation. The hypothetical classification of second-generation outcomes constructed by sociologists Alejandro Portes and Ruben Rumbaut illustrates ways in which these factors intersect (see Table 1).

CHILD AND ADOLESCENT IMMIGRANTS AND WHERE THEY LIVE

The United States admitted more than 17 million immigrants during the period from 1971 to 1995, with most of these immigrants coming from Asia and Latin

While the older generation of immigrants often bemoans the loss of traditional values among their offspring, adolescent newcomers—like these Cambodians at a "heavy metal" party—frequently enjoy the freedom American culture brings. *(Leah Melnick/Impact Visuals)*

America. This has given rise to a record number of child immigrants and children raised in immigrant families (with children defined as being under eighteen years of age). The U.S. census of 1990 identifies about 13 million such children, accounting for about 15 percent of the total U.S. child population. In terms of ethnic breakdown of the foreign-born component, 52 percent are Latinos and a further 27 percent are Asians; in all, 90 percent of Asian-American children and 59 percent of Latin American children belong to the first or second generation. More specifically, the top nine sending countries during the 1980s were Mexico, the Philippines, China/Taiwan, South Korea, Vietnam, the Dominican Republic, India, El Salvador, and Jamaica.

The various groups have not settled randomly across America. Many states and cities have experienced very little immigration, while the demographic fabric of others has been altered dramatically. In 1993, the seven principal metropolitan areas favored by immigrants arriving that year were New York (128,000), Los Angeles/Long Beach (107,000), Chicago (44,000), Miami (30,000), Washington, D.C. (27,000), Houston (23,000), and San Francisco (21,000). Of these destinations, Miami was dominated by Cuban immigration (34 percent of the 1993 influx); Houston, Los Angeles/Long Beach, and Chicago by Mexican immigration (19–27 percent); New York by Dominicans (20 percent); San Francisco by Chinese and Filipinos (17 and 16 percent, respectively); and Washington, D.C., by Salvadorans (13 percent). Within these cities, groups tend to be segregated from one another, and especially from the white population, forming distinctive enclaves, such as Chinatowns, barrios, and ghettos. Spatial concentration was previously thought to hinder social mobility, although it is accepted now that some groups, such as Chinese, Vietnamese, and Koreans, are benefiting from employment opportunities embedded in ethnic enclave economies, where the tendency for coethnic recruitment protects immigrants from what they see as a closed and discriminatory mainstream labor market.

Table 1
Types of Acculturation, Social Context, and Predicted Second-Generation Outcomes

Type of Acculturation	Social Context		Segmented Assimilation Outcomes
	(I) Discrimination High; Family/Community Resources Low	(II) Discrimination Low; Family/Community Resources High	
Consonant Resistance to Acculturation	X		Downward: probable return to home country
		X	Stagnant: perpetuation of distinct ethnic subculture
Consonant Acculturation	X		Downward: blocked entry into American mainstream; reactive ethnicity
		X	Upward: integration into mainstream and gradual abandonment of parental culture
Dissonant Acculturation	X		Downward: socialization into urban underclass roles; adoption of adversarial stance toward the mainstream
		X	Uncertain: contingent on individual traits and resources
Selective Acculturation	X		Upward: slow mobility into white-collar occupations
		X	Upward: rapid mobility into professional and managerial occupations

Source: Portes and Rumbaut 1996: Figure 10, p. 252.

The children of these immigrants now constitute America's fastest growing and multiethnic sector of the total child population. To understand why the adjustment of this new generation is potentially problematic, it must first be remembered that differences exist between children and adolescents, and between the foreign- and native-born. Adolescent immigrants (that is, those age thirteen to seventeen years) will have different adjustment experiences compared with younger children who emigrate. It is important, then, to treat these two segments of the first generation as separate cohorts. In the research literature, adolescent immigrants are considered members of the pure first generation. Meanwhile, younger child migrants are identified by the recently coined term "one-and-a-half generation." This distinction is drawn because the one-and-a-half generation should, theoretically, have similar adjustment experiences as the pure second generation (that is, those born in the United States), because both parties lack meaningful connections to the homeland.

IMPACT OF IMMIGRATION ON FIRST-GENERATION ADOLESCENTS AND OLDER CHILDREN

The upheaval associated with immigration is, in the case of adolescents, superimposed upon the more general condition of adolescence, a phenomenon that most developmental psychologists assert is a time of increased self-awareness and desire for autonomy from family members and a period of rebellion against adult norms and values. The process of immigration, then, is a highly demanding one for adolescents, even if they are accompanied by family members and are departing to a destination that offers better living standards. Such displacement can result in homesickness and feelings of insecurity. In this sense adolescents may be more vulnerable than adults because they perhaps lack the necessary information to permit comprehension of their changing circumstances. Indeed, sociologist Bryan Roberts's use of the concept of "socially expected durations" illustrates how a high degree of doubt surrounding the permanence of settlement results in low levels of premigratory preparation and low inclinations for social and economic investment upon settlement. For the immigrant adolescent, this can translate into social isolation from new peers, disinterest in the life and functioning of the new community, slow educational progress, and disinclination toward English-language acquisition.

In the case of adolescent refugees fleeing war or natural disaster, the firsthand experience of such events can lead to extreme forms of stress that extend well into adulthood. Adolescents may be less able to articulate personal anxieties than adults, or may conceal them for fear of becoming a burden to their family. It is also notable that many families emigrate in stages (chain migration), and it is not uncommon for parents to be separated geographically from each other for many years. One parent or the extended family may raise the child in the homeland, but it is sometimes the case that the adolescent has grown up among strangers. Thus the upheaval associated with immigration can commence well before the adolescent leaves the homeland, and subsequent reunification with a missing parent may prove no less unsettling in an emotional sense. Chain migration may also result in custody-style battles between geographically separated parents, or between a parent and the extended family. In 2000 the Elian Gonzalez case attracted considerable media attention around the world. This boy set sail from Cuba with his mother, who died en route to Florida. He was then cared for by extended-family members in Miami against the wishes of his father, who remained in Cuba. After months of intense media attention and eventual intervention by the national government, the boy returned to Cuba to live with his father.

CHALLENGES CONFRONTING IMMIGRANT CHILDREN AND CHILDREN OF IMMIGRANTS

Immigrant adolescents have to adjust to their new society in much the same way as adult immigrants and are therefore expected to make similar socioeconomic progress. This is not the case for the one-and-a-half and second generations, whose formative years are spent in the new society, and whose connections with the homeland may be based purely on distant memories or on stories recited by parents and elders. These children are inclined to evaluate themselves in relation to native-born youth and are more likely to challenge and manipulate their ascribed ethnic identities in relation to their perceptions of the "ideal" American identity. This process of identity negotiation is often accompanied by acculturative stresses, which manifest themselves in many different aspects of everyday life and in a range of settings including home, school, and community. It has been argued that such children experience confusion because they are situated precariously between two cultures (the homeland and the new society, or the culture of the home and that of the school). This view, however, assumes that immigrant children are passive victims of circumstance, lacking in their own agency and will. It is therefore more acceptable and valid these days to refer to such children as "cultural navigators" or "code switchers," that is, social actors who modify visible expressions of their identity according to the perceived identity of the observers. Nevertheless, under conditions of nonacceptance by observers, oppositional (that is, anti-American) cultures can develop. This reactive ethnicity has become known as "second-generation rebellion/revolt," and the term has been applied to the largely ghettoized African-American population.

Furthermore, children of the one-and-a-half and

second generations tend to have higher educational and occupational aspirations and expectations than first-generation immigrants, and there is a propensity for them to develop an adversarial stance toward the "immigrant" pay and working conditions associated with their parents' generation. The problem is exacerbated because many of these children lack the skills needed to gain professional or white-collar employment and are more susceptible than earlier white immigrants to racial discrimination. Moreover, the increasingly hourglass structure of the U.S. labor market means that it is harder for all persons of low status to attain occupational mobility. The most likely outcome of this is a widespread failure to fulfill aspirations, which can result in subcultural retreat and downward mobility, a phenomenon termed "second-generation decline."

DIVIDED FATES: VARIABLE ADJUSTMENT AMONG TODAY'S CHILD AND ADOLESCENT IMMIGRANTS

Some of the more quantifiable challenges facing America's diverse immigrant children have been measured in recent research projects. The following analysis traces children from various origins (particularly Asians and Hispanics) and explores issues such as English-language acquisition, educational attainment, and psychological well-being. In some cases, comparisons between the first generation, the one-and-a-half generation, and the second generation can be made.

Table 2 presents findings for children from selected countries of origin on English-language use at home, English-language ability, and linguistic isolation. The data originate from the 1990 U.S. census. In almost all cases, the probability that a first-generation child lives in a non–English-speaking household is greater than 90 percent (the exceptions being children of German, Italian, Indian, and Filipino origin). It is also the case that second-generation children are more likely to live in English-speaking households than first-generation children, providing support for the generational succession model. There is, however, considerable variation. For example, 95 percent of first-generation children of Thai origin do not speak English at home, compared with just 32 percent for the second generation. The case for children of Japanese origin is very similar. However, second-generation children who originate from Laos, Cambodia, the Dominican Re-

public, Mexico, and El Salvador are almost as likely as first-generation children to not speak English at home. This may suggest the strength of intergenerational cultural maintenance within the household, rather than the child's ability to speak English.

Regarding English-language ability among first-generation children, it is mainly Asian children who are the least likely to speak English exclusively or very well: 66 percent for Japanese children, followed closely by Thais (65 percent), Chinese (63 percent), and Cambodians (62 percent). Second-generation children of Thai and Japanese origin perform much better, with just 9 percent of Thai children and 10 percent of Japanese children not speaking English exclusively or very well. This suggests successful acquisition of English through schooling and through less formal socialization such as the media. The generational succession model is less convincing with respect to Lao, Cambodian, Dominican, Salvadoran, and Mexican children, where only slight improvements in English-language acquisition are evident in the second generation. In terms of linguistic isolation, similar patterns emerge. A linguistically isolated household is defined as one in which no household member age fourteen or above speaks English very well or exclusively. The succession model applies to Thai, Japanese, and Cuban children but fits less well for Lao, Cambodian, Dominican, Vietnamese, Guatemalan, Salvadoran, and Haitian children.

Table 3 presents findings on aspects of educational attainment. The data are derived from two sources: the 1990 U.S. census and a 1992 survey of second-generation children in southern California and south Florida. The first main column refers to the proportion of foreign-born adolescents from selected countries of origin enrolled in school. Two periods of immigration are used, to permit comparison between the first generation and the one-and-a-half generation. Among the first-generation immigrants, those of Mexican origin perform much less favorably than any of the other groups, with just 22 percent of eighteen- and nineteen-year-olds enrolled at school. Salvadoran, Guatemalan, and Honduran adolescents are also more likely not to be enrolled at school as eighteen- and nineteen-year-olds. At the other end of the scale, it is adolescents with Asian origins that perform better; those from Hong Kong, Japan, Thailand, and Taiwan have enrollment rates exceeding 90 percent. Rates of enrollment are generally higher for the one-and-a-half generation, with the exception of Mexicans and Guatemalans. The adolescents of Nicaraguan, Filipino, and Salvadoran origin made substantial gains between the first and one-and-a-half generations,

Table 2
English-Language Use at Home and English-Language Ability Among First- and Second-Generation Immigrant Children from Selected Countries of Origin, 1990

Country of origin	Number of children (thousands)		Children who do not speak English at home (percent)		Children who do not speak English exclusively or very well (percent)		Children who live in linguistically isolated households (percent)	
	Generation							
	First	Second	First	Second	First	Second	First	Second
Cambodia	30	34	97	87	62	54	58	63
China	34	97	97	74	63	23	59	35
Colombia	29	88	96	78	38	17	44	27
Cuba	27	184	98	77	36	15	39	13
Dominican Republic	48	131	97	91	55	31	49	38
Ecuador	12	52	98	80	38	20	42	26
El Salvador	77	126	98	90	53	35	48	45
Germany	16	243	69	14	15	4	11	1
Guatemala	35	66	98	83	56	26	53	38
Haiti	28	77	91	67	47	21	39	32
Honduras	17	35	93	69	48	18	49	26
Hong Kong	17	39	97	66	54	22	54	26
India	45	130	84	53	24	10	18	9
Italy	8	171	85	35	21	7	23	6
Japan	32	68	94	34	66	10	63	12
Korea	67	163	92	50	38	14	48	28
Laos	49	64	97	95	57	65	55	63
Mexico	643	1,975	97	88	59	32	52	33
Nicaragua	39	35	97	75	58	22	54	30
Philippines	83	316	75	21	27	5	16	7
Poland	18	62	96	55	31	9	44	16
Taiwan	32	65	96	68	41	16	47	31
Thailand	36	33	95	32	65	9	67	15
Vietnam	99	33	97	76	52	34	46	44

Source: Hernandez and Charney 1998: Table B-2A, p. 236, and Table B-2E, p. 264.

whereas some groups fell back considerably, such as the adolescents from Thailand and Panama.

The remaining columns in Table 3 offer findings from the 1992 survey. The first of these columns examines performances in the Stanford Reading Test. The average score is 41.2 across ten Latin American, Caribbean, and Asian groups (for which data are available). Filipino, Jamaican, Cuban, and Colombian adolescents perform better than average, and considerably better than their Cambodian, Lao, and Mexican counterparts. In terms of performance in math, the Stanford average is 52.9 for the fourteen groups surveyed. Once again, the Filipino, Cuban, and Colombian children perform well, while the Mexican, Cam-

bodian, Lao, and Haitian adolescents underperform. The final measure of educational attainment, grade-point average, has a mean of 2.52 for all ten groups. The maximum value is 4. As the third column of the 1992 survey shows, adolescents of Asian origin all perform above average, while the adolescents of Latin American and Caribbean origin all perform below average, with the highest and lowest achievers being the Vietnamese and Mexican adolescents, respectively.

Table 4 explores various aspects of poverty and psychological well-being, using the same combination of data sources. The poverty and overcrowding variables represent useful surrogates for examining physical health, for the link between poor health and pov-

Table 3
Enrollment in Education and Educational Attainment After Age 17 for Immigrant Children from Selected Countries of Origin, 1990 and 1992

Country of Birth	1990 U.S. Census		1992 Survey of Second-Generation Adolescents in Southern California and South Florida			
	Percent foreign-born 18- and 19-year-olds enrolled in school *Immigration period*		Stanford Reading Test (percentile)	Stanford Math Test (percentile)	Grade Point Average (0–4)	Sample Size
	1987–90 1st gtn.	1980–81 1.5 gtn.				
Cambodia	74	84	14.0	35.7	2.72	96
China	86	93	NA	NA	NA	NA
Hong Kong	95	95	NA	NA	NA	NA
India	82	92	NA	NA	NA	NA
Iran	82	80	NA	NA	NA	NA
Japan	92	96	NA	NA	NA	NA
Korea	86	88	NA	NA	NA	NA
Laos	68	76	22.3	42.1	2.86	155
Philippines	56	82	51.1	59.1	2.93	818
Taiwan	90	99	NA	NA	NA	NA
Thailand	92	79	NA	NA	NA	NA
Vietnam	77	89	37.6	60.4	3.04	371
Mexico	22	30	26.6	31.9	2.24	757
Cuba	67	67	47.5	58.5	2.28	1,227
Dominican Republic	57	61	NA	NA	NA	NA
Haiti	81	77	30.4	45.0	2.31	178
Jamaica	70	73	47.8	55.5	2.58	155
Trinidad/Tobago	63	53	NA	NA	NA	NA
El Salvador	37	60	NA	NA	NA	NA
Guatemala	38	48	NA	NA	NA	NA
Honduras	48	60	NA	NA	NA	NA
Nicaragua	57	87	38.0	55.4	2.28	344
Panama	80	68	NA	NA	NA	NA
Colombia	64	75	44.7	58.4	2.33	227
Ecuador	65	72	NA	NA	NA	NA

Sources: Hirschman 1996: Table 4.4, p. 74; Rumbaut 1996: Table 7.3, p. 140.

erty is widely documented. More than 50 percent of first-generation Thai, Cambodian, and Lao adolescents live in conditions of official poverty, compared with less than 20 percent for Filipino, Indian, Japanese, Jamaican, Taiwanese, and Colombian adolescents. Among the second generation, official poverty remains widespread for Lao, Cambodian, and Dominican adolescents. Thai and Vietnamese adolescents made the most substantial improvements between the first and second generation. In terms of household overcrowding (that is, more than one person per room), the highest levels are experienced by first-generation Nicaraguans, Mexicans, and Salvadorans, and in all cases except the Lao and Cambodians, levels of overcrowding fall significantly among the second generation. Thais, Nicaraguans, Chinese, and Indians improved most.

The remaining columns in Table 4 are based on the 1992 survey. The first of these columns makes use of the Rosenberg ten-item self-esteem scale. The scale runs from 1 to 4, with higher values reflecting higher self-esteem. Relatively low levels of self-esteem prevail among second-generation Lao, Cambodian, and Vietnamese immigrants. Jamaicans, Colombians, and

Table 4
Poverty and Well-Being Among First- and Second-Generation Immigrant Adolescents from Selected Countries of Origin, 1990 and 1992

Country of origin	1990 U.S. Census						1992 Survey of Second-Generation Adolescents in Southern California and South Florida			
	Number of children (thousands)		Children in official poverty (percent)		Children in crowded homes (percent)		Self-esteem scale, 1–4	CES-D depression subscale, 1–4	Percent discriminated against	Sample size
	Generation									
	1st	2nd	1st	2nd	1st	2nd				
Cambodia	30	34	52	41	76	73	3.07	1.66	59.6	96
China	34	97	25	10	59	32	*NA*	*NA*	*NA*	*NA*
Colombia	29	88	19	16	59	36	3.41	1.66	45.3	227
Cuba	27	184	27	13	48	25	3.40	1.60	38.1	1,227
Dominican Republic	48	131	41	42	63	48	*NA*	*NA*	*NA*	*NA*
Ecuador	12	52	26	19	60	39	*NA*	*NA*	*NA*	*NA*
El Salvador	77	126	32	25	82	71	*NA*	*NA*	*NA*	*NA*
Guatemala	35	66	36	27	79	61	*NA*	*NA*	*NA*	*NA*
Haiti	28	77	30	24	68	47	3.36	1.68	62.7	478
Honduras	17	35	37	25	71	49	*NA*	*NA*	*NA*	*NA*
Hong Kong	17	39	26	3	57	24	*NA*	*NA*	*NA*	*NA*
India	45	130	10	3	42	18	*NA*	*NA*	*NA*	*NA*
Jamaica	40	92	18	14	39	25	3.49	1.70	74.2	155
Japan	32	68	11	6	14	12	*NA*	*NA*	*NA*	*NA*
Korea	67	163	20	9	49	27	*NA*	*NA*	*NA*	*NA*
Laos	49	64	51	50	78	79	3.07	1.59	72.1	155
Mexico	643	1,975	44	32	83	64	3.17	1.68	64.9	757
Nicaragua	39	35	36	18	84	57	3.37	1.68	51.2	344
Philippines	83	316	9	4	58	33	3.25	1.68	63.5	818
Taiwan	32	65	19	7	34	19	*NA*	*NA*	*NA*	*NA*
Thailand	36	33	59	5	79	16	*NA*	*NA*	*NA*	*NA*
Vietnam	99	33	42	23	67	50	3.10	1.69	67.2	371

Sources: Hernandez and Charney 1998: Table B-2A, p. 236, and Table B-2B, p. 246; Rumbaut 1996: Table 7.3, p. 140.

Cubans fare better. The CES-D (Center for Epidemiological Studies—Depression) subscale measures depression and also ranges from 1 to 4, with higher values reflecting higher levels of depression. Variations are very small, ranging from 1.59 for the Lao immigrants to 1.70 for the Jamaicans. It should be noted that self-esteem and depression are not different sides of the same coin, and hence the results for Jamaicans do not contradict one another. The findings on discrimination reveal significant variability between groups: 74.2 percent of Jamaicans (the group with the highest level of depression) had been discriminated against, compared with 38.1 percent of Cubans and 45.3 percent of Colombians—two groups that scored high on the Rosenberg self-esteem scale.

LIKELY WINNERS AND LOSERS

Given the diversity of origins of the children of the post-1965 immigrants and the relative recentness of their arrival, it is not surprising that group-by-group incorporation scenarios are currently open to speculation. All that can be said for now is that some groups, notably Thais, Koreans, and Japanese, appear to be adjusting more quickly than others, in particular Mexicans, Nicaraguans, Lao, and Cambodians. Parental origins remain important in shaping adjustment patterns but are less crucial determinants of success and failure than was previously thought. It is anticipated that the data from the 2000 U.S. census will offer the prospect of even more vigorous social, economic, and geographic analyses, since a greater number of the second generation will have reached adulthood by this stage. More urgent, though, is the need to examine processes of adjustment and adaptation as they occur, instead of guessing at the mechanics of incorporation by looking solely at outcomes. It is only via this approach that policies can be developed that will effectively assist the most vulnerable groups. It is hoped, then, that more projects in the style and spirit of the 1992 southern California/south Florida survey will emerge over the coming decade.

Martin D. Smith

See also: Adoption (Part II, Sec. 2); Family (Part II, Sec. 4); Public Schools (Part II, Sec. 9); Amerasian Children Act, 1997, *Lau v. Nichols,* 1974, *Plyler v. Doe,* 1982, California Proposition 63, 1986 (Part IV, Sec. 1); New York State Report on Multicultural Textbooks, 1991 (Part IV, Sec. 2).

BIBLIOGRAPHY

Ballard, Roger, ed. *Desh Pardesh: The South Asian Presence in Britain.* London: Hurst and Company, 1994.

Fernández-Kelly, María Patricia, and Richard Schauffler. "Divided Fates: Immigrant Children in a Restructured U.S. Economy." *International Migration Review* 28 (1994): 662–89.

Gans, Herbert J. "Second-Generation Decline: Scenarios for the Economic and Ethnic Futures of the Post-1965 American Immigrants." *Ethnic and Racial Studies* 15 (1992): 173–92.

Hernandez, Donald J., and Evan Charney, eds. *From Generation to Generation: The Health and Well-Being of Children in Immigrant Families.* Washington, DC: National Academy Press, 1998.

Hirschman, Charles. "Studying Immigrant Adaptation from the 1990 Population Census: From Generational Comparisons to the Process of 'Becoming American.' " In *The New Second Generation,* ed. Alejandro Portes, pp. 54–81. New York: Russell Sage Foundation, 1996.

Massey, Douglas. "American Apartheid: Segregation and the Making of the Underclass." *American Journal of Sociology* 96:2 (1990): 329–57.

Portes, Alejandro, ed. *The New Second Generation.* New York: Russell Sage Foundation, 1996.

Portes, Alejandro, and Rubén G. Rumbaut. *Immigrant America—A Portrait.* 2d ed. Berkeley: University of California Press, 1996.

Roberts, Bryan R. "Socially Expected Durations and the Economic Adjustment of Immigrants." In *The Economic Sociology of Immigration: Essays on Networks, Ethnicity, and Entrepreneurship,* ed. Alejandro Portes, pp. 42–86. New York: Russell Sage Foundation, 1995.

Rosenberg, Morris. *Society and the Adolescent Self-Image.* Princeton, NJ: Princeton University Press, 1965.

Rumbaut, Rubén G. "The Crucible Within: Ethnic Identity, Self-Esteem, and Segmented Assimilation Among Children of Immigrants." In *The New Second Generation,* ed. Alejandro Portes, pp. 119–70. New York: Russell Sage Foundation, 1996.

Zhou, Min. "Growing Up American: The Challenge Confronting Immigrant Children and Children of Immigrants." *Annual Review of Sociology* 23 (1997): 63–95.

ELDERLY

Elderly immigrants represent the fastest-growing segment of the American population. This growth is due to several mutually reinforcing demographic trends: the overall aging of the American population, including immigrants, a result of better medicine and healthier lifestyles; the explosive growth of the immigrant population generally; and the slightly higher percentages of older people among immigrants. Approximately 13 percent of all immigrants in the 1990s were 65 and over; among native-born Americans, the percentage of seniors is 12 percent. Of course, immigrant ages vary widely among different groups. For example, the median age of immigrants from El Salvador, Mexico, and Vietnam is just thirty years old, while the median for immigrants from most European countries is well over fifty, including a record fifty-nine for Italians. Overall, however, the Asian elderly—along with the white elderly—were the fastest-growing segment of the American population in the 1990s, a trend that is expected to continue in the next decade.

ELDERLY AND THE IMMIGRANT FAMILY

Most elderly immigrants come to the United States for one simple reason: they want to remain close to their family—some for reasons of affection, others for fear of being left without any financial support in their homeland, and most, undoubtedly, for a combination of the two. According to several sociologists, the Hong Kong elderly were frightened of moving to America because they worried about separation from their children there, financial problems, and ending up in nursing homes. The family connection has deep roots in many cultures from which the immigrants come. The Confucian tradition that is central to Chinese culture, for example, emphasizes human rela-

tions as the key to the smooth running of families, communities, and nations. Confucian philosophy includes the Five Cardinal Relationships, which dictate the terms of the relationship between human beings, both within families and societies. In all these relationships, there is a hierarchy that is based on age, giving the elder member of the relationship certain authority and privilege. Within the family, the father is the highest authority, and respect must be paid to him.

According to the psychologist K. K. Hwang, social interactions within Chinese culture are based on four concepts: *guanxi* (relationships), *renqing* (kindness), *mianzi* (face, or dignity), and *bao* (reciprocation of favors). Guanxi is the critical element for understanding Chinese family life, says Hwang, and it dictates that children support their parents when their parents can no longer support themselves. Of course, to support a parent requires being able to support oneself first. Here, too, filial respect comes into play in many Asian immigrant cultures, both among the Chinese and those—as in Korea and Japan—that have been influenced over the centuries by Chinese culture. Filial respect means achieving a career and a financial status that brings respect to the parents and the family. This, say many scholars, is a major factor behind the extraordinary educational and career successes of many Asian immigrants. Thus, in the end, filial duty contributes to the capacity for taking care of elderly parents as well as imposing the requirement to do so.

Not surprisingly, then, many Asian elderly follow their children to America because they believe they will be properly taken care of. And they are generally not mistaken in this belief. A study of Korean- and Anglo-American families conducted by the sociologist T. K. Sung in the early 1990s found that while both groups cited obligation, affection, and reciprocity as important family values, the Koreans emphasized respect for parents, family harmony, and filial sacrifice as the critical motivation behind these values. In addition, elderly immigrants follow their family to

When elderly immigrants, like this Sikh man from India, have a difficult time adjusting to a new culture and a new language, they often find themselves isolated and, if lacking a supportive family, impoverished as well. *(Rommel Pecson/Impact Visuals)*

Table 1
Elderly Asian and Pacific Islander Immigrants in 1995

Group	Percentage of Group 65 and Over
Mainland Chinese	13.6
All Chinese[a]	8.1
Japanese	12.5
Filipino	7.4
Korean	4.4
Samoan	3.3
Asian Indian	2.8
Vietnamese	2.8
Hmong	2.8
Cambodian	2.5
Laotian	2.5
Thai	1.6
Total Asian/Pacific Islander	6.2
Total U.S. population	12.5

Source: Bureau of the Census, *Statistical Abstract of the United States, 1996*. Washington, DC: Bureau of the Census, 1996.
[a] Hong Kong, Taiwan, and Southeast Asia.

panics are more likely to live in the same communities as their children than are white Americans and less likely to be institutionalized. In general, it is safe to say that Hispanics are less willing to turn to support outside of their families when they are older. Still, a number of trends are leading to the disruption of traditional extended families among immigrant Latino populations. For example, as younger members of the family move up the socioeconomic ladder, they often tend to look for better housing in the suburbs, leaving elderly parents and grandparents isolated in the urban barrios.

Table 2
Elderly Latino Immigrants in 1990

Group	Percentage of Group 65 and Over
Cuban Americans	14.8
Puerto Ricans	4.7
Mexicans	4.4
Central and South Americans	3.0
Total Latinos	5.1
Total U.S. population	12.1

Source: Bureau of the Census, *Statistical Abstract of the United States, 1992*. Washington, DC: Bureau of the Census, 1992.

America for more than just financial support. Because of the centrality of family to one's identity and one's social life, older adults often prefer not to stay behind even if they have the monetary wherewithal to do so, for by being removed from their family they are removed from a web of relationships that gives their life meaning.

In Latino families, of course, there is no Confucian philosophy, but there is a tradition of strong extended families that bring into one grouping—if not under one roof—many disparate relatives, including grandparents (known affectionately as *abuelitos*). Roughly 15 percent of Hispanics age sixty-five to seventy-four live with their children, while nearly 25 percent of those over seventy-five do so. Moreover, elderly His-

Of course, in both Latino and Asian cultures, there is evidence of a growing trend of intergenerational conflict between the younger, Americanized members of families and the older members who remain rooted in their traditional cultures and ways of thinking. Several components exist to this disjunction of cultures. First, the nuclear family is the norm within American culture, and the degree to which social norms influence either first-generation immigrant children raised in America or second-generation children born here is the degree to which older ideals of filial duty wither. Individualism is also the central ideology of American life, and this runs counter to the ideals of guanxi, in Chinese and Chinese-influenced cultures and to family loyalty within Hispanic cultures.

In many respects, American culture tends to place an emphasis on youth and the young, often de-emphasizing and degrading the value of the elderly, which surely affects both older adults—in not asking for as much from their offspring—and the children who imbibe that youth-oriented message. And, of course, unable to speak English or barely capable of understanding the way society operates in America, the elderly are less in a position to advise younger members of the family, a situation that undermines the ideal of wisdom that is at the core of Confucian philosophical ideas about respect for the older persons within the family.

Finally, there are more substantial financial and career considerations. The American economy is geared to dynamic geographic mobility, which tends to undermine communities and make it difficult to keep families together. In addition, family connections are often far less important in America in getting into schools and good-paying jobs than they are in the immigrants' homeland, thereby undermining the value of the family and parents. Finally, young people in America have far greater opportunities to support themselves and to find alternative living arrangements—dorms, roommates, and the like—all of which undermines the dependence young people feel on their parents. And with young people feeling less dependent in their most vulnerable early years of adulthood, they are less likely to support their parents in the latter's most vulnerable years of seniority.

ECONOMIC, HEALTH, AND SOCIAL PROBLEMS

Despite a higher likelihood than native-born Americans of being taken care of by their children finan-cially and being supported psychologically by a family social support network, many older adult immigrants suffer from a number of economic, health, and psychological difficulties. First, there is the matter of finances. While Asian elderly have incomes comparable with white elderly (in 1990, roughly $14,000 and $14,900, respectively), this was an average, meaning that over half lived below this relatively low income level. Of course, there is great variety among different Asian groups, with Chinese and Vietnamese elderly most likely to be living in poverty.

In general, several factors contribute to financial problems among the elderly immigrant population. One is that many have never been part of the legitimate U.S. workforce—or at least not for long—and are therefore less entitled to Social Security and other benefits that accrue to the older adults. Furthermore, most elderly immigrants did not develop the skills in English to find the good-paying jobs and careers that would have provided them with the savings to pay for an easy retirement, and indeed many elderly immigrants are forced to continue in low-paying jobs long after native-born Americans retire. A frequent sight on urban streets are elderly immigrants picking through garbage and recycling bins for cans and bottles that can be redeemed at local groceries. In 1996, approximately 30 percent of Hispanic elderly over the age of sixty-five relied on Medicaid, the federal health insurance for poor Americans. Adding to the problem of impoverishment is the reluctance of many elderly immigrants—and particularly the Asian elderly—to take advantage of social services that may be available to them. Language barriers, lack of information, and past discrimination have kept many Chinese, Japanese, and Filipino elderly from seeking various public services, according to S. M. Fujii.

Health problems face many elderly persons, but they differ considerably between various ethnic groups. Life expectancy is one example. According to the Bureau of the Census, both Hispanics and Asians age sixty-five could expect to live longer than the same group of whites, with Asians outpacing both. This anomaly—an anomaly, given the fact that Hispanic and Asian elderly tended to be poorer than white elderly—can be partially explained by the lower stress of having better social and familial networks.

According to the sociologist Monit Cheung, elderly Chinese are more likely to maintain—through a close-knit peer group of friends—values and customs from their youth than are white elderly. In addition, most belong to many cultural associations. These many connections allow them to avoid the stress of isolation that contributes to health problems among

Table 3
Predicted Life Expectancy of 65-Year-Olds in 1995

Ethnic Group	Male	Female
Asian	83.9	88.0
Hispanic	83.9	87.2
Non-Hispanic White	80.9	84.5

Source: Bureau of the Census, *Current Population Reports,* no. P25–1130. Washington, DC: Bureau of the Census, 1996.

the elderly. Moreover, many Chinese continue to seek out alternative health remedies from Chinese health specialists, a familiar, comforting, and perhaps efficacious set of health practices that lower stress levels. Other scholars have found that elderly Chinese had higher levels of social competence—within the confines of their ethnic community—than did whites, thereby further contributing to lower stress levels and better health.

Latino elderly also frequently enjoyed better community and social support than their Anglo counterparts. Senior citizens of Latino background are generally more likely to attend community center groups geared to their age. And while at these community centers, many Hispanic elderly are put in touch with health information and health care professionals. In addition, there is the familiar relationship between lowered stress levels and better health. By sustaining close social relationships with peers, Hispanic elderly experience less of the stress associated with isolation among older adults.

Still, many elderly immigrants face severe problems of isolation and the psychological and somatic problems associated with isolation. Studies of Chinese elderly in Los Angeles have revealed large numbers of persons living in isolation, with little or no contact with their families. Many lived in impoverished conditions and had little access to social activities. In addition, they were often reticent to seek out aid from the government or nonprofit groups, seeing it as charity and therefore shameful after a lifetime of hard work and economic self-sufficiency. While this attitude is less prevalent among Hispanic elderly, language problems often make it difficult for this group to find means to break out of their social and psychological isolation. Perhaps the elderly group most affected by this problem, however, are Southeast Asian refugees. Having been forced to leave jobs and careers behind abruptly, many have had a hard time adjusting to their new homeland, especially because many were cut off from their family during the process of emergency relocation in the mid-1970s that occurred in the wake of the Vietnam War.

In general, the majority of elderly immigrants enjoy a relatively healthful, comfortable, and socially fulfilling life in their new U.S. home. Traditions of filial respect and extended family support run deep in most Hispanic and Asian cultures, making care of the elderly both an obligation and a duty for adult children. In addition, many elderly immigrants find social fulfillment through the many peer groups in their ethnic enclaves. Overall, elderly immigrants experience less social stress than their white counterparts, a factor that helps explain greater life expectancies, despite having fewer financial means. Still, problems exist for elderly immigrants. Those who do not have family often live in poverty. Lacking a work track record in the United States, many are not eligible for Social Security and other programs designed to help the elderly. Finally, many elderly immigrants, shackled by a lack of familiarity with U.S. customs and with the English language, cannot take full advantage of those programs which are available to them.

Patricia Cedeño-Zamor

See also: Sponsorship (Part II, Sec. 2); Health Care, Social Services (Part II, Sec. 9).

BIBLIOGRAPHY

Bacerra, Rosina. "The Mexican-American: Aging in a Changing Culture." In *Aging in Minority Groups,* ed. R. L. McNeely and J. N. Colen. Beverly Hills, CA: Sage Publications, 1983.

Cheung, Monit. "Elderly Chinese Living in the United States: Assimilation or Adjustment." *Social Work* 34 (1989): 457–61.

Fujii, S. M. "Older Asian Americans: Victims of Multiple Jeopardy." *Civil Rights Digest* (Fall 1976): 22–29.

Hwang, K. K. "The Dynamic Processes of Coping with Interpersonal Conflicts in a Chinese Society." *Proceedings of the National Science Council* (Taiwan) 2 (1978): 198–208.

Mahara, R. "Elderly Puerto Rican Women in the Continental United States." In *The Psychosocial Development of Puerto Rican Women,* ed. Cynthia T. García Coll and María de Lourdes Mattei. New York: Praeger, 1989.

Sung, T. K. "Cross-Cultural Comparison of Motivations for Parent Care: Americans and Koreans." *Journal of Aging Studies* 8 (1994): 195–209.

Torres-Gil, Fernando M. *Politics of Aging Among Elder Hispanics.* Washington, DC: University Press of America, 1982.

ETHNIC INTERMARRIAGE

The United States has earned the title of "melting pot" partly because of the high instance of intermarriage, or the marriage or legal partnership of two people from different racial or ethnic groups. Ethnic intermarriage is a central indicator of interethnic group relations. It is a reflection of the social distance between groups and of the extent to which a group has become incorporated into a host society. Furthermore, patterns of intermarriage indicate the extent to which groups are generally open to social interaction with one another, as well as the extent to which groups actually do interact.

It is important to clarify what is meant by "racial" and "ethnic" categories. The Bureau of the Census considers White, Black (African American), Asian, and Other to be racial categories, whereas Hispanic is treated as an ethnic category. There is no consensus, however, about which groups of people should be classified as a racial group and which should be called an ethnic group. These distinctions are often arbitrary, as various organizations, scholars, and popular media have divided groups into "racial" and "ethnic" categories in myriad ways. For purposes of simplification and clarity, reference to any combination of marriages between whites, African Americans, Asians, and Hispanics in this entry will be called an *ethnic* intermarriage.

SIGNIFICANCE OF INTERMARRIAGE

Intermarriage is thought to be an indication of a minority group's incorporation into a host society. Large-scale ethnic intermarriage signals the incorporation of a minority group into the most fundamental institutions and structures of the host society. Intermarriage also influences the quality of social relations between ethnic groups. Once intermarriage takes place, individuals often lose negative feelings that they may have for other ethnic groups. Furthermore, intermarriage decreases the salience of cultural distinctions in the children of intermarried couples, since these children are less likely to identify strongly with one group. In sum, says Matthijs Kalmijn, "what makes intermarriage sociologically relevant lies in its inherent dynamic: It is not just a reflection of the boundaries that currently separate groups in society, it also bears the potential of cultural and socioeconomic change."

FACTORS FOR ETHNIC INTERMARRIAGE: PREFERENCE FOR CERTAIN PARTNERS

Research has highlighted three factors that account for intermarriage: preference for certain partners, social group influences, and the availability of marriage partners. Ethnic intermarriage often takes place because individuals have a preference for partners who embody certain characteristics. One such characteristic that attracts members of different ethnic groups to one another is status. Some observers point out that ethnic minorities may exchange their monetary and educational status for their partner's higher social status.

Preference for certain partners also depends on the cultural characteristics that may attract partners to one another. Similar customs, attitudes, values, norms, religious practices, and language that are associated with cultural backgrounds facilitate attraction between partners. For example, people of European ancestry tend to intermarry across ethnic lines more often when their spouse is of the same religious background.

SOCIAL GROUP INFLUENCE

The extent to which members of an ethnic group intermarry also depends on influence of social groups. One such social group influence is the feeling of attachment to one's own ethnic ancestry. When members of an ethnic group have a strong affinity for their ethnic background, or strong sense of "peoplehood," they may be more likely to seek partners from the same ethnic group.

Choice of marriage partners is not entirely a function of free choice, however. Individuals may also be constrained in their choice of partners by sanctions imposed by the social groups. Sanctions may stem from the norms and attitudes associated with marrying members of certain other groups. Prejudicial attitudes, stereotypes, and discrimination toward some groups may discourage intermarriage. To illustrate, it is not surprising that marriages between African Americans and whites are relatively uncommon, given the history of prejudice and discrimination that African Americans have experienced. However, as whites' attitudes have become more liberal with respect to interethnic relations, the instance of intermarriage between whites and African Americans has increased.

There are also formal sanctions on intermarriage that have historically impeded unions between members of different ethnic backgrounds. Antimiscegenation laws—laws prohibiting marriage between whites and members of another race—were on the books for years in the South and other parts of the United States. In 1967, the Supreme Court ruled that state statutes prohibiting intermarriage were unconstitutional. At the time of the 1967 Supreme Court decision, nineteen states still had antimiscegenation laws in effect, posing a major impediment to interethnic unions.

AVAILABILITY OF MARRIAGE PARTNERS

The frequency of ethnic intermarriages also depends on the extent to which individuals have the opportunity to meet potential partners. One factor that influences such opportunities is the probability of contact between groups. Members of smaller ethnic groups may be more likely to intermarry with members of larger ethnic groups simply because there are more members of the larger ethnic groups that one

can potentially meet. Likewise, members of larger ethnic groups will intermarry less, because there are more opportunities to have social contact with members of their own ethnic group.

A second factor that influences opportunities for social contact between ethnic groups is the geographic dispersion, or heterogeneity, of ethnic groups. Greater ethnic heterogeneity increases the likelihood that members of different ethnic groups will meet. Thus, when an ethnic group is dispersed heterogeneously throughout a population, that group will tend to intermarry more often. Conversely, when an ethnic group is distributed homogeneously in a population, that group will tend to intermarry less. African Americans represent a prime example of the latter case. The degree of spatial isolation that African Americans have experienced is unparalleled by any other racial or ethnic group in the United States. As a consequence, African Americans have had fewer opportunities for social contact with other ethnic groups. Thus, spatial isolation, or geographic homogeneity, has impeded intermarriage between African Americans and other ethnic groups.

A final structural factor influencing ethnic intermarriage is status. The degree of status distinctions between groups influences the extent to which different ethnic groups have social contact in venues where people of similar status interact, such as the neighborhood, schools, and work. With greater opportunity for social contact, there is an increase in the likelihood of ethnic intermarriage.

In sum, ethnic intermarriage depends on a combination of individual preferences, normative and formal sanctions, as well as the availability of marriage partners. No single factor can account entirely for intermarriage among certain ethnic groups. Rather, it is a combination of these factors that influences the extent to which ethnic groups intermarry.

TRENDS IN ETHNIC INTERMARRIAGE

It is important to note that data on ethnic intermarriage indicate the prevalence of intermarriage, or the number of intermarried couples at the time the data were collected. Thus, the data provide no information on the incidence of intermarriage or the total number of intermarriages that ever take place.

Historically, the very definition of ethnic intermarriage has changed. For much of American history, intermarriage between identity groups usually meant intermarriage between persons of differing religious backgrounds. Racial intermixing was viewed as so taboo until the post–World War II era that it was not even considered in discussions of identity intermarriage. In the colonial era, religious intermarriage could even mean marriage between persons of differing Protestant backgrounds, particularly if one of the partners was a member of a minority sect or one considered to be radical by mainstream Protestants, such as Quakers. There was also a certain taboo against intermarriage between members of so-called high (Anglican or Episcopalian) and low (Baptist, Methodist) churches.

With its emphasis on religious freedom and a nonsectarian civic order, intermarriage between various Protestant sects increased, even as the taboo against it faded. What remained, however, were strong feelings against intermarriage between Protestants and Catholics. This was especially the case after the great wave of poor Irish immigration in the mid-nineteenth century and the corresponding reaction against it by Protestant Americans. This taboo against Protestant–Catholic intermarriage persisted through much of the nineteenth and early twentieth centuries. However, ethnic intermixing in the immigrant neighborhoods of the great Northern and Midwestern cities—as well as the subsequent move by second- and third-generation white ethnic immigrants to the suburbs in the post–World War II era—tended to diminish the hostility toward Protestant–Catholic intermarriage. To a lesser extent, the same process applied to Christian–Jewish intermarriage in the postwar era, although taboos continue here, but more because minority Jews fear the loss of heritage implied by marriage to non-Jews.

Over the past few decades, as hostility toward intermarriage between religious groups has faded, the question of identity-group intermarriage has focused on ethnic and racial intermarriage. Even here, however, the numbers show an unmistakable trend toward more intermarriage, as the overall rate in the United States has risen for nearly all ethnic groups over the past forty years. In 1960, .37 percent of all married couples were interethnic. That figure rose to .7 percent and 1.92 percent in 1970 and 1980, respectively. By 1990 the number of interethnic couples had climbed to more than 1.6 million, constituting 4 percent of all married couples. Most intermarriages are between whites and nonwhites, as interethnic marriages in the United States seldom involve members of two nonwhite groups.

Consistent with trends in intermarriage in general, the intermarriage rate for whites has climbed steadily. In 1960, only .35 percent of marriages were between a white and a nonwhite. That figure grew to .67 per-

cent in 1970 and to 1.83 percent in 1980. By 1990, 2.67 percent of all marriages were between a white and a nonwhite. Similarly, the number of African-American intermarriages has steadily increased. In 1960, .15 percent of all marriages were between an African American and a non-African American; by 1990, these unions constituted .56 percent of all marriages. Intermarriage rates for Asians have grown slightly more compared to African Americans and slightly less compared to whites. In 1960, .14 percent of marriages were between an Asian and a non-Asian. By 1990, 1.02 percent of all marriages were between an Asian and a non-Asian. Hispanics, or Spanish-origin groups, have shown the most dramatic increase in intermarriage. In 1970, Spanish-origin/non-Spanish-origin marriages made up 1.31 percent of all marriages. The number of Spanish-origin intermarriages nearly tripled between 1970 and 1990, making up 2.55 percent of all marriages in 1990.

Although marriages across ethnic groups have increased, the overwhelming majority of marriages are between members of the same racial or ethnic group. In 1992, 95 percent of all marriages were between members of the same ethnic group. Among all ethnic groups, whites and African Americans are more likely than other groups to marry members of the same group. In 1990, 94 percent of all African-American couples were same-ethnicity couples and 93 percent of all white couples were same-ethnicity. Asians and Hispanics, on the other hand, marry members of the same ethnic group with slightly less frequency. Seventy percent of all Asian couples and 70 percent of all Hispanic couples were same-ethnic group couples in 1990.

Although the racial and ethnic divide remains fairly rigid with respect to intermarriage, men and women do not experience this divide equally. In particular, gender differences among African Americans are quite striking. In 1998 there were nearly twice as many couples in which the male partner was African American and the female partner was white than couples in which the female partner was African American and the male partner was white (210,000 compared to 120,000). Asians also show a marked difference between men and women: 52,000 couples involved an Asian/Pacific Islander male and a white female in 1980, compared to 181,000 couples in which the male was white and the female was Asian/Pacific Islander.

In sum, intermarriage rates have risen over time for nearly all racial and ethnic groups. However, an overwhelming majority of unions are between members of the same racial or ethnic group, indicating that racial and ethnic barriers remain fairly rigid where intermarriage is concerned. This divide is most clear among whites and African Americans and slightly less pronounced among Asian and Hispanic groups. With respect to gender, African-American men intermarry much more often than their female counterparts. Among Asian Americans, women intermarry far more often than do men.

INTERMARRIAGE AND THE FUTURE OF ETHNICITY

What is the influence of intermarriage on ethnicity? The hypothesis that mass-scale intermarriage weakens a strong sense of ethnic identity has largely held true, especially for descendents of European immigrants. Many whites now trace their ethnic roots to multiple sources. For those who do have multiple ethnic roots, there is generally a symbolic or superficial attachment to any particular group, and ethnic identity is often a matter of choice.

The trajectory of ethnicity for immigrants who have come to the United States in the last thirty years may be different from that of earlier European immigrants for a number of reasons. First, many of these immigrants have darker skin, making them more visibly distinct. Second, immigration from major sending regions, particularly Latin America and Asia, is ongoing. Third, the more recent immigrants enter an economy in which there are diminishing prospects for mobility for those who are unskilled, as are most of the recent immigrants.

As a result of these differences, intermarriage patterns and the fate of ethnicity for more recent immigrants may differ from that of European ethnic groups. The low skills that many of the newer immigrants bring to the U.S. economy may hinder upward social mobility and thus lessen the extent to which immigrants interact and intermarry with the native population. Also, the increase in the number of immigrants increases the probability of in-group marriages among immigrants as well as between native coethnics and immigrants. Additionally, perpetual immigration maintains and rejuvenates culturally distinct ethnic markers, such as language, among both immigrants and coethnic natives. Finally, the racial distinctiveness of more recent immigrant groups may influence the way in which immigrants and the children of immigrants incorporate into the native population. For example, Caribbean and West Indian immigrants may be perceived by the native population as African Americans because of their dark skin. Thus, prejudices against African Americans are

transferred to these immigrants and their children, and barriers between with these immigrant groups and other ethnic groups remain. Combined, these mitigating factors suggest that intermarriage rates may remain low and that ethnic distinctions will endure.

However, similar speculations were made about European immigrants at the beginning of the twentieth century. These immigrants were thought to be unassimilable because of their racial distinctiveness and strong ties to their ethnic group, but their eventual full assimilation into American social, political, and economic life and their high rates of intermarriage proved otherwise. In fact, the extent to which European-ancestry groups assimilated into American society has led some to proclaim an "ethnic miracle." There are some indications that the more recent immigrant groups and their descendents may be on the way to an "ethnic miracle" of their own. According to a recent Gallup Poll, 47 percent of white teens, 60 percent of African-American teens, and 90 percent of Latino teens said that they had dated someone of another race. Additionally, recall that intermarriage rates have shown an increase in the last forty years. While one can only speculate, these figures suggest that a second "ethnic miracle" may indeed be on the horizon.

Tomás Jiménez

See also: Marriage Market, Sponsorship (Part II, Sec. 2); Family, Gender (Part II, Sec. 4).

BIBLIOGRAPHY

Alba, Richard D. *Ethnic Identity: The Transformation of White America.* New Haven, CT: Yale University Press, 1990.

Blau, Peter M. *Inequality and Heterogeneity.* New York: The Free Press, 1979.

Bureau of the Census. *Subject Reports on Marital Status and Living Arrangements,* 1960, 1970, and 1980.

———. *Current Population Reports,* P20, nos. 461 and 468, 1991 and 1992.

———. "Marital Status and Living Arrangements: March 1998 (update)," in *Current Populations Reports,* Series 20: 514, 1998.

Davis, James F. *Who Is Black: One Nation's Definition.* University Park, PA: Pennsylvania State University Press, 1991.

Gans, Herbert. "Symbolic Ethnicity: The Future of Ethnic Groups in America." *Ethnic and Racial Studies* 2 (January 1979): 1–20.

Gordon, Milton. *Assimilation in American Life: The Role of Race, Religion and National Origins.* New York: Oxford University Press, 1964.

Greeley, Andrew. *Ethnicity, Denomination, and Inequality.* Beverly Hills, CA: Sage, 1976.

Harrison, Roderick J., and Claudette Bennett. "Racial and Ethnic Diversity." In *State of the Union: America in the 1990s. Volume Two: Social Trends,* ed. Reynolds Farley, pp. 141–210. New York: Russell Sage Foundation, 1995.

"How Times Have Changed." *Chicago Sun-Times,* February 28, 1999, 17.

Kalmijn, Matthijs. "Intermarriage and Homogamy: Causes, Patterns, and Trends." *Annual Review of Sociology* 24 (1998): 395–421.

Lieberson, Stanley, and Mary C. Waters. *From Many Strands: Ethnic and Racial Groups in Contemporary America.* New York: Russell Sage Foundation, 1988.

Massey, Douglas S., and Nancy A. Denton. *American Apartheid: Segregation and the Making of the Underclass.* Cambridge, MA: Harvard University Press, 1993.

Merton, Robert K. "Intermarriage and Social Structure: Fact and Theory." *Psychiatry* 4 (1941): 361–74.

Schumann, Howard, Charlotte Steeh, Lawrence Bobo, and Maria Krysan. *Racial Attitudes in America: Trends and Interpretations,* rev. ed. Cambridge, MA: Harvard University Press, 1997.

Waters, Mary C. *Ethnic Options: Choosing Identities in America.* Berkeley: University of California Press, 1990.

———. "Ethnic and Racial Identities of Second-Generation Black Immigrants in New York City." *International Migration Review* 28 (1994): 795–820.

FAMILY

No institution is more central to the immigrant experience than the family, as it plays a critical role in every facet of the immigration process, from the decision to make the journey through the ultimate assimilation—or acculturation—into American society. Once considered an archaic vestige from the Old Country that hampered the newcomer's ability to adjust to American culture and society, the traditional immigrant family—with its extended relations and many internal obligations—is now widely viewed by sociologists as perhaps the most important mechanism by which immigrants establish themselves in their new homeland.

FAMILIES AND RELAY IMMIGRATION

The critical nature of the family begins with the process of immigration itself. Many immigrant families—both historically and today—move to America in stages, through a process known as "relay" or "chain" immigration. By this process, one member of the family makes his or her way to America, establishes a household, achieves some kind of economic stability, and then sends for further members of the family. This was common among Italian immigrants at the beginning of the twentieth century and has been a feature familiar to Asian immigrants at the end of the twentieth century.

Traditionally, relay immigration began with an adult male, often the father of the family. More recently, however, the order has often been reversed, particularly among middle-class immigrants from such East Asian countries as Taiwan and the Philippines. A common pattern now is for the wife and children to go on ahead, establishing residency and schooling for the children, while the husband stays behind and continues to work, occasionally visiting his family in the United States, before making the final

move himself. Another new pattern of relay immigration involves sending elder children, particularly boys, to America. They are enrolled first in university until they graduate and get a job. Once they have established themselves economically in America, they send for their parents and their younger siblings.

For Hispanic and Caribbean immigrants, who often have fewer economic resources than most Asian immigrants, more traditional patterns persist. The tendency among these groups is for the husband and father to go on ahead and establish an economic foothold in the United States before sending for his wife and family. This process is aided by the geographic proximity between the United States and the immigrant's native country. Fathers can often go back and visit, thereby lessening the emotional strains of separation.

Regardless of the shape relay immigration takes, the process has been aided over the past few decades by changes in American law. The landmark Immigration and Nationality Act of 1965 ended the old national quotas established in the 1920s, replacing them with an emphasis on family reunion. Relay immigration not only becomes possible but is actually encouraged by this law that places those with family already in the United States at the front of the immigration queue.

MARRIAGE AND GENDER ISSUES

While somewhat diminishing as a cultural custom—particularly among the urban and more Westernized segments of the population—arranged marriages remain the norm in most Asian cultures and among many Asian immigrant communities. While young people—especially those more fully acculturated to life in the United States—may reject the principle of arranged marriage, they often lack an alternative. Few

Asian cultures offer a tradition of dating and courtship, and so even more Westernized young persons may feel at a loss about how to proceed in finding a mate of their own. Moreover, given the traditionally strong obligations to family, many Asian immigrants of marriageable age may not feel comfortable resisting arrangements made by their parents. Most Hispanic and Caribbean immigrants, however, do not come from cultures where arranged marriages prevail and this adjustment to the dating and courting style typical in the United States is less alien to them.

Still, regardless of the means by which partners are found, immigrant marriages—particularly among those less acculturated to U.S. social norms—tend to follow traditional patriarchal patterns, wherein the husband assumes ultimate authority over virtually all decision making concerning the couple and eventually their family. The traditional Hispanic family, for instance, was essentially patriarchal, in which the husband and father took on the macho persona of virility, strength, authority, and self-reliance. Fathers were supposed to be authority figures in the lives of their children, while mothers were supposed to be the loving nurturers.

This model, of course, was more often honored in the breach. Hispanic women have frequently been strong figures of authority in the household, particularly in the immigrant household where they have provided a major share—if not the majority share—of the family's economic well-being. At the same time, there has been a marked change in the behavior of many Hispanic fathers in recent years whereby they establish more emotional and loving relationships with children.

Equally significant to the changing gender roles within Hispanic families has been the rise of female-headed households, particularly among Puerto Ricans and Dominicans in New York. With the husband out of the picture, the mother is required to take on both the traditional authoritarian role of the male and the loving and nurturing role of the female. As of 1995, approximately 30 percent of all Hispanic children in America were living in households headed by a mother only.

While Asian cultures vary greatly from country to country, there are a few patterns that run throughout. Like many Hispanic societies, Asians also tend to emphasize patriarchal families. Confucianism—the central philosophy of traditional Chinese society (and adapted in various ways to Japanese, Korean, and Vietnamese cultures as well)—is premised on the idea that a well-functioning family, like a well-functioning society, is one in which every member knows his or her place and role. As far as marriage was concerned,

the male's role was the dominant one, and women were expected to follow their husband's lead in all decisions.

Of course, under Communist rule, old Confucian ideas were combated, and Chinese revolutionary leader Mao Zedong—with his adage that "women hold up half the sky"—emphasized equality of the sexes. Meanwhile, though Confucianism does not hold sway in other Asian cultures—such as those from the subcontinent of India or the Middle East—a similar view of marriage relations predominates among immigrants from those regions as well. Both Hindu and Muslim scripture prescribes a clearly subordinate role for wives within a marriage.

Still, both the move to and life in America has a tendency to wear down such traditional relationships. Removing people from the cultural milieu in which they grow up tends to undermine traditional rules, a process exacerbated by being exposed to the relatively liberal norms of American marital relations. In addition, there is the matter of economic survival. To survive economically in the new country, both husband and wife are required to work outside the home. This working role for women often enhances their sense of independence, as well as their stature within the marriage relationship. And among Asian immigrants, for example, the workforce participation rate is relatively high, with approximately 60 percent holding jobs outside the home in the 1990s, slightly higher than the rate among non-Asian women.

TYPES OF FAMILIES AND FAMILY RELATIONS

Unlike the nuclear family typical among native-born Americans, the immigrant family is often more complex and extended. Sometimes this implies various generations living under one roof. However, this pattern tends to disappear with growing urbanization, even in the home country and certainly once the family emigrates to the United States. More typical is a close-knit extended family living in several different households in close geographic proximity to one another. And even where the family is scattered across various cities and even countries, the sense of obligation that ties extended kin to one another applies to a stronger degree than is the case in nuclear-type American families.

In addition, many Hispanic immigrant families have relationships altogether different from those common in native-born American ones. There is, for example, the institution of *compadrazgo*, or godparenthood. While godparents exist in many cultures—including Italian-American homes—it is generally a stronger ideal in the Hispanic family. Essentially, compadrazgo involves a relationship between the parents of a child and close friends or even relatives, whereby the *compadre*, literally the coparent, takes on the obligation of helping to raise the child in event of the parent's death. But it is also more than that. A compadre will often contribute financially to the child's upbringing and education and will frequently spend a good deal of time with the child as she or he is growing up.

Another Hispanic family ideal is that of *parentesco*, or kinship sentiment. This is, in a sense, the bond that ties many disparate wings of an extended family together. Like compadrazgo, although without its formalities and rituals, it requires various uncles, aunts, grandparents, elder cousins to come together in the raising of children by different parents within the family. Thus, the son or daughter of one couple will essentially be viewed as the son or daughter of the entire extended family. Oftentimes, children from one couple will spend extended periods of time in the household of an uncle or an elder cousin. Parentesco, then, while common in Hispanic countries, is also a useful mechanism for immigration because the process of moving from one country to another often involves the temporary breakup of households and economic hardship. By spreading out the obligation to raise children among many different family members, the chance of raising the child in a loving and supportive home is increased.

ASIAN FAMILIES: A HISTORY

The history of Asian immigration to the United States begins with the Chinese, who began coming to the United States in large numbers after the discovery of gold in California in the mid–nineteenth century. At first, virtually no females came to this country. According to the 1890 census, less than a decade after the Chinese Exclusion Act made further immigration virtually impossible, there were twenty-seven male Chinese to every female Chinese. Under these conditions, the development of Chinese-American families was, for all intents and purposes, impossible. Moreover, intermarriage between Chinese men and non-Chinese women was made illegal by antimiscegenation laws in most states where there were significant Chinese populations.

Japanese and Koreans were the next large Asian group to immigrate to the United States (Korea was considered a part of Japan for immigration purposes and was indeed taken over as a colony by Tokyo in 1910); they began to come in significant numbers, mostly as agricultural workers, beginning around the turn of the twentieth century. Like the Chinese, most of these immigrants were male. But unlike the Chinese, they found a way—if only temporarily—to create families. The method was the picture bride. For a fee, agencies in the home countries would send brides—chosen by the male immigrants through the perusal of photographs—to America. While the fee was somewhat steep for a worker, it was doable with much financial sacrifice, and thus a nucleus of Japanese- and Korean-American households was formed in this period. However, even this avenue was closed off by the Gentlemen's Agreement of 1907, reached between the U.S. and the Japanese governments, which cut off almost all immigration from Japan.

Filipinos, as American colonial subjects, were therefore the only significant Asian group eligible to emigrate to this country in the first few decades of the twentieth century. Beginning with the 1900s, increasing numbers of Filipino males made their way to the agricultural regions of California. Although there were few females among them, Filipino males had the good fortune of coming from the only Catholic country in Asia, making intermarriage with Catholic Mexican women an option.

With World War II and the Korean and Vietnamese wars, many American servicemen met and became involved with Asian women. Under the War Brides Act of 1946, it became easier for these men to bring back these women as brides. Ultimately, tens of thousands of Japanese, Korean, and Vietnamese women immigrated to the United States as partners in interethnic marriages from the 1940s through the 1970s. Most of these women dispersed around the country to the various communities in which their husbands settled and were quickly acculturated into American life. This acculturation process was even more pronounced among their offspring, who had virtually no connection to their home culture, as they were unlikely to live in communities surrounded by people from their mother's ethnic background.

With the 1965 Immigration and Nationality Act, which eliminated the extremely low quotas for Asian immigrants (barely over 100 annually from most countries), a new wave of Asian immigrants made their way to this country. And because of the emphasis on family unification, the arrival of a few immigrants from an Asian society often led, as noted earlier, to the arrival of many more family members. This

The contrast between traditional customs and a modern American lifestyle does not seem to bother this Laotian family in Long Island, New York. *(Mel Rosenthal)*

Table 1
Living Arrangements of Hispanic Children Through Age 17 (1995)

Arrangement	Percentage[a]
Living with both parents	65.8
Living with mother only	29.8
Mother never married	10.8
Divorced	8.1
Separated	9.5
Widowed	1.3
Living with father only	4.4
Father never married	1.9
Divorced	1.4
Separated	0.8
Widowed	0.2

Source: Bureau of the Census, *Marital Status and Living Arrangements: March 1995.* Washington, DC: Bureau of the Census, 1996.

[a] Because numbers are rounded off, percentages do not always add up to totals.

made it possible for Asian communities to develop in the United States beginning in the 1970s. (In addition, the wave of refugees following the Vietnam War, of course, created instant Vietnamese-, Cambodian-, and Laotian-American communities of significant size after 1975.) With their emphasis on strong family obligations and an almost religious commitment to education, Asians have done relatively well for themselves and for their offspring. At the same time, however, increasing wealth and education levels among the second-generation Asians have tended to undermine extended family obligations and have created a tension between them and older Asian immigrants.

HISPANIC-AMERICAN FAMILIES

MEXICAN-AMERICAN FAMILIES

By far the largest Hispanic immigrant group in the United States—indeed, the single largest immigrant group in America from any country—Mexican Americans have a long history in the United States and have lived in the Southwest for centuries. More recently, although Mexicans are increasingly moving to cities in the Midwest and the Northeast, they remain largely in the Southwest, their traditional zone of settlement. Because of their close proximity to the home country—and because of the relative isolation of the Southwest, until recently, from the major population centers of the United States—Mexican-Americans have retained many of their historical family institutions, a phenomenon further enforced by the segregation of Mexican-American neighborhoods by Anglo neighbors.

The Mexican family is usually a very tightly bonded one and is based in the agrarian tradition of the family as a single economic unit, supporting itself collectively. This pattern was then reinforced by the fact that many Mexicans continued to work in agriculture once they moved to the United States. Indeed, the need for these families to put every member to work to survive financially reasserts the traditional ideal that obligation to family comes before individual success. Mexican Americans are often forced to pull children out of school and thus have one of the highest dropout rates of any immigrant group in America.

Increasingly, of course, as more and more Mexicans settle in urban areas—and as generations become more Americanized—the ideal of family cohesiveness begins to give way to individualistic values. Many Mexican households today have adopted the nuclear form, although the ideal of *parentesco* remains strong and the rituals of life—weddings, funerals, coming-of-age ceremonies—are times when the extended family reasserts itself, even among the most modern and urban of Mexican nuclear households.

PUERTO RICAN FAMILIES

The second-largest Hispanic immigrant group in America, Puerto Ricans have largely settled in the urban centers of the Northeast and most particularly in the New York City metropolitan area. Because Puerto Rico is a colony of the United States, immigrants—technically, migrants—need not worry about immigration controls, and as a result, there is a lot of coming and going between the homeland and America. Thus, the extended family ideal typical of Hispanic cultures often ties households in Puerto Rico and the U.S. mainland together, with children frequently being raised in both places by different branches of the family. Indeed, there is a pattern in Puerto Rican families in which mainland parents—fearing the bad influences of urban life—send their children back to the

island to inculcate traditional values of respect for parents.

At the same time, Puerto Rican families face difficulties of their own. One of these is the crowded housing conditions of their adopted country. Because most Puerto Ricans live in New York City, which suffers from one of the tightest housing markets in the nation, their families are often forced to live in crowded and substandard conditions, a situation exacerbated by one of the highest ethnic poverty rates in the country. In addition, Puerto Rican families also have one of the highest rates of separation and divorce of any Hispanic group, a result of their longer history in the United States and the stress of poverty and crowded living conditions. Indeed, more Puerto Rican children live in households headed by a single woman than do those of any other Hispanic group.

CUBAN-AMERICAN FAMILIES

Cubans—the third largest of the Hispanic immigrant groups in America—share many characteristics with other Hispanic family groups. They, too, tend to fuse the nuclear and the extended family into a unique form suitable to life in the United States. In addition, Cuban families also make use of the institution of compadrazgo and place an emphasis on parentesco. However, there are elements in the Cuban-American experience that make their families unique among Hispanic immigrant groups.

Among these elements, perhaps the most important is the unusual history of Cuban immigration. Essentially, Cuban immigrants have come to this country in three waves. The smallest of these includes those Cubans who came to the United States before the Castro revolution. Along with those who came immediately before and during the revolution—that is, the second wave—these early Cuban immigrants tended to be far more educated and better off financially than other Hispanic immigrants. In addition, they tended to be more Americanized, or Westernized, in their family arrangements, often living in nuclear households both before and after they moved to the United States.

The third wave of Cuban immigrants are those who have come to the United States long after the Castro revolution took hold in their homeland. Among these later immigrants, often referred to as Marielitos—after the massive boat lift from the port of Mariel in Cuba, which saw over 100,000 Cubans flee their homeland in 1980—were far more poor and less-educated persons. In addition, there is the matter of race. Most of the Marielitos were of black or mixed-race backgrounds, whereas earlier Cuban immigrants tended to come from families with European ancestry. Notably, this racial difference was reflected in familial relations. Earlier Cuban immigrants tended to be more individualistic in outlook, whereas later ones tended to emphasize obligation to family.

Moreover, for reasons of class and racial snobbery, many elderly Cubans place an emphasis on the "good family." That is, they tend to divide the community into those who came from families with good backgrounds—usually meaning lighter skinned, better educated, and with more financial resources—and those from families without proper pedigrees. Thus, earlier Cuban immigrant families often continue to try and assert greater control over their children as far as finding a mate is concerned.

DOMINICAN-AMERICAN FAMILIES

Dominicans represented the fourth-largest and the most recent of large-scale Hispanic groups in the United States. And like other Hispanics, Dominican-American families often fuse nuclear and extended forms. While most Dominicans—both in the island and in the United States—tend to live in nuclear households, they still maintain the forms and ideals of the extended family. As immigration to the United States rose in the 1970s and 1980s, the ideal of parentesco was utilized to help Dominicans both make their way to the United States and adjust themselves to life in their adopted homeland. Moreover, to a large degree, Dominicans maintain connections between various branches of the family in the island and the United States. Indeed, one of the largest sources of foreign exchange in the Dominican Republic comes from family members in the United States sending money back to their extended kin on the island.

As with Puerto Rican families, most Dominicans have settled in the large urban centers of the Northeast, especially in the New York City metropolitan area. Here, they experience the overcrowded housing conditions and high cost of living. This financial burden has created the need for both parents to work and has led to rising levels of family breakups through separation and divorce. As women go to work or raise families on their own, they tend to break free from older patterns of subservience to male heads of households. Yet, where a father can

support his wife staying home, he often does, though this is inevitably changing among younger and more acculturated Dominicans.

The family has always been a crucial factor in immigration and the most critical institution in the acculturation process. The extended immigrant family—with its interlocking obligations and support networks—offers both a financial and psychological safety net for newcomers to America. While the old perspective—that the extended family sheltered the immigrant from American society and thereby hampered his or her ability to assimilate—has disappeared, the immigrant family is not without its problems. Most important are the tensions that exist between generations, as a younger members adjust more rapidly to life in America while parents and older relations try to impose values from the native country.

Daniel James

See also: Chain Migration (Part II, Sec. 1); Adoption, Sponsorship (Part II, Sec. 2); Elderly, Ethnic Intermarriage, Gender (Part II, Sec. 4); Immigration and Nationality Act, 1965, Illegal Immigration Reform and Immigrant Responsibility Act, 1996, Amerasian Children Act, 1997 (Part IV, Sec. 1).

BIBLIOGRAPHY

Abalos, David T. *The Latino Family and the Politics of Transformation.* Westport, CT: Praeger, 1993.

Agarwal, Pankaj. *Passage from India: Post-1965 Indian Immigrants and Their Children—Conflicts, Concerns, and Solutions.* Palos Verdes, CA: Yuvati Publications, 1991.

Ambert, Alba N., and Maria D. Alvarez, eds. *Puerto Rican Children on the Mainland: Interdisciplinary Perspectives.* New York: Garland, 1992.

Chan, Sucheng. *Asian Americans: An Interpretative History.* Boston: Twayne, 1991.

Georges, Eugenia. *The Making of a Transnational Community: Migration, Development, and Cultural Change in the Dominican Republic.* New York: Columbia University Press, 1990.

Karnow, Stanley, and Nancy Yoshihara. *Asian Americans in Transition.* New York: Asia Society, 1992.

Ready, Timothy. *Latino Immigrant Youth: Passages from Adolescence to Adulthood.* New York: Garland, 1991.

GAY AND LESBIAN IMMIGRATION

Until recently, gay and lesbian immigrants have received little attention from the media and even less from immigration scholars. Despite the recent progress of the gay rights movement globally, heterosexuality remains the standard by which "normal" sex is defined (a concept referred to as "heteronormativity" by academics). Gays and lesbians face discrimination and violence throughout the world, and while many men and women flee their home countries seeking greater freedoms, American society is far from ideal. Normative definitions of sexuality have long been an important dimension of U.S. immigration policy and the state's attempts to control the "desirability" of those who cross its borders. Thus, to understand contemporary gay and lesbian immigration to the United States, it must be examined as one particular way in which sexuality shapes immigration policy in general.

HISTORY

United States immigration restrictions and exclusions have historically been organized along the five distinct but intersecting dimensions of race, class, gender, ideology, and sexuality. Thus, restrictions and exclusions have been biased against not only non-European groups but also those who posed a political or ideological threat (such as communists and anarchists), those of lower socioeconomic status who might become a "public charge," women (who potentially posed a double threat of economic liability and sexual menace by reproducing "inferior races"), and "sexual deviants."

At the turn of the twentieth century, the growing influence of science and the medical establishment, which employed the rhetoric of science to justify social inequalities (including those of race, gender, and sexuality) was utilized to justify restrictions on and exclusions of "deviants" in immigration policy. In 1917, the Immigration and Naturalization Service (INS) banned the entry of "constitutional psychopathic inferiors," a category that included those with "abnormal sexual instincts." But "sexual deviants," such as prostitutes and homosexuals, might also be prevented entry by moral reasoning or criminal histories.

If any ambiguities had existed, Congress passed legislation in 1952 which attempted to identify and categorize all manner of immigrant—to identify the desirable immigrant, the undesirables had to be named as well. According to section 212(a), subsections 1182 (a) (4) and (9) of the McCarran-Walter Act, also known as the Immigration and Nationality Act (INA), "aliens" (i.e., a person not a citizen or national of the United States) could be denied entry if they were found to be "afflicted with psychopathic personality, or sexual deviation" or "convicted of a crime involving moral turpitude." Lesson 3.2 of the INS's Extension Training Program titled "Grounds for Exclusion" explains: "Crime involving moral turpitude refers to a criminal act which is basically wrong (malum per se), evil, depraved, and offensive to society. . . . It is not criminality that creates moral turpitude, but the inherent evil or offensiveness of the action. Moral turpitude for the purpose of our law must be judged by American standards." Thus, even if the "crime" was not a crime as such, in the country of origin, an act or, more important, a characteristic could be judged to be a "crime of moral turpitude" by American standards.

Yet, not all morally offensive acts were to be considered "crimes involving moral turpitude." Rape, incest, prostitution, and polygamy were defined as such, but "fornication" and "extra-marital relations" were not. Homosexuality was also included, but to make things perfectly clear, in 1967, the U.S. Supreme Court determined in *Boutilier v. Immigration and Naturalization Service* that the subsection of the McCarran-Walter Act was meant to prohibit all homosexuals

Protesters at the Gay Pride parade in New York City in 1999 demand that the U.S. government stop deporting their AIDS-infected partners. *(Wanderlan P. Silva, Impact Visuals)*

from immigration to the United States. Writing for the Court, Justice Thomas Clark asserted:

> It has long been held that the Congress has plenary power to make rules for the admission of aliens and to exclude those who possess those characteristics which Congress has forbidden. Here Congress commanded that homosexuals not be allowed to enter. The petitioner was found to have that characteristic and ordered deported. . . . It may be, as some claim, that "psychopathic personality" is a medically ambiguous term, including several separate and distinct afflictions. But the test here is what the Congress intended, not what differing psychiatrists may think. It was not laying down a clinical test, but an exclusionary standard which it declared to be inclusive of those having homosexual and perverted characteristics. It can hardly be disputed that the legislative history of 212 (a)(4) clearly shows that Congress so intended.

The emphasis on characteristics, rather than conduct, was particularly important for the logic of homosexual exclusion at this historical period. Following the 1948 publication of *Sexual Behavior in the Human Male*, in which Alfred Kinsey estimated that at least 37 percent of the American male population had had at least one homosexual experience, an exclusion based on homosexual conduct was dangerous. In fact, the Supreme Court cited Kinsey in its argument and thus helped to affirm the exclusion based on an essential characteristic. But while the logic supported the exclusion, it did not solve the problem of determining resolutely who had this characteristic—that is, who exactly was the "homosexual"?

The process of identifying "homosexuals" depended on various filters, some of which were criminal records, psychiatric records and examinations (which also included physical exams), and self-disclosure. Criminal records were not "full proof" simply because not all "sexual perverts" had criminal records, despite the criminality of their behavior, and they could more easily avoid detection. Thus, a second filter aided in detection. In the first half of the century, as immigrants were required to take physical and psychiatric evaluations, the psychomedical model of homosexuality was thought to be an effective mechanism of detection. Over time, however, a decreasing number of mental health professionals subscribed to the "homosexuality as mental illness" paradigm, and in 1973, the American Psychiatric Association removed homosexuality from the DSM II. The third filter depended on self-disclosure. Following the passage of the INA in 1952, immigrants were directly asked about their moral character in immigration forms and explicitly asked if they were "homosexuals." These filters tended to detect and in fact targeted more men than women because of the gendered ways in which homosexuality was constructed and understood.

Despite these filters, in the opinion of some, detecting homosexual immigrants was still problematic, and with the advent of acquired immunodeficiency syndrome (AIDS) in the 1980s; detection seemed all the more important amid the homophobic reaction that followed the spread of the disease. Thus, immigration became even more exclusive in 1987 when Congress enacted a law preventing the immigration of those infected with the human immunodeficiency virus (HIV). In a surprising turnaround, however, in 1990 Congress dropped the exclusion of gays based on the old moral reasoning of the INA.

CONTEMPORARY ISSUES

Accurately describing the contemporary U.S. gay and lesbian immigrant population is a nearly impossible task. This results in part because the INS does not keep data based on sexual orientation but also because of the fluidity of sexual identity itself. Sexual identities are shaped by a number of factors including culture, social class, context, and time. Thus, "gay" immigrants in the United States are not a homogeneous group. And while some might believe that discrimination against gay and lesbian immigrants no longer exists, a fourth exclusionary "filter" remains firmly intact.

Today, gay and lesbian immigrants face overt discrimination through the heteronormativity of U.S. immigration in law by the following means: family definition, HIV status, and political asylum. Immigrants who apply for U.S. residency based on a family petition must be the parent, child, sibling, or spouse of a U.S. citizen. While ten countries currently permit same-sex partners to immigrate (Australia, Belgium, Canada, Denmark, the Netherlands, New Zealand, Norway, South Africa, Sweden, and the United Kingdom), in the United States, gay relationships are not recognized as a legitimate means by which an American "spouse" can claim citizenship rights for his or her non-American partner. Proponents of gay immigrant rights argue that gay and lesbian immigrants have the right to maintain loving and supportive relationships, which they demand be recognized as legitimate by the state—that is, via same-sex marriage or by extending the definition of family to include gay and lesbian families.

As previously mentioned, individuals who are HIV-positive are also excluded from immigrating to the United States. But this exclusionary policy may be waived for heterosexual spouses. No such waiver exists for same-sex partners, as those relationships are not recognized by the state. Several national and international organizations, including the National Commission on AIDS, the Centers for Disease Control, the American Medical Association, and the World Health Organization, have publicly denounced this ban.

In 1994, Attorney General Janet Reno recognized homosexuality as a persecuted class for claims of political asylum, and a growing number of exiles are seeking asylum based on that claim. The move toward recognizing sexual orientation as a persecuted class actually began in 1986 when a Houston immigration judge barred the INS from deporting a gay Cuban man based on the threat of persecution due to his sexual orientation. In 1993, another immigration judge in San Francisco granted asylum to a Brazilian man. And in 1994, for the first time, the INS granted asylum directly to a gay Mexican man, prompting Reno's announcement.

Yet while the INS has officially recognized sexual orientation and HIV status as membership in a persecuted class for granting political asylum, this status is difficult to prove and available only to immigrants from specific countries who can demonstrate "well-founded fears of persecution." Countries that have fit such a definition to date include Cuba, Brazil, Mexico, and several Islamic countries. Between 1994 and 1997, approximately sixty petitioners were granted asylum by U.S. judges, but there were reportedly over one thousand petitions in this same time frame.

FIGHTING FOR LESBIAN AND GAY IMMIGRANT RIGHTS

Gay and lesbian immigrants do resist the constraints placed on them by U.S. immigration laws and policies through either individual or organized efforts and by utilizing a variety of strategies. For example, in 1982, Anthony Sullivan, an Australian citizen, and Richard Adams, an American citizen, sued the INS to have their marriage to each other recognized for legal purposes. Although the couple lost the case, it became a rallying cry for the future struggles of binational gay couples. Currently, two main organizations deal with gay and lesbian immigration issues in the United States: the International Gay and Lesbian Human Rights Committee (IGLHRC) and the Lesbian and Gay Immigration Rights Task Force (LGIRTF).

Founded in 1991, IGLHRC is a nongovernmental human rights organization. The main objective of the San Francisco–based organization is to protect and advance the human rights of all people and communities subject to "discrimination or abuse on the basis of sexual orientation, gender identity, or HIV status." The international monitoring that the group conducts has been an essential resource for gay and lesbian immigrants who seek political asylum based on their sexual orientation around the world.

The Lesbian and Gay Immigration Rights Task Force has focused on another aspect of gay immigration—binational same-sex relationships. The LGIRTF was created in 1992 through the joint efforts of the International Lesbian and Gay Association and the Lambda Legal Defense and Education Fund, which believed that the repeal of homosexual exclusion from U.S. immigration policy in 1990 was an "opportunity" for action. The group was actually begun by gay and lesbian immigrants in New York who felt that their concerns were not being addressed. Thus, the mission of the LGIRTF from its inception was to "challenge the discrimination against gay and lesbian immigrants, recognizing that these issues were rarely discussed within the gay and lesbian or immigrant communities." Other organizations also monitor immigration—though not as a main concern—such as Amnesty International, the Human Rights Campaign Fund, the Lambda Legal Defense and Education Fund, and the Freedom to Marry Coalition.

Gay and lesbian immigration to the United States is only beginning to be studied. Little is known on the subject and much research remains to be done. The study of gay and lesbian immigrants is a difficult project due to the lack of data and the fluidity of sexual identity.

Lionel Cantú

See also: Gender (Part II, Sec. 4).

BIBLIOGRAPHY

Argüelles, Lourdes, and Anne M. Rivero. "Gender/Sexual Orientation Violence and Transnational Migration: Conversations with Some Latinas We Think We Know." *Urban Anthropology* 2:3–4 (1993): 259–76.

Boutilier v. Immigration and Naturalization Service, 387 U.S. 118 (1967). Reproduced in *Lesbians, Gay Men, and the Law*, ed. William B. Rubenstein. New York: New Press, 1993.

Cantú, Lionel. "Border Crossings: Mexican Men and the Sexuality of Migration." Ph.D. diss., University of California at Irvine, 1999.

Dorf, Julie, director of International Gay and Lesbian Human Rights Commission. Interview by author, 1998.

Harvard Law Review Editors. *Sexual Orientation and the Law*. Cambridge: Harvard University Press, 1990.

Immigration and Naturalization Service. "Grounds for Exclusion." Lesson 3.2 of Extension Training Program, U.S. Dept. of Justice, Immigration and Naturalization Service, 32: 10. Washington, DC: Government Printing Office, 1987.

International Gay and Lesbian Human Rights Committee. Mission Statement. 1996. http://www.iglhrc.org/about/index.html

Kinsey, Alfred. *Sexual Behavior in the Human Male*. Bloomington, IN: Indiana University Press, 1998.

Luibheid, Eithne. "Racialized Immigrant Women's Sexualities: The Construction of Wives, Prostitutes, and Lesbians through U.S. Immigration." Ph.D. diss., University of California at Berkeley, 1998.

Soloway, Lavi S. "Challenging Discrimination against Gays and Lesbians in U.S. Immigration Law: The Lesbian and Gay Immigration Rights Task Force," 1996. http://www.lgirtf.org/html/about.html

GENDER

Immigration processes and patterns are shaped by gender roles and gender socialization. Gender roles and socialization can also be altered in the process of immigration. "Gender roles" refer to behavior that is influenced by the society's conception of differences between men and women and how these differences contribute to people functioning in society. "Gender socialization" is the process in which people of a given society or culture are taught to learn appropriate roles, aspirations, and social interaction based on gender difference. The society as a whole works to teach these gender norms. To understand the connection of the two terms to immigration, one must consider the variation of gender and immigration.

Often the immigrant must assimilate to new ideals of gender roles and socialization. The concept of "assimilation" refers to absorbing the cultural traditions and practices of a population or group. Typically, this characterizes a minority immigrant population absorbing the cultural practices of the dominant ethnic group in their new home.

Throughout American history, the assimilation of minority groups has often been resisted by dominant groups owing to the challenge to their power from such integration. There are three major mechanisms of resistance to integration: prejudice, discrimination, and institutional racism. "Prejudice" is the act of prejudging or making assumptions about an individual based on preconceived ideas about the group of which they are a member. "Discrimination" is the actual practice of treating people in an unequal fashion. Usually prejudice and discrimination are linked to each other, though it is important to see that the terms are also distinct. "Institutional racism" refers to discriminatory practices that are built into the structure and conduct of everyday activities.

Only a few scholars have attempted to outline the dimensions of assimilation and integration for immigrant women. Perceptions of these women, along with their education, religious beliefs, and fertility and childbearing practices, have been the subjects of much research. Additional scholarly work has outlined how family and kinship have served as important sources of support in immigrant neighborhoods for maintaining cultural traditions and adapting to a new life.

The two primary means of analyzing immigrant women's and men's experiences are "the push-pull effect" and the "systems approach." The push-pull effect focuses on the "push" factors that forced individuals to emigrate, and the "pull" factors that drew the immigrants to a particular destination. This analysis is confined to whether the migrants are pushed out of their home country by unfavorable circumstances or pulled toward another country by greater opportunity. The systems approach focuses on a multiplicity of social factors that aid in the immigration decision. These include social networks, life course, religion, and local politics. Both theories are helpful in thinking about how immigration and gender are interconnected and how different systems and push and pull factors affect the process of immigration for both men and women.

CONTEXT AND CULTURAL DIFFERENCE IN IMMIGRATION AND GENDER

Although generalizations can be made about the experiences of immigrant women and men or about the effects of gender on immigration, it is impossible to do so accurately without accounting for cultural difference. "Cultural difference" refers to the variation in the specific practices and beliefs of men and women immigrants from different nations.

Culture plays a big role in determining the relationship between gender and immigration. Different cultures have different conceptions of gender and the

Women immigrants—like these protesting East Indians—often find themselves shunted into the lowest paying domestic jobs. *(Stacy Rosenstock/Impact Visuals)*

process of immigration. Therefore, to address gender and immigration, it is important to include analysis of individuals from many cultures who immigrate, to highlight the similarities and differences of the immigration experience as gendered from all nations to America.

Contexts shape understanding of gender, and experience of immigration varies based on differences in groups, attitudes of the receiving community, reasons for leaving, and contribution of the immigrants in the new society. It is crucial to situate in history the immigrant group and the norms concerning gender relations pertinent to the particular immigrant group. All these factors involve gender, because both the sending country and the receiving country will have an understanding of gender roles and socialization. Sometimes these attitudes and perceptions of gender are complementary. But in most cases, there is some amount of conflict. In addition, immigration shapes gender in terms of work, education, family, and voluntary association. Immigrant strategies for success in the new country have been important to some degree

for all immigrant groups, but ethnic circumstances are equally relevant.

Throughout the nineteenth century in America, the increase in immigration was largely a product of poverty and religious persecution in Europe. The industrialization, urbanization, and cultural diversity of America, particularly in such metropolitan centers as New York City, were huge draws for male and female immigrants. The rural to urban migration of women introduces additional elements of choice, offering legitimate alternatives for women.

The socialization of these European women who came from rural areas was challenged upon arriving in urban centers of America. Ideal of "appropriate" or "expected" behavior of women from their original countries often stood in contrast to American urban ideals of the roles and attitudes of women and men. This includes differences in ideas about education, work, and participation in activities both outside and within the home.

By the end of the twentieth century, both the immigrant populations and the reasons for emigrating had changed drastically. This often forced men to re-think the roles of women. For example, unlike the exodus from Europe a century before, more recent immigrants to the United States have come from both rural and urban Asia and Latin America. In 1980 in New York City, approximately 50 percent of immigrants were from the Caribbean, Asia, and Latin America. Dominicans were the largest group, followed by Jamaicans, Chinese, Haitians, Italians, immigrants from Trinidad and Tobago, Colombians, Ecuadorians, immigrants from the Soviet Union, and Guyanese. Of the Asians in New York City in 1980, more than one quarter were Chinese. The Asian immigrant population made up 24 percent of the total immigrant population in 1980. By 1990, Russians had again become as a high proportion of immigrants to New York City. These more recent groups bring with them ideas about gender socialization that often contrast with mainstream American life today, especially in work and education. However, the differences in gender socialization focus more on the conflicting Western attitudes and values that Latin American and Asian immigrants confront on arrival.

Large-scale political realignments in the 1990s increased the pace of change across Europe. The collapse of Eastern European state socialism, massive immigration into Western Europe, and the emergence of a federated Europe with a common market all bring renewed attention to issues of national histories and transnational futures. This period has a greater focus on political exile rather than on economic interests alone.

IMMIGRATION PATTERNS OF MEN AND WOMEN

Over the last 200 years, the ratio of male to female immigrants has varied greatly. The differences in rates of immigration for men and women can be explained by two factors. The first factor has to do with the division of labor, which is the breakdown of skills and tasks required to make one product based on the perceived or actual attributes of individual workers. The concept commonly entails the division of work based on gender difference. Men's work and women's work are divided, often into complementary tasks. The second factor that shapes the ratio of male to female immigrants are laws that have regulated immigration for particular peoples, consequently increasingly institutionalizing American assumptions about proper gender relations. Gender relations in the United States

changed because of expectations at home and at work that differed from those in the home country included women working outside of the home for the economic survival of the family, as opposed to men working outside of the home as the sole "family breadwinner" while the women maintained the household. Rural immigrants such as the Italian and Irish, for examples, settled in cities where agricultural skills were irrelevant and family survival depended on adapting to new circumstances, with both men and women typically working in the industrial sector. Immigrant women shared many attributes and aspirations. However, they immigrated for different reasons and had various perceptions of women's economic contribution to the family. In addition, men who traditionally had been the sole economic provider had to readjust to the financial need for women to participate in the workplace.

IMMIGRATION AND THE FAMILY

Immigrant families have distinctive patterns of marriage, family formation, and fertility. The distinctions are connected to the conflicting expectations of men and women as they moved from their country of origin to their new country. These patterns also reflected extensive differences from families of different national backgrounds. The age at which women marry varies considerably between cultures, as does the age of childbearing. Variations in immigrant fertility patterns also reflect social and economic factors. Urban birthrates for instance, have generally been lower than for immigrant women from rural areas. This has been more common for the second generation than for the first.

Regardless of whether they arrived in family units, reconstituted separated families, or formed new ones in the United States, immigrants usually organized their household in ways similar to those of native-born Americans, except during periods of temporary stress such as an influx of new immigrants. This is connected to the process of acculturation and assimilation present in immigrant communities. Historically, however, there has been great variation of family strategies for economic survival, due to ethnic difference and traditions in the place of origin.

Throughout the nineteenth century in the United States, most Irish families were among the poorest in the nation. More Irish immigrant families took in boarders and lodgers or lived with other people than did other immigrant populations. More-recent research has challenged the early analysis of Irish immigrant women as stereotypes of passive, rural European women who faithfully followed their husbands into a future over which they had no control.

A somewhat larger number of women than men emigrated form Ireland to America in the 1800s. (In fact, more men than women emigrated in the first half of the century, and more women than men in the second half.) Irish women left for the United States in droves for many reasons: most Irish girls had little hope that marriage would provide anything more than subsistence living, Irish women had more to gain than men economically from emigrating, and the freedom and independence promised by a paying job in a distant city was more attractive than a subordinate role as unpaid helper in one's own family. Irish women were more certain of obtaining employment in the United States than were Irish men. "Women's work" was more plentiful for these immigrants, particularly in domestic services.

Married Irish women in America typically contributed to the family income. The traditionally family-centered Irish peasant women adapted to the economic pressures of urban life by combining their economic activity with the functions of childrearing and housekeeping—many took in boarders. Uprooted physically from the land of their birth, their cultural roots continued to shape their responses and adaptation to their new environment. These immigrants were coming to identify themselves as Irish, to discover the values that bound them together and separated them from the the host society. At the same time, they were learning what values were similar to those in their new home country, occasionally going so far as to modify some of their practices and institutions to conform to general cultural norms. This produced a very complex set of relationships between a changing national culture and a changing Irish-American culture.

Italians immigrated in a more condensed period than did the Irish and Jews and arrived with few resources that prepared them for urban and industrial work. Italian women used family networks of female relatives and neighbors to survive economically and shifted behavior in response to changing economic and social conditions. Very few of these women set out for independence or autonomy as women or to take the roles of Italian men. Rather, they contributed to the family economy out of necessity, with the aim of eventually leaving paid work to care for their family in the home.

More recent immigrants, such as those from Southeast Asia, have faced different issues in family life after arriving in America and trying to reestablish their lives. There is much controversy and debate over gender relations within families and communities for these populations. Family issues concerning the care and disciplining of children have been problematic for immigrant South Asian women and men; many of these new immigrants argue that their home cultures express tenderness and love, as well as discipline, in more physical terms than is the standard in U.S. culture. This difference has caused conflicts between immigrants' choices in childrearing and American laws that are designed to protect children. Many first-generation South Asian immigrants do not fully agree with prevailing American ideals and definitions concerning domestic violence and child abuse. Moreover, this immigrant community strongly believes that society should not interfere in family life.

Another concern of family life to recent South Asian immigrants that particularly affects women is America's propensity toward more open sexuality. Female virginity and arranged marriages are integral to gender socialization of many South Asian immigrants, which, of course, contrasts with American ideas of sexuality and marriage choice. This causes concern because it directly challenges the structure of the family as well as gender roles and gender socialization for both girls and women. Among most of these immigrants, modesty is expected for daughters. In particular, many South Asian fathers believe it is their duty to protect their daughters, often through extreme measures. Among Muslims, daughters might put on the *hijab*, or head scarf, when they enter adolescence. Many women wear this traditional clothing as a defense against U.S. conditions that they see as threatening.

IMMIGRATION, WORK, AND GENDER

In the literature concerning women and work, paid work has always received more attention than home work. "Paid work" refers to any work conducted outside the home for wages; "home work" refers to the nonpaid work involved in maintaining a home. This includes cooking, cleaning, and caring for children, a husband, and elderly parents and relatives. However, home work is starting to receive more attention, with emphasis on how different immigrant communities create various household settings.

To address paid work and immigrant women, it is crucial to situate this issue in terms of class difference. Although immigrants come from a variety of economic backgrounds, the bulk of American immigrants have historically included many from the working classes. This was particularly true before World War I but still continues at the millennium. Therefore, studies of working-class women are often studies of immigrant women.

There is the dual burden of being both an immigrant and a woman worker. When the immigrant worker is a woman, her adjustment to conditions of American industrial life often requires assistance from female relatives or friends to acquire the job. The dual burden is the combination of the problem of the immigrant in industry with that of the woman in industry. This increases the likelihood of discrimination. Immigrant women often end up in the least-skilled, lowest-paying jobs. Immigrant men often have greater ease than do women in finding industrial work, which is typically considered "men's work."

Divisions of labor by gender varied considerably in each American locality and industry. A clear division of labor by gender developed in immigrant efforts to build community through ethnic association. In the United States, immigrant men and women have been very active in building community life, both in and beyond the workplace. For example, many Jews left Russia during the late nineteenth and early twentieth centuries because of harsh conditions and threats of pogroms. They brought with them a strong sense of community structure, which helped them create a network for obtaining work and enabled them to organize. This was facilitated by the level of industrial skills possessed by many Jewish women and men, compared with other immigrant groups of the same time period. By 1920, two-thirds of entering Jewish immigrants were skilled workers compared with 20 percent of other immigrant groups. Although Jewish men and women also faced gender segregation at work, they experienced greater opportunities due to their skills. Skilled positions in the workforce were more available to men than women, across immigrant groups. Many women had to resort to piecework. This involved bringing pieces of work home to complete there and being paid only for the piece, rather than by the hour, or for overall production. Piecework was the lowest-paid work, yet it was still quite competitive.

The Italian women were seen as a threat to working-class solidarity because of their prevalence in piecework and willingness to work for less money during the first two decades of the twentieth century. As a result, many Italian women encountered hostility in the workforce and continued to bring work home for pay. Although the Italian immigrant women working in their homes did not encounter the poor conditions of the workplace, as did other female immigrants, they worked in their cramped home while trying to care for their family. Often their husband or

sons would bring home additional work for the family to complete.

A growing body of empirical research indicates that immigrant women arriving more recently are less skilled and have been less successful in the labor market than were earlier immigrants and that important links exist between the shifts in national origin and declining immigrant skills. This implies that both the entire population of recent immigrants are less skilled than earlier immigrants, as well as that the particular nationalities of recent immigrant groups are connected to their lack of skill. When drawing these differences between immigrant men and women of the later nineteenth century as compared with the late twentieth century, however, it is important to highlight the change in the economic structure of America, which has moved from a manufacturing economy to a service economy. Therefore, the conception of skill will be different, as different tasks are being performed by new immigrants.

The manufacturing economy consisted of production of material goods for the United States and beyond. Throughout the twentieth century, many industrial and manufacturing plants have moved to other parts of the world, resulting in a decrease in manufacturing and an increase in service-related work. The shift of the economy to a service economy has resulted in a loss of good-paying, blue-collar jobs, which consequently has had a negative effect on the more recent immigrants. Therefore, new skills are needed, and many immigrant groups have become involved in the service sector in order to advance in the American economy. In fact, several immigrant groups have come to be identified with a type of business or service. By the mid-1990s, natives from more than one hundred nations lived in America's large cities, carving out an occupational niche for themselves and their communities. An example of this can be seen in the rise of independent supermarkets catering to inner-city neighborhoods in New York, New Jersey, and Connecticut by Dominicans. For the most part, men are more likely to be the employers in immigrant-owned businesses in the United States. In the case of Dominicans, the average owner is a Dominican-born, middle-aged married man. Businesswomen in the Dominican community are mostly in the service sector, owning small businesses that cater to other women, such as beauty parlors.

According to the 1990 census, no major ethnic group in the United States had exceeded Korean Americans in the percentage of self-employed or unpaid family workers. Traditionally, the family is the basic social unit in Korean culture. For this reason, it is not uncommon for many family members to work at family-owned stores without pay. Although the businesses are technically "owned" by the husband or male head of household, the wife will work as many hours as does he to assist the family. As the businesses expand, they hire nonfamily members. Many Korean-American women also work in manufacturing, outside both the home or family store. With Vietnamese family businesses in California, husbands hold other full-time jobs while wives open and run grocery stores, restaurants, or boutiques. Indian grocery stores are often managed by wives while husbands work as engineers or in other specialized positions for American-owned companies. Collectively, the women in these groups make more business and family decisions than they would have back home. This is an adjustment for both female and male immigrants.

Men are overrepresented as emigrants from countries that send relatively few immigrants. This includes African countries and Islamic nations. Sex-specific conditions in particular countries explain why some countries send more men. For example, much of the literature on recent immigrant women involves their leaving to find work, as a short-term endeavor. Often, these women do not refer to themselves as immigrants but as "migrants," a term that more accurately denotes someone who moves temporarily, usually for work. For example, many women from developing countries have migrated "temporarily" to the United States to participate in the domestic service industry.

Foreign-born maids became a big industry toward the end of the twentieth century, due to the growth in the service economy and decrease in the manufacturing economy. Out of economic necessity, women leave their homes to be maids in other, more developed regions of the world. Therefore, migration is gendered as well, with a greater number of women than men migrating for the benefit of their families.

The jobs available to migrants are female-specified jobs, such as domestic service, which explains the greater number of female migrant workers. The availability of "female jobs" over "male jobs" often refers to feminization of the workforce. This feminization of international labor migration has heightened the way gender issues intersect with economic, social, cultural, and political concerns.

The impact of international labor migration on sending and receiving communities has dominated the Asian and Pacific landscape during the 1990s. Migrant workers often become informal leaders—advisers in their country of origin—as they move in and out of the community. Men often migrate before their family to provide stability and the means to bring the family to America. Women independently migrating

for work encounter their own set of problems, distinct from those of migrating families or migrating single men. These problems include discrimination as women immigrants, as well as overall issues of safety.

VOLUNTEERISM AND POLITICAL ACTIVISM OF IMMIGRANTS

Most immigrant voluntary associations began as networks of friends and family members and were originally designed to celebrate events of the life cycle (birth, marriage, and so on). Over time, various immigrant groups have developed more cultural or political underpinnings to their voluntary associations. However, a component that each of the immigrant groups share in their associations is an effort to aid newer immigrants and to retain their cultural heritage.

The Irish produced an American political style of their own during the nineteenth century. For Irish women, this meant an involvement in the direction of the Roman Catholic Church in the United States. Volunteerism by Irish immigrant women was strongest in Catholicism, where volunteerism helped form a unique blend of community building. These Irish immigrant women were joined by Italian immigrant women during the first two decades of the twentieth century. Irish men were more prominent in local and national politics, particularly in the Democratic Party.

The distinctiveness of eastern European Jewish culture was critical for the experience of immigrant women for two reasons: the broad cultural orientation that Jews brought to the United States concerning issues of social change, and a conception of gender different from other groups. These young Jewish women do not fit neatly into established models of labor, immigration, and women's history. For immigrant Jewish women, volunteerism took the form of political activism, and labor protest represented a form of civic participation. There was a search for self-esteem through political involvement as part of a larger transformation of feminine social identity—one that had been evolving before they left home. The experiences of Jewish women in the garment industry, for example, suggest that work, activism, and domesticity were never clearly demarcated stages in the life cycle. These women moved in and out of work and politics, rather than organize their life around one identity. Although many Jewish immigrant women practiced their activism in the workplace, there were other organizations formed for specific social and political purposes.

An example of a social grassroots movement in which immigrant women were involved was the Citizen Wives' Organization (CWO). The CWO was founded in the United States between World War I and World War II. Members of the group were new women citizens who were trying to obtain visas for their husbands so they could immigrate to the United States and join them. This was the main purpose of the organization, and the immigrant women used their status as citizens to achieve their desired goal. Even though these women were steeped in their activism, gender discrimination complicated the lives of the Citizen Wives. A combination of factors worked against these women, including national origin, potential for employment, and gender. Even though these women had legitimacy as citizens, these other obstacles were often too difficult to overcome. They used their family reunification issue to develop strategies to overcome gender discrimination. Therefore, their appeal to family values and the importance of marriage, as well as a male head of household, was their best means to attain visas for their husbands, rather than aggressive political activism.

Muslim immigrant women have more recently urged linkages with broader community services as well as the mobilization of women alongside of men within Islamic communities. Mosques are being used for publicizing women's support groups and as meeting places for groups dealing with such "women's issues" as domestic violence. But contention exists here due to the conflict between the Islamic tradition of the separation of men and women and the new American culture in which men and women work together. Both immigrant men and women in the Muslim communities have resisted the inclusion of women in public affairs.

The political activism and volunteerism of more recent immigrants often involve their reasons for emigrating. Often, the activism of more recent groups highlights issues of political persecution throughout the world or especially in the country of origin. This can be exemplified by Eastern European immigrant women who are raising consciousness about ethnic cleansing in their homeland, or Mexican immigrant women who are protesting *maquiladoras*, factories for women on the United States/Mexico border where women work for little money and are often exposed to violence.

Women immigrants have always been involved in some form of activism and volunteerism in the United States. The difference in the subject and form of activism from the end of the nineteenth century to the beginning of the twenty-first century is between issues that affect the immigrant community in the United States and efforts now to inform Americans of issues affecting those who still live in the immigrant's country of origin, such as female genital mutilation.

Female genital mutilation (FGM) is believed to have originally developed independently among certain ethnic groups in sub-Saharan Africa as part of a practice in puberty rites. Over 80 percent of FGM today occurs in Africa, with the remaining 20 percent largely accounted for in regions of the Middle East. The commonality of all ethnic groups practicing FGM is that they are patrilineal societies. In other words, the most frequent occurrences of FGM are in male-dominated societies, where resources and power are under male control. Reasons for the continued practice of FGM include the need for "the attenuation of desire," the belief that the clitoris could cause danger to the baby during childbirth, and the preservation of family honor and premarital chastity of the woman. Throughout the Western world, it is interpreted as a practice that suppresses and controls the sexual behavior of both women and girls. Today, the ceremonial aspects of FGM have decreased and are being performed at a young age, which does not correlate with entry into adulthood or marriage.

Besides being a human rights issue, FGM is also an immigration refugee issue, as the practice of FGM sends many women fleeing their home communities and countries. International interest in FGM peaked during the United Nations Decade for Women (1975–85). But concern from the Western community (Europe, America, and Canada) has also been interpreted as outside interference and the promotion of colonialism. Still, health care officials do confirm that FGM is being practiced on children in the West and that it does have considerable health risks. Few public accounts exist of FGM practiced in the United States. In a documentary on FGM titled *Scarred for Life*, shown on American television in 1993, a Somali couple living in Atlanta, Georgia, were interviewed about whether they planned to have their daughters genitally mutilated. The husband opposed the practice, but his wife favored it, citing concern that her daughters would be "different" from her and others in the Somalian community if they did not go through the alteration. As of 1993, there was no child care policy on FGM in Georgia, so there is no public knowledge on what happened to the daughters. Although FGM is practiced in America, it is largely silenced. More recently, there have been social service organizations established throughout major U.S. cities having large African and Middle Eastern immigrant communities to aid women fleeing countries that demand they undergo FGM and to aid women who have undergone FGM and are in need of aid. In addition, as of January

26, 1998, there is a United States Code (Title 18, "Crimes and Criminal Procedure") forbidding the practice of FGM within the United States. Organizations also exist for American men of both Middle Eastern and African descent who oppose genital mutilation. In most cases, it is older women who have had the procedure themselves who encourage it, and fathers, husbands, and brothers who oppose the practice. There is a growing concern in America about breaking the silence surrounding FGM and educating people about the prevalence and health and human rights issues of FGM.

IMMIGRANT WOMEN AND EDUCATION

Only in the context of familial need and work opportunities for immigrant women can we understand attitudes about girls' education, largely because education has historically been seen as a site of male privilege. Disparities in completed years of school can aid in explaining a substantial share of the differences in labor market outcomes. In countries where education is scarce and children are needed in the workforce to help support the family, boys are more likely to receive an education. For example, during the early decades of the twentieth century, Italian families faced pressures to turn children into wage earners as soon as possible, often forfeiting their children's chance to obtain an education. This was particularly true for girls, who were needed to assist their mothers in piecework performed at home.

Attitudes toward women gaining literacy in English upon arriving in America have changed over the century. Many work opportunities in the service sector require some amount of literacy and communication in English. Therefore, for survival strategies, literacy has become more acceptable for newer female immigrants. In some cases, families depend on it. This is particularly true of the second-generation children of immigrants, as parents may rely on those children for communicating in English and navigating through American social systems and institutions.

For South Asians, first-generation immigrants want their daughters to be well educated, and many encourage them to pursue careers. However, particularly among Muslims, there is often some controversy about unrestrained mixing with men through school and work. Therefore, even though education is a priority for young women, it often is replaced by more traditional roles, to protect young women from American acculturation. In 1990 in New York City, Dominicans had the highest proportion of persons twenty-

five years of age or older who had not completed high school. The high dropout rate of newer Dominican immigrants has also led to difficulties in the workforce, for both men and women.

TRANSFORMATIONS OF GENDER DUE TO IMMIGRATION

The process of immigration changes women's and men's lives in the public sphere of work, education, and volunteerism, as well as in the private sphere of the household. Often, the changes in the public lives of women, due to immigration, create a transformation in the domestic lives of immigrant women. Some of the public changes that shape the private sphere could include a change in economic structure, political rule, and religious tolerance. These public changes transform women's private lives because the expectations of women will change as a result of the public transformations, causing mutations of previously understood gender roles and socialization. Although such factors as political subordination and economic inequality most often spark immigration, the immigrant must have the power to move. This means that the immigrants must have a sufficient source of initial support to emigrate in the first place. This support could come in the form of financial aid or as an extension of a social support system, either in the country of origin or within a community in the United States. The support system is particularly relevant for immigrant women.

Two decades or more of social historical analysis has shown that European immigrants throughout the nineteenth century and at the start of the twentieth century came from villages that were not isolated, not untouched by the modern social, economic, and political change that was occurring in their countries as well as around the world. Women began their transformation from female of one country to female immigrant in response to the demands of capitalist expansion that caused economic imbalance, as well as changes in political rule and colonialism. Overall, the history of women immigrants in the United States points to the flexibility of American identities and the mutations of ethnic definitions of American womanhood.

In studying a group of Mexican women immigrating to Atlanta, Georgia, Jennifer S. Hirsch shows a change in gendered behavior of the immigrants. The changes she witnessed through interviews of Mexican immigrant women and their husbands had a profound effect on the private sphere of the household. Hirsch analyzes the shift occurring in this immigrant population in terms of marital ideals. She found that during and after the process of immigration, the ideal changed from one based on respect between marital partners to one based on mutual trust. She refers to respect as appreciation for the complementary tasks performed by the partners. Therefore, this notion of respect implies a rigidity in gender roles. The transformation of marital relations to a relationship based on trust implies that more cooperative decision making and a less rigid division of labor is occurring in the household. It is important to address the cultural changes that accompany migration, but these changes can be understood only in the broader historical context of how the sending communities are changing. Such understanding highlights the ambiguity in the process of immigration. And this ambiguity can be seen in the slipping of gendered task boundaries. In this way, men view women as autonomous and more independent because they work.

Latin American immigrants to the United States have also experienced transformations in gender socialization and gender roles. Immigrant Latino men in large cities have been found to be more likely to favor a continuity in patterns of socialization and organization among men and women. Contrary to these ideals, immigrant Latina women are more likely to favor change for both men and women. Latinas have developed alternative economic strategies on their own through state aid and kin and work networks and communities. This gives Latina women a broader community to draw from, which keeps them more involved in political issues, while Latino men are less likely to develop alternative economic strategies.

In other instances, the gender roles and gender socialization that was in place prior to leaving continued to be practiced upon arrival in America. A continuation of gender ideals can be seen in the case of Jamaican immigrants. It was common for Jamaican women to migrate to such large cities as New York first, to be followed by their husbands after they had established themselves. Most of the immigrant women who went to United States worked outside the home before leaving Jamaica. This gave the women more financial independence and made the transition of their men coming to America less stressful, due to there being less of a drastic change in terms of gender roles for both the men and the women.

Although many differences exist among various groups in terms of gender and immigration, all immigrant groups possess a clear understanding of gender roles and gender socialization before leaving their homeland and go through a period of adjusting to American conceptions of gender roles and gender socialization as part of the immigration process. In some cases, the adjustments will be more explicit, while other immigrant groups will experience only nuances of what it means to be a male or a female in America.

Teal Rothschild

See also: Marriage Market (Part II, Sec. 2); Fertility (Part II, Sec. 3); Family (Part II, Sec. 4); New U.S. Rules on Asylum for Women, 1995 (Part IV, Sec. 2).

BIBLIOGRAPHY

Alba, Richard, Douglas S. Massey, and Ruben G. Rumbaut. *The Immigration Experience for Families and Children.* Issue Series in Social Research and Social Policy. Washington, DC: American Sociological Association, 1999.

Bergland, Betty. "Immigrant History and the Gendered Subject: A Review Essay." *Ethnic Forum* 8:2 (1988): 24–39.

Bredbenner, Candace Lewis. "The Case of the 'Lovelorn Jewish Workers': Gender Bias and the Response to Immigration during the Great Depression." *Prologue* 31:1 (1999): 37–52.

Cohen, Miriam. *Workshop to Office: Two Generations of Italian Women in New York City, 1900–1950.* Ithaca: Cornell University Press, 1992.

Diner, Hasia. *Erin's Daughters in America: Irish Immigrant Women in the Nineteenth Century.* Baltimore: Johns Hopkins University Press, 1983.

Donato, Katharine M. "Understanding United States Immigration: Why Some Countries Send Women and Others Send Men." In *Seeking Common Ground: Multidisciplinary Studies of Immigrant Women in the United States,* ed. Donna Gabaccia, pp. 159–84. Westport, CT: Greenwood Press, 1992.

Dorkenoo, Efua. *Cutting the Rose: Female Genital Mutilation: The Practice and Its Prevention.* London: Minority Rights Publications, 1996.

DuBois, Ellen Carol, and Vicki Ruiz, eds. *Unequal Sisters: A Multicultural Reader in U.S. Women's History.* New York: Routledge, 1990.

Foner, Nancy, ed. *New Immigrants in New York City.* New York: Columbia University Press, 1987.

Furio, Colomba M. "An Abstract of Immigrant Women and Industry: A Case Study—the Italian Immigrant and the Garment Industry, 1880–1950." Ph.D. diss., New York University, 1979.

Gabaccia, Donna. *From the Other Side: Women, Gender, and Immigrant Life in the United States, 1820–1990.* Bloomington: Indiana University Press, 1994.

Glenn, Evelyn Nakano. *Issei, Nisei, War Bride: Three Generations of Japanese American Women in Domestic Service.* Philadelphia: Temple University Press, 1986.

Glenn, Susan A. *Daughters of the Shtetl: Life and Labor in the Immigrant Generation.* Ithaca: Cornell University Press, 1990.

Groneman, Carol. "Working-Class Immigrant Women in Mid-

Nineteenth-Century New York: The Irish Woman's Experience." *Journal of Urban History* 4:3 (1978): 255–74.

Harzig, Christiane. *Peasant Maids, City Women: From the European Countryside to Urban America.* Ithaca: Cornell University Press, 1997.

Hirsch, Jennifer S. "En el Norte la Mujer Manda: Gender, Generation, and Geography in a Mexican Transnational Community." *American Behavioral Scientist* 42:9 (1999): 1332–49.

Hurh, Won Moo. *The Korean Americans.* The New Americans. Ed. Ronald H. Bayor. Westport, CT: Greenwood Press, 1998.

Leonard, Karen Isaksen. *The South Asian Americans.* The New Americans. Ed. Ronald H. Bayor. Westport, CT: Greenwood Press, 1997.

Licuanan, Patricia. "The Socio-Economic Impact of Domestic Worker Migration: Individual, Family, Community, Country." In *The Trade in Domestic Workers: Causes, Mechanisms, and Consequences of International Migration,* ed. Noeleen Heyzer, Geertje Lycklama, and Nijeholt and Nedra Weerakoon, 103–15. London: Zed, 1994.

Morawska, Ewa. *For Bread with Butter: The Life-Worlds of East Central Europeans in Johnstown, Pennsylvania, 1890–1940.* New York: Cambridge University Press, 1985.

Mortimer, Delores M., and Roy S. Bryce-Laporte. *Female Immigrants to the United States: Caribbean, Latin American, and African Experiences.* Washington, DC: Research Institute of Immigration and Ethnic Studies, Smithsonian Institution, 1981.

Schoeni, Robert F. "Labor Market Outcomes of Immigrant Women in the United States: 1970–1990." *International Migration Review* 32:1 (1998): 57–78.

Seller, Maxine, ed. *Immigrant Women.* Philadelphia: Temple University Press, 1981.

Smith, Judith E. *Family Connections: A History of Italian and Immigrant Lives in Providence, Rhode Island, 1900–1940.* Albany: State University of New York Press, 1985.

Torres-Saillant, Silvio, and Ramona Hernandez. *The Dominican Americans.* The New Americans. Ed. Ronald H. Bayor. Westport, CT: Greenwood Press, 1998.

Turbin, Carole. *Working Women of Collar City: Gender, Class, and Community in Troy, New York, 1864–1886.* Urbana: University of Illinois Press, 1992.

Vernez, Georges. *Immigrant Women in the U.S. Workforce: Who Struggles? Who Succeeds?* Lanham, MD: Lexington Books, 1999.

SEGMENTED ASSIMILATION

The theory of segmented assimilation is an attempt to explain the ways in which immigrant children and U.S.-born children of immigrants adapt to American society. The theory arose in response to the unique experiences of second-generation Americans after 1965 in counterdistinction to theories of assimilation formulated decades earlier to explain the adaptation process of immigrants who arrived in the United States during the late nineteenth and early twentieth centuries. Proponents of the theory of segmented assimilation argue that the post-1965 second generation faces a social reality that widely diverges from the social reality immigrants had to contend with before the 1960s. Prior to the 1960s, most research on immigration advanced the idea that immigrants to the United States followed a path of straight-line assimilation to the dominant Anglo-American culture.

As the thinking went, immigrants, along with their children and grandchildren, found success and entered the middle class only as they gave up the language and culture of their homeland. The language and culture of the country of origin was associated with ignorance and poverty, implicitly inferior to Anglo-American linguistic and cultural norms.

Segmented assimilation theory posits a more complex process of cultural adaptation by immigrants and their children to U.S. society. Sociologists Alejandro Portes and Min Zhou identify three patterns of adaptation among post-1965 immigrants. The first pattern follows the expectations of traditional pre-1965 theories of assimilation. Accordingly, immigrants and their children and grandchildren steadily abandon the language and culture, in an effort to enter mainstream, middle-class America. Their success in entering the middle class is in direct proportion to their assimilation of the linguistic and cultural norms of this class.

The second pattern is one of assimilation to the norms of the U.S. underclass. Immigrants who follow this pattern typically live in the inner city and fall into permanent or semipermanent poverty as they acculturate to the dominant norms of their social milieu. To immigrants and children of immigrants following this pattern of adaptation, the American Dream, in which America is a land of opportunity for all, reveals itself to be an illusory myth. According to the third pattern of assimilation, immigrants who deliberately hold to the values embedded in their native culture and maintain tight solidarity within their ethnic community in the United States make rapid socioeconomic advancement. For immigrants following this pattern of adaptation, full assimilation to American cultural norms is not necessarily a prerequisite to upward mobility, as it had been for immigrants in earlier decades. The maintenance of an internally cohesive cultural and ethnic community distinct from native-born Americans can serve the interests of community members, reinforcing those ethnic cultural values that enhance academic and economic success and providing ladders of socioeconomic advancement within the ethnic community and not otherwise available in the larger host society. These three patterns of adaptation stand in contrast with earlier theories of straight-line assimilation to the white middle class.

The main reason for the different patterns of assimilation between pre- and post-1965 immigrants lies in differences in the compositions of the two waves of immigrants and in changes in American society during and after the 1960s. Between the years 1882 and 1965, U.S. immigration policy was designed to create and maintain a white, northern European-based America. With large numbers of Chinese and Japanese immigrants settling on the West Coast prior to 1882 and additional Japanese immigrants soon thereafter, many native Anglo-Americans feared being overtaken by people perceived to be different and nonassimilable. Nativist concerns led to the passage of the Chinese Exclusion Act in 1882 and the Gentlemen's Agreement with Japan in 1907, thereby restrict-

Many immigrants—like these Russians at a seaside café in Brighton Beach, New York—try to retain old ways of life even as they make their way in their adopted land. *(Mel Rosenthal)*

ing most immigration to the United States to Europeans. Between 1880 and 1930, more than 20 million Europeans immigrated to the United States. As white immigrants, the main barriers to full participation in American society were related to language, culture, and religion. Hence, the main pattern of cultural adaptation was one of nearly complete assimilation to Anglo-American, middle-class norms. Furthermore, the U.S. economy was in a period of rapid expansion, providing avenues for socioeconomic advancement to immigrants and their children. The pre-1965 immigrants and their children, enjoying abundant economic opportunities, except during the years of the Great Depression, and suffering from few or no racial barriers to mobility relative to blacks and Asians, shed the language and culture of their country of origin in as brief a period as one generation. Moreover, failure to adopt the language and culture of the new country was often met by hostility and disdain by a nativist American public, complicating the adaptation process. With language and culture the main factors differentiating the otherwise similar European immi-

grants and Anglo-American natives, assimilation was nearly universally adopted as a desirable group goal by the immigrants.

IMMIGRANTS AND POST-1965 AMERICAN SOCIETY

After 1965, both the composition of immigration flows and the nature of American society changed, departing markedly from their pre-1965 counterparts. In 1965, U.S. immigration policy underwent dramatic revisions designed to eliminate differential restrictions on immigration by country of origin. As a result, immigrants arriving in the United States after 1965 are exceedingly diverse in terms of national origin, language, origin, and culture in comparison with the earlier, predominantly European immigrants.

While during the 1950s and early 1960s Europeans made up one-half of all immigrants to the United

States, they composed only 10 percent of all immigrants in the late 1980s. Immigration from Asia, Latin America, and the Caribbean, in particular, rose dramatically in the 1970s, 1980s, and 1990s, adding new layers of ethnic and racial diversity to American society. As early as the 1970s, for example, fully 1.5 million immigrants from Asia arrived in the United States. Only 840,000 immigrants from Europe arrived during the same period. Between 1965 and 1990, the number of Chinese living in the United States rose from 360,000 to 1,645,000; the number of Filipinos grew from 200,000 to 1,400,000; Koreans skyrocketed from only 45,000 to nearly 800,000; and Asian Indians saw their numbers grow from 50,000 to more than 800,000.

Moreover, political instability in Southeast Asia encouraged the immigration of hundreds of thousands of Vietnamese, Cambodian, and Laotian refugees to the United States, furthering the growing ethnic and cultural diversity of American society. It is noteworthy to add that the experiences of adaptation to U.S. life are as varied as the Asian immigrant groups themselves, belying attempts at across-the-board generalizations.

Census figures show Hispanics as one of the fastest growing minorities within the United States, reflecting, in part, high levels of Latin American immigration in the post-1965 period. The term "Hispanic," however, masks the great diversity in race, ethnicity, and national origin that Latin American immigrants add to U.S. society. Mexicans, predominantly mestizo in race, represent by far the largest immigrant group in the United States and fully 60 percent of all U.S. Hispanics. Puerto Ricans are the second largest Hispanic population living in the United States, followed by Cubans and Dominicans, Colombians, Salvadorans, and Guatemalans. Smaller numbers of other Central Americans and South Americans have also immigrated. Each group faces unique experiences in adapting to life in the United States, conditioned in part by the skills they bring to the country and where they settle. Moreover, in the 1960s and 1970s, greater numbers of immigrants from the Caribbean decided to make their home in the United States. The West Indians, like the Asians and Latin Americans, are a diverse group. English-speaking Jamaicans make up the largest contingent among West Indian immigrants and are often among the most educated of Jamaican society. French and Creole-speaking Haitians, many of whom come to the United States impoverished and with low levels of education and few marketable job skills, now comprise the second largest group of West Indian immigrants. West Indian immigrants, who are predominantly African in ethnic origin, must also

learn to navigate the racialized context of American society, in a manner different from their European immigrant predecessors and contemporaries and independent of country of origin, levels of education, and profession.

Contemporary U.S. immigrants are culturally, ethnically, and racially diverse without parallel in U.S. immigration history, with important consequences for the adaptation of these immigrants and their children. Furthermore, before the 1960s, American society placed a much greater emphasis on the need for the cultural assimilation of immigrants, stressing cultural uniformity over cultural pluralism. During the 1960s, however, commonly held notions about the role of ethnicity and minority cultures in public life underwent reevaluation. The civil rights and black power movements of the 1960s encouraged a revival in the importance of ethnicity within American society. African Americans began celebrating their culture, integrating their experiences into the larger American nation. Hispanics, too, began asserting their identity as a linguistic and cultural minority, pushing for the creation of bilingual education programs. Native Americans, Hawaiians, and the French speakers of Louisiana—minority peoples that settled American territory before the imposition of Anglo-America—also pushed their cultural identities and created educational programs designed to teach the histories, languages, and cultural values of their people to their children.

Since the 1960s, as a result of ethnic revival activities by African Americans, Hispanics, and indigenous peoples, multiculturalism has emerged as a dominant ideology in the United States, and it competes with the century-old ideology stressing the importance of complete assimilation to Anglo-American norms, altering the playing field for post-1965 immigrants and their offspring. No longer does American society expect nor can it expect immigrants and their children to follow traditional patterns of cultural adaptation, according to which the culture, language, and values of the country of origin are entirely abandoned for those of the United States. The United States, as more people are aware than ever before, is composed of a diversity of ethnic peoples and cultures without rival in the world. Many Americans now hold multiple ethnic and cultural identities. Anglo-American monolingualism and monoculturalism, once the mainstay of white, middle-class America, are no longer prerequisites to upward mobility. To the contrary, complete assimilation to Anglo-American norms may work against the socioeconomic advancement of immigrant children and U.S.-born children of immigrants.

The U.S. and world economies have also undergone great transformations since the 1960s, further altering the social reality with which immigrants and their children must contend in adapting to American life in the post-1965 era. After the Second World War, the U.S. economy rapidly expanded, providing manufacturing jobs and avenues of socioeconomic mobility to a great proportion of the American population. The middle class grew quickly, and the disparities in wealth between the richest and poorest fifths of the U.S. population diminished. It was a time of great optimism. People expected the economy to continue expanding and individual economic opportunities to continue improving. The children of earlier immigrants could land relatively well paying manufacturing jobs with relatively low levels of education. The strong manufacturing sector of the U.S. economy, in addition to white racial status, facilitated the earlier second generation's entry into the white middle class. However, between the mid-1960s and the 1970s, many of the United States's manufacturing industries moved their operations overseas, where the costs of labor were lower. Through the 1970s, the manufacturing base of the United States diminished, gradually being replaced by service sector jobs. The manufacturing jobs that were lost to relocation overseas had supported a large middle class. Without these jobs, the middle class entered a period of crisis, from which it has yet to recover.

Moreover, the majority of the service sector jobs that replaced the lost manufacturing jobs were relatively low paying, leaving jobholders little opportunity for economic advancement. The few high paying service sector jobs that were created during and after the 1970s typically required high levels of education and specialized professional skills. The post-1965 U.S. economy has been characterized as an "hourglass" economy, with many low paying, labor-intensive jobs at the bottom; high paying, knowledge-intensive jobs at the top, and few of the jobs in the middle that historically served as stepping-stones in the path toward upward mobility. The gap in income and wealth between the richest fifth and the poorest fifth of the U.S. population began to grow during the 1970s, increased rapidly during the 1980s, and continued to widen during the 1990s. The paths of adaptation that the contemporary second generation must take are complicated by the demands and constraints of a highly stratified society. American society currently suffers from levels of stratification that have historically characterized much of Latin America. While earlier immigrants and their descendants gained requisite education for social mobility over several generations, immigrants today must ensure that their American-born or American-raised children get the high levels of requisite education to enter affluent society within a single generation. Otherwise, their children and grandchildren may remain at or near the bottom of the U.S. social hierarchy.

As the United States has lost its domestic manufacturing base abroad to countries with lower costs of labor and as the U.S. economy has become increasingly service-oriented and "hourglass" in occupational structure, technologies of communications and transportation have facilitated the exchange of news and information and the movement of people at relatively low costs and rapid speeds. Many current immigrants in the United States, unlike earlier immigrants, can communicate with family, friends, and business partners in their country of origin and can travel back and forth between the United States and their country of origin with relative ease. In a host society where a plurality of social and cultural identities compete for the allegiance of the second generation and where the opportunities for the socioeconomic mobility of the second generation are limited to those individuals who possess highly specialized knowledge and skills, the paths of cultural adaptation that immigrants and their children must follow are fraught with challenges and tough choices. Furthermore, in a world that is ever more integrated, where immigrant parents and their offspring have greater opportunities to maintain and cultivate links with their country of origin, the process of cultural adaptation may include selectively holding on to those ethnic values and cultural attributes that encourage success.

CULTURAL ADAPTATION IN THE FACE OF SOCIAL PRESSURES TOWARD DOWNWARD MOBILITY

The social environment in which immigrants settle and raise their children has potentially enormous consequences for the cultural adaptation of the children. Most contemporary immigrants to the United States take up permanent residence in relatively large cities. Many settle in inner-city neighborhoods where housing is within financial reach and access to public transportation is assured. In the inner city, however, immigrants live in close proximity to native residents who tend to be already isolated from affluent Anglo-American society as a result of a history of institutional racial discrimination and segregation. In the inner city, often inhabited by poor, native-born blacks or Latinos who have suffered a history of socioeconomic deprivation, ladders of socioeconomic mobility are few and far between. Inner-city residents often carry the burden of chronic unemployment or underemployment. Moreover, due to social isolation, inner-city residents tend to lack the social networks through which other Americans routinely advance. In the inner city, a history of social isolation and deprivation has given rise to an adversarial culture among disaffected minority and lower-class youth. In a chaotic urban environment where opportunities are few and expectations for socioeconomic mobility are low, many poor, minority youth reject the values middle-class America strives to promulgate, adopting instead attitudes and values in opposition to those of the middle class.

The schools that serve marginalized, socially isolated urban communities are often burdened by limited resources, underpaid teachers, and overcrowded classrooms in addition to an adversarial student culture in relation to teachers, administrators, and the formal learning process in general. In many schools throughout the United States and especially in the country's inner cities, little formal learning is achieved. American youth culture is profoundly antiacademic, regarding "studious" as a socially undesirable epithet. The strong antiacademic nature of mainstream American youth culture is compounded by the rejection of middle-class values by many urban, minority youth. In the schools, the students strongly influence one another's values, attitudes, and expectations; they downplay the importance of education and perpetuate an oppositional culture that hinders them from acquiring the skills needed to succeed in American society. Immigrant children often get their first exposure to the American host culture through attendance in public schools. In the absence of strong immigrant parent and community control over and influence on immigrant children's social, cultural, and educational development, extensive contact with native peers may do the work of assimilating immigrant youth into a culture that belittles academic achievement and fosters distrust of and opposition to authority, including the authority of parents, the ethnic community, the schools, and national institutions.

In New York City, for example, one sociologist found that children of Puerto Rican migrants were put down by their native-born peers for aspiring to upward mobility via the channels historically condoned by middle-class America, namely, via strong academic performance in school. The pressure of the native-born peers was so great that many of the Puerto Rican

children lowered their aspirations and expectations in an effort to fit into the dominant school culture, forgoing their earlier dreams and the dreams of their parents and lowering their academic achievement. Moreover, evidence suggests that poor inner-city environments negatively affect the rates of school completion among foreign-born and second-generation Mexican-American students. Social environments outside the inner city are more conducive to completing high school among both foreign-born and second-generation Mexican-American students. Third-generation Mexican Americans drop out of high school at rates higher than the first and second generations, which offers evidence of downward mobility as the process of cultural adaptation advances. In many inner-city environments, U.S.-born and acculturated Mexican Americans negatively affect their foreign-born and second-generation counterparts in terms of values supportive of academic perseverance, progress, and performance.

The children of West Indian immigrants, because of their black racial status, are also exposed to pressures to assimilate to the norms of a native U.S. minority, African Americans. Miami is home to some 100,000 Haitian immigrants, many of whom arrived illegally and with very little or no money. First-generation Haitians hold a strong national identity, which enables them both to maintain the community solidarity and to cultivate the ethnic social networks that aid in promoting individual success. First-generation parents, however, struggle to instill their sense of national identity and the importance of maintaining group solidarity to their children, who attend predominantly inner-city schools with primarily native-born, African-American peers. As self-identified Haitians, Haitian students tend to be ridiculed by their native-born peers as subservient to whites. Native students also make fun of Haitian language and dress, subjecting their Haitian peers to ostracism and occasionally violence. Many Haitian students, in an effort to fit into their school environment, yield to the culture of the native school majority, adopting attitudes that devalue education as a means of socioeconomic advancement. However, other second-generation, Haitian-American students, who are strongly motivated to excel academically, assimilate only partially to the culture of their African-American peers, consciously retaining a Haitian ethnic identity as a tool for social mobility. Other children of West Indian immigrants have also consciously held to a West Indian identity in an effort to distance themselves from the stigmatized African-American minority and to make educational and socioeconomic gains.

THE ROLE OF ETHNICITY IN SOCIAL MOBILITY

Ethnicity, as an independent factor, may be either negatively or positively associated with the academic achievement and social mobility of immigrants and their children, which lends support to the theory of segmented assimilation that asserts differential paths of cultural adaptation by distinct ethnic groups. The cultural values and degree of cohesiveness of an ethnic group are potentially vital determinants in the socioeconomic advancement, leveling, or demotion of immigrant children. Chinese-American children, for example, even those with low social status and low competence in English, tend to maintain considerably higher grade point averages than their native-born, non-Chinese schoolmates. One sociologist attributes the consistent academic success of Chinese-American youth to the influence of the family and the ethnic community and to cultural values that emphasize education and encourage study. Children of a particular immigrant group benefit from the central importance that group places on education as the means to success. Typically, education-oriented parents make tremendous sacrifices and exert continual parent-to-child reinforcement to afford their children a solid education. Even when the factors of social class, family structure, and the place of birth of parents are controlled for, ethnicity remains a significant factor explaining success in school. Asian-American students consistently outperform European-American students, who, in turn, consistently outperform African-American and Hispanic-American students. Ethnic groups differentially emphasize the importance of education and differentially prepare their children for academic success.

There is great diversity in the outcomes of cultural adaptation by members of pan-racial groups. Among Southeast Asians, for example, ethnicity, independent of all other factors, is an important determinant of academic performance, one whose effect varies from one national-origin group to another. Vietnamese high schools students outperform Cambodian and Laotian students in grade point averages and test scores. One sociological study attributes the academic success of the Vietnamese over the Cambodians and Laotians to ethnic adaptability and durability. In rural northern California, Punjabi immigrant parents and the Punjabi ethnic community have successfully instilled in their children values supportive of education, effective study skills, and the need to adhere to the norms of and share an identity with the Punjabi ethnic group. The northern Californian Punjabis, like the Vietnamese, have a high degree of ethnic resilience relative to other ethnic groups who are otherwise poorly prepared to meet the demands required for upward mobility in American society. Punjabi immigrant parents came to northern California as farm laborers and occupy a low socioeconomic position within local society. Yet, in spite of the modest social status of their parents and in the face of an antagonistic white host society, Punjabi students outperform native white students academically. Punjabi parents, continually stressing the importance of education, insist that their children avoid intensive contact with the native white students. In an unfriendly social climate, the cohesiveness of the Punjabi family and community and the high value that Punjabis place on education translate into academic success and upward social mobility for American-born Punjabi children.

SOCIAL CAPITAL IN THE PROCESS OF CULTURAL ADAPTATION

Individual members of immigrant communities characterized by a high degree of solidarity can use the social networks of the ethnic community to garner the resources or to make the contacts so essential to social mobility, particularly when confronted with a negative environment in the host society. Shared experiences of adversity, typically in the form of discrimination by native members of the host society, tend to reinforce a sense of belonging by immigrants to a larger immigrant community. Moreover, a common culture and language serve to delineate group boundaries, distinguishing the immigrant group from the native-born Americans. Taken together, the ties reinforced by shared experiences of adversity and a common culture and language work in favor of the formation of immigrant group solidarity. With a high degree of group solidarity within an immigrant community, immigrants and their children are under less pressure and have a reduced need to assimilate entirely to the culture of the host society. Social capital, or the ability to muster resources by virtue of membership in social networks or larger social structures, which in the case of the immigrant are often found within the ethnic community, enables immigrant group members to circumvent the ladders of social mobility provided and sanctioned by the dominant social group of the host culture.

In Miami, in sharp contrast with the city's relatively impoverished Haitian community, the Cuban community offers newly arriving Cuban immigrants immediate opportunities for employment and subsequent opportunities for socioeconomic advancement, thereby buffering the immigrants from the often hostile reception immigrants receive from the native, Anglo-American establishment. A shared ethnicity, encouraging tight in-group solidarity, has equipped Miami's Cuban Americans, regardless of social class, with a level of collective social organization to overcome economic hardship and discrimination and to provide ladders of social mobility to ethnic group members. Cuban immigrants with poor English-language skills and educational credentials that are not recognized by the larger American society benefit from an ethnic community that has achieved high levels of economic prosperity and institutional development independent of the Anglo-American establishment. Furthermore, with the arrival of the Cubans in the 1960s and the increasing integration of the global economy, Miami has emerged as the United States's commercial and cultural window to Latin America. A thriving Spanish-speaking, Cuban-American community both enhances and benefits from Miami's unique position as gateway between the two Americas. As a result of having rewarding access to two cultural worlds, Cuban-American children are less likely to abandon completely the Spanish language and a Cuban-American identity. Instead, children of Cuban immigrants tend to assimilate selectively to the culture of the larger Anglo-American society, while retaining those elements of Cuban identity that enhance their success within the context of Latin-oriented Miami.

Social capital works in favor of other immigrant communities as well. The Korean-American community of Los Angeles, for example, firmly established by the late 1970s, provides its members with networks of social relations through which they can obtain low-interest loans to start businesses, thereby allowing Korean-American entrepreneurs, often with little or no credit history in the United States, to bypass the stringent regulations and lending practices of the American banking and credit industry. As a result of a strong entrepreneurial drive and access to credit through the ethnic community, Korean Americans created a multitude of businesses in which members of the Korean-American community, including newly arrived immigrants with limited English-language skills, could find employment. Furthermore, as with Cubans, Korean-American group solidarity buffered community members from hostility by native-born Americans, resentful of the Korean-American business presence, which in some parts of the city was the predominant presence and tended toward monopoly over retail trade. Confronted with rising violent crime against Korean-American merchants, the community enlisted the help of the Los Angeles Korean Chamber of Commerce, which campaigned against rising crime, and when efforts to obtain additional police protection failed, the community collected public subscriptions to pay for a bilingual police post and anticrime patrols in Koreatown.

Social capital, in the form of social support and social control, accounts for much of the "ethnic effect" on high school achievement by children of immigrants. In Los Angeles, Korean-American parents' expectations and support of and control over their children are largely responsible for the success of Korean-American students in the public school system and at the University of California at Los Angeles, where their relative numbers are much greater than their proportion of the population of Los Angeles County would suggest. Among Vietnamese-American youth attending public school, maintenance of a strong, traditional Vietnamese family structure in the home, which emphasizes respect for older family members and a responsibility on the part of the older members to guide and supervise younger family members, is positively associated with high academic performance and upward mobility. More assimilated Vietnamese-American youth who have intensive social contact with native-born American peers tend to devalue education; show less respect toward their older siblings, parents, and grandparents; and perform more poorly in school. Among contemporary immigrants and their children, complete assimilation to the cultural norms of the immediate American context in which they find themselves may not be in their best interests. Selective assimilation, holding on to the more positive attributes of traditional culture while adapting to the best of American culture, provides many immigrants and their offspring the path most conducive to securing a brighter, more prosperous future.

Aonghas Mac Thòmais St.-Hilaire

See also: Connections to Homeland (Part II, Sec. 2); Settlement Patterns (Part II, Sec. 3); English as a Second Language, Language (Part II, Sec. 10).

BIBLIOGRAPHY

Bankston, Carl, and Min Zhou. "The Social Adjustment of Vietnamese American Adolescents: Evidence for a Segmented-Assimilation Approach." *Social Science Quarterly* 78 (1997): 508–23.

Bourgois, Philippe. "In Search of Respect: The New Service Economy and the Crack Alternative in Spanish Harlem." Paper presented at the Conference on Poverty, Immigration, and Urban Marginality in Advanced Societies, Maison Sugar, Paris, May 10–11, 1991.

Fernández-Kelly, Maria Patricia. "Social and Cultural Capital in the Urban Ghetto: Implications for the Economic Sociology of Immigration." In *The Economic Sociology of Immigration: Essays on Networks, Ethnicity, and Entrepreneurship*, ed. A. Portes, pp. 213–47. New York: Russell Sage Foundation, 1995.

Gibson, M. A. *Accommodation without Assimilation: Sikh Immigrants in an American High School.* Ithaca: Cornell University Press, 1989.

Hing, Bill. "Asian Immigrants: Social Forces Unleashed after 1965." In *The Immigration Reader: America in a Multidisciplinary Perspective*, ed. David Jacobson, pp. 144–82. Malden, MA: Blackwell Publishers, 1998.

Landale, Nancy, R. S. Oropesa, and Daniel Llanes. "Schooling, Work, and Idleness among Mexican and Non-Latino White Adolescents." *Social Science Research* 27:4 (1998): 457–90.

Light, Ivan. "Immigrant Entrepreneurs in America: Koreans in Los Angeles." In *The Immigration Reader: America in a Multidisciplinary Perspective*, ed. David Jacobson, pp. 265–82. Malden, MA: Blackwell Publishers, 1998.

Ogbu, J. U. *Cultural Models and Educational Strategies of Non-Dominant Peoples: The 1989 Catherine Molony Memorial Lecture.* New York: City College Workshop Center, 1989.

Portes, Alejandro. "Children of Immigrants: Segmented Assimilation and Its Determinants." In *The Economic Sociology of Immigration: Essays on Networks, Ethnicity, and Entrepreneurship*, ed. A. Portes, pp. 248–80. New York: Russell Sage Foundation, 1995.

———. "From South of the Border: Hispanic Minorities in the United States." In *The Immigration Reader: America in a Multidisciplinary Perspective*, ed. David Jacobson, pp. 113–43. Malden, MA: Blackwell Publishers, 1998.

Portes, Alejandro, and Robert Manning. "The Immigrant Enclave: Theory and Empirical Examples." In *Majority and Minority: The Dynamics of Race and Ethnicity in American Life*, ed. Norman Yetman, pp. 319–32. Boston: Allyn and Bacon, 1991.

Portes, Alejandro, and Min Zhou. "The New Second Generation: Segmented Assimilation and Its Variants among Post-1965 Youth." *Annals of the American Academy of Political and Social Science* 530 (1993): 74–98.

Rumbaut, Ruben, and Kenji Ima. *The Adaptation of Southeast Asian Refugee Youth: A Comparative Study.* Washington, DC: Office of Refugee Resettlement, 1988.

Sowell, Thomas. *Ethnic America: A History.* New York: Basic Books, 1981.

Steinberg, Laurence. *Beyond the Classroom.* New York: Simon and Schuster, 1996.

Ueda, Reed. "The Changing Face of Post-1965 Immigration." In *The Immigration Reader: America in a Multidisciplinary Perspective*, ed. David Jacobson, pp. 72–91. Malden, MA: Blackwell Publishers, 1998.

———. *Postwar Immigrant America.* Boston: St. Martin's Press, Bedford Books, 1994.

Warner, William, and Leo Srole. *The Social Systems of American Ethnic Groups.* New Haven: Yale University Press, 1945.

Waters, Mary. "Ethnic and Racial Identities of Second-Generation Black Immigrants in New York City." *International Migration Review* 28: 4 (1994): 795–820.

Zhou, Min. "Segmented Assimilation: Issues, Controversies, and Recent Research on the New Second Generation." *International Migration Review* 31: 4 (1997): 975–1008.

LAW AND LEGISLATION

INTRODUCTION

$\mathcal{S}$ection 5 of Part II of the *Encyclopedia of American Immigration* is devoted to law and legislation. The entries in this section cover the issues of amnesty, civil rights, crime, naturalization, dual citizenship, and state, county, and municipal legislation. In addition, the section includes two longer general entries that cover legislation on immigration and legislation that affects immigrants already in the United States.

In her entry on amnesty, Susan González Baker explores the amnesty policy option before moving on to offer a brief review of amnesty in the United States. She then gives data on amnesty applicants and implementation of amnesty rules. Baker also discusses the effects of legalization on host communities.

The entry on civil rights by Scott Zeman lays out the contending schools of thought on the subject, before going into an examination of the historical development of immigrants' constitutional rights. Next, the author looks at the issue of immigrants and civil rights since the 1980s and concludes with a discussion of refugees and deportations.

The entry on crime by Paul Magro covers the subject as it pertains to immigrants from two angles: immigrants as perpetrators of crimes and immigrants as victims of crime. Magro begins with a discussion of the history of early immigrant crime groups, including the Irish Molly Maguires and Italian-American crime. He then moves on to discuss the theories of crime causation among immigrant groups, in both their historical and contemporary contexts. In exploring crime among immigrant groups today, the author focuses on two groups: Chinese Americans and Mexican Americans. Finally, Magro takes a look at crimes against immigrants, including discrimination by institutions and hate crimes by individuals.

In the first general survey entry on legislation affecting immigrants, James R. Edwards Jr. looks at those laws that affect the immigration process itself. The author begins with a look at the history of the subject, starting with a discussion of antebellum federal immigration legislation, before moving on to discuss legislation from the Civil War era and the late nineteenth century. Edwards then explores the subject of restrictive legislation passed around the turn of the twentieth century, including the literacy and quota laws of 1910 through the 1920s. Finally, the author looks at the liberalization of immigration laws in the 1960s, followed by further restrictions—as well as amnesty laws—in the 1980s and 1990s.

In his entry on legislation regarding immigrants already in America, A. James Vázquez-Azpiri begins by discussing the legal question of what an immigrant is before exploring the government's power to control the administration of aliens in this country. Vázquez-Azpiri also looks at the issues of permanent residency, employment, naturalization, and taxation, as well as legislation concerning the removal of immigrants, the property rights of immigrants, and criminal activity by immigrants. Finally, the author explores the question of immigrant legal rights, including constitutional rights and access that immigrants have to the judicial process and government benefits. In addition, Vázquez-Azpiri looks at how selective service, or the draft, affects immigrants and what laws affect the sponsorship of families for permanent residency and the renouncing of immigrant status.

In his entry, Luis F. B. Plascencia discusses the critical but little-known subject of state, county, and municipal legislation that affects immigrants. He begins with a constitutional and historical background to the topic before looking at state, county, and municipal immigrant policies, which include occupational and professional licensing and overall immigrant restrictions.

$\mathscr{A}$MNESTY

In 1986, the U.S. Congress passed an immigration reform bill with an ambitious goal: to restore control over burgeoning undocumented immigration. The 1986 Immigration Reform and Control Act (IRCA) offered two new policy tools. First, IRCA created civil and criminal penalties for U.S. employers who knowingly hired undocumented immigrants. Second, IRCA authorized a set of temporary, one-time-only immigration benefits programs to "legalize" certain undocumented immigrants already living in the United States—programs that came to be known in the immigrant community as "amnesty."

This reform produced some dramatic short-term changes in immigration dynamics. In the year following IRCA's passage, some undocumented immigrants went home; some delayed coming; and many came forward to adjust to legal status. Contemporary evidence suggests, however, that over the long haul, undocumented immigration persists virtually undaunted. For instance, U.S. Border Patrol apprehensions dropped nearly 50 percent in the three years after IRCA's passage but now exceed pre-IRCA levels. Similarly, although IRCA's legalization options reached nearly 3 million undocumented immigrants, recent estimates by the Immigration and Naturalization Service (INS) of the current undocumented immigrants—some 4 million—imply that IRCA did little to reduce undocumented settlement.

Post-IRCA scholarly attention has focused on INS law enforcement efforts to control immigration. However, only a few projects have assessed U.S. legalization programs. Shortly after IRCA's passage, policy analysts evaluated the amnesty efforts as they unfolded in the field, focusing on emerging challenges to street-level bureaucracies implementing the program. Subsequent efforts extracted some general themes about immigration reform from the legalization experience and examined how legalization affected settlement experiences in particular immigrant communities. Finally, preliminary results are emerging that assess the labor market experiences of those newly legalized and the implications of IRCA legalization for specific sectors of the U.S. industrial structure. Still, a comprehensive assessment has simply had to wait until most applications have been adjudicated and data could be gathered, both quantitative data on the nation's "amnestied" cohort and qualitative data on the dynamics unfolding in communities where that cohort is settling.

THE "AMNESTY" POLICY OPTION

The American satirist Ambrose Bierce wryly defined "amnesty" as "the state's magnanimity toward those offenders whom it would be too expensive to punish." Truly, amnesty offers an expedient way out of the heavy costs involved in fully prosecuting systematic rule violation, be it tax evasion, the committing of war crimes, widespread avoidance of military service obligations, or the circumventing of immigration law. But amnesty also represents the state's admission that its policies have been honored in the breach. Not surprisingly, it is rarely a popular option among policymakers.

To counter this image of vulnerability, amnesty is usually introduced together with either new policies or redoubled efforts at enforcing old policies aimed at the undesirable actions the "amnesty" targets have already taken. Policymakers may fear, understandably, that these new enforcement threats ring hollow alongside an expansive, well-publicized amnesty for the very behavior being sanctioned. Such has been the case throughout the world in the case of amnesty directed toward undocumented or irregular migration. Amnesty, it is argued, implies capitulation to those migrants who, collectively, have taken the migration and settlement process into their own hands, often as a result of changes in or cessation of "temporary"

Amnesty, like that granted to many undocumented immigrants under a 1986 law, allows people to come out of hiding, like this Mexican alien living in an Arizona orchard. *(Philip Decker/Impact Visuals)*

guest-worker programs that encouraged their entry into the host country but seek to constrain the possibility of settlement.

Case studies in Spain, France, Japan, Italy, Belgium, Canada, and Venezuela cohere into a portrait of governments adopting the amnesty option reluctantly, if at all, and only on the heels of renewed efforts to limit irregular immigration. In every case, the primary concern is not fear of the numbers who might come forward but fear of the precedent that amnesty sets regarding the legitimacy of the institutions controlling entry and settlement into the host country. Although turnout never exceeded a few hundred thousand in these cases (and more typically leveled off at less than 100,000 applicants), policymakers consistently voiced concerns that amnesty created a perverse incentive for increased undocumented immigration through its seeming reward for bypassing legal routes to foreign residence.

As bad as this dilemma has been for countries with small to moderately sized undocumented populations, it has proved all the more nettlesome for the

United States, where these themes intersect with a numerically large population of potential amnesty-eligibles. The interaction of the ever-present "undermining of the state's authority" theme and the real possibility of big numbers served to stall U.S. amnesty proposals for more than a decade. In the mid-1970s, the INS began issuing estimates of the resident illegal immigrant population on the order of 12 million. By the time 1980 census figures substituted these estimates with more reasonable alternatives of from 2 million to 4 million, the social construction of a nation losing control of its borders was well entrenched in public sentiment, making border control a popular policy theme and amnesty a very hard political sell.

But the invasion metaphor, with its implication that new immigration control efforts were necessary, shed little light on the problem of what should be done about those undocumented immigrants already living in the United States. Several alternatives existed: wholesale efforts at deportation; a broad, "slate-cleaning" amnesty that would wave a "legalization" wand over the U.S.-resident undocumented immi-

Bangladeshi immigrants demand more grants of amnesty and the extension of Immigration and Naturalization Service rules that allow immigrants to stay in the United States while their legal status is being decided. *(Rommel Pecson/Impact Visuals)*

grants and let the United States concentrate resources on discouraging and interdicting new undocumented flows; or a more targeted pathway to legal residence and full citizenship open only to those undocumented immigrants with "firm equities" built up during their years of U.S. residence, coupled with the hope that ineligibles would find the new immigration law enforcement climate so inhospitable that they would leave.

In the end, IRCA's legalization programs represented an amalgam of the "firm-equities" and "slate-cleaning" options in its two major legalization programs. The main amnesty program offered a chance at legal status to those undocumented immigrants who could prove they had been in the United States continuously since January 1, 1982, and who could surmount several intermediate obstacles to permanent resident status, including a "temporary" residence period and fulfillment of English language and civics education requirements. A separate, much more liberally structured program for undocumented farmworkers with recent experience harvesting U.S. crops (the Special Agricultural Worker, or SAW, program) made its way into IRCA in the closing weeks of congressional debate.

A BRIEF REVIEW OF AMNESTY IN THE UNITED STATES

The IRCA amnesty programs emerged from a byzantine series of cleavages and coalitions wheeling and dealing their way through Congress. The eleventh-hour introduction of SAW legalization, for example, both saved the IRCA package and condemned it to its worst criticism. Well-documented elsewhere, the SAW amnesty bears special mention here as an example of the hard bargains that characterized the IRCA debate.

All observers recognized that IRCA would not see daylight without support from California, home to and employer of most U.S. undocumented immigrants, including a large share of undocumented farmworkers. Throughout the debate over IRCA, California growers and their advocates sought agricultural "guest-worker" provisions and exemptions from employer sanctions to ease IRCA's impact. Farmworkers and their advocates wanted, instead, a generous amnesty that would not condemn them to second-class guest-worker status. Immigration restrictionists throughout Congress insisted on the strong enforcement of sanctions across the board in exchange for their votes supporting amnesty provisions. Immigration advocates mobilized along ethnic lines to insist on generous amnesty in exchange for their support of sanctions against the major employers of their ethnic compatriots. Congressional power brokers attempted to balance both the restrictive and inclusionary impulses of all the players with increasingly complex tinkering with sanctions and legalization parameters.

These machinations produced a fairly involved set of statutory requirements for longer-term undocumented immigrants seeking legalization, including continuous residence since 1982, significant burdens of proof imposed on their petitions, an application process that took place in multiple stages, educational requirements, and bans on access to social services following successful completion of the process. In contrast, as a final compromise intended primarily to shut out a deal-breaking agricultural guest-worker provision being promoted by Senator Pete Wilson of California, SAW legalization offered full-fledged legal resident status to farmworkers whose migration history was as limited as ninety days of employment in the previous growing season, promising growers uninterrupted access to their traditional workforce. Gritting their teeth, employer sanctions supporters accepted these legalization programs as part of the IRCA deal (though amnesty survived the final House battle by only four votes), and the package reached President Ronald Reagan's desk on November 6, 1986.

DATA ON APPLICANTS AND IMPLEMENTATION

To monitor the IRCA implementation effort, the Ford Foundation sponsored a nationwide research project codirected by the Rand Corporation and the Urban Institute. During 1988 and 1989, researchers conducted field interviews in eight sites where legalization was expected to draw a significant response: Los Angeles, San Jose, El Paso, San Antonio, Houston, Chicago, New York, and Miami. Respondents included local INS officials, immigrant advocates, trade and union representatives, public officials, and employers. In addition, interviews took place with regional and national-level respondents. Approximately six hundred interviews were conducted. My analysis of early legalization implementation draws from this database.

Immigration and Naturalization Service statistical

analysts estimated that up to 2.1 million persons might be eligible for pre-1982 legalization. Demographers estimated that another 250,000 farmworkers might be eligible for SAW status. Ultimately, the 107 INS legalization offices around the country processed approximately 1.7 million pre-1982 applications. However, SAW applications dwarfed all reasonable estimates, with 1.3 million applicants coming forward and claiming to have worked in U.S. agriculture in as little as a single growing season.

Census Bureau estimates of the undocumented population resident in the selected standard metropolitan statistical areas (SMSAs) in 1980 should be treated with some caution. First, the estimates do not include the 1981 additions to the undocumented population who were also eligible for legalization. Furthermore, the estimates may vary in quality across sites. Nor can we account for post-1980 migration within the United States, which may have affected the potential population that might apply in each site. Nonetheless, the estimates serve as a baseline for program turnout comparisons.

Los Angeles hosted the largest legalization program, and its turnout was close to preimplementation estimates. Each Texas SMSA took in far more applications than predicted. Chicago and San Jose corresponded closely to preimplementation estimates. New York City and Miami are notable in their relatively low legalization showing. Statewide totals mirror the profiles for the individual SMSAs, with high turnout in Texas; California and Illinois falling between the "high" and "low" range; and New York and Florida demonstrating relatively modest turnout. Across the board, in every site, SAW turnout burst through the roof of INS planning estimates.

Miami's low pre-1982 numbers are obviated somewhat by the 50,500 additional immigrants who applied under the SAW program, some of whom may also have been eligible for the pre-1982 program. In New York City, however, all indications are that pre-1982 legalization turnout was modest. Field interviews with New York respondents identify several reasons. First, the diversity of the immigrant community in New York made legalization outreach particularly difficult. No single national-origin group constitutes more than 10 percent of the foreign-born population in New York City. Second, INS district leadership expressed less enthusiasm for legalization than for other district priorities, particularly in light of the modest resources afforded to the district. Only two legalization offices operated inside the SMSA boundaries, versus sixteen Los Angeles offices.

In contrast, Houston boasted one of the most organized, proactive advocacy communities in the country, working in concert with a highly motivated INS district. This community, drawing together private immigration lawyers, refugee resettlement programs, religious organizations, and human rights groups, mounted its own publicity campaign and took advantage of the INS district's interest in rehabilitating its public image by meeting regularly with district leadership under the auspices of an immigration task force. The result was a turnout twice the expected total in the SMSA's single legalization office. In addition, the Texas undocumented population was much more homogeneous than that of New York, and this largely Mexican population was exactly whom the framers of IRCA had in mind as they designed and implemented the program.

Evidence for IRCA's tilt toward Mexicans (and, to some extent, other Latino immigrants) can be seen in several key INS implementation decisions. For example, throughout legalization, the INS battled in the courts to exclude applicants who did not fit the typical profile of the Mexican undocumented immigrant "entering without inspection" (INS parlance for crossing the border surreptitiously). Visa overstayers, for example, were much more likely to hail from a wide range of countries. Court challenges to INS regulations proved necessary before many of these undocumented immigrants were allowed to apply for legalization. In addition, INS respondents in several key sites—Houston and Los Angeles, for example—reported making a special effort to hire temporary employees for legalization office duty who either were Hispanic or spoke Spanish. No mention was made of such effort on behalf of other ethnic groups. Immigration attorneys complained that this misled non-Hispanic eligibles, with one Houston attorney reporting, for example, that a Zambian client failed to apply because he "thought that program was only for Mexicans."

Given these observations, how closely did the demographic, social, and economic characteristics of legalized aliens match the expectations of policymakers and researchers? Answering this question requires a closer look at the composition of the legalized population and a comparison of those features with policy assumptions.

Years after the legalization window closed, questions have emerged regarding the fate of those legalized and the lessons of the program for policymakers. These questions include the following themes:

1. Who was permitted in, and who was not? As we shall see in the next section, some sociodemographic groups were more successful than others in availing themselves of the amnesty opportunity.

2. What did the "amnestied" gain? Policymakers assumed that legal status would promote economic and civic integration of its beneficiaries and that the residual undocumented population would leave the United States. Field evidence indicates that some assumptions were more plausible than others.

3. What did host communities gain? Legalization produced new economic and political constituencies in some of the largest labor markets in the United States. I examine how these constituencies have produced new social and economic dynamics, as well as new conflict points, in the communities where they now reside.

4. What does legalization offer for the future of host communities in general and their labor market dynamics in particular? Legalization imposed a new set of economic rights and responsibilities on an extant group of workers. Preliminary evidence on the legalized population's position in U.S. labor markets can offer some guidance on how this cohort will operate in the future and what that might mean for its U.S.-born counterpart.

5. What lesson does legalization offer for the making of immigration policy? As a policy tool for coping with illegal immigration, legalization was virtually unprecedented in the United States. Evaluating whether legalization met its goals can allow us to assess whether it merits consideration in other immigration contexts.

I employ two data sources to address these research questions. First, I use the results of federally sponsored data collection projects: administrative data on the entire legalized alien population, known as LAPS data (from the Legalization Application Processing System), and a more detailed survey of 6,193 persons drawn from that sampling frame. The survey, conducted by Westat, Inc. in two waves, one in 1989 under the direction of the INS and a second in 1992 under the Department of Labor, identifies key sociodemographic and economic characteristics of the legalized population. Because these data are restricted to the pre-1982 cohort, evaluations of SAW characteristics are not possible. Therefore, the demographic overview is restricted to the 1.7 million recipients of legal status through the main amnesty program. Second, I employ the results of updated field interviews conducted in late 1993 and early 1994 in the same implementation sites that served as the sample for an earlier review of legalization.

Disaggregating total amnesty turnout by region of origin and implementation site reveals useful information. First, it is clear that Mexicans were the overwhelming winners. Preimplementation estimates placed the Mexican share at roughly half the undocumented total, according to R. Warren and J. Passel, yet Mexicans accounted for 70 percent of all legalization applicants and greater shares in California, Texas, and Illinois. Interestingly, the Mexican share was more modest in Houston, where a particularly active advocacy community concentrating on Central Americans conducted extensive outreach among the Salvadoran and Guatemalan constituencies and brought thousands into the program. Active legalization outreach among Polish immigrants accounts for much of the Eastern Hemisphere showing in Chicago, while Caribbean migrants—Dominicans, Haitians, Jamaicans—were significantly represented in New York and Florida.

If this national-origin composition reflects implementation bias, it may be the case that legalization cleaned some parts of "the slate" better than others. Legalization may well have altered the immigration-status composition of the Mexican-origin community in the United States while leaving other national-origin subgroups relatively untouched. Indeed, recent estimates of the resident undocumented population show a dramatic shift in national-origin composition. Whereas pre-IRCA estimates placed the Mexican share at roughly half, new INS estimates place it at one-third. To the extent that non-Mexican subgroups are concentrated in particular geographic areas—New York, for example—the labor market dynamics of undocumented immigration for those local areas are unlikely to evince much change as a result of amnesty.

Rather than assuming that the gender patterns in legalization accurately reflect population composition, it is important to consider how implementation affected the gender distribution. In each site visited during early implementation immigrant advocates and INS officials noted that undocumented women faced great difficulty in trying to adjust to legal status. Legalization required a paper trail demonstrating U.S. residence since 1982—for example, rent receipts, paycheck stubs, utility bills. Women were less likely to have such evidence, particularly when (1) they were partnered with men whose names appeared alone on leases, bank accounts, and the like, and (2) when they were employed in the underground economy of domestic service. In sum, the concentration of males among the legalized likely reflects both migration dynamics and program implementation decisions.

Further evidence that women were present in the networks of legalized aliens comes from the high proportion of amnesty recipients who reported being married or living with a partner as if married in the 1989 Westat survey. While many of these spouses/partners may not have been eligible for legalization, it is clear that a portrayal of the undocumented immigrant who legalized through IRCA as a solitary earner is incomplete.

Along with basic demographic characteristics, the Legalized Person Survey provides human capital profiles that are useful in anticipating labor market incorporation. Clearly, the legalized population lags far behind other groups of U.S. workers on education. Median education level is seven years for the entire legalized population, with lower educational attainment in Texas. Higher education levels emerge in New York and Florida, in keeping with the greater diversity of national-origin backgrounds evident in these sites. English-language skills vary across sites. Overall, 15 percent of legalized adults reported speaking English "well" in the Westat survey. That proportion was much lower in Texas (8 percent) and considerably higher in New York and Florida.

Thus, it appears that the most numerous amnesty beneficiaries did not rank high on orthodox indicators of human capital. That is, the largely low-education, non-English-speaking undocumented immigrants in the southwestern United States were the most numerous applicants, and it is in that region, and among the job and industry categories where those workers are found, that the effects of legalization are likely to be greatest.

Again, implementation decisions facilitated the ability of these modestly educated immigrants to complete the legalization process successfully. One important decision was the creation of alternatives to the IRCA-mandated "English/civics" test for permanent residence. The act also provided for adjustment to permanent residence if an applicant could demonstrate attendance at an English/civics course of study approved by the INS, for a minimum of forty hours, even if proficiency levels were insufficient to pass the test. Roughly three-quarters of the legalizing immigrants surmounted the English/civics barrier through these alternate routes.

These amnesty "Phase II" classes, as they were called in most sites, brought thousands of legalizing immigrants into the classrooms of adult education providers, even prompting one Houston respondent to call the program "the largest Hispanic adult education program ever mounted in this city." Still, forty hours of instruction could not promote true English literacy among a population starting with so little educational background. Although IRCA originally authorized $1 billion a year for four years to be returned to states and localities for the expenses incurred in delivering such services as English/civics classes, follow-up field interviews in 1993 indicated that the moneys actually disbursed dropped so dramatically over time that many course providers in the nonprofit community simply closed up shop. In Los Angeles, where respondents from L.A. Unified School District reported IRCA adding approximately 270,000 students to the adult education caseloads, federal reimbursement was limited to those first forty hours of instruction necessary to meet the permanent residence requirement. The "amnesty coordinator" for the school district noted that IRCA students were then "forced into the general student population and had to compete with our non-IRCA students for slots. Most of them require at least 90 to 150 hours of English training for even the most limited skills. All 40 hours does is keep them in their present low-wage job and social position." Thus, IRCA's goal of strengthening the connection of legalized aliens to their host society may have been undercut by the inability of program directors to implement English/civics as part of a meaningful educational opportunity.

Legalized aliens were much more likely to be living in households with family members than living alone. This was particularly true of legalized aliens living in California, where over 80 percent of the applicants reported family members sharing their U.S. households.

Respondents to the Westat survey identified persons living in their households at the time of their application and whether each person was either a U.S. citizen or a legal permanent resident. The residual household members in the legalized alien's household who were neither U.S. citizens nor permanent residents may serve as a proxy for part of the post-IRCA residual undocumented population. As many as 710,000 presumably undocumented persons were living in the United States with legalized aliens in 1989.

This phenomenon of mixed immigration status within families proved to be one of the thorniest implementation issues facing legalization. Early in the program, it became apparent that one of the factors chilling application rates was the immigrants' concern that their ineligible family members would come to the attention of the INS as a function of their own applications. As a result, the INS issued implementing regulations instructing district offices to grant administrative relief through such mechanisms as "voluntary departure" status to the undocumented minor children and, ultimately, the spouses of legalizing ali-

ens. In addition, the Immigration Act of 1990 created a temporary allotment of 55,000 extra visa slots in fiscal years 1993 and 1994 to be applied to spouses and minor children of legalized aliens.

In sum, both regulatory and statutory relief was brought to bear on the problem of mixed immigration status so as to avoid resorting to the deportation of undocumented family members attached to legalized aliens. Still, by 1989, for every 100 legalized aliens, 41 family members remained in the United States without either citizenship or permanent resident status having been secured through their relationship to their "amnestied" relative.

Considerable variation exists across implementation sites in the labor market position of the legalized population. In Florida, one in three legalized aliens worked in a white-collar occupation. Legalized aliens, in Texas, by contrast, were highly concentrated in blue-collar work and were more dispersed across industries, including a much higher share in construction work. Legalized aliens were more concentrated in the manufacturing and service sectors in California and New York.

Wage rates and individual earnings confirm the assumption that legalized aliens were a low-wage group. Median wages for legalized aliens at the time of application stood at roughly 60 percent of that for the total U.S. workforce, and median earnings were less than half. These dollars earned were also being stretched beyond the boundaries of the U.S. households. Fully two-thirds of the 1989 Westat survey respondents reported sending an average of 7 percent of their family income back to their country of origin through remittances. These figures were higher in Texas, with greater shares of the sample (over 70 percent) sending greater amounts (roughly 10 percent of family income), and lower in Florida. Thus, although legalized aliens had demonstrated firm ties to the United States through their extended residence, they still connected with their countries of origin.

This observation yields one of the more important themes in IRCA legalization. Field interviews with advocates indicate that one of the strongest incentives for legalizing, from the immigrant perspective, was the right to travel internationally. Another was the right to petition for relatives to immigrate legally. In sum, rather than fully integrating aliens into their identities as U.S. residents, legalization was a way to keep their ties alive with the country of origin.

With this profile, we can reevaluate some of the research questions outlined above. Who won? Clearly, the undocumented Mexican and Central American populations of the southwestern United States availed themselves most thoroughly of the legalization opportunity. The legalized population is also heavily male and concentrated in the ages of young adulthood. These results are due to both the composition of the eligible population and the implementation decisions made throughout the program. From its regulations to the nature of legalization publicity, the program targeted the undocumented border crosser from a Spanish-speaking country.

With these demographic characteristics come human capital repertoires reflecting low levels of education and English proficiency, and these characteristics translate into an unsurprising occupational, industrial, and income profile. As would be expected, legalized aliens work in lower-skill, lower-pay jobs in the U.S. labor markets where they settle.

The legalized cohort is tied significantly to both U.S.-resident kin and family members abroad. Not only do legalized immigrants demonstrate this through ongoing remittances, but they also continue to share U.S. households with both legally resident and undocumented family members.

The next question is, what did the immigrants win? Legalization brought work authorization, travel authorization, and authorization to petition for relatives to immigrate. Although the transition to legal status did not translate immediately into dramatic economic gains for the legalized cohort, both INS data and field data indicate that legalized aliens took advantage of the opportunity to immigrate their relatives and to maintain ties to their countries of origin.

Thus, the relationship between the legalized alien and identity-construction as a U.S. resident may be more complex than policymakers had anticipated. While legal U.S. residence is the first step toward full citizenship and participation in U.S. civic culture, legalized aliens appear to be using this resource, in the short term, as a bridge between home and host countries. In the words of one New York INS official, "The most valued card is the Employment Authorization Card. The 'Green Card' is no longer important." The opportunity to work, regardless of formal immigration status, is paramount. Additionally, little evidence exists to support the claim that the residual undocumented population has been chilled from staying in the United States or that new flows have been halted. Rather, legalization has introduced a wider variety of possibilities in the building of international immigrant social networks and the strategies of work and household formation.

THE EFFECTS OF LEGALIZATION ON HOST COMMUNITIES

The legalization program extends beyond the boundaries of the legalized. It also affects the social, economic, and political landscape on which immigrant and U.S.-born groups come together. Field interviews in key legalization sites yield several themes that allow us to assess how effectively legalization accomplished its policy goals.

A decade after IRCA's passage, field respondents report very little concrete labor market change. However, two trends did emerge in California: an increase in immigrant day labor; and a gradual transition from farm labor to low-wage manufacturing and service work. Immigration and Naturalization Service officials and advocates in Los Angeles noted that day-labor pools had expanded and often included IRCA-legalized aliens whose petitions for permanent resident status were still pending. Respondents from the INS attributed this day-labor increase to their enforcement of employer sanctions, which reduced opportunities in the formal sector, although sanctions enforcement should not have affected the job search process for legalized aliens, who are authorized to work wherever they manage to get a job offer. Advocates pegged the trend, instead, to the stagnant California economy. In San Jose, advocates and employment training program directors noted that clients were beginning to come in from agricultural work to seek assistance in finding manufacturing jobs. "But," as a training director noted, "they're still low-wage, unskilled jobs . . . as long as their education level is so low, they won't move too far up the ladder."

Across the country, respondents noted that, in lieu of job changes, IRCA-legalized aliens evinced changes in awareness regarding their rights in the workplace. An immigration program director in San Jose remarked that legalized aliens were making inquiries about union jobs. This kind of awareness fulfilled the expectations of a Houston carpenter's union local that sought Qualified Designated Entity (QDE) status during early implementation in an effort to reach undocumented construction workers. (A QDE is a community organization approved by the INS to process legalization applications.) As the union director noted, "We knew they were there, but we didn't have a way to reach them . . . By helping with legalization, we didn't have to preach unionism to them . . . we had them at a time when they were going to be receptive." Although union officials did not identify dramatic increases in their membership as a function of IRCA (and, indeed, very little change was noted in such key union strongholds as the garment workers in New York), they did identify legalization as a force reducing the barriers to successful organizing.

Nonetheless, the removal of "undocumented" status altered other constraints very little, such as the dour state of the economy, particularly in California, during the postimplementation period. Respondents repeatedly noted that the full effect of legalization on the labor market could not be seen separately from the lack of job growth characterizing the entire economy. In Los Angeles, an immigrant advocate noted that the office had seen the highest levels of unemployment among its immigrant constituency in recent memory. Again, this perspective coincided with the observations of INS officials who saw an upsurge in informal, irregular employment. With nearly 1 million legalized people residing in California, little economic mobility was anticipated by respondents for the population as a whole.

Another constraint on economic mobility cited frequently was the low education level among IRCA-legalized aliens. Here, educational service providers were particularly adamant about the disjuncture between the amnesty promise and its realization. The IRCA program for state reimbursement of social service costs—State Legalization Impact Assistance Grants (SLIAG)—came under particular fire. In Houston, a nonprofit service organization reported its frustration at the low level of reimbursement for its IRCA clients. Its SLIAG-funded services shut down in 1992 because, according to the director, "it just wasn't cost-effective." What had been touted in 1988 by a Houston respondent as the biggest Hispanic adult education program in the city's history had by 1993 become a program whose funding limitations removed providers with strong ties to the immigrant community from the pool of those to whom immigrants could go for educational assistance.

In sum, the legalization program has not produced significant labor market change. Rather, information is the resource identified in the short-term as accruing to legalized aliens. That is, linkages to social service providers and advocates have improved, so that the IRCA-legalized possess better information about their rights as permanent legal residents. But this integration into the host community infrastructure was clouded by a simultaneous theme emerging in the field: the anti-immigration backlash.

In August 1993, California governor Pete Wilson (who had been instrumental in the design and passage of IRCA as a U.S. senator) mobilized immigration restrictionists by placing an "open-letter" advertisement directed at President Bill Clinton in several leading newspapers calling for an end to citizenship rights for the U.S.-born children of undocumented immigrants and an end to federal mandates providing health and education services to undocumented immigrants. The letter touched off a firestorm of controversy surrounding both legal and undocumented immigration, ultimately leading to the passage of a referendum known as Proposition 187, and its effects are abundantly evident in the field interviews conducted for this project.

Without exception, every respondent reported the "backlash" as a key immigration issue facing the local community. From the INS in Los Angeles, whose respondents stated that legal and illegal immigrants were being "lumped together unfairly," to a reporter in New York, who portrayed the community as consumed by "the politics of hysteria," respondents noted that anti-immigrant sentiment was commanding most of the media attention on immigration.

Although most observers agreed that anti-immigrant sentiment was strongest toward the currently undocumented, many noted an IRCA-related issue contributing to the anti-immigration milieu—the secondary migration of legalized alien family members. In site after site, respondents noted the increasing presence of whole families among their client populations. "The pre-1982 applicants started petitioning for family members as soon as they could. We estimate that 60 percent of our clients have done so, and this appears among all nationalities," stated a San Jose educator. A Houston advocate explained the same dynamic in different terms: "We see, particularly among Central Americans, the tendency to leave the kids at home, or even to send them back home when they're born here. . . . Now that the parents are legalized, they've got Grandma calling them up saying, 'Hey, when are you coming to get the kids?'" The large cohort of IRCA beneficiaries, overwhelmingly from Mexico and Central America, all coming eligible at the same time to petition for their immediate relatives, has produced an upswing in the salience of immigrant families in key sites and thus has produced an upswing in concerns about their use of such services as health care and education. In response to the "anti-immigration/anti-immigrant" sentiment, a variety of policy actors have now come together to promote another immigration benefit for the newly legalized: naturalization.

Both government and private advocacy group respondents identified naturalization as a top priority in immigration policy in the coming years—particularly for the IRCA-legalized cohort, which one advocate described as a "special client community," given its unique entry into legal status. The IRCA-legalized are seen as likely candidates for a break from the traditionally low naturalization rates characteristic of Mexican immigrants, for reasons outlined by a private nonprofit group attorney: "They can bring their relatives more easily if they're citizens. But, just as importantly, in this climate, the lines are being drawn in ways that further incentivize naturalization. The ante is upped now. If you're not a citizen, you're going to have to be concerned about changes in criminal rights that are coming up in the Senate crime bill, you're going to have to worry about your eligibility under welfare reform, under health reform. Citizenship is self-protection. I hate to make it a defensive tactic, but there's a real sense among the advocates that we don't know what's coming next."

Immigration and Naturalization Service officials echoed this sentiment. Los Angeles officials noted that the next step should be to "close the door on illegal immigration, but bring legal immigrants in completely. Help us help them become citizens." In sum, the resources of the advocacy community and the INS are in alignment and directed toward naturalization, and respondents were optimistic about their chances of persuading the IRCA cohort to naturalize. As legalization itself demonstrated, varied organizations marshaled toward a common goal in the implementation of immigration policy can have a profound impact on immigrant behavior.

Yet, this element—immigrant behavior—remains as the unknown factor. Will IRCA immigrants avail themselves of the naturalization benefit? Evidence from the field is mixed. During early implementation, one immigration researcher noted that the immigrant community, particularly the Latino immigrant community "has the least possible contact necessary with the government . . . they tend to want to deal with the government only as much as they have to in order to survive." Today, respondents identify the backlash itself as producing a perverse incentive for IRCA immigrants to align themselves more deeply with their U.S. identity by naturalizing as a survival strategy, one that is facilitated, for example, by the economic crisis in Mexico and changes in Mexican policy that allow for dual-nationality status.

Should IRCA beneficiaries naturalize in great numbers, we are left to ponder economic and political implications. Ironically, some evidence suggests that the transformation to legal status may exacerbate competition effects with native-born workers. That is, the presence of legal immigrants has demonstrated more consistent, albeit mild, depressing effects on wage rates and earnings in local labor markets than has the presence of undocumented workers. As the IRCA cohort moves up the job ladder, it may set off

new competition dynamics with native-borns and, particularly, with other legal immigrants.

But will these dynamics become more pronounced with the acquisition of U.S. citizenship? Here, again, we return to the issue of immigrant policy, rather than immigration policy. The legacy of legalization, economic and political, will depend on both the human capital repertoires of the IRCA cohort and the fit between those repertoires and the labor market. With such modest skill levels, and few opportunities for education and training, amnestied citizens are likely to remain largely where they were as legal resident aliens—among the ranks of the working poor.

Thus, concern about their use of public assistance entitlements for poor people becomes the new immigrant policy battleground. The field interviews conducted in this project highlight a growing political tendency for the distinction among immigration status groups to be drawn in broader and broader terms. Whereas the political rhetoric surrounding IRCA focused on *undocumented* migration, the political debates today are much more inclusive, with concerns being voiced about the overall level of immigration to the United States. With renewed emphasis on domestic reform in the areas of health, education, and welfare, immigrants are finding themselves caught in a protracted battle over benefits eligibility and state/federal division of the cost for delivering those services.

The impact of naturalization on this dynamic is uncertain. While facilitating access to public services may exacerbate the backlash, it can also facilitate the incorporation of the IRCA cohort by affording it the full array of social services intended to promote economic mobility. This is certainly the appeal being made to permanent resident aliens by naturalization advocates. If, instead, those who have been legalized remain outside the boundaries of programs to enhance human capital, they will likely continue on their current economic path—occupying lower-wage, lower-skill niches; subject to dislocation in times of economic downturn; and incurring the wrath of local political actors when their demands on the public coffers appear to outstrip their contributions.

On its own terms, legalization worked well. It reached and successfully adjusted the status of millions of undocumented immigrants, who are now more connected to the institutions of the host society and are the focus of an INS-sponsored campaign encouraging their further incorporation through naturalization.

But as immigrant-focused policy promoting social and economic adaptation, IRCA left much to be desired. Field respondents strongly critique the arrangements to assist states in financing immigrant incorporation. The legacy is a new battlefield, pitting immigrants against natives once again.

At present, the negative incentives of increased border enforcement, employer sanctions, and a reduction in funds for immigrant-serving social programs appear to have done little to stem immigration. At the same time, political energy is now being marshaled toward a package of positive incentives—citizenship and increased adult education opportunities, for example—that can channel legally resident immigrants more rationally into their U.S. communities. The legalization experience illustrates that public agencies, partnered with trusted private organizations, can attract immigrants to use services. Although such efforts will not combat the continued flow of undocumented immigrants seeking to improve their economic life chances, they increase the odds that legally resident immigrants, including the IRCA cohort, will succeed in their efforts to settle successfully in the United States.

Susan González Baker

See also: Immigration Legislation of the 1980s and 1990s (Part I, Sec. 5); The Immigration and Naturalization Service, Legal and Illegal Immigration: A Statistical Overview (Part II, Sec. 2); Legislation I: Immigration (Part II, Sec. 5); Immigration Reform and Control Act, 1986 (Part IV, Sec. 1); New U.S. Rules on Asylum for Women, 1995 (Part IV, Sec. 2).

BIBLIOGRAPHY

Baker, S. G. "California and Catalunya: The Politics of Immigration Control in the United States of America and the Kingdom of Spain." Unpublished manuscript, 1995.

———. *The Cautious Welcome: The Legalization Programs of the Immigration Reform and Control Act.* Washington, DC: Urban Institute Press, 1990.

———. "Immigration Reform: The Empowerment of a New Constituency." In *Public Policy for Democracy*, ed. H. Ingram and S. Rathgeb-Smith, pp. 136–58. Washington, DC: Brookings Institution, 1993.

Bean, Frank D., B. Edmonston, and J. Passel. *Undocumented Migration to the United States: IRCA and the Experience of the 1980s.* Washington, DC: Urban Institute Press, 1990.

Bean, Frank D., B. Lindsay Lowell, and Lowell J. Taylor. "Undocumented Mexican Immigrants and the Earnings of Other Workers in the United States." *Demography* 25 (1988): 35–52.

Bean, Frank D., R. Chanove, R. G. Cushing, R. de la Garza, G. Freeman, C. W. Haynes, and D. Spener. *Illegal Mexican Migration and the United States/Mexico Border: The Effects of Operation Hold-the-Line on El Paso and Juarez.* Washington, DC: U.S. Commission on Immigration Reform, 1994.

Bierce, Ambrose. *The Devil's Dictionary.* New York: A. & C. Boni, 1925.

Borjas, G. *Friends or Strangers: The Impact of Immigrants on the U.S. Economy.* New York: Basic Books, 1990.

Borjas, G., and M. Tienda. "The Employment and Wages of Legalized Immigrants." *International Migration Review* 27:4 (1993): 712–47.

Calavita, K. "Italy and the New Immigration." In *Controlling Immigration: A Global Perspective*, ed. W. Cornelius, P. L. Martin, and J. F. Hollifield, pp. 303–26. Stanford: Stanford University Press, 1994.

Cornelius, W. A. "Spain: The Uneasy Transition from Labor Exporter to Labor Importer." In *Controlling Immigration: A Global Perspective*, ed. W. Cornelius, P. L. Martin, and J. F. Hollifield, pp. 331–70. Stanford: Stanford University Press, 1994.

Cornelius, W. A., P. L. Martin, and J. F. Hollifield. "Introduction: The Ambivalent Quest for Immigration Control." In *Controlling Immigration: A Global Perspective*, ed. W. Cornelius, P. L. Martin and J. F. Hollifield, pp. 3–42. Stanford: Stanford University Press, 1994.

Donato, K. "Current Trends and Patterns of Female Migration: Evidence from Mexico." *International Migration Review* 27:4 (1993): 748–71.

Donato, K., J. Durand, and D. Massey. "Stemming the Tide? Assessing the Deterrent Effects of the Immigration Reform and Control Act." *Demography* 29:2 (1992): 139–58.

Fix, M., and P. Hill. *Enforcing Employer Sanctions: Challenges and Strategies.* Washington, DC: Urban Institute Press, 1990.

Freeman, G. "Can Liberal States Control Unwanted Migration?" *Annals of the American Academy of Political and Social Science* 534 (July 1994).

Garcia y Griego, M. "Canada: Flexibility and Control in Immigration and Refugee Policy." In *Controlling Immigration: A Global Perspective*, ed. W. Cornelius, P. L. Martin, and J. F. Hollifield, pp. 119–40. Stanford: Stanford University Press, 1994.

Hagan, J. M. *Deciding to Be Legal.* Philadelphia: Temple University Press, 1994.

Hagan, J. M., and S. G. Baker. "Implementing the U.S. Legalization Program: The Influence of Immigrant Communities and Local Organizations on Immigration Policy Reform." *International Migration Review* 27:3 (1993): 513–36.

Hollifield, J. F. "Immigration and Republicanism in France: The Hidden Consensus." In *Controlling Immigration: A Global Perspective*, ed. W. Cornelius, P. L. Martin, and J. F. Hollifield, pp. 143–76. Stanford: Stanford University Press, 1994.

Hondagneu-Sotelo, P. *Gendered Transitions: Mexican Experiences of Immigration.* Berkeley: University of California Press, 1995.

Immigration and Naturalization Service. *The Immigration Reform and Control Act: Report on the Legalized Alien Population.* Washington, DC: Government Printing Office, 1992.

Immigration and Naturalization Service. "INS Estimates of Nonimmigrant Overstays, Resident Illegal Alien Population." Unpublished memorandum, April 22, 1994.

Koussoudji, S. "Playing Cat and Mouse at the U.S.-Mexican Border." *Demography* 29:2 (1992): 159–81.

Loe v. Thornburgh. No. 88 Civ. 7363 (PKL) (S.D. New York). In *Litigation Update: Legalization/Special Agricultural Workers*. Washington, DC: American Immigration Lawyers Association, 1989.

Lowell, B. Lindsay, and Z. Jing. "Unauthorized Workers and Immigration Reform: What Can We Ascertain from Employers?" *International Migration Review* 28:3 (1994): 427–48.

Martin, P. L. "Good Intentions Gone Awry: IRCA and U.S. Agriculture." *Annals of the American Academy of Political and Social Science* 534 (July 1994): 44–57.

Massey, D. "The New Immigration and Ethnicity in the United States." *Population and Development Review* 21:3 (1995): 631–52.

Massey, D., K. Donato, and Z. Liang. "Effects of Immigration Reform and Control Act of 1986: Preliminary Data from Mexico." In *Undocumented Migration to the United States: IRCA and the Experience of the 1980s*, ed. Frank D. Bean, B. Edmonston, and J. Passel. Washington, DC: Urban Institute Press, 1991.

Meissner, D., and D. Papademetriou. *The Legalization Countdown: A Third-Quarter Assessment*. Washington, DC: Carnegie Endowment for International Peace, 1988.

Meissner, D., D. Papademetriou, and D. North. *Legalization of Undocumented Aliens: Lessons from Other Countries*. Washington, DC: Carnegie Endowment for International Peace, 1986.

North, D. *Decision Factories*. Washington, DC: Transcentury Development Associates, 1988.

North, D. "IRCA Did Not Do Much to the Labor Market: A Los Angeles County Case Study." Immigration Policy and Research Working Paper 10. Washington, DC: Department of Labor, 1991.

North, D., and A. M. Portz. *The U.S. Legalization Program*. Washington, DC: Transcentury Development Associates, 1989.

Sorensen, E., and F. Bean. "Immigration Reform and the Wages of Mexican Origin Workers: Evidence from Current Population Surveys." *Social Science Quarterly* 75:1 (March 1994): 1–17.

Snowden, L. "Collective versus Mass Behavior: A Conceptual Framework for Temporary and Permanent Migration in Western Europe and the United States." *International Migration Review* 24 (1990): 577–90.

Warren, R., and J. Passel. "A Count of the Uncountable: Estimates of Undocumented Aliens Counted in the 1980 U.S. Census." *Demography* 24:3 (1987): 375–93.

CIVIL RIGHTS

The Constitution forms the bedrock of civil rights guarantees in the United States. The specific prohibitions against state power over American citizens outlined in the first ten amendments include the protection of free speech, freedom from illegal searches and seizures, the right to bear arms, and other rights American citizens consider their birthright. Later amendments, such as the Fourteenth Amendment, guarantee that all Americans receive equal protection under the law. Key U.S. Supreme Court decisions have also served to expand constitutional protections. And while the Supreme Court has shifted interpretations of the specifics of these protections, often reversing previous decisions, all American citizens are considered equally protected under the Constitution. But questions about whether some or all of these rights apply to immigrants continue to be debated.

This is a more complex issue than it appears on the surface. At certain times in American history the answer has been a qualified yes, at other times a qualified no. Historically, there have been a variety of interpretive models put forth concerning immigrants and the Constitution. One model contends that the Constitution applies universally to all people residing in the United States and that it should safeguard the rights of anyone residing within the nation's boundaries, whether an immigrant living on American soil or a native-born citizen. A different model holds that the Constitution applies only to members of the "social contract"—in other words, those who constitute the actual body politic of the United States. Yet another interpretation, the mutual-obligation model, argues that when the government requires certain obligations of immigrants, such as subjecting them to military draft or taxation, then it also must extend to them constitutional protection of their civil rights. A more recent global model holds that constitutional rights may be applied to citizens and noncitizens alike in accordance with international laws and treaties.

In addition to the various interpretive models developed over time is added the complicating issue of state sovereignty. There is the question of the relationship between the various states and the federal government regarding immigrants. In some cases, especially before the twentieth century, the federal government deferred to state governments in formulating immigration policy and defining immigrant rights. This has given the states a significant role both in immigration policy and in the question of immigrants' civil rights.

HISTORICAL DEVELOPMENT

The question of immigrants' civil rights first received national attention at the close of the eighteenth century. The young American republic found itself torn externally between the warring powers of England and France and internally between the warring political factions of Federalists and Democratic-Republicans. In 1798, a Federalist congress enacted the Alien and Sedition Acts. The sedition portion of the acts targeted speech and actions that might cause the government, and in particular the Federalist president John Adams, disrespect. The primary targets of the sedition aspect of the Alien and Sedition Acts were Democratic-Republican newspaper editors supportive of their party's leader, Thomas Jefferson. The alien portions of the act, on the other hand, targeted "aliens" (immigrants residing in the United States); most important in the minds of the authors of the legislation were French citizens residing in the United States and agitating for American intervention in their hostilities with England. What is important for the purpose of examining the historical development of immigrants and civil rights are the two different models of immigrants and the Constitution raised by the measures. Federalists contended that the civil rights guarantees applied only to American citizens, while

Jeffersonian Democratic-Republicans favored a more inclusive interpretation. They believed that "alien friends" in residence in the United States enjoyed the same constitutional protections as citizens.

This Jeffersonian interpretation has been called the mutual-obligation model: The government obliges immigrants to abide by the laws of land, and in return, the government is obliged to protect their civil rights. This model remained the dominant interpretation in the United States until the latter decades of the nineteenth century, when the courts returned to the so-called social-contract interpretation. According to scholar Gerald L. Neuman, since the turn of the century developments "have produced a mosaic of inconsistent rules and rationales."

The image of a mosaic of inconsistency is an appropriate one to describe immigrants and civil rights since the turn of the century. Policies began to be im-

Asian immigrants in California organized a counter-demonstration against Proposition 187, a 1994 referendum that would have cut off almost all social services to legal and illegal immigrants. *(Slobodan Dimitrov/Impact Visuals)*

plemented that restricted both the ability of immigrants to enter the country and the rights they enjoyed once arrived. In 1882, Congress passed the first racially based immigrant exclusion law, the Chinese Exclusion Act, which denied entrance to most Chinese immigrants.

Despite the harsher anti-immigrant tone of the period, the U.S. Supreme Court moved counter to the dominant trend. In 1903, the Supreme Court ruled in *Yamataya v. Fisher* that the Immigration and Naturalization Service (INS) must conduct hearings that abide by due process, a nod to the notion that immigrants are indeed protected by at least portions of the Constitution.

In the 1920s, President Woodrow Wilson's attorney general, A. Mitchell Palmer, spearheaded a program of mass deportation of suspected subversives, a period known as the Red Scare. Thousands of immigrants, particularly eastern Europeans, were deported without hearings and without due process, in clear violation of the *Yamataya v. Fisher* ruling. Accused of having communist, socialist, anarchist, and other leftist ties, these immigrants were simply rounded up and shipped out of the United States.

The 1920s also witnessed the creation of the U.S. Border Patrol, an agency specifically charged with the mission of protecting the U.S.-Mexico border from illegal immigration. This agency, more so than any other, has been accused of violating immigrants' civil rights. In the latter decades of the twentieth century, the Border Patrol was charged with abuses against both documented and undocumented immigrants ranging from unnecessary detention to sexual abuse to unlawful death.

In the Depression years of the 1930s, the INS launched a massive program of deportation of Mexican immigrants, the so-called Mexican Repatriation Program. Thousands of legal as well as undocumented immigrants were rounded up and sent back to Mexico. For many of them the United States was home and Mexico but a distant childhood memory. In most cases these immigrants were deprived of basic constitutional protections of equal treatment under the law and due process.

One of the most egregious abuses of immigrants' civil rights occurred during World War II. In 1942, President Franklin D. Roosevelt signed Executive Order 9066, ordering the internment of persons of up to one-eighth Japanese ancestry living in a zone along the West Coast. Before the internment camps closed just before the end of the war, over 110,000 Japanese immigrants and American-born citizens of Japanese descent had been interned in the camps. At the time, organizations and concerned individuals pointed to the violation of internees' civil rights, especially those of the American citizens among them. In the 1980s, the government acknowledged the abuses and began proceedings to extend reparations to some of the camp survivors.

The federal government shifted the focus of immigration policy in 1965. The government instituted policies that favored families and skilled workers in place of the older quotas based on national origin. Since the 1960s, the majority of immigrants to the United States have come from Latin America and Asia.

IMMIGRANTS AND CIVIL RIGHTS SINCE 1980

In the 1990s, estimates of the annual number of immigrants to the United States varied from 700,000 to 900,000. This number does not include an estimated 400,000 undocumented immigrants. The estimated immigration to the United States, of both documented and undocumented immigrants, averaged about 1 million. Foreign-born residents accounted for about 10 percent of the American population. Since 1965, an estimated 26 million immigrants have come to call the United States home.

In the two decades since 1980, major areas of concern with immigrant civil rights have been constitutional protections of due process, equal protection under the law, and First Amendment guarantees of free speech and religious freedom. Again the issues raise more questions than they provide answers, including whether immigrants are entitled to due process. This question is most relevant to the deportation of immigrants. In many cases, immigrants have been deported based upon secret evidence. Deportees do not have the right to see this evidence against them, but only a brief and general summary. For those who subscribe to a universalist model of immigrant constitutional rights, this is an obvious violation of due process. In the view of those favoring a more restrictive interpretation, for security reasons, not all evidence can or should be divulged. Because of the person's status as a noncitizen, the civil rights guaranteed by the Constitution are deemed to have not been violated.

Another question concerns whether the Fourteenth Amendment guarantee of equal protection under the law encompasses noncitizens residing in the United States. If deportation hearings raise issues of due process, they also raise serious concerns about the Four-

teenth Amendment's equal protection clause. In most cases, immigration judges' rulings are not subject to judicial review, and the immigrant has either a very limited ability or no ability at all to appeal such decisions.

Added to these measures restricting immigrants' rights were "English-only" laws adopted by several states in the 1980s and 1990s. These laws typically restrict state agencies to using only the English language for official documents. The concern is that the English-only laws tread on immigrants' First Amendment right to free speech. For example, Arizona's amendment to its state constitution, Article 28, which mandated that state agencies "act in English and in no other language," was challenged by the American Civil Liberties Union (ACLU) and other concerned groups on the basis that it violated the equal protection guaranteed by the Fourteenth Amendment. In 1995, the Ninth Circuit Court of Appeals declared the Arizona law unconstitutional. In other states, English-only laws have also been challenged on the grounds that they violate First Amendment protection of free speech.

Far-reaching changes to an immigrant's ability to access health care also came up in the 1990s. Access to quality health care has been another major concern of immigrants to the United States in recent years. Immigrants share several problems with other groups in the United States associated with low income levels. To this are added issues of language barriers, fear of the INS, little or no insurance, and a lack of knowledge of what health care services are available at the local, state, and federal levels. The Personal Responsibility and Work Opportunity Reconciliation Act of 1996 (PRWORA) restricted immigrant access to Medicaid and other federal programs. Prior to this national legislation, immigrants had been entitled to participate in most federal health care programs. PRWORA restricted access to federal health care benefits that immigrants had previously enjoyed. Most notably, the legislation restricted immigrants' access to Medicaid benefits. Thus, PRWORA represented a major shift in immigrant health policy. It gave the states the majority of the responsibility in deciding who qualifies for federal aid. If access to at least minimal health care is considered a basic right in the United States, then PRWORA has strengthened the general trend in the 1980s and 1990s toward further limiting immigrants' rights in the United States.

Of the states, only California has included immigrants in all of its state health programs. As of 2000, federal law prohibited children and pregnant women who had arrived in the United States after August 1996 from receiving Medicare and state children's health insurance. California's Children's Health Insurance Program (CHIP) provides the main source of immigrant health benefits along with Medicaid (Medi-Cal in California). This fact has led some Californians to feel that they shoulder an unfair burden. Partly as a backlash to this, California voters approved Proposition 187 in 1994, which eliminated access to health care, education, and other social services for noncitizens and undocumented immigrants. Most of the provisions of Proposition 187 were subsequently declared unconstitutional by a U.S. district court judge.

To counter this trend in restricting immigrants' rights, in 1985 the ACLU initiated its Immigrant's Rights Project to protect immigrants' civil rights. The ACLU takes a universalist approach to the Constitution, arguing that while the federal government should have the power to regulate the entrance of immigrants into the United States, once here the immigrants should enjoy the full protection of the law and of constitutional safeguards of their civil rights. By law, immigrants are entitled to hearings before an immigration judge, the right to an attorney (although not at government expense), reasonable notice of hearing date and fees, reasonable opportunity to see evidence against themselves, and an interpreter.

REFUGEES AND DEPORTATIONS

The United States has traditionally accepted refugees fleeing persecution in their home countries. Yet since 1980, when laws regarding political refugees were enacted, the federal government has increased restrictions on refugees. The Reagan administration rejected the vast majority of petitioners from Guatemala and El Salvador, despite knowledge of the extensive repression in those countries. President George H. Bush followed suit in denying safe haven to over twenty thousand Haitian refugees, ordering the Coast Guard to intercept them and turn them back to their troubled island nation. In the 1990s, changes in immigration laws, as well as the passage of new antiterrorism legislation, gave the government wider latitude in deporting immigrants and forbade class-action lawsuits on the part of refugee groups, such as Salvadorans. It also allowed for the use of secret evidence in deportation cases, a clear rejection of the more inclusive models of the relationship between immigrants and the Constitution.

Another significant change in immigrant rights came with the Illegal Immigration Reform and Immigrant Responsibility Act of 1996 (IIRIRA). This legislation allowed for the deportation of legal immigrants, even if they have resided in the United States for a lengthy period, if they are convicted on drug charges. In such cases, an immigrant facing deportation cannot appeal an unfavorable decision because the law proscribes review by a higher court. This law was modeled on the concept that immigrants are not protected by the Constitution in the same ways U.S. citizens are, a refutation of the universalist approach.

The Illegal Immigration Reform and Immigrant Responsibility Act also restricted the ability of immigrants to challenge INS activities in court. This measure, also based on an exclusionary model of immigrants and the Constitution, has raised serious concerns about immigrants' rights to due process. In some of these cases, the issue of double jeopardy has also been raised. A legal immigrant may be convicted and serve the required sentence or pay the required fine but later be subject to INS review and possible deportation.

One of the major constitutional concerns at the close of the twentieth century, therefore, was the restrictions on judicial review of immigration judge rulings. IIRIRA effectively eliminated judicial review. Immigrants subjected to deportation, on whatever grounds, have little or no ability to appeal INS decisions. If immigrants were considered protected by the Constitution, then this is a violation of due process and basic fair legal treatment. It is also a violation of habeas corpus review of whether or not the government is holding an immigrant in custody in violation of the law. Prior to 1996, immigrants had retained the right to judicial review of deportation cases.

One case in the late 1990s highlighted the fact that certain gross abuses of immigrants are deemed to be clearly in violation of their civil rights. On August 9, 1997, Abner Louima, a Haitian immigrant, was taken into custody in Brooklyn, New York, following an altercation outside a nightclub. Louima was handcuffed and beaten by police, and later taken into a bathroom, where he was again beaten and violated with a sharp object. The attack resulted in a ruptured bladder, rectal lacerations, and other serious injuries that required hospitalization. Four of the police officers were indicted on charges that they had violated Louima's civil rights. The court found that such violence against an immigrant obviously violated that person's civil rights.

If immigrants such as Louima have avenues for redressing civil rights violations, they also have means to seek justice for suspected cases of employment discrimination. The Office of Special Counsel for Immigrant-Related Unfair Employment Practices in the U.S. Department of Justice was established to examine cases of alleged job discrimination against immigrants. Immigrants can request an investigation of claims that they were denied employment or fired because of their citizenship status or national origin, or were requested to provide unusual or unnecessary documentation.

The question of immigrants' civil rights and the relationship between immigrants and the Constitution is a complicated one, fraught with inconsistency and even caprice. The exact relationship was ill-defined at the time of the framing of the Constitution and remained so at the close of the twentieth century. At certain times in American history immigrants were believed to enjoy most of the rights guaranteed in the Constitution. At other times they were considered largely outside constitutional protection. If there has been one consistent feature in conceptions of immigrants' civil rights, it is that they are subject to trends in American society. At times of national insecurity and war, tensions that gave rise to the Alien and Sedition Acts and Japanese internment, immigrants' civil rights have been seriously circumscribed. At other times of national growth and security, such as the first half of the nineteenth century, the definition of immigrants' civil rights has been expanded. There is no reason to believe that this historical trend of shifting visions of immigrants' rights will not continue well into the future.

Scott Zeman

See also: Immigrants and the Red Scare, Japanese Internment (Part I, Sec. 4); Immigration Legislation of the 1980s and 1990s (Part I, Sec. 5); Immigration and Crime, Legislation II: Immigrants in America (Part II, Sec. 5); Anti-Immigrant Politics (Part II, Sec. 6); *United States v. Bhagat Singh Thind,* 1923, *Hirabayashi v. United States,* 1943, *Lau v. Nichols,* 1974, *Plyler v. Doe,* 1982, *LULAC et al. v. Wilson et al.,* 1995, California Proposition 63, 1986, California Proposition 187, 1994, California Proposition 227, 1998 (Part IV, Sec. 1); Reparations for Japanese-American Internees, 1988, U.S. Report Under the International Covenant on Civil and Political Rights, 1994 (Part IV, Sec. 2).

BIBLIOGRAPHY

Bader, Veit-Michael, ed. *Citizenship and Exclusion.* New York: St. Martin's Press, 1997.

Carlimer, David. *The Rights of Aliens and Refugees: The Basic ACLU Guide to Alien and Refugee Rights.* Carbondale: Southern Illinois University Press, 1990.

Jonas, Suzanne, and Dod Thomas, eds. *Immigration: A Civil Rights Issue for the Americas.* Wilmington, DE: Scholarly Resources, 1999.

Neuman, Gerald L. *Strangers to the Constitution: Immigrants, Borders, and Fundamental Law.* Princeton, NJ: Princeton University Press, 1996.

United States Congress. *Border Violence.* Washington, DC, 1993.

United States Immigration and Naturalization Service. *Brutality Unchecked: Human Rights Abuses Along the U.S. Border with Mexico.* Washington, DC, 1992.

IMMIGRATION AND CRIME

As a nation of immigrants since its founding, the United States has a long and complex history of crime perpetrated both by and against immigrants. Fear of crime and criminal behavior from immigrants has long led immigration officials to screen incoming aliens for criminal records and to deny admission or deport those with criminal backgrounds. From the Irish Molly Maguires through the Italian Mafia to the Eastern European and Asian organized crime groups in the 1990s, immigrants have played a prominent role in the annals of crime and criminology.

A multiplicity of problems appears when addressing the subject of immigrants and crime. It can be a somewhat difficult task to speak of such things as "crime" and "immigration" in such general terms; surely the culture, background, history, and demographics of each immigrant group that has come to America is unique and as diverse as America itself. Some data sources attempt to divide and classify groups into general categories that can make the problem even tougher. For example, "Hispanic" groups can include Mexicans, Puerto Ricans, Colombians, Cubans, and so on; "Asian" groups include Japanese, Chinese, Filipinos, Indians, Pakistani, Thai, Vietnamese, Laotians, Cambodians, and Koreans. Further complications arise with questions of first-generation and subsequent immigrants and matters of "assimilation." Yet, at the same time, the diversity of the country itself makes it difficult to narrow the study of some groups and then generalize those narrow findings to an entire group and an entire country.

Moreover, defining "crime" can be equally as frustrating and ambiguous. Crime can range from such things as petty theft and vandalism to gangs, organized crime, and today's global networks and drug cartels. For some, the only crime involved is being arrested for being in the country illegally. With all these issues in mind, the caution must be issued that the discussion to follow, as any discussion of this type, is necessarily incomplete.

Lastly, a discussion of immigrants and crime necessarily carries the caveat that the majority of people of any immigrant group are law-abiding people with no criminal involvement and no criminal propensity. Although at various periods of U.S. history and continuing up through the present day, immigrant groups have often been feared and unjustly accused of being criminal, no such evidence exists that any group is inherently more criminal than any other. In fact, most immigrants are model citizens.

Criminal involvement by immigrant groups is most often a blend of behavior of both the first-generation immigrants and subsequent generations and a product of the social milieu in which they find themselves. Criminal behavior has sometimes resulted when immigrants have been isolated; faced with poverty, low education levels, and unemployment; at odds with the dominant culture, and dealing with concerns over assimilation and acceptance.

EARLY IMMIGRANT CRIME GROUPS

Examination of the history of crime shows that immigrant criminals came from virtually every group that emigrated. Although criminals sometimes operate as individuals, best known are immigrant gangs and organized crime groups that have dominated in large cities and metropolitan areas, including, among others, Jewish, Irish, Italian, French, German, Polish, Slavic, Mexican, Puerto Rican, Cuban, Colombian, Chinese, and Filipino groups. Two prominent groups, the Irish Molly Maguires and the Italian Mafia, are examined below.

THE MOLLY MAGUIRES

The Molly Maguires were perhaps the best known of the early immigrant crime groups. The nature of the

Members of a Filipino chorale group in Seattle sing during a memorial service for slain postal worker Joseph Ileto, a victim of anti-immigrant hate crime, in 1999. *(Associated Press)*

Mollies depends on which account one reads. To some, they were the epitome of a cutthroat, murderous gang that terrorized eastern Pennsylvania around the time of the Civil War, while to others, they were crusaders fighting the business barons in defense of the coal miners and other oppressed Irish immigrants of the region.

According to legend, a woman in Ireland named Molly Maguire had killed several of the despised landlords and their agents who had terrorized and oppressed the workers of the region, at about the same time as a vigilante group of men were formed for more or less the same purpose. Sharing the same principles and methods as Molly herself, the men began calling themselves the Molly Maguires (or were so called by others in the area) and dressing as women for disguises when carrying out their murders.

Reportedly, the Mollies were a branch of the secret fraternal organization of the Ancient Order of Hibernians. Emigrating to the United States at the same time as the majority of Irish immigrants in the 1850s,

the Mollies left behind the women's clothing but continued fighting what they saw as the oppression of the poor, this time the coal miners in eastern Pennsylvania. Throughout the 1850s, 1860s, and 1870s, the Mollies continued to remain a dominant force in the region, involved primarily in the labor conflict involving coal, railroads, and workers. Conflict and strikes characterized the region for years, with the Molly Maguires always in the thick of it. Working conditions were so miserable at the time that the workers took the law into their own hands at any opportunity they could, usually in secret and by stealth. Crime ran rampant among the Irish immigrants but, oddly, not among many of the other immigrant groups of the region that were subject to the same conditions, primarily the English, Welsh, and German miners.

A series of strikes and lockouts occurred during the late 1860s and early 1870s, with the Mollies immersed in the troubles. Terrorizing the "scab" laborers and as well as the Irish workers "recruited" into their midst, the Mollies grew stronger and bolder, becom-

Like all Americans, immigrants can be both victims and perpetrators of crime. Here the Immigration and Naturalization Service displays weapons confiscated from immigrant gangs in Los Angeles. *(Donna DeCesare/Impact Visuals)*

ing so powerful that some members of the Molly Maguires were elected to public office in the region as public officials, commissioners, and even chiefs of police.

The beginning of the end of the Molly Maguires came in the person of iron, coal, and railroad magnate Frank B. Gowan. Knowing that the Mollies could not be broken through "official" channels, Gowan brought in the services of the famous Pinkerton Detective Agency. The main operative for the Pinkertons was an Irish immigrant from County Armagh named James McParlan. McParlan changed his name to McKenna and set about to infiltrate the Molly Maguires. Within three years, McKenna presented enough evidence to indict twenty of the local Irish immigrants, with many of them, it was later claimed, upstanding men with no criminal ties. McKenna's work culminated in what later became known as "Black Thursday" or "the day of the rope," when seven repudiated members of the Mollies met their death by hanging.

The debate and the controversy surrounding the Molly Maguires continue to this day. To some, the Mollies were a band of dangerous thugs and got what they had coming on Black Thursday. To others, Mc-

Kenna, Gowan, and the Pinkertons were the thugs who destroyed a group of innocent men in the anti-Irish, anti-immigrant sentiment of the day.

ITALIAN-AMERICAN CRIME

Italian-American crime groups have been known by various names in the popular media: the Mafia, the Black Hand, L'unione Siciliana, the Neapolitan Camorra, and La Cosa Nostra. While the existence of the crime groups themselves is not in question, their level of formal organization and importation to America has been debated for years.

The earliest mention of a secret Italian society in America begins with the murder of New Orleans police superintendent David Hennessey in 1890. With his dying breath, Hennessey is reported to have named "Sicilians" or "dagoes" as his assassins. Nineteen Italian immigrants were arrested and charged with being part of a secret organization of assassins responsible for Hennessey's murder. Although the defendants were found not guilty, an angry mob gathered and stormed the jail, killing eleven of the defendants by either shooting or hanging them.

In reality, there was no secret organization of assassins. Hennessey supported the Provenzano family in a business feud between them and the Matranga family for control of the New Orleans docks. After Hennessey's murder, an investigation by authorities found that less than 1 percent of the Italian immigrants of New Orleans had any type of criminal record, most of them for petty offenses. But rumors persisted of the secret society, and debate has arisen as to its origin: whether it was imported, evolved, or was a new creation patterned after the Italian Mafia.

Although there are many theories as to the origin of the name, the word "mafia" in Italian means to strut or swagger, and criminals known as mafiosi began to appear in western Sicily in the early nineteenth century. Sicily and southern Italy, a region known as the Mezzogiorno, had been an oppressed region for centuries, under the control of various conquerors, one after the other. After feudalism had been abolished, a power broker system of absentee landowners with middlemen/overseers began to take form, and peasants who owned no land of their own courted their favor to lease the land in small plots or become sharecroppers. These middlemen became powerful people, and without official recourse from their conquerors, peasants often turned to them for help and for protection. Growing even more in strength and stature, these power brokers evolved into a means of extorting "protection" from the local populace and, at the same time, providing goods and services for them that were unattainable through legal channels. Thus there are many who believe that mafia, with a small *m*, is more a method than a formal organization.

It does not seem likely that any formal crime organization was imported with the Italian immigrants that began coming to the United States in the 1880s. Rather, the power broker system, coupled with the natural distrust and secretiveness that was necessary for survival by everyone in coping with the centuries of conquerors and oppressors, was imported along with the immigrants. "Black Hand" gangs began springing up, particularly in the large urban ghettos inhabited by the immigrants, with extortion and protection as their main enterprise. The Black Hand gangs were independent in nature, however, and while they may occasionally have cooperated with or at least tolerated one another, there is no evidence that they were a secret, formal, organized group.

It was not until the advent of Prohibition—the Volstead Act—that the smaller gangs began to coalesce into large, organized crime groups. The sale and distribution of illegal alcohol made the crime groups rich and necessitated a greater degree of cooperation between the Italians in their competition with the other ethnic gangs involved in bootleg liquor, especially the Irish and Jewish gangs. In Chicago, for example, typical of the competition among gangs across the nation, a line of succession through Big Jim Colosimo, Johnny Torio, and Al Capone wrested control from Dion O'Bannion and his gang, while in New York, the so-called Castellemarese War culminated in the rise to power of those such as Charley "Lucky" Luciano and Vito Genovese. Intent on ridding themselves of the first-generation immigrant gangsters they called "greaseballs" or "Mustache Petes," Luciano, Genovese, and others took control and set up the five-family system still in existence in New York today.

Interestingly, while the press paid close attention to the gang activities of the 1920s and 1930s, the word "Mafia" hardly ever appears in the media, being cited only four times in the *New York Times* between 1918 and 1943. In the 1950s, however, "Mafia" became embedded in the national consciousness as a synonym for organized crime. Senate hearings chaired by Estes Kefauver concluded that "the Mafia" was a "sinister criminal organization" that had been imported from Italy and operated globally.

In 1957, fearing a takeover by Albert Anastasia and seeking to increase his own power, family boss Vito Genovese reportedly engineered Anastasia's murder, causing a "conference" of nationwide Mafia leaders to be called for in the small, upstate New York town of Appalachin. Noting the constant parade of black limousines, a conscientious New York state trooper formed a roadblock and called for reinforcements to investigate the possible illegal activity. When word of the roadblock and possible raid spread through the "conference," dozens of crime bosses were sent scrambling through the woods in their silk suits in an attempt to get away and avoid investigation. The incident made national headlines and once again brought the issue of the Mafia and "Italian gangsters" into the forefront of the public eye, stepping up efforts by both the Justice Department and local officials in combating organized crime.

In 1963, Mafia "soldier" turned informant Joe Valachi gave America a look inside the secret organization he called La Cosa Nostra. Literally translated as "this thing of ours," Valachi testified as to the never-before-revealed structure and organization of the Cosa Nostra, which many saw as the proof of its existence. Still, there are many who present well-founded arguments that the Mafia, La Cosa Nostra—or whatever name is used—is merely a loose confederation of localized crime groups, not a national, formal, and secret organization.

IMMIGRANTS AND THEORIES OF CRIME CAUSATION

With the earliest waves of immigrants, feelings of xenophobia caused most Americans through the early twentieth century to think that the "foreigners" coming to America's shores were simply more criminal in nature. Seen as sinister and morally degenerate, this view was reinforced by early academic theorists who posited theories of crime as stemming from hereditary and biological causes, as well as evolutionary "throwbacks" who were less developed on the evolutionary scale in the popularity of the Darwinist thought of the day.

The advent of sociology as an academic discipline in the early twentieth century gave rise to new thoughts as to the social causes of crime. Especially popular was the Chicago school of sociology pioneered at the University of Chicago. Using the methods of the Chicago school, crime and other social problems were studied in an ecological context, using Chicago and its many immigrant populations as a laboratory in which social ills could be studied in their natural environment.

In one of the most prominent studies begun in the 1920s, Clifford Shaw and Henry McKay expanded on the work of other Chicago sociologists Robert E. Park and Ernest W. Burgess. They noted that urban areas grew in a series of concentric zones resembling a bull's-eye: the older, decaying areas with higher crime rates lay toward the center of the city, and newer areas with fewer social problems lay in the outer zones, furthest away from the center of the city. A series of immigrant groups had lived in the neighborhoods closest to the center that Shaw and McKay had studied, including Czechoslovakians, Germans, Greeks, Italians, Irish, Poles, and Russians. As one group gained economic advantage and moved further away from the center of the city into a new zone, a new immigrant group succeeded them as occupants of the neighborhood.

The significance of Shaw and McKay's study was that no matter which immigrant group occupied the neighborhoods closest to the center of the city, the crime rate remained high, while the crime rate of the immigrant group moving away from the city declined. Shaw and McKay then concluded that it was the social disorganization of the neighborhood that caused the high crime rate, not the immigrant group within it. Shaw and McKay's work, however, was not without its flaws. Most notably, later sociologists have

determined that some immigrant groups do vary in their rates of crime, but Shaw and McKay began the process of showing that crime was more of a social product and not inherent in any one immigrant group.

A rise in juvenile delinquency and gangs brought a new awareness to the subject of crime causation in the 1950s and 1960s. Most of these theories did not focus directly on immigrants or ethnicity as a cause of delinquency, but retained them as an issue by default, instead concentrating on social class, subcultural concerns, and the social construction of law itself. Thorsten Sellin, for example, in his book *Culture Conflict and Crime*, puts forth the idea that the law is created by the dominant culture as a reflection of its own values and that ethnic and racial minorities clash with those values when their own conduct norms are in opposition. When the conduct norms of the original culture are upheld by immigrants over the norms of the new culture, a conflict develops that can, in effect, create a criminal out of an immigrant who is doing what has always been, to him or her, the right thing to do. Sellin uses the example of an immigrant Sicilian father who finds and kills his daughter's seducer. The father is outraged by his subsequent arrest for doing what his culture said was the right and honorable thing to do in that situation.

Albert Cohen, another prominent social theorist of the day, saw delinquency as a form of culture conflict between the lower and the middle class. In his 1955 book *Delinquent Boys*, Cohen noted that such authority figures as schoolteachers held lower-class youth to middle-class standards, which were difficult or impossible to achieve, a concept he termed the "middle-class measuring rod." These boys undergo a "status frustration" that they protest by involving themselves in street gangs and behavior that he termed "nonutilitarian, malicious, and negativistic."

A number of social theorists have focused on the conflict in cultures and on social class, inequality, and ecological concerns of residential areas to the present day. While none has established a definitive and universally accepted theory of "the" cause of crime, ethnic or otherwise, some general conclusions about ethnic crime can be drawn. Most notably, street gangs are ethnically and racially homogeneous, are products of lower socioeconomic backgrounds, and are primarily young and male. Reflecting the characteristics of immigration itself, the white European immigrant youth gangs of earlier days have now largely disappeared.

IMMIGRANT CRIME TODAY

As difficult as the problems of studying, defining, and determining the causes and issues of immigrant crime in the past have been, they pale in comparison with many of the concerns that exist today. The ethnic street gang of yesteryear still exists, to be sure, albeit in a modern and more sophisticated context, aided by modern and up-to-date technology, better armed with a variety of sometimes very sophisticated weaponry, and engaged in more sophisticated types of crime than just the turf wars of earlier days. In today's global society, immigrant crime takes on much more serious proportions than just local neighborhoods of high crime, entering the realm of such things as transnational drug cartels, money laundering, international terrorism, smuggling, and gunrunning. As international business ventures and the global market become more lucrative and more attractive for legitimate enterprise, so too are they for illegitimate and illegal activity. These illegal enterprises have surfaced in a variety of common and everyday places and everyday walks of life. Allegations have even surfaced in the 1990s of criminal involvement in such things as professional sports, most notably of Russian organized crime involvement in the National Hockey League in Canada and the United States. While the scope of such problems and immigrant groups are beyond what can be discussed in detail here, I will attempt to describe the history and involvement of two such groups, those of Chinese and Mexican origin.

CHINESE AMERICANS

As noted above, the term "Asian" is a general one, including Japanese, Chinese, Filipino, Indian, Pakistani, Thai, Vietnamese, Laotian, Cambodian, and Korean groups. While, to some, evaluating several different cultures as "Asian" may be a handy and convenient categorical means of evaluating several groups, it is unfair to do so in terms of cultural diversity and especially in terms of criminal patterns and behavior.

For example, Asian Americans have sometimes been called a "model minority," having lower arrest and incarceration rates than whites, African Americans, or Native Americans. Japanese Americans, for example, have historically had very low crime rates, attributable in part to the structure of the family in Japanese culture.

Patterns of criminal offense among Chinese immigrants show a much different and more clouded picture. Much of the crime in Chinese communities in the late nineteenth and early twentieth centuries has been attributable to a high number of arrests on vice charges, particularly gambling, opium, and prostitution. Chinese men first came to work in gold mines and on railroads, and after the Chinese Exclusion Act of 1882 was passed and immigration from China shut off, Chinese men outnumbered women, and the number of brothels in many Chinese neighborhoods flourished. Gambling, long a staple of Chinese society, was at odds with U.S. culture, particularly in the Victorian era.

Historical reports of Chinese crime, however, have been ambiguous, at best. At various times and by various reports, Chinese crime rates have been described as both extremely high and extremely low. One such report, by the Wickersham Commission in 1931, for example, stated that the Chinese had the highest arrest rate of any foreign-born ethnic group in San Francisco. In 1938, only seven years later, a report by Judge Helen MacGill of the juvenile court in Vancouver, British Columbia, addressed the extremely low crime rates among Chinese and Japanese youths of that area. Judge MacGill remarked that this low rate was achieved despite the high rate of poverty when compared with other ethnic groups having much higher crime rates.

Several events in the latter half of the twentieth century have contributed to a resurgence of Chinese immigration. Repeal of the Exclusion Act and the Chinese War Brides Act in the 1940s began the flow of immigration once again. In the mid-1960s, with relaxation of immigration laws in general, more Chinese immigrants began arriving from Taiwan and Hong Kong. Many refugees of Chinese ethnic origin entered the United States from Southeast Asia after the fall of Saigon in 1975, and the reestablishment of diplomatic relations with China has also contributed to Chinese-U.S. immigration in recent years.

Much of the rise in crime in Chinese communities is attributable to gang activity, and much of the gang activity is rooted in the particular social structure of Chinese culture. Except for the commerce in catering to the tourist industry, many American Chinatowns were enclaves left to themselves and largely ignored by mainstream American society. Life in American Chinatowns followed the practices and customs that had long been a part of Chinese culture. This social order include Chinese voluntary associations of varying types. Enmeshed in a complex web of political, business, and regional alliances, one type of voluntary organization, the *tongs*, is most closely linked with illegal activities; the tongs employ members of youth gangs as bouncers, enforcers, and helpers in territorial disputes.

This gang activity began to flourish with the influx of immigrants in the 1960s and 1970s. Due in large part to high unemployment, social conditions, and adjustments that these immigrants made, gang activity was generally ignored by the American population at large for a long while, until several incidents made the American public and law enforcement officials take notice. In the first of these, three Chinese gunmen walked into the Golden Dragon Restaurant in San Francisco's Chinatown in 1977 and opened fire, mistakenly believing they were killing rival gang members. Five customers were killed and eleven wounded, all innocent victims. On Christmas Eve of 1982, three gunmen opened fire at random in a Chinatown bar in New York City, and three months later, in February 1983, fourteen customers of the Wah Mee Club, a Chinese gambling house in Seattle, were taken hostage, tied up, and shot at pointblank range during a robbery. Several other incidents followed, including rape, robbery, and murder of innocent tourists. With violence no longer restricted to Chinatown residents, law enforcement officials reacted to the public outcry, and a host of anti–Chinese gang task forces were formed to combat the problem.

Ko-Lin Chin, in his study of Chinese gangs, finds little or no evidence to support the theory of a Chinese Mafia in New York but that the characteristics of Chinese gangs parallel those of other ethnic gangs. Chin found that Chinese crime, largely a result of gang activity, includes such things as gambling, prostitution, robbery, heroin trafficking, human smuggling, and extortion. Although Chinese gangs can be violent in other crimes, Chin finds little violence involved in the extortion of money from Chinese businesses and merchants by the gangs. Partly rooted in Chinese culture, the extortion is often seen as a more serious offense by law enforcement than by the business owners themselves.

Despite the task forces that were formed to combat the outbreak of Chinatown violence in the late 1970s and early 1980s, Chinese gangs still exist in Chinatowns across the nation. Perhaps not seen as the same degree of social problem when Chinatown residents are victimized as when outsiders are attacked, Chin offers three policy recommendations at the conclusion of his book to solve the pervasive problem of Chinatown gangs: curb illegal immigration, crack down on unlicensed businesses, and discourage tong membership.

MEXICAN AMERICANS

Mexican Americans comprise the largest Spanish-speaking immigrant group in the United States. As with most other immigrant groups, criminal involvement remains a matter of involvement of both the immigrant generation and subsequent generations. Sharing a border with Mexico and a history that includes much of the western United States as one-time Mexican territory, Mexican influence and immigration have long been a part of U.S. history. Los Angeles and many other U.S. cities had their beginnings as Mexican pueblos.

Along with African Americans, Mexicans share the unfortunate distinction of having the largest ethnic involvement in gang activity in the United States, while southern California, with its large Mexican-American population, carries the dubious distinction of "gang capital of the U.S." As with some other immigrant groups, many Mexicans who came to the United States to settle in the first half of the twentieth century were poor and uneducated. Finding work in both rural agricultural areas and manufacturing jobs in the cities, Mexican immigrants often settled into the cheapest—and therefore poorest—areas.

As early as the 1920s, many of what were labeled as Mexican "gangs" were no more than traditional social groups of young males hanging out together in the barrios, or neighborhoods. These social groups were extremely territorial in nature and often clashed with the young men from other barrios at dances, parties, and similar social events, earning them the "gang" moniker. The effects of immigration and poverty drove many of these youths to petty crime and minor skirmishes with the law, deepening the "gang" labels that had already been applied.

Mexican gangs gained national notoriety in the so-called Zoot Suit Riots of 1942 in Los Angeles. So named for the flashy zoot suits that were the fashion of the day, a young Chicano was killed in a gang-related incident that resulted in the arrest and conviction of seventeen gang members on various charges stemming from the killing. A panic broke out as the news media warned about the Mexican zoot suit gangs and police dragnet-raids swept the area, resulting in hundreds of arrests. Caught up in the vigilante-type atmosphere, a number of U.S. servicemen on leave were involved in a series of fights with groups of young Mexican males, most of whom had no gang involvement at all but were chosen at random and beaten up by the servicemen.

The Zoot Suit Riots created a moral panic among local Anglo residents in areas with large Mexican-American populations, but Mexican-American gang activity was minimal for a period of years. Most researchers and social scientists of the day expected that Mexican-American gang problems would fade as older gang members aged and the Mexican-American population was assimilated into the larger society, much as had happened with many other, earlier ethnic gangs. But many of the social problems that other ethnic and immigrant gangs had experienced did not fade away for a large portion of the Mexican-American population, and by the late 1960s, many Mexican-Americans were caught up in the social unrest that swept the country among African Americans and other minorities.

Throughout the 1970s and 1980s, gang problems grew among Mexican-American populations, particularly in southern California and especially in Los Angeles. Many feel that the gang "problem" grew in proportion and in response to the underlying social problems of Mexican Americans and the newer Mexican immigrants of the area. Mexican Americans had always played an important role in the economy of the southwestern United States, but for many, the gradual assimilation and acculturation predicted in earlier days never took place. Continuously isolated and marginalized in the poorest barrios, the *cholos*, or dress and demeanor peculiar to Mexican gangs, continued to live in the forefront of life for many Mexican-American youths. As the American economy changed throughout the 1970s, 1980s, and into the 1990s and America changed into more of a service-sector economy, young Mexican Americans, both male and female, continue to face the high unemployment, high dropout rates, and continued marginalization that contribute to the proliferation of the attractiveness of gang life for many Mexican-American youths.

CRIMES AGAINST IMMIGRANTS

The United States is a country in which immigration has played a major role in its founding, shaping, and population as a nation, but the history of the United States is littered with xenophobia, nationalist, and nativist sentiment, and an abundance of crimes perpetrated against its immigrants. Almost without exception, all major immigrant groups settling in the United States have been the objects of persecutions and discrimination and the victims of assaults, rapes, lynchings, and homicides.

Such crimes were common against immigrant populations and sometimes were even encouraged. Some newspapers, for example, ran editorials encouraging lynchings and beatings at the height of the anti-Chinese sentiments of the nineteenth century. Often immigrants were swept up in anti-immigrant frenzies, their only crimes a matter of being in the wrong place at the wrong time. In the Zoot Suit Riots described

above, for example, Mexicans with no gang involvement whatsoever were attacked, beaten, and killed by American servicemen only because they were Mexican. There are several incidents of lynchings and beatings of Italians, Jews, Chinese, and others who were singled out and attacked solely on the basis of their ethnic origin.

Labor unrest was also a major form of violence against many immigrant groups. Whether one believes that members of the Molly Maguires constituted a cutthroat gang of thugs or were protectors of the innocent, the lynchings that occurred were certainly typical of the labor strife that surrounded many immigrants. In one such labor incident, twenty-one Hungarian and Slavic immigrants were killed and forty wounded when a sheriff's posse fired into a group of striking miners in Pennsylvania in 1897.

Such events were not uncommon in the past and to some degree have continued in the present. Harassment of Iranian, Iraqi, and other Middle Eastern immigrants has been reported, for example, in the wake of recent American conflicts with those nations, most recently over U.S. involvement in Serbia and the Balkan nations. Hate crimes, discussed below, have been a long-term social problem in America and have been cast into the forefront of American culture as the country moves into the twenty-first century.

INSTITUTIONAL CRIMES

Institutional racism and discrimination have long been a form of crime perpetrated against immigrant populations. Until the mid-1960s, when civil rights legislation made discrimination illegal based on race or national origin, immigrant populations were restricted and regulated in various aspects of life.

Many immigrant populations voluntarily confined themselves to ethnic neighborhoods and enclaves as a means of convenience and survival upon their arrival in the United States. Faced with strange customs, hostility, and language barriers, these enclaves provided a degree of security and familiarity for many of the immigrants in a strange land. But for many, the opportunities to better themselves and provide improved housing for themselves and their children were blocked by legislation that did not allow them to live in certain areas. Some people were not allowed to sell their homes to members of certain ethnic or immigrant groups. Typical, for example, were legal clauses written into real estate contracts forbidding sale to "Negroes, Jews, Italians, Poles, Chinese, or any other member of a non-white race."

Miscegenation was also a form of institutional discrimination that made it a crime for many immigrant groups to marry or even be in the company of persons of the opposite sex that were outside their ethnic group. Some immigrant groups were predominantly male when they came to the United States, for example, Filipinos, Chinese, and Mexicans, but were legally prohibited from intermarriage with American women.

Discrimination in the criminal justice system is another form of institutional crime perpetrated against immigrants and ethnic groups. Sometimes ignored by the criminal justice system and deemed not worthy of official attention, many immigrant groups were often left to handle legal and justice issues on their own, without official recourse from the system. But oftentimes, immigrants were victims of police brutality, judicial bias, and abuses of the correctional system. The issue of human rights violations and criminal justice bias remains in the forefront of immigrant issues but is a hotly debated topic. Some social science researchers and criminal justice experts maintain that discrimination in the modern-day system is a matter of individual bias, offering data and evidence that no systematic and institutional bias exists. Others, however, maintain that criminal justice bias and human rights violations are as rampant as ever and offer support for their arguments as well. Whichever side is more correct, it remains an emotional issue, spurred on by media reports such as that of the brutalizing of a Haitian immigrant in 1997 in a Brooklyn police precinct headquarters and the 1999 shooting of an unarmed African immigrant who police thought was reaching for a gun, both incidents that made national headlines.

HATE CRIMES

Many of the incidents described above of crimes perpetrated against immigrants are now classified as hate crimes. Congress defines hate crimes as those "in which the defendant's conduct was motivated by hatred, bias, or prejudice, based on the actual or perceived race, color, religion, national origin, ethnicity, gender, or sexual orientation of another individual or group of individuals."

Even with the many positive gains in civil rights in the twentieth century, prejudice, discrimination, and hatred of out-groups persist in American society. Membership in "skinhead" gangs and neo-Nazi and white supremacist groups has grown since the 1970s, and in 1990, Congress passed the Hate Crime Statistics Act, which was signed into law by President Bush to keep track of the problem of hate crimes. Typically,

hate crimes are extremely vicious and brutal acts that are often perpetrated on strangers at random by multiple offenders. Including intimidation, brutal beatings, and murder, hate crimes have steadily increased throughout the last years of the twentieth century.

Various explanations have been offered for the proliferation of hate crimes. One details a "culture of hate" in which those who are different are singled out and become the objects of scorn of those in the in-group. While hate crimes are perpetrated against a number of different groups, immigrants make up a large proportion of hate crimes. In recent years, large numbers of immigrants from Latin America, Eastern Europe, Asia, and Africa have faced the same xenophobia and nativist sentiment that have plagued immigrants in the United States since its inception.

Of the immigrant issues that have been with the United States since colonial times, the intertwining of crime and immigration has been one that has been present and prominent from the beginning. In seeking a better life for themselves and their families, immigrants to America have not only had to adjust to the strange language and customs of a new homeland but the strange languages and customs they brought with them have also sometimes been seen as evil, sinister, and criminal by those who were already here. Living in overcrowded ghetto conditions, plagued by poverty, high unemployment, and lower educational levels, the vast majority of immigrants from all nations have endured, eventually realizing a better life. But for some, the living conditions and social problems they have faced have blocked legitimate opportunities and forced immigrants to explore other opportunities, among them criminal activities.

While some immigrants undertook criminal opportunities as individuals, most prominent and most visible were those who turned to crime groups. Offering solace and understanding to their members, some crime groups arose from social groups whose only social outlets were the streets; others viewed themselves as latter-day Robin Hoods, protecting themselves from the oppression by others; still others found crime to be their opportunity for financial and social gain.

Also important is consideration of crime against immigrant groups. Plagued by random acts of violence almost from the day of arrival, immigrants have been beaten, tortured, intimidated, lynched, and murdered, often for the sole "crime" of being immigrants. Most immigrant groups have had to endure institutional crimes and discrimination from the very institutions they turned to for help in bettering their lives. And despite the many strides that have been made in social, cultural, and legal equality, sadly there are still many immigrants who endure the hate crimes today.

Paul Magro

See also: Legislation II: Immigrants in America (Part II, Sec. 5).

BIBLIOGRAPHY

Alba, Richard D. *Italian Americans: Into the Twilight of Ethnicity.* Englewood Cliffs, NJ: Prentice Hall, 1985.

Albini, Joseph L. *The American Mafia: Genesis of a Legend.* New York: Meredith Corporation, 1971.

Barlow, Hugh D. *Criminal Justice in America.* Upper Saddle River, NJ: Prentice Hall, 2000.

Chin, Ko-Lin. *Chinatown Gangs: Extortion, Enterprise, and Ethnicity.* New York: Oxford University Press, 1996.

Cohen, Albert. *Delinquent Boys: The Culture of the Gang.* New York: Free Press, 1955.

H. R. 4797, 102d Cong. 2d sess., 1992.

Jacobs, James B., and Kimberly Potter. *Hate Crimes.* New York: Oxford University Press, 1998.

Klein, Malcom W. *The American Street Gang: Its Nature, Prevalence, and Control.* New York: Oxford University Press, 1995.

Kleinknecht, William. *The New Ethnic Mobs: The Changing Face of Organized Crime in America.* New York: Free Press, 1996.

Levin, Jack, and Jack McDevitt. *Hate Crimes: The Rising Tide of Bigotry and Bloodshed.* New York: Plenum Press, 1993.

Liska, Allen E., and Steven F. Messner. *Perspectives on Crime and Deviance.* Upper Saddle River, NJ: Prentice Hall, 1999.

Mays, G. Larry, ed. *Gangs and Gang Behavior.* Chicago: Nelson-Hall, 1997.

Marshall, Ineke Haen, ed. *Minorities, Migrants, and Crime: Diversity and Similarity Across Europe and the United States.* Thousand Oaks, CA: Sage, 1997.

Moore, Joan W. *Going Down to the Barrio: Homeboys and Homegirls in Change.* Philadelphia: Temple University Press, 1991.

Parrillo, Vincent N. *Strangers to These Shores: Race and Ethnic Relations in the United States.* New York: Macmillan, 1990.

Reynolds, C. N. "The Chinese Tongs." *American Journal of Sociology* 40:5 (1935): 612–23.

Rodriguez, Luis J. *Always Running: La Vida Loca: Gang Days in L.A.* Willimantic, CT: Curbstone Press, 1993.

Sampson, Robert F., and Janet L. Lauritsen. "Racial and Ethnic Disparities in Crime and Criminal Justice in the United States." *Crime and Justice: A Review of Research* 21 (1997): 11–74.

Sellin, Thorsten. *Culture Conflict and Crime.* New York: Social Science Research Council, 1938.

Shaw, Clifford Robe, and Henry McKay. *Delinquency Areas.* Chicago: University of Chicago Press, 1929.

Sutherland, Edwin H., Donald R. Cressey, and David F. Luckenbill. *Principles of Criminology.* New York: General Hall, 1992.

Thrasher, Frederic Milton. *The Gang: A Study of 1,313 Gangs in Chicago.* Chicago: University of Chicago Press, 1927.

Tonry, Michael, ed. *Ethnicity, Crime, and Immigration: Comparative and Cross-National Perspectives.* Chicago: University of Chicago Press, 1997.

Vigil, James Diego. *Barrio Gangs: Street Life and Identity in Southern California.* Austin: University of Texas Press, 1988.

Walker, Samuel, Cassia Spohn, and Miriam DeLone. *Race, Ethnicity, and Crime in America: The Color of Justice.* Belmont, CA: Wadsworth, 2000.

Waters, Tony. *Crime and Immigrant Youth.* Thousand Oaks, CA: Sage, 1999.

LEGISLATION I: IMMIGRATION

At the beginning of the American republic in the 1770s, states wrote their own immigration laws, which followed the practice of colonial days. Further, the U.S. Constitution does not enumerate federal responsibility for immigration law; however, it does specify in article 1, section 8 that the Congress shall make a uniform rule of naturalization. Thus, the earliest immigration-related federal legislation dealt with becoming a citizen, rather than the grounds for admitting prospective immigrants. The understanding was that the Constitution reserved jurisdiction over immigration to the states.

States enacted laws, such as the colonial-era statute Massachusetts adopted in 1788, which required foreigners to register and which refused admittance to aliens who were likely to become a public charge—that is, unable to support themselves without dependence on charity. Others, such as criminals and those lacking republican virtues, were excluded from entering most states. As Thomas West of the University of Dallas has pointed out, "Americans were struggling, however clumsily, with a real problem: how to maintain a population with the moral and religious qualities to keep itself free." In other words, the founders' view of immigration's role was not merely utilitarian, to fill up an expanding nation; they also wished to ensure that the people of the United States would have the qualities of character to govern themselves as necessary under the newly constituted federal, republican government. And some aliens came to America as agents of foreign nations, such as France and England, for which they would exploit American resources and send the profits to their home governments. This underhanded activity occurred at a time when the new nation was seeking to establish its laws, society, and order.

ANTEBELLUM FEDERAL IMMIGRATION LEGISLATION

Early federal legislation relating to immigration, then, had to do with naturalization and with aliens present in the United States. The Naturalization Act of 1790 set a uniform residence requirement of two years before an alien could gain citizenship. The 1798 Aliens Act authorized the president to deport any foreigners he determined to be engaged in treasonous activities against the U.S. government. In force for two years it also called for the collection of information on immigrants upon their arrival. The Alien Enemies Act of 1798 authorized the president to hold or remove aliens from foreign nations with which the United States was at war. However, foreigners' property rights were preserved under various treaties. The Alien Enemies Act was in force for only two years and not renewed.

The first federal legislation that dealt directly with immigration passed in 1819 and regulated passenger ships. It represented the first significant assertion of federal authority over the conditions of immigration. The law restricted the number of passengers on both foreign and American vessels. Only two passengers per five tons of vessel burden would be allowed; this provision adopted the British carrying capacity standard of the time. The law also required the delivery of a manifest, or list, of the names of all passengers, as well as other information about the passengers. The law carried penalties for failure to comply. Another provision, unrelated to immigration, prescribed the amount of food ships must carry for each passenger when departing from U.S. ports for Europe.

In 1836, Congress embarked on an inquiry into the importation of poor immigrants. The states had long been addressing this problem, and the policy generally was to reject public charge immigrants. Some Americans alleged that Britain was sending many of its poor to the United States, and the Massachusetts legislature passed a resolution asking Congress to write a federal law "to prevent the introduction of foreign paupers into this country." The U.S. Senate adopted a resolution directing the secretary of the treasury to investigate. Five months later, the treasury secretary sent the Senate a report, based on inquiries made of diplomatic and commercial agents in Europe, who said they had no knowledge of or denied participation in the deportation of poor immigrants to America. Therefore, Congress took no further action.

In 1837 and 1838, Congress received more petitions asking for federal laws to prevent poor and criminal foreigners from immigrating to the United States. The House Judiciary Committee considered these proposals and launched an investigation into executive branch activity on the pauper immigrant issue. Some evidence was discovered of the systematic immigration of the poor and convicts. The special investigative committee reported out a bill to fine a ship's master for bringing to the United States any alien who was mentally ill, infected with an incurable disease, convicted of a crime, or unable to support himself or herself. However, the legislation died without action by the full House.

This issue of undesirables surfaced again in 1845. A Senate resolution sought any additional information from the secretary of state regarding the dumping of foreign criminals and the poor in America. The secretary reported having no additional information. Meanwhile, the House Judiciary Committee, pursuant to a resolution sponsored by Representative Hamilton Fish of New York, undertook an investigation into this concern. The committee held hearings in Baltimore, New Orleans, New York, and Philadelphia and delivered to Congress a report of its findings. The committee report included much evidence that foreign nations were dumping their "undesirables" on U.S. shores. However, the report came on the last day that Congress met that session.

In 1847, Congress revisited the Passenger Shipping law of 1819. Amid the Irish potato famine exodus, ships were being overcrowded with passengers. This resulted in the arrival of numerous sick immigrants, many of whom had to be hospitalized once here. Rather than basing passenger limits on tonnage, the new law would base the limits on deck space. Congress passed the law and later enacted a second law that prescribed improved ventilation standards for passenger vessels, as well as cooking, food, water, and sanitation requirements.

The arrival of large numbers of Irish Catholic immigrants in the mid- to late 1840s sparked the formation of the American Party, a secret organization that came to be called the Know-Nothings. Especially prominent in homogeneous New England, the anti-immigrant Know-Nothing movement rose to political power. Its candidates won control of the Massachusetts legislature in 1854, as well as six governorships and several congressional seats. But a split in its offshoot, the American Party, between northern and southern members over slavery sealed its fate in 1856,

A marcher's sign mockingly uses American history to protest California's Proposition 187, a 1994 ballot initiative that would have severely limited undocumented immigrants' access to social services. *(Mark Ludak/Impact Visuals)*

and many northern Know-Nothings joined the recently organized Republican Party.

In 1855, Congress approved another passenger ship law. It included steamships under passenger capacity and safety laws already on the books or under consideration. The legislation took into account the Fish report, produced by a select committee formed pursuant to a Senate resolution by the former New York representative and now senator Hamilton Fish. The committee investigated the nature of the illness and death of immigrants while on board ships and found that the greatest health problems among ship-borne immigrants were cholera, smallpox, and typhus.

Congress also reconsidered the issue of "undesirables" and this time nearly passed legislation. The House Commerce Committee reported out legislation in 1855 to prevent the immigration of "foreign criminals, paupers, idiots, lunatics, and insane, and blind persons." The Senate passed such a measure; the House considered an amended bill but tabled it. Immigration also became mixed up in the states' rights debate. Tennessee senator James C. Jones had introduced legislation that squarely rejected federal jurisdiction over immigration policy, leaving states free to determine how to deal with the problem of immigrant paupers and criminals. The Senate opted for the other bill that presumed some level of federal authority over immigration.

Congress took up the issue in 1855, with the House Foreign Affairs Committee reporting out a bill to prohibit the immigration of foreign undesirables. The committee report cited the connection between mass immigration and the rise of poverty and crime. Both the Senate and the House resolutions inquired into a new immigration problem that had arisen after the California gold rush and the settlement of western territory: accusations of Chinese coming as contract laborers.

Chinese increasingly immigrated during the second half of the nineteenth century, first, to join the gold rush and, then, to build the transcontinental railroad. A declining empire at home and industrialization and expansion abroad matched the supply of laborers with demand. Many Chinese immigrants found work on farms, in factories, and in construction. Some Chinese immigrants secured passage either by agreeing to repay a middleman their fare or by signing a contract to work for an agreed time in another country in exchange for passage. This latter arrangement was known as the "coolie trade" and predominantly occurred in Hawaii, Peru, and Cuba. Many contract laborers were coerced and mistreated.

In 1860, the House Commerce Committee reported out legislation to prohibit American vessels from being involved in the Chinese coolie trade. However, no action was taken on the House floor. Still, the House adopted a resolution seeking new information on the issue from the executive branch. Also, a passenger protection bill amended the law. It sought to protect female passengers from crew members who might try to seduce them.

Thus ended the federal legislation relating to immigration during the antebellum period. Most legislation concerned public health during transit of immigrants and the exclusion of immigrants who would likely fail to be self-supporting or who might present a threat to public safety. A subtle shift occurred from very limited federal jurisdiction over immigration policy to certain uniform protection of all Americans against "undesirable" aliens who might pose more of a threat than a benefit to the nation.

WARTIME, RECONSTRUCTION, AND WESTWARD EXPANSION

The next thirty years saw legislation regularly introduced and sometimes considered in Congress that ad-dressed passenger vessels, immigrant health and safety, the coolie trade, and Chinese immigration, along with the encouragement or limitation of immigration. In 1862, Congress enacted a bill to end the coolie trade. In 1863, President Abraham Lincoln noted in his annual message that with the Northern soldiers off fighting in the Civil War, the nation required laborers, especially in agriculture and mining. In July 1864, Congress passed a law authorizing labor contracts, in which prospective immigrants could agree to pay a portion of future wages in exchange for transportation to America. The law created a new office, Commissioner of Immigration, overseen by the secretary of state, that would administer the labor contracts. A joint resolution was passed in 1866 that protested the practice of several foreign governments that pardoned criminals who agreed to emigrate to America.

When the Civil War ended, the necessity of foreign labor dropped, while concern over the continued immigration of convicted criminals grew, dampening sentiment for immigration. In 1868, Congress repealed the contract labor law. Meanwhile, postwar pressures to relieve the war debt and settle the West were a counterweight. Thus, the House Foreign Affairs Committee reported a bill, which was recommitted to committee, to encourage immigration of "persons of capital, industry, or skill." Especially on the Pacific Coast, Chinese immigration increased owing to the building of the transcontinental railroad. In 1869, President Ulysses S. Grant asked Congress to close off contract labor immigration, which many Americans compared to slavery. In 1870, the House considered a joint resolution by a California congressman to limit Chinese immigration and declare state authority to use nuisance laws to prohibit various Chinese customs. Throughout the 1860s and 1870s, legislation would be introduced either to promote or to restrict immigration. These bills usually died in committee without action taken on them.

Soldiers returning from the Civil War, an influx of immigrants bringing different ways and different religions, and a severe economic depression in the 1870s sparked unrest against competing foreign labor. Native-born workers feared not only job competition but also depressed wages due to contract foreign laborers. American workers' discontent resulted in protests or worse, such as a Los Angeles riot in 1871 that cost nineteen Chinese their lives.

In 1874, the House requested and received from the secretary of state information about the immigration of foreign convicts. This and other problems relating to immigration were addressed in the Immigration Act of 1875. An early direct federal regulation of immigration, this law gave the first designation of "excludable aliens," or named classes of foreigners ineligible to immigrate. Excluded were convicted criminals and prostitutes; most Chinese women on the West Coast at this time were prostitutes. However, political prisoners were exempt. The law made supplying coolie labor a felony.

During the 1860s and 1870s, problems associated with Chinese immigration caused greater concern. An 1877 joint committee report cited evidence that many Chinese were not immigrating to stay or to become U.S. citizens (though many were ineligible for citizenship). Western states increasingly called on Congress to restrict Chinese immigration. In 1879, Congress passed a bill to restrict Chinese immigration, by large margins in each house. However, President Rutherford B. Hayes vetoed the legislation because it encroached on the executive's treaty and diplomatic powers, saying the measure violated the Burlingame Treaty of 1868, which opened up immigration between the United States and China. A congressional committee reported in 1880 on problems with Chinese immigration and recommended renegotiating the Burlingame Treaty with China.

Congress updated the ship passenger laws in 1882. The new law regulated carrying capacity by cubic foot and specified requirements to ensure passenger health, safety, and protection.

However, the more significant immigration legislation of 1882 was the Immigration Act. This law added categories to exclude those who were mentally ill and those unable to care for themselves. It imposed a federal head tax on immigrants to help pay for the return fare of excluded foreigners. Another major law that year was the Chinese Exclusion Act. This precedent-setting law banned practically all Chinese immigration for ten years and barred Chinese immigrants from becoming citizens. The Chinese Exclusion Act marked the first time that the United States had restricted immigration on the basis of race or nationality. Future anti-immigration laws against Asians in the early 1900s and Europeans in the 1920s would draw on this act.

The passage of laws did not end the problems they were designed to solve. European governments continued to dump their "undesirables" on America, and the Chinese government violated the new exclusion law. Subsequent legislation passed Congress to clarify the Chinese exclusion. The contract labor issue rose again. While the facilitation of contract labor had been repealed years before, current foreign laborers under contract to work continued to threaten to take American jobs. Enacted in 1885, the Alien Contract Labor Act prohibited bringing foreigners under contract to

work in the United States and voided all such contracts made before immigration. The law excepted certain immigrants, including laborers whose skills were unavailable in this country. The Contract Labor Law of 1887 amended the 1885 law, empowering the treasury secretary to enforce the law and to order that excludable persons be returned home upon arrival.

The number of immigrants began to rise in the 1880s, causing domestic concerns over the impact on the nation. An 1888 law ended the issuance of reentry certificates for Chinese workers and nullified all existing documents. Congress received petitions to restrict immigration levels, and a select committee was established to study the problems associated with immigration regulation and enforcement. The committee identified difficulties with inspecting new arrivals and called for admission only of worthy foreigners "who in good faith desire to become citizens."

THE TURN OF THE CENTURY

Attempts to curb immigration gained steam in the 1890s. Ethnic Chinese not technically subjects of the Chinese Empire continued to emigrate to the United States. In 1891, both houses of Congress drafted broad legislation to exclude various "undesirables" and to encourage the immigration of skilled and talented persons. The final version, the Immigration Act of 1891, added to excludable categories polygamists, those likely to become public charges, and those with a contagious disease. Exempted from the contract labor ban, however, were professionals, professors, and ministers. It also contained deportation provisions for those who had broken the law to immigrate or who became public charges in their first year in the United States.

With the approach of the ten-year expiration of the 1882 act, Congress passed the Chinese Exclusion Act of 1892. It extended the exclusion ten more years and required Chinese workers to get residence certificates or face deportation. It did not address the problem of excludable Chinese entering through Canada. Meantime, hundreds of petitions arrived on Capitol Hill from many states, labor organizations, churches, and citizens calling for immigration restriction. The introduction of bills both to regulate and to suspend immigration followed.

President Benjamin Harrison continued quarantining certain ships with immigrants because of a cholera epidemic overseas. In 1893, Congress empowered the president to quarantine any vessel or to prohibit any person or property from entry when infectious diseases threatened. Also, the Immigration Act of 1893, while ultimately limited in scope to inspection information and procedure, had nearly included new excludable grounds: illiteracy and advocating anarchy. Another bill that year extended by six months the one-year period for Chinese immigrants to obtain residence certificates. Many Chinese had been counseled that the requirement would be struck down as unconstitutional; however, the Supreme Court upheld the provision.

In 1894, Congress wrestled with finding a practicable way to inspect prospective immigrants abroad in order to exclude undesirables while still in their home country. While this idea went unresolved, Congress doubled the immigrant head tax to one dollar. Congress also considered several versions of a literacy test for immigrants. Congress passed such a requirement in 1897, but President Grover Cleveland vetoed it. As the twentieth century dawned, Americans became increasingly concerned about mass immigration. Throughout the 1890s, Congress gave renewed attention to the literacy issue but never resolved it. Instead, Congress established a commission to investigate broadly the immigration question and make recommendations. Problems with Chinese immigration were highlighted by China's Boxer Rebellion in 1900, bringing Chinese exclusion to the forefront. The Boxers reacted against Western nations' new "open-door" trade policy with China. Along with a weakened, sympathetic Chinese government, the Boxers' antiforeign backlash drew Western troops to quell the fighting and protect their nations' traders, diplomats, and missionaries. Congress enacted a law in 1901 for U.S. commissioners to hear cases about the smuggling of Chinese aliens.

The commission made its report to Congress late in 1901, recommending among other things a tripling of the head tax, land border inspection, and the penalizing of shipping companies that brought contagious foreigners. In 1902, Congress extended the Chinese exclusion laws until a new treaty could be made, as well as applying the law to certain U.S. territories. In 1903, Congress passed a broad immigration bill largely based on the commission's recommendations. The list of exclusions grew to include political radicals. Otherwise, previous immigration laws were codified, and the head tax increased to two dollars and was charged to nearly every alien passenger. Chinese exclusion was made permanent in 1904.

The Immigration Act of 1907 addressed President Theodore Roosevelt's consistent call for improving the immigration system to favor promising foreigners likely to become good Americans. The exclusion list now included mentally ill and physically disabled,

unaccompanied children, and tuberculosis carriers. The head tax doubled again to four dollars in order to keep out those deemed less desirable and to reduce the number of immigrants. The manifesting of alien passengers would now occur at the point of departure from the United States. This manifesting would help alleviate illegal return by fraudulent schemes. However, a literacy test had been stricken by amendment.

Japanese immigration to the U.S. mainland rose significantly between 1890 and 1907, with nearly all individuals settling in California. This rapid influx fanned nativist sentiment, and the state and localities restricted Asians' rights, such as to landownership. San Francisco's 1906 segregation of Asian school children angered the Japanese government. In 1907, President Roosevelt negotiated the "Gentlemen's Agreement." Japan agreed to a voluntary quota limiting emigration of Japanese people to the United States. This agreement also bound immigrants from the Japanese colony, Korea.

In 1909, Congress granted an exception to the departure manifesting provision for vessels sailing exclusively between U.S. ports and those of Canada and Mexico. A year later, it enacted the White Slave Traffic Act, or Mann Act, which prohibited the importation or interstate transportation of women to engage in prostitution. A similar act expanded the grounds for exclusion and deportation of prostitutes, adding their procurers and transporters for punishment. In 1911 and 1912, Congress expended much energy trying to craft a broad bill with a literacy test and additional exclusions, as well as deportation of criminal aliens. However, President William Taft vetoed the legislation, which barely survived an override vote in the House, because of the literacy test. In 1913 and 1914, Congress worked on similar legislation, which met the same fate: President Woodrow Wilson vetoed the bill because of the literacy test and its failure to allow political asylum.

From 1915 to 1917, Congress passed yet another immigration bill, which Wilson also vetoed, but this time both houses of Congress overrode the veto. The 1917 Immigration Act included a literacy test for prospective immigrants, with exceptions for certain close family members and for those unable to read but facing religious persecution. The head tax was doubled to eight dollars. The list of grounds for exclusion grew to include persons from much of Asia, "psychopaths," alcoholics, vagrants, and those attempting to return within a year of deportation. The act also provided for the immigration of skilled laborers if native workers were not available in the occupations these immigrants were skilled in.

The combination of World War I and mass immigration led Congress in 1918 to enact a law clarifying that anarchists were excludable aliens. They became subject to deportation at any time, and the return of deported anarchists became a felony.

THE MOVE TOWARD RESTRICTION

With a number of postwar issues reinforcing sentiment for restriction of immigration, Congress acted on several fronts. It passed a law giving the president authority to protect public safety with whatever rules and regulations on alien entry he deemed necessary. Another act deported alien enemies of the United States; another excluded anarchists, terrorists, advocates of anarchy or terrorism, and those associated with subversive organizations or publications. Yet another law was enacted to grant an exception to the literacy test for the foreign fiancée petitioned for by a U.S. World War I veteran; this law would expire after five years.

Several bills were introduced that called for a moratorium on immigration. One, providing for a fourteen month suspension, passed the House in 1920. However, the Senate took up a bill to set immigration quotas at 3 percent per year of a nationality's U.S. residence as counted in the 1910 census. The quotas applied only in the Eastern Hemisphere, and preference was given to wives and minor children of naturalized U.S. citizens and those who had applied for naturalization. In conference committee, the House accepted the Senate quota approach; President Wilson pocket vetoed the legislation in 1921.

Congress quickly took up a similar bill, which President Warren G. Harding signed on May 19, 1921. This was the first quota law. It set a yearly quota for each nationality at 3 percent of the number of foreign-born persons from a nation of origin as found in the 1910 census. The law exempted certain foreigners from the quota, such as government officials and the minor children of U.S. citizens. Further, it gave general preference for admission to family members of citizens, resident aliens applying to naturalize, and aliens who had honorably served in the military in World War I and were eligible for citizenship. This law was to be effective for just over a year. Congress extended the life of the law by two years.

The 1921 act nearly included a provision exempting from the quota refugees fleeing persecution because of their religious beliefs. The House passed its version of legislation containing this provision, but it was removed by the conference committee.

As the 1924 expiration date approached, Congress turned to immigration again. Sentiment continued to run high for restricting immigration. The House passed a bill to reduce the national quotas, scale back the nonquota exemption categories, and put the burden of proving one's admissibility on prospective immigrants. The bill included the close relatives of citizens and skilled laborers in the nonquota categories but excluded those not eligible to become citizens from immigrating. This latter provision affected foreign policy with Japan because it broke the Gentlemen's Agreement allowing entry of Japanese. The Senate crafted a similar bill, but it opted for preferences of admission and had no nonquota entries.

The Quota Act of 1924 established a national origins quota system. The quotas were based on 2 percent of a nation's presence in the U.S. population according to the 1890 census. Each nation had a minimum annual quota of one hundred, and Eastern Hemisphere nations were limited to an annual total of 150,000. Some types of immigrants were exempt from the quotas, such as nuclear family members, students, returning travelers, ministers and professors, and female former citizens who lost their citizenship through former marriages. Western Hemisphere nations enjoyed no quota restrictions. Preference was given within country quotas, first, to citizens' spouses, unmarried children under twenty-one, and parents and, next, to skilled agricultural workers and their family. Now, consular officers would issue visas abroad and control immigration processing and evaluation from foreign shores. Those ineligible for citizenship—particularly Japanese—were inadmissible. And the immigrant now bore the burden of proof in determination of admissibility and in deportation proceedings. This law served the purpose of preserving the existing makeup of the U.S. population.

Congress also passed a joint resolution allowing 10,000 aliens previously admitted above the quota limit to remain in the United States, if they were admissible and not subject to deportation. Congress later enacted legislation to facilitate admission of wives and minor children of alien professors and ministers entering the country before July 1, 1927. And foreigners who were World War I veterans, along with their families, received preferential ship passage rates. Additionally, Congress postponed the date on which the national origins quota system would take effect until 1929 because the quotas were still being computed.

THE YEARS OF LIMITED IMMIGRATION

The Great Depression sank in just as the new, restrictive immigration system came into operation. With the number of unemployed Americans soaring, keeping out immigrants who were likely to become public charges became a major concern. In 1930, Herbert Hoover instructed consular officers to keep an applicant's public charge likelihood in mind in visa issuance decisions. Congress considered other immigration measures during the 1930s, such as reducing the quotas, granting nonquota status to certain classes of foreigners, emphasizing skilled immigrants more in admissions, and placing quotas on Western Hemisphere nations. None of these became law.

As the 1930s ended and the 1940s began, hostilities in Europe and Asia caused American concern over foreigners to grow. In 1940, Congress enacted the Alien Registration Act, part of which required aliens and resident aliens seeking a visa to register and give fingerprints. Congress in 1941 passed a law for consular officers to deny aliens visas if they suspected the aliens of threatening American public safety. To ease the wartime labor shortage the Roosevelt administration negotiated an agreement, called the Bracero Program, to bring in temporary foreign workers, especially Mexicans. To counteract Japanese propaganda, Congress repealed the Chinese Exclusion Act in 1943, giving China, a wartime ally, a 105-visa annual quota and making Chinese persons eligible for naturalization.

After World War II ended, other immigration concerns won Congress's attention. The War Brides Act of 1945 facilitated the immigration of foreigners betrothed to American servicemen and -women. Another bill was enacted to make Filipinos and Indians admissible and eligible for naturalization. In 1948, Congress passed the Displaced Persons Act. This law allowed the admission of 205,000 persons displaced by war or Communist takeover of their homeland, in fear of persecution on account of their religion, race, or political beliefs. In 1950, Congress amended the Displaced Persons Act, admitting nearly two hundred thousand more refugees.

With the Cold War intensifying, American vigilance against Communist subversives rose. The Korean conflict only added to the intensity. The 1950 Internal Security Act, which established a Subversive Activities Control Board, broadened the grounds for excluding foreigners who posed a threat to national security and required all aliens to register their addresses each year. Another law was enacted to allow war veterans who were U.S. citizens to gain admission for their alien spouses and minor children, regardless of racial restrictions. Early in 1952, Congress passed a law addressing illegal immigration, following a Supreme Court decision striking down earlier statutes. The 1917 act and a 1948 law had made aiding the illegal entry of aliens a federal crime. After the Court's ruling, Congress, in response to the growing problem of immigration from Mexico, reinstated the assisting of illegal entry and the transporting or harboring of illegal aliens as felony offenses and boosted the Border Patrol's enforcement powers. (The Border Patrol is an agency within the Immigration and Naturalization Service.)

Congress labored in the early 1950s to reconstitute the immigration laws, with the House and Senate each crafting its own comprehensive bills. A conference committee ironed out the differences between the two bills, and the McCarran-Walter Act, named for its primary sponsors, Senator Patrick McCarran (D-NV) and Representative Francis Walter (D-PA), was sent to President Harry Truman, who vetoed it. Congress overrode the veto, and the Immigration and Nationality Act of 1952 became law.

The new law preserved the national origins quota system and adjusted the quota formula. It opened up immigration to all races by striking racial barriers to naturalization. The law expanded the application of people from Asian-Pacific countries, rather than country of birth, for quota purposes. The law set a new preference system, shifting the first preference for half of a country's quota to skilled workers instead of citizens' family members. It also broadened the list of excludable categories; these fell into general classes of those with diseases threatening public health, convicted criminals, communists, potential public charges, and those apt to flood a particular occupation's labor market.

Unsatisfied with the outcome, Truman appointed a commission to quickly finish a report before the next Congress convened. The commission presented a report whose findings were in line with Truman's policy preferences. However, in the short run, the report had minimal influence on Congress, given its predetermined findings and recommendations. Bills were introduced incorporating many of the commission's recommendations, but none was acted on.

Yet, Congress gave attention to another problem with the Refugee Relief Act of 1953. This law provided 205,000 nonquota visas for fourteen eligible groups of refugees, in addition to the existing quotas.

It was amended in 1954 to aid the adjustment of refugees' status to permanent resident if they were unable to go home for fear of persecution because of race, religion, or political views; the amendment also required certain refugees and immigrants to prove to a consular officer that the individual would have housing and a job without displacing someone else.

In 1956, President Dwight D. Eisenhower requested changes in immigration law to loosen its restrictiveness and to give the executive branch more discretionary power. In 1957, Congress passed a law that aided the admission of foreign stepchildren and the adoption of orphans. It also loosened the rules for aliens in certain circumstances. Throughout the 1950s, various bills were introduced to heavily reshape or repeal the 1952 law, such as one by Senator Philip Hart (D-MI); alternatives were based on either the Truman commission's recommendations or those of the Eisenhower administration. None gained consideration because the makeup of Congress had not changed appreciably from the 1952 coalition. However, Congress in 1959 passed a law modifying the preference system, moving certain family members up in preference order. And the "T.B.-Orphan bill" of 1959 excepted from exclusion certain family members of U.S. citizens, in spite of infection with tuberculosis, for a year; this extended the 1957 law cited above. In 1960, another refugee law passed that provided visas for certain groups, such as Indonesians living in the Netherlands and "refugee-escapees," as well as adding as a criterion for exclusion and deportation the violation of marijuana laws.

With the 1960 election of President John F. Kennedy, a former senator and author of *A Nation of Immigrants*, congressional sentiment was changing to a more favorable view toward immigration. A 1961 law made permanent immigration legislation concerning adopted children; granted a minimum 100-visa quota to new, independent nations; and authorized the Public Health Service to decide which diseases warranted grounds for exclusion. Congress in 1962 passed legislation to enhance the immigration of skilled foreigners by speeding their spouse's and children's entry. In 1963, Kennedy proposed changes in the immigration law, principally to end the national origins quota system in favor of focusing on an individual's skills to meet U.S. needs and on certain relatives. In 1964, the Bracero Program was ended. And Lyndon B. Johnson continued to press for Kennedy's immigration reforms.

THE END OF NATIONAL ORIGINS QUOTAS AND THE START OF MASS IMMIGRATION

Early in 1965, President Johnson called on Congress to change the immigration laws, in conjunction with the civil rights movement. More than seventy reform bills were introduced, including the administration's bill. The Immigration and Nationality Act Amendments of 1965 broadly reflected the Kennedy-Johnson proposals. This legislation replaced the national origins quota system with a selection procedure based on individual qualities, particularly family relations. Now, immigrants would be admitted largely if related by blood or marriage to a U.S. citizen or permanent resident alien. One's skills, education, and ability fell to a much lower priority, and a new labor certification requirement posed a barrier to skilled immigrant admission. A preference system with seven categories determined the order of admission for immigrants from Eastern Hemisphere nations; each Eastern Hemisphere country had a maximum annual quota of 20,000 visas, and an overall yearly quota of 170,000 applied to that hemisphere. The Western Hemisphere now had an overall quota of 120,000 visas annually, but visas were distributed on a first-come, first-served basis instead of by a preference system. Nonquota admissions were broadened to include more family relations. Refugees would gain admission as a category of the preference system. The Asia-Pacific triangle was abolished, thus opening up immigration from those nations.

In 1969 and 1970, Congress provided for admission of especially skilled immigrants and counted employees of international firms and certain betrothed aliens as nonimmigrants. Congress worked in 1973 and 1974 to limit Western Hemisphere immigration, achieving this goal by extending the 20,000 per-country quota and the seven-category preference system to the Western Hemisphere in 1976. As the Vietnam War ended and Saigon fell, Congress acted quickly in 1975 to provide assistance for resettlement of refugees. Refugee assistance was expanded with the Indo-Chinese Refugee Act of 1977 and the Refugee Parolees Act of 1978. In 1978, Congress also combined the two hemispheric quotas into a single, worldwide quota of 290,000. In 1980, Congress passed the Refugee Act, which removed refugees from the preference system, set annual admissions at 50,000 for refugees, lowered the immigrant quota to 270,000, defined "refugee" clearly, and established admission procedures and the Office of Refugee Resettlement.

The Select Commission on Immigration and Refugee Policy, established by legislation in 1978, issued its report in March 1981. Titled *U.S. Immigration Policy and the National Interest*, the report formed the basis for immigration legislation considered in the next three Congresses and passed in 1986. It recommended penalizing employers who hired illegal aliens, strengthening border enforcement, granting amnesty to untold millions of illegal aliens living in the United States, and opening up legal immigration. The Simpson-Mazzoli Bill, named for Senator Alan Simpson (R-WY) and Representative Romano Mazzoli (D-KY), incorporated these provisions. It also created a special agricultural workers program and provided for those workers' legalization under the amnesty. Failing in the 1981–82 and 1983–84 sessions of Congress, Simpson-Mazzoli passed in 1986 as the Immigration Reform and Control Act (IRCA).

The next Congress attended to implementation of IRCA. In 1990, Congress passed another large bill, this time expanding legal immigration. The 1990 act raised the annual quota to 700,000 for three years and to 675,000 thereafter. It also expanded the terms of the 1986 amnesty. The preference system was modified to create a diversity visa program that issued visas by lottery in countries sending few immigrants and a special immigrant category for those investing $1 million in a new business in the United States that employed at least ten people. Other provisions included "temporary protected status" for illegal aliens from designated countries in which there was warfare, repression, or natural disaster; establishment of new nonimmigrant, or temporary, visa categories; revision of the grounds for exclusion and deportation and elimination of some grounds for exclusion; and the chartering of another immigration commission.

While immigration issues received little congressional attention in the next two Congresses, the issue was bubbling up from the grass roots, especially in California, the most populous state and the top destination for immigrants. In 1994, Proposition 187, a California ballot initiative, passed with 59 percent of the vote. This proposition would have denied illegal aliens a variety of government services, including nonemergency health care, public education, and welfare benefits. However, a federal court swiftly issued an injunction against the referendum's implementation. In 1997, a federal judge ruled that the state law encroached on federal jurisdiction over immigration. California governor Gray Davis refused to appeal the decision.

The U.S. Commission on Immigration Reform, authorized by Congress and also known as the Jordan Commission after its chairman, former representative Barbara Jordan, issued its first report in 1994. In 1995 and 1996, Congress based broad immigration reform bills on many of the commission's recommendations. The Illegal Immigration Reform and Immigrant Responsibility Act of 1996 strengthened border enforcement against illegal immigration. It provided improved investigatory and prosecutorial tools for tough punishment against alien smuggling rings and identification document fraud, as well as stiffer penalties for illegal entry or overstay of a nonimmigrant visa. The law closed loopholes in the processes to deport and exclude aliens. It built on the employer sanctions already in the law to improve the quality and speed of verification of new employees' legal work eligibility; strengthened the requirements for the sponsors of immigrants to fulfill their pledged responsibilities to provide for the needs of the immigrants they sponsored; and streamlined the asylum process so that those truly fleeing political or religious persecution in their home country would gain asylum, while perpetrators of asylum fraud could not tie up the system with false claims.

Congress then oversaw implementation of the 1996 act. In 1998, Congress also raised the quota of H-1B nonimmigrant visas, issued to skilled foreigners and popular with the high-technology industry. The annual quota for those visas was temporarily increased from 65,000 to 115,000 for three years.

Immigration legislation has always addressed the problems and challenges at hand. Sometimes, the perspective of the majority in Congress has shifted as to the nature of those problems and challenges. And at some times the view from Capitol Hill has aligned more closely with popular opinion than at others. But the focus of the legislative process has always been to promote the national interest of the United States and to address the needs of the particular period, whether these were to increase or decrease the labor force, emphasize certain qualities or characteristics of the immigrant flow, or protect the citizenry against threats to the nation.

James R. Edwards Jr.

See also: Changes in the Law, Immigration Legislation of the 1980s and 1990s (Part I, Sec. V); Legal and Illegal Immigration: A Statistical Overview (Part II, Sec. 2); Amnesty (Part II, Sec. 5); Immigration and Nationality Act, 1965, Immigration Reform and Control Act,

1986, Illegal Immigration Reform and Immigrant Responsibility Act, 1996 (Part IV, Sec. 1).

BIBLIOGRAPHY

Baseler, Marilyn C. *"Asylum for Mankind": America, 1607–1800.* Ithaca: Cornell University Press, 1998.

Congressional Quarterly. "Immigration Reform." In *Congress and the Nation, 1965–1968*, 2:57–61. Washington, DC: Congressional Quarterly Service, 1969.

Gimpel, James G., and James R. Edwards Jr. *The Congressional Politics of Immigration Reform.* Boston: Allyn and Bacon, 1999.

Gyory, Andrew. *Closing the Gate: Race, Politics, and the Chinese Exclusion Act.* Chapel Hill: University of North Carolina Press, 1998.

Heer, David. *Immigration in America's Future: Social Science Findings and the Policy Debate.* Boulder, CO: Westview Press, 1996.

Hutchinson, E. P. *Legislative History of American Immigration Policy, 1798–1965.* Philadelphia: University of Pennsylvania Press, 1981.

LeMay, Michael C. *From Open Door to Dutch Door: An Analysis of U.S. Immigration Policy since 1820.* New York: Praeger, 1987.

Reimers, David M. *Still the Golden Door: The Third World Comes to America.* 2d ed. New York: Columbia University Press, 1992.

Thernstrom, Stephen, ed. *Harvard Encyclopedia of American Ethnic Groups.* Cambridge: Harvard University Press, Belknap Press, 1980.

West, Thomas G. *Vindicating the Founders: Race, Sex, Class, and Justice in the Origins of America.* Lanham, MD: Rowman and Littlefield, 1997.

LEGISLATION II: IMMIGRANTS IN AMERICA

United States law recognizes four classes of persons within its territory, in descending order of privilege: (1) U.S. citizens; (2) immigrants or lawful permanent residents; (3) aliens admitted to the United States in nonimmigrant status; (4) aliens present in the United States without authorization. The Immigration and Nationality Act (INA) of 1965 defines an immigrant by exclusion as every alien except those who hold nonimmigrant status in one of the enumerated classes of nonimmigrants. The INA does not elaborate upon this definition, other than to define a "special immigrant" as an immigrant "lawfully admitted for permanent residence in the United States." The INA further defines lawful admission as "the privilege [not *right*] of residing permanently in the United States as an immigrant." The touchstone of immigrant status in the United States, is then, the ability to live in this country for an indefinite period. Often referred to by the synonymous terms of "permanent resident" or "green card holder," immigrants constitute a class of persons who, although they retain the citizenship of a foreign state and remain subject to that nation's laws, have been allowed to live in the United States on an indefinite basis and are expected by the U.S. government to make their permanent homes here. The coveted green card (probably the most notorious misnomer in immigration lexicon, since it is no longer green, but blue and pink), more properly known as Form I–551, the Permanent Resident Card, is the immigrant's proof of this privilege and must be carried by all immigrants at all times.

The public policy of the United States in creating this class of persons who may live in this country but are not entitled to share fully in the body of rights granted to U.S. citizens dates back to the earliest days of this country and is reflected in the text of the federal Constitution, which carefully distinguishes between "citizens" and "persons," and differentiates the entitlements and protections that can be granted to each. Such a policy is, of course, not unique; virtually every sovereign state, whether a democracy or a dictatorship, has designated such a class of persons. The reasoning generally underlying this policy is that citizenship is a benefit that must be earned by persons born outside the state's territory, and that (since immigrants are generally afforded the opportunity to become citizens after a given period of time) a grant of permanent residence provides aliens with a means of earning this benefit after a probationary period and also enables the state to assess whether or not such persons can meet the tests imposed for citizenship. By establishing fairly rigid distinctions between citizens and immigrants, and depriving immigrants of some of the rights granted to citizens, this policy also creates an incentive for immigrants to become citizens and thereby promotes a state's interest in reducing the number of persons within its territory who owe allegiance to foreign nations.

THE POWER TO CONTROL THE ADMISSION OF ALIENS

It has become axiomatic that Congress and the federal government have plenary power to regulate the admission of aliens to this country and to control their activities once they are here. The administration of the immigration laws are shared between the Department of Justice, primarily through the Immigration and Naturalization Service (INS) and the Department of State. The former generally regulates the admission to the United States of aliens and the ability of aliens to remain here; the latter regulates the ability of aliens to apply for admission by granting or denying visas at U.S. consulates abroad. In general, attempts by states to regulate the activities of aliens, whether immigrants or nonimmigrants, or to control the entitlements of aliens (such as their right to receive government benefits), will fail, since they are an infringement

Lawyers trained at Peoples College of Law in Los Angeles have been defending immigrant rights for decades. *(Donna DeCesare/ Impact Visuals)*

on the plenary federal power in this area. The U.S. Constitution voices this power, granting Congress, in Article I, Section 8, the authority to "establish a uniform Rule of Naturalization." The Supreme Court has traditionally recognized the federal plenary power and has shown extreme deference to federal measures that pertain to the activities of aliens, whether immigrants or nonimmigrants.

PERMANENT RESIDENCE IN THE UNITED STATES

The most significant benefit accorded to immigrants is the ability to reside permanently in the United States, or, in other words, to live in this country for an indefinite period. This ability provides the fundamental distinction between immigrants and nonimmigrants: The latter class of persons is admitted to the United States for a temporary period, whose duration is generally determined before admission to this country, and must leave the country once this period expires. The term "permanent residence" is misleading, however, inferring that the immigrant's ability to remain in the United States is not subject to change. Although immigrants are granted the ability to remain in the country for an open-ended period, they do not enjoy a right to stay here for as long as they live, and the U.S. government, through the INS, retains the authority to remove or exclude immigrants from its territory, without regard to how long the immigrant has lived here, to the ties that he or she may have developed to this country, or to the fact that he or she has children who are U.S. citizens. U.S. citizens are, of course, not subject to this authority and may reside in the United States on a truly permanent basis. It is sometimes a source of confusion to immigrants that their green cards, which ostensibly empower them to remain here permanently, have an expiration date; they are generally valid for ten years and can usually be reissued almost automatically for a further ten-year period. No affirmative showing of a continuing entitlement to permanent-resident status need be made to receive a new green card, but the INS has the discretion not to renew the card if it has reason to believe that an immigrant is no longer entitled to this status.

In practice, an immigrant's ability to reside in the United States "permanently" operates as much as an obligation as a privilege. Immigrants have the ability to travel in and out of the United States as frequently as they wish and to remain abroad for extended periods of time, but only if they continue to maintain their primary residence in the United States or establish an intention to return to the United States to live here on a permanent basis. The INS may, and frequently does, revoke an immigrant's status as a permanent resident or bar his or her readmission to the country if it has reason to believe that the immigrant has abandoned his or her permanent residence (or intention to reside permanently) in the United States. Such abandonment may be inferred if the immigrant has spent long periods abroad without returning to the United States. Thus, if an immigrant has been abroad for a period of longer than twelve months, he or she may not use a green card to be readmitted to the United States. Immigrants who plan to spend a period longer than one year outside the United States must obtain a reentry permit, a document issued by the INS only after the requisite intention to reside permanently in the United States, together with the necessary proof of continuing ties to this country, have been shown. The prohibition on reentering the United States as an immigrant after a twelve-month absence has given rise to the misconception that immigrants living abroad may continue to maintain their lawful permanent resident status in the United States by visiting the country for a brief period once every year. An immigrant who has been outside the United States for over a year and does not have a reentry permit may apply for a special immigrant visa as a returning resident at a U.S. consulate or embassy abroad.

Every permanent resident who returns to the United States after a trip abroad is classified as a special immigrant under the INA and must meet two requirements: (1) he or she has been lawfully admitted for permanent residence, and (2) he or she is returning from a temporary visit abroad. Federal courts and the INS will generally consider several factors in assessing whether or not a returning immigrant's visit abroad was temporary. The most compelling factor is the immigrant's intent. The Board of Immigration Appeals (BIA) takes a very fact-specific approach to determining this intent and looks to the following issues: (1) the immigrant's reason for departing the United States. The immigrant should generally have a definite and specific reason for proceeding abroad temporarily; (2) the termination date of the immigrant's trip abroad. This visit should be expected to terminate within a relatively short period that is fixed by some event. If unforeseen circumstances cause an unavoidable delay in returning, the trip may retain its temporary character, as long as the immigrant continues to intend to return home as soon as his or her original purpose is completed; and (3) place of employment or actual home. The immigrant must intend to return to the United States as a place of employment or business or as an actual home. Of particular importance to the INS's determination that permanent residence has been maintained is the immigrant's continued filing of annual income tax returns in the United States.

Immigrants have complete mobility in the United States and may live anywhere in this country they please. However, the INA requires all immigrants to keep the INS informed of their address and to notify the INS of any change of address within ten days. A failure to notify the INS within this period provides a basis for removal from the United States.

EMPLOYMENT IN THE UNITED STATES

In addition to enjoying the privilege of residing in the United States for an indefinite period, immigrants are allowed to accept employment in the United States, however, they are not required to maintain gainful employment in this country. Although applicants for permanent resident status must generally provide proof that they have adequate funds or employment opportunities to avoid becoming public charges, persons who have been granted permanent resident status are not required to maintain such funds or employment in order to maintain that status and will not risk removal from the United States if they fall on hard times and become unemployed after arriving in the country.

The permission granted to immigrants to accept employment in the United States is not guaranteed explicitly by the INA, but is not subject to dispute. The green card itself states that the bearer is "entitled to reside permanently and work in the United States." This document is one of the few documents enumerated in the 1986 Immigration Reform and Control Act as probative of an unrestricted right to work in this country.

Immigrants therefore stand on a different footing from nonimmigrants, who may generally only work for employers that have sought, and received, the appropriate authorization from the INS, and who may generally only remain employed in the United States for a finite period of time.

Immigrants are not granted complete latitude in their choice of employment opportunities, however. The office of president of the United States is closed to immigrants and naturalized citizens by the U.S. Constitution, which requires, in Article II, Section 1, that the president be a "natural born Citizen." The Constitution also mandates that all U.S. senators have been citizens for at least nine years (Article I, Section 3), and that all U.S. representatives have been citizens for at least seven years (Article 1, Section 1). Both sections therefore exclude recent immigrants from Congress, but explicitly make provision for immigrants to become senators or representatives once they have become naturalized citizens.

The federal government denies employment for most positions to aliens, whether immigrants or nonimmigrants. However, immigrants may be able to work for various governmental agencies under specific exemptions provided by statute, regulation, or other authority. The U.S. Postal Service originally prohibited the employment of aliens but, as a result of litigation, abandoned its citizenship requirement for all positions except those in sensitive or policy-making positions. The Department of Defense, the Atomic Energy Commission, the National Aeronautics and Space Administration, and the Foreign Claims Settlement Commission may also employ immigrants for most positions. The Department of State and the Department of Agriculture also employ immigrants for specific positions.

The U.S. Supreme Court has visited the issue of the right of immigrants to be employed by examining the constitutionality of various state statutes and regulations that denied employment to immigrants by limiting membership in professions to U.S. citizens. In 1973, in *In Re Griffiths*, the Supreme Court invalidated a Connecticut court rule that excluded all aliens (including immigrants) from membership in the state bar. In this case, a permanent resident alien married to a U.S. citizen who had graduated from a U.S. law school applied to take the state bar examination to become licensed as an attorney. Although the immigrant was qualified in every other respect, the county bar association refused her application because she was not a U.S. citizen. The Supreme Court found this rule to be unconstitutional, reasoning that a lawfully admitted immigrant is a "person" under the Fourteenth Amendment and that classifications based on alienage are inherently suspect as probably violative of the equal protection guarantee and subject to close judicial scrutiny. The Court also decided that the state bar's interest in ensuring that all members possessed the character and general fitness required for the practice of law, while valid, did not justify the practice of excluding immigrants from membership. In 1973, the Court also held invalid a New York statute that barred immigrants from the competitive classified civil service, a category that embraced the vast majority of government positions.

In 1984, in its most extensive treatment of the constitutionality of legislation prohibiting the employment of noncitizen immigrants, the Supreme Court in *Bernal v. Fainter* struck down a Texas statute that denied aliens the opportunity to become notaries public. In this case, an immigrant applied to become a notary public but was denied on the basis that the statute required all Texas notaries public to be U.S. citizens. The Court observed, under an equal protection analysis, that state laws that discriminate on the basis of alienage can be sustained only if they can withstand strict judicial scrutiny. To withstand strict scrutiny, such laws must advance a compelling state interest by the least restrictive means available. The Court also noted, however, that there was a narrow "political function" exception to the rule that discrimination based on alienage triggers strict scrutiny. This exception applies to laws that exclude immigrants from positions intimately related to the process of democratic government. The Court noted that states have the right to establish their own forms of government and to limit the right to govern to those

who are fully fledged members of the political community (i.e., U.S. citizens) and also observed that some public positions are so closely bound up with the formulation and implementation of self-government that states are permitted to exclude from those positions persons outside the political community (i.e., noncitizens). Accordingly, the Court stated that the strict scrutiny standard may be lowered when evaluating the validity of exclusions that entrust only to U.S. citizens important elective and nonelective positions whose operations "go to the heart of representative government." The Court nevertheless found that the "political function" exception was inapplicable to this case, since a notary's duties are essentially clerical and ministerial, and not political in nature. Applying the strict scrutiny standard, the Court found that the state's interest in ensuring that notaries are reasonably familiar with state law and institutions was not compelling and noted that there was no evidence that resident aliens, as a class, are so incapable of familiarizing themselves with Texas law as to justify the state's absolute and class-wide exclusion.

The Supreme Court has used the "political function" exception to uphold state statutes and regulations that limit employment to U.S. citizens. In 1978, in *Foley v. Connelie*, the Court held that a state may require police officers to be citizens, since police officers perform a fundamental obligation of government. In 1979, in *Ambach v. Norwick*, the Court held that a state may bar aliens who have not declared their intent to become citizens from teaching in public schools, because teachers, like police officers, possess a high degree of responsibility and discretion in the fulfillment of a basic governmental obligation. In 1982, in *Cabell v. Chavez-Saldo*, the Court held that a state may bar immigrants from positions as probation officers because such officers routinely exercise discretionary power involving a basic government function.

NATURALIZATION

Arguably the most valuable benefit accorded to immigrants is the opportunity to become U.S. citizens. In fact, many immigrants consider themselves to be citizens-in-waiting and regard their permanent resident status as a temporary purgatory before admission to the citizenry of the United States. The INA allows immigrants to become eligible for naturalization as U.S. citizens once five years have elapsed from the date they initially became permanent residents.

Naturalization does not follow automatically from completing the first five years of permanent residence, however, and the immigrant is free to choose whether or not to embark upon the naturalization process.

To become a U.S. citizen, an immigrant must file the required application with the INS and must establish that he or she fulfills the requirements for naturalization. Under the INA, to be eligible for naturalization, an immigrant must establish that he or she (1) has been a permanent resident for five years (or three years if married to a U.S. citizen and living with the citizen spouse in the United States); (2) is able to read, write, and speak simple English; (3) has a basic knowledge and understanding of the fundamentals of the history, principles, and form of government of the United States; and (4) during the period of residence, has been, and still is, a person of good moral character, attached to the principles of the Constitution of the United States, and well disposed to the good order and happiness of the United States.

To be eligible for naturalization, then, an immigrant must have resided continuously in the United States for at least five years immediately before the date on which he or she files the naturalization application (although an application for naturalization may be submitted up to ninety days before the five-year anniversary). Additionally, during the five years immediately before this filing, the immigrant must have been physically present in the United States for periods totaling at least half of the five-year period (i.e., thirty of sixty months). He or she must also have resided for at least three months in the state or INS district in which the application is filed and must reside continuously in the United States from the date of the application until the date of admission to citizenship. In scrutinizing the absences from the United States of a naturalization applicant, the INS is guided by the following standards: (1) an absence from the United States of less than six months will generally not affect the continuity of residence requirement; (2) an absence from the United States of more than six months but less than one year presumptively breaks the continuity of residence, but this presumption can be overcome by the applicant if he or she shows evidence that residence in the United States was not abandoned; (3) an absence from the United States of a year or longer conclusively breaks the continuity of an applicant's residence, although an exception does exist for immigrants stationed abroad by the U.S. government, a U.S. corporation or research institution, or a public international organization.

TAXATION OF IMMIGRANTS

All immigrants employed in the United States must, like U.S. citizens, declare their income to the U.S. government and pay the appropriate taxes. Under the Internal Revenue Code (IRC), an immigrant is deemed a resident of the United States for taxation purposes under the "green card test." Since all immigrants remain citizens of another nation until becoming U.S. citizens, this exposes them to the possibility of double taxation, that is, having the obligation of paying taxes to two nations on a single income. The United States has entered into tax treaties with a number of foreign nations in order to protect its citizens and immigrants (and other aliens subject to double taxation) from such an obligation. These tax treaties provide relief to aliens who are tax residents of the United States and of another country by implementing a "tie breaker" rule that, for tax purposes, assigns the residence of such aliens to one country only. Tie breaker rules operate by assessing various factors, such as permanent residence, center of vital economic interests, habitual abode, and nationality or citizenship, and assigning residence on these bases. Since these factors are very similar to those scrutinized by the INS to determine whether or not an immigrant has abandoned his or her intention to reside in the United States permanently, an immigrant who wishes to be considered a tax resident of another country under the tie breaker rule does so at the peril of losing his status as a permanent resident of the United States. Indeed, as discussed above, one of the most important factors for the INS in evaluating a returning immigrant's maintenance of permanent resident status is the immigrant's continued filing of income tax returns in the United States. An immigrant who, by virtue of the application of a tie breaker rule, has been deemed a tax resident of another country is unlikely to convince the INS that he or she intends to continue to reside permanently in the United States. Similarly, an application for a reentry permit asks specifically whether or not the applicant has failed to file an income tax return because he or she considered himself or herself a nonresident. An affirmative answer is likely to result in the denial of the application.

REMOVAL OF IMMIGRANTS

All aliens in the United States, whether immigrants, nonimmigrants, or undocumented aliens, may be removed or expelled from United States territory. To be removed from the United States, an immigrant must be within one or more of the classes of deportable aliens enumerated in the INA. These classes include aliens who have committed criminal acts, are drug abusers, have failed to register with the INS or have falsified immigration documents, or have falsely claimed U.S. citizenship. Also included are aliens who have become public charges from causes not shown to have arisen since entry to the United States, who have voted, whose presence or activities in the United States are considered by the secretary of state to have potentially serious adverse foreign policy consequences, and aliens who have engaged in any activity intended to oppose the U.S. government by force, violence, or other unlawful means.

Aliens removed from the United States are barred from reentering the country for five years. If removed from the United States on a second or subsequent occasion, they are barred from reentering for twenty years. If removed on the basis of a conviction for an aggravated felony, they are barred from ever reentering.

Although immigrants are not shielded by their permanent resident status from being removed as a result of falling into a class of deportable aliens, they may, unlike nonimmigrants, be eligible for the remedy of Cancellation of Removal under the INA. Cancellation of Removal allows the INS to withhold the removal of an alien who is removable from the United States as long as the following three conditions are met:

1. The alien has been a permanent resident for five years or more;

2. He or she has resided in the United States continuously for at least seven years;

3. He or she has not been convicted of an aggravated felony.

This relief is granted at the discretion of the INS, which is not required to provide it even though these three criteria may have been met. Indeed, case law has held that an applicant for Cancellation of Removal must establish that he or she merits the favorable exercise of the INS's discretion. It should be noted that a showing of extreme hardship to the immigrant or to a person dependent upon the immigrant need not be made for Cancellation of Removal to be granted.

CRIMINAL ACTIVITY BY IMMIGRANTS

All immigrants must abide by U.S. law and are subject to the same penalties, including imprisonment, as U.S. citizens for failing to do so. In no case will an alien's immigrant status protect him or her from liability for committing a criminal offense. Indeed, most aliens convicted of crimes in the United States will find that such convictions carry the added penalty of causing them to violate the immigration laws of this country and therefore become removable. Of particular seriousness are convictions for the new strain of "aggravated" felonies created by Congress through the Illegal Immigration Reform and Immigrant Responsibility Act of 1996. An immigrant who is convicted of such an aggravated felony will be automatically removed from the United States without recourse to any discretionary relief, including Cancellation of Removal. Over fifty crimes or classes of crimes are now classed as aggravated felonies in the INA. These include crimes of violence carrying a sentence of at least one year, crimes involving the sale (but not possession) of drugs, theft offenses carrying a sentence of one year or more, fraud involving a loss of more than $10,000 to the victim, and a number of prostitution-related offenses. The INS has held that certain felony Driving While Intoxicated offenses are crimes of violence classifiable as aggravated felonies. The penalties for committing an aggravated felony operate retroactively, and immigrants may be removed for convictions for aggravated felonies without regard to when these convictions occurred, even if the convictions occurred many years before the introduction of these penalties in 1996. In view of the harshness of these provisions and the perceived unfairness to immigrants who have resided in the United States for most of their lives, legislation has been introduced in Congress to mitigate the new law's most severe provisions.

CONSTITUTIONAL RIGHTS OF IMMIGRANTS

Aliens who are physically present in the United States, whether immigrants or nonimmigrants, are entitled to many of the protections and rights offered by the U.S. Constitution. These include the rights guaranteed by the First Amendment (the rights of religious freedom, free speech, and assembly), the Fourth Amendment (the right to be free of unreasonable searches and seizures), the Fifth Amendment (the rights against double jeopardy, self-incrimination, and the taking of private property for public use, and the right to due process), the Sixth Amendment (the rights to a jury trial, to confront adverse witnesses, and to legal counsel), the Eighth Amendment (the right against cruel and unusual punishment), and the Fourteenth Amendment (the right to due process and the right to equal protection). Courts have traditionally held that the Constitution's granting of such rights and protections to "persons" or "people," rather than "citizens" should be interpreted to mean that aliens present in the United States should share in these rights and protections.

The most important right guaranteed to U.S. citizens, but denied to immigrants, is the right to vote. No aliens may vote in local, state, or federal elections, regardless of how long they have been permanent residents of this country. The original thirteen colonies did grant suffrage to aliens, as did states later admitted to the Union. Only in 1926, when Arkansas enacted a citizenship requirement for voters, were immigrants prohibited from voting in all jurisdictions. The fact that aliens have no constitutional right to vote has never been addressed by the Supreme Court, but is a proposition that is so self-evident that no legal challenge to it appears possible.

PROPERTY RIGHTS

The property rights of aliens, whether immigrants or nonimmigrants, are considered to be protected by the constitutional guarantee of equal protection, as well as by the Constitution's prohibition on the taking of property without just compensation. The rights of aliens outside the United States to own property here are therefore much more limited than the property rights enjoyed by aliens who are physically present here, since this guarantee is generally held to apply only within U.S. territory. Restrictions upon alien ownership of personal property are highly unusual, and immigrants may own all types of tangible personal property. With respect to intangible personal property such as licenses, the property rights of immigrants are less than absolute. In a number of states, for example, only U.S. citizens may hold liquor licenses. This limitation has not been tested under the equal protection analysis discussed above, but it is arguable that under the Twenty-first Amendment a state's power to regulate alcohol would allow the bar to stand. The federal government denies licenses to

aliens to operate atomic power plants and radio stations, or to lease oil or mineral lands. The fact that it is the federal government, rather than a state government, that is imposing the restriction tends to insulate such limitations from legal challenges, by virtue of the plenary power of the federal government over aliens. Thus, in *Campos v. FCC* (1981), a Federal Communications Commission (FCC) bar on the granting of commercial operator licenses to aliens or foreign corporations was upheld on the basis that the federal control of aliens is a political question that requires only minimal judicial scrutiny on equal protection grounds.

Immigrants also enjoy intellectual property rights in the United States, and no restrictions exist on the right of aliens to own patents or trademarks. An alien's work may also be protected by the Copyright Act of 1976 if the alien is domiciled here when the work is first published.

Limitations on the rights of aliens to own real property in the United States were upheld in the early part of the last century through a line of cases (the most important of which is *Terrace v. Thompson* [1923]) in which the Supreme Court held that states could confine the ownership of land to U.S. citizens. Although the 1948 case of *Oyama v. California* indirectly overruled this line of cases, *Terrace v. Thompson* has never been explicitly overruled, and many prohibitions on alien ownership of real property appear in state statutes. Such prohibitions are rarely exercised and would be likely to be voided by a court as violative of the equal protection clause.

ACCESS OF IMMIGRANTS TO THE JUDICIAL PROCESS

The Civil Rights Act of 1870 allows "all persons within the jurisdiction of the United States" to have the same right in every state to make and enforce contracts, to sue, to be parties to a lawsuit, to give evidence, and to have access to the full and equal benefit of all laws and proceedings. This guarantee has traditionally been interpreted to embrace aliens physically present in the United States and therefore within its jurisdiction. The right of aliens to bring judicial actions is not in question and is recognized to extend to undocumented aliens. The right or obligation to serve on juries is reserved to U.S. citizens exclusively.

GOVERNMENT BENEFITS

Immigrants are generally eligible for most benefits granted by federal, state, and local governments to the same extent as U.S. citizens. In particular, a federal statute specifically prohibits discrimination on the grounds of race, color, or national origin under any program receiving federal financial assistance, and the Supreme Court in *Graham v. Richardson* (1971) and *Rok v. Legg* (1939) has declared unconstitutional state legislation that denied welfare and other benefits to resident aliens, since such restrictions violate the equal protection clause and infringe on the exclusive federal authority to control the entitlements granted to aliens. The entitlement of immigrants to Social Security benefits appears not to be questioned, although no case has yet addressed this issue. Although various initiatives designed to deny welfare benefits to aliens have, and continue to be, debated in state legislatures, such initiatives apply only to undocumented or nonimmigrant aliens, and do not embrace immigrants admitted for lawful permanent residence.

SELECTIVE SERVICE REGISTRATION

All immigrants who were under twenty-six years of age on the date they became permanent residents must register for Selective Service. A failure to do so may be a basis for denying the immigrant's naturalization application. Nonimmigrants are not required to register, but undocumented aliens, strangely, are required to do so.

SPONSORSHIP OF FAMILY MEMBERS FOR PERMANENT RESIDENCE

Immigrants are entitled to file applications to allow their relatives abroad to be admitted to the United States as immigrants. In this respect, their opportunities are much more limited than the opportunities granted to U.S. citizens. Citizens may sponsor their spouses, unmarried children under twenty-one, and parents (as long as the petitioning citizen is over twenty-one) as "immediate relatives," and may also sponsor adult sons, daughters, and siblings. Immigrants may only sponsor their spouses and unmarried children for permanent residence, and must also wait many years before these persons can be admitted.

RENOUNCING IMMIGRANT STATUS

An immigrant may renounce his or her permanent resident status in the United States for whatever reason, and the INS provides a formal mechanism for doing so. For practical purposes, an alien who wishes to relinquish his or her immigrant status may do so only at a consulate or INS office abroad, since a renunciation of immigrant status in the United States would immediately result in the ex-immigrant being considered to be out of status and therefore technically removable. Immigrants who have relinquished their permanent resident status are not barred from returning to the United States, but must seek and obtain valid nonimmigrant or permanent resident status before doing so. It should be noted that immigrants who renounce their immigrant status to avoid taxation in the United States may not be penalized for doing so, unlike U.S. citizens who renounce their citizenship for this reason.

Without attempting to be polemical, it is accurate to describe immigrants as second-class citizens. They are part of the American family, in the sense that they may live here "permanently," hold jobs, pay taxes, and participate extensively in the life of their communities. In certain key respects, however, immigrants stand in an inferior position to U.S. citizens, who may vote, hold federal jobs, serve on juries, and can almost never be expelled from this country. The upward mobility of immigrants is possible, however, and immigrants can change their situation by exercising their privilege to become naturalized citizens.

A. James Vázquez-Azpiri

See also: Immigration Legislation of the 1980s and 1990s (Part I, Sec. 5); Legal and Illegal Immigration: A Statistical Overview (Part II, Sec. 2); Civil Rights (Part II, Sec. 5); California's Farm Labor Law, 1975, Illegal Immigration Reform and Immigrant Responsibility Act, 1996, Personal Responsibility and Work Opportunity Reconciliation Act, 1996, *LULAC et al. v. Wilson et al.*, 1995, California Proposition 63, 1986, California Proposition 187, 1994, California Proposition 227, 1998 (Part IV, Sec. 1); Title IV: Restricting Welfare and Public Benefits for Aliens, 1996 (Part IV, Sec. 2).

BIBLIOGRAPHY

Aleinikoff, Alexander, and David Martin, eds. *Immigration and Nationality Laws of the United States. Selected Statutes, Regulations, and*

Forms as Amended to March 6, 1990. Saint Paul, MN: West Publishing, 1990.

Ambach v. Norwick, 441 US 68 (1979).

Bernal v. Fainter, 467 US 216 (1984).

Cabell v. Chavez-Salido, 454 US 432 (1982).

Campos v. FCC, 650 F2d 890 (7th Cir 1981).

Code of Federal Regulations, Title 8, Aliens and Nationality.

Commission on Immigration Reform. *Becoming an American: Immigration and Immigrant Policy.* Washington, DC: Government Printing Office, 1997.

Department of Justice, Immigration and Naturalization Service. *An Immigrant Nation. United States Regulation of Immigration, 1798–1991.* Washington, DC: Government Printing Office, 1991.

Foley v. Connelie, 435 US 291 (1978).

Immigration and Nationality Act, 8 U.S.C.A. 1–1434 ("Aliens and Nationality").

In re Griffiths, 413 US 717 (1973).

Martin, David. *Major Issues in Immigration Law.* (Washington, DC: Federal Judicial Center, 1987).

Mathews v. Diaz, 426 US 67, 77 (1976).

Motomura, Hiroshi, et al. "Alienage Classifications in a Nation of Immigrants: Three Models of 'Permanent' Residence." In *Immigration and Citizenship in the Twenty-First Century*, ed. N. Pickus. Lanham, MD: Rowman & Littlefield, 1998.

———. "Whose Alien Nation? Two Models of Constitutional Immigration Law." *Michigan Law Review* 94 (1996): 1927.

Neuman, Gerald. *Strangers to the Constitution: Immigrants, Borders, and the Fundamental Law.* Princeton, NJ: Princeton 1996.

Oyama v. California, 332 US 633 (1948).

Rok v. Legg, 27 F. Supp. 243 (D.C.Cal. 1939).

Rosberg, Gerald. "Aliens and Equal Protection: Why Not the Right To Vote?" *Michigan Law Review* 75 (1977): 1092.

Terrace v. Thompson, 263 US 197 (1923).

STATE, COUNTY, AND MUNICIPAL LEGISLATION

This entry draws attention to the largely overlooked role of states and local governments in the regulation of immigrants. It suggests that the tendency of researchers, advocates, and policymakers to focus on federal immigration policy has obscured the shared authority between states and the federal government in enacting immigrant policies. Consequently, we lack a comprehensive understanding of the articulation between federal and state policies and between immigration and immigrant policies.

The phrase "immigration policy" is ambiguous. This ambiguity stems from its dual use. On one hand, it is used to refer to all policies that impact persons wishing to enter the United States, as well as those already within its territory. On the other hand—and the one adopted here—it is used more specifically to refer to the powers defined by the U.S. Constitution (art. 1, sec. 8) and Supreme Court decisions. Under the latter use, federal immigration powers include the authority to determine how many immigrants should be allowed to enter, define conditions for their entry and removal (formerly known as deportation), and grant national citizenship. In all four of these policy areas, the federal government has a preemptive authority. Customs and Border Patrol functions are here considered primarily as activities related to entry control and thus are not listed as separate areas of authority.

Additionally, Congress, the president, and federal agencies have the power to regulate the activities of immigrants within the nation. This federal policymaking power encompasses the duties and benefits of immigrants in relationship to such issues as military conscription, federal taxes, ownership of federally regulated resources, and eligibility for federal employment and public assistance programs. Such policies are referred to as federal immigrant policies.

The federal formulation of immigration and immigrant policies has dominated public debate and research agendas on these issues over the past three decades. Experts and public alike, as a result, have largely ignored state and local immigrant policymaking. An important shift, however, was brought about by the passage of the 1996 Personal Responsibility and Work Opportunity Reconciliation Act (PRWORA). Several efforts, such as the Urban Institute's New Federalism project, were started that focused on the devolution of federal authority to states regarding the eligibility of lawful permanent residents for key public assistance programs. Although these efforts have raised the public profile of state immigrant policymaking, they have done so in a narrow way by focusing solely on state decisions regarding such federal/state programs as TANF (Temporary Assistance to Needy Families), Medicaid, and food stamps. In fact, states, with respect to their noncitizen residents, legislate in numerous other policy areas, as they have done since the colonial period. In other words, states have always shared authority over immigrants with the federal government and have never lost any of that authority.

The important role that states have in making immigrant policies is here highlighted through two related analyses. The first examines the licensing of twenty-three occupations and professions in six states (California, Florida, Illinois, New Jersey, New York, and Texas) over approximately fifty years. The second examines the 1999 statutes that restrict noncitizens from state resources in these same six states along with Louisiana and Virginia. According to the Immigration and Naturalization Service and the Bureau of the Census, the first six states are among the nine most populous states as well as the destination of 68 percent of the immigrants admitted in 1997, as well as the state of residence for 73 percent of the nation's foreign-born population. The latter two states were included in this study to provide a contrast to the six states that dominate discussion on immigrants and immigration. Although municipal immigrant policies are evident, the absence of a comprehensive analysis of these prevents a fuller discussion; consequently, only a small number of examples are cited in this essay.

BACKGROUND

The Tenth Amendment to the U.S. Constitution gives the states powers not explicitly delegated to the federal government. Consequently, states are entitled to exercise wide powers in formulating occupational, political, educational, and other policies regarding immigrant and nonimmigrant residents within their boundaries. The state powers, however, are limited by Fourteenth Amendment guarantees of equal protection and due process, as well as other constitutional protections.

From the colonial period through the late 1880s, the colonies and later the states actively specified conditions on the entry of immigrants into their dominion (such as excluding those likely to become a public charge), taxing vessel owners and immigrants, ordering deportations, as well as granting naturalization. Gradually, however, the erosion of their authority began with the 1790 Immigration Act, which established a uniform rule for naturalization but not a federal mechanism. This was followed by the 1882 Immigration Act, the first general immigration law, which established a central control system, though it operated through state boards. The first comprehensive law for national control of immigration implemented through a federal bureau was not established until the passage of the Immigration act of 1891. None of these acts, however, eliminated or reduced the states' authority over immigrant policymaking.

Moreover, the states have also played an important role in shaping the nation's federal immigration policies and their administration. A significant part of the early federal statutes was modeled on existing state statutes. Additionally, federal efforts to control immigration relied on the states to implement federal policies. The 1882 Immigration Act, for example, established a federal system for control of immigration that relied on state boards for its implementation. But with the creation of the federal Bureau of Immigration under the 1891 act, states ceased to have this sort of direct role in federal immigration policy. Yet they continued to exercise uninterrupted authority to legislate on matters relating to immigrants residing within their territories. States also gave local governments parallel authority to regulate immigrants in such areas as public employment and business and professional licenses.

STATE IMMIGRANT POLICIES

For over one hundred years, as evident from state and federal court cases filed by lawful permanent residents, states and local governments have restricted a wide range of ordinary economic activities to U.S. citizens. Some of the policies specifically excluded noncitizens from a wide array of activities such as collecting garbage, cutting hair, driving a taxi, operating a pool hall, inspecting plumbing, serving as a peace officer, operating a pawn shop, teaching in public schools, and working at pari-mutuel racetracks. Such prohibitions, however, affected lawful permanent residents as well as other noncitizen immigrants.

In addition to economic activities, states and municipalities have placed restrictions on voting and political appointments. All states and almost all cities now limit voting to U.S.-born and naturalized citizens. This was not always the case. During the period of westward expansion, for example, voting rights was an important element in the recruitment of immigrants to settle in new territories such as Oregon. In 1926, the state of Arkansas, for example, became the last state to remove the noncitizen franchise rights that had existed previously in twenty-two states.

To a small degree, the pendulum now appears to be swinging back the other way. In 1992, Takoma Park, Maryland, amended its charter to allow permanent residents to vote in local elections. By this action, Takoma Park joined a handful of cities, such as New York and Chicago, that have allowed noncitizens to vote in local elections. In 1999, Cambridge, Massachusetts, considered extending the franchise in local elections to permanent residents.

Voting restrictions in several states and municipalities are sustained more by tradition than by statute. In cases where it is not explicitly prohibited, there appears to be a presumption that U.S. citizenship restriction in federal and state elections directly apply to local elections. The outcome in both instances is the exclusion of permanent residents from local elections.

OCCUPATIONAL AND PROFESSIONAL LICENSES

States have a long-established interest in regulating employment, particularly the licensing of occupations and professions. Figure 1 provides a review of twenty-three occupations for six states (California, Florida, Illinois, New Jersey, New York, and Texas) between

1946 and 1999. (It should be noted that the year 1999 represents the legislative cycle covering sessions from 1997 to 1999.) These occupations are accountant, architect, attorney, barber, chiropractor, cosmetologist, dental hygienist, dentist, embalmer, engineer, manicurist, midwife, nurse, optician, optometrist, pharmacist, physical therapist, physician, podiatrist, practical nurse, psychologist, teacher, and veterinarian. Figure 1 shows that while overall there has been a significant reduction between 1946 and 1999 in the number of professional and occupational licenses restricted to U.S. citizens, states continue to maintain certain restrictions. It also shows the variability in immigrant policymaking by state legislatures: while some states relaxed the number of restrictions within the 23 occupations, others tightened them. In Florida, Illinois, New Jersey, and Texas, the number of restrictions increased between 1946 and 1977—a perplexing development against the backdrop of the civil rights movement and Supreme Court decisions barring discrimination against immigrants.

By 1999, three of the six states no longer restricted any of the twenty-three occupations to U.S. citizens. Illinois and New York still require applicants for a teaching license to be U.S. citizens; otherwise, the applicant is given a temporary license and required to become a citizen within a specified period of time. If the applicant fails to acquire U.S. citizenship, the license is revoked. New Jersey, on the other hand, maintains restrictions for six of the twenty-three occupations.

Multiple factors account for the significant decrease in number of restricted occupations after 1997. There are three principal factors: (a) the multiple federal court decisions that ruled that such restrictions are unconstitutional under the Fourteenth Amendment; (b) these judicial decisions and subsequent opinions by state attorneys general that discouraged legislators from expanding citizenship-based restrictions; and (c) the actions of state legislators and state agencies to remove some of the existing restrictions.

The decisions of the Supreme Court were central to the state legislative changes. Between 1973 and 1984, the Supreme Court ruled on cases involving U.S. citizenship restrictions on attorneys (*In re Griffiths*, 413 US 717), architects and engineers (*Re Examining Board v. Flores de Otero*, 426 US 572), state troopers (*Foley v. Connelie*, 435 US 291), public school teachers (*Ambach v. Norwick*, 441 US 68), probation officers (*Cabell v. Chávez-Salido*, 454 US 432), and notary publics (*Bernal v. Fainter*, 467 US 216). Other than the cases dealing with teachers and state troopers, the Supreme Court ruled that the restrictions were unconstitutional under the guarantees of equal protection of the Fourteenth Amendment. Citizenship restrictions for teachers and state troopers were allowed to stand on the theory that both occupations were central to the definition of "political community" in the states. On this basis, states were permitted to restrict such politically sensitive occupations, as well as voting and appointive positions, to U.S. citizens.

The Supreme Court also addressed the constitutionality of such restrictions in other areas. Over the past 100 years, the Supreme Court ruled on twenty-

Figure 1
State Citizenship-Based Restrictions on Professional and Occupational Licenses, 1946 to 1999

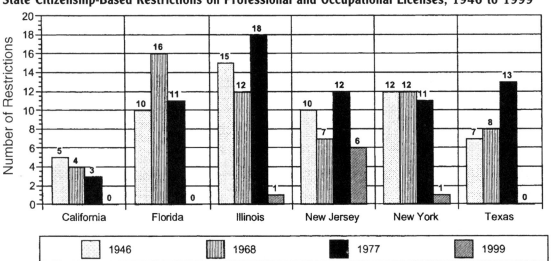

Source: G. Sanders. "Aliens in Professions and Occupations: State Laws Restricting Participation." *I&N Reporter* (1968): 37–40.

six cases regarding local and state citizenship-based restrictions such as public employment, use of public resources, receipt of public benefits, and ownership of agricultural land. The Court has thus declared that states have the authority to continue to make policies regarding immigrants within their territories, as long as they do not violate constitutional protections.

OVERALL STATE IMMIGRANT RESTRICTIONS

State immigrant policymaking is not limited to professional and occupational licenses but includes a broad set of activities and resources. These can be summarized as encompassing economic, political, and other resources and activities. "Economic issues" are here defined as those activities related to the operation of a business, eligibility for state resources (e.g., a farm loan), and employment-related areas (including occupations and professional licenses). "Political issues," on the other hand, relate to activities such as holding appointive office, voting, jury service, judgeships, and holding a public administrative appointment. The category of "other" corresponds to activities of a more general nature such as obtaining a fishing license, receiving a scholarship, serving on the state militia, and obtaining a special license plate.

Rather than list all the three types of restrictions that exist in the eight states—the same six states discussed above as well as Louisiana and Virginia—I summarize these in Table 1. Several clarifications, however, should be made about the table. First, the table presents a summary of the statutory citizenship-based restrictions; it does not include restrictions that may exist in the respective state constitutions. Second, the data in the table represent the direct legislative restrictions and thus do not include indirect restrictions. In other words, the table summarizes the presence of a particular statute that restricts a particular resource; it does not present other restrictions that may exist but are not apparent because they cross-reference another statute. An example of this would be a statute for a public housing security guard that does not indicate that the applicant be a U.S. citizen, yet because the position is defined as a "peace officer," the individual must meet the U.S. citizenship requirement in the statute specifying the conditions for "peace officers."

Third, the table should be interpreted with some caution, being read as representing a relative picture of the restrictions in each state and not as an absolute comparison of their restrictiveness. For example, a particular statute can be written to encompass a single entity (e.g., that the members of a particular state board must be U.S. citizens)—and this is the case in most such statutes—or it can be written as a more comprehensive statute covering multiple entities. Virginia's statute regarding "regulatory" boards exemplifies the latter: that statute requires that all members of "regulatory" boards be U.S. citizens. However, it should be noted that some ambiguity exists within Virginia's secretary of State's office about which boards and commissions are considered "regulatory."

Table 1 allows certain important insights about immigrant policymaking in the eight states. It is clear that states show a differential emphasis in the area about which they are most concerned, with respect to citizen-based restrictions. In three of the states, the largest number of restrictions are in economic activities; the other three states, on the other hand, appear most concerned with political issues. Interestingly enough, Louisiana, a state not generally invoked in national immigrant or immigration debates, has the most numerous political restrictions, as well as overall total number of restrictions (99). Among the first six states, Florida emerges as the least restrictive and Texas as the most restrictive.

In summary, while space does not allow a detailed description of the citizenship-based restrictions that exist in each of the eight states, Table 1 offers a glimpse of the extent and variation of the immigrant policymaking roles that are found in the six major immigrant-receiving states. The restrictions are the product of a long history of state involvement in the regulation of political, economic, and other resources within each state. Yet, as was noted in the discussion of the trends in the licensing of the twenty-three occupations, citizenship-based restrictions are not fixed and can undergo significant changes.

Table 1			
State Citizenship-Based Restrictions, 1999			
State	Economic	Political	Other
California	5	19	12
Florida	3	6	12
Illinois	37	14	6
New Jersey	27	12	14
New York	20	27	31
Texas	20	58	7
Louisiana	14	68	17
Virginia	8	7	2

Source: Lexis-Nexis, State Codes (1997–99 legislative sessions).

Although the above discussion has focused on the role of states in the formulation of immigrant policy, we should not overlook the parallel role that exists among municipal and county governments. Unfortunately, this dimension remains largely ignored. Aside from occasional newspaper stories (such as the recent *Philadelphia Inquirer* story about the elimination in 1999 of the 1969 restriction in Lindenwold, New Jersey, of taxi licenses to U.S. citizens) that report on specific ordinances, very little has been produced regarding this issue. A recent comprehensive analysis of municipal restrictions does not appear to exist. Francis Kalnay's brief summary of multiple cities, though outdated, remains unique in the immigration literature.

While their role in the formulation of immigrant policies has generally been overlooked by experts and the public alike, states and local governments have been active in such policymaking from colonial times to the present. Recent evidence of this role is clear from the analyses of licensing practices of twenty-three occupations over a fifty-year period in the six major immigrant-receiving states and of the 1999 citizenship-based restrictions in those same states. The important role of the states in immigrant policymaking has been eclipsed by the attention given to the federal role in immigration and immigrant policy.

While the passage of the 1996 welfare act (PRWORA) had the important consequence of drawing attention to the role of states in the making of immigrant policy, this attention, however, was narrowly focused on decisions regarding public assistance benefits. Analyses such as those presented here suggest a starting point for the development of a broader understanding of state and local immigrant policy and their articulation with federal immigrant and immigration policy.

Luis F. B. Plascencia

See also: Legislation II: Immigrants in America (Part II, Sec. 5); Welfare and Public Benefits (Part II, Sec. 9); *LULAC et al. v. Wilson et al.,* 1995, California Proposition 63, 1986, California Proposition 187, 1994, California Proposition 227, 1998 (Part IV, Sec. 1).

BIBLIOGRAPHY

Carliner, D. *The Rights of Aliens.* New York: Avon Books, 1977.

Immigration Commission. *Immigrants in Industries,* vol. 20. Washington DC: Government Printing Office, 1911.

Kalnay, F. *The New American.* New York: Greenberg Publishers, 1941.

Konvitz, M. *The Alien and the Asiatic in American Law.* Ithaca: Cornell University Press, 1946.

Lexis-Nexis. State Codes. 1997–99 Legislative Sessions.

"Lindenwold to Repeal Law on Taxis." *Philadelphia Inquirer,* August 11, 1999.

Plascencia, L. F. B., G. P. Freeman, and M. Setzler. "Restricting Immigrant Access to Employment: An Examination of Regulations in Five States." In *Policy Brief.* Rev. to include New Jersey. Claremont, CA: Tomás Rivera Policy Institute, 1999.

Sanders, G. "Aliens in Professions and Occupations: State Laws Restricting Participation." *I & N Reporter,* 1968, 37–40.

POLITICS

INTRODUCTION

Section 6 of Part II of the *Encyclopedia of American Immigration* is devoted to the subject of immigrants and politics. Three of the entries deal with the role of immigrants within politics. Two of these focus on the role of immigrants within American politics—both in terms of electoral participation and activism—and one looks at the role immigrants play in the politics of their home country. The remaining two entries in this section focus on how American politics and public opinion affect immigrants and the immigration process.

In his entry, Brian N. Fry examines the recent history of anti-immigrant politics in America. He begins with a discussion of how increasingly partisan the subject has become and how the choice of language and description determines political positions. Next, Fry goes into the various immigration-related interest groups before making a comparison between so-called expansionists and restrictionists. The author then turns to a brief history of anti-immigration politics and discusses the dichotomy between the political viewpoints that see immigrants as "capital" and immigrants as "costs." A discussion of restrictionists and the question of American nationalism is followed by a look at how globalization supporters are often expansionists on the immigration question.

In "Immigrant Politics I: Activism," S. Karthick Ramakrishnan begins with a discussion of early immigrant activism, going back to the wave of East European Jewish immigration in the early twentieth century. The author then discusses the role of immigrant activism during World War II, before moving on to examine the subject within the context of the Civil Rights movement of the 1950s and 1960s. Finally, Ramakrishnan updates the discussion by exploring the role of immigrants in activist politics in the post–Civil Rights era.

"Immigrant Politics II: Electoral Politics," also by S. Karthick Ramakrishnan, begins with a history of immigrant electoral politics going back to the Irish of the mid-nineteenth century, taking it through the great wave of southern and eastern European immigration beginning in the 1880s, and concluding with a discussion of Mexican-American electoral politics in the decades leading up to the immigration reform law of 1965. Ramakrishnan then turns to a discussion of immigrant electoral politics in the contemporary period before examining how the growth and change in the immigrant population in recent years has affected American electoral politics. Next, the author provides a step-by-step review of how immigrants become involved in electoral politics, beginning with naturalization and then moving on to registration, voting, establishing partisan identification, and, finally, contributing to campaigns.

The final entry on immigrant politics, also by S. Karthick Ramakrishnan, explores the role of immigrants in the politics of their home country. Once again, the author begins with a discussion of the history of the subject, looking first at the role of Irish immigrants in the nineteenth century before moving on to discuss the role of immigrants in the many anticolonial movements of the twentieth century. Next, Ramakrishnan examines contemporary home country politics and how immigrants in America interact with political activists back in their homeland and how those political activists look at individuals who have left for America.

In his entry on public opinion and immigration, Thomas J. Espenshade begins with an examination of the subject in a historical context, before moving on to discuss modern public opinion on immigrants and immigration. Espenshade then breaks down the question of public opinion into attitudes about various immigrant groups. In addition, he also discusses the question of public opinion in terms of how it relates to immigrants and the economy and illegal immigration, among other things. The author also examines a variety of public opinion polling methods and several specific polls to understand what they say about Americans' attitudes toward immigrants and immigration.

ANTI-IMMIGRANT POLITICS

In the United States, the politics of immigration reform spin on an axis where conservative and liberal positions are sometimes hard to see. Partly because immigration and refugee policies are starting to resemble redistributive policies, congressional policymaking on immigration has become increasingly partisan since the late 1970s. The issue of immigrant admissions, however, seldom separates voters by party or ideology. In high-immigration states such as California, politicians are attentive to their constituents' attitudes toward immigration, but most members of Congress can comply with the views of interest groups without jeopardizing their reelection bids.

Since 1965, public opinion polls reveal America's restrictionist leanings, but Congress has moved steadily in the opposite direction. Why? Scholars offer a variety of interpretations, but one explanation highlights the policymaking process. Issues such as abortion, gun control, and civil rights frequently divide voters, but immigration rarely elicits the kind of passion that pushes voters to choose one candidate over another. Recognizing this, lawmakers hesitate to campaign on immigration reform. Their reluctance, rooted in the reality of the public's relative indifference, opens up the policymaking process to the expertise and strategies of advocacy groups.

CHOOSING SIDES BY CHOOSING TERMS

In partisan issues, choosing words is like choosing sides. The terms used by immigration reformers routinely disclose their opinions of immigration and the U.S. management of it. The entry of *illegal* aliens should presumably be *impeded*, but the status of *undocumented* aliens, who also entered the United States illegally, should apparently be *regularized*. Is immigration a crisis or a management problem? Should the

United States accommodate, assimilate, incorporate, or integrate immigrants? And the people who use these terms—are they pro-immigrant or anti-immigrant, pro–open borders or nativists? When used indiscriminately, this terminology obscures an already complex set of issues.

There are five basic questions, however, that split immigration reformers into two conflicting camps: (1) Why does the United States want immigrants? (2) How many immigrants should the United States admit each year? (3) On what basis should immigrants be admitted? (4) How should immigrants be treated once they arrive? (5) How should the government enforce the laws (especially those related to illegal immigration)? Immigration reformers regularly address one or more of these questions, but given the complexities of immigration policy, how should their proposals be characterized?

Paul Donnelly, organizer of the Immigration Reform Coalition, uses the terms "expansionist" and "restrictionist" to minimize misunderstanding. These terms do not represent immovable, all-or-nothing postures, but merely signify *tendencies*. Expansionists generally want to maintain or expand the number of visas available to legal permanent residents, and restrictionists generally want to see the numbers reduced. There are many differences besides immigration quotas that make it difficult to draw a sharp line between the two sides (e.g., some expansionists favor recent attempts to further restrict the number of programs and benefits available to noncitizens, but some restrictionists oppose these measures), but restrictionists are generally more or less restrictionist and expansionists are usually more or less expansionist.

In a figurative sense, expansionists and restrictionists also view the impact of immigrants on the economy, population, and culture of the United States in terms of expansion and restriction. For example, restrictionists generally see the economy in zero-sum terms. Immigrants entering the labor force compete with native-born workers for a fixed number of jobs, thereby restricting the opportunities of American citizens and residents. Expansionists, on the other hand, visualize an expanding economy. American opportunities are expanded by immigrants: jobs that would have otherwise been lost are retained and new jobs are created. "Expansionist" and "restrictionist" are not flawless, but less ideological than conventional depictions.

IMMIGRATION-RELATED INTEREST GROUPS

There are basically seven kinds of immigration-related advocacy groups involved in immigration reform: (1) labor unions and business groups (e.g., American Businesses for Legal Immigration, National Association of Manufacturers); (2) immigration lawyers (e.g., American Immigration Lawyers Association); (3) ethnic and immigrants' rights organizations (e.g., National Council of La Raza, National Immigration Forum); (4) population–environmental groups (e.g., Zero Population Growth, Population–Environment Balance); (5) environmental–cultural groups (e.g., Federation for American Immigration Reform, American Immigration Control Foundation); (6) think tanks (Center for Immigration Studies, Cato Institute); and (7) religious lobbies (Council of Jewish Federations, U.S. Catholic Bishops Conference). A number of bipartisan and nonpartisan organizations are also involved, such as the International Migration Program of the Carnegie Endowment for International Peace, the Center for Migration Studies, Lewis Center for Regional Policy Studies, House and Senate immigration subcommittees, and of course, the Immigration and Naturalization Service (INS).

COMPARING EXPANSIONISTS AND RESTRICTIONISTS

The immigration debate is overflowing with empirical and moral arguments, with myriad values and interpretations. The worldviews of expansionists and restrictionists frame immigration in contrasting ways and assign different meanings to immigrants and the changes they generate.

To restrictionists, immigration is more of a national question than a human one. The health of the American culture, economy, environment, and polity supersedes the desires of immigrants to enter the United States. Immigration is not a solution to the world's problems of overpopulation, government corruption, and weak economies, but in fact, contributes to each of these problems. The notion that the United States is somehow exceptional or exempt from natural laws must be debunked, restrictionists argue, if America is ever going to establish immigration policies in harmony with human nature and the environment. Until then, the country can expect higher levels of illegal immigration, interethnic tension, and environmental degradation. In short, restrictionists argue that the time has come to temporarily end the "American experiment."

To expansionists, immigration is more of a humanitarian and economic question than a national one. The national interest is significant, but other aspirations also deserve special consideration, such as the rights of refugees, desires of immigrants, and needs of business. These objectives are interconnected and complementary in the expansionist vision. For example, the United States acquires generosity by giving it away, and American businesses profit from immigrant proficiencies just as immigrants gain from American deficiencies. The list could go on, but the point is this: By and large, immigration benefits the United States and the people it accommodates. The national interest is achieved by expanding immigration, not by restricting it. The American experiment with immigration is not an empty tradition, but part of a broad, imprecise strategy to synchronize the extension of democracy with the unceasing march of capital.

Comparing the worldviews of expansionists and restrictionists (based on publications, agency documents, and interviews with immigration activists, lobbyists, policymakers, and researchers) necessitates understanding the values and beliefs underpinning their efforts. In short, their differences stem from different *values* (e.g., is a sustainable environment, or a strong economy, more important?) and *assumptions* about how the world works (e.g., can humans exceed natural limits, or are they bound by the laws of nature?). Not surprisingly, these differences lead to seemingly incompatible recommendations (e.g., immigration levels should stabilize population growth versus immigration levels should meet the needs of business). The following comparisons are presented from the vantage points of immigration reformers (expansionists and restrictionists), and uses their words (enclosed by quotation marks without names attached), ideas, and interpretations to convey their respective logics.

American-born demonstrators voice their support for Proposition 187, a 1994 California referendum that would have cut off many social services to immigrants. *(Slobodan Dimitrov/Impact Visuals)*

IMMIGRATION HISTORY

According to expansionists, repeated investments in immigration have generated valuable returns. Like a mutual fund brochure, they caution that historical performance does not guarantee future results, but emphasize the strengths of the prospectus. Unlike many countries, the United States transforms diversity into a strength and enjoys an almost unrivaled level of prosperity and political stability. True, immigration is an experiment, but it is also one supported by a reassuring history of overall success. Throughout its short history the United States has benefited greatly from immigration—why discontinue a successful tradition?

Expansionists generally see past achievements as indicative of future success. The status of "experiment" should not dissuade Americans from venturing a small risk because the experiment has worked out rather well. Immigration carries a degree of risk, but so does postponing or ending it. Restrictionist arguments for a temporary moratorium or replacement-level policy strike expansionists as risky, unnec-

essary, selfish, or simply unrealistic. From the perspective of expansionists, the American experiment with immigration benefits immigrants and the United States. Immigrants are afforded unparalleled opportunities and the country receives a return that is, in many respects, immeasurable. Compared to the risks of discontinuing the tradition, the risks of continuing it are negligible.

But restrictionists see a history unlikely to repeat itself. The American experiment worked, in large part, because the last great wave of immigration at the turn of the century was followed by a forty-year breather from 1924 to 1965 and because assimilation, not multiculturalism, was the *modus operandi*. Comparisons of the past and present are misleading because the current stream of immigration continues unchecked. People point to the benefits of immigration, but forget that the last great wave of immigration was brought to an end. Arguably, the only reason Americans can wax nostalgic about how good immigration has been for the country is because the United States closed the gates for a while. It gave immigrants and their children a chance to get ahead.

With no end in sight, meaningful comparisons between the past and present are few and far between. Unlike the last great wave, today's flow is entering a country brimming with people. To use the metaphor of one restrictionist, Americans are no longer advancing on the frontier, "but the frontier is now advancing on us." Apples-to-apples comparisons are hard to come by and the country is full of people—so, restrictionists ask, what is there to be optimistic about?

IMMIGRANTS AS CAPITAL VERSUS IMMIGRANTS AS COSTS

Expansionists usually see immigration in terms of augmentation (e.g., immigrants contribute to the economy and enhance American culture), whereas restrictionists normally view it in terms of depletion (e.g., immigrants deplete natural resources and strain race relations) largely because they focus on *different phenomena*. Expansionists are generally more interested in vigorous economic growth and ethnic diversity, perhaps at the expense of the environment, whereas restrictionists are generally more interested in the environment and cultural homogeneity, perhaps at the expense of the economy. Viewed from their respective vantage points, the vocabularies of capital and costs are understandable.

To expansionists, immigrants represent a medley of resources. By strengthening the economy, enriching American culture, stimulating innovation, and revitalizing traditional American values, immigrants satisfy national needs and stimulate beneficial change. Expansionists regularly make these claims, but libertarian expansionists are especially fond of the economic advantages. They ask, why should the United States accept only some kinds of capital and not others? In this race for human capital and investment capital, the United States is well positioned to import both. It is no accident, they argue, that Americans are more inventive than other nationalities. The bringing together of diverse peoples expands the innovation process. Immigrants bring in skills and talents that the United States needs.

The very act of migration signifies a bright future. Immigrants, they say, are "self-selected" in that they already possess characteristics indicative of future success—risk taking, motivation, and a willingness to work hard. This, along with their propensity to exert more effort than natives, enhances their overall attractiveness. This is especially true of highly skilled immigrants, who solidify America's technological edge and (among other things) keep Silicon Valley on the San Francisco peninsula. Immigrants strengthen American businesses and contribute to the economy's overall health.

Expansionist observations sometimes portray America as a leaky bucket and immigrants as stoppers. Immigrants arrest the seepage of values and ultimately become a part of the bucket, reinforcing its strengths and moderating its deficiencies. More than being beneficial, their values and perspectives are almost vital. Unlike many native Americans, immigrants capitalize on available opportunities. They perpetuate and revitalize traditional American values, work hard, and appreciate their newfound freedoms and opportunities. If the American work ethic cannot be restored from within, then an external solution must be sought.

Restrictionists disagree. Immigrants are not the solution—they are a problem. Because mass immigration threatens the natural environment and the life it sustains, it must be stopped or least reduced substantially. In their eyes, the world's resources cannot sustain the world's current population. The problem is more than a resource shortage or distribution problem. The *real* problem is overpopulation. Humans, they insist, are not exempt from natural laws. For restrictionists, the resource base is finite. The United States sits, just like every other country in the world, on top of a fixed resource base. Every additional person born in, or admitted to, the United States represents a subtraction of some kind, and in the absence of a technical solution, this situation will not change. The population problem is, to use Garrett Hardin's term, a "no-technical-solution problem," a problem that cannot be solved by scientific advances, but only by changing human nature, which is a practical impossibility.

Accepting "surplus" populations and intervening in a country's affairs (e.g., by sending foreign aid) cannot solve the population problem. These well-intentioned efforts, in fact, usually exacerbate the situation. Hardin argues that American survival depends not on sharing ethics but on "lifeboat ethics." Because sharing produces a "commons" (see below), each government should govern its activities by the ethics of a lifeboat. The world's rich and poor reside in comparatively rich and poor countries—about one-third and two-thirds, respectively. Metaphorically, each rich nation is a full lifeboat and each poor nation an overcrowded one. The poor continuously fall out of their lifeboats, swim to the rich lifeboats, and ask to come aboard (i.e., the right to immigrate) or for "handouts" (i.e., foreign aid).

Hardin asks people to imagine that the American

These native-born American protesters demonstrate at an "America for Americans" rally outside the Republican Party National Convention in 1996. *(Donna Binder/Impact Visuals)*

lifeboat contains fifty people, but that the carrying capacity of the lifeboat, just to be generous, is sixty. This leaves little room for natural disasters or new plant diseases. How should Americans respond to the 100 people treading water outside the lifeboat? Hardin believes they have three options: (1) allow all of the needy to board (result: pure justice, complete catastrophe); (2) discriminate among the needy and allow only ten of the 100 to board (result: jeopardize entire lifeboat for the sake of ten more people); and (3) preserve the small safety factor (result: survival of lifeboat occupants is now possible).

More room cannot be created on the lifeboat, because it takes only a few people to spoil the commons. A voluntary system in which people restrain their consumptive and reproductive habits in order to admit a few others is hardly possible in a world of imperfect human beings. More room cannot be made, and exceeding the carrying capacity of each nation will only lead to ruin. Hardin is perhaps best known for his metaphors—lifeboat ethics, carrying capacity, and tragedy of the commons. All three metaphors, and their connected logic, portray immigrants as costs

and exert a profound influence on the worldviews of restrictionists.

The tragedy of the commons, for example, depicts an unmanaged economy in a crowded world. The system is tragic because the logic of the system compels people to maximize their gains—at the expense of others—in a world of finite resources. The system, and the logic it encourages (each person acting in his or her best interest), ultimately destroys things held in common (e.g., natural resources).

Hardin depicts a publicly shared pasture in which every rancher is allowed to manage and maximize his herd. This arrangement works fine until the number of cattle eventually exceeds the pasture's carrying capacity. "At this point," Hardin argues, "the inherent logic of the commons remorselessly generates tragedy." Each rancher decides that he should add an animal to his herd because he can share the costs of overgrazing with the other herders, and still enjoy most of the proceeds from the sale of additional animals. But because nearly every rancher makes this same decision, they lock themselves into an arrangement that pressures them to maximize their herds on a limited resource base. "Ruin is the destination toward which all men rush," Hardin concludes, "each pursuing his own best interest in a society that believes in the freedom of the commons. Freedom in a commons brings ruin to all."

Restrictionist estimates of natural resources, overpopulation, and quality of life are a natural extension of Hardin's metaphor. Their arguments and projections are usually based, either implicitly or explicitly, on the concept of "carrying capacity." According to David Durham, carrying capacity refers to the number of people "who can be supported without degrading the natural, cultural and social environment, i.e., without reducing the ability of the environment to sustain the desired quality of life over the long term." For example, if the carrying capacity of a given area is 1,000, then approximately 1,000, people can enjoy a specified quality of life within that area without reducing the environment's ability to sustain that level of living over the long term. Restrictionists admit that the concept is variable and somewhat vague, but argue that Americans are already exceeding the environmental carrying capacity of the United States. A noted restrictionist, Roy Beck, contends that "if sustainable living can be defined as enjoying the fruit without harming the tree that produces it, then there is ample evidence that 260 million Americans are already hacking vigorously at the trunk."

HUMAN INGENUITY VERSUS NATURAL LIMITS

For some expansionists, natural resources and national economies are not bound by the rules of a zero-sum game, where losses equal winnings. Technological progress, nurtured by human intelligence and ingenuity, creates positive-sum (win–win) situations. Expansionists tend to see more "nurture" than "nature" in human potential. Because there is a clear, positive-sum element to natural resources, humans can exceed natural "limits" by nurturing inventiveness—by enabling people to tap the "ultimate resource"—the human mind. Over time, and in terms of decreasing prices and increasing substitutability (of resources), humans have been *expanding* the world's resource base, not depleting it.

To restrictionists, banking on human ingenuity is an unnecessary risk. Instead of relying on the human ability to get "out of tight fixes," they ask: Why not accept the scientific truism that growth cannot occur forever on a finite resource base? However, some ex-

pansionists are not convinced. Their skepticism is based largely on the data and logic of the late economist Julian Simon, who maintained that "natural resources are not finite in any economic sense."

Scientists cannot conclusively "prove" or "disprove" these assumptions, because they are metaphysical claims. Hardin and Simon both concede that their arguments are built, respectively, on assumptions of finiteness and infiniteness. Scientists simply cannot measure all of the world's natural resources. Nor can they "test" the metaphors of positive and zero-sum scenarios. They can amass piles of studies to demonstrate the plausibility of each perspective, but they cannot "prove" the existence of either. A seemingly zero-sum situation (immigrants displacing native-born workers) might have positive-sum results (the creation of additional jobs, which expands opportunities for native-born workers). Or, a positive-sum event (immigrant entrepreneurs creating additional jobs) might be only a passing development in an otherwise zero-sum scenario (the creation of additional jobs is achieved at the expense of competitors, who must then downsize their workforces in order to stay in business).

The human mind, to Simon, is the "ultimate resource." Through supply and demand mechanisms, a larger population creates a short-term demand for more resources, which in turn raises prices. A larger population (in a free society) will eventually hit upon a solution because, all things being equal, a larger population produces a larger amount of knowledge. In many cases, humans have apparently filled their niche (i.e., seemingly reached a natural limit), only to expand it. Unlike other animals, humans can expand limits.

Simon agrees with Hardin (and other population restrictionists) that population growth does cause some problems. However, the agreement ends here. Hardin sees population growth as a problem in and of itself because (1) there is a fixed resource base, and (2) the relationship between humans and natural resources cannot be solved technically. Simon, on the other hand, sees population growth as a *temporary* problem. Population-induced problems encourage new developments that, in the end, leave people better off than if the problems never occurred. Population growth contributes (directly and indirectly) to progress.

Not surprisingly, Simon viewed immigration in additive terms. Immigrants stimulate demand and innovation because improvements in productivity spring from human ingenuity and because immigrants enlarge the U.S. population (via migration and fertility). They create cultural variety, "a key ingredient of invention," and transport innovative ideas. Recognizing that human progress ultimately hinges on the output of human nurture, and not the initial input (or regenerative capacity) of nature, why tamper with this win–win scenario? Expansionists argue that immigrants expand the country's strength and creativity. Restrictionists may not realize it, but the key to American success is indeed immigration.

Restrictionists acknowledge that humans are very resourceful, but why risk exceeding a country's carrying capacity? The prudent approach is to stay below maximum carrying capacity. The logic of "Pascal's wager" is applied to population problems: If a country wants more people and later on learns that it can support a larger population without harming the environment or quality of life, it can always let more people in. But reducing a population that is already exceeding its carrying capacity is a much more difficult, if not impossible, task.

Human ingenuity—while impressive—simply cannot trump natural laws. Beliefs in American "magic" and "exceptionalism" are impediments to change. This "antiscientific, antilogical, antireality strain" promotes a utopian belief that technological advances will solve all of our problems, including overpopulation. Technology cannot "fix" the population problem, and even if it could potentially solve it, why take the chance? Why not live within nature's limits and experience its dividends rather than wager it all at the technology table? In a world of limited resources, America should decrease consumption and slow its population growth, but other countries have to do the same. Population policies are the "sort of very sensitive policies that can only be established nation by nation."

RESTRICTIONISTS AND NATIONALISM

Expansionists and restrictionists contend for public approval and governmental policies congruent with their worldviews, yet both are nationalistic in that the national interest is ostensibly at the heart of their reforms. They legitimize their claims by demonstrating how their ideas are in the country's best interests.

Restrictionists emphasize boundaries and the drawing of lines. In a world of limits, lines have to be drawn—not the kind synonymous with isolationism, but the kind that clarify and advance national interests. The United States should assert its sovereignty in the face of stark inequalities, international policy frameworks, and migrations. The United States cannot serve as the world's soup kitchen or population

safety valve, but can assist sending countries by holding them responsible for their own demographic futures. Siphoning off their dissidents, professionals, and excess populations only circumvents self-sufficiency and responsibility. By providing them with foreign aid (either directly or indirectly), the United States unwittingly contributes to the very problems it is trying to relieve.

The United States cannot welcome every aspiring immigrant or admit all of the world's dispossessed if it hopes to avoid the tragedy of the commons. Drawing lines is not a cruel exercise, but necessary and compassionate. Some people say it is unkind, but restricting immigration is not unkind—it is a responsible choice in a world of limits.

Restrictionists often stress that national borders represent, in some sense, the outskirts of a nation's obligations. They are not indifferent to the needs and desires of foreigners, but maintain that their sense of responsibility generally ends at the U.S. border. As one lobbyist put it, in a world of limits "you've got to demark what your responsibility is to the group." Some restrictionists argue that foreign governments should assume responsibility for their own environmental and economic futures. Until they learn to stabilize their populations, they cannot become self-sufficient.

Even if the United States has historically meddled in a nation's affairs, it has to take some responsibility. If a country refuses to acknowledge that its resource base cannot keep up with its growing population, and if it is not willing to work toward stabilizing population growth, then the United States should not admit its extra people. A country has to feel the back-pressure of population growth before it is willing to deal with its population problem. If you are worried about population growth as a contributing factor in environmental decline, controlling the international movement of people is imperative. Most environmental problems are local in nature—that is why it is so important for each country to stabilize its own population.

An ethical system sensitive to this reality is needed because lines are an inescapable fact of life. The Golden Rule (do unto others as you would have others do unto you) needs to be contextualized. If a beggar doesn't have a coat, and you tear your coat in half, and if both of you can stay warm, then that's the right thing to do. But if you have to tear your coat into a billion worthless fragments, what good is that? Each person has to figure out just who it is that has a claim on his or her conscience. The fact that a man loves his wife more than other women does not mean that he hates other women. According to restrictionists, people who say they love everybody and want a border-less world are really saying that they are above normal attachments.

This greater sense of responsibility requires one to think about the present and future. Preferences are natural in the sense that we love some people more than others. Hard choices have to be made, but they are not only in the interest of the United States, but also in the interest of other countries. The emigration of highly skilled individuals from poor countries to rich countries, for example, widens the gap between rich and poor nations. Affluent countries benefit at the expense of poor countries. Some expansionists question the ethics of "brain drain" migration, but most of the reservations are voiced by restrictionists. The United States, they argue, not only siphons off the "best and brightest," but also robs countries of their change agents.

If the outlet of migration did not exist, people might actually improve their situations at home rather than try to figure out how to leave. Is it really legitimate, restrictionists ask, to take a country's change agents? Admitting a country's best and brightest actually widens the economic and social gap between the United States and less developed countries. The best kind of foreign aid that the United States can give is the kind that keeps the best and brightest at home. By characterizing immigrants and countries as self-seeking, restrictionists acknowledge the value of some immigrants, but indirectly dispute expansionist depictions of immigrants as "survivors." Migrating to a more advantageous locale is a rational decision, but that does not mean it is honorable or in the sending country's best interest.

For restrictionists, boundaries between natives and aliens are unavoidable: "Life is a series of drawing lines and you have to draw lines with respect to whom you want to be kind." The paired categories of citizen/noncitizen and national/international are fundamental to their mindset. This is especially true of environmental and population restrictionists. Their solutions for minimizing population growth and environmental degradation rely heavily on such distinctions. As one restrictionist put it, "population policies are the sort of very sensitive policies that can only be established nation by nation." In a stratified and overpopulated world, sovereignty is a precondition for drafting efficacious policies. The nation-state is used by restrictionists to mitigate the presumed problems of overpopulation and environmental decline. In their minds, the United States can only stabilize its population by maintaining replacement-level fertility (births = deaths) and migration (immigration = emigration) ratios. These goals are national-level goals,

and their success hinges largely on the reformulation of national immigration laws.

EXPANSIONISTS AND GLOBALISM

In a very general sense, globalism signifies the countless streams of information, people, resources, and goods crossing national boundaries on a regular basis. Tough to define, yet easy to spot, expansionists see it as an inevitable force in national and international affairs. From their perspective, the activities comprising globalism are basically benign and governable if international agreements and immigration policies are adjusted to its inner workings and varied impacts. To expansionists, globalism is something to engage—as much as possible—on one's own terms. Their views on border enforcement and various immigration policies demonstrate a desire to manage immigration, not with open borders, but with fair and flexible policies.

The cross-border circulation of people and products, expansionists argue, should be accommodated, not resisted. Besides, fighting the inevitable makes no sense. Immigration is a fact of life, so why not manage it with better policies and programs? As the world's drawstrings are pulled tighter by international linkages, immigration becomes increasingly important to the health of the American economy. The United States prospers by engaging immigration, not by resisting it. This idea of "engaging" is central to the expansionist perspective on globalism. Almost every policy decision radiates from this midpoint in some way.

If the United States is to engage the world, its policymakers must recognize that severing immigration policy from other policies is not only imprudent but also impractical. The historical and economic links welcoming capital also invite people. One expansionist explains: "There's a very, very small difference between closing the doors on immigration and closing the doors to international trade because they both respond to the same impulse." According to business expansionists, the United States needs to align its policies with the realities of globalization. Because some companies no longer see themselves as American companies (they think of themselves as global companies), the United States should welcome immigrants. If America does not accommodate immigrants, other countries will—and reap the advantages.

The United States has to *manage* immigration. The option of cutting it off does not exist: "Whether you're pro-immigration or anti-immigration—the immigrants are coming one way or the other." This view is representative of most expansionists. One way or the other, immigrants will continue to come. First, as long as there is a low-wage market in need of workers, employers are going to recruit cheap labor. Second, in some countries, the United States contributed to the conditions that encouraged people to emigrate in the first place.

Given these realities, some expansionists believe that the United States should assist immigrants and refugees who are, in some way, responding to contexts created, at one time or another, by the American government. Other expansionists recommend adapting national immigration laws to the rudiments of international agreements and norms. Similarly, some argue that the employment side of immigration policy needs immediate updating. If immigration law does not keep up with the ever-evolving strategies and procedures of business, the global competitiveness of U.S.-based international firms will be undermined.

This does not mean that expansionists necessarily favor open borders. Without being put to the question, most expansionists regularly assert their commitment to a regulated border. "I don't think you'll find barely a person who opposes some kind of orderly, systematic...limitation on immigration.... You may find an open border person somewhere or another, but pretty much not in most of the groups who are working on this issue." The idea of a *more* open border, however, does appeal to some expansionists. As intimated earlier, why should outmoded, fatiguing INS regulations slow the flow of human capital when investment capital is allowed to cross without inspection?

Brian N. Fry

See also: Nativist Reaction (Part I, Sec. 4); Anti-Immigrant Backlash (Part I, Sec 5); Public Opinion and Immigration (Part II, Sec. 6); California Proposition 63, 1986, California Proposition 187, 1994, California Proposition 227, 1998 (Part IV, Sec. 1).

BIBLIOGRAPHY

Beck, R. *Re-charting America's Future.* Petoskey, MI: Social Contract Press, 1994.

Donnelly, P. "Statement by Paul Donnelly, Organizer Immigration Reform Coalition, to the National Research Council Committee on IT [Information Technology] Workforce Needs," http://immigrationreform.com/donnelly2.html, February 29, 2000.

Durham, D. F. "Fatal Challenges: Prospects for Real Solutions." *Focus* 7 (1997): 10–13.

Fry, B. N. *Alien Notions: Varieties of Nativism and Perceptions of the Threat.* Ph.D. diss., Michigan State University, 1998.

Geyer, G. A. *Americans No More.* New York: Atlantic Monthly Press, 1996.

Gimpel, J. G., and Edwards, J. R., Jr., *The Congressional Politics of Immigration Reform.* Boston: Allyn & Bacon, 1999.

Hardin, G. *The Immigration Dilemma: Avoiding the Tragedy of the Commons.* Washington, DC: Federation for American Immigration Reform, 1995.

LeMay, M. C. *Anatomy of a Public Policy: The Reform of Contemporary Immigration Law.* Westport, CT: Praeger, 1994.

Light, I. "Nationalism and Anti-Immigrant Movements." *Society* (1996): 58–63.

———, and S. J. Gold. *Ethnic Economies.* San Diego, CA: Academic Press, 2000.

Salins, P. *Assimilation, American Style.* New York: Basic Books, 1997.

Sassen, S. *Losing Control? Sovereignty in an Age of Globalization.* New York: Columbia University Press, 1996.

Simon, J. L. *The Economic Consequences of Immigration.* Oxford: Basil Blackwell (in association with the Cato Institute), 1989.

———. *The Ultimate Resource 2.* Princeton, NJ: Princeton University Press, 1996.

Stefancic, J. "Funding the Nativist Agenda." In *Immigrants Out! The New Nativism and the Anti-Immigrant Impulse in the United States,* ed J. Perea, 119–35. New York: New York University Press, 1997.

Teitelbaum, M. S., and Winter, J. *A Question of Numbers: High Immigration, Low Fertility, and the Politics of National Identity.* New York: Hill & Wang, 1998.

Weiner, M. *The Global Migration Crisis.* New York: HarperCollins, 1995.

_I_MMIGRANT POLITICS I: ACTIVISM

_S_ince the waves of immigration in the early 1900s, immigrants have been portrayed either as bulwarks of apolitical conservatism or as instigators of radical activism. Neither generalization seems to hold true for immigrants to the United States, either across time or across nationality groups. During some historical periods and for some groups, immigrants have played an active role in defending their interests and emphasizing their unique identities. Other times, however, groups have been forced to downplay their activism in the face of hostility from the larger society. In this section on immigrant activism, we shall examine changes in the level of immigrant activism from the early years to the contemporary period.

EARLY ACTIVISM

During the early twentieth century, activism among European immigrants was heavily influenced by their association with socialist parties and movements. In New York, Jewish needle trade workers formed the core of the union movement and the American Socialist Party. Radical newspapers such as the _Jewish Daily Forward_ and _The Call_ bolstered support for political radicalism among Jewish immigrants. Support among Jewish immigrants for socialist organizations and parties rose even further after the Russian Revolution of 1917. Radicalism among European immigrants was not confined to New York. In the Midwest, Finnish socialists were the backbone of the Socialist Party and tried to promote radical activism among other immigrant groups. Despite these instances of strong radicalism among some immigrant groups, activism during the early twentieth century was not widespread. Irish immigrants were strongly integrated into the Democratic Party machines in such cities as Boston and New York, while Italian immigrant workers tended to stay away from political radicalism. Even among Jewish immigrants, support for the

Socialist Party waned after the early 1920s as many Jewish immigrants became small entrepreneurs. More important, the Democratic Party under President Franklin Roosevelt responded to the threat of a growing Socialist Party by adopting some of its less radical positions. Mobilization of immigrant voters under the New Deal effectively ended the tradition of independent radicalism among European immigrants, who now found themselves fully aligned with the Democratic Party.

Political organizations among Mexican immigrants in the United States originally consisted of several _mutualistas_, self-help organizations that included both the native-born and the foreign-born. After World War I, the strength and nature of Mexican-American political organizations changed dramatically. As veterans returning from World War I, many community leaders sought to combat racial discrimination by creating such organizations as the Order of the Sons of America and the League of United Latin American Citizens (LULAC). These organizations were different from the previous mutualistas in that they were composed only of U.S. citizens and focused their attention on proving the patriotism and cultural assimilation of Mexican Americans.

The Great Depression only served to exacerbate the split between Mexican-American organizations and recent immigrants from Mexico. As unemployment levels soared to 11 million by the end of 1932, several communities and government agencies pressured Mexican immigrants and their children to return to Mexico. In reaction to this rising tide of nativism, many Mexican Americans became politically active by joining LULAC. Organization members defended the interests of Mexican Americans by intensifying their efforts to prove their community's patriotic credentials and assimilation into American society. The group also sought to combat discrimination by organizing voter registration drives and fighting segregation in public schools and public facilities

Protesters in New York City demand amnesty so that many undocumented immigrants can get legal status to live and work in the United States. *(Carlos Villalon/Impact Visuals)*

through the legal system. At the same time, LULAC distanced itself from the Mexican immigrant population and gave qualified support to legislation that restricted the flow of immigration from Mexico. So, even though Mexican-American organizations were becoming stronger and more active during the 1920s and early 1930s, immigrants from Mexico increasingly found themselves excluded from such activism.

Asian immigrants began to organize politically as early as 1891, when Chinese agricultural laborers in Hawaii protested cuts in wages. Although Asian immigrants organized themselves separately along lines of national origin, they soon began to see the advantage of reaching across ethnic lines to fight for higher wages and better working conditions. In 1903, Japanese agricultural laborers in California joined forces with Mexican immigrant workers to form the Japanese-Mexican Labor Association. Similarly, in

1920, the Federation of Japanese Labor reached out to Filipino, Chinese, and Portuguese workers in calling a strike against Hawaiian plantation owners.

As second-generation Asian immigrants came of age during the 1920s and 1930s, they saw their stay in the United States as more secure and permanent. Like their Mexican-American counterparts, second-generation Japanese immigrants formed organizations that emphasized the American aspects of their political and social identities. The Japanese American Citizens League (JACL), formed in Seattle in 1930, focused on strategies that emphasized the patriotism of Japanese Americans and their educational and business achievements. Although JACL conferences and social activities would stress the need for ethnic solidarity, the organization shied away from protests and strikes, actions that it deemed to be too militant.

During this period, many first- and second-

These Haitian-American demonstrators are calling on the Immigration and Naturalization Service to extend rule 245-I, which allows immigrants to remain in the United States while their legal status is decided. *(Rommel Pecson/Impact Visuals)*

generation Chinese immigrants responded to widespread discrimination by turning inward. Instead of mass mobilization, most returned to their ethnic enclaves to seek employment opportunities. Indeed, some ethnic Chinese newspapers even urged immigrants to return to China, where they would find better opportunities than in the United States. There were a few voices of Asian immigrant activism during the 1930s. For instance, some Japanese Americans organized Democratic clubs in San Francisco, Oakland, and Los Angeles to provide support for the New Deal and for legislation that would eliminate racial discrimination. For the most part, however, Asian-American activism was limited during the years before World War II.

WORLD WAR II

World War II was a watershed for activism among Asian Americans and Latinos in the United States.

The war encouraged political incorporation by raising the status of some immigrant groups while it entailed a loss of legal rights and social status for others. Some Asian immigrants saw an improvement in their status as a result of the war. For example, Filipino immigrants realized an increase in job opportunities in war-related industries. The war also enabled Filipinos to attain U.S. citizenship. In 1943, Filipino soldiers who served in the United States military were allowed to become citizens, and in 1945, the right to naturalize was extended to all Filipino immigrants. Similarly, Korean immigrants became involved in the war effort against Japan by serving as translators and broadcasters, volunteering for the National Guard and purchasing defense bonds. Although these efforts increased the level of acceptance of Korean immigrants in American society, they did not attain the right to naturalize. The reliance of the United States on cooperation with China also benefited Chinese immigrants with the repeal of Chinese exclusion laws. Finally, World War II also benefited Asian Indians, who were successful in their efforts to increase immigrant admissions and to secure rights to citizenship in 1946. Indian intellectuals in the United States argued effectively that America's principles of self-determination and opposition to Nazi ideology necessitated a change in its own policies toward the Indian immigrant population.

Although arguments equating American racism with Nazi ideology may have swayed the U.S. Congress at the end of the war, they had little impact on its decision to intern Japanese Americans during the early 1940s. Soon after the attack on Pearl Harbor on December 7, 1941, Navy Secretary Frank Knox suggested that Japanese immigrant laborers in Hawaii had aided Japan in its attack on the Hawaiian military base. He recommended the internment of Japanese immigrants in Hawaii by placing them on a separate island. The proposal to intern Japanese immigrants in Hawaii soon foundered, not because of activism among Japanese-American groups but because the governor and economic groups in Hawaii argued that internment would have a severely negative impact on the islands' wartime economies.

In the mainland United States, however, several segments of society amplified the call to place the so-called Japs in concentration camps. Prominent newspaper columnists such as Walter Lippmann reiterated Secretary Knox's assertion that Japanese Americans were a fifth column of the Japanese army on the West Coast of the United States. Organizations such as the American Legion, farmer associations, and state and local governments in California and Oregon called for the removal of Japanese Americans. On February 19, 1942, President Franklin Roosevelt signed Executive Order 9066, which authorized the military to relocate groups deemed to be a "military threat." When a few Japanese Americans tried to resist military orders for evacuation and internment, they were sent to prison. Although they tried to challenge the military order through the judicial process, their convictions were upheld by the Supreme Court, which ruled that government policies were based on military necessity. Although support for internment declined as many second-generation Japanese Americans enlisted in the draft and fought valiantly in Europe and Asia, Japanese Americans continued to face discrimination from the government and the larger society.

World War II had a different effect on Mexican Americans. The war and its aftermath intensified the efforts of Mexican-American organizations to combat discrimination and violence against their communities. In 1942, the Los Angeles police arrested and charged twenty-two members of a Mexican-American gang with the murder of a fellow Mexican American, José Díaz. Based on highly circumstantial evidence, an all-white jury convicted seventeen of the members on charges that ranged from assault and battery to first-degree murder. In reaction to the ruling, several local leaders formed the Sleepy Lagoon Defense Committee, enlisting the support of union organizers and Hollywood actors. The committee succeeded in overturning the convictions on appeal, arguing that the conviction was rooted in racial prejudice. Furthermore, members of the committee linked the fight against discrimination at home with the country's wartime effort against Germany and its policies of racial extermination.

One of the most significant impacts of World War II on political activism among Mexican Americans was the creation of the GI Forum in 1948. Mexican-American veterans of the war found upon their return to the United States that they were still subject to exclusion from residential neighborhoods and public spaces. When a funeral parlor in Three Rivers, Texas, refused to bury the remains of a Mexican-American veteran, fellow veterans organized the GI Forum in protest. They enlisted the aid of the then senator Lyndon Johnson and succeeded in having the remains interred at Arlington National Cemetery with full military honors. Soon afterward, the GI Forum spread quickly to other parts of Texas and the American Southwest. Like LULAC, it focused exclusively on the concerns of citizens of Mexican origin in their attempts to overcome poverty and fight racial discrimination. It also advocated the end of legal and illegal immigration from Mexico, blaming much of the poverty and underemployment among Mexican Americans on the influx of agricultural workers that had begun with wartime measures such as the Bracero Program. So, World War II and the period that immediately followed saw a continuation and intensification of efforts among Mexican-American organizations to defend the interests of citizens of Mexican-American origin, at the same time as they advocated an end to immigration from Mexico.

CIVIL RIGHTS ERA

The Civil Rights era produced a dramatic shift in activism among both Mexican Americans and Asian Americans. Already by 1960, community organizations such as the Mexican American Political Association were beginning to advocate political mobilization along ethnic lines. This marked a shift from previous stances by groups such as LULAC that had pushed for assimilation of the Mexican-American population. At the same time, such groups as the

Community Service Organization (CSO) began to address the needs and concerns of both Mexican immigrants and the native-born, Mexican-American population. Unlike the GI Forum and LULAC, the CSO did not require American citizenship from its members. Furthermore, it did not insist on cultural assimilation among its members and often conducted Spanish-language workshops on issues such as health and nutrition, naturalization, and voter education.

The Community Service Organization also spawned one of the most celebrated Mexican-American activists of the Civil Rights era, César Chávez. Chávez joined the CSO in 1952 in its campaign to register and mobilize Mexican Americans. Within six years, he became national director of the organization. However, when the CSO refused to take up the cause of organizing migrant farmworkers, he resigned from the organization in 1962 and created a new union for farmworkers—the National Farm Workers Association (NFWA). By 1965, the group had organized over seventeen hundred families in the Delano area. When a largely Filipino union, the Agricultural Workers Organizing Committee (AWOC), struck against growers over low wages, Chávez and the NFWA decided to join the struggle.

In March 1966, César Chávez led the NFWA on a 300-mile march from Delano to the state capitol building in Sacramento. The march, which was inspired by the 1964 Freedom March from Selma to Montgomery, Alabama, drew national attention to the plight of farmworkers. Even before the protestors reached Sacramento, one of the major producers of table wine formally recognized the NFWA and agreed to refrain from hiring farmworkers through labor contractors. For the next two years, the union signed contracts with a few other vineyards in central California. It also bolstered its strength by affiliating with the American Federation of Labor–Congress of Industrial Organizations (AFL-CIO) to form the United Farm Workers (UFW).

Despite these early gains, the largest table-grape growers in California still refused to negotiate with the group, and they circumvented the union's boycott by shipping grapes under different labels. Faced with increasing resistance from the state's major grape growers, Chávez called for a nationwide boycott of California table grapes beginning in January 1968. The boycott drew support from labor unions, Chicano associations, civil rights activists, and college students. The UFW set up boycott organizations in over forty major cities, and mayors of several cities endorsed the campaign against California table grapes. The grape boycott was a tremendous success for César Chávez and the UFW. Public opinion polls found that over 17

million Americans had stopped eating grapes because of the boycott. Faced with significant losses in revenue, many growers acceded to the demands of the UFW, including higher wages, health insurance, formal grievance procedures, and safe working and living conditions.

During the same time as the grape boycott, there arose several other efforts by Mexican-American activists that fell under the label of the "Chicano movement." The Alianza Federal de Pueblos Libres was a movement organized in 1962 by Reies López Tijerina, an uneducated immigrant and Protestant revivalist. The Alianza sought to secure land for Mexican and Native Americans based on past U.S. treaties with Spain and Mexico. It also raised demands based on the Treaty of Guadalupe Hidalgo, which stated that Mexicans in the American Southwest would be given citizenship and rights to their land and culture. Another organization, the Crusade for Justice, championed the needs of the urban poor and advocated the creation of alternative institutions based on cultural consciousness and principles of humanism.

The Crusade for Justice activated progressive elements within the Mexican-American community and played an important role in civil rights protests and the creation of ethnic activist organizations. For example, the group was prominent in the creation of the National La Raza Unida Party. In 1970, Mexican-American leaders in south Texas created the La Raza Unida Party (LRUP) to elect Mexican Americans to school board and council seats. Within two years, Rudolfo "Corky" Gonzales, the lead organizer of the Crusade for Justice, called for a national convention in El Paso to create a national LRUP. Student activists, ethnic journalists, and members of the Alianza and the Crusade for Justice participated in a four-day convention that culminated in the establishment of a national party for Mexican Americans. Although the party succeeded in garnering 215,000 votes in the 1972 Texas state election (nearly 7 percent of the total), it soon began to decline. Faced with internal dissent, resource shortages, and the defection of members to the Democratic Party, the National LRUP disintegrated by the late 1970s.

Another important aspect of the Chicano movement was the student movement that gained force in colleges and universities from the mid-1960s to the early 1970s. Working-class students in California, Texas, Arizona, and New Mexico formed groups such as the United Mexican American Students and the Mexican American Youth Organization. The initial purpose of these organizations was to increase educational opportunities and to establish academic programs on the study of Mexican immigrant and

Mexican-American communities. These movements soon spread to college campuses in other parts of the country. By 1970, many student organizations had changed their name to El Movimiento Estudiantil Chicano de Aztlan (MECHA). Rejecting the accommodationist stance of mainstream political organizations such as LULAC, these new student organizations took a militant posture in the attempt to eliminate social inequality and to reject assimilation into the dominant society. Some organizations, such as the Brown Berets, went even further, emphasizing the right to armed self-defense and national self-determination. Finally, Chicanos mobilized in large numbers against the war in Vietnam. After President Richard Nixon declared war on Cambodia in 1970, thousands of Mexican Americans joined millions of student demonstrators in protesting the expansion of the war. In August 1970, over thirty thousand protestors in Los Angeles participated in the national Chicano Moratorium.

Protests against the war in Vietnam also had a profound impact on activism among Asian Americans. To many second- and third-generation Asian Americans, the war in Vietnam represented not only American imperialism but also racism against Asian peoples. Many perceived this racism firsthand when other Americans indiscriminately labeled them as "gooks." So, Asian-American activists often differentiated themselves from the majority of antiwar protestors by denouncing the war as racist and proclaiming solidarity with their "brothers and sisters" in Vietnam. For example, many Asian Americans refused to join the 1971 antiwar march in Washington, D.C., because the organizers failed to adopt a statement denouncing the war as racist. When they did take part in marches, many passed out their own leaflets and carried Vietnamese and Chinese flags proclaiming solidarity with their coethnics in Asia.

Student mobilization in the late 1960s and early 1970s also spawned movements promoting a pan-ethnic Asian-American identity. Until the 1960s, most Asian immigrant populations had identified with their own particular nationalities. Nationality differences among Asian immigrants were reinforced not only by residential segregation into ethnic enclaves but also by wars in immigrant homelands. This was especially true during World War II, when Chinese, Filipino, and Korean immigrants wore buttons and displayed signs that indicated that they were not Japanese. After the war, residential segregation among Asian immigrants of different nationalities began to decline. Many Asian immigrants began moving out of urban enclaves into the suburbs, while some enclaves began to house multiple Asian immigrant groups. Fi-

nally, the pull of national identity and homeland politics became less salient to second-generation Asians, who were emerging as an increasingly important part of the Asian immigrant community.

While demographic changes lay the groundwork for a pan-ethnic identity, it was the civil rights struggle in the 1960s that prompted the articulation of an Asian-American identity. Following the example of the Black Power and Brown Beret movements, Asian-American activists began to call for a Yellow Power movement that would unite all Asian immigrant nationalities. This "yellow" reference was soon dropped in favor of an Asian-American label that accommodated the demands of Filipino student activists, who argued that the original label excluded "brown" Asians. The first pan-Asian organization, the Asian American Political Alliance (AAPA), was founded at the University of California, Berkeley in 1968. Shortly afterward, organizations cropped up at the University of California at Los Angeles and other college campuses on the West Coast, as well as such universities on the East Coast as Columbia and Yale. Concurrent with the creation of pan-Asian political organizations, students at university campuses across the country began to push for Asian-American studies departments and programs. Although their initial successes were exclusively in West Coast universities, activists were later successful in achieving programs and departments in a few East Coast universities such as Cornell University, Brown University, and Boston College.

POST–CIVIL RIGHTS ERA

Latino and Asian-American activism since the Civil Rights era has been profoundly influenced by the consequences of the Immigration and Nationality Act of 1965, which led to a massive increase in the level of immigration to the United States. As the national origin of immigrants shifted from Europe to Latin America and Asia, first-generation immigrants began to constitute a larger and larger proportion of the Latino and Asian-American populations. Not surprisingly, activism among Latinos and Asian Americans began to shift toward greater advocacy of the rights of immigrants, including those of undocumented workers. At the same time, activist organizations used policy instruments of the Civil Rights era to press for improvements in education and affirmative action in employment. Many also pushed for strong enforcement of provisions in the Voting Rights Act, which included the institution of multilingual ballots in counties with high proportions of residents speaking a language other than English.

Among Latinos, the Mexican American Legal Defense Fund (MALDEF) played a prominent role in advocating for the rights of legal residents and undocumented immigrants. Founded in 1968 with a $2.2 million grant by the Ford Foundation, MALDEF has used litigation to challenge workplace raids by the Immigration and Naturalization Service and to defend the educational rights of immigrant children. Expanding beyond the concerns of Mexican immigrants, MALDEF supported political asylum for undocumented immigrants from Nicaragua, Guatemala, and El Salvador. Other groups, such as the National Council of La Raza and LULAC, also played a significant role in advocating for the rights and interests of immigrants from Latin America. Dropping its earlier requirement that all members be citizens of the United States, LULAC advocated for the rights of all Latino residents in the United States—citizens, legal residents and undocumented immigrants. Finally, even though the UFW continued to oppose temporary guest-worker programs, it advocated worker protection for all agricultural laborers and dropped its earlier support for the deportation of undocumented workers. Although the major Latino advocacy organizations began to differ on the specifics of immigration reform during the 1980s, they were able to secure an amnesty program for undocumented agricultural workers in the Immigration Reform and Control Act of 1986 (IRCA).

During the 1990s, Latino activism was defined primarily in reaction to a series of legislative measures that were perceived to be against the rights and interests of Latino immigrants and native-born citizens. In 1994, California passed Proposition 187, a measure intended to bar illegal immigrants from accessing public services such as means-tested benefits and public education. Even though most Latino voters opposed the measure at the ballot box, a sizable proportion of Latino immigrants had initially supported the measure. Groups such as LULAC and MALDEF signaled their opposition to Proposition 187 and produced reports detailing the punitive consequences of the measure. After several months of voter education and mobilization through television advertisements and community service organizations, Latino activists were able to crystallize opposition to Proposition 187 among immigrants and nonimmigrants alike. Soon after the passage of Proposition 187, both LULAC and MALDEF filed suits against the anti-immigrant measure. The groups were successful in blocking implementation of the initiative, pending resolution of the

constitutionality of its provisions. Finally, various community organizations and student groups carried out protests in several cities and university campuses during the months following the passage of Proposition 187. They also mobilized new Latino voters into the electorate, a trend that increased in 1996 with the passage of anti-immigration legislation at the national level. Many of these new voters in California voted for Gray Davis in 1998, the Democratic candidate for governor who finally ended the implementation of Proposition 187 once he took office.

Just as the new waves of immigration after 1965 had profound effects on political activism among first- and higher-order immigrants from Latin America, it also led to a significant shift in political activism among Asian Americans. First, the predominance of first-generation immigrants in the Asian-American community meant that national differences often proved to be significant barriers to political organization. The "new" immigrants from Asia were still attached to politics and political developments in their countries of origin. This homeland attachment made it more difficult for Asian-American activists to make an impact on domestic politics. Thus, even though the number of Asian immigrants had grown remarkably, it was difficult for community activists to organize immigrants along pan-ethnic lines.

Another significant consequence of the post-1965 immigration to Asian immigrant activism was the labeling of Asian immigrants as "model minorities." Sociologist William Petersen initially coined the term "model minority" in 1966 when referring to the economic success of second-generation Japanese immigrants. Petersen used the example of Japanese Americans as a model for the advancement of other racial and ethnic groups in America. Although the term "model minority" was coined in the mid-1960s, it did not pervade the public consciousness until the early 1980s. The new set of immigration laws since 1965 made the Asian immigrant population more high-skilled than African Americans or immigrants from Latin America. As professional Asian immigrants and their children showed signs of economic and educational success in the United States, many journalists and scholars began to hold up Asian immigrants as the model minority that other groups should emulate. Many Asian-American activists persisted in pointing out the flaws in the "model minority" argument— many immigrants from Laos, Cambodia, and the Philippines were not highly skilled professionals, and academic success still did not dispel the reality of racism against Asian Americans. Despite these efforts, the model minority myth has continued to hamper the efforts of Asian-American activists to draw attention to prejudice against Asian immigrants and to build alliances with African Americans and Latinos.

At the same time, there have been two other forces that have led to greater activism among the Asian-American community since the 1970s: the activist legacy of the Civil Rights movement and the rise in violence against Asian immigrants. While the radicalism of the late 1960s dissipated after a few years, community service organizations grew in number and in membership. Prompted by the political activism of the Civil Rights era, Asian-American social workers lobbied successfully for public welfare funding from the federal government as well as the ability to administer welfare services to Asian-American communities. They were also successful in establishing training centers to address the specific needs of Asian Americans in areas such as mental health. Although many grassroots community activists began to challenge the legitimacy of professional social workers, community organizations were able to secure public and private funding to meet the needs of an increasingly diverse population with a fast-growing immigrant population.

The activist legacy of the Civil Rights era was felt more directly in the attempt of Japanese Americans to seek redress for internment during World War II. Beginning in the early 1970s, Japanese Americans waged a successful campaign to declare as historical landmarks the relocation centers in California. Dissident activists within and outside the Japanese American Citizens League began to call for legislation on redress and reparations for the internment during World War II. Soon, a redress committee was formed within the JACL. In 1978, the group came up with a proposal that asked for $25,000 per capita payments to formerly displaced individuals or their heirs, as well as $100 million to establish a Japanese-American community fund.

Conservative forces within the JACL and the Japanese-American community reacted negatively to the recommendations. Senator S. I. Hayakawa, a Japanese American from California, admonished the group, telling it to concern itself only with issues of the present and future. Indeed, he even suggested that the internment and subsequent dispersion of Japanese Americans actually benefited them by forcing them out of their segregated existence in California. Others insisted that money could never compensate them for their suffering and that it was best not to reopen the wounds of the past. Faced with such opposition, the JACL changed tactics in 1979, calling for a federal commission to determine "whether a wrong was com-

mitted" against those interned in World War II. Soon, such a commission was indeed established under the administration of President Jimmy Carter—the Commission for Wartime Relocation and Internment of Civilians (CWRIC). After several months of public hearings and discussions, CWRIC issued its recommendations to Congress in 1983. Among other things, the commission called for a formal apology by the federal government, as well as $20,000 to each of the estimated sixty thousand survivors of the relocation. Although Congress agreed with most of the recommendations of CWRIC, it did not approve the monetary payments until January 1990.

During the 1980s and 1990s, activism among Asian Americans also grew as a response to violence against Asian immigrants. Initial targets of anti-Asian violence were refugees from Vietnam, Laos, and Cambodia. Many refugees faced physical threats and found their homes and cars vandalized. Immigrant entrepreneurs also found themselves the targets of vandalism and physical intimidation. The problem was particularly acute for Korean immigrants, who faced tense and hostile reactions from black and Latino residents of the low-income areas in which the entrepreneurs operated. Finally, violence against first- and higher-generation Asian Americans increased during the 1980s in reaction to the mainstream media's portrayal of Japan as a rising economic power and possible threat to the United States.

The various instances of violence have drawn a united response from immigrants of various Asian nationalities. In 1982, community activists mobilized Asian Americans in the Midwest and nationwide in response to the killing of Vincent Chin. Chin, a twenty-seven-year-old Chinese American, was beaten to death with a baseball bat by two automobile employees in Detroit. The assailants had mistaken Chin for a Japanese national and had wanted to exact revenge for Japan taking away American jobs. Although one assailant pleaded guilty to second-degree murder and the other plea-bargained for manslaughter, the Wayne County Circuit Court judge sentenced both to three years' probation and $3,000 in fines. In response to the lenient sentence, Asian-American activists and community groups such as American Citizens for Justice called for a retrial and prosecution under civil law. Although this effort also ultimately failed in providing just compensation for the life of Vincent Chin, Asian-American advocates learned from the process and were able to mobilize against other cases of hate crime against Asian immigrants and Asian Americans.

In addition to the Vincent Chin case, the Los Angeles riots of 1992 prompted Asian-American activists to focus their efforts on problems of racial misunderstanding and violence. During the riots, groups oriented toward the home country lost their standing and credibility because they were unable to articulate the domestic needs and concerns of the Asian immigrant community. After the riots, there emerged a new set of leaders from the second generation who advocated interracial cooperation and pushed Asian immigrant organizations to pay more attention to domestic needs and interests.

Finally, just as anti-immigrant legislation led to increased activism among Latino immigrants, the passage of Proposition 187 in 1994 led to a surge in activism among Asian Americans. Organizations such as the Asian Pacific American Legal Center (APALC) and the Chinatown Service Center in Los Angeles joined Latino and African-American advocacy organizations in forming the Coalition for Humane Immigrant Rights of Los Angeles (CHIRLA). The coalition opposed the anti-immigrant measure by mobilizing citizens and by raising constitutional challenges through litigation. Finally, Asian-American activism on immigration issues continued in 1996, as organizations such as the National Asian Pacific American Legal Consortium (NAPALC) attempted to modify restrictionist provisions in the national legislation relating to immigrants.

Immigrant involvement in political activism or radicalism has not remained constant over time or across national groups. Until the Civil Rights era, Latino and Asian immigrant groups were largely assimilationist in their orientation. Indeed, the major Mexican-American organizations excluded Mexican immigrants and ignored their needs and interests. During the Civil Rights era, both Asian-American and Latino groups took on a more activist and separatist orientation. Furthermore, many ethnic organizations began to address the needs of immigrant workers and to include immigrants as members. This trend has continued in the post–Civil Rights era as immigrants constitute an increasingly large portion of the Asian-American and Latino populations. Mobilization against anti-immigrant measures during the 1990s has served only to strengthen the partnerships in activism between first- and higher-generation immigrants. De-

spite attempts by the Republican and Democratic Parties to draw immigrant voters, independent activism among immigrants is likely to endure in the upcoming decades.

S. Karthick Ramakrishnan

See also: Legislation II: Immigrants in America (Part II, Sec. 5); Immigrant Politics II: Electoral Politics, Immigrant Politics III: The Home Country (Part II, Sec. 6); Central America, Cuba, Haiti and French-Speaking Caribbean (Part III, Sec. 2).

BIBLIOGRAPHY

Acuña, Rodolfo. *Occupied America: A History of Chicanos.* 2d ed. New York: Harper and Row, 1981.

Chen, Sucheng. *Asian Americans: An Interpretive History.* New York: Twayne Publishers, 1991.

Daniels, Roger. *Asian America: Chinese and Japanese in the United States Since 1850.* Seattle: University of Washington Press, 1988.

Dunne, John Gregory. *Delano: The Story of the California Grape Strike.* New York: Farrar, Straus and Giroux, 1967.

Espiritu, Yen L. *Asian American Panethnicity.* Philadelphia: Temple University Press, 1992.

Gómez-Quiñones, Juan. *Chicano Politics: Reality and Promise, 1940–1990.* Albuquerque: University of New Mexico Press, 1990.

Griswold del Castillo, Richard, and Richard A. Garcia. *César Chávez: A Triumph of Spirit.* Norman: University of Oklahoma Press, 1995.

Gutiérrez, David. *Walls and Mirrors: Mexican Americans, Mexican Immigrants, and the Politics of Ethnicity.* Berkeley: University of California Press, 1995.

Jenkins, J. Craig. *The Politics of Insurgency: The Farm Worker Movement in the 1960s.* New York: Columbia University Press, 1985.

Muñoz, Carlos, Jr. *Youth, Identity, Power: The Chicano Movement.* New York: Verso, 1989.

Portes, Alejandro, and Rubén Rumbaut. *Immigrant America: A Portrait.* 2d ed. Berkeley: University of California Press, 1996.

Ramos, Henry A. J. *The American GI Forum.* Houston: Arte Publico Press, 1998.

Suro, Roberto. "Two California Judges Block Anti-Immigrant Measure at the Start." *Washington Post,* November 10, 1994.

Takaki, Ronald. *Strangers from the Different Shore: A History of Asian Americans.* Boston: Little, Brown and Company, 1998.

Villareal, Roberto E., and Norma G. Hernandez, eds. *Latinos and Political Coalitions: Political Empowerment for the 1990s.* New York: Praeger, 1991.

ℐMMIGRANT POLITICS II: ELECTORAL POLITICS

The past two decades have witnessed a remarkable increase not only in the number of immigrants living in the United States but also in the number of naturalizations among immigrants. The share of the foreign-born among the American voting-age population has grown by more than 20 percent since 1994 and now stands at 6 percent of the overall population. If we also take into account second-generation adults, immigrants account for nearly 14 percent of the electorate today. The importance of immigrants to the political process has not been lost on either the Republican or Democratic party, as each tries to win the support of newly naturalized citizens and swing voters among Latinos and Asian Americans. While the importance of immigrants to the electoral process is something that is gaining attention from politicians and scholars alike, the issue has its precedents among earlier waves of immigrants.

EARLY IMMIGRANT INCORPORATION

At the turn of the century, when Europeans arrived in large numbers to the United States, party organizations played a large role in the political incorporation of immigrants. Republicans largely dominated the national government as well as state governments outside the Confederate South, while Democrats controlled most city-level governments. Known as "machines," local party organizations in cities such as New York and Boston had successfully mobilized Irish immigrants in the late nineteenth century to gain control of city governments. The mobilization of Irish immigrants was also crucial to the maintenance of Irish control, as party bosses relied on systems of patronage to ensure their continued dominance in city government.

Faced with the influx of immigrants from southern and eastern Europe, both Republicans and Democrats sought to minimize the influence of new entrants on the political system. The Republican Party, fearful that the new immigrants would vote for Democrats at the state and national level, pushed for a series of legal barriers to citizenship and voting. Republicans in Congress passed the Naturalization Law of 1906, which required immigrants to provide stringent proof of lawful entry and continuous residence in their applications for citizenship. At the same time, several Republican-controlled state governments passed laws requiring literacy tests in English and banning the practice of alien suffrage, whereby immigrants who had filed their first naturalization papers could vote. Under the new set of regulations, the denial rate of naturalization rose from 3 percent to 15 percent and the average duration of naturalization doubled to eleven years.

Although local Democratic machines did not support restrictions on citizenship and voting, they too were reluctant to register and mobilize new immigrants during the early twentieth century. Local party bosses had already ensured dominance over city government by mobilizing Irish voters through patronage networks. With the exit of middle-class "Yankee" voters to the suburbs and the association of Republicans with anti-immigrant policies, Irish Democratic machines in most major cities did not fear competition from local Republican parties. What they did fear were demands from new immigrants to have a share in the distribution of power and patronage at the local level. So, even though the incorporation of new voters would have cemented the control of Democrats over city governments, party bosses were reluctant to register and mobilize immigrant voters because new constituencies would undermine the control of Irish Americans over government patronage. Only in a few cities where Irish Americans had not consolidated their hold over city governments were local Democratic organizations eager to aid immigrants in the processes of naturalization and registration.

Participation of Asian immigrants in the political process has increased in recent years, thanks to pioneers like Michael Woo, the first Asian American elected to the Los Angeles City Council. (© Michael Woo. Photo by Jason Jem)

Immigrant groups reacted to political demobilization and neglect in different ways. For Italian immigrants, exclusion by party machines reinforced political apathy and alienation. For Jewish immigrants, political exclusion bred radical and reformist strategies. As the Irish-dominated labor movement ignored the needs of less skilled workers, Jewish socialists began to organize the garment industry, which employed over one-half of the Yiddish-speaking population in New York City. Working-class Jewish immigrants also began to vote for the Socialist Party, which accounted for an increasing share of the opposition. Still, radical politics did not lead to the massive incorporation and mobilization of immigrants into American politics; such a task would be left to the Great Depression and the New Deal. The Great Depression weakened local party machines by severely curtailing the amount of patronage that city governments could provide. The depression also increased demands for greater political voice by immigrant groups excluded from the spoils of government. Finally, the massive increase in immigrant support for Democrat presidential candidates Al Smith (1928) and Franklin Roosevelt (1932) enabled Italian and Jewish

immigrant voters finally to overcome the grip of Irish political machines in cities such as Boston and New York.

While Italian and Jewish immigrants may have gotten a belated entry into electoral politics, immigrants from other groups found themselves excluded from American citizenship during the first half of the twentieth century. With occasional exceptions, the exclusion of Asian immigrants from electoral politics stretched as far back as the Naturalization Act of 1790, which conferred the privilege of citizenship only to free white males. Thus, unlike their European counterparts, early immigrants from Asia could not vote or hold elected office. Furthermore, laws preventing Asian immigrants from owning agricultural land forced many to remain migrant laborers, isolating them from the larger labor movement and hindering their capacity to form stable political organizations. Some immigrants responded to the legal restrictions by turning to the legal system, pushing cases for naturalization all the way to the Supreme Court. Most, however, took a defensive stance that was nonpartisan and nonpolitical, seeking to show the rest of the American community that Asian Americans were loyal members of American society who intended to make the United States their permanent home.

Mexican-American organizations in the 1930s and 1940s took a similar stance when faced with the forced repatriation of tens of thousands of Mexican immigrants. As unemployment levels soared to 11 million by the end of 1932, several communities and government agencies pressured Mexican immigrants and their children to return to Mexico. Reluctant to have their precarious status endangered even further, many Mexican Americans turned to organizations such as the League of United Latin American Citizens (LULAC), which emphasized the American side of the Mexican-American identity and distanced itself from the concerns of Mexican immigrants. At the same time, LULAC sought organized registration drives and supported local campaigns to combat discrimination against Mexican Americans in public schools and public facilities. Still, Mexican-American politics was limited by policies of discrimination and intimidation. Furthermore, electoral barriers such as the poll tax and race-based districting ensured the continued marginalization of Mexican Americans from electoral politics. Indeed, it was not until the rise of the civil rights movement and the 1965 abolition of the poll tax, and passage of the Voting Rights Act that Mexican and Asian immigrants were able to fully participate in electoral politics.

ELECTORAL POLITICS IN THE CONTEMPORARY PERIOD

The year 1965 marked a turning point in the participation of immigrants in electoral politics. Not only did it signal the end of an era of poll taxes and racial gerrymandering (i.e., the drawing of districts to dilute the impact of votes by racial minorities), it also inaugurated a new era in American immigration. The passage of the Immigration and Nationality Act of 1965 set the stage for a massive increase in the level of immigration to the United States and a significant change in the national origin of immigrants. Both of these changes, in conjunction with the passage of landmark civil rights legislation, eventually led to a fundamental transformation in the participation of immigrants in electoral politics.

GROWTH AND CHANGES IN THE IMMIGRANT POPULATION

The number of immigrants in the United States has nearly tripled since 1965, from 9.7 million to over 26 million today, or 10 percent of the U.S. population. At the same time, changes in the national origin of immigrant groups has led to an ethnic composition that is dramatically different from earlier waves of immigration. While most immigrants in the early twentieth century were from southern and eastern Europe, the overwhelming majority of immigrants since 1965 have come from Latin America and Asia. These changes have had a significant impact on ethnic politics in the United States, as the foreign-born constitute a growing portion of the ethnic vote among Latino and Asian-American groups. Furthermore, immigrants today tend to be concentrated in a few states and metropolitan areas, thereby increasing their potential to influence state and local elections. However, it is not simply demographic changes that have led to differences in the electoral politics of immigrants to the United States.

Just as important as the changing level and composition of immigrant streams have been processes related to the political incorporation of such groups: naturalization, registration and voting, partisan identification, and political contributions. Unlike the early period of immigrant political incorporation, the contemporary period is not marked by the power of local party machines. With the consolidation of the national welfare state and its civil bureaucracy, party machines play a limited role in encouraging or limiting the participation of contemporary immigrants in electoral politics. Thus, processes such as naturalization and mobilization operate under different political contexts today than during the early part of the previous century.

NATURALIZATION: THE FIRST STEP IN ELECTORAL POLITICS

Naturalization is a necessary first step in the participation of immigrants in electoral politics. While immigrants may choose to acquire citizenship for a variety of reasons, they cannot participate in most elections unless they have first become citizens. During the 1990s, the annual number of naturalizations rose dramatically. It shot up from almost 300,000 in 1990 to a peak of over 1 million in 1996 before declining to 870,000 by the end of the decade. Despite this recent rise in naturalizations, the pool of naturalized citizens is considerably smaller than the total number of immigrants in the United States. Even though immigrants may account for 10 percent of the total population in 2000, their electoral impact is diminished by the fact that they account for only 6 percent of adult citizens in the country. This is due both to regulations that make immigrants wait a minimum of five years before attaining citizenship and to the ability and willingness of eligible immigrants to naturalize.

There are several factors that influence the rate at which immigrants acquire U.S. citizenship, the most important of which is the time immigrants spend in the United States. Regardless of how old an immigrant is at the time of arrival, he or she is more likely to naturalize the longer he or she stays in the country. This is due primarily to the fact that longer stays in the United States lead to a stronger attachment to social networks in this country and a higher ability to speak English. In addition to duration of stay, an immigrant's socioeconomic status plays an important role in shaping the decision to naturalize. Those with high levels of educational attainment and high levels of income are more likely to naturalize than those with lower levels of education or income. High levels of education and income are also usually associated with higher proficiency in English, which in turn leads to greater rates of naturalization. Finally, immigrants who have spouses or children who are U.S. citizens are more likely to naturalize than those who have noncitizen family members. This is due not only

The impact of Latino voters is growing in the United States. Here a Latina woman from San Diego casts her ballot in the 1996 presidential election. *(David Maung/Impact Visuals)*

to the fact that the process of naturalization is quicker but also to the fact that such immigrants are more open to forces of assimilation that encourage the acquisition of American citizenship.

Even after taking into account factors related to length of stay and socioeconomic characteristics, there remain considerable differences in naturalization across national origins. This is reflected not only in the proportion that become U.S. citizens but also in the speed with which they attain citizenship. Immigrants from Asia are more likely to become U.S. citizens than those who come from Europe or Latin America. Asian immigrants have also tended to naturalize quicker than immigrants from other regions, although the gap has narrowed considerably since the 1980s. Overall, immigrants from Vietnam, China, and the Philippines have the highest rates of naturalization (over 65 percent), while those from Canada, the United Kingdom, and Mexico have the lowest rates of citizenship acquisition (below 35 percent).

Distance to the home country plays a significant role in accounting for differences in the rate of naturalization across national origins. Immigrants who come from nearby countries such as Canada or Mexico are less likely to naturalize because of the ease with which they can make periodic returns to their home country. In addition to proximity to the home country, the type of political regime left behind also has a significant influence on the propensity to naturalize. Immigrants who come from nondemocratic regimes are more likely to become U.S. citizens, either because of ideological reasons or because they lack the ability to return or to maintain close ties with their countries of origin. So, even though Cuba is in close proximity to the United States, Cuban immigrants naturalize early and in great numbers because they cannot entertain hopes of returning to their home country. Finally, immigrants are more likely to naturalize when their home countries institute policies of dual nationality or dual citizenship.

Naturalizations, 1907–1998

Year	Naturalizations	By Year	Naturalizations
1907–97	15,936,733	1975	141,537
		1976	142,504
By decade		1976, TQ*	48,218
1907–10	111,738	1977	159,873
1911–20	1,128,972	1978	173,535
1921–30	1,773,185	1979	164,150
1931–40	1,518,464	1980	157,938
1941–50	1,987,028	1981	166,317
1951–60	1,189,946	1982	173,688
1961–70	1,120,263	1983	178,948
1971–80	1,464,772	1984	197,023
1981–90	2,214,265	1985	244,717
1991–99	4,774,762	1986	280,623
		1987	227,008
By Year		1988	242,063
1961	132,450	1989	233,777
1962	127,307	1990	270,101
1963	124,178	1991	308,058
1964	112,234	1992	240,252
1965	104,299	1993	314,681
1966	103,059	1994	434,107
1967	104,902	1995	488,088
1968	102,726	1996	1,044,689
1969	98,709	1997	598,225
1970	110,399	1998	474,177
1971	108,407	1999	872,485
1972	116,215		
1973	120,740		
1974	131,655		

*TQ = third quarter.
Source: 1997 Statistical Yearbook of the Immigration and Naturalization Service and Monthly Statistical Reports; September Year End Reports for FY 1999 and 1998.

With such policies in place, immigrants no longer have to face the loss of legal or even voting rights in the home country when deciding to adopt U.S. citizenship.

The remarkable growth in naturalizations during the 1990s can, in part, be attributed to the increasing number of countries offering dual citizenship and dual nationality. By the late 1990s, immigrants from Colombia, Mexico, and the Dominican Republic no longer had to choose between political participation in the United States and participation in the homeland. However, the rise in dual citizenship can account for only part of the dramatic rise in naturalizations during the 1990s.

Also leading to the rise in naturalizations was the decision of the Immigration and Naturalization Service (INS) to institute a Green Card Replacement Program, which cost permanent residents slightly less than an application for naturalization. The Green Card Replacement Program was instituted by the Immigration and Naturalization Service in 1993 to remove old and fradulent green cards from circulation. Those who had obtained green cards before 1978 had to pay $70 and fill out a form to obtain the newer tamper-proof cards. At the time, the cost of application for naturalization was comparable to the cost of obtaining a replacement green card. Thus, many long-time residents chose to naturalize instead of obtaining a green card that would have to be renewed every ten years. Another important factor in the rise of naturalizations was that many of the 2.7 million undocumented immigrants who were granted permanent resident status in 1986 became eligible for naturalization. Finally, many immigrants chose to naturalize after the passage of measures such as Proposition 187 in California and the welfare reform bill at the national level. Both measures denied legal immigrants access to means-tested public benefits. Some had speculated that the rise in naturalization came primarily from welfare recipients who stood to lose benefits due to the new legislation. Evidence from the late 1990s indicates, however, that immigrants receiving public benefits were actually less likely to naturalize than those not receiving such benefits. Instead, anti-immigrant legislation seems to have created a hostile environment in which all immigrants (welfare recipients as well as nonrecipients) chose naturalization in order to preserve their sense of security.

REGISTRATION AND VOTING

While naturalization is a necessary first step in the process of domestic political participation, it is not all that is required: Naturalized citizens also have to register in order to vote in domestic politics. In the late 1990s, only 52 percent of naturalized Asian immigrants and 58 percent of Latino immigrants were registered to vote. After taking into account the effects of age and socioeconomic status, first-generation Latino citizens were one-third less likely to have registered than their native-born peers. Similarly, first-generation Asian-American citizens were 54 percent less likely to have registered than native-born Asian Americans. Part of the problem of low registration is due to limitations in outreach efforts by ethnic organizations. Despite their various efforts to mobilize citizens from the first generation and higher, registration drives seem to penetrate less than a third of the Latino and Asian-American electorate. Another reason for low levels of registration seems to stem from the recent rise in naturalizations following the passage of anti-immigrant legislation. Many immigrants seem to have naturalized less out of a desire to participate in politics than out of a determination to secure their place in American society.

After registration, turnout at the polls is the next and final step in voting participation. Among Asian immigrants, turnout seems to be yet another hurdle at which naturalized citizens fall behind native-born citizens. During the late 1990s, turnout among registered Asian Americans was 35 percent lower for naturalized citizens than it was for native-born Asian Americans. Among Latinos, however, higher turnout among naturalized citizens seems to counter the negative effect of lower rates of registration. Indeed, in

1996, higher turnout among registered Latinos in the first generation canceled out the "registration disadvantage" they faced in relation to Latinos of the second generation and higher.

In addition to intergenerational differences in voting among Latino and Asian immigrants, there are also differences in voting within the first generation. For example, a longer stay in the United States makes an immigrant not only more likely to naturalize but also more likely to vote after becoming a citizen. Also, differences in national origin lead to differences in voting participation. Among Latino immigrants, Cubans in Florida have unusually high rates of political participation. This is due, in large part, to their intense concern over relations between the United States and Cuba and to their wish for the downfall of the Castro government. In the past two decades, however, Cuban immigrant participation has also been motivated by a desire to gain power and control in local politics in Miami and state politics in Florida. There does not seem to be a clear instance of high levels of voting participation among immigrants from Asia. Unlike their counterparts from Cuba, refugees who fled communist regimes in Vietnam and Laos do not have high levels of voting participation. Indeed, when the question of communist country origin is examined more systematically across different ethnic groups, coming from a communist country does not increase the likelihood that an immigrant will participate in electoral politics.

Finally, turnout among first- and second-generation immigrants has also been influenced by anti-immigrant legislation at the state and national levels. In 1994, immigrant rights was a prominent campaign issue in California, as Proposition 187 sought to deny public benefits to undocumented immigrants. The anti-immigrant initiative propelled many first- and second-generation immigrants in the state to register and vote for the first time as U.S. citizens. Although there were a sizable number of naturalized citizens who supported the principles of Proposition 187, most immigrants mobilized against the measure. By 1996, legislation had moved from California to the national level. As the Republican Congress passed national legislation in 1996 to curtail illegal immigration and to deny public benefits to all immigrants, immigrant mobilization shifted to the national level. Ethnic and immigrant organizations across the country conducted registration drives and mobilized registered voters to the polls. In California, the mobilization of newly naturalized citizens helped Latinos in Orange County to elect Loretta Sanchez to Congress. In addition to encouraging naturalized citizens to go to the polls, mobilization over anti-immigrant legislation also had important longer-term effects on the partisan identification of newly naturalized citizens.

PARTISAN IDENTIFICATION

Some of the same factors that influence voting behavior among immigrants in elections also influence their adoption of political attitudes and partisan identifications. For example, the longer Latino immigrants stay in the United States, the more likely they are to identify themselves as Democrats. Identification with the Democratic Party grows even stronger in the second generation and remains strong among third-generation Latinos. Because Latino immigrants are likely to experience economic and social discrimination, they are more apt to favor political parties and candidates who are perceived as being more supportive of policies favoring minorities and other disadvantaged groups. During the mid-1990s, this partisan shift seemed to occur even earlier among naturalized citizens. As Republicans became associated with anti-immigrant legislation, newly naturalized citizens voted overwhelmingly for Democrats in 1996 and 1998. In the 2000 election, Republicans sought to woo Latino voters back to the Republican Party with presidential candidate George W. Bush and a party platform that appealed to the social-conservative values among Latino immigrants.

The most notable exception to the pattern of Democratic Party support among Latino immigrants has been among Cuban Americans, who have had a strong Republican Party orientation since the failure of the Bay of Pigs invasion in 1961. Cuban immigrant support for the Republican Party strengthened under the Reagan presidency, as the president took a firm stance against communism around the world. Organizations such as the Cuban American National Foundation (CANF) found a receptive ear in the administration to policies aimed at undermining the rule of Fidel Castro in Cuba. Since the 1980s, the strength of Cuban-American identification with the Republican Party has diminished somewhat, as second-generation Cuban immigrants are more likely than their parents to be party independents or Democratic Party supporters. Still, Cuban Americans remain exceptional among Latino immigrants in their strong support for Republican candidates.

Asian immigrants tend to have much weaker partisan affiliation than immigrants from Latin America. About one-fifth of Asian Americans are registered as independents, and the rest have split their loyalty between the two major parties. Just as in the case among Cuban Americans, during the 1980s and 1990s, Asian immigrants from communist countries such as China, Vietnam, and Laos were more likely to identify with the Republican Party, which was seen as taking a tough stance against communism. Homeland politics seems to play a much stronger role in shaping the partisan identification of Asian immigrants, who often divide even within national groups on matters related to foreign policy. The diversity of Asian national origins, when combined with educational and occupational differences, has made it difficult for Asian Americans to have a unified political agenda. However, recent issues such as anti-Asian violence and opposition to Asian-American quota limits in some university admissions have served to mobilize Pan-Asian support. Finally, the passage of anti-immigrant legislation during the mid-1990s has tended to shift the party identification of Asian immigrants toward the Democratic Party.

CAMPAIGN CONTRIBUTIONS

Contributions to political candidates and parties help immigrants to overcome political disadvantages that stem from their geographic dispersion across different cities or states. Political contributions also enable immigrant candidates to mount a credible run for elected office. Finally, until recently, campaign contributions were one of the few ways in which all immigrants, citizens as well as noncitizens, could participate in the electoral process. Since the controversy over political contributions by foreign governments to the Democratic Party during the 1996 election, legal permanent residents in the United States are severely limited in their ability to make campaign contributions to major political candidates.

There have not been many studies of political contributions among immigrants from Latin America. The Latino National Political Survey, conducted in 1990, revealed that even though Cuban Americans enjoyed the highest levels of socioeconomic status, they were less likely than other Latino groups to make political contributions. Contributions by Latino immigrants to political campaigns have, in general, been relatively sparse because most lack the financial resources to make such donations. Furthermore, the need to make such donations is not as strong as it is among Asian immigrants because Latinos possess strength in numbers in cities such as Miami and Los Angeles and states such as Texas and California.

Although there is no comprehensive data on

campaign contributions among Asian immigrants, data from the 1980s and early 1990s indicate that they were among the heaviest contributors to political campaigns. The rate of contribution among Asian Americans was often disproportionate to their numbers in the population. This was especially true among first-generation immigrants: citizens as well as noncitizens. Despite contributing money disproportionate to their numbers, Asian immigrants did not contribute money disproportionate to their wealth. Furthermore, differences in the political contributions across different Asian nationalities mirrored differences in socioeconomic status. Immigrant groups that were relatively well off, such as ethnic Chinese, Indians, and Koreans, were more likely to contribute to political campaigns than less-well-off groups such as Filipino and Vietnamese Americans. Although political contributions did not grant Asian immigrants access to high-level appointments, they did increase the extent to which political candidates listened to the concerns of Asian Americans. Furthermore, they helped Asian-American candidates such as Michael Woo in Los Angeles and S. B. Woo in Delaware in their successful bids for city councilman and lieutenant governor, respectively.

Since 1996, however, political contributions by Asian immigrants have received intense national scrutiny. Congressional investigations of John Huang, a top Asian-American fund-raiser for the Democratic National Committee, brought the issue of Asian immigrant political contributions to the national spotlight during the 1996 presidential campaign. As Congress moved to investigate the campaign finance abuses by John Huang and other Asian Americans, President Clinton announced in January 1997 that the Democratic National Committee would no longer accept donations from permanent residents who are not U.S. citizens. Later, Huang pleaded guilty to funneling millions of dollars from foreign companies and individuals, and Maria Hsia, a longtime fund-raiser for Al Gore, was convicted of funneling campaign contributions through a Buddhist temple in Los Angeles. It is still unclear what effect, if any, the campaign contribution scandals have had on the level of campaign contributions by Asian immigrants. Asian Americans still face considerable hurdles in attaining political power through mechanisms such as voting and other forms of political participation. With a population that is dispersed across different cities, and with first-generation immigrants still concerned about influencing politics in the homeland, Asian Americans may have to continue to rely on political contributions as a means of gaining influence in the electoral process.

During the mid- to late 1990s, the processes of electoral incorporation have been fundamentally affected by such political developments as the passage of anti-immigrant legislation and the Asian-American campaign finance scandal. And yet, it is still too early to tell what the final outcome of such events will be on the propensity of immigrants to naturalize and vote in domestic elections, their party identification, or their monetary contributions to political campaigns. One development that is certain is that immigrants will play an increasingly important role in electoral politics. With continued high levels of immigration to the United States and high numbers of applicants for citizenship, as well as the second-generation children becoming of voting age, the importance of immigrants in elections will continue to grow during the next few decades.

S. Karthick Ramakrishnan

See also: Civil Rights, Legislation II: Immigrants in America (Part II, Sec. 5); Immigrant Politics I: Activism, Immigrant Politics III: The Home Country (Part II, Sec. 6); California Proposition 63, 1986, California Proposition 187, 1994, California Proposition 227, 1998 (Part IV, Sec. 1).

BIBLIOGRAPHY

Arvizu, John R., and F. Chris Garcia. "Latino Voting Participation: Explaining and Differentiating Latino Voting Turnout." *Hispanic Journal of Behavioral Sciences* 18:2 (1996): 104–28.

Bonner, Raymond. "Donating to the First Lady, Hoping the President Notices." *New York Times*, March 14, 2000.

Cain, Bruce E., D. Roderick Kiewiet, and Carole J. Uhlaner. "The Acquisition of Partisanship by Latinos and Asian Americans." *American Journal of Political Science* 35:2 (1991): 390–422.

Carnegie Center for International Peace. "New Americans and Co-Ethnic Voting." *Research Perspectives on Immigration* 1:3 (1997).

de la Garza, Rudolfo O., Louis DeSipio, F. Chris Garcia, John Garcia, and Angelo Falcon. *Latino Voices: Mexican, Puerto Rican and Cuban Perspectives on American Politics.* Boulder, CO: Westview Press, 1992.

DeSipio, Louis. *Counting on the Latino Vote: Latinos as a New Electorate.* Charlottesville: University Press of Virginia, 1996.

———. "Making Citizens or Good Citizens? Naturalization as a Predictor of Organizational and Electoral Behavior among Latino Immigrants." *Hispanic Journal of Behavioral Sciences*, 18:2 (1996): 194–213.

DeSipio, Louis, and Rudolfo O. de la Garza. "Immigrants, Immigrant Policy and the Foundation of the Next Century's Latino Politics." Paper presented at *The Crisis in Latino Civil Rights Conference,* sponsored by the Civil Rights Project at Harvard University and the Tomás Rivera Policy Institute. Los Angeles, CA, 1997.

Erie, Stephen P. *Rainbow's End: Irish-Americans and the Dilemmas of Urban Machine Politics 1840–1985.* Berkeley: University of California Press, 1988.

Espiritu, Yen L. *Asian American Panethnicity.* Philadelphia, PA: Temple University Press, 1992.

Frisby, Michael K., and John Harwood. "Democrats and Clinton, in Surprise Move, Curb Contributions, Vow to Refuse Aliens' Donations." *Wall Street Journal,* January 22, 1997.

Gutiérrez, David. *Walls and Mirrors: Mexican Americans, Mexican Immigrants, and the Politics of Ethnicity.* Berkeley: University of California Press, 1995.

Hill, Kevin, and Dario Moreno. "Second-Generation Cubans." *Hispanic Journal of Behavioral Sciences* 18:2 (1996): 175–93.

Immigration and Naturalization Service. *Statistical Yearbook of the Immigration and Naturalization Service.* Washington, DC: Government Printing Office, 1997.

Lewis, Neil A. "Longtime Fund-Raiser for Gore Convicted in Donation Scheme." *New York Times,* March 3, 2000.

Liang, Zai. "Social Contact, Social Capital, and the Naturalization Process: Evidence from Six Immigrant Groups." *Social Science Research* 23:4 (1994): 407–37.

Lien, Pei-te. *The Political Participation of Asian Americans: Voting Behavior in Southern California.* New York: Garland Publishing, 1997.

———. "Who Votes in Multiracial America? An Analysis of Voting Registration and Turnout by Race and Ethnicity, 1990–1996." Paper presented at the Annual Meeting of the American Political Science Association, 1998.

Márquez, Ben. *LULAC: The Evolution of a Mexican American Political Organization.* Austin: University of Texas Press, 1993.

Pachon, Harry, and Louis DeSipio. *New Americans by Choice: Political Perspectives of Latino Immigrants.* Boulder, CO: Westview Press, 1994.

Portes, Alejandro, and John W. Curtis. "Changing Flags: Naturalization and Its Determinants Among Mexican Immigrants." *International Migration Review* 21:2 (1987): 352–71.

Portes, Alejandro, and Rafael Mozo. "The Political Adaptation Process of Cubans and Other Ethnic Minorities in the United States: A Preliminary Analysis." *International Migration Review* 19:1 (1985): 35–63.

Portes, Alejandro, and Rubén Rumbaut. *Immigrant America: A Portrait,* 2d ed. Berkeley: University of California Press, 1996.

Rosenbaum, David E. "A Day of Spin Follows a Month of Hearings." *New York Times,* August 2, 1997.

Takaki, Ronald. *Strangers from a Different Shore: A History of Asian Americans.* Boston: Little, Brown and Company, 1998.

*I*MMIGRANT POLITICS III: THE HOME COUNTRY

*I*mmigrants have not only become involved in electoral politics and political activism in the United States but have also remained active involved in the politics of their homeland. Immigrant involvement in homeland politics has increased considerably in the past two decades, thanks to reductions in the costs of transportation and communication, as well as efforts by homeland governments to engage with their overseas populations. Despite this recent increase in homeland politics the phenomenon is not something that is unique to the contemporary period. Immigrants and immigrant organizations in the United States have been interested and involved in the politics of their home countries for well over a century.

EARLY IMMIGRANT NATIONALISTS

During the nineteenth and early twentieth centuries, immigrant groups engaged in various types of involvement in the politics of their home countries. The type of homeland politics that immigrants engaged in depended in large part on the type of political system they left behind. In the late nineteenth and early twentieth centuries, immigrants came from different types of political systems: nations that were struggling for independent statehood, states that did not yet have a unified nation, democratic nation-states, and authoritarian nation-states. During this period, immigrant involvement also waxed and waned depending on political turmoil in the home country and the immigrants' economic situation in the United States. Immigrants were more likely to participate in homeland politics during time of war or civil strife in the home country. They were also more likely to participate when they had a relatively secure economic foothold in the United States, but less likely to participate during times of economic crisis such as the Great Depression. Finally, immigrant involvement during the early period was both direct (contributing funds or personnel to fight in the nationalist cause) and indirect (urging U.S. intervention or neutrality during times of war or civil strife).

Some of the earliest examples of immigrant mobilization around homeland politics involved immigrants from nations that were struggling for independent statehood. Once they secured an economic foothold in the United States in the mid-1800s, Irish immigrants set up local clubs to give financial support to independence movements in Ireland. Irish Americans also began to pressure the United States after the Civil War to move in an anti-British direction. Some even went so far as to invade Canada in 1866, hoping to draw the United States into a war with Britain. Only after Ireland achieved independent statehood following World War I did Irish Americans scale back their involvement in homeland politics. Similarly, Cuban immigrants in the late 1800s used the United States as a base of operations from which to mount a battle for independence from Spain. The leader of the Cuban Revolutionary Junta, José Martí, organized the war of independence from the group's headquarters in New York, raising substantial sums of money, arms, and soldiers among Cuban immigrants in the United States. Even after Martí died in battle in 1895, Cuban immigrants in New York continued their campaign of agitation and mobilization through the press, eventually prompting the United States to intervene in the war against Spain.

There were also examples of nationalist participation among Asian immigrants during this period. Soon after their arrival in the United States in 1902, Korean immigrants formed several political organizations to aid the resistance effort against Japanese imperialism in Korea. Korean immigrant involvement in homeland politics escalated after 1908, when a Korean nationalist in Seattle assassinated Durham Stevens, an American lobbyist hired by Japan. After the assassination, Korean-American organizations raised

Cuban Americans are perhaps the best example of an immigrant group that retains its focus on politics in the homeland. *(Tom McKitterick/Impact Visuals)*

vast sums of money for the independence struggle, and some groups even trained soldiers for the resistance effort against Japanese rule. Similarly, Asian Indians in California formed the Ghadr, or "revolutionary," Party in 1911 to provide intellectual and financial support for Indian independence from Britain. After the outbreak of the war in Europe, about four hundred members of the Ghadr Party left the United States to participate in revolutionary activities in India. However, the movement soon collapsed in India, and the federal government effectively destroyed the Ghadr base in the United States by prosecuting several Indian immigrants for violating America's laws of neutrality.

Immigrants who came from states that were not yet nations had a kind of involvement in homeland politics different from those who came from nations seeking independent statehood. When Italian peasants immigrated to the United States, they had a stronger sense of local or familial identity than any kind of unified national identity. But once they began living in the same neighborhoods, attending the same churches, as well as facing the same kind of discrimination as other Italians, they began to feel more and more like Italians. External events such as wars strengthened the feeling of national identity among Italian Americans. After Italy declared war on Ethiopia, Italian Americans came to the defense of their home country, vigorously lobbying the Roosevelt administration to refrain from imposing an embargo on trade with Italy. Similarly, Mexican peasant immigrants had a strong sense of regional identity when

they arrived in the United States. Once in the United States, however, they adopted a national identity after interacting with Mexicans from different regions, as well as being treated as Mexicans by Anglos in the American Southwest. This sense of national identity was strengthened in the early twentieth century during the Mexican Revolution, as hundreds of Mexican Americans contributed money and service to different factions in the struggle.

Immigrants who came from consolidated nation-states generally did not get involved in homeland politics because many had immigrated to the United States for purely economic reasons. Those who did participate had fled oppressive regimes and were trying to subvert authoritarian rule at home. For example, Russian-Jewish immigrants strenuously lobbied the United States government in 1913 to drop trade relations with Russia over the country's maltreatment of its Jewish population. Indeed, many Jewish organizations initially supported Germany during the First World War because of their members' deep hatred for czarist Russia. Only after they celebrated the Bolshevik overthrow in 1917 did many Russian Jews shift their sympathies away from Germany and become full supporters of American entry into the war.

Wartime also provoked many immigrant groups from both nation-states and stateless nations to raise money for refugee relief funds in their homeland. For example, during World War I, such organizations as the Lithuanian Central War Relief Committee and the Polish War Relief Committee raised hundreds of thousands of dollars from various immigrant organizations across the United States. Wartime also sparked nationalist fervor among immigrants whose homelands were consolidated nation-states. The most prominent example of early overseas nationalism occurred during World War I, when German Americans supported Germany's policies of nationalist expansion and pressed for American neutrality during the war. Although the German American National Alliance was initially established to fight forces of prohibition in the United States, it soon got caught up in the war in Europe. After Britain entered the war, the alliance attacked the press and President Woodrow Wilson as being pro-British. By 1916, several newspapers and politicians began to question the patriotism of German Americans. Even the president declared that groups such as the alliance had "injected the poison of disloyalty into our most critical affairs" and that such disloyalty "must be absolutely crushed." German-American involvement in homeland politics finally came to an end after the United States entered the war, as the alliance disbanded itself

While Cuban émigrés failed to overthrow their former island home's revolutionary government during the Bay of Pigs invasion in 1961, the spirit lives on, as this paramilitary group practicing in the Florida Everglades demonstrates. *(Jim Tynan/Impact Visuals)*

and donated all its proceeds to the American Red Cross.

HOMELAND POLITICS TODAY

Immigrant involvement in homeland politics today may not match the scale or intensity of efforts such as German-American mobilization during the First World War. Immigrant involvement in homeland politics is more regular today than in the past, however, continuing beyond moments of war or civil strife. The regular participation of immigrants in homeland politics can be partially explained by improvements in technology that have dramatically reduced the costs of transportation and communication for immigrants. But not all immigrants participate in homeland politics in the same manner. One of the critical factors that distinguishes various forms of immigrant participation in homeland politics is the kind of treatment immigrant communities receive from their sending

countries: antagonism, paternalistic engagement, or indifference. Another important factor that influences the ways in which immigrants participate in homeland politics is the extent to which they possess political power in the United States. If immigrant groups lack political power in the United States, they may turn toward their homeland, where they can wield a significant amount of power. Turning to homeland politics poses the risk of perpetuating the immigrant group's marginal status in American politics. It is also possible that participation in homeland politics empowers immigrants to become more active in domestic politics.

TREATMENT BY SENDING COUNTRIES

In cases in which immigrants come fleeing from repressive regimes such as Cuba and El Salvador, they tend to hold antagonistic relationships with such regimes and may even campaign actively for their overthrow. By contrast, some immigrants come from countries such as South Korea that actively engage with their émigré communities, sponsoring cultural and political organizations in the United States. In such instances, immigrants initially participate in homeland politics in ways that are carefully managed by the home country. Finally, for such individuals as Indian and Colombian immigrants, the sending country is indifferent to the departure of immigrants and their fortunes in the United States. Over time, however, even indifferent countries may shift their stance toward active engagement during periods of economic turmoil or political transition in the home country.

Antagonism

Cuban Americans represent the quintessential example of high involvement in homeland politics that springs from an antagonistic relationship between the immigrant community and the government in its home country. When the first wave of Cuban refugees arrived in the United States in 1959, they viewed their stay in the United States as purely temporary. They were convinced that, with the help of the U.S. government, they could overthrow Fidel Castro and return to a free Cuba. It was only after the failure of the Bay of Pigs invasion in 1961 and the Cuban Missile Crisis in 1962 that Cuban exiles diminished their hopes to liberate Cuba. As the Cuban-American community lengthened its stay in the United States, an increasing portion of the community began to view its stay in the United States as permanent and started to become involved in local political contests.

Still, the community's intransigent opposition to the Cuban government continued to shape the group's political adaptation in the United States. Founded in 1981, the Cuban American National Foundation (CANF) soon became a powerful lobbying group in Washington, pressing the United States government to pass policies aimed at undermining the Castro regime. Under the powerful leadership of Jorge Mas Canosa, CANF pushed the government to maintain its trade embargo with Cuba and to establish *Radio Martí* and *TV Martí*—broadcasting operations that transmit news and anticommunist propaganda toward Cuba. The group even went so far as to sponsor anticommunist forces outside Cuba, such as the (Union for Total Independence of Angola) (UNITA) movement in Angola. By the mid-1990s, Cuban-American involvement in homeland politics had declined considerably, as the second generation began to focus its attention on domestic affairs. However, events in early 1996 and in 2000 strengthened the hand of anti-Castro organizations once again. In 1996, Cuba shot down two planes belonging to a Cuban-American group called Brothers to the Rescue after

members of the group dropped anti-Castro pamphlets over Cuba. In reaction to the shooting, such organizations as CANF waged an intense lobbying campaign to pass the Helms-Burton law, a measure that enables the United States to sue foreign companies that do business with Cuba. Similarly, the custody battle over Elián Gonzalez in early 2000 between the boy's father in Cuba and his distant family in Miami served to rally the Cuban-American community, encouraging the second generation to remain interested in homeland politics and to renew the community's antagonistic stance toward the Castro regime in Cuba.

Salvadorans in the United States are another example of immigrants whose initial involvement in homeland politics was propelled by an adversarial relationship between the government in El Salvador and immigrant communities in the United States. During the civil war in El Salvador, immigrant associations in the United States criticized American foreign policy toward El Salvador, condemned human rights abuses in their homeland, and supported various factions of the leftist group Farabundo Martí National Liberation Front (FMLN). The end of the civil war in 1992 and the resumption of democratic politics did not signal an end to homeland politics among Salvadoran immigrants. There was indeed an initial vacuum in Salvadoran transnational politics as the FMLN began to contest elections in El Salvador. Some organizations reacted to the transformation by starting to pay more attention to the needs of immigrant communities in the United States. But this did not diminish immigrant involvement in the homeland, for organizations initiated projects of reconstruction and development in El Salvador. The Salvadoran government also actively began to reach out to its expatriate communities, offering help with legal services for immigrants and business deals for Salvadoran entrepreneurs, as well as coordinating the efforts of cultural and relief organizations in the United States. Thus, while the initial relationship between Salvadoran immigrants and their homeland government may have been antagonistic, the end of the civil war in El Salvador has led to mutual engagement and cooperation between the immigrant community and the Salvadoran government.

Paternalistic Engagement

While antagonism was the driving factor that compelled Cuban Americans to remain involved in homeland politics, paternalistic engagement was the primary factor in the participation of Korean Americans during the 1960s and 1970s. Although the Korean government did not sponsor the emigration of its nationals, it soon saw the opportunity to promote its economic and political agenda in the United States by engaging with Korean-American communities. Beginning in the late 1960s, the government managed such communities by creating official umbrella organizations for Korean-American groups and discouraging alternative ones by stressing the need for cultural unity. This type of paternalistic engagement worked well for several years. The government's involvement provided financial and organizational support to community activities and helped resolve intracommunity struggles. It also provided Korean-American business leaders the opportunity to gain privileges from the Korean government and to advance in homeland politics. Finally, the paternalistic arrangement enabled the Korean government to have a set of loyal advocates for its interests in the United States.

Over time, however, Korean Americans began to see the limits of relying on the Korean government as a basis for community organization. As local problems cropped up and as such scandals as the 1976 "Koreagate" surfaced, Korean Americans in New York began to create autonomous associations that dealt primarily with their immediate domestic concerns. Still, many prominent Korean-American groups such as the Korean Federation in Los Angeles retained close connections to the homeland government. It was only after the Los Angeles riots in 1992 that major Korean-American organizations reoriented themselves exclusively toward domestic politics. During the riots, the Korean Federation, among other groups, lost their standing and credibility among the Korean-American community, as homeland-oriented community leaders were unable to articulate the domestic needs and concerns of Korean Americans. After the riots, there emerged a new set of leaders from the second generation who advocated interracial cooperation and pushed Korean-American organizations to focus exclusively on the needs and interests of Korean Americans.

So, the Korean-American case suggests that although groups may initially benefit from paternalistic engagement from the home country, this relationship is likely to change over time. As immigrant groups stay longer in the United States, they begin to see political conflicts in the United States as more pressing than homeland politics. No longer believing that the government from the home country can solve their problems, immigrant organizations begin to reduce their dependence on homeland political actors. They may still retain their connection to homeland politics, but political crises in the United States may finally prompt the group to sever those ties completely.

Mutual Indifference

For many other groups, relationships between immigrant communities and the government in the home country are initially characterized by relative indifference. Colombian and Indian immigrants come to the United States not to flee political persecution but to advance their individual and familial economic interests. As a result, such communities do not initially engage in homeland politics. They do form ethnic organizations, but such associations are primarily cultural or recreational, as immigrants seek to reconstruct and maintain their homeland lifestyles within the United States. Over time, however, political and economic changes in the homeland may prompt homeland governments to engage with émigré communities.

Relations between Colombian immigrants and the homeland government were initially characterized by mutual neglect. The Colombian government did little to encourage political or cultural organization among its immigrant community in the United States. At the same time, immigrants and immigrant associations in the United States generally disassociated themselves from both domestic and homeland politics because of the predominantly negative portrayal in the media of Colombians as drug traffickers. Since the early 1990s, however, there has been a marked shift in political relations between Colombia and its immigrants in the United States. When the homeland government created a National Constituent Assembly to propose constitutional reforms, immigrant groups in New York and Miami created a task force and mounted a vigorous lobbying campaign to promote the interests of the overseas Colombian community.

Thanks in large part to immigrant efforts, Colombia announced in 1991 that it would grant dual citizenship to all nationals living outside the country. Furthermore, the Constituent Assembly allowed for the political representation of émigrés in the Colombian congress by creating a global overseas district. In 1997, the Colombian government also passed a law granting nationals living abroad the right to vote for representatives in their region of origin. Finally, the government also instituted various programs in its American consulates, all intended to provide legal assistance to and strengthen political organization among Colombian émigrés. In response to greater efforts at engagement by the homeland government, Colombian immigrants in the United States have increased their political involvement in their homeland.

Asian Indians in the United States are another example of an immigrant group whose political relations with the home country were initially characterized by mutual indifference. Indians who immigrated after 1965 were largely professionals or entrepreneurs seeking to advance their individual and familial economic interests. Although many analysts in India complained of a brain drain, the government did little to prevent the out-migration of its professionals. Also, even though overseas Indians sent millions of dollars in remittances to their relatives in India, the government did not actively engage with its overseas communities. During the late 1980s and early 1990s, economic and political developments in India prompted the government to increase its engagement with Non-Resident Indians (NRIs) in the United States. The Indian economic crisis in 1991 prompted the government to pay more attention to NRIs who had been sending remittances to their families. Faced with an acute shortage in foreign currency, the government implemented several policies aimed at increasing direct investment by NRIs in their home country. Also during this period, the Hindu nationalist Bharatiya Janata Party (BJP) was making a strong bid to wrest power from the ruling Congress Party. In its attempt to gain power, the BJP turned to overseas organizations for political contributions. As a result of outreach efforts by homeland political actors, the Indian immigrant community in the United States has now become highly involved in Indian politics. In addition to making contributions to political parties in India, they lobby the U.S. government on American policies that affect Indian national security and economic development. Furthermore, they contribute heavily to legislators who promote India's interests in the U.S. Congress.

POLITICAL POWER AND HOMELAND POLITICS

Involvement in homeland politics can relate to political power in the United States in one of several ways. First, immigrant groups may turn toward homeland politics as a way to compensate for the lack of political influence in the United States. For example, Indian Americans became involved in homeland politics not only because of political developments in India but also because the Indian-American community felt relatively disenfranchised in the United States. Even though Indian Americans represent less than 1 percent of the U.S. population, they expect to exert a significant degree of political influence based on their high levels of income and educational attainment. However, because Indian Americans are not geographically concentrated in the United States, they cannot hope to elect any Indian Americans to Congress or state legislatures. So, many have turned to

homeland politics to compensate for the lack of political power in the United States. A similar dynamic can be found among Colombian immigrants, who do not exert significant political power in the United States because of smaller numbers and relatively low levels of naturalization when compared with other Latino groups. Thus, while outreach efforts by homeland political actors give immigrants the *opportunity* to participate in homeland politics, the *demand* for such participation often springs from frustrated expectations of political power in the United States.

By turning to homeland politics, the immigrant group incurs the risk of perpetuating its marginal status in American politics. Some scholars and community activists have argued that the focus of immigrant populations on homeland politics prevents them from taking an active role in U.S. politics. This may especially be true for groups whose home countries do not allow for dual citizenship. In such cases, immigrants may forgo opportunities to attain U.S. citizenship with the hope of maintaining political ties to the homeland. Participation in homeland politics may also close off opportunities for pan-ethnic mobilization in the United States. For example, active political engagement between Colombian immigrants and the Colombian government has dampened the appeal of pan-Latino issues among Colombian political activists in the United States. After the increase in homeland political participation during the 1990s, Colombian immigrants are now more likely to mobilize around issues pertaining to Colombia and their particular ethnic communities in the United States.

In many cases, however, that participation in homeland politics actually empowers immigrants to increase their involvement in domestic politics. First, immigrant activism in homeland politics can prompt the home country to revise its constitutions to allow for dual citizenship. This is especially true for such groups as Dominican and Colombian immigrants, who send home millions of dollars in remittances and who represent a significant proportion of their homeland's population. With the establishment of dual citizenship, immigrants no longer have to choose between political participation in the United States and participation in the homeland. Such participation can include voting, lobbying or making political contributions, and also running for political office. Thus, for example, it was possible for Jesús Galvis to run for a congressional seat in Colombia in 1998 while being a member of the city council in Hackensack, New Jersey.

Over time, immigrant empowerment from homeland political participation can reinforce or increase participation in domestic politics. For instance, Dominican immigrants' participation in the politics of the home country does not seem to have detracted from their involvement in U.S. politics. After the Dominican Republic instituted a policy of dual citizenship in 1994, the number of naturalizations soared among Dominican immigrants in New York. The rise in naturalizations rose even further after the passage of anti-immigrant policies in 1996, for Dominicans no longer needed to worry about losing citizenship rights in their homeland in order to fight for their interests in the United States. After naturalization, Dominican immigrants in New York registered and mobilized in large numbers for domestic politics as well as homeland politics. The passage of dual citizenship thus enabled Dominicans in New York to elect Guillermo Linares to the city council in 1992 and Adriano Espailat to the state legislature in 1996.

Immigrant involvement in homeland politics is clearly not something that is unique to the contemporary period. During the nineteenth and early twentieth centuries, immigrants got involved in their home country during periods of nationalist struggle or world war. What is unique about the contemporary period is the regularity of immigrant involvement in homeland politics. Reductions in the costs of transportation and communication have enabled immigrants to stay informed and involved in the politics of their home countries. At the same time, consolidated nation-states have shown an increasing willingness and ability to engage with their overseas populations to promote their interests in the United States and to ensure the steady flow of American dollars through immigrant remittances. Immigrant involvement in homeland politics may initially lead to a reduction in domestic political participation. As more and more countries pass laws granting dual nationality and dual citizenship, however, we can expect to see an increase in immigrant involvement in both domestic and homeland politics.

S. Karthick Ramakrishnan

See also: Impact on the Home Country Economy (Part II, Sec. 7); Cuba, Dominican Republic, Mexico (Part III, Sec. 2).

BIBLIOGRAPHY

Axtman, Kris. "New Energy, and More Unity, for Cubans in US." *Christian Science Monitor*, January 13, 2000.

Boswell, Thomas D, and James R. Curtis. *The Cuban-American Experience*. Totowa, NJ: Rowman and Allanheld, 1984.

Child, Clifton. *The German-Americans in Politics, 1914–1917*. Madison: University of Wisconsin Press, 1939.

Clarke, Ida. *American Women and the World War*. New York: D. Appleton and Company, 1918.

Fritz, Mark. "Pledging Multiple Allegiances." *Los Angeles Times*, April 6, 1998.

Glazer, Nathan. "Ethnic Groups in America." In *Freedom and Control in Modern Society*, ed. Monroe Berger, Theodore Abel, and Charles Page, pp. 158–73. New York: Van Nostrand, 1954.

Guraniso, Luis Eduardo, and Luz Marina Díaz. "Transnational Migration: A View from Colombia." *Ethnic and Racial Studies* 22:2 (1998): 397–421.

Itzigsohn, José, Carlos Dore Cabral, Esther Hernandéz Medina, and Obed Vázquez. "Mapping Dominican Transnationalism: Narrow and Broad Transnational Practices." *Ethnic and Racial Studies* 22:2 (1998): 316–339.

Jones-Correa, Michael. *Between Two Nations: The Political Life of Latin American Immigrants in New York City*. Ithaca: Cornell University Press, 1998.

Kanawada, Leo. *Franklin D. Roosevelt's Diplomacy and American Catholics, Italians, and Jews*. Ann Arbor, MI: UMI Research Press, 1982.

Kim, Ilsoo. *New Urban Immigrants: The Korean Community in New York*. Princeton: Princeton University Press, 1983.

Landolt, Patricia, Lilian Autler, and Sonia Baires. "From Hermano Lejano to Hermano Mayor: The Dialectics of Salvadoran Tansnationalism." *Ethnic and Racial Studies* 22:2 (1998): 290–315.

McCaffrey, Lawrence. *The Irish Catholic Diaspora in America*. Washington, DC: Catholic University of America Press, 1997.

Morga, Dan, and Kevin Merida. "South Asia Rivals Had Money on South Dakota Senate Race." *Washington Post*, March 24, 1997.

Ojito, Mirta. "Castro Foe's Legacy: Success, Not Victory." *New York Times*, November 30, 1997.

Park, Edward. "Competing Visions: Political Formation of Korean Americans in Los Angeles." *Amerasia Journal* 24:1 (1998): 41–57.

Portes, Alejandro, and Rubén Rumbaut. *Immigrant America: A Portrait*. 2d ed. Berkeley: University of California Press, 1996.

Sachar, Howard. *A History of the Jews in America*. New York: Alfred A. Knopf, 1992.

Shankar, Lavina Dhingra, and Rajini Srikanth, eds. *A Part, yet Apart*. Philadelphia: Temple University Press, 1998.

Takaki, Ronald. *Strangers from the Different Shore: A History of Asian Americans*. Boston: Little, Brown, 1998.

$\mathcal{P}$UBLIC OPINION AND IMMIGRATION

$\mathcal{R}$alph Waldo Emerson once said, "Consistency is the hobgoblin of little minds." Many Americans appear to share this view when it comes to immigration. While Americans pride themselves in being a nation of immigrants, seldom have they displayed an overwhelming enthusiasm for immigrants—especially new immigrants. Americans say they want levels of U.S. immigration reduced, but they keep on rising. And, while Americans frequently express negative views about the abstract concept of "immigration," they can extend much hospitality toward those immigrants they know personally.

Some of these apparent contradictions arise because, as we shall see later, attitudes about immigration typically are not strongly held. Equally important, however, is the fact that the immigration landscape is constantly changing, being reformed by larger and larger arrivals of immigrants from new and varied lands. In the twenty years beginning with 1981, more immigrants will have been admitted for legal permanent residence in the United States than in any other twenty-year period in American history. This rise has been accompanied by important shifts in source countries. In the early part of the twentieth century, the five most important sending countries for legal immigrants were Italy, Austria-Hungary, Russia, Canada, and the United Kingdom. In the 1980s and 1990s, this list was headed instead by Mexico, the Philippines, China, the Dominican Republic, and India. To make the point more explicitly, during fiscal year 1997 (the last year for which we have data), 147,000 immigrants from Mexico were admitted for legal permanent residence in the United States out of a total of 798,000 migrants from all countries combined. Mexico's share of 18.4 percent was not only greater than that of any other country but also exceeded by nearly 25,000 the total number of European immigrants to the United States (147,000 versus 122,000).

As a result of rapidly rising levels of immigration, the number of foreign-born persons living in the United States stood at 25.8 million in March 1997. This is the largest foreign-born population in U.S. history and represents a 30 percent increase over the 1990 census figure of 19.8 million. An estimated 9.7 percent of the U.S. population is now foreign-born. This percentage is substantially above the 4.7 percent figure registered in 1970 but still considerably below the peak during the twentieth century—14.7 percent in 1910.

Mexico accounts for 7 million or 28 percent of the total foreign-born population. Six states had foreign-born populations of 1 million or more in 1997: California (8.1 million); New York (3.6 million); Florida (2.4 million); Texas (2.2 million); New Jersey (1.2 million); and Illinois (1.1 million). Nearly three-quarters of all foreign-born individuals lived in one of these six states. Moreover, more than 40 percent of all foreign-born individuals are recent arrivals, having come to the United States within the past ten years. Finally, the shift from predominately European source countries to those in Asia and Latin America has also been accompanied by a rise in the number of illegal or undocumented migrants living in the United States—now estimated at more than 5 million. Mexican nationals account for more than one-half of this total.

An understanding of immigration-related attitudes is important because Americans live in a representative democracy, and these attitudes have the potential to shape policy. We know that the early part of the twentieth century frequently played host to strong anti-immigrant sentiment. One author, for example, wrote in 1920 in the *Saturday Evening Post*, "If the United States is the melting pot, something is wrong with the heating system, for an inconveniently large portion of the new immigration floats around in unsightly indigestible lumps." How are views about immigrants expressed today? What role does the state of the economy play, the racial and ethnic identifica-

This liquor store sign in Miami makes light of a serious problem, the many Haitian and Cuban refugees arriving on Florida shores aboard unseaworthy rafts. *(Jack Kurtz/Impact Visuals)*

tion of respondents, immigrants' country of origin, and whether respondents are themselves immigrants?

We will answer these questions with two kinds of data. First, even though most public opinion surveys are snapshots of the population taken at a given point in time, some questions have sufficient salience that they are asked repeatedly across numerous surveys. Assembling responses to these aggregate questions allows us to have some historical perspective on changing immigration attitudes. Second, some surveys are sufficiently unique and also rich in the kinds of data they convey that they are worth considering in their own right. Oftentimes, these surveys have been subjected to more rigorous statistical analyses which permit tests of hypotheses and which isolate the impact of selected factors such as age, income, and education on public opinion. We will discuss three of these studies in particular.

HISTORICAL PERSPECTIVES ON IMMIGRATION ATTITUDES

GENERAL IMMIGRATION ATTITUDES

Growing anxiety over the presence of immigrants has accompanied the rise in immigration. One question frequently asked in public opinion polls is whether respondents would like to see U.S. immigration increased, decreased, or kept the same. When the proportion responding "decreased" is graphed, the trend is relatively flat at about 40 percent until sometime after 1975, when it rises abruptly. The evidence suggests that the United States has entered a *neorestrictionist era* in the past two decades. The proportion wanting fewer immigrants reached nearly 70 percent in the early 1980s, fell back to less than 50 percent in the late 1980s, rose again to more than 60 percent in the early 1990s, and then fell once more by the mid-1990s to close to 50 percent. Some understanding of these trends is gained by comparing immigration attitudes with changes in the U.S. unemployment rate. When this rate is put onto the same graph as immigration attitudes, they fluctuate roughly in parallel fashion, which suggests that Americans' attitudes toward immigrants are partially conditioned by the state of the economy and that these attitudes harden when employment prospects for native workers dim. Similar patterns have emerged in Canadian data.

Rita Simon, a longtime student of immigration attitudes, examined more than a century's worth of magazine articles, media editorials, and books on immigration attitudes. She has concluded that the most remarkable thing about immigration is that so many people were admitted to the United States when there was demonstrably little enthusiasm for them for such long periods of time. This contradiction is all the more poignant during the neorestrictionist period, because an apparent divide has opened up between federal initiatives that have continued to liberalize legal immigration policy and American public opinion, which has become more restrictionist toward immigrants. To understand this paradox, three additional factors must be considered: (1) American attitudes toward immigration are often ambivalent; (2) even when opinions are negative, they are typically not strongly held; and (3) federal policymakers are frequently more influenced by vocal pro-immigrant interest groups (including business interests) than by the general public, which is often not well organized.

ATTITUDES TOWARD MEXICAN IMMIGRATION

In the remainder of this section, four main issues will be examined: (1) attitudes toward particular kinds of immigrants; (2) the perceived economic consequences of immigration; (3) policies toward legal and undocumented (or illegal) immigration; and (4) the relative importance of immigration issues. Results are based on data derived from the Public Opinion Locator Library (POLL) database, a comprehensive online retrieval system for polling data provided by Dialog Information Services, Inc. and constructed from survey data collected and archived by the Roper Center for Public Opinion at the University of Connecticut. These data are typically drawn from national surveys conducted by a variety of polling organizations during a thirty-year period from the mid-1960s to the mid-1990s. Because Mexican immigration to the United States is so prominent, some of our findings relate directly to attitudes about Mexican immigrants or to policies for controlling Mexican immigration. In other instances, given the growing richness of the POLL database, we are able to isolate the attitudes of Hispanic respondents.

Preferences for Immigrants by Country of Origin

In general, when they are presented with a choice, the American public prefers European immigrants over those from Asia or from Latin America. And when the choice is restricted to Asian and Latin American immigrants, Asian migrants typically rank higher. In 1965, the vast majority of Americans mentioned European immigrants as those toward whom they felt most favorably, and only one in ten cited Mexico, Latin America, or Asia. By 1993, however, the proportion feeling most favorably toward Latin America or Asian migrants surpassed the percentage citing Europe. During this period, the racial and ethnic composition of the U.S. population also changed, and this change may have had some bearing on aggregate responses.

When respondents are asked to identify the immigrants that they like the least, immigrants from Mexico and the Caribbean receive the largest share of votes. In 1965, for example, the number of respondents citing Europe as their least favorite immigrant homeland was less than half of the number who cited Europe as their preferred source country. On the other hand, the number who gave Mexico, Latin America, or Asia as their least favorite country of origin outnumbered those preferring immigrants from these regions by three to one. Moreover, when direct comparisons are made between Mexico and countries in

Asia, a specific Asian country is mentioned twice as often as Mexico as a favorite source of immigrants. Similar responses are elicited when people are asked about which immigrant groups have benefited the United States and which have caused problems. European immigrants were viewed most favorably in 1993, followed by migrants from Asia, then Latin America and the Caribbean. In addition, among Latin American/Caribbean migrants, Mexicans "did better" than Cubans and Haitians. Some of the negative attitudes toward the latter two groups may be related to extensive media coverage of the Cuban and Haitian boat lifts and to fear of Acquired Immunodeficiency Syndrome (AIDS) among these immigrants.

Other questions probe into immigrants' perceived characteristics, including welfare use, criminal behavior, work ethic, degree of competitiveness, school performance, and family values. Latin American immigrants are believed to be more welfare dependent than Asian migrants and also more likely to add to the crime problem. Asians are more likely than Latinos to be seen as hardworking, and whereas a majority of respondents disagree with the depiction of immigrants as too competitive, Asians were 50 percent more likely than Latinos to be seen in this light. Asian competitiveness is presumed to pay dividends in terms of school performance, especially in comparison with Latinos. Moreover, recent immigrants are believed by the American public to possess strong family values, with no apparent differences between Asians and Latinos.

Perhaps one way of summarizing the public's views about Asian and Latino migrants is to ask whether the United States is admitting too many, too few, or about the right number from these regions. Based on surveys taken between 1984 and 1995, at least one-half of survey participants feel we are letting in too many in both categories. With these categories, however, there is a greater likelihood of responding "too many" when Latin American immigrants are mentioned. This suggests in yet another way that immigrants from Latin America are seen in some sense as less desirable than Asian migrants.

Perceived Economic Consequences

Two central concerns about the economic impacts of immigrants are that (1) immigrants adversely affect the employment and earnings opportunities of natives and (2) immigrants exert an unfavorable "fiscal" impact on natives by using more publicly provided services (for example, public schooling) than they pay for with their taxes. In public opinion polls, a minority of respondents feel that immigrants take jobs from

American citizens. Half or more of all respondents feel that immigrants are filling jobs that natives do not want. Generally, Hispanic respondents have more positive assessments than do all respondents about the labor market impact of immigrants. Americans have a different perception, however, about the labor market effects of undocumented immigrants. Survey participants are more likely to believe that illegal immigrants are competing with natives; typically, between 50 and 70 percent of all respondents view undocumented immigrants as competitors with native workers in the labor market.

With respect to the fiscal impacts of immigrants, some surveys ask whether the United States can still "afford" to keep its door open to newcomers. In general, small majorities feel that America should keep the welcome mat out for immigrants. Responses do not differ appreciably between questions that make reference to all immigrants versus legal immigrants. In this case, the responses of Hispanic participants are quite similar to those of all respondents. When more direct questions are asked about immigrants' fiscal impacts, a slight majority of all respondents tend to view immigrants today as a burden on the United States. Survey participants appear much better equipped to respond to questions that are generally worded than to narrower matters that they may consider too esoteric (for example, whether immigrants "use up more than their fair share of tax dollars and government services"). Such questions elicit a high proportion of the response "don't know." In contrast to all respondents, Hispanic respondents typically feel that immigrants strengthen the U.S. economy. Here is another instance in which Hispanic respondents have more optimistic assessments.

Illegal Immigrants: Attitudes and Policies

Because Mexican immigration to the United States is so prominent and because an estimated 40 percent of Mexican immigrants living in the United States are in undocumented status, it is important to consider different perceptions of legal versus illegal immigrants. Many opinion surveys tend to characterize immigration as a "problem." Nevertheless, the American public is more likely to view illegal immigration as problematic than legal immigration. Rather consistently in a series of polls, when asked how much of a problem legal immigration is, Americans' responses are generally evenly distributed across the categories "major," "moderate," "minor," and "no problem." Hispanic responses are similar to those of all participants when the top two and bottom two categories are com-

bined, but within those groups, Hispanics are less likely than all adults to consider legal immigration a problem.

By contrast, survey participants are more than twice as likely to say that illegal immigration is a major problem. Approximately two out of every three individuals see illegal immigration this way. Hispanic respondents are just as likely as all respondents to consider undocumented immigration as either a major problem or a moderate problem. It could be that undocumented immigration, much of it from Mexico or otherwise from Latin America, stigmatizes Latinos whether they themselves are legal or not.

The American public is generally supportive of measures such as those encompassed in California's Proposition 187 to deny education, health care, and other social services to illegal migrants. At the same time, the extent of support depends crucially on question wording. Support is strongest when questions are framed in terms of denying welfare, and weaker when only schools and hospitals are cited. References to denying "public assistance" muster strength that is midway between these categories. Furthermore, agreement with measures to deny social services to undocumented immigrants weakens whenever children may be harmed and strengthens if adults are the only group likely to be affected. Typically, Latinos are considerably less enthusiastic about denying social services to illegal immigrants than are all respondents.

As a result of federal reforms to the welfare system that were enacted in 1996, legal immigrants now face greater limits on their access to means-tested public benefits. Surveys have asked respondents how they feel about measures to deny welfare to *legal* immigrants as part of a package of measures to tighten eligibility criteria. Answers depend very much on question wording. Respondents seem most against blanket prohibitions that make no exceptions and more supportive when questions are framed to differentiate between "deserving" and "undeserving" immigrants. For example, persons who fall into the deserving category include immigrants who work hard, pay taxes, and have become U.S. citizens. Having lived in the United States for more than five years also matters. By and large, the American public is most supportive of welfare cuts to legal immigrants if these cuts are targeted to immigrants who have not become U.S. citizens and have lived in the United States for fewer than five years. In comparison with all respondents, Latino respondents profess either the same or lower levels of agreement with proposals to restrict benefits for legal immigrants.

When asked, the American public usually says

that the United States has a problem with southern border security. In a 1990 survey, three out of five respondents believed that the United States has a serious problem with illegal aliens coming across the border, and 80 percent agreed that the United States was doing either a fair or poor job controlling illegal immigration. Most respondents also felt that the federal government can and should be doing more to cope with the problem. The remainder of this section deals with the public's views about different ways to control illegal immigration across the (southern) border. To preview the findings, whereas many Americans support the general notion of controlling undocumented immigration, this support often wavers in the face of proposals about specific tactics.

Roughly nine out of ten people believe that "patrolling U.S. borders and coastlines more strictly" is a good idea as a way of curbing illegal immigration, although support declines dramatically when respondents are reminded that increased border security will mean higher taxes. Approximately 80 percent of respondents support adding more Border Patrol agents as a way to increase enforcement personnel along the border. Support drops when using the military is proposed as an alternative to the Border Patrol, but two-thirds of respondents still agree with this option. Unsurprisingly, persons who believe that illegal immigration is a serious problem give more enthusiastic endorsements to both the Border Patrol and the military proposals.

Two-thirds of respondents favor erecting fences or digging ditches in high-traffic areas to discourage illegal immigrants who cross the border on foot or in vehicles. On the other hand, a proposal to build a fence along the entire U.S.-Mexico border is opposed by a majority of respondents. An even larger majority opposes building a wall along the Mexican border. What these responses seem to suggest is that people are willing to support token or symbolic measures to control illegal immigration, but enthusiasm declines for measures that are seen as too extreme or draconian (even if they might work).

Three-quarters of respondents favor the idea of charging a small $2 fee to cross U.S. borders if the money is used to enhance border security. Another approach to controlling illegal immigration is to penalize employers who hire undocumented workers. In fact, the 1986 Immigration Reform and Control Act (IRCA) did just that for employers who exhibit a "pattern and practice" of violations. Three out of every four individuals surveyed believe that hiring an illegal alien should be against the law, but support drops to 65 percent when respondents are presented with penalizing employers as a specific means of enforcing

IRCA. Amnesty for undocumented immigrants who had lived in the United States since January 1991 was another feature of IRCA, proposed in order to gain sufficient support for the employer sanctions provisions. In survey after survey, a slim majority of Americans consistently opposes amnesty. Numerous survey questions about amnesty specify different residency requirements (zero, two, or seven years). This variation has little effect on participant responses. People seem instead to be reacting to the general principle of forgiveness.

A final set of proposals for limiting undocumented immigration revolves around computerized data systems that would permit employers to check the legal status of job applicants. When individuals are asked whether they believe it is a good idea to issue national identification (ID) cards to every U.S. citizen at birth or when they become naturalized, support for the proposition is very mixed. The measure is supported by roughly half of all respondents; one-third oppose it; and the remainder either have mixed feelings or are unsure how they feel. When stronger wording (such as "require" or "carry") is used, support typically goes down. Conversely, support increases if words such as "carry" are softened to "have." Limiting the use of a national ID card to employment-related purposes does not augment its popularity. A slightly larger majority (about two-thirds) favor the use of a forge-proof Social Security card. This higher level of support may be due to the American public's greater familiarity with Social Security cards and to the fact that U.S. residents use Social Security numbers routinely for identification purposes.

Relative Importance of Immigration Issues

So far our discussion of polling data on immigration suggests that the American public is genuinely concerned about the issue, that illegal immigration especially is viewed as a serious problem, and that the federal government can and should take stronger action to curb immigration. These responses, however, are typically elicited when respondents are cued to think about immigration, when immigration is portrayed as a problem in survey questions, or when migrants are cast as being in the United States largely in illegal status. It is of interest to know how the public feels about immigration in relation to other social issues that may be equally or more pressing, especially when respondents are not prompted to consider one particular issue or another.

When respondents are faced with a variety of open-ended questions designed to assess the relative importance of a variety of potentially important issues, the results are striking. Numerous surveys have asked questions about "the most important problem" facing the United States today or facing that part of the country where the respondent lives, or (even more narrowly) the most important problem "that you and your family are most concerned about." The three most commonly cited concerns—mentioned by roughly 50 to 60 percent of all respondents—include crime, followed by concerns over jobs and the state of the economy, followed by high taxes and government spending. Immigration is nowhere near the top of any of these lists. In fact, it typically ranks lower than "don't know."

STAND-ALONE SURVEYS OF IMMIGRANT ATTITUDES

In contrast to surveys that ask more or less the same questions at frequent intervals, other surveys are special purpose and designed to capture attitudes about one facet or another of immigration. Typically, questions from these surveys are sufficiently unique that they are not repeated over time. Moreover, some of these special-purpose opinion polls have been subjected to sophisticated statistical analyses designed to test a variety of hypotheses related to immigration.

UNDOCUMENTED MIGRANTS IN SOUTHERN CALIFORNIA

In June 1983, the Field Research Corporation conducted interviews with 1,031 individuals living in the six urban counties of Southern California. The questions focused primarily on attitudes toward undocumented immigration but included as well a series of questions about the demographic, socioeconomic, and other characteristics of respondents. These data contain the most comprehensive set of respondent characteristics and other attitudinal information relevant to an examination of opinions about undocumented U.S. migration ever assembled, including opinion polls from the 1990s. When asked, "How serious a problem do you believe the illegal immigration situation is in Southern California at the present time?" 60 percent of respondents indicated "very serious" and another 28 percent said "somewhat serious." Likewise, 39 percent of survey participants felt that the "influx of illegal or undocumented immigrants into Southern California" has a "very unfavorable" effect on the state as a whole, and another 30 percent felt the effect was "somewhat unfavorable." Just 20

percent believed that the effect was favorable (including "very" and "somewhat").

These data were then used to test five hypotheses about undocumented immigration. They include (1) a "labor market competition hypothesis" which suggests that individuals with the lowest levels of socioeconomic achievement have the most to fear from job competition with new immigrants and are therefore most likely to express negative attitudes toward illegal immigration and undocumented immigrants; (2) a "cultural affinity hypothesis" that predicts that individuals with the strongest pro-immigrant attitudes will be persons whose own cultural attributes are most similar to those of undocumented migrants; (3) an "education hypothesis" that suggests that individuals with the most education will be most sympathetic toward undocumented migrants; (4) a "utilitarian hypothesis" that emphasizes the costs and benefits associated with immigration and predicts that negative attitudes toward undocumented immigration will be associated with anxieties over one's material well-being; and (5) a "symbolic politics hypothesis" according to which challenges to conventional views about what constitute important symbols of American nationality may evoke anti-immigrant attitudes.

There is only weak support in the data for a labor market competition hypothesis. Household income is unrelated to immigrant attitudes. The results for employment status and living in a household containing a union member are either mixed or statistically weak. There is greater support for the cultural affinity story. Hispanics are more likely than non-Hispanics to have favorable immigrant attitudes, as are first-generation immigrants. Blacks, on the other hand, are substantially more likely to view illegal immigration as a serious problem.

Some of the strongest associations in the data are with educational attainment. Respondents with any amount of college education have more favorable attitudes toward undocumented migrants than persons who have not gone beyond high school, and the more education respondents have, the less they appear to be concerned about potential problems associated with illegal immigration. Age and gender are additional respondent characteristics that are associated with attitudes toward illegal immigration. In general, older respondents—especially those beyond age thirty-five—have more pessimistic outlooks than younger persons about the consequences of illegal immigration. Females have somewhat more negative attitudes than males, a finding that parallels other studies suggesting that females are more likely than males to value those traits that "define a true American." Chief among these are believing in God, standing up for one's country, economic self-reliance, speaking English, and voting in elections—characteristics that women may consider lacking in undocumented migrants.

Cost-benefit considerations have a clear influence on attitudes toward illegal immigration. Individuals who believe that illegal migrants are more likely to receive welfare benefits, more likely to commit crimes, or more likely to impose a fiscal burden on other taxpayers are themselves significantly more likely to feel that illegal immigration is a serious problem. On the other hand, pro-immigrant views emerge when respondents perceive that immigrants enhance their economic well-being as, for example, in lowering prices for consumer goods.

Finally, evidence suggests that illegal immigration to Southern California evokes normative reactions related to the use of English and to egalitarianism as symbols of what it means to be an American. Threats to those symbols are viewed negatively. In particular, respondents in Southern California who believe that the number of non-English-speaking persons will grow or who feel that an increase in the number of such persons will have a bad effect on ethnic relations are more likely to be concerned about illegal immigration as a serious problem.

PRESENCE OF IMMIGRANTS IN NEW JERSEY

New Jersey is an important state for immigration. In 1997, an estimated 1.2 million foreign-born persons lived in New Jersey, up from 967,000 in 1990. New Jersey ranks fifth among all states in the number of foreign-born residents and fourth in the proportion of all residents who are foreign-born (15.4 percent in 1997). Adults in New Jersey were polled in September 1994 about their attitudes toward immigrants. Roughly half of those interviewed believed that the current number of immigrants was about right, and another 40 percent thought this number should be reduced. Only a small minority (less than 5 percent) felt the number needed to be increased. Foremost in the minds of those who wanted fewer immigrants was anxiety about whether there were enough jobs to go around. Concerns about higher taxes and overcrowding were also prominent.

A regression analysis demonstrated that respondents' demographic and socioeconomic characteristics were closely linked to how they felt about immigrants. In particular, older, less-educated, central-city, and Catholic residents were more likely to want fewer immigrants, whereas married persons and members of minority groups were more tolerant. A separate

analysis of survey participants' attitudes about a variety of narrower immigration issues showed that New Jersey residents were least tolerant when immigrants were believed to affect adversely the labor market opportunities of native workers, to represent a drain on the welfare and social service system, and to undermine the primacy of the use of English both for instructional purposes in schools and in public discourse. The importance of respondents' perceptions about the impact of immigrants on the state cannot be explained away by the demographic makeup of sample members. A combined analysis of the joint influence of respondents' beliefs and characteristics showed that both are significant predictors of attitudes about the appropriate number of immigrants in New Jersey.

A NATIONWIDE POLL INCORPORATING TESTS OF NEW HYPOTHESES

In June 1993, respondents to a CBS News/*New York Times* poll were asked whether they would like to see the level of immigration to the United States increased, decreased, or kept the same. Answers to these questions were combined with respondents' demographic and socioeconomic characteristics and their opinions to a range of other (sometimes nonimmigration) questions to test conventional theories and also a novel set of hypotheses about the sources of immigration attitudes. Conventional issues focused on the labor market competition hypothesis, the cultural affinity hypothesis, and the cost-benefit (or utilitarian calculus) hypothesis.

Three new theories were also examined: (1) a hypothesis focusing on the health of the economy, according to which respondents who feel that the economy is in the best current condition and likely to grow rapidly in the future are most likely to prefer higher immigration levels; (2) a social and political alienation hypothesis which predicts that residents who are marginalized from mainstream social and political institutions are likely to blame immigrants for part of their problems and to want lower levels of immigration; and (3) a hypothesis related to economic and political isolationism which expects that respondents whose views could most properly be characterized as isolationist will prefer lower levels of immigration than participants with a more global perspective.

Each of these hypotheses received empirical support in the data. Respondents who believed the U.S. economy was getting worse had more negative attitudes toward immigration than those who felt the economy was improving. In addition, believing that the United States would be an economic superpower in the twenty-first century was also correlated with a preference for higher immigration levels. Second, a sense of alienation is an important determinant of immigration attitudes. For example, having a favorable view of Ross Perot or having voted for Perot—taken as signs of alienation from the political mainstream—is associated with a desire for lower levels of U.S. immigration. Finally, having an isolationist mentality has a negative influence on immigration attitudes. For example, those who believe that trading with other countries is bad for the United States, who oppose the North American Free Trade Agreement (NAFTA), and who feel that German and Japanese products are generally inferior to those produced in the United States generally desire lower levels of immigration.

This brief review of the literature on polling data and American attitudes toward immigration supports five main conclusions:

1. When the American public is given a choice, it expresses a preference for European immigrants over those from Asia or Latin America. And when the choice is restricted to the latter two groups, Asian immigrants are generally considered preferable along a number of different dimensions.

2. Whereas the American public is concerned about illegal U.S. immigration, they are generally willing to support only the mildest measures to try to control it. Measures that might have a greater chance of being effective are generally viewed as too unattractive to the majority of American adults.

3. Attitudes often appear ambivalent. In particular, quite disparate responses can be triggered to seemingly similar questions by slight changes in question wording. Some words or phrases appear to have acquired symbolically important meanings to many Americans, and the invocation of these phrases can predispose respondents to react in predictable ways. For example, in each of the following paired comparisons, the category or group that is mentioned first seems to have acquired a quasi-protected status: (a) children versus adults as targeted populations; (b) legal versus illegal immigrants as potentially affected groups; (c) education and health benefits versus welfare benefits; and (d) citizens versus noncitizens.

4. Comparing the responses of all Americans to those of Hispanic Americans reveals that Latinos usually have either the same or more positive assessments about immigration and its consequences than does the general public. This conclusion lends additional support to the cultural affinity hypothesis.

5. Those who have studied the relevance of public opinion to U.S. immigration policy have concluded that foreign policy or business considerations usually dominate, especially when public opinion is not tightly organized into well-defined pressure groups; that sustained public opinion on an issue counts for more than sporadic manifestations of concern; and that the state of the economy shapes the views of policymakers and the general public. Despite professing strong concerns over immigration issues, especially when illegal immigration is presented as a "problem" to survey participants, the general public is substantially more concerned about crime, job opportunities, and family economic security. Perhaps the most surprising finding to emerge from the data is that immigration ranks below "don't know" among the most important problems facing the United States today.

Thomas J. Espenshade

See also: Legislation I: Immigration, Legislation II: Immigrants in America (Part II, Sec. 5); Anti-Immigrant Politics (Part II, Sec. 6); Welfare and Public Benefits (Part II, Sec. 9); Value of an Immigrant, 1871 (Part IV, Sec. 2); Emigration, Emigrants, and Know-Nothings, 1854 (Part IV, Sec. 3).

BIBLIOGRAPHY

Espenshade, Thomas J. "Taking the Pulse of Public Opinion Toward Immigrants." In *Keys to Successful Immigration: Implications of the New Jersey Experience*, ed. Thomas J. Espenshade, pp. 89–116. Washington, DC: Urban Institute Press, 1997.

Espenshade, Thomas J., and Charles A. Calhoun. "An Analysis of Public Opinion Toward Undocumented Migration." *Population Research and Policy Review* 12 (1993): 189–224.

Espenshade, Thomas J., and Katherine Hempstead. "Contemporary American Attitudes Toward U.S. Immigration." *International Migration Review* 30:2 (Summer 1996): 535–70.

Espenshade, Thomas J., and Maryann Belanger. 1998. "Immigration and Public Opinion." In *Crossings: Mexican Immigration in Interdisciplinary Perspectives*, ed. Marcelo M. Suarez-Orozco, pp. 365–403. Cambridge: Harvard University Press, 1998.

———. "U.S. Public Perceptions and Reactions to Mexican Migration." In *At the Crossroads: Mexican Migration and U.S. Policy*, ed.

Frank D. Bean, Rodolfo O. de la Garza, Bryan R. Roberts, and Sidney Weintraub, pp. 227–61. New York: Rowman and Littlefield Publishers, 1997.

Immigration and Naturalization Service. *Statistical Yearbook of the Immigration and Naturalization Service, 1997.* Washington, DC: Government Printing Office, 1999.

Schmidley, A. Dianne, and Campbell Gibson. "Profile of the Foreign-Born Population in the United States: 1997." In Bureau of the Census, *Current Population Reports,* series P23–195. Washington, DC: Government Printing Office, 1999.

Simon, Rita J., and Susan H. Alexander. *The Ambivalent Welcome: Print Media, Public Opinion, and Immigration.* London: Praeger, 1993.

ECONOMICS

INTRODUCTION

*S*ection 7 of Part II of the *Encyclopedia of American Immigration* examines the question of immigrants, immigration, and the economy. Entries in this section include those on immigrant entrepreneurialism, housing and consumption, immigration and immigrants' impact on the American economy, the impact of immigration and immigrants on the economies of the home countries, income and wealth, poverty, and taxation and government spending.

"The Economic Debate over Immigration" by John Herschel Barnhill begins by looking at how the Immigration and Naturalization Act of 1965 changed the profile of immigration to America, and the impact the new wave of immigration would have on government spending. He then examines the political reaction to these immigrants and the perception that they were draining government resources. Finally, he analyzes this argument, as well as those that show that immigrants contribute more to government coffers than they take.

In her entry on entrepreneurialism, Zulema Valdez looks at the various theories concerning ethnic and immigrant entrepreneurship, including the neoclassical, structural, ethnic-network, cultural, and interactive approaches. In addition, she offers a section entitled "Ethnic Entrepreneurship Revisited," where the latest controversies concerning the subject are discussed, including the question of economic mobility versus survival-strategy ethnic entrepreneurship. Finally, Valdez examines some of the negative consequences of ethnic entrepreneurship.

The entry on housing by Nancy Haekyung Kwak examines homeownership versus renting among contemporary immigrants, as well as the history of immigrant housing. She also looks at how immigrants mix their immigrant heritage and their newfound American identity in the ways they furnish and decorate their housing.

In the entry entitled "Impact of Immigration on the American Economy," Tom Macias examines who the "winners and losers" are in an American economy so heavily impacted by immigration. He also studies the diversity of American immigrants and how they affect the nation's overall economic outlook. Finally, he takes a look at how this impact has changed over the years and what the new century will bring.

In the entry entitled "Impact on the Home Country Economy," Rafael Alarcón discusses the various elements implicit in the title, including the effects that remittances have on the economy of the immigrant's country of origin. This includes the uses to which these remittances are put.

In her entry on income and wealth, Rose Ann M. Rentería discusses immigrants in high- and low-income groups before moving on to the question of poverty among immigrants. All of these various levels of income and wealth are looked at in terms of the immigrant's country of origin. In addition, Rentería examines the subject of median income, earnings for year-round workers, labor force participation, and remittances to the home country.

In the entry on poverty by Enrique S. Pumar, the author offers the trajectory of poverty among immigrants, as well as some of the current arguments among scholars concerning immigration and poverty. In addition, the author looks at immigration within the context of the world economy and transnational immigrant communities. Finally, Pumar explores the question of poverty and segmented assimilation of immigrants and some further directions research on the subject is taking.

THE ECONOMIC DEBATE OVER IMMIGRATION

For two hundred years, America has weighed the economic costs and benefits of immigration. As the twentieth century ended, the welcome mat was out, but pressure had been rising since the mid-1960s to reduce the hundreds of thousands of illegal immigrants and the 1 million legal immigrants who come to this country annually.

Until the 1920s, America had been a nation of immigrants. Changes in immigration law in the 1920s made immigration less of an issue for the next forty years. Immigration dropped from 800,000 in 1921 to less than 150,000 in 1929. Then came the Great Depression of the 1930s, and only 23,000 immigrants came in 1933. There were refugees in the 1930s and 1940s, of course, but not many, and most of these were European. After World War II, immigrants were again welcome: America was in a Cold War competition with the Soviet Union for the allegiance of the emerging nations. Initial numbers were small, and the immigrants fit America's style, as many were refugees from wars or totalitarian states.

IMMIGRATION REFORM LEGISLATION

The Immigration and Nationality Act (INA) of 1965 reduced national quotas and shifted emphasis to immigrant family members and those with needed skills. At the time of its passage, most experts thought that the majority of immigrants entering under the new law would be Europeans. But in the 1960s, Europe prospered. At the same time, many Latin American, Asian, and African immigrants came seeking relief from changing political, economic, and social conditions in their home nations. During the ten years after passage of the INA, Asian immigration soared 663 percent, while European immigration fell 38 percent. Total immigration rose 60 percent. Congress set quo-

tas for Latin American countries in 1976. In 1986, Congress imposed penalties on employers of illegal aliens but amnestied illegal aliens in residence before 1982.

Some immigrants seemed undesirable to many Americans. Among these were poor Cubans, Haitians, and Vietnamese. Cubans had been emigrating since Fidel Castro's revolution in the late 1950s. From 1959 to 1973, they were mostly anti-Castro, white, successful, middle class, and skilled. In 1980, as many Americans perceived it, Castro opened his prisons and let go all his prisoners and drug abusers, many of whom were black. These people, known as the Marielitos, because of the Cuban port from which they embarked, mostly moved to established Cuban communities, especially in the Miami area. Then, into neighborhoods unsettled by the newly arrived Marielitos, came Haitian boat people in flight from government repression and hard economic times. They too tended to be black and poor.

Immigrants from Vietnam and Southeast Asia at first were the elite that came after American troops left and Saigon collapsed in 1975. The next wave was still middle class. The third wave was another group of impoverished boat people. Other Asian and Latin American immigrants came as well. Many of these immigrants were easier for native-born Americans to accept. Colombians, Salvadorans, and the Irish were culturally and economically compatible with American ways, and their goals, sanctuary or economic opportunity, fit the mainstream. But some were illegal aliens, part of the 250,000 to 750,000 per year who came through porous borders, most noticeably from Latin America via Mexico to California and the American Southwest. Although Hispanics established ethnic enclaves in many midwestern cities, their major presence and its associated controversy were in the Southwest.

American policy was consistently inconsistent. Amnesties in 1982, 1986, and the late 1990s accomplished little beyond legitimating large numbers of illegal immigrants while leaving larger numbers illegitimate. Inevitably, in the 1990s, a backlash came from Americans who felt that the welcome mat had worn thin.

REACTION

Californians took the lead as the problems that faced Americans generally—a growing gap between rich and poor, rampant crime, moral decay, weakening communities, and increasing racial tensions—appeared in their state first. California, destination for many of the Hispanic immigrants, defined the debate: Bilingual education, required since the 1960s, was unfair and expensive. Immigrants went on welfare, many Californians argued, and ate up taxpayer money. At the same time, a contradictory view arose. Many native-born Americans believed that immigrants were taking jobs and putting native-born Americans on welfare.

California Proposition 187, passed in 1994, denied education, health care, and other public services to illegal immigrants. Immigration supporters claimed that immigrants took the undesirable, low-paying jobs that Americans spurned and moved rapidly from economic burden to economic benefit, eventually bringing additional growth to the economy. The debate was inconclusive in California, after courts overturned many of the proposition's provisions. Nationally, although Congress spent the 1990s passing an average of one immigration reform law per year, the debate was equally inconclusive.

ARGUMENTS FOR RESTRICTION

The harshest anti-immigrant rhetoric had dissipated somewhat by the year 2000 in the face of the nation's longest economic growth period. But it remains below the surface, many experts say, ready to boil over at the first hint of a recession-driven spike in unemployment. Overall, the Bureau of the Census projects a U.S. population in 2050 of 390 million to 520 million under late 1990s immigration policy and enforcement levels. Already, since 1970, the country's population has increased by 60 million, and over half of the increase is from immigrants and their offspring. Restrictionists assume that each new immigrant takes an American job. They note, for example, that black American hotel workers in California decreased by 30

percent while immigrant hotel employment increased 166 percent in the 1980s.

Opponents of immigration argue that unfair immigrant competition puts poor American-born citizens on welfare, increases the income gap, and enables American businesses to get by on cheap labor. Furthermore, restrictionists say, even though the country tightened welfare and excluded new immigrants and illegal aliens, natives are half as likely as immigrants to be on welfare. The annual financial drain of immigration will likely range between $67 and $87 billion a year in the first half of the twenty-first century, an annual tax burden of $166 to $226 a year for each American household.

Welfare for immigrants costs $75 billion per year, not counting the expense of the native poor who end up on welfare after losing their jobs to low-wage immigrants. Restrictionists argue that illegal immigrants commit a criminal act by merely coming. Their arrest rate is higher than average, say anti-immigrant activists, even as the cost to society of imprisonment rises. The State Criminal Alien Assistance Program (SCAAP), which dates from 1994, compensates states and local governments for housing illegal aliens serving time for two misdemeanors or a felony. In 1999, state and local governments filed SCAAP claims of $1.5 billion for 69,502 illegal alien detention-years, an average of over $21,000 per prisoner per year. The program reimbursed slightly under $573 million, only 39 percent of the claimed expenses, leaving nearly $911 million unreimbursed. In 1998, the reimbursement rate was 40 percent.

ARGUMENTS FOR IMMIGRATION

Supporters of immigration contend that America has more jobs than people and that the native population is getting older. The nation needs young immigrants who are willing and able to take on low-end jobs and who bring to America new blood, new ideas, and new perspectives. To maintain the 1989 population level through 2010, the United States will need 500,000 immigrants per year. Even then, the country's median age will still rise.

Supporters of immigration point out that blacks, overrepresented at the low end of the American job ladder, have no fewer problems with immigrants than the majority white population. They recognize that, rather than competing for the same jobs, low-scale immigrants bring new energy that pushes natives up the economic ladder. New black immigrants move into old black neighborhoods as Vietnamese tend initially to cluster near Chinatown. Immigrants bring to the old neighborhoods their vitality, solid family structure, and determination to get ahead and revitalize. The neighborhood turns around, and the old residents benefit, say immigrant supporters in the black community. Statistically, blacks in gateway cities do tend on average to be better off than those in nonimmigrant cities.

Another argument put forward by immigration advocates is that immigrants create their own jobs when they have to. Between 1987 and 1992, minority-owned businesses in New York City proliferated. At the same time, black business ownership rose to almost 36,000 from 17,400; Hispanic businesses more than tripled from 10,000 to over 34,000; and Asian ownership increased from 27,000 to 46,000. In all these statistics, immigrants accounted for 90 percent of these new businesses.

Admittedly, note supporters of immigration, these businesses were not major manufacturing establishments. Immigrants started small, many in service jobs or low-profit businesses that Americans were unable or unwilling to handle. Immigrants established a viable service economy that included delivery services, phone parlors, and remittance shops (where immigrants send money home). Import establishments specialized in the products and novelty items of the immigrants' homeland. Immigrants willingly became day laborers and labor contractors. Many work as grocers and taxi drivers. One examination of taxi licenses showed the pattern of upward mobility, as the predominant nationality of drivers changed—first Russian, then Haitian, then Pakistani. A case of creative hole-filling in the system was when unlicensed Dominican and African cabbies gave ethnic neighborhoods cheap transportation through unlicensed cabs when the legitimate companies would not serve their area. Although small, the businesses have a multiplier effect, with an around-the-clock jitney cab providing three jobs directly, as well as an unknown number to meet the increased demand for gasoline, tires, and maintenance. Jitneys also get the otherwise stranded unemployed affordably out of the community and into the job market. For pro-immigrationists, each employed immigrant is a potential buyer of a house, car, and services. Immigrants, they say, are a boon to the economy.

Although many immigrants work for lower wages, they often take home more pay. The 1990 census recorded a New York City median household income of just under $30,000, about the same as the average for single wage earners. Either there were a lot of overpaid singles or a lot of native-born households

getting by on only one income regardless of racial and ethnic group. For immigrants, individual income was below average, but household income was above by as much as 50 percent. In the Guyanese, Jamaican, Korean, Indian, and Filipino communities, one household might have two, three, or even four earners living together. They may not be related, just strangers becoming family who share costs, economize, and reduce demand for city services.

Restrictionists cite a mid-1990s study by Donald Huddle of Rice University. Huddle found that, on balance, legal and illegal immigration imposed a tax burden of at least $29 billion. Pro-immigrationists counter that immigrants are an asset to the tax rolls, paying more in taxes than they cost in government services. Immigrants pay the same federal and state withholding, sales, property, and transaction taxes that natives do. Critics have charged that Huddle based his conclusions on incomplete data. Pro-immigrationists note that immigrants generally are undercounted. For one thing, censuses are ten years apart; for another, immigrants are not as prompt as natives in reporting changes of address. Because states and localities get federal reimbursement based on the inaccurate census data and because immigrants are undercounted for federal reimbursement to states and localities, the cost may appear greater than it truly is. In actuality, immigrants pay more, but the bookkeeping delays mean that state and local government short-term costs are higher than the federal government reimburses.

Immigrants are in a different labor market than the native population. They are younger—in their teens to thirties—than the graying native population. From this different and otherwise unfilled labor market comes another unquantifiable economic benefit to the native population: Immigrants provide inexpensive services that support natives in maintaining and improving their higher standard of living. For instance, immigrants make possible the cheap day care and low-cost lunches that allow a mother to leave the house and enter the economy. Immigration increases opportunity.

Rather than raising prison costs, immigrants save money because they lower the crime rate. New York City statistics show that immigrant teens commit fewer crimes than natives from similar ethnic or racial groups. Immigrants have a better family support system and live in more vibrant neighborhoods with higher population densities. High population density lowers crime: there is less empty and hidden territory and more people watching the community.

WELFARE REFORM AND IMMIGRANTS

Anti-immigrant forces are well organized. The largest organization is the Federation for American Immigration Reform (FAIR), which dates from 1979 and claimed around seventy thousand members in the late 1990s. Anti-immigration lobbies had some national success in the 1990s. For instance, in 1996, Congress increased funding for border patrols, tightened asylum rules, and encouraged the Immigration and Naturalization Service (INS) to be more aggressive in deporting alien criminals. Welfare reform that same year had a major negative impact on immigrants, denying them access to food stamps and disability assistance. Its harshness toward immigrants led to pressure on governments. States and the federal government restored some welfare benefits for pre-1996 immigrants, but in 2000, the U.S. Supreme Court upheld the welfare restriction laws. One impact of the tightened immigration and welfare rules was a rush by many aliens finally to become citizens. Naturalizations grew from a 1980s average of around 200,000 to a 1993 total of over 950,000. By the time the federal government countered by tightening citizenship procedures in 1998, the new citizens were securely ensconced on the voter registration rolls.

American immigration policy in the 1990s was inconsistent, ebbing and flowing in a futile attempt to accommodate competing pressures and find an equitable solution. Immigration continues at a rate greater than 1 million people each year. As long as the numbers remain high, anti-immigration groups will agitate for tighter controls and lower quotas. Pro-immigrationists will continue to cite economic benefit and economic need. The debate is without end because there is no way of telling how many people the United States can hold without degrading its quality of life, straining its political and economic systems and its social welfare arrangements. Congress modified immigration policy in 1965, 1976, 1978, 1980, 1986, and 1990. Each time, more immigrants came. Asylum law became more liberal nearly every year in the 1990s. At the same time, the INS toughened enforcement, increased border patrols, and deported more people. The immigrants continued to come. More than 10 million legal immigrants came in the 1990s, the largest immigration decade ever. Another 275,000 to 500,000 illegal aliens came each year.

The nonnative population nearly doubled as a percentage of the total between 1970 and 1996; in the latter year, almost one in ten were nonnative. The new mix brought on a revival of the old restrictionist sentiment that had largely disappeared in the 1920s. Still, the door has in no measure begun to close. The debate about the economic costs and benefits shows no sign of ending. As long as the economy holds and the immigrants come, the debate will persist.

John Herschel Barnhill

See also: Collapse of Communism (Part I, Sec. 5); Political, Ethnic, Religious, and Gender Persecution (Part II, Sec. 1); New York City (Part II, Sec. 12); Immigration to Canada, Immigration to Western Europe (Part II, Sec. 13).

BIBLIOGRAPHY

Bennett, David. *The Party of Fear: From Nativist Movements to the New Right in American History.* Chapel Hill: University of North Carolina Press, 1988.

Bodnar, John. *The Transplanted.* Bloomington: Indiana University Press, 1985.

Countryman, Edward. *Americans, a Collision of Histories.* New York: Hill and Wang, 1996.

Dinnerstein, Leonard, and David M. Reimers. *Ethnic Americans.* 4th ed. New York: Columbia University Press, 1999.

Fleming, Donald, and Bernard Bailyn, eds. *The Intellectual Migration: Europe and America, 1930–1960.* Cambridge: Harvard University Press, Belknap Press, 1969.

Handlin, Oscar. *The Uprooted.* 2d ed. Boston: Little, Brown and Co., 1973.

Huddle, Donald. *The Net National Cost of Immigrants.* Washington, DC: Government Printing Office, 1996.

Isbister, John. *The Immigration Debate: Remaking America.* West Hartford, CT: Kumarian Press, 1996.

Immigration and Naturalization Service. *Characteristics of Immigrants: Statistical Yearbook of the Immigration and Naturalization Service.* Washington, DC: Government Printing Office, 1998.

Lacey, Dan. *The Essential Immigrant.* New York: Hippocrene Books, 1990.

Millman, Joel. *The Other Americans.* New York: Viking, 1997.

Olson, James Stuart. *The Ethnic Dimension in American History.* New York: St. Martin's Press, 1979.

Portes, Alejandro, and Rubén G. Rumbaut. *Immigrant America: A Portrait.* Berkeley: University of California Press, 1990.

Reimers, David M. *Still the Golden Door: The Third World Comes to America.* 2d ed. New York: Columbia University Press, 1992.

Salins, Peter D. *Assimilation, American Style.* New York: Basic Books, 1997.

Takaki, Ronald. *A Different Mirror.* Boston: Little, Brown and Co., 1993.

ENTREPRENEURS

While ethnic entrepreneurs have been studied historically—Jewish peddlers and tailors in New York, Japanese restaurant owners and farmers in the western states, and Chinese businessmen located in Chinatowns at the turn of the twentieth century—renewed interest has been sparked in recent years. The current focus and abundant literature on ethnic entrepreneurship reflect the reversal of a trend toward declining business ownership that has taken place since the mid-1970s. Especially apparent has been the increase in small business ownership among the foreign-born, who after ten years in the United States, surpass the native-born in self-employment participation. Small businesses have flourished and self-employment has increased by over 2.1 million between 1975 and 1986. In 1980, 9.2 percent of the foreign-born population in the nation's largest cities was self-employed, as compared to only 7.1 percent of the native-born. Ethnic enterprise participation varies greatly, however, across ethnic groups. While less than 6 percent of foreign- and U.S.-born Mexican males and only 3.1 percent of African Americans engaged in self-employment in 1990, close to 18 percent of foreign- and U.S.-born Korean Americans and Russians (10 percent) were self-employed during this same period.

The Immigration Act of 1965 lowered strict immigration constraints and resulted in the growth of Latinos, Asians, and other immigrants to the United States from every country in the world. According to the 1990 census, almost 20 million people, or 7.9 percent of the total population in the United States, was foreign-born. The Hispanic population in the United States increased by 50 percent from 1980 to 1990, and presently accounts for almost 9 percent of the total population. Blacks increased by 4 million (largely Dominican and Caribbean immigration), and an astonishing 99 percent increase in the Asian population took place in the ten-year period from 1980 to 1990. The contemporary immigrants largely come for eco-

nomic reasons, but there are other reasons as well. Immigrants are not usually from the poorest segments of their countries, since those who seek a better economic future for their family require the means to move. Some immigrants are educated, skilled professionals who find themselves unable to advance in their own country to the extent they can in the United States. The opportunities for socioeconomic mobility and the ability to enjoy the fruits of their labor in the United States elicit a strong pull among these upwardly mobile immigrants. In the United States, the economic structure facing the new immigrants has changed over time, as well. The combination of increasing immigration since the 1970s, the restructuring of the economy, and the increasing competition between the United States and foreign countries in the globalized economy has had a profound effect on the U.S. economy and society. In this context, it has been argued that ethnic entrepreneurship provides opportunities for the economic absorption of ethnic groups who are in the otherwise difficult position of integrating into the U.S. economy.

Social scientists define entrepreneurialism differently. Economists highlight the role of the entrepreneur as a risk-taking, talented innovator who recognizes and pursues new opportunities, thereby altering the existing market economy toward greater efficiency. Most scholars of ethnic entrepreneurship emphasize business ownership by a member of an ethnic or immigrant group and stress individual or group awareness of and participation in extant market opportunities. Ethnic entrepreneurship is broadly defined and may include managers, the pure self-employed (those who have no employees), or business owners who hire workers and work in part for themselves.

The ethnic economy is understood in two ways. Some scholars suggest that the general economy is made up of primary and secondary labor markets. While the primary market consists of good-paying white-collar jobs that reward human capital and afford room for advancement and promotion, the secondary labor market is understood as part-time, seasonal, and low-wage employment with limited advancement opportunities. Some scholars place the ethnic economy in the secondary market. From this perspective, immigrant entrepreneurs are business owners participating in risky business ventures of limited capital, growth, and appeal. Others describe the ethnic economy as existing alongside or as an alternative to the general labor market. Included is the more spatially concentrated ethnic enclave, as well as businesses owned outside the entrepreneur's ethnic neighborhood, such as those owned and operated by middleman minorities. The term ethnic economy is a more general concept of ethnic business ownership that includes the more specific ethnic enclave, business owners and their co-ethnic employees, and self-employed business owners (with no employees).

In this explanation, business ownership is not assumed to be a survival strategy; rather, it may provide an avenue of economic mobility. There is great variation with respect to actual employment and occupations among entrepreneurs in an ethnic economy. Included is marginal, low-skilled, and part-time self-employment—for instance, people who work as domestic workers or gardeners. Additionally, full-time, midrange occupations are often studied, such as the owner or manager of a small retail business or garment factory. Finally, highly skilled technological occupations or those requiring specialized knowledge are included, for example, the owner of a large firm, a physician in private practice, or a freelance computer technician.

THEORIES OF ETHNIC ENTREPRENEURSHIP: NEOCLASSICAL APPROACH

Social scientists and economists concerned with immigrant adaptation and settlement processes have provided competing explanations for ethnic group participation and differences in entrepreneurship. Most focus on the individual or group, socioeconomic or cultural characteristics, or structural determinants.

Neoclassical economists highlight individual-level determinants or structural opportunities in the market to explain ethnic entrepreneurship. The human capital model is often employed by economists, who argue that each individual has an equal opportunity to work based on his education, training, and work experience in a free and competitive labor market. Ethnic entrepreneurs are those ethnic or immigrant group members who have the necessary human capital attainment to translate skills into entrepreneurial opportunities. According to this approach, foreign-earned human capital (acquired in the country of origin) may contribute to entrepreneurial opportunities. The acquisition of technological, professional, or managerial skills and education gives immigrants with foreign-earned human capital an advantage in starting a business in the receiving country. Therefore, immigrants with high human capital attainment will participate in enterprise in above-average numbers, while groups with low educational attainment and skills will not.

To illustrate, foreign-born Mexicans on average have low levels of human capital and face discrimination in the general economy and unequal returns on their human capital investments. Low levels of human capital may limit entry into entrepreneurship, as less than 6 percent of Mexican immigrants in greater Los Angeles (where the largest concentration of Mexicans is found, outside of Mexico City) are self-employed, far below the average rate of entrepreneurship for immigrant groups in the United States. In contrast, Korean immigrants come to this country with many more years of education and professional and managerial experience. High human capital attainment endows Koreans with the knowledge and skills necessary to organize and facilitate business ownership, according to this model. Self-employment of Koreans greatly exceeds that of Mexicans and most other immigrant groups. While the examples presented here lend support for the neoclassical approach, other studies have shown that when controlling for human capital, differences persist in self-employment participation across ethnic groups.

Scholars in support of a second and related position argue that immigrants who participate in ethnic enterprise fare better financially than their worker counterparts in the general labor market, and for this reason, ethnic participation in self-employment may be explained. Simply put, those involved in business ownership will reap bigger financial rewards than they would as wage or salary workers. Again, scholars have found contradictory evidence. Economists argue that discrepancies in income disappear once human capital attainment is accounted for, while others present evidence that suggests that even when holding human capital constant, groups differ with respect to returns on entrepreneurship. Moreover, education and work experience have unequal outcomes on earnings of the foreign-born relative to the native-born, with the native-born consistently generating larger re-

Many immigrant entrepreneurs create niche businesses that serve their own community, like this San Francisco immigrant who creates dresses for the Latino celebration of *quinceanera*, or coming-of-age ceremony. *(Gary Wagner/Impact Visuals)*

turns on their human capital investments than the foreign-born. Finally, among those ethnic groups whose returns are higher, members are more likely to be self-employed, regardless of their individual human capital attainment.

STRUCTURAL APPROACH

Labor market theorists argue that blocked mobility—the discriminatory practice of employers limiting access to opportunities for advancement and promotion among immigrants, minorities, and women—explains ethnic-group entry into self-employment. Scholars argue that limited English, racial discrimination, and few opportunities for employment provide the nec-

essary push toward self-employment. Yet, while blocked mobility can successfully explain particular ethnic-group participation in self-employment—those that enter into ethnic enterprise in above-average numbers relative to the U.S. population—it does not explain those groups with low rates, such as Mexican immigrants or African Americans. Hence, blocked mobility faced by ethnic groups cannot entirely explain participation in self-employment, because disparities exist between groups.

A "demand-side" structural approach suggests the combination of residential segregation and need for businesses providing immigrant services, combined with limited majority-owned businesses in areas of immigrant settlement, culminate in the development of entrepreneurial immigrants. They benefit from opportunities available due to the absence of majority-owned businesses in the area. Middleman minorities, typified by sojourning groups whose ultimate goal is to return to the home country, take on the role of business owner to fill these marginal enterprise opportunities. While in the United States, these groups are willing to face the arduous and antagonistic relationships that often emerge between the larger supplier on one side and the impoverished immigrant customer base on the other. The trade-off for entering into this antagonistic business relationship is the ability to accumulate more financial capital over a shorter period of time than can be gotten in the general labor market. Considered a classic middleman minority, Chinese entrepreneurs can be found catering to residents (co-ethnic or not) in low-income urban areas where opportunities for business ownership are available as a result of majority-group occupational succession.

In response to the neoclassical approaches to economic action that stress methodological individualism or the structural perspective that couches entrepreneurial participation as the outgrowth of market mechanisms and external structural opportunities, social scientists present a different perspective. They claim that to fully understand ethnic entrepreneurship, one must understand the social structure of the ethnic group itself.

ETHNIC NETWORKS

Migrant networks are defined as social relationships between people who share kinship, friendship, or work experience, which develop and adapt to the circumstances of international migration. In migrant networks, the connection between the sending country and receiving country allows for the network to exist.

The Sahadi food market in Brooklyn is run by Palestinian immigrants who import many nuts and dried fruits from their homeland.
(Hazel Hankin/Impact Visuals)

Migration networks produce social capital (relationships between actors that facilitate group or collective action). The support can be economic or noneconomic in character. During the settlement process, a reciprocal relationship pattern develops, in which the new arrivals, once established, take on the role of settled immigrants and maintain the link to the sending country. They provide support such as information on housing, job opportunities, and financial support and other aid to the new arrivals. Social scientists argue that ethnicity may emerge from situations that require the maintenance of networks. Thus, through migration networks, adaptation, and settlement processes, ethnic awareness evolves and ethnic networks form.

The ethnic network provides for the accumulation of financial capital (as well as other types of aid) from its group members. For example, while scholars have shown that the majority of immigrant business owners use personal savings as start-up capital for their fledgling businesses, many others rely on family or their ethnic community to acquire loans, either semiformally or through co-ethnic–owned loan companies

and banks. The ethnic network serves as a source of mutual aid. It benefits borrowers economically through the compensating mechanisms of the network, which ultimately contributes to the advancement of the group as a whole.

Social scientists argue that ethnic networks facilitate ethnic entrepreneurship. An ethnic group can emigrate to a new country and through the use of its network, generate social capital that provides opportunities and resources to establish businesses. Some scholars elaborate on this further and include structural opportunities that exist within the economy as interactive forces that when combined explain ethnic participation and differences in ethnic entrepreneurship.

CULTURAL APPROACH

Professors Ivan Light and Edna Bonacich suggest that class and ethnic resources provided by the ethnic network have played an important role in facilitating ethnic entrepreneurship. Class resources refer to previous wealth or capital, business knowledge or contacts gained through social class position, and bourgeois values. Ethnic resources refer to cultural values, solidarity, attitudes, and specific ethnic group features and identities brought over from the country of origin. Class and ethnic resources combine to propel particular groups into ethnic enterprise. While Light and Bonacich acknowledge that class and ethnic resources are different phenomena, the definitions overlap. Thus, self-employment participation is explained by a combination of inherent ethnic-specific and class-specific characteristics of a particular ethnic group that originate prior to and develop upon arrival to the host society.

Ethnic networks provide class and ethnic resources that serve to provide opportunities for entrepreneurship. To illustrate, Light discusses the formation of rotating credit associations (RCA) among the Japanese (*Ko*) and Chinese (*Hui*), and more recently, among Korean immigrants. Korean immigrants participate in the voluntary rotating credit association known as the *Kye*, created and maintained by the Korean ethnic network. The organization serves to provide money to individual Koreans who join in an effort to accumulate financial capital with which to purchase a business. In RCAs, a sum of money is collected from participating members in a fund and is usually distributed to one participant at a time until all participants receive the sum. Members who receive their share are obligated to remain in the *Kye* until all members take their turn. The creation of the *Kye* is only possible through the ethnic and class resources the network provides. Within the network, social capital in the form of solidarity and trust shapes the behaviors of the individual participants. Trustworthiness and a sense of obligation are critical for the maintenance of *Kyes*, because they depend on the participation of members until the cycle is complete. The closure of ethnic networks creates trustworthiness and thereby ensures the effectiveness of obligations to the *Kye* by clearly defining the group that can benefit from it.

Similar to the ethnic network that provides opportunities for capital accumulation in the form of RCAs, Cuban "character loans" provide the means to accumulate capital among Cuban immigrant recipients. Small loans are granted to Cuban immigrants, without the need for collateral. The character loan is approved or denied by the Cuban bankers based solely on an individual's reputation in Cuba. Again, the use of the ethnic network allows Cuban bankers to lend money backed by ethnic and class resources.

While bankers do not require financial collateral, lenders should not be perceived as performing an irrational or purely altruistic act. Instead, through the mechanisms of mutual obligations and expectations, bankers are making solid business decisions: Cuban bank sources in Miami reported no losses in lending of these character-based loans. The trust bankers put in the co-ethnic recipients of the loans stemmed from the sanctions that recipients could expect if they failed to repay; thus there is an enforceable quality to the trust. The network permits the accumulation of resources among Cuban exiles—individuals who might not have been approved for loans from other sources for the establishment of their businesses.

Moreover, the ethnic network provides a source of cheap labor, as immigrant business owners often hire family and co-ethnic members. The immigrant business sector benefits directly by having access to low-wage labor. Family members experience the obligation to work in family businesses and are often not paid for their labor. However, family employees have their own self-interested motives in the success of the collectively owned business, from which they will actively benefit. Co-ethnic employees provide an easily exploitable low-wage labor pool, since they will not be discriminated against by their employer due to their immigrant status or lack of proficiency in the English language (a very real threat in the general economy). A co-ethnic or family employee may also benefit in rewards conferred by the reciprocal relationship with the employer, as he or she also learns the necessary business and managerial skills to open up a business in the future.

While the cultural approach appears to explain the entrepreneurial pursuits of some groups, such as Cuban and Korean immigrants, a critique can be made that the class and ethnic resources that facilitate entrepreneurship are only deemed ethnic resources in retrospect. Hence, when a member of an ethnic group owns a business, strategies and resources the owner employs to promote business are then labeled as ethnic and ascribed to the entire group. Sociologist Roger Waldinger offers two more criticisms of this approach. First, ethnic groups whose values appear oriented toward entrepreneurship readily become salaried employees in only one or two generations, as they quickly adapt to the host society. This calls into question the suggested primordial quality of the entrepreneurial-oriented ethnic characteristics. Second, he argues that there is weak evidence to link these "business-relevant" values and beliefs to premigration experiences in the country of origin.

INTERACTIVE APPROACH

In *Ethnic Entrepreneurs: Immigrant Business in Industrial Societies*, Waldinger and his colleagues present three sets of characteristics necessary to explain variations in ethnic enterprise: premigration characteristics, circumstances of migration, and postmigration characteristics. Premigration characteristics include the skills that the immigrant group brings with it from its country of origin and include characteristics such as human capital, as well as experience in business or conditions that may contribute to entrepreneurial behavior within a group. Settlement processes, especially whether a group is classified as temporary or permanent, define circumstances of migration. Finally, postmigration characteristics refer primarily to the occupational position of the immigrant group upon entry in the receiving country. Strategic occupational positions—those that provide business opportunities—are explained by prior skills, "random factors," and "cumulative social advantage."

These three factors interact with specific ethnic-group strategies to explain ethnic entrepreneurship, and while premigration characteristics, circumstances of migration, and postmigration characteristics may be different across groups, the strategies employed are very similar. This comprehensive approach has been used to explain entrepreneurship among a variety of ethnic groups in the United States, including African Americans, Chinese, Koreans, and Cubans, as well as ethnic groups in a number of Western industrialized countries.

A similar argument has been presented suggesting that the contextual effects surrounding a particular ethnic group need to be accounted for in any explanation of immigrant entrepreneurship. Important are the characteristics of the immigrant group with respect to human capital attainment, the ethnic community, existing opportunities for entrepreneurship within the economy, and finally, the standing governmental policies of the host society. The combination of contextual effects provides differing "modes of incorporation" necessary to explain the differences that prevail across various immigrant groups.

Important in the interactive model or contextual effects approach is the social structure of the ethnic network itself, which may actually precede ethnic-group awareness. In this interpretation, it is suggested that ethnicity is a response by some ethnic groups to blocked mobility, limited opportunities, or unequal returns on human capital investments in the general labor market. This notion of emergent ethnicity describes resource mobilization as a precursor to

ethnicity, which then becomes instrumental in facilitating ethnic business opportunities for future members within an ethnic group. This approach to ethnicity addresses previous cultural arguments that explain ethnicity as primordial or inherent. The interactive approach and analysis of contextual effects are comprehensive in that they combine structural, cultural, and individual-level factors to explain ethnic entrepreneurship.

ETHNIC ENTREPRENEURSHIP REVISITED

Social scientists concerned with ethnic entrepreneurship have provided competing explanations yet face some similar problems in their arguments. First, in this literature, ethnicity is often treated as monolithic. Further, the social capital, ethnic, and class resources scholars attach to a particular ethnic group are often assumed to be characteristic of and available to the entire ethnic group. Differentiation within an ethnic group—the possibility that members of an ethnic group face different opportunities or experience ethnicity differently—is not entertained. Ethnicity, and therefore ethnic networks, are attributed to the entire group.

Second, scholars of ethnic entrepreneurship have failed to successfully explain why ethnic entrepreneurship is, in fact, "ethnic." A general critique can be made by the creation of the category of "ethnic entrepreneurship." By ascribing ethnic groups to a particular kind of entrepreneurship—that is, an ethnic type—theorists stress the primacy of ethnicity as facilitating and contributing some component part to entrepreneurship. Ethnic entrepreneurship scholars agree that ethnicity provides sources of social capital in the form of bounded solidarity and enforceable trust crucial for ethnic entrepreneurship (in Light's formulation, ethnic and class resources) but in so doing, suggest that those groups who do not engage in self-employment are somehow culturally deficient. Thus specific ethnic groups with high self-employment rates, such as Koreans, are attributed an entrepreneurial advantage stemming from the social solidarity provided by the ethnic identity of the group, while low self-employment rates are explained as due to individual or cultural shortcomings.

In addition, scholars assume a homogeneous group of entrepreneurs emerges from within a single ethnic group. In other words, they suggest members from a particular ethnic group face the same opportunity structures, have similar human capital attainment, and operate within the same kinds of kin and ethnic networks. And there is the assumption that members of the same ethnic group will experience similar entrepreneurial attitudes based on ethnicity, thereby constraining members within an ethnic group to similar entrepreneurial fates. A reformulation of existing theories is needed to account for a variety of individual ethnic experiences. In sum, the literature on ethnic entrepreneurship has neglected to specify the distinct contributions of economic, ethnic, and structural factors on enterprise, while overemphasizing the importance of ethnicity, treated as inherent and monolithic.

While social scientists agree that entrepreneurship may provide opportunities for the economic absorption of ethnic or immigrant groups, they disagree on the extent to which ethnic entrepreneurship succeeds at this task. Two major theoretical approaches dominate the scholarly work in this area. Some scholars argue that ethnic enterprise provides an avenue of socioeconomic mobility among "entrepreneurial immigrants" whose efforts over time realize entry into the middle class. Koreans and Chinese in the United States and Pakistanis in Britain are some examples of groups ascribed this type of entrepreneurial success. In contrast, other social scientists and economists argue that immigrant entrepreneurship is a survival strategy, a response to disadvantage in the labor market that results in peripheral and marginal enterprises plagued with high risks, low returns, and limited growth. West Indians in Britain and Mexicans in the United States have been mentioned in this context.

ECONOMIC MOBILITY VS. SURVIVAL STRATEGY ETHNIC ENTREPRENEURSHIP

Chinese immigrants and their descendants provide a classic example of economically mobile ethnic entrepreneurs. Historically and contemporaneously, Chinese entrepreneurs are found in businesses catering to their own community as well as to the general population. In addition to acting as a middleman minority in depressed areas, Chinese-owned businesses are also found in ethnic enclaves called "Chinatowns" and provide specialty goods and services to their co-ethnic communities. More recently, Chinese entrepreneurs can be found in advanced technology occupations, such as computer consulting and engineering. In sum, this group dominates the market in Chinese consumer products and has also established itself as owners and managers of professional and highly skilled businesses. Consequently, the Chinese are considered highly entrepreneurial, with businesses that range from no employees to one hundred and that are, on average, larger than other ethnic minority businesses. The concentration in above-average jobs among the Chinese has provided strong evidence for scholars to categorize this group as economically mobile, entrepreneurial immigrants, and to conclude that this group has reached socioeconomic parity with whites.

Similarly, Cubans and their descendants are generally described as thriving economically in the Cuban ethnic enclave in Miami. Avenues for entrepreneurship arise from the combination of access to capital—accumulated from their kin and ethnic networks—the available cheap labor from the concentration of immigrants in the area, and finally, business opportunities resulting from the need for specialty goods and services and the rise of manufacturing in the area. Cuban businesses are flourishing, indeed, businesses have grown beyond the enclave in size and amount. By 1982, Cuban-owned businesses had climbed to 21,000 firms, up from 900 in the late 1960s. At the present time, this group has reached socioeconomic levels that are comparable to those of the general population.

In comparison, Mexican immigrants are considered to engage in survival self-employment in response to disadvantage in the labor market. Mexicans face discrimination by employers, a language barrier, low skills, and for many, undocumented status, all of which limit employment options. According to the 1990 census, only 6 percent of the foreign-born population of Mexicans can be found in managerial and professional occupations, while the majority can be found in labor-intensive, low-wage, low-skill jobs. Similarly, self-employed Mexicans are found in marginal enterprises, including labor-only subcontracting or temporary, flexible, and part-time self-employment. They also concentrate in peripheral light manufacturing that includes garment and furniture-making industries, and in the service industry, such as in restaurants and hotels. Moreover, scholars provide some evidence that many Mexicans participate in the informal economy, in unregulated occupations that are generally temporary or poorly paid. Mexicans are largely involuntary entrants, preferring marginal self-employment to the alternative low-wage work or unemployment. The types of occupations in which Mexicans engage lead scholars to conclude that self-employment among this group cannot be considered entrepreneurial, in the sense that there is little hope for growth or mobility.

A reconsideration is necessary to fully understand the implications of ethnic enterprise on economic mobility. First, ethnic entrepreneurship is not a guarantee of economic success, as much of the literature posits. Many have equated high entrepreneurship participation rates with economic mobility or success, yet this relationship has not been fully explored. For example, Koreans in the United States are considered successful entrepreneurial immigrants because their rates of self-employment far surpass that of the general population, more than 17 percent compared to 6.9 percent. However, the emphasis on the types of jobs these entrepreneurs fill is rarely discussed beyond considering in what industry a specific group may cluster. While Koreans may enjoy high rates of entrepreneurship, labeling them as entrepreneurial immigrants who over time will enter the middle class may be premature, unless the type of self-employment in which they are involved provides opportunities that will eventually afford them socioeconomic mobility. Contradictory findings show that while some Koreans have entered professional and skilled businesses, most remain in small businesses and work long hours, with uncertain futures. For example, Light and Bonacich conducted a telephone survey and found Korean proprietors in Los Angeles worked, on average, seventy-nine hours a week in their businesses and suffered physical and mental exhaustion. Similarly, Professors Lucie Cheng and Philip Yang find that although one-third of Korean immigrants in Los Angeles are entrepreneurs, firms "tend to be small, to use family members or a few employees, and are concentrated in retail trade, manufacturing, and services." Although it may be argued that groups with high self-employment rates like Cubans in Miami and the Chinese (7.3 percent and 7.2 percent, respectively) have established patterns of mobility through entrepreneurship, mixed findings for Koreans cannot be readily interpreted as that this group is following in their footsteps.

Similar indeterminate information has been found among Asians (Indians and Pakistanis) in Britain, where many engage in entrepreneurial activities but are found overwhelmingly in small workshops and are not the entrepreneurial elite. These examples illustrate that groups with high entrepreneurship rates vary in their capacity to achieve mobility within the economy.

Scholars have neglected to realize the implications of self-employment participation rates among ethnic groups. By hastily presenting two outcomes—that immigrants exhibiting high entrepreneurship rates will achieve economic mobility while those with low rates will not—the two trends of ethnic entrepreneurship are reinforced and presented as separate phenomena,

each trend necessary to explain the circumstances of particular ethnic groups. In so doing, the actual relationship between an ethnic groups' self-employment rate and economic mobility is overlooked, and those within-groups differences are not examined at all. While in some cases high entrepreneurship and economic mobility are analogous, for example, among the Chinese, the Korean case remains ambiguous.

Depending on their market position, members of specific self-employment networks face different opportunities and resources that are available to them through their networks. Economic mobility is not ensured by virtue of becoming self-employed. Rather, some networks use self-employment as a "survival strategy" or "economic lifeboat"—an alternative to the labor market where none may exist. Although Koreans enter into self-employment in above-average numbers and their earnings are better than Korean workers in the general labor market, they are not assured economic mobility. More research on this topic is necessary in order to illuminate this discussion.

While ethnic entrepreneurship provides an avenue of upward mobility for some and is limited to a strategy of survival for others, the predominant trend of ethnic entrepreneurship today is the small-business owner who enlists the help of an unpaid family laborer (much like their nonethnic counterparts). The majority of small businesses do not hire employees, and those that do hire very few, usually co-ethnics. Therefore, while instances of ethnic entrepreneurship do exist (for instance, the Chinese immigrant who turned his small family-run Chinatown restaurant into a successful and lucrative business that will be passed down to his son), this is the exception rather than the rule.

NEGATIVE CONSEQUENCES

Social capital, ethnic, and class resources provide opportunities for entrepreneurship among some groups, however, some scholars argue that while internal social structures benefit members of ethnic group networks, others experience negative consequences. Moreover, questions have been raised about the ramifications of a group that depends on internal dynamics of that group for support, thereby effectively closing itself off from the "outside world."

Negative effects on integration with the greater society at large may occur for group members as a result of ethnic network constraints. For example, the closure of social networks is important for the group because it creates trustworthiness and ensures the effectiveness of obligations. Social closure defines the group that can gain access to the benefits of membership. However, breaking trust or not fulfilling an obligation does occur, with contrary effects for group members. One example of this is linked to rotation credit associations. Individuals who join an RCA may benefit from membership by acquiring an amount of financial capital otherwise unattainable. However, there have been instances where a participating member acquires the capital and breaks the trust by forfeiting payment, leaving other participants empty-handed. Legal recourse is limited, since RCAs are not legal or advertised by the group. Sanctions may be imposed upon the individual member, although retribution is rare.

Fundamental to the successful network is the ability of actors to control actions of members through sanctions, which benefit the group as a whole but may have consequences for the individual. The importance of closure within the confines of particular industries should not be dismissed. For example, the construction industry is one that requires contractors to form social networks for business opportunities, since many contractors know each other, share business opportunities or leads, and often share the same suppliers and employees. Here contractors, subcontractors, and suppliers benefit from closure, in that the trust generated between individuals is critical to their economic survival. Becoming known for quality craftsmanship, paying employees and suppliers in a timely manner, and finishing a job on time are all factors that contribute to establishing a good reputation. A good reputation is necessary, as it allows credit to be established between the contractor and suppliers, which is crucial in order to stay in business. A contractor may have difficulty establishing these key requirements, effectively locking himself out of job opportunities. In addition, a contractor who fails in his obligation to pay a supplier, risks future job opportunities.

While the ethnic network provides economic and noneconomic support for its members, unintended consequences may result. By maintaining and reproducing an alternative system of support within the ethnic network, integration into mainstream society (including the greater economy) may be hindered. Segregation, whether imposed from without or stemming from within, can result in detrimental effects for the group. For example, some evidence has shown that Cuban immigrant employees in Miami—where the highest concentration of Cubans reside and work—receive less wages than Cuban immigrants who live outside Miami when controlling for human capital. Moreover, the types of jobs employees hold and pos-

sibilities for advancement may be more limited in ethnic economic arrangements. Diminished returns and opportunities among these Cuban immigrant employees suggest that exploitation of workers by co-ethnic employers may be greater within the network structure than outside of it.

In addition, a "free-riding" problem may erupt in the community, whereby membership in the group allows for excessive expectations and obligations made by members on the more successful member—often the entrepreneur. The expectations of mutual aid for employment and financial support leveled at employers may turn a promising business into a private charity. In other situations, some individual members of the ethnic group, or sometimes the entire group, experience what amounts to censorship or restrictions on individual freedoms. Thus, the constraints and expectations placed on individuals by the group can manifest both positive and negative consequences.

It has been argued that social constraints within the ethnic network may have an impact on those individuals or groups that are external to it. Outsiders who attempt to enter into situations where ethnic networks are situated may be banned (although that is often not acknowledged publicly) from job opportunities. In sum, migrant and ethnic networks serve as positive sources of mutual aid that ease settlement and provide opportunities for adaptation for individuals who have met with adverse consequences in the external society. However, negative consequences may occur as a result of these same network processes affecting individuals who are constrained by their community or individuals and groups located outside them.

Ethnic networks provide expectations and obligations of mutual aid along with information channels to find work and a place to live—crucial elements for successful incorporation into a new society. Similarly, family and co-ethnic networks provide sources of ethnic and class resources that facilitate entrepreneurial opportunities. Through solidarity and enforceable trust, immigrants and ethnic-group members provide alternative means for labor-market participation in the face of limited opportunities or provide new ones for entrepreneurial endeavors. Social closure, sanctions, and the excessive demands mutual aid places on the more successful members of the group may also result in detrimental effects, stalling integration of the group and sometimes barring individuals outside the group from the benefits of membership, thereby limiting opportunities.

The research on ethnic networks in facilitating entrepreneurship contributes to an understanding of group processes in the face of adversity. While not entirely optimistic, since critical reflection has uncovered negative consequences both within and outside the group, ethnic networks are clearly important in creating opportunities in a market economy to realize both economic and noneconomic gains.

If the current economic trend continues—with respect to the globalization of the world economy, the effects of economic restructuring felt in the U.S., and the patterns of immigration, including the settlement and adaptation strategies of immigrant groups—ethnic entrepreneurship will continue to furnish opportunities for economic integration. Yet, participation in entrepreneurship varies dramatically by ethnic group and effect—that is, whether it provides an avenue of economic mobility or a survival strategy for particular groups. Among the factors important to consider in explaining diversity in entrepreneurial outcomes are individual-level determinants such as human capital attainment, the social structure of the ethnic group—including the contributions of ethnic and class resources and social capital found in particular ethnic networks—and structural opportunities found in the economy. Ultimately, the more comprehensive explanations combine structural, cultural, and individual-level analyses. However, while the literature presents many perspectives with which to understand ethnic enterprise, much of the research to date treats ethnicity as monolithic and of primary importance in determining ethnic-group participation and differences in entrepreneurship. Hence, few attempts have been made to explain the origin of ethnicity or the characteristics that are ascribed to it in a particular ethnic network. Hence, more research is needed to reveal the specific contributions of ethnicity and replace monolithic interpretations of ethnicity with alternative, dynamic definitions that can begin to account for within-group differences.

Zulema Valdez

See also: Economics I: Pull Factors (Part II, Sec. 1); Income and Wealth (Part II, Sec. 7).

BIBLIOGRAPHY

Aldrich, Howard, Trevor P. Jones, and David McEvoy. "Ethnic Advantage and Minority Business Development." In *Ethnic Communities in Business: Strategies for Economic Survival*, ed. Robin Ward and Richard Jenkins, pp. 189–210. Cambridge: Cambridge University Press, 1984.

Aldrich, Howard E., and Roger Waldinger. "Ethnicity and Entrepreneurship." *Annual Review of Sociology* 16 (1990): 111–35.

Bonacich, Edna, and John Modell. *The Economic Basis of Ethnic Solidarity: Small Business in the Japanese-American Community*. Berkeley: University of California Press, 1980.

Borjas, George J. *Friends or Strangers: The Impact of Immigrants on the American Economy*. New York: Basic Books, 1990.

Cheng, Lucie, and Philip Q. Yang. "Asians: The 'Model Minority' Deconstructed." In *Ethnic Los Angeles*, ed. Roger Waldinger and Mehdi Bozorgmehr, pp. 305–41. New York: Russell Sage, 1996.

Chiswick, Barry R. *Income Inequality: Regional Analysis Within a Human Capital Framework*. New York: National Bureau of Economic Research: Columbia University Press, 1974.

Coleman, James S. "Social Capital in the Creation of Human Capital." *American Journal of Sociology* 94 (1988):S95–S121.

Fairlie, Robert W., and Bruce D. Meyer. "Ethnic and Racial Self-Employment Differences and Possible Explanations." *The Journal of Human Resources* 31 (1996):757–91.

Granovetter, Mark. "Economic Action and Social Structure: The Problem of Embeddedness." *American Journal of Sociology* 91 (1985):481–510.

Hakim, Catherine. "Self-Employment in Britain: Recent Trends and Current Issues." *Work, Employment and Society* 2(4) (1988): 421–50.

Light, Ivan Hubert. *Ethnic Enterprise in America: Business and Welfare Among Chinese, Japanese and Blacks*. Berkeley: University of California Press, 1972.

Light, Ivan, and Edna Bonacich. *Immigrant Entrepreneurs: Koreans in Los Angeles*. Los Angeles: University of California Press, 1988.

Portes, Alejandro, and Robert Bach. *Latin Journey: Cuban and Mexican Immigrants in the United States*. Berkeley and Los Angeles: University of California Press, 1985.

Portes, Alejandro, and Ruben G. Rumbaut. *Immigrant America: A Portrait*. Berkeley and Los Angeles: University of California Press, 1990.

Portes, Alejandro, and Julia Sensenbrenner. "Embeddedness and Immigration: Notes on the Social Determinants of Economic Action." *American Journal of Sociology* 93 (1993): 1320–50.

Sanders, Jimy M., and Victor Nee. "Limits of Ethnic Solidarity in the Enclave Economy." *American Sociological Review* 52 (1987): 745–73.

———. "Social Capital, Human Capital, and Immigrant Self-employment: The Family as Social Capital and the Value of Human Capital." *American Sociological Review* 61 (1996): 231–49.

Schumpeter, Joseph A. *Essays on Entrepreneurs, Innovations, Business Cycles, and the Evolution of Capitalism*. New Brunswick, NJ: Transaction Publishers, 1989.

Swedberg, Richard, and Richard Granovetter, eds. *The Sociology of Economic Life*. Boulder, Co: Westview Press, 1992.

Tilly, Charles. "Migration in Modern European History." In *Human Migration, Patterns and Policies*, ed. William S. McNeill and Ruth Adams, pp. 48–72. Bloomington: Indiana University Press, 1978.

Waldinger, Roger. "Immigrant Enterprise: A critique and reformulation." *Theory and Society* 15 (1986):249–85.

Waldinger, Roger, Howard Aldrich, Robin Ward, and associates. *Ethnic Entrepreneurs: Immigrant Business in Industrial Societies*. Newbury Park, CA: Sage Publications, 1990.

HOUSING

Housing represents more than a roof overhead or shelter from the elements. Housing patterns reflect and maintain the occupants' vision of their own family, their financial prospects, their educational resources, and their livelihood. Although Americans generally participate in a cultural valuation of the single-household suburban home as a source of morality, clean living, freedom, and family unity, immigrants have exhibited different housing needs, preferences, and patterns of consumption.

HOMEOWNERSHIP

Immigrants have typically demonstrated less interest in homeownership than native-born consumers, though this varies between different nationalities. Using New York City as an example, European and Chinese immigrants exhibit the highest rates of homeownership, and Dominicans and Puerto Ricans the lowest. Moreover, immigrants face particular housing needs, as they usually arrive with a limited commitment to homeownership in the new country, a need for alternative credit and mortgage financing systems, diverse housing preferences, and oftentimes language and cultural barriers to overcome. These problems are not to be underestimated; the extremely low rate of Latino homeownership in urban centers has been often attributed to the discrimination toward Spanish-speakers, to the development of Spanish-speaking ethnic enclaves, and to the difficulty in acquiring information, credit, and fair housing without fluency in English.

Immigrant patterns of housing consumption and, most particularly, home ownership vary widely depending on length of stay. As the length of residency extends, the likelihood of homeownership increases. By the thirty-sixth year of residence, demographic statistics demonstrate that the immigrant is just as likely as the native-born to be a homeowner. As immigrants stay in the country longer, assimilate into the larger culture, learn more English (if necessary), acquire more financial flexibility and capital, and learn more about the local housing market, they are more likely to purchase homes and discontinue rentals.

According to the Fannie Mae Foundation's 1997 study of immigrant housing, in 1975–80, only 37 percent of the 2.44 million immigrants maintained separate households, and 78 percent of these households rented; ten years later, these same immigrants had a 42 percent separate-household rate and a 47 percent rate of home ownership. According to this same study, immigrants also tended to quickly close the homeownership rate gap between themselves and native-born contemporaries. Obviously, as immigrants became acclimated to the American housing market and culture, they chose to participate in more economically profitable housing investments.

At the same time, immigrants tend to spend disproportionately more of their income on housing than native-born residents, whether they are renters or homeowners. The disparity seems to come more from unequal wage earnings than housing costs; as immigrants assimilate, and as their wage earnings rise to comparable levels, the percentage of their income devoted to housing drops. Housing consumption increases rapidly with assimilation into American society (see Figure 1).

When immigrants do manage to overcome these difficulties and purchase homes, they tend to buy homes predominantly in urban centers. Whether they own or rent, immigrants tend to gravitate toward heavily immigrant cities such as Miami, Los Angeles, New York, Chicago, San Francisco, Houston, and San Diego. In 1980, four out of every ten immigrants lived in either the New York or Los Angeles area, and New York, Los Angeles, Chicago, San Francisco, and Miami held 46 percent of the total immigrant population from 1965 to 1980.

Owning one's own home is a part of the American dream that draws immigrants to this country. This achievement is aided by bilingual real estate brokerages like this office in New York's Chinatown. *(Anne Burns)*

These urban immigrants are more likely to occupy crowded housing units in these cities; housing researchers Nancy McArdle and Kelly S. Mikelson have demonstrated that from 1980 to 1989, immigrants were ten times more likely than the native-born to occupy housing with more than one occupant per room. Besides crowded quarters, immigrants tend to share housing with more than one family. A number of reasons can account for this housing pattern: Immigrants may need to share housing because of limited financial resources, they may be helping or receiving help from other newly immigrated families, or they may be planning and saving for future residential upward mobility. As homeowners—or, more commonly, as renters in primarily urban settings—immigrant's choice of housing has proved crucial to the maintenance of local economies. The widespread and ever-increasing demand for accommodation has consistently revitalized housing production and the local

tax base, despite concerns that immigrants threaten the cultural identity of the city and of the nation at large.

HISTORY OF IMMIGRANT HOUSING

To the extent that almost all Americans were at one point immigrants, the history of immigrant housing is, in effect, the history of American housing writ large. However, immigration did not become a focus of such rampant and historically important nativist reaction until the nineteenth century, when the numbers of continental European, Irish, and, to a lesser extent, Chinese immigrants began to disturb the previous, primarily British immigrant population. The coinciding industrial revolution did not ease American anxiety, and industrialists and moralists

Figure 1
Housing Ownership/Rental Rates for Immigrant Population in United States—1980–2010

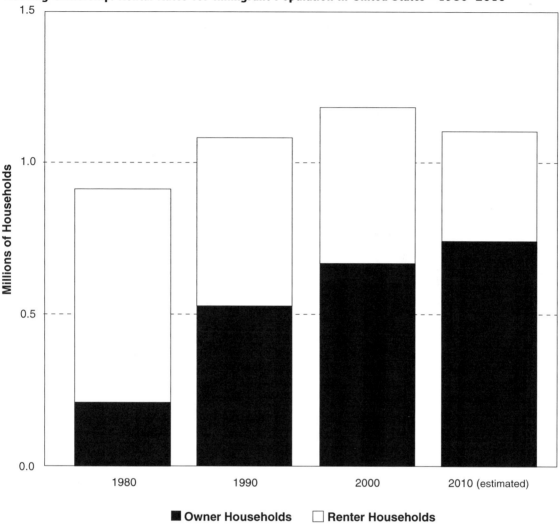

■ **Owner Households**   □ **Renter Households**

Source: John R. Pitkin, Dowell Myers, Patrick A. Simmons, and Isaac F. Megbolugbe. "Immigration and Housing in the United States: Trends and Prospects. Report of Early Findings from the Fannie Mae Foundation Immigration Research Project." Washington, DC: Fannie Mae Foundation, 1997.

attempted to establish an Americanization program through model housing in the early 1820s and 1830s. By developing model housing for newly immigrant factory workers, these reformers hoped to establish an American identity through architecture.

These attempts quickly deteriorated in the face of the huge influx of Irish workers in the late 1840s, and German, Irish, Slavic, and other immigrants found themselves increasingly occupying shantytowns and tenements in the factory towns and large cities of the Northeast and Midwest. Shantytowns and tenements were especially prevalent in big immigrant urban centers such as New York and Boston, as well as in New England and Pennsylvania mill towns. The typical home in these factory towns consisted of a tiny parlor,

a slightly larger family space, and extremely limited sleeping quarters (often a single bedroom in the back for an entire family). Despite the already overcrowded condition of most homes, immigrants often had to accommodate more than their nuclear family in their residential space. Slavic steelworkers in Pennsylvania, for example, could not subsist on their daily wage of $1.65 and had to take in boarders to make the rent.

Tenement flats were even less welcoming than some factory-town homes, consisting of singularly cramped quarters with poor ventilation, and extremely hazardous health conditions. Most early housing for immigrant workers, whether in factory towns or large cities, shared the common traits of poor sanitation, limited light, and extreme overcrowding. The Lower East Side in New York typified the densely packed housing of immigrant households throughout the nineteenth century. Nonetheless, immigrants more often than not invested both emotionally and financially in their homes, saving carefully and adorning even the simplest homes with such items as a piano or lace curtains.

If European immigrants encountered extremely crowded housing conditions, Asian immigrants, most of whom flocked to urban centers in California, fared no better. Angry white Californians (including recent Irish immigrants) opposed Chinese and Japanese immigrants' occupation of housing outside designated ethnic ghettos throughout the nineteenth and twentieth centuries. Mexicans, blacks, and Jews likewise encountered discrimination, with restrictive laws prohibiting certain housing sales throughout the early 1900s. In 1948, the Supreme Court ruled that such discriminatory contractual agreements were illegal, though discrimination continued under various guises. For example, zoning measures continued to discriminate against immigrants, banning such typically immigrant behaviors and needs as multiple-family dwelling units and immigrant food stands in residential areas. Although the Fair Housing Act of 1968 attempted to address some of this discrimination by making it illegal for landlords, mortgage providers, realtors, and others in the housing industry to discriminate based on race and national origin, such segregation continues even today. As sociologists Douglas Massey and Nancy Denton point out, 98 percent of housing in the United States is private and therefore more open to the possibility of residential segregation.

PRESERVING AMERICAN IDENTITY IN IMMIGRANT HOUSING

Concern over the American identity is not a recent phenomenon, and neither is its appearance in the debate over immigrant housing. From the early nineteenth century on, Americans of varying backgrounds and status have exhibited a profound concern over the increasing influx, first of southern and eastern Europeans, and then of Asians, Latinos, Middle Easterners, and Africans. This concern manifested itself in early-nineteenth-century debates over architecture. That century witnessed one of the first concerted efforts to "save" a preindustrial, unified, wholly American past, as Colonial Revivalists celebrated and encouraged a "pure" nationalist American architectural

style. This historic revivalist fervor struck a chord with many architects and architectural firms. Peabody and Stearns, J. Frederick Kelly, George Howe, Charles Morse Stotz, William Lawrence Bottomley, Thomas Tileston Waterman, Richard Koch, John Gaw Meem, and A. Page Brown are only a few of the architects who fully embraced a return to previous architectural styles and community ethos. These architects hailed from locales as divergent as New England, the old South, the Southwest, and the West Coast. While they varied in origin and in where they built, these architects all shared a belief that architecture needed to emphasize and celebrate a declining white past, one that did not bear witness to the many difficulties of nineteenth- and twentieth-century immigration. Charitable institutions likewise began adopting these revivalist styles in the mid-nineteenth century, hoping to Americanize immigrants through their choice of building structure.

At the same time, immigrants themselves attempted to claim a traditional landscape in the design of their homes. Dell Upton, an architectural historian, describes this construction of tradition as an attempt on the part of immigrants to establish some claim to the United States. The Chinatowns in both New York City and San Francisco were originally designed by white architects and populated by Asian residents primarily to promote ethnotourism, "exotic" appeal, and the inevitable profits that could be made from such stratagems. (San Francisco's Chinatown, for example, regularly featured opium tours during the early years of Chinese immigration in the nineteenth century.) Asian immigrants have since relied upon, celebrated, protested, and otherwise engaged with their Chinatowns, Japantowns, and Koreatowns. African Americans have likewise engaged in this complicated process of myth making and reconstructing tradition; in Washington, D.C., the local community chose to decorate a side street with commemorative Ndebele housing decorations, calling upon a mythicized immigrant past in their choice of ornament. Although most slaves were stolen and bought from West Africa, African Americans claimed a southern African (Ndebele) and pan-African identity in their choice of housing decoration.

Throughout American history, immigrants have faced discriminatory and financial limits on their housing options. Often arriving with little money and unfamiliar with America's system of home financing, they have generally opted for rental housing, at least at first. At the same time, they have usually been shunted—or they have chosen, for cultural reasons—to live in overcrowded urban ghettos where miserable housing conditions prevailed. However, over time, immigrants displayed the same desire and capacity for homeownership as native-born Americans, oftentimes blending a mix of traditional and newly acquired styles in decorating their homes.

Nancy Haekyung Kwak

See also: Settlement Patterns (Part II, Sec. 3); Family, Segmented Assimilation (Part II, Sec. 4); Income and Wealth (Part II, Sec. 7).

BIBLIOGRAPHY

Halpern, Robert. *Rebuilding the Inner City: A History of Neighborhood Initiatives to Address Poverty in the United States.* New York: Columbia University Press, 1995.

Krivo, Lauren J. "Immigrant Characteristics and Hispanic-Anglo Housing Inequality." *Demography* 32:4 (1995): 599–615.

Massey, Douglas S., Andrew B. Gross, and Kumiko Shibuya. "Migration, Segregation, and the Geographic Concentration of Poverty." *American Sociological Review* 59 (1994): 425–45.

Massey, Douglas S., and Nancy A. Denton. "American Apartheid: Segregation and the Making of the Underclass." *American Journal of Sociology* 96 (1990): 329–58.

Pitkin, John R., Dowell Myers, Patrick A. Simmons, and Isaac F. Megbolugbe. "Immigration and Housing in the United States: Trends and Prospects. Report of Early Findings from the Fannie Mae Foundation Immigration Research Project." In *Fannie Mae Foundation Working Paper.* Washington, DC: Fannie Mae Foundation, 1997.

Schill, Michael H., and Samantha Friedman. "The Housing Conditions of Immigrants in New York City." In *Fannie Mae Foundation Working Paper.* Washington, DC: Fannie Mae Foundation, 1998.

Upton, Dell. *Architecture in the United States.* Oxford: Oxford University Press, 1998.

Waldinger, Roger. "Immigration and Urban Change." *Annual Review of Sociology* 15 (1989): 211–32.

Warner, Sam Bass, Jr. *The Urban Wilderness: A History of the American City.* Berkeley: University of California Press, 1995.

Wright, Gwendolyn. *Building the Dream: A Social History of Housing in America.* Cambridge: MIT Press, 1981.

$\mathcal{I}$MPACT OF IMMIGRATION ON THE AMERICAN ECONOMY

$\mathcal{T}$he surge of anti-immigration politics that erupted in the mid-1990s brought back into the limelight the ongoing debate over the economic impact of immigration on American society. At the national level, the principal anti-immigration legislation approved by Congress during this period was the Illegal Immigration Reform and Immigrant Responsibility Act (IIRIRA) of 1996, which increased restrictions on illegal immigrant access to federally funded welfare benefits and provided greater resources to the U.S. Border Patrol, allowing it to double its staff from five thousand to ten thousand in a four-year period. Another federal law passed in 1996, the Personal Responsibility and Work Opportunity Act, also known as the Welfare Reform Act, excluded even legal immigrants, that is, permanent residents, from participating in most social welfare programs.

Despite the national scope of IIRIRA and the Welfare Reform Act, the one attempt at lawmaking that stands out as most emblematic of the immigration controversy during the 1990s was at the state level. Proposition 187, approved by 59 percent of California voters in 1994, called for measures much more severe than those specified nationally, including restricting the access of illegal immigrant children to public schools, prohibiting illegal immigrants from attending community colleges or institutions in either of the two California university systems, limiting the use of public health facilities by illegal immigrants to emergency care, and requiring that state-run offices report suspected illegal immigrants to law enforcement authorities. Shortly after its approval, lawsuits filed by opponents of Proposition 187 questioning the proposition's constitutionality blocked its implementation.

Popular political support for restrictive legislation such as IIRIRA and Proposition 187 suggests a general belief among Americans in the 1990s that immigration, especially illegal immigration, has a negative impact on the United States economy and, perhaps more important, on the life chances and opportunities of nonimmigrants who must function within it. Though part of the broader discussion of the effects of immigration revolves around noneconomic questions such as English-language acquisition and cultural assimilation, what follows here is a summary of current socioeconomic research on the economic impact of immigration on American society. As will be shown, this is a topic upon which even the experts cannot entirely agree.

THE NEW IMMIGRATION

The legal immigration of nearly 10 million persons into the United States during the 1990s surpassed the previous peak of 8.8 million reached during the first ten years of the twentieth century, making the past ten years the decade with the highest amount of immigration in the nation's history. Including some 3 million undocumented individuals who have come to stay, immigrants have added nearly 5 percent to the United States population since the 1990 census. Between 1991 and 1997, the countries sending the largest amount of immigrants were Mexico (1,800,576), the Philippines (400,952), and China (306,640). The current origin of immigrants, 45 percent of whom come from Latin America and 31 percent of whom come from Asia, contrasts greatly with immigration at mid-century, when over half of the immigrants entering the United States came from Europe. This massive shift in the countries of origin is directly related to the Immigration and Nationality Act of 1965, which repealed a highly restrictive quota based on national origin and gave preferences based on family reunifi-

Many native-born Americans fear labor competition from immigrants, but numerous studies find that unskilled immigrants, like these Guatemalan day laborers in Brooklyn, tend to take jobs that Americans do not want. *(Catherine Smith/Impact Visuals)*

cation and skills needed in the U.S. economy. At least one prominent economist has argued that in addition to changing the racial and ethnic composition of the U.S. immigrant population, the shift in immigrants' countries of origin since 1965 has negatively affected the "quality" of immigrants and their descendants in the U.S. labor force. By this, immigration scholar George Borjas means that the "relative skills of successive immigrant waves declined over much of the postwar period," and "it is unlikely that recent immigrants will reach parity with the earnings of natives during their working lives." Beyond the implications this has for the lives of immigrants themselves, Borjas believes the presence of these lower-skilled immigrants in the U.S. labor market may explain in part the lower earnings of unskilled native workers during the 1980s. Moreover, the higher rates of participation among recent immigrant waves in welfare programs and their use of public services present additional fiscal costs that must be paid eventually by all Americans through taxation.

GAINERS AND LOSERS

Other research in this area, most notably that conducted by the National Research Council (NRC) in 1997, takes a more circumspect approach to the overall impact immigration has had on the U.S. economy, finding that although there is good reason to be concerned about the rising costs of immigration, it is clear that much of American society benefits both directly and indirectly from the presence of immigrant labor. Put in crude economic terms, immigration produces both gainers and losers. On the winning side are business owners, highly skilled workers, and the consumers of goods and services produced by immigrant labor. Of these three categories, the benefits accruing to business owners and consumers are perhaps most obvious: Service providers and producers of goods may cut costs and increase profits by hiring less-skilled immigrant labor, while part of the savings, as it were, may be passed on to the consumer as well. The benefits earned by highly skilled employees are

Many immigrants contribute to urban economies by opening modest businesses, like this Pakistani immigrant in front of his newsstand.
(Donna Binder/Impact Visuals)

somewhat more indirect and depend upon their degree of job specialization and their complementary relationship with immigrant labor. Put simply, another way business owners may use the money they save through immigrant employment is by hiring highly trained workers and professionals with specialized skills who will, presumably, also work to increase profits.

On the losing side of the immigration bargain are those domestic workers for whom immigrant workers represent a close substitute in the labor market, that is, less-skilled workers who compete directly with immigrants for jobs and who may find their wages lowered because of this. Occupying this category are native-born workers with low levels of education, immigrants from earlier waves of immigration, and native-born members of minority groups. Regarding the last category, there is some debate over the impact immigration has had on the lives of African Americans in particular. The NRC finds that although it is likely some blacks have lost jobs to immigrants in areas where there is a large concentration of immi-

grants, most blacks do not live in these areas and thus find their economic opportunities tied largely to other factors. Other researchers, such as Frank Bean and Stephanie Bell-Rose, have been less sanguine about the question of labor substitution and argue that although many native-born U.S. workers receive positive economic benefits from immigration, these benefits generally do not extend to African Americans. Generally, econometric studies conducted in U.S. cities find the impact of immigration on domestic wages to be negligible, with a 10 percent increase in the immigrant workforce associated with a reduction in average wages of less than 5 percent.

Balancing the positive and negative effects described above, the NRC concludes that the U.S. economy as a whole benefits, if only slightly, from immigration, with its gross domestic product gaining anywhere from $1 billion to $10 billion a year from immigrant labor participation, a modest contribution to an annual total of roughly $7 trillion. Even this narrowly positive assessment, however, must be tempered with other research that finds the benefits of immigration to be highly concentrated among farmers, hotel and restaurant owners, and other business owners who benefit directly from the lower input costs of immigrant employment. In addition, the fiscal impact of immigrants' use of public services and their ability to contribute to government revenue through taxation has caused many to question the value of what they consider to be liberal immigration policy. In sum, the macrolevel benefit of present immigration on the U.S. economy appears to be marginal, at best.

IMMIGRANT DIVERSITY

An aggregate snapshot of the economic impact of immigration tends to gloss over two important factors central to the immigration debate, namely, the diversity within the present population of immigrants entering the United States, and changes that may take place within this population over time. As already noted, the composition of the immigrant population in the United States has shifted over the course of the twentieth century from being primarily of European origin to being primarily of Latin American and Asian origin. Beyond these obvious national differences, however, the truly significant increase in diversity among the new immigrants derives from the fact that they bring with them greater variation in occupational skills than did their predecessors. Today's immigrants as a group occupy both high-skill and low-skill positions, with Asians often entering the workforce with high levels of training and education, some of which they may have received in the United States, and Latin Americans tending to bring with them few skills and little formal education. In contrast to the European immigrants of the early part of the twentieth century, who arrived at the bottom of the skills hierarchy, and contrary to the assertions that immigrant quality has decreased, evidence from the 1990 census suggests that the contemporary immigrant population in the United States is exceptional for its level of socioeconomic diversity, which in some aspects is similar to that of the native population. At 20 percent, the rate of college completion among immigrants is just shy of that for Americans in general (23 percent). Among some groups, levels of educational attainment are extraordinary. Sixty-five percent of Asian Indians entering the United States, for example, are college graduates, and in regions where immigrants concentrate, such as southern California, highly educated

immigrants occupy a large portion of professional positions in pharmacy, dentistry, and engineering.

On the other end of the scale, approximately 3 percent of the children of Mexican immigrants live in a household headed by a college graduate. Lower levels of education combine with proximity to their country of origin to make Mexicans one of the immigrant groups least likely to become U.S. citizens. Not coincidentally, many Mexican immigrants occupy low-paying jobs in agriculture, an industry dependent on undocumented labor—somewhere between 20 and 40 percent of the nation's 2 to 3 million farmworkers work in the country illegally. Given the size of the Mexican immigrant population—22 percent of the foreign-born population in the United States in 1990—if Mexicans were not included in the calculation, immigrants in the United States would actually be more likely to reach college than native-born Americans. As two sociologists specializing in this area have recently observed, "Mexicans loom large among the foreign-born population" and make the position of immigrants as a group seem more precarious than that of native-born Americans.

CHANGE OVER TIME

Another factor easily overlooked in aggregate accounts of economic impact is the length of time that immigrants reside in the United States. Related to the question of duration is the impact the descendants of immigrants have on the U.S. economy over generations. As regards employment status—that is, whether a person is employed, unemployed, or not a member of the workforce—immigrants experience on average a five-year trajectory during which they begin with relatively low levels of labor force participation (85 percent for men, 55 percent for women) but end with levels that converge with those of the native-born population (91 percent for men, 69 percent for women). New immigrants thus appear to go through an adjustment process in which they acquire both formal knowledge, through additional schooling and language training, and informal knowledge, from on-the-job training and social networks through which labor market information may be obtained and employment contacts established.

Individual earnings, defined as the annual sum of wage, salary, and self-employment income, is another area where convergence over time between immigrants and native-born Americans has been observed. Though, as would be expected, there is much variation in average immigrant earnings, depending on country or region of origin ($38,800 for European and Canadian immigrants, $32,000 for Asians, and $16,100 for Mexicans), when other relevant variables such as age and education are controlled, the earnings of non-refugee male immigrants reach parity with those of native males within a ten- to twenty-year period.

A positive take on current research in this area is that, despite greater diversity in terms of both country of origin and occupational skills, there is still considerable evidence that the labor force participation and occupational attainment of immigrants tend to converge over time with those of native-born workers. On the other hand, considering both the remarkably low level of formal education of immigrant groups such as Mexicans and their relatively high rates of fertility (U.S. women averaged 1.85 children in 1990, whereas Mexican immigrant women averaged 4.6), some researchers fear that immigration is but the first phase in a multigenerational process through which the American labor force will be gradually deskilled.

Some social scientists also raise concern about the strong correlation between the skills of immigrants and the skills of their second-generation descendants, which suggests that the skill differentials observed among contemporary immigrant groups will eventually be reflected in the skill differentials of future American-born ethnic groups. Others are less pessimistic when they argue that, even for European Americans, "catching up" with the native population was a process that spanned longer than two generations. Moreover, rates of intermarriage with other groups become so high by the third generation that the question of individual ethnic identity becomes an important factor when considering exactly which groups are being measured. Significantly, this last point is not unique to the descendants of European immigrants, as both Asians and Hispanics become increasingly likely to marry people outside their group over the course of generations. Thus, the question of the long-term impact of immigration on the U.S. economy hinges on the ability to actually count individuals as descendants of immigrants, which for two major reasons is not always a straightforward endeavor: First, it depends on a subjective sense of self-identity that is complicated by the options created through intermarriage, and second, the overwhelming majority of Americans, whether they admit it or not, are themselves descendants of immigrants. If this last point is taken seriously, it becomes clear that in a very real sense, the principal long-term effect of immigration on the U.S. economy has been the perpetuation of the U.S. economy.

IMMIGRATION IN THE NEW MILLENNIUM

As the twenty-first century begins with the United States experiencing the longest period of economic growth in the nation's history, it is perhaps not surprising that the impassioned anti-immigration politics of the mid-1990s has waned considerably. With unemployment at near-record lows, the threat of ongoing immigration, which has not itself waned, seems to have once again faded into the background of the American collective consciousness. Meanwhile, immigrants find themselves working in one of the more welcoming labor environments in recent history. There is ample evidence, for example, that the Immigration and Naturalization Service, though still closely policing the southern border with Mexico, is become increasingly tolerant of the presence of undocumented workers in U.S. industry, with arrests for deportation dropping from 22,000 in 1997 to just 8,600 in 1999. It may be argued, in fact, that the increased leniency toward illegal immigrants during this period of rapid economic expansion has helped keep inflation below expectations by lowering the pressure for wage increases among low-skilled workers. The expansion-with-low-inflation model of economic growth that we have seen in the U.S. economy through the 1990s is thus very likely related to the close-substitution and complementary-worker statuses described above. Native-born workers with skills and educational attainment levels close to those of recent immigrants have probably not received great benefit from the recent economic boom, or, put another way, have seen their wages stagnate as they compete directly with immigrant labor. Professionals and workers with highly specialized skills, on the other hand, have done quite well and owe, in part, the lack of an inflationary economy to the presence of immigrants in the workforce.

But perhaps the most notable change in tone has come from Washington, D.C., where in October 2000 Congress approved a modification of the H-1B visa, which increases the number of college-educated, foreign-born workers allowed into the United States from 115,000 to 195,000 a year for the next three years. Still waiting in the wings are proposed changes to the federal H2A program that, if approved in the form envisioned by some lawmakers, would transform it into the biggest guest worker legislation since the Bracero Program, which brought waves of Mexican agricultural workers into the United States between 1942 and 1964. Increased levels of immigration in recent years have, unfortunately, also been met with increased violations of federal labor laws, with many employers refusing to pay workers' compensation, minimum wage, or time-and-a-half for immigrants working overtime. Immigrant workers, however, are not standing idly by; many have accepted the call of the American Federation of Labor–Congress of Industrial Organizations (AFL-CIO), the Farm Labor Organizing Committee, and other groups to organize and bargain collectively with their employers for better working conditions and wages. How this will affect the U.S. economy remains unknown, but it seems that for the moment, immigrants, who were only very recently the target of harsh exclusionary politics, are beginning to challenge their status as political outsiders, and in doing so are becoming all the more integrated into American society.

Tom Macias

See also: Anti-Immigrant Backlash (Part I, Sec. 5); Economics I: Pull Factors (Part II, Sec. 1); Anti-Immigrant Politics, Public Opinion and Immigration (Part II, Sec. 6); The Economic Debate over Immigration (Part II, Sec. 7); Report on the Shortage of Technology Workers, 1997 (Part IV, Sec. 2).

BIBLIOGRAPHY

Alvarez, Lizette. "Congress Approves a Big Increase in Visas for Specialized Workers." *New York Times,* October 4, 2000, p. A1.

Bean, Frank, and Stephanie Bell-Rose. "Introduction: Immigration and Its Relation to Race and Ethnicity in the United States." In *Immigration and Opportunity: Race, Ethnicity, and Employment in the United States,* eds. Frank Bean and Stephanie Bell-Rose, pp. 1–28. New York: Russell Sage Foundation, 1999.

Borjas, George J. "The Economics of Immigration." *Journal of Economic Literature* 32:4 (1994): 1667–717.

———. *Heaven's Door: Immigration Policy and the American Economy.* Princeton, NJ: Princeton University Press, 1999.

Chiswick, Barry R., and Teresa A. Sullivan. "The New Immigrants." In *State of the Union: American in the 1990s,* vol. 2, *Social Trends,* ed. Reynolds Farley, pp. 211–70. New York: Russell Sage Foundation, 1995.

DePalma, Anthony. "Farmers Caught in Conflict over Illegal Migrant Workers." *New York Times,* October 3, 2000, p. C1.

DeSipio, Louis, and Rodolfo O. de la Garza. *Making Americans, Remaking America: Immigration and Immigrant Policy.* Boulder, CO: Westview, 1998.

Greenhouse, Steven. "Foreign Workers at Highest Level in Seven Decades." *New York Times,* September 4, 2000, p. A1.

Martin, Philip, and Elizabeth Midgley. "Immigration to the United States: Journey to an Uncertain Destination." *Population Bulletin* 49 (September 1994): 1–47.

Perlmann, Joel, and Roger Waldinger. "Second Generation Decline? Children of Immigrants, Past and Present—a Reconsideration." *International Migration Review* 31:4 (1997): 893–922.

Qian, Zhenchao. "Breaking the Racial Barriers: Variations in Interracial Marriage Between 1980 and 1990." *Demography* 34:2 (1997): 263–76.

Reimers, David M. *Unwelcome Strangers: American Identity and the Turn Against Immigration.* New York: Columbia University Press, 1998.

Schaefer, Richard T. *Racial and Ethnic Groups.* New York: Longman, 1998.

Sierra, Christine Marie, Teresa Carrillo, Louis DeSipio, and Michael Jones-Correa. "Latino Immigration and Citizenship." *Political Science and Politics* 33:3 (2000): 535–40.

Smith, James P., and Barry Edmonston. *The New Americans: Economic, Demographic, and Fiscal Effects of Immigration.* Washington, DC: National Academy Press, 1997.

Uchitelle, Louis. "I.N.S Is Looking the Other Way as Illegal Immigrants Fill Jobs." *New York Times,* March 9, 2000, p. A1.

*I*MPACT ON THE HOME COUNTRY ECONOMY

*M*oney remittances are the transfers in cash or in kind from immigrants working abroad to household residents living in their country of origin. According to the United Nations Population Fund 1996 estimate, 125 million people live in a country different from the one in which they were born. An estimate of official remittance flows based on balance of payment statistics reveals that migrants remitted home about $71.1 billion in 1990. These remittances have increased substantially since 1980, when they were estimated at $43.3 billion.

It is very difficult to estimate the actual volume of remittances. The main sources of official data on migrant remittances are the annual balance of payments records of countries that are compiled in the *Balance of Payments Statistics Yearbook* published by the International Monetary Fund. These sources have many limitations. First, it is very difficult to distinguish between individuals who are "residents" or "nonresidents" of an economy. Second, countries apply different criteria to classify the transactions involving international migrants. Third, a significant proportion of remittances are sent through "informal" channels. As a result, specialized surveys are necessary to gather more detailed information on migrants' remittances.

Due to excessive fees or lower exchange rates, many migrants do not use the services of banks, the post office, or money-wiring companies. Rather, they employ "informal" mechanisms: they carry money personally when they go to the home country, send cash or documents through relatives or friends, or send in-kind remittances of clothes and other consumer goods.

In such countries as Bangladesh, India, Pakistan, and the Philippines, many migrants use the Hundi system whereby the migrant delivers a sum in foreign currency to an agent in the destination country under the agreement that the equivalent amount in the currency of the country of origin would be given by the agent's counterpart to the migrant's family. Similarly, documented Mexican migrants living in U.S. border cities exchange their dollars for pesos, cross the border, and wire the money to relatives through banks or by telegraph.

It is estimated that in Asia, remittances sent through unofficial channels at least double or even triple the official figures. On average, almost 16 percent of total remittances by Pakistani workers is sent through informal methods, but this figure could be as high as 48 percent for workers from some regions where banking facilities are not widely available. In Tonga and Western Samoa in the South Pacific, only 43 percent of the remittances were sent through official channels in 1992. The rest arrived in the form of goods sent by mail and goods and money carried personally by migrants in their visits. According to scholar Fernando Lozano, Mexicans living in the United States sent $3.867 billion in 1995. From this amount, 80.5 percent was transferred while the migrants were in the United States, and 19.5 percent was carried by them when they returned to Mexico. A study of the money remittance industry conducted by researchers at the University of California at Los Angeles, reveals that there is a very competitive market for money transfers to Mexico and that migrants in Los Angeles who are members of hometown associations send relatively large amounts of money, pay high transaction fees, and receive poor service when they send money through the formal mechanisms. The most important finding of the study reveals that these migrants send cash through relatives and friends more often than mailing money orders and checks or sending money through banks or money-wiring companies.

IMPACT OF REMITTANCES IN COUNTRIES OF ORIGIN OF MIGRANTS

Although most remittances are sent by individuals, a portion is transferred by migrant organizations that raise money in the United States to fund the construction of public infrastructure and the creation of social projects that benefit the poor in the community of origin through the support of health care clinics, childcare centers, convalescent homes for older adults, and schools. For twenty-five years, migrants from the Dominican Republic residing in Boston have raised funds to support the construction of many public facilities in their locality of origin. Between 1992 and 1994, they raised approximately $70,000 through dances, fairs, and private donations to continue investing in public works. Mexican migrants in the United States have formed a large number of hometown associations that try to promote the well-being of their communities in Mexico. In partnership with the Mexican government, the Zacatecas Federation of Hometown Associations in Los Angeles committed up to $600,000 for fifty-six public projects in thirty-four towns of Zacatecas in 1995.

The remittances that migrants send are often very significant in relation to their country's gross domestic product (GDP) and merchandise exports. For instance, in 1992, according to the World Bank using official data, the money that migrants from Lesotho in Africa sent home was equivalent to 85 percent of the country's GDP. Mexico, with a large number of migrants in the United States, received the equivalent of 1 percent of its GDP and 12 percent of its merchandise exports the same year. This is also the case of the Dominican Republic, whose remittances accounted for 4.5 percent of its GDP and 61 percent of the value of its merchandise exports.

The extent of the economic impact of remittances on the sending country depends on factors such as the size of its economy, the volume of the migrant flow, the composition of the migrant population (temporary workers versus settled immigrants), and the wages they obtain in the host society. In El Salvador remittances are either the primary or one of the most important sources of foreign exchange, often approaching or surpassing revenues from exports and foreign aid. The Economic Commission for Latin America and the Caribbean estimated that Salvadorans in the United States sent $760 million in 1987. Interestingly, a Salvadoran researcher calculated this flow at $1.3 billion, a figure estimated to be close to double the national budget for fiscal year 1987. In the case of Cuba, remittances from and visits by the

Cuban-American community in 1985 produced $400 million. This amount almost equaled the $500 million earned through the country's sugar sales and exceeded the $300 million generated by tourism. In the case of Mexico, the money that migrants sent in 1990 nearly equaled Mexico's 1990 earnings from export agriculture, and represented 59 percent of revenues from tourism and 56 percent of its earnings from maquiladora production. In 1995, in the context of increased Mexican exports, remittances represented 96 percent of Mexico's earnings from export agriculture, 63 percent of revenues from tourism, and only 13 percent of earnings from maquiladora production.

Migrants send an important portion of their incomes. A study conducted among Salvadoran and Filipino migrants in Los Angeles shows that while Salvadorans send home 10 percent of their annual incomes, Filipinos send 4 percent. The two groups display different socioeconomic characteristics. Salvadorans are much younger and have much lower levels of education and income than Filipinos. The mean family income for Salvadorans is $15,412, and for Filipinos, $52,631. Among those who remit, the mean annual amount of money sent home is larger for Filipinos ($2,161) than for Salvadorans ($1,531).

The decision to remit money is influenced by family income in the United States. The higher the earnings potential, the more money migrants send home. Another important factor is family obligations. Having children in the United States decreases the likelihood of remitting, but having more children in the country of origin increases the likelihood and the amount of remittance. Finally, investments in the United States, especially homeownership, are associated with reduced remittances.

USE OF REMITTANCES

Research conducted all over the world reveals that remittances are primarily used to meet such basic needs as food, clothing, and shelter. Generally, after these needs are covered, housing improvements are the most popular target. For this reason, very little money is left for productive investments.

According to a study conducted in 1982 in four Mexican localities, the money that migrants to the United States saved on their last trip was used primarily on current consumption, which includes family sustenance, housing, and the acquisition of a home. Migrants to the United States displayed a preference for investing their savings in housing, therefore a significant share of their home was bought with money earned in the United States. In the rural locality of Chamitlan, 41 percent of homes purchased by international migrants were bought with money earned in the United States. In Altamira, the other rural locality, the respective figure was also 41 percent. In the urban localities of San Marcos and Santiago, the figures were 26 percent and 20 percent, respectively. As a result of this, migrants to the United States were more successful in becoming homeowners than were nonmigrants. Relatively few savings go to productive investment. Among the four communities, the percentage of migrants spending a potentially productive way varied from only 9 percent in Chamitlan to 21 percent in San Marcos.

The use of remittances by migrant households in Asia parallels the patterns observed in other parts of the developing world. After meeting basic needs, there is a heavy concentration of investment in real estate. Business investments are undertaken mostly in trade, transport, and other services, and investment in manufacturing and agriculture is relatively rare. This investment pattern could be explained by the fact that in many sending countries, starting a small business or buying land enables the return migrant to compete, at least symbolically, with the established capital owners of the community of origin.

In a small community in Pakistan, most of the money that family members working in the Middle East send home is used to meet basic family needs, which include health care, education, housing, and other necessities. While the highest proportion of remittance income (42 percent) went into meeting basic needs, 13 percent was used in a business investment, and 16 percent was spent on agriculture.

The scholars Demetrios Papademetriou and Phillip Martin consider that the literature on the relationship between migration and economic development suggests that although individual migrants benefit from international labor markets, this does not mean that remittances and returning migrant skills promote local economic development in sending regions. In opposition to this, the sociologist Richard Brown contends that evidence from his study in Tonga and Western Samoa does not support the view that remittances are used exclusively for consumption purposes. He found that most remittance-dependent households save and/or invest a significant part of their remittances domestically. Migrants not only remit to support their families but also to invest in housing and in more productive spheres, including agriculture. Remittances in kind often take the form of investment goods such as building materials, light machinery, and vehicles. In the same vein, the scholars Jorge Durand, Douglas Massey, and E. Parrado contend that

results from a multiplier model suggest that the inflow of remittances stimulates economic activity in Mexico, both directly and indirectly, and that it leads to higher levels of employment, investment, and income within specific localities and the nation as a whole. The sociologist German Zarate-Hoyos reached similar conclusions in his study of the effects of remittances on Mexico using an economy-wide model.

Increasingly, governments, the private sector, and nonprofit organizations are participating in the movement of migrant remittances in order to channel them into the formal sector and make them play a pivotal role in economic development schemes. For instance, in the early 1990s, the Commission for the Study of International Migration and Cooperative Economic Development, created by U.S. Congress, recommended using migrant remittances in a strategy to foster economic development as a way to diminish the pressures for undocumented migration in sending countries. The commission recommended that individual migrant remittances be complemented by other financial resources from public and private institutions to support the development of the small business sector.

Some sending countries have attempted to require that a certain percentage of the remittances be deposited into a national fund. Korea has succeeded in this endeavor, but the effort has failed in the Philippines, Pakistan, Thailand, and Bangladesh. The Pakistani government has tried to encourage migrant workers to invest their earnings in productive activities through the Overseas Pakistani Foundation, offering information on investment opportunities, tax exemptions, and access to sites in newly created industrial parks. In Mexico, state governments are increasingly working with migrant organizations to channel remittances to more productive uses.

Rafael Alarcón

See also: Immigrant Politics III: The Home Country (Part II, Sec. 6).

BIBLIOGRAPHY

Alarcón, Rafael, David Runsten, and Raul Hinojosa Ojeda. *Migrant Remittance Transfer Mechanisms between Los Angeles and Jalisco, Mexico*. Research Report Series no. 7. Los Angeles: North American Integration and Development Center, University of California, Los Angeles, 1998.

Bilsborrow, R. E., Hugo Graeme, A. S. Oberai, and Hania Zlotnik. *International Migration Statistics: Guidelines for Improving Data Collection Systems*. Geneva: International Labor Office, 1997.

Brown, Richard. "Migrants' Remittances, Savings, and Investment in the South Pacific." *International Labour Review* 133:3 (1994).

Diaz-Briquets, Sergio, and Jorge Perez. "Refugee Remittances: Conceptual Issues and the Cuban and Nicaraguan Experiences." *International Migration Review* 31:2 (1997).

Durand, Jorge, Douglas Massey, and E. Parrado. "Migradollars and Development: A Reconsideration of the Mexican Case." *International Migration Review* 30:2 (1995).

Goldring, Luin. "The Power of Status in Transnational Social Fields." In *Transnationalism from Below: Comparative Urban and Community Research*, ed. Luis Guarnizo and Michael P. Smith. New Brunswick: Transaction Publishers, 1998.

Levitt, Peggy. "Transnationalizing Community Development: The Case of Migration between Boston and the Dominican Republic." *Nonprofit and Voluntary Sector Quarterly* 26:4 (1997): 509–26.

Lozano, Fernando. "Migracion internacional y remesas: Cambios en el Quinqueno 1990–1995." Coloquio Internacional Sobre Migracion Mexicana a Estados Unidos, Mexico City, 1996.

Massey, Douglas, Rafael Alarcón, Jorge Durand, and Humberto Gonzalez. *Return to Aztlan: The Social Process of International Migration from Western Mexico*. Berkeley: University of California Press, 1987.

Menjivar, Cecilia, Julie DeVanzo, Lisa Greenwell, and R. Burciaga Valdez. "Remittance Behavior among Salvadoran and Filipino Immigrants in Los Angeles." *International Migration Review* 32:1 (1998).

Papademetriou, Demetrios, and Phillip Martin, eds. *The Unsettled Relationship: Labor Migration and Economic Development*. New York: Greenwood Press, 1991.

Puri, Shivani, and Tineke Ritzema. "Migrant Worker Remittances, Micro-Finance, and the Informal Economy." Working Paper no. 21. Geneva, Switzerland: Social Finance Unit, Enterprise and Co-operative Development Department, International Labor Organization, 1999.

Russell, S. S., and M. S. Teitelbaum. "International Migration and International Trade." World Bank Discussion Papers, 160. Washington, DC: World Bank, 1992.

Sofranko, A. J., and Khan Idris. "Use of Overseas Migrants' Remittances to the Extended Family for Business Investment: A Research Note." *Rural Sociology* 64:3 (1999): 464–81.

Zarate-Hoyos, German. "A New View of Financial Flows from Labor Migration: A Social Accounting Matrix Perspective." *EIAI* 10: 2 (1999).

*I*NCOME AND WEALTH

There are several key theoretical positions concerning the earnings of foreign-born individuals in the United States, and these positions are supported by competing sets of empirical evidence. Researchers have attempted to understand how and if the earnings of foreign-born individuals change over time, as they continue to live and work in the United States. On the one hand, Barry R. Chiswick has suggested that the relative earnings of foreign-born adult white men eventually surpass those of comparable native workers. Using cross-sectional data from the 1970 *Current Population Survey*, Chiswick indicates that five years after immigration, foreign-born white males have weekly earnings 10 percent lower than the native-born. The earnings of the two groups are approximately equal after thirteen years, however, and the earnings of foreign-born white males are 6 percent higher than those of natives after 20 years. This evidence suggests that immigrants need not be economically disadvantaged. Instead, they have the opportunity to fare relatively well in the U.S. economy—perhaps even better than native-born persons with comparable characteristics—as time progresses and as they obtain job skills and human capital.

According to Chiswick, one major cause of the economic mobility of immigrants is that they face relatively strong incentives (compared with native workers) to make human-capital investments such as education and postschool training. Also, immigrants encounter the expectation of greater job mobility than the native-born, and immigrants receive little firm-specific training from employers. This occurs because employers do not generally invest in immigrant workers, which creates the propensity for immigrants to find better jobs and keep moving toward their most productive, high-wage occupation. Chiswick argues that these findings support the ability-motivation hypothesis, which posits that the foreign-born have greater innate ability, are more highly motivated to-

ward the achievement of labor-market success, and self-finance larger investments in postschool training.

One limitation of this type of empirical work is its reliance on cross-sectional data sets, which raises doubts about the finding that as years elapse following immigration, the earnings of immigrants converge on if not surpass the earnings of the native-born. George J. Borjas has advanced a different theoretical position, along with contrasting empirical findings that rely on longitudinal data sets. In one particular study of immigrant scientists and engineers, Borjas found that (1) the rate of convergence between the age/earnings profiles of immigrants and natives was relatively small, to the extent that recent immigrant scientists and engineers did not achieve earnings parity during their working lives, and (2) the average earnings capacity of the 1970 cohort of immigrants was at least 7 percent lower than the earnings capacity of the 1960 cohort. Moreover, the average hourly wage gap between immigrants who had been in the country for less than five years has widened over the last several decades—from 12 percent in 1960 to 15 percent in 1970 and 26 percent in 1980.

In a recent empirical analysis using the 1970 to 1990 Public Use Microdata Samples of the U.S. census, Borjas uncovers no evidence that more recent immigrant cohorts, who have lower entry wages, experience faster wage growth. Instead, he finds that, on average, recent immigrants earn about one-third less than natives and have greater use of the welfare state because of their poverty status. For example, the 1970 census indicates that immigrant households were less likely than native households to receive cash benefits such as cash welfare and supplemental security income. In contrast, the 1990 census shows that immigrants were more likely to receive cash welfare benefits than native households. This type of analysis clearly shows that wage gaps and poverty are economic realities for many immigrants. Thus, experience in the U.S. labor market following immigration

The growing income and wealth of many immigrant communities has attracted the interest of the business community, as this bank advertisement in New York's Chinatown indicates. *(Anne Burns)*

does not easily close the wage gap for many foreign-born workers.

LOW TO HIGH INCOME

Nancy Cleeland considers the economic realities of immigrant workers who work for the minimum wage. She uses the phrase "stuck at *el minimo* (the minimum)" to describe how Mexican and Central American immigrants in Los Angeles, California, are trapped in minimum-wage employment. Cleeland provides an extensive profile of one minimum-wage worker named Gladys Vitro, a thirty-five-year-old widow from Honduras. In 1999, had Vitro worked forty hours a week for fifty-two weeks straight, she would have earned less than $12,000 for the year. Her jobs featured strenuous, repetitive activities: pulling

glass, plastic, and cardboard from a garbage-laden conveyer belt; coring and peeling an average of fifteen heads of lettuce per minute in a food-processing factory refrigerated to thirty-five degrees; and finally, packing sugar-free candy bars. In the Los Angeles area, 11 percent of workers earned the minimum wage or something close to it in 1999, compared with 8.7 percent nationwide. Of those Los Angeles workers, 28 percent were in manufacturing.

Cleeland's study shows how immigrants can be part of the working poor without accumulating meaningful skills that raise their incomes over time. In addition, undocumented immigrants face an additional hurdle in the form of U.S. immigration law, which prohibits them from working legally in the U.S. labor market. Although many undocumented workers are able to evade these restrictions through the use of false documents, they still tend to get trapped in the secondary labor market, which is marked by low wages, limited job security, little to no health insurance, and few questions asked.

Thomas Muller provides further evidence of how immigrant and undocumented workers are found in low-paying jobs, especially those which require limited use of the English language and few advanced work skills. In 1980, almost one-third of new immigrants worked in manufacturing, a much higher rate than for nonimmigrants. Immigrants, especially undocumented workers, were also represented disproportionately in certain service industries, such as restaurants, hotels, hospitals, and domestic services. In 1980, about 7 percent of all hotel and restaurant jobs were held by undocumented workers, according to John K. Hill and James E. Pearce (as cited by Muller). Hill and Pearce argue that among undocumented workers, more than one-half are employed in the production of apparel and other manufactures.

At the same time, Muller observes that immigrants occupy a wide variety of economic positions in the U.S. labor market. For example, some immigrants are skilled craftworkers or professional workers who bring needed skills to the U.S. economy and further develop those skills as they reside in the United States. In the 1960s, the United States attracted many well-educated professionals, most of whom settled in California and New York. In the New York area, more than eleven thousand of those who arrived during the 1970s were employed as craftworkers in manufacturing, such as jewelers. The 1980 census enumerated 23,300 Asian-born engineers and natural scientists living in such central cities as Washington, D.C., and New York City. Among New York's recent Asian immigrants, the proportion of professionals is almost as high as that among the native white population. The 1990 census revealed that the economic experiences of immigrants continued to vary greatly. For instance, the proportion of employed foreign-born workers sixteen years old and over in managerial and professional occupations ranged from 40 percent for immigrants from the United Kingdom to just 6 percent for immigrants from Mexico.

Muller reports that a disproportionate share of non-Hispanic immigrants work as entrepreneurs, with most in retail trade or services. In 1987, Asians owned 4 percent of all retail stores in the United States, a percentage in excess of their share of the population, and about 20 percent of all Cubans are self-employed. Muller describes the variety of entrepreneurs in New York: Greeks own coffee shops; Koreans, fruit and vegetable markets; Dominicans, construction companies; Asian Indians, travel agencies; and Chinese, restaurants. In Los Angeles, the scenario varies, as Korean entrepreneurs own gasoline stations, liquor stores, and hamburger stands, and Indians own motels and dry cleaning businesses. In Houston, 39 percent of all commercial buildings are owned by foreign investors, mostly Asians. In the early 1990s, Asians were estimated to own two-fifths of all retail stores in Los Angeles County and one-third in the San Francisco metropolitan area. Finally, there are a dozen or more Asian Indian, Chinese, and Korean businesses in every state of the union.

POVERTY

Census data describing the poverty rate and median family income of various immigrant groups help us to understand the current economic status of immigrants. In 1990, about one-third of the U.S. population age sixty-five or over who were born in Cuba, Germany, or the United Kingdom lived in poverty, as did 25 percent of elderly persons born in Canada and 56 percent of elderly persons born in Italy. However, a slightly smaller proportion of households maintained by a foreign-born female with no husband present lived in poverty, compared with similar households maintained by a U.S.-born female.

Poverty continues to be a pressing social problem for many immigrants, even though the United States is in the midst of its longest economic expansion ever. In 1996, the poverty rate was 21 percent for the foreign-born population, compared with 14 percent for natives. For both males and females, the poverty rate was higher among the foreign-born population than the native population. Region of birth is associated with striking differences in poverty rates for the foreign-born population: 13 percent of European immigrants, 15 percent of Asian immigrants, and 28 percent of Latin Americans were poor.

The children of immigrants also encounter poverty. In 1996, the poverty rate for related children under age eighteen in families with foreign-born members was 32 percent, or 3.4 million of the 10.5 million youths in this category. For foreign-born children, the poverty rate was 39 percent, or 900,000 of 2.3 million youths.

COUNTRY OF BIRTH

The U.S. Census Bureau defines income as money income received (including capital gains), before deductions for income taxes, Social Security, union dues, Medicare deductions, and does not include the value of noncash benefits such as food stamps, Medicare, public housing, and employer-provided fringe benefits. Among immigrant families, median income varies widely by country of birth. In 1989, the median income of the nearly 6 million families headed by a foreign-born person was $37,785, compared with $35,225 for all U.S. families. However, the median income for households with a member born in the Philippines was $47,794. Medians among household members born in Mexico and El Salvador were the lowest at $21,585 and $21,818, respectively.

The income of foreign-born households also varied by region in 1996 (see Table 1). Households with at least one Asian-born member had a median income of $42,900, while households with a member born in Latin America had a median income of $24,100. One factor for this difference is the relatively low proportion of householders from Asia who are age sixty-five or older. Another factor is that a relatively high proportion of foreign-born workers in managerial and professional specialty occupations are from Asia.

As region of birth is linked to occupational status, workers from certain parts of the world are less likely to vie for higher-income jobs. In March 1997, managerial and professional occupations accounted for 38 percent of jobs held by European immigrant workers, 36 percent of Asian immigrant workers, but only 11 percent of Latin American immigrant workers (see Table 2). Among Mexican immigrants, these jobs accounted for only 6 percent of workers. Over 50 percent of Mexican-born workers were employed as operators, fabricators, laborers, or service workers.

The occupational profiles of immigrants also differ from those of the native-born. For example, managerial and professional occupations accounted for 24 percent of jobs held by foreign-born workers, compared with 30 percent of native workers, while technical, sales, and administrative support occupations accounted for 22 percent of foreign-born workers, compared with 31 percent of native workers. In sum, these two occupational groups, which are relatively high-paying, accounted for 46 percent of foreign-born workers and 61 percent of native workers. Also, higher proportions of the foreign-born were in the following three occupational groups: service occupations (19 percent versus 13 percent); operators, fabricators, and laborers (also 19 percent versus 13 percent); and farming, forestry, and fishing occupations (5 percent versus 2 percent). In contrast, the occupational distributions of naturalized-citizen workers and native workers were relatively similar: managerial and professional specialty occupations accounted for 33 per-

Table 1 **Median Income of Foreign-Born Households by Region of Birth of the Householder, 1996**		
	Households (in millions)	Median income ($)
Europe	2.2	31,300 (4)
Asia	2.7	42,900 (Highest)
Africa	0.3	31,300 (4)
Latin America	4.9	24,100
Caribbean	1.2	23,900
Central America	3.0	23,000
Mexico	2.4	22,400 (Lowest)
Other	0.6	25,400
South America	0.6	31,800 (3)
North America	0.3	35,000 (2)
(U.S. and Canada)		
Total[1]	10.4	30,000

Source: Census Bureau, 1999.
Note: Households as of March 1997. Includes civilian non-institutional population plus armed forces members living off-post or with their families on-post.
[1]Total includes Oceania and region not reported, not shown separately.

cent of naturalized-citizen workers and 30 percent of native workers; service occupations accounted for 15 percent of naturalized-citizen workers and 13 percent of native workers; and technical, sales, and administrative support occupations accounted for 28 percent of naturalized-citizen workers and 31 percent of native workers.

MEDIAN INCOME

In 1996, the median income for all U.S. households was $35,500. The median income for households with a foreign-born householder equaled $30,000, compared with $36,100 for native householders (see Table 3). The length of U.S. residence appears to be closely correlated to the median income of foreign-born households. The median income in 1996 ranged from $33,100 when the householder's length of residence in the United States was twenty years or more to $25,900 when then length of residence was less than ten years. Also, the median income was considerably higher when the householder is a naturalized citizen: $37,400 for naturalized citizens compared with $25,700 for noncitizens.

The Census Bureau has also found that 43 percent

Table 2
Major Occupation Groups of Foreign-Born Workers 16 Years Old and Over by Region of Birth, 1997

		Occupational Group					
	Workers (in millions)	Managerial and professional specialty (%)	Technical, sales, and administrative support (%)	Service occupations (%)	Precision production, craft, and repair (%)	Operators, fabricators, and laborers (%)	Farming, forestry, and fishing (%)
Europe	2.1	37.8	25.7	16.4	10.4	8.7	0.9
Asia	4.1	35.8	29.5	13.0	7.0	13.4	1.3
Africa	0.4	26.1	32.2	25.1	5.4	10.5	0.7
Latin America	7.4	11.4	16.5	23.6	14.2	26.2	8.1
Caribbean	1.5	19.0	25.4	24.5	9.5	19.3	2.4
Central America	5.0	7.0	12.2	23.4	16.6	29.8	11.1
Mexico	3.8	5.8	10.9	21.9	17.5	30.7	13.2
Other	1.1	11.0	16.7	28.3	13.3	26.7	3.9
South America	0.9	23.3	25.8	23.4	8.8	17.4	1.3
North America	0.3	46.5	28.5	10.5	10.4	3.8	0.3
Total	14.5	23.7	22.3	19.1	11.3	18.9	4.7

Source: Census Bureau, 1999.

Table 3
Median Household Income by Nativity, Length of Residence in the United States, and Citizenship Status of the Householder, 1996

	Households (in millions)	Median Income ($)
Native	90.6	36,100
Foreign-born	10.4	30,000
Length of residence in the U.S.		
Less than 10 years	3.0	25,900
10–19 years	3.1	30,200
20 years and up	4.3	33,100
Citizenship status		
Naturalized	4.6	37,400
Not a citizen	5.8	25,700
Total	101.0	35,500

Source: Census Bureau, 1999.
Note: Households as of March 1997. Includes civilian non-institutional population plus armed forces members living off-post or with their families on-post.

of foreign-born households fall below $25,000, compared with 35 percent of native households. When incomes above $50,000 are studied, we find that 29 percent of foreign-born households had median incomes

of $50,000 or more, compared with 35 percent of native households.

Marital status is another way to view income. In 1996, the median income of married-couple families with a native householder was $50,800, significantly more than the $38,800 of the 6 million married-couple families with a foreign-born householder (see Table 4). At the same time, the amount of $38,800 was more than twice the median income of the 1.4 million families maintained by a foreign-born female with no husband.

EARNINGS FOR FULL-TIME, YEAR-ROUND WORKERS

According to the census, earnings are defined as money wage or salary income from work performed as an employee, net income from nonfarm self-employment, and net income from farm self-employment before deductions, including taxes. A full-time, year-round worker is one who has worked 35 or more hours per week for 50 or more weeks during the previous calendar year.

Three distinct patterns exist in the earnings levels of full-time, year-round immigrant workers compared with similar native workers. First, these earnings are

Table 4
Median Family Income by Nativity of Householder, Type of Family, and Presence of Related Children under Eighteen Years, 1996

	Families with foreign-born householder (in millions)	Median family income ($)	Families with native householder (in millions)	Median family income ($)
Total	7.9	33,000	62.3	43,400
No related children	3.0	36,400	30.1	44,700
One or more related children	5.0	31,300	32.2	42,200
Married-couple family	6.0	38,800	47.6	50,800
No related children	2.2	40,300	25.2	47,400
One or more related children	3.8	38,000	22.4	53,800
Female householder, no				
husband present	1.4	16,800	11.4	20,200
No related children	0.4	28,900	3.4	30,700
One or more related children	0.9	13,400	8.0	16,800

Source: Census Bureau, 1999.
Note: Families as of March 1997. Includes civilian noninstitutional population plus armed forces members living off-post or with their families on-post.

lower for foreign-born workers than for their native counterparts. In 1996, the median earnings of full-time, year-round workers were $32,100 for males and $23,700 for females. At the same time, the median earnings of foreign-born male and female workers were $25,000 and $20,800. Second, the earnings of naturalized citizens are slightly higher than the earnings of other foreign-born workers. For foreign-born male workers, median earnings in 1996 were $35,600 for naturalized citizens and $20,500 for noncitizens. The corresponding figures for foreign-born female workers are $25,500 and $17,200, respectively.

Finally, the median earnings of workers from Asia and Europe exceeded the median earnings of all foreign-born workers. For males, these medians were $35,300 for naturalized citizens and $40,500 for noncitizens, and for females, $24,600 and $23,400, respectively. The median earnings of Caribbean-born workers was $23,900 for males and $20,200 for females, while the median earnings of workers from South America was $25,200 for males and $21,100 for females. At the same time, the median earnings of workers from Latin America were below the median earnings of all foreign-born workers. The median for male workers from Latin America was $18,600 (compared with $25,000 for all foreign-born workers), and the median for female workers from Latin America was $16,700 (compared with $20,800). Among workers from Mexico, the median earnings of both males ($16,800) and females ($13,700) were below the me-

dians for workers from the Caribbean, South America, Asia, and Europe.

LABOR FORCE PARTICIPATION

According to the March 1997 *Current Population Survey*, the foreign-born population accounted for 11.5 percent, or 15.6 million, of the total civilian labor force of 135 million in the United States. There was little difference between the labor force participation rates of the foreign-born population (66 percent) and the native population (67 percent). Likewise, foreign-born men ages twenty-five to fifty-four participated in the labor force at roughly the same rate as native males (92 and 91 percent, respectively).

Female labor-force participation, however, differed substantially. Foreign-born women ages twenty-five to fifty-four had a much lower labor-force participation rate than native women (66 percent versus 78 percent). There were also differences within the foreign-born group according to citizenship status and country of birth. Specifically, naturalized women were more likely to work than noncitizen women (77 percent versus 60 percent), and foreign-born women from Mexico were less likely to work than other foreign-born women (52 percent versus 66 percent).

In terms of the unemployment rate, the 1997 data showed a higher rate for foreign-born workers (6.9

percent) compared with native workers (5.4 percent). Among women, the unemployment rate was also higher for the foreign-born: 7.4 percent for foreign-born women versus 4.9 percent for native women. Yet men experienced a similar unemployment rate: 6.5 percent for foreign-born men and 5.9 percent for native men.

REMITTANCES

One interesting question about immigrant income concerns how immigrants spend their income. Many immigrants send money back to family members who continue to live in the immigrants' country of origin. These transmitted moneys are usually called "remittances," although some researchers use the more informal term "migradollars." According to Dennis Conway and Jeffrey H. Cohen, Mexican immigrants in the United States may remit between $4 and $6 billion to their family members in Mexico each year. This process usually entails transmitting the money via Western Union, Moneygram, the United States Postal Service, or some other means. Once remittances arrive at their intended destination, the persons who continue to reside in the country of origin decide how to use this money. In the case of Mexican migration to the United States, the persons who remain in Mexico are more likely to be women, including the wife or partner of the migrant, along with the migrant's mother, sisters, and aunts.

Two consequences result from remittances, according to Richard C. Jones. On the one hand, migrants can invest the money—in agricultural land, a family business, or educational expenses for younger family members—and reduce inequality among migrant households, assuming that the investments occur disproportionately in poorer households. Or remittances may be used primarily to purchase consumption goods, such as unnecessary gifts, the accumulation of dowries, and household embellishments. Such purchases would tend to increase inequality among migrant households, as wealthier households would be likely to have more left over for any investments.

Rose Ann M. Rentería

See also: Housing, Poverty (Part II, Sec. 7).

BIBLIOGRAPHY

Borjas, George J. "The Economic Progress of Immigrants: Working Paper 6506." Working Paper Series. Cambridge, MA: National Bureau of Economic Research, April 1998 (www.nber.org/papers/w6506).

———. "Immigrant and Emigrant Earnings: A Longitudinal Study." *Economic Inquiry* (January 1989): 21–37.

———. "Immigration and Welfare: Solving the Welfare Problem Will Solve the Welfare Problem—Not the Immigration Problem." *National Review,* June 16, 1997.

———. "Immigrants—Not What They Used to Be." *Wall Street Journal,* November 8, 1990.

Census Bureau. *The Foreign-Born Population of the United States: March 1997.* Washington, DC: Department of Commerce, 1999.

———. *We the American . . . Foreign Born.* Washington, DC: Department of Commerce, 1993.

Chiswick, Barry R. "The Effect of Americanization on the Earnings of Foreign-Born Men." *Journal of Political Economy* (October 1978): 897–921.

Cleeland, Nancy. "Workers Trapped at el Minimo: For a Growing Class of Workers in L.A., the Minimum Wage Isn't a Beginning but a Dead End." *Los Angeles Times,* March 9, 2000.

Conway, Dennis, and Jeffrey H. Cohen. "Consequences of Migration and Remittances from Mexican Transnational Communities. *Economic Geography* (January 1998): 26–45.

Hill, John K., and James E. Pearce. "Enforcing Sanctions against Employers of Illegal Aliens." *Economic Review* (May 1987): 1–15.

Jones, Richard C. "Introduction: The Renewal Role of Remittances in the New World Order." *Economic Geography* (January 1998): 1–7.

Muller, Thomas. *Immigrants and the American City.* New York: New York University Press, 1993.

Schaefer, Richard T. *Racial and Ethnic Groups.* Upper Saddle River, NJ: Prentice Hall, 2000.

POVERTY

Most scholars today agree that immigration and poverty go hand in hand. According to a study from the Center for Immigration Studies, "immigration is one of the primary factors causing the nation's overall poverty rate and the number of people living in poverty to be higher today than they were 20 years ago." In addition, this same study shows an alarming trend. The rate of poverty among immigrant-headed households continues to increase despite a robust economic cycle in the United States. The poverty rate for people living in immigrant households grew from 15.5 percent in 1979 to 18.8 percent ten years later and to 21.8 percent in 1997. These figures are well above the national average for nonimmigrant households during the same period. In the 1990s, according to figures from the same study, the poverty rate for children living in immigrant-headed households fluctuated between 24.8 and 30.9 percent. Moreover, every new wave of immigrants dramatically contributes to the poverty trend. Around one-third of the new arrivals to the United States live in poverty, and the rate of immigrants who remain in poverty today after ten years of residence is double that of natives.

These findings have been validated by other research. Labor economists and demographers working on immigration issues are quick to point out that income differentials also vary disproportionally among immigrant groups. George J. Borjas and Marta Tienda have closely scrutinized occupational data to find that Latin American immigrants are positioned on the bottom of the occupational scale when compared with other nationalities. In general terms, Borjas and Tienda establish a correlation between occupational attainment and place of origin. Immigrants from the developing regions show lower employment potential than those from industrial societies. Dudley L. Poston has corroborated these results, among others. Poston finds that refugees turned immigrants do not compare well in terms of socioeconomic status with those who immigrate voluntarily to the United States. Additionally, according to the 1990 census, of the nearly 32 million Americans who live in poverty, the proportion of poor people identified as Hispanic expanded by 7 percent during the 1980s from 11 percent in the beginning of the decade to 18 percent toward its end. This trend holds true for different strata of the population. In 1990, while the percentage of "elderly" (those sixty-five and over) whites living in poverty has been cut almost by half to 10 percent, 23 percent of the Hispanic elderly continue to live in poverty. Among Americans under eighteen years old, the poverty rate for Hispanics was approximately 38 percent in 1990 as compared with 16 percent among whites. And, according to figures computed by Paul A. Jargowsky, close to 30 percent of Hispanics live in high-poverty neighborhoods. Hispanics account for one of the higher rates of poverty among immigrants.

While it is true that many immigrants live in poverty or close to it, some fare better. The research on second-generation immigrants suggests that poverty is not a permanent condition for newcomers. Many more in the first generation live in deprivation than do subsequent generations. The children of immigrants profit from parental capital accumulation and their own segmented assimilation into the way of life in the host country. Moreover, it has been suggested that not only do some groups of immigrants fare better than others, but even intragroup disparities exist. For instance, Hispanics' median income trailed that of Asians, non-Hispanic whites, and blacks. At the same time, the median income among Cubans is typically higher than that of Mexicans and Puerto Ricans. These and other studies suggest there is no simple answer when it comes to the correlation between poverty and immigration. The diverse number of positions regarding this factious issue merits further investigation.

A member of a Phoenix church group distributes free food to impoverished Guatemalan migrant farm workers. *(Jeffry D. Scott/Impact Visuals)*

POVERTY AND IMMIGRATION: A CONCEPTUAL TRAJECTORY

After two decades of stable immigration flows and relative postwar prosperity in the United States, the 1960s witnessed a renewed interest among social scientists on the issue of ethnic poverty. Several reasons account for this boom. During the decade, there was a shift in the pattern of immigration as the proportion of immigrants from less developed nations sought a better standard of living and political refuge in the industrialized countries. A concomitant effect of this radical change was that a large number of the newcomers were not well equipped to adapt to the new demands of more-industrial societies, and many ended up among the ranks of the dispossessed. The distinct cultural identity of the new immigrants presented another challenge. Cultural and language barriers made the adaptation period strenuous. In short, the 1960s witnessed a demographic revolution only comparable to the great immigration wave of the turn of the century in the United States.

Social scientists also became interested in the question of poverty because they tried to assess the impact of the newly institutionalized government initiatives highlighted by such programs as the War on Poverty and the Great Society in the United States and, internationally, the First United Nations Development Decade. In addition, many of the immigrants arriving from developing nations also brought the legacies of underdevelopment to the forefront of American and European politics.

Mounting difficulties associated with immigrant adaptation, coupled with a renewed interest in poverty alleviation, generated one of the most intense debates on immigration and poverty among social scientists. At the core of the first wave in the immigration debate is the question of how to understand the different rates of prosperity among various ethnic communities. On one end of the spectrum in this debate is the paradigm of assimilation, on the other is the research on ethnic enterprise.

Many consider assimilation to be one of the grand themes in immigration research. At the core of the classical assimilation perspective is the assumption that the gradual substitution of ethnic identity with newly embraced social values from the host nation is the most significant factor determining the capitalization of opportunity structures and rate of welfare. The natural process by which diverse minorities assimilate to new cultural and behavioral patterns is factored by such intangibles as social class, language of origin, religion, and educational attainment at the time of arrival. In addition, one researcher in this tradition, Milton Gordon, has postulated an assimilation typology that attempts to capture the complexity of assimilation. In Gordon's view, cultural adaptation is the first step in the process of immigrant assimilation. This linear process goes through different stages, eventually leading to intermarrying into the mainstream population and melting into the civic life of the host nation. Other researchers, such as Richard Alba, Stanley Lieberson, and Mary Waters, have more recently suggested that language proficiency and the immigrants' prior exposure to new cultural values progressively increase the social mobility among ethnic minorities.

Classical assimilation was influenced by the culture of poverty research, which dominated the social sciences, and the discourse on poverty during the early half of the 1960s. Like the culture of poverty paradigm, assimilation underlines the role of values in relation to social deprivation. Those immigrants who managed to escape poverty did so by adapting to the new social environment, leaving behind their cultural identity. Moreover, assimilation theorists anticipate that marginality is an individual condition that cannot be legislated. Therefore, this body of research pays little attention to the adverse impact of public policy and other structural conditions that may contour the chances of prosperity. This is an approach whose focus is on the intersubjective capacity for human action.

Some of the predictions from the classical assimilation approach did not match the experience of non-European immigrants. Detractors of the assimilation perspective identified at least three major problems with this literature. First, proponents of assimilation characterize this process as a one-way street—that is, they believe that when immigrants assimilate, they give up their background. This is not necessarily the case. The incorporation of many immigrants into host societies is characterized by many blends of assimilation. Some immigrants choose to mesh their particular values and behavioral patterns with those of the mainstream, resulting in what the critic Gustavo Perez Firmat calls "life on the hyphen." Others opt for re-

sisting adaptation altogether. And a few immigrants also embrace the culture and values of their adopted homeland without much hesitation. The main point is that assimilation is complex and varies radically among ethnic groups, and today there are multiple assimilation scenarios, not a single path to incorporation that the assimilation perspective articulates.

More important with respect to poverty, another shortcoming of this perspective is that, as subsequent research has shown, there is not sustained correlation between poverty rates and the ability or willingness to adapt to a new environment. Some immigrants adapt well only after enduring relative economic success. Finally, focus on the behavior of individuals or groups of individuals has resulted in the neglect until recently of other structural factors that play a role in the process of ethnic incorporation, such as labor market structures, social networks, and the effects of the social composition of enclave communities.

A competing perspective to assimilation research is the "ethnic enclave hypothesis." The intellectual manifestation of this research also dates back to the labor market studies of the 1960s. The basic goal of ethnic enclave research is to prove the industrious character of immigrants even when they face adverse situations and language barriers. In this sense, this research is a refutation of the negative stereotypes that some cultural research generated about ethnic groups. The enclave research also conceptualized ethnic enterprises, which many dubbed as a failure and a source of exploitation, as apprenticeship. In a seminal study published in 1980, Franklin Wilson and Alejandro Portes found that a sizable proportion of newly arrived immigrants work for coethnic firms. The data for this study were generated from a longitudinal study of Cubans in Miami between 1973 and 1976. The results of this study reveal that recent immigrants who worked for other immigrants were doing much better than those Cubans who worked for white-owned secondary firms. This seminal study by Wilson and Portes single-handedly recasted immigration research toward enclave economies. In *Latin Journey*, Portes and Robert Bach seem to critique at least one of the premises of the assimilation perspective by underlining the positive correlation between the levels of education that immigrant workers bring with them and the occupational gains during the resettlement experience.

The enclave hypothesis also generated its own controversy among immigration scholars. Among them, Victor Nee and Roger Waldinger in their respective research question the validity of the claim that immigrant workers are better off working for other minority firms. Waldinger, for example, takes into account the positive impact of training in primary-sector industries. He makes the notable point that immigrant firms cannot match the training systems of mainstream firms. Therefore, the relative prosperity of immigrants in enclave economies is only because recruitment in this sector is through ethnic networks that improve skill transfer from one employer to another. Prosperity among immigrant workers is a function of human capital beyond acquiring self-employment skills. Nee and his associates dispute the measurement of enclave by Portes and Bach and, by comparing minority workers in enclave economies with those outside, are able to illustrate that the relative prosperity of the former is not as notable as previously stated.

CONTEMPORARY POSITIONS

Despite the early pitfalls and controversies associated with theories of immigration despair, there is reason to believe that contemporary positions will contribute noble ideas to understanding the persistent poverty rates in immigrant communities. In many ways, current theories employ a more sophisticated methodological approach and propositions. For instance, one of the most promising areas of research incorporates insight from transnationalism into the question of ethnic identity and economic ties. While the list of recent research agendas is numerous, I have selected four positions to map the diverse theoretical terrain and the rich findings that the more contemporary interpretations offer.

IMMIGRATION AND THE WORLD ECONOMY

Two scholars who have linked the fate of urban immigrants to changes in the world economy are Saskia Sassen and William J. Wilson. In her *Cities in the World Economy*, Sassen asserts that structural changes in the world economy are having a profound effect among immigrants concentrated in major cities. At the same time that the pattern of immigration movement changed from east-west to north-south, major cities among industrial nations began to experience a structural transformation from a manufacturing-based to a service economy. This means that immigrants with low skill attainment had a high probability of becoming marginalized because they do not possess the required skills to compete for the more lucrative jobs in the service economy. Ironically, the new international division of labor also generates demands for remedial employment to support the lifestyle of the more affluent. In essence, Sassen asserts that one of the consequences of globalization is a new urban stratification, hence the agglomerations of low-skilled immigrant labor in most major cities. The expansion of low-wage jobs has also reorganized capital-labor relations by constraining the capacity of organized labor to successfully represent low-wage workers in the new service economy.

William J. Wilson, not normally regarded as an immigration scholar, builds on Sassen's idea to posit that levels of poverty among immigrants in the inner cities is the result of a simultaneous shift in the urban job structures and demographic patterns. The migration of low-skilled labor into the inner cities coincided with the structural shift toward a more technology intensive economy. Wilson asserts that the new immigrant underclass, like blacks before them, does not possess and cannot afford to acquire the skills needed to take advantage of the current economic boom in the United States. Poverty reproduces itself in part because the successful middle class settles to the more affluent suburbs, further shrinking the revenue base and denying the underclass a chance to socialize with role models.

TRANSNATIONAL COMMUNITIES

This line of research, most prominently proposed by Alejandro Portes and Douglas Massey, builds on the observation that the struggle for economic advancement and the social recognition of immigrants is shaped by the formation of tense networks across political borders. While the world economy perspective accentuates structural changes to account for the rise of the urban underclass, proponents of the transnational view examine both rural and urban immigrant communities. The difference between these two positions goes beyond scope. Transnationalists also propose a middle-range conceptual position and stress the role of the web of social ties to understand the incorporation of waves of immigrants.

One implication of the transnational research perspective is that immigrants who come from poor communities may in fact find it hard to overcome poverty in the host nation precisely because transnational ties may reproduce social values and expectations so prevalent in their native society. As Portes asserts, "As money and goods flow through transnational communities, so do cultural influences and even politics." The irony of this situation is that immigrants who leave their native communities in search of a better life abroad may find themselves further isolated when they become embroiled in local politics back home and vulnerable to the social enigmas in the home country.

Attaining a better standard of living and status in the host society may also be susceptible to the social obligations reinforced by existing transnational ties. Immigrants are often expected to send remittances to family relatives back home. In some cases, immigrants underwrite civic projects back in their hometowns as a way to solidify their solidarity with those left behind. Finally, in other instances, immigrants set up microenterprises and self-employment arrangements to sell merchandise bought in the home country in enclave communities. All of these ethnic niches strengthen transnational social ties and personal identity at a very high price, because very few of these economic activities can successfully compete outside enclave communities, and the skills acquired from these activities may not necessarily be transferable to the sophisticated world of venture capitalism.

SEGMENTED ASSIMILATION

A third research program attempts to correct some of the perils of the classical assimilation position by investigating the longitudinal attainment of the second-generation immigrant in relation to the first. Advocates of this research propose that the different patterns of incorporation of immigrants' descendants depend to a greater extent on such individual attributes as education attainment and acculturation, particularly the ability to acquire language proficiency, as well as more-structural variables such as social stratification, place of residency, and racial composition. Scholars often point to mitigating factors, such as multiculturalism and transnationalism, to account for the experiences of the second generation.

In her review of this literature, Min Zhou proposes three factors that transect classical assimilation to determine the adaptation of the second generation. First, the kinds of blue-collar employment usually available to newly arrived immigrants are fewer in number than in previous years. For this reason, the economic situation of less-skilled immigrants today is usually bleaker than in the past. Second, the racial composition and class status of contemporary immigrants add to their hardship during the adaptation period because many of them experience prejudice that adds barriers to economic attainment. Minorities face unequal distribution of resources and opportunities that curtails their chances to escape the difficult conditions

of enclaves. Third, in some cases, as with Asian Americans, immigrants can overcome disadvantages in the host society by establishing strong group solidarity. Segmented assimilation scholars have expended considerable effort identifying the conditions that promote social capital and group solidarity in the midst of ethnic diversity and competitions within and among ethnic groups.

CONTEMPORARY LABOR STUDIES

Labor economists and their colleagues from sociology analyze trends in real wages and earnings potential of immigrants with sophisticated quantitative techniques. Unlike some of the most interpretative counterparts, this perspective strikes at measuring relationships with precision. The statistical approach of these studies has not hampered the amount of controversy surrounding some of these findings. In fact, the ability to quantify relations has actually provided an incentive to explore very contentious questions somewhat neglected by the previous body of theories discussed earlier. One such question concerns the effects of new immigrants' labor on labor market segmentation. According to the research by Gregory DeFreitas, recent Hispanic immigration has not had a significant effect on wages except for those of black women. George Borjas, Robert Lalonde, and Robert Topel, on the other hand, have debated the effects of education attainment on long-run earning potentials.

Perhaps one of the most significant contributions from this literature is the willingness to tackle questions on the public sector cost of immigration. Marta Tienda and Leif Jensen have found that while the poverty rate of recent immigrants surpasses that of the native-born, the propensity to solicit public assistance is relatively similar. This finding is significant not only to dispel the popular perception of immigration as a social burden but also because it opens a line of interesting research to account for the reasons behind the apparent hesitation to seek public assistance in spite of overwhelming deprivation.

FURTHER RESEARCH

Immigration studies have become more sophisticated with time; however, a variety of research themes persist. One of them is the effect of education attainment on incorporation. Another is the process of skill acquisition by immigrants. Are immigrants better off working for mainstream firms or within the enclave business sector? Yet a third remaining question concerns how to measure the relative prosperity of immigrant families. While these questions are likely to remain as part of this line of research for the foreseeable future, it is time to contemplate other research questions. I suggest three areas that potentially could dominate the ethnic poverty scholarship in the near future.

1. What are the effects of deportation and asylum denial on developing nations? This question is important because, increasingly, industrialized nations are closing legislative loopholes and deporting individuals requesting political asylum after a short stay in the country. It seems that either these individuals may decide to vent their anger at the United States and become a possible threat to our security or they could assimilate back into their societies.

2. From a policy point of view, how can one operationalize the difference between political and economic immigrants? The end of the Cold War and the new wave of democratization have blurred the distinction between economic and political refugees. Besides, many immigrants from developing regions may actually be able to make both claims. The current cases of female genital mutilation constitute a recent example of the difficulties posed by this question.

3. Within immigrant communities, it is worth paying close attention to new grassroots efforts to improve life in the enclave. Also, one should pay attention to the fragmented and infant mobilization of immigrant groups without a community political voice.

Poverty among immigrants has been a major preoccupation of social scientists for a long time. An analysis of the intellectual trajectory of this field suggests that immigration studies have undergone a profound epistemological transformation in recent years. In the 1960s, the focus of attention was on the capacity of immigrants to adopt to the host environment as a precondition to social attainment and economic success. Today, scholars pay particular attention to mitigating factors that shape the rate of prosperity among newcomers. Studies of immigrant poverty are rich in interpretation and controversy.

Despite thematic diversity, poverty across immigrant communities still is a burgeoning field of research. Many scholarly controversies have not been settled, and in many cases, the debate has opened new

areas of research. Besides the traditional issues of education, enclave economies, and economic restructuring, immigration studies will do well to scrutinize mobilization efforts and how new immigrant social movements are changing the local political terrain. Witness the political struggle between the Dominican and Puerto Rican communities in New York City. As we progress into the new millennium and transnational immigration becomes more prevalent, social tensions related to immigration will become national issues.

Enrique S. Pumar

See also: Economics II: Push Factors (Part II, Sec. 1); Welfare and Public Benefits (Part II, Sec. 9); Illegal Immigration Reform and Immigrant Responsibility Act, 1996, Personal Responsibility and Work Opportunity Reconciliation Act, 1996 (Part IV, Sec. 1); Title IV: Restricting Welfare and Public Benefits for Aliens, 1996 (Part IV, Sec. 2.).

BIBLIOGRAPHY

Alba, Richard. *Italian Americans: Into the Twilight of Ethnicity*. Englewood Cliffs, NJ: Prentice Hall, 1985.

Bailey, Thomas, and Roger Waldinger. "Primary, Secondary, and Enclave Labor Markets: A Training System Approach." *American Sociological Review* 56 (1994): 432–45.

Borjas, George J. "The Economics of Immigration." *Journal of Economic Literature* 32 (1994): 1667–1717.

Borjas, George J., and Marta Tienda. "The Employment and Wages of Legalized Immigrants." *International Migration Review* 27 (1993): 712–42.

Camarota, Steven A. *Importing Poverty: Immigration's Impact on the Size and Growth of the Poor Population in the United States*. Washington, DC: Center for Immigration Studies, 1999.

DeFreitas, Gregory. "Hispanic Immigration and Labor Market Segmentation." *Industrial Relations* 27 (1988): 195–214.

Gordon, Milton. *Assimilation in American Life: The Role of Race, Religion, and Natural Origins*. New York: Oxford University Press, 1964.

Jargowsky, Paul A. *Poverty and Place*. New York: Russell Sage, 1997.

Lalonde, Robert, and Robert Topel. "Immigrants in the American Labor Market: Quality, Assimilation, and Distributional Effects." *American Economic Review* 81 (1991): 297–302.

Lieberson, Stanley, and Mary Waters. *From Many Strands: Ethnic and Racial Groups in Contemporary America*. New York: Russell Sage, 1988.

Massey, Douglas, and L. Goldring. "Continuities in Transnational Migration: An Analysis of Nineteen Mexican Communities." *American Journal of Sociology* 99 (1993): 1492–1533.

Perez Firmat, Gustavo. *Life on the Hyphen*. Austin: University of Texas Press, 1994.

Portes, Alejandro. "Global Villagers: The Rise of Transnational Communities." *American Prospects* 25 (March–April 1996).

———. "Social Capital: Its Origins and Applications in Modern Sociology." *Annual Review of Sociology* 24 (1998): 1–24.

———. "Transnational Communities: Their Emergence and Significance in the Contemporary World-System." In *Latin America in the World Economy*, ed. Roberto P. Korzeniewidcz and William C. Smith, pp. 151–68. Westport, CT: Greenwood Press, 1996.

Portes, Alejandro, and Robert Bach. *Latin Journey*. Berkeley: University of California Press, 1985.

Poston, Dudley L., Jr., "Patterns of Economic Attainment of Foreign-Born Male Workers in the United States." *International Migration Review* 27 (1993): 478–500.

Roberts, Sam. *Who We Are: A Portrait of America*. New York: Times Books, 1983.

Sanders, Jimmy, and Victor Nee. "Limits of Ethnic Solidarity in the Enclave Economy." *American Sociological Review* 52 (1990): 745–73.

Sassen, Saskia. *Cities in a World Economy*. 2d ed. Thousand Oaks, CA: Pine Forge Press, 2000.

———. *The Global City*. Princeton: Princeton University Press, 1991.

Tienda, Marta, and Leif Jensen. "Immigration and Social Program Participation: Dispelling the Myth of Dependency." *Social Science Research* 15 (1986): 372.

Wilson, Franklin, and Alejandro Portes. "Immigrant Enclaves: An Analysis of the Labor Market Experience of Cubans in Miami." *American Journal of Sociology* 99 (1993): 295–319.

Wilson, William J. *The Truly Disadvantaged*. Chicago: University of Chicago Press, 1987.

Zhou, Min. "Segmented Assimilation: Issues, Controversies, and Recent Research on the New Second Generation." *International Migration Review* 31 (Winter 1997): 975–1008.

LABOR

INTRODUCTION

The entries in Section 8 of Part II of the *Encyclopedia of American Immigration* explore the question of immigrants, immigration, and labor. Articles focus on the role of immigrants and immigration in various sectors of the economy, including agriculture, the professions, factory work, the service sector, and the underground economy. In addition, the section includes articles on labor markets and unions and union organizing among immigrant workers.

In his entry on agriculture, Ronald L. Mize begins with the role immigrants play in what he calls the "three systems of U.S. agricultural production." The author also discusses the ethnic and racial shifts in the agricultural labor force that have occurred in the twentieth century. Mize goes on to look at how the public perceives the plight of migrant farmworkers and what effect this perception has on the actual working conditions of immigrant agricultural laborers. Finally, the author considers what effects changes in immigration law have had on the agricultural sector, as well as the impact of farmworker social movements and contemporary trends in migrant farm labor.

Michael B. Aguilera's piece on labor markets largely focuses on a series of studies on the subject conducted in the 1980s and 1990s by the U.S. government. These studies offer data on various aspects of immigrant labor markets, including such questions as English fluency and economic well-being among immigrants.

In his entry "Professionals and the Brain Drain," Philip Q. Yang examines the controversial subject of professional immigration and its effects on both the U.S. economy and the economies of developing countries around the world. He begins with a world history of "brain drains," going back to classical times and continuing through the globe in the first few decades following World War II. Next, Yang looks at the levels and types of professional immigrants to the United States today, before considering the determi-

nants of the brain flow. Finally, the author examines the impact of this immigration of professionals on the U.S. economy and sending countries' economies, both today and in the immediate future.

Judith Warner's entry on the service sector opens with an examination of economic restructuring in America's new global cities before discussing income polarization within the service sector. Warner then looks at economic informalization, ethnic enclaves, and urban development. In addition, she provides specific case studies of immigrants and the service sector in various American cities, including San Diego, Los Angeles, and Philadelphia, as well as the country's suburban communities. She closes with a look at the unionization movement within the immigrant service sector.

In her entry on sweatshops and factories, Teal Rothschild begins with a discussion of the origins of sweatshops in the United States before moving on to explore the role that immigrant workers have played in the development of sweatshops. The author also goes into some detail on sweatshops in the nineteenth century and sweatshops in the garment industry yesterday and today. In addition, Rothschild looks at union organizing among immigrant garment workers and what the future holds for sweatshops and the immigrants who labor in them. The author also examines the question of women and sweatshops, as well as the legal issues concerning immigrants and sweatshops, both today and in the near-term future.

Judith Warner's entry on immigrants in the "underground economy" examines how globalization, economic restructuring, and what the author calls "informalization" affect the phenomenon. Next, the author discusses the numbers of persons involved in this economy before focusing on several specific communities, including New York City and Miami. She also looks at various sectors such as sweatshops and homework, especially in the garment industry. She explores law enforcement in this area, especially surrounding household service and street vending. There is also a discussion of unions, immigrants, and the underground economy. Finally, she offers a detailed discussion of immigrants and organized crime.

In their essay on unions and union organizing, Immanuel Ness and Nick Unger focus on unionization within the New York City labor market, with discussions of industrial restructuring and informalization, ethnic flux and volatility, and union organizing. They then go on to describe various types of union organizing strategies for immigrant workers.

$\mathcal{A}$GRICULTURE

In many respects, the history of large-scale agricultural production in the United States developed concurrently with the use of immigrant labor. The majority of marginalized ethnic and racial groups who entered the United States often found their economic start in the fields. California quickly became the agricultural center of both America and the world. By 1929, California had become the largest producer of fruits and vegetables in the southwestern United States. This region, often referred to as Mex-America, accounted for 40 percent of the total output of agricultural goods in the United States. Currently, agriculture in California accounts for nearly one-half of all profits generated from agricultural goods throughout the entire globe.

Understanding the characteristics of U.S. agriculture requires an explanation of the different agricultural regions. The three systems of agricultural production, as defined by sociologist Max Pfeffer, are first delineated. Then the discussion will focus on large-scale agribusiness, or the factories in the field, which has traditionally employed the vast majority of immigrant laborers. Of particular interest are the ethnic and racial shifts in the composition of the agricultural labor force. For the most part, the plight of the migrant farmworker has gone unnoticed by the U.S. public, but a small number of significant fictionalized accounts, social histories, news reports, and union-organized boycotts have periodically thrust the struggles in the fields onto the public stage.

One of the most important facets of agriculture and migration is the role that U.S. immigration law has played in shaping the agricultural labor force. In addition, social movements (in the form of both unionization efforts and strikes) on the part of laborers have also served to challenge the negative aspects of agricultural work. Finally, the current situation of migrant farmworkers will be discussed in light of U.S. immigration law and the farmworker social movements.

THE THREE SYSTEMS OF U.S. AGRICULTURAL PRODUCTION

The prototypical image of U.S. agriculture is the family farm. Television programs such as *The Waltons* and *Little House on the Prairie* have taken this image to represent the totality of rural America. But Max Pfeffer notes that this model fits well with the geographic area of the Great Plains after the Homestead Act of 1862 parceled small plots of prairie land to individual families. In fact, European immigrant families were able to capitalize on the prospect of owning land in the midwestern United States. But there are two other forms of U.S. agricultural production that do not fit the family farm mythos: sharecropping in the southern United States and corporate farming (otherwise referred to as agribusiness) in California. Sharecropping is a remnant of the slave plantation economy, and particularly in the regions where cotton was cultivated, the children and grandchildren of slaves often became sharecroppers for the same families who had owned their ancestors, working the same land.

Scale is one feature of the corporate model of agricultural production that distinguishes it from the family farming and sharecropping models. Agribusiness, by its very definition, coordinates production on a large scale. As early as 1939, the social critic and historian Carey McWilliams referred to the agribusiness mode of production as "factories in the field." Even though California is the penultimate in corporate agriculture, this system of production has a long historical formation in the southwestern United States and is quickly expanding to the geographic areas that had previously embodied the family farm and sharecropper systems.

The origins of large-scale agricultural production in the Southwest arise from the colonial settlement pattern of issuing land grants to develop *ranchos*. These plots of land were established for agricultural

Low-wage agriculture often provides the only work available to many immigrants, like this Haitian farmworker in Putnam County, New York. *(Mel Rosenthal)*

and livestock purposes but were also granted in large tracts to expand private property in the name of the Spanish empire. The Spanish land grants that fueled the rancho movement had one particular effect that persists: The land grants were designed to establish private property claims to ensure that the frontier could be expanded to the greatest possible extent. In the Southwest and particularly California, this resulted in the parceling out of large tracts of land concentrated in the hands of the few.

To understand the scale of California agribusiness, one must look at the history of land tenure in California that concentrated such large landholdings within the ranks of the elite class of landowners. Elite Spanish landowners were replaced by wealthy Anglo land speculators (through fraud, theft, and changing legal structures) after the U.S.-Mexico War of 1846–48. Mexico ceded nearly one-half of its northern territory to the United States for the purchase price of $15 million. The Treaty of Guadalupe Hidalgo secured the peace agreement between the two nations as well as defining the rights of Mexican citizens who found themselves suddenly on U.S. soil—foreigners in their own land. Article 10 of the treaty specifically stated that the United States would honor all Spanish and Mexican land grants in the U.S. territories. The U.S. Senate removed this article from the treaty. As historian Lawrence Cardoso notes, "Beginning during the periods of Spanish and Mexican sovereignty over the area, grants of land from crown or republican governments had frequently conveyed huge plots to private parties. . . . With the advent of irrigation projects many of these same properties, and others conveyed subsequent to 1848, were converted to intensive agricultural use. The sheer size of the new farmlands obviated the possibility of a resident labor force."

California was the most extreme example of land concentration and Anglo control. In 1900, farms with more than 1,000 acres accounted for more than 60 percent of all agricultural acreage. California governor Henry Haight stated that the land system was designed to "facilitate the acquisition of large blocks of land by capitalists or corporations either as donations or at nominal prices." California soon became a state whose Anglo landowners became dependent entirely on migrant labor from Asia and Mexico.

ETHNIC AND RACIAL SHIFTS IN AGRICULTURAL LABOR

Corporate agribusiness in the United States is one sector that has traditionally been filled by the most desperate and destitute of internal and international migrants. Carey McWilliams's 1939 *Factories in the Fields* traces the succession of ethnic groups who provided the preponderance of the labor for California capitalist agriculture. First used by agribusiness were the indentured servants of Japan and China who were forced into California agriculture in exchange for passage. Chinese immigrants provided the majority of manual labor in California agriculture from the 1860s to their prohibition in 1882. In addition, the Chinese also provided the expertise in fruit cultivation that moved the California agricultural economy from a wheat producer to a fruit and vegetable producer. The Chinese Exclusion Act of 1882 and subsequent acts of 1892, 1902, and 1904 barred further immigration from China and cut off the stream of cheap labor that flowed eastward. Due to the anti-Chinese sentiments, it is impossible to provide an accurate assessment of the percentage of Chinese laborers employed in the fields. The anti-Chinese California Bureau of Labor estimated that in 1870, 90 percent of the agricultural labor of the state was performed by Chinese immigrants. This percentage is probably an exaggeration, but it does point to the heavy reliance of California agribusiness on Chinese laborers.

After passage of the Chinese Exclusion Act, Japanese migrants were recruited to fill the void. The rising importance of the combined cultivation of sugar beets and strawberries at the turn of the century relied most heavily on Japanese immigrants. The model of factory farming followed the agricultural developments in Hawaii. Utilizing Japanese laborers in Hawaii to cultivate the sugarcane and strawberry crops, large-scale growers such as John D. Spreckles lobbied the federal and California state governments to apply a similar production model with the same labor pool. The introduction of sugar beet cultivation brought the processing factories closer to the fields, thus beginning large-scale corporate farming in California. In 1907, the Gentleman's Agreement was arranged between the federal governments of Japan and the United States to bar Japanese laborers from entering the United States. The final action that was fueled by the nativist sentiments of the time was the 1924 Quota Act, which completely barred migration from Asia and limited migration from southern and eastern Europe. Due to the limited successes of East Indian, Japanese, and Chinese laborers to purchase land and begin cultivation, California also enacted a series of "alien landholding" acts that sought to ban Asians from owning land. Due to the colonial status of the Philippines, Filipino immigrants were admitted as U.S. citizens and started working in the fields as early as 1923, but they too met the exclusionary measures. When the Philippines called for independence in 1934, the islands were subject to the 1924 Quota Act, and further migration was halted. McWilliams estimated that fifty thousand Filipinos, mostly working as agricultural laborers, remained in the United States at the end of the 1930s.

With the passage of laws that restricted migration from Asia, Mexican labor was contracted to work the fields during the first part of the twentieth century. The major influx of Mexican laborers took place during World War I, when a labor shortage was officially identified by the U.S. government. With the sanction from the government, U.S. growers sent *enganchadores* (labor contractors) to the U.S. border towns and the interior of Mexico to recruit laborers. El Paso, Texas, became the central way station for the labor recruitment and distribution of Mexican migrants. The termination point of the Mexican Central Railroad, which originated in central Mexico, was El Paso. Most U.S. rail lines that headed westward, such as the Southern Pacific Railroad, went through El Paso. The heavy recruitment of Mexican laborers came to a complete halt during the Great Depression when an estimated five hundred thousand Mexicans (a portion were even U.S. citizens) were repatriated to Mexico. President Hoover even went as far as to blame the Great Depression on the influx of Mexican immigrants taking jobs from citizens. The nativist sentiment had found a new target: the Mexican population residing in the United States.

In some ways, the Mexican population was displaced during the depression to make room for white citizens fleeing the Dust Bowl of Oklahoma and Arkansas. The New Deal programs and industrial development, which were both geared toward the white destitute population, provided the white working class two means of leaving the fields for better opportunities. It was in the late 1930s to the 1960s that a mix of European, African-American, Filipino, Mexican-American, and Mexican immigrant laborers toiled in the fields.

But Mexican migrant workers also were able to locate work in other parts of the Southwest. In Colorado, the rise of the sugar beet industry paralleled the growth of monopoly capitalists that controlled entire regions of production. The Great Western Sugar Company controlled most of northern Colorado, Wyoming, and the western portions of Nebraska and Kansas owing to the economic significance of its processing plants. Great Western and other large-scale agribusiness firms began to recruit seasonal labor from the predominately Chicano areas of the rural Southwest, urban trade centers such as El Paso, and rural villages in Mexico. The enganchadores were institutionalized as the central means of recruiting labor to harvest the vast tracts of land devoted solely to the production of sugar beets.

A major shift occurred as capitalist social relations became firmly entrenched into the local south Texas communities. Douglas Foley describes the shift as a move from the rancho era of semifeudal relations (1900–1930) to the *colonia* era of capitalism (1930–60). "As agriculture became fully capitalist in character, a major recomposition of the community's class structure occurred. The old semifeudal relationships of patrons to their peons were transformed into a modern, more impersonal, wage-labor relationship during the Colonia era." The social historian David Montejano refers to Texas agricultural production as encompassing labor controls and discipline imposed by Anglo farmers on Mexican farmworkers as a set of repressive labor relations: "Labor repression refers basically to the use of compulsion for organizing the recruitment, work activity, and compensation of wage labor." These labor relations were indicative of the corporate agricultural system of production and were codified by the United States at the start of World War II.

The Bracero Program extended the employment of Mexican nationals to every region of the United States. From 1942 to 1964, the United States and Mexico arranged a set of accords that supplied U.S. agricultural growers, and for a brief time the railroad industry, with a steady stream of Mexican labor. Initially intended to serve as a wartime relief measure, the temporary-worker arrangements were allowed to continue until 1964. The vast majority of workers were sent to three states (California, Arizona, and Texas), but a total of thirty states participated in the program. In the contemporary situation, an almost total reliance on Mexican nationals (legal, undocumented, and contracted) can be traced back to its origins in the Bracero Program.

A rise in undocumented migration from Mexico occurred when the number of contracts issued to braceros was reduced. In 1954, an Immigration and Naturalization Service measure to repatriate undocumented workers was implemented under the name of Operation Wetback. The patterns of undocumented migration followed earlier recruitment patterns by labor contractors and stemmed from the regions of Mexico that sent the largest number of braceros to the United States during the program. It was not until 1986 that the United States took an active stance against undocumented migration.

PUBLIC AWARENESS OF THE PLIGHT OF THE MIGRANT FARMWORKER

Unfortunately, the plight of the migrant agricultural worker has rarely found its way into the popular imagination. A handful of works have periodically shattered the silences surrounding the issues facing agricultural labor. In the 1930s, John Steinbeck's *Grapes of Wrath* was the first and single most important fictionalized account of the migrant condition during the depression. Through the Okie family of the Joads, Steinbeck dramatized an account of poverty and limited life chances of the agricultural laborers in California agribusiness. Following on the heels of the best-seller, McWilliams's *Factories in the Fields* was another best-seller focused on California agribusiness. McWilliams offered a historically informed analysis of land tenure patterns, ethnic and racial discrimination, and the advent of capitalist social relations in agriculture. Two other successful works of nonfiction—Dorothea Lange and Paul S. Taylor's *An American Exodus* and *Let Us Now Praise Famous Men* by James Agee and Walker Evans blended eloquent prose and stark photographic images to offer two realist texts on the deplorable living conditions of white migrants and sharecroppers. Each of these novels had the effect of inserting the lives of agricultural laborers into the consciousness of the U.S. public.

As quickly as migrant workers were thrust onto the public stage, they were returned to obscurity until a *CBS Reports* special aired on Thanksgiving in 1960. Edward R. Murrow's "Harvest of Shame" chronicled the lives of migrant farmworkers in the United States and exposed their dire living conditions and abject poverty. The documentary wove interviews with growers in California and Florida, Secretary of Labor James Mitchell, the president of the American Farm Bureau, Representative Harrison Williams (D-NJ), a journalist, a teacher of migrant children, a crew boss, a reverend who lived with migrants, and several white and black migrant families with images of migrant camps, shakedowns, unsafe transportation practices, an Agricultural Workers Organizing Committee

(AWOC) union rally for striking cherry pickers, and, for approximately twenty-eight seconds, Mexican braceros crossing the border into the United States for agricultural work.

The stated purpose of "Harvest of Shame" was to introduce those forgotten, or invisible, workers who harvested the food that found its way to the Thanksgiving dinner tables in the United States. As Murrow states, "These are the forgotten people. Were it not for the labor of the people you are going to meet, your table would not be laden with the luxuries that we have all come to regard as essential. We should like you to meet some of your fellow citizens who harvest the food for the best-fed nation on earth."

The focus on "citizens" is laden with assumptions that persist in the United States about the Mexican-origin population that resides within U.S. boundaries. "Harvest of Shame" succeeded in shedding light on the black and white citizens whose labor put food on the table for the U.S. public. At the same time, it relegated the Mexican and other immigrant groups residing in the United States even further into obscurity despite the fact that their labor was equally responsible for feeding "the best-fed nation on earth."

Issues surrounding migrant agricultural workers were again returned to their invisible status until the United Farm Workers organized a successful and publicly recognized grape boycott. In January 1968, "the union began its legendary boycott against all California table grapes—a campaign that cut across all age, class, and regional differences, and became the most ambitious and successful boycott in American history." Targeting California growers of table grapes and national grocery supermarket chains, the boycott was very successful in bringing a public eye to the lack of union representation for agricultural laborers. "*Uvas, NO!*" became the rallying cry that found its way into the national newspapers and evening news reports.

HISTORY OF U.S. IMMIGRATION LAW

United States immigration law did not take on its restrictionist cast until the Chinese Exclusion Act was passed in 1882. Before then, the only immigrants who were likely to be barred from entry were those "likely to become a public charge" or "enemies of the state." The Chinese Exclusion Act began a long history of targeting and restricting ethnic groups from entering the United States. Anti-Chinese conventions were held in California, and the Chinese communities in Tacoma, Washington, and Denver, Colorado, faced

acts of mob violence. One of the worst episodes occurred in Rock Springs, Wyoming, in 1885. In that mining community a white mob drove Chinese workers out of town and burned their homes and killed twenty-eight Chinese immigrants.

The next targeted group to draw the ire of nativist restrictionists was the Japanese immigrant community. Owing to their relative success in moving from agricultural laborers to farm owners, Japanese immigrants were charged with undercutting citizen workers. As the sociologist Thomas Archdeacon writes, "Through a series of notes exchanged between Tokyo and Washington in 1907–8, Japan promised not to issue passports to laborers desiring to emigrate to the United States. Tokyo also recognized the Americans' right to turn back Japanese who attempted to enter on documents issued initially for travel to other places, including Hawaii, Mexico, and Canada."

The Gentlemen's Agreement was aimed at Japanese male laborers, the majority of whom worked in California agriculture, and coincided with the alien landholding laws that restricted Asian immigrants from owning and leasing land. These acts were formally codified in the 1924 act barring all immigrants from Asia with the exception of the U.S. colony of the Philippine Islands. Coinciding with the Quota Acts that were aimed at restricting southern and eastern European immigrants from entering the country, the year 1924 represented the legislative pinnacle of nativist sentiments and immigration restriction.

With the barring of Asian immigrants, Mexican citizens were actively recruited to fill the void. The history of U.S. immigration law, as it relates to Mexican migrant laborers, is associated with the corporate farming system. This system, which relies almost exclusively on migrant workers, was associated with agribusiness in California and was the major recipient of Mexican workers. The sociologists George Kiser and Martha Kiser refer to two bracero eras: the first associated with World War I and the second associated with World War II. Both the two wartime invitations that the United States extended to Mexican citizens to meet labor-shortage needs were accompanied by episodes of mass repatriations. Lawrence Cardoso notes that the United States officially sanctioned the importation of laborers, and growers recruited Mexican nationals during World War I. Later mass unemployment of the Great Depression was perceived to be "partially remedied" by the large-scale repatriation of Mexican citizens. During times of labor surpluses or economic downturns, a number of Mexican nationals and U.S. citizens of Mexican descent either voluntarily returned or were forced to return to Mexico. In Los Angeles alone during the 1930s, nearly one-third of the Mexican population returned to Mexico. These episodes of mass repatriation were highly symbolic of the status of Mexicans in U.S. society.

The first and most significant "guest-worker program" of the U.S. government was the Bracero Program, 1942–64. The Bracero Program began on August 4, 1942, in Stockton, California, as a result of the U.S. government responding to requests by southwestern agricultural growers for the recruitment of foreign labor. The agreement, arranged between the federal governments of Mexico and the United States, stated the following four terms, which served as the general guidelines for its twenty-two-year existence:

1. Mexican contract workers would not engage in U.S. military service.

2. Mexicans entering the U.S. under provisions of the agreement would not be subjected to discriminatory acts.

3. Workers would be guaranteed transportation, living expenses, and repatriation along the lines established under Article 29 of Mexican labor laws.

4. Mexicans entering under the agreement would not be employed either to displace domestic workers or to reduce their wages.

Nine months later, under many of the same agreement guidelines, though utilizing different administrative channels, the railroad industry secured the importation of Mexican laborers to meet wartime shortages.

The first guideline was meant to quell Mexican popular discontent and apprehensions about how earlier uses (during World War I) of Mexican labor were thought to have occurred during the first bracero era. Without government interference, U.S. growers directly recruited Mexican laborers from Mexico to meet wartime labor shortages. After the First World War, the citizens of Mexico heard a number of rumors that Mexican laborers, brought to the United States to work in the agricultural fields, were forced into the military to fight in the war. The governments of both the United States and Mexico denied that the practice ever occurred. Nevertheless, the first article was meant to reduce Mexican popular apprehensiveness and to allay fears.

The second article was designed to explicitly ban discrimination against Mexican nationals and served as the key bargaining chip by the Mexican government to safeguard the treatment of braceros by Anglo growers. The arrangements of the first bracero program, during World War I, were conducted without the input of the Mexican government. As a result, Mexican nationals worked in the United States without protections, and subsequently, workers were subject to a number of discriminatory acts.

From 1942 to 1947, no braceros were sent to Texas because of the documented mistreatment of Mexican workers by Texas growers and other citizens. A series of assurances by the Texas state government were secured before growers were allowed to import labor from Mexico. The states of Colorado, Illinois, Indiana, Michigan, Montana, Minnesota, Wisconsin, and Wyoming were also blacklisted by the Mexican government until the 1950s due to discriminatory practices documented in each of the states.

The third article was intended to guarantee workers safe passage to and from the United States as well as decent living conditions while working in the United States. The costs associated with transportation, room, and board would be covered by someone other than the workers if Mexico's labor laws were followed to their exact wording. But these costs were subject to negotiation by the Mexican government, and as a result, workers had a number of these expenses deducted from their paychecks.

The final article was designed to reduce competition between domestic and contracted labor, and the United States government played two roles in assuring that competition would not arise. The first role was the determination of the "prevailing wage" in each region of the country. To ensure that braceros were receiving the same rate as domestics, the prevailing wage was determined prior to the harvest season in each locale, and braceros were to receive that wage. Labor activist Ernesto Galarza notes that the prevailing wage was approved by the Department of Labor, but it was growers who got together before the harvest and fixed the pay rates to determine the prevailing wage they were willing to pay.

It was also the responsibility of the Department of Labor to designate when a certain region had a labor shortage of available domestic workers. Again, growers were the key to this determination because they were responsible for notifying the department when they expected labor shortages to occur. Growers would often set a prevailing wage rate so low as to effectively discourage domestics from working at wage levels at which one could not live in the United States.

The historical record of the treatment of braceros developed contrary to the guidelines put forth by the Mexican government. Galarza documented the lack of adequate housing; substandard wages; exorbitant prices for inedible food; illegal deductions for food, insurance, and health care; inadequate transportation; and a lack of legal rights. The historian Erasmo Gamboa found in his study of braceros working in the Pacific Northwest that "although the workers had contracts guaranteeing minimum job standards, their employers unilaterally established rock bottom and discriminatory wage rates. In doing so, growers reduced the workers to a state of peonage.... In addition, the farmers' reckless abandon of human considerations was shocking and led to numerous job-related accidents."

One of the main results of the program was a steady increase in the number of Mexican undocumented workers, which was dealt with in three ways. The most common means of dealing with growers using noncontracted labor on the part of state authorities was to ignore undocumented workers and allow them to seek work in the United States. These undocumented workers were usually directly recruited in Mexico by farm labor contractors or other intermediaries on behalf of growers. In particular, those growers near the border were able to recruit Mexican laborers directly and avoid the bureaucratic channels of the Bracero Program. The illegal status of undocumented farmworkers was an advantage to growers because the rights guaranteed to braceros did not have to be met. At no time were growers held responsible for directly recruiting "illegal" labor. It was not until 1986 that growers could be held legally responsible for hiring undocumented workers.

The second way of dealing with illegal immigration was to legalize undocumented workers by giving them bracero contracts. From the period of 1947–54, undocumented workers were contracted as braceros at the U.S. sites where they were already working. The bureaucratic regulations of the Bracero Program were then applied ex post facto to legalize illegal workers. As scholar Manuel García y Griego describes the process: "Legalization was a process by which deportable Mexicans who had been in the United States for a certain number of weeks were given bracero contracts, usually to work for the same employer, without the laborer having to return to Mexico and undergo the screening process in the interior, or the employer having to pay transportation to the United States."

The third way of dealing with illegal immigration was deportation. In 1954, Commissioner Joseph Swing of the Immigration and Naturalization Service mounted a mass repatriation campaign of illegal Mexican workers, dubbed Operation Wetback, which resulted in a return of 1.3 million workers to Mexico. The means of repatriation varied—migrants forced to return, voluntary leavers—but the effect was the same: "Operation Wetback did not bring an end to illegal immigration from Mexico. It did slow the influx for a short time but it brought no permanent solution to the problem. It was a stop-gap measure," says historian Juan Ramon García. Operation Wetback sent a strong message to the Mexican people about their rights to live and work in the United States. It also sent a strong message to Anglo growers, stating that they would not be held responsible for the mass migration that they initiated and perpetuated by actively recruiting and employing undocumented labor. This mass repatriation of Mexicans occurred at a time when the Bracero Program was running at its peak. At the same time, the contradictory message was sent to Mexican immigrants that they were not wanted in the United States yet their labor would be remunerated and rights protected if they had a bracero contract.

The 1986 Immigration Reform and Control Act (IRCA) sought to provide a comprehensive set of provisions to deal with the agricultural labor situation as well as the issue of undocumented immigration. The employer sanctions provision was designed to hold accountable employers who knowingly hired undocumented laborers. Verification of citizenship status became a lasting feature for all new hires. The legalization provision was designed to grant U.S. citizenship for undocumented immigrants who could prove they had lived in the United States continuously for at least the previous ten years. Special rules were enacted in regard to the undocumented migrant and seasonal worker population owing to the circular migration trends that predominated. The H-2A Program is in many ways an extension of the Bracero Program. Designed to meet the needs of U.S. growers, the program was written into the law to guarantee the option of employing immigrant workers if citizens are not willing to work in agriculture.

FARMWORKER SOCIAL MOVEMENTS

A long history of labor struggle in the fields has been documented by a number of scholars. Throughout the Southwest, episodes of labor strikes, retaliatory measures, and unionization efforts define the legacy of labor relations in the agribusiness industry. The earliest successful organizing campaign and strike was conducted by the Japanese-Mexican Labor Association (JMLA). In 1903, growers in Oxnard, California, formed their own labor-contracting association to exclude Japanese labor contractors from providing workers. Wages were reduced, often by one-half, by the grower-controlled Western Association Contracting Company (WACC). On February 11, 1903, writes the historian Tomás Almaguer, "approximately 800 Japanese and Mexican workers organized the Japanese-Mexican Labor Association, electing as officers Kosaburo Baba (president), Y. Yamaguchi (secretary of the Japanese branch), and J. M. Lizarras (secretary of the Mexican branch)."

This is all the more impressive because collective bargaining and the right to unionize were not granted to U.S. workers until 1935. The National Labor Relations Act (NLRA) established the rights of workers to join unions. The National Labor Relations Board (NLRB) was a victory for industrial workers, but not all workers. Agriculture was specifically exempted from the NLRA. Agricultural employers were also exempt from minimum wage laws with which other U.S. employers were legally bound to comply. Given these obstacles, the JMLA represents a very important early victory in the assertion of immigrant worker rights.

The sociologists Richard Griswold del Castillo and Arnoldo de León note other obstacles to labor organizing: antilabor passions, the deliberate strategy undertaken by management to divide and rule workers, and the power of employers to use scabs, violence, police authority (Texas Rangers in Texas), and threats of deportation or incarceration. In spite of the obstacles, farmworkers in other regions were able to organize and strike for better working conditions. La Unión de Trabajadores del Valle Imperial led a successful campaign for better wages and working conditions in the cantaloupe farms of California's Imperial Valley. An organized work stoppage in the fields of Wheatland, California, resulted in violence and the calling in of the National Guard. The mainstream union movement was not particularly interested in organizing the racialized Mexican immigrant community, so early labor struggles depended on the tenuous support of the Mexican consulate and the more steady support of the *mutualistas* (mutual aid societies) and ladies' auxiliaries.

The drive for union representation for migrant farmworkers was always ancillary to the industrial labor movement. Fringe unions, such as the Southern Tenant Farmer's Union, attempted to organize in the fields under the leadership of Ernesto Galarza and the National Farm Labor Union (NFLU). Recruitment was limited strictly to U.S. citizens, based on U.S. labor laws, so many immigrant workers were automatically excluded from joining the ranks. In 1959, the American Federation of Labor-Congress of Industrial Organizations (AFL-CIO) finally took an active interest in organizing farmworkers and created the Agricultural Workers Organizing Committee (AWOC). Unfortunately, AWOC seemed to be designed, based on Ernesto Galarza's perspective, to replace the NFLU, and the union infighting assured its eventual failure in recruiting workers and improving conditions. Publicly, a libel suit filed by DiGiorgio Farms over the AWOC showing of the banned documentary *Poverty in the Valley of Plenty* had disastrous consequences, says Galarza. "In the working code of agribusiness the test of this strategy was that it worked. The obnoxious film was suppressed, a strike was broken, a labor organizing campaign in the Central Valley was repulsed, DiGiorgio freshened his laurels as the champion of farmers big and little, and a scorching indictment of agricultural unionism passed unchallenged." It was not until the rise of the United Farm Workers (UFW), led by Cesar Chavez and Dolores Huerta, that farmworkers were able to call a union their own and see tangible results from the organizing, boycotting, and strike efforts. In terms of public consciousness, the UFW succeeded by bringing the plight of the migrant farmworker into the everyday lives of U.S. citizens. With their boycott of California table grape growers and supermarket chains, the march to Sacramento, and Chavez's hunger strike, the UFW became part of a much larger movement that called for social justice for Chicanos. The UFW also was closely aligned with the Filipino migrant community, and both Cesar Chavez and Larry Itliong helped organize the AWOC and were both present at the signing of the first union contract by Giumarra Farms.

One of the principal means of organizing workers was through the theatrical productions performed by El Teatro Campesino. The group found great success well beyond the fields and traveled extensively in Europe, to college campuses, and city auditoriums to dramatize publicly the issues confronting migrant workers. The director, Luis Valdez, has become a successful motion picture director but recently stated that "the cultural root is the campesino, the farmworker. I don't care how sophisticated we get in the city, we share the communal remembrance of the earth. This goes for Chicanos as well as anyone else." In addition to these efforts, the UFW also branched out to other regions of the country. A sister organization, the Farm Labor Organizing Committee (FLOC), was founded in 1967 to represent migrant farmworkers of the Midwest. Currently, the UFW is present in Washington, California, Florida, Pennsylvania, Texas, Oregon, Arizona, and other agricultural states.

CONTEMPORARY TRENDS IN MIGRANT FARM LABOR

The National Agricultural Workers Survey (NAWS) was the first systematic attempt on the part of U.S. government data collection agencies to survey the migrant worker population. Conducting interviews with over 7,200 workers from 1989 to 1992, the survey notes that farm labor forces are increasingly reliant on Latino immigrants. Seventy percent of those surveyed are Latino, and of the immigrant population, 96 percent of the foreign-born are Latino. The increasing reliance on Mexican immigrant workers in agriculture is evidenced by the trend in California. In 1965, 46 percent of farmworkers were Latino. In 1988, 88 percent of farmworkers were Latino, and from 1989 to 1991, 92 percent.

This increasing reliance on Mexican labor has resulted in the development of migrant streams to the different areas of the United States that currently employ migrant labor. Workers in the established migrant streams travel from Mexico, through the border states of California, Arizona, New Mexico, and Texas, to the Pacific Coast, Mountain States, Upper Midwest, or the Atlantic Coast. A number of agricultural communities in California and southern Texas also send migrant workers along these same routes as well as to the Ozark/Appalachian region.

The NAWS survey found that the migrant labor force is overwhelmingly male (73 percent) and relatively young (median age 31). This result has the effect of separating the costs associated with reproducing the conditions necessary for family survival (health care, education services, food, shelter, clothing) from the costs of production for profit. In effect, the sending communities of Mexico bear the costs of maintaining the family, while the receiving communities of the United States reap the benefits of cheap labor who come for strictly production purposes (to make enough money to send back to Mexico for sustenance).

This situation is only liken to worsen given the political climate of today and the public worries about the "Latinization" of U.S. society. In 1994, California voters overwhelmingly passed Proposition 187 in order to deny public services to undocumented immigrants. Not recognizing the social costs of reproduction that are paid in Mexico, the mass media and immigration commentators clamored about how undocumented immigrants were purportedly draining the social services of the United States. The amount of sales tax dollars that Mexican immigrants contribute to the economy were ignored in favor of focusing on Mexican women having children in U.S. hospitals or highly publicized welfare fraud campaigns. In many ways, the economic recession, which California was enduring as a result of deindustrialization and the state's reliance on shrinking military contract dollars, was much easier to blame on undocumented immigrants. Using the Mexican immigrant as a scapegoat represents a return to the nativism that had disastrous consequences on prior generations of immigrants.

Ronald L. Mize

See also: Unions and Union Organizing (Part II, Sec. 8); Rural America (Part II, Sec. 12); Mexico (Part III, Sec. 2); "Bracero Program" Act, 1949, California's Farm Labor Law, 1975 (Part IV, Sec. 1).

BIBLIOGRAPHY

Agee, James, and Walker Evans. *Let Us Now Praise Famous Men.* Boston: Houghton Mifflin, 1941.

Almaguer, Tomás. "Racial Domination and Class Conflict in Capitalist Agriculture: The Oxnard Sugar Beet Workers' Strike of 1903." In *From Different Shores: Perspectives on Race and Ethnicity in America,* ed. Ronald Talcaki, pp. 128–38. 2d ed. New York: Oxford University Press, 1999.

Archdeacon, Thomas J. *Becoming American: An Ethnic History.* New York: Free Press, 1983.

Barger, W. K., and Ernesto Reza. *The Farm Labor Movement in the Midwest.* Austin: University of Texas Press, 1994.

Cardoso, Lawrence. *Mexican Emigration to the United States.* Tucson: University of Arizona Press, 1980.

Department of Labor. *U.S. Farmworkers in the Post-IRCA Period: Based on Data from the National Agricultural Workers Survey (NAWS).* Washington, DC: Department of Labor, 1993.

Ferris, Susan, and Ricardo Sandoval. *The Fight in the Fields: Cesar Chavez and the Farmworkers Movement.* New York: Harcourt Brace Jovanovich, 1997.

Foley, Douglas. *Learning Capitalist Culture: Deep in the Heart of Tejas.* Philadelphia: University of Pennsylvania Press, 1990.

Foley, Douglas, et al. *From Peones to Politicos.* Austin: University of Texas Press, 1988.

Galarza, Ernest. *Merchants of Labor: The Mexican Bracero History.* Santa Barbara, CA: McNally and Loftin, 1964.

———. *Spiders in the House and Workers in the Fields.* South Bend, IN: University of Notre Dame Press, 1970.

———. *Strangers in Our Fields: Based on a Report regarding Compliance with the Contractual, Legal, and Civil Rights of Mexican Agricultural Contract Labor in the United States.* 2d ed. Washington, DC: United States Section, Joint United States-Mexico Trade Union Committee, 1956.

Gamboa, Erasmo. *Mexican Labor and World War II: Braceros in the Pacific Northwest, 1942–1947*. Austin: University of Texas Press, 1990.

García, Juan Ramon. *Operation Wetback: The Mass Deportation of Mexican Undocumented Workers in 1954*. Westport, CT: Greenwood Press, 1980.

García y Griego, Manuel. "U.S. Importation of Mexican Contract Laborers." In *The Border That Joins*, ed. Peter Brown and Henry Shue, pp. 49–98. Totowa, NJ: Rowman and Littlefield, 1983.

Griswold del Castillo, Richard, and Arnoldo de León. *North to Aztlán: A History of Mexican Americans in the United States*. New York: Twayne Publishers, 1996.

Kiser, George C., and Martha W. Kiser. *Mexican Workers in the United States*. Albuquerque: University of New Mexico Press, 1979.

Lange, Dorothea, and Paul S. Taylor. *An American Exodus*. New York: Reynal and Hitchcock, 1939.

McWilliams, Carey. *Factories in the Fields: The Story of Migratory Labor in California*. 1939; Berkeley: University of California Press, 1999.

Montejano, David. *Anglos and Mexicans in the Making of Texas*. Austin: University of Texas Press, 1987.

Pfeffer, Max. "Social Origins of Three Systems of Farm Production in the United States." *Rural Sociology* 48:4 (1983): 540–62.

Reimers, David. *Still the Golden Door: The Third World Comes to America*. New York: Columbia University Press, 1985.

Sanchez, George J. *Becoming Mexican American*. New York: Oxford University Press, 1993.

Steinbeck, John. *The Grapes of Wrath*. New York: Viking, 1935.

LABOR MARKETS FOR RECENT IMMIGRANTS: A STATISTICAL PORTRAIT

The labor markets for immigrants living and working in the United States are an important consideration, because this population constitutes an increasing proportion of the U.S. population and workforce. The 1992 U.S. Labor Department's Legalized Population Survey (LPS) indicates how immigrants adapt to labor markets in the United States after obtaining lawful permanent residence. The survey—with its several measures of labor market outcomes—also allows illustration of how the legalized population is faring within the U.S. labor market, as economic adaptation is perhaps the most important form of adaptation. In addition, the survey provides a way to assess how education and English fluency influence immigrants' labor market experiences.

The survey employs such conventional measures of labor market experience as income and wages. But it also includes other measures of immigrant economic well-being, including occupation employment status, hourly wage, yearly income, the number of hours worked per week, and formal or informal labor market participation. These variables provide a comprehensive statistical picture of immigrants in the workforce.

SURVEY DATA

With the passage of the Immigration Reform and Control Act (IRCA) in 1986, the United States granted permanent residency to about 2.7 million undocumented immigrants who were living in the United States. The act legalized undocumented immigrants living in the United States, imposed sanctions on employers of undocumented immigrants, and increased the number of Immigration and Naturalization Service (INS) agents. According to a 1996 Department of Labor study, IRCA allowed 1.6 million undocumented immigrants who had resided in the United States prior to 1982, as well as 1.1 million migrant farmworkers, to become lawful permanent residents. The LPS contains data about the labor market experiences of the 1.6 million immigrants who were granted lawful permanent residency, and these immigrants will be the focus of this essay. The LPS data provide a valuable opportunity to study formerly undocumented immigrants, as the survey was able to collect data about undocumented immigrants who are typically underrepresented in other surveys, such as the census.

Most respondents included in the LPS are Mexican immigrants, who represent the largest portion of the undocumented population living in the United States. In total, Mexican immigrants account for 69 percent of the undocumented immigrants legalized through IRCA. About 15 percent were from Central America, and the remaining 16 percent represent nations throughout the world.

Survey interviews were first conducted in 1989 by the INS. Three years later, the Department of Labor conducted follow-up interviews, which provided information about the immigrants after they received lawful permanent residency. Lawful permanent residency meant that immigrants could legally remain in the United States and would be eligible for citizenship after five years.

FINDINGS

Table 1 illustrates the labor market outcomes of the legalized population. It includes only immigrants eighteen to sixty-four years of age, as those younger or older are not likely to be fully incorporated into the labor market. For employment status, all immigrants

A Salvadoran immigrant is fingerprinted in Washington, D.C., in order to file papers for temporary legal working status. *(Donna DeCesare/Impact Visuals)*

eighteen to sixty-four years of age are included. For the remaining labor market outcomes, including constructed hourly wage, individual yearly income in 1991, number of hours worked in the previous week, formal or informal labor market participation, and occupation, only those eighteen to sixty-four years of age who were employed at the time of the survey are examined.

Studies by sociologists Pierrette Hondagneu-Sotelo, Tony Tam, and others suggest that male and female workers differ in many respects. Thus Table 1 includes three classifications: all workers, male workers, and female workers.

Differences between the total number of respondents included in the measures of labor market outcomes are the result of missing cases. "Missing cases" signify information that the respondent was unable or unwilling to provide to interviewers. Thus, small discrepancies exist between the total number of respondents included in the employment outcomes.

LABOR MARKET OUTCOMES

The first labor market outcome in Table 1 is employment status. Employment status is one of the most important measures of the labor market, for workers who are unemployed and out of the labor market are excluded from earning a living. People who do not want to work because they are occupied with other activities such as schooling or raising children, or those who simply have given up seeking employment, are considered out of the labor market. The "All Workers" column shows that 76 percent of the workers are employed, 8 percent are unemployed, and 17 percent are out of the labor market. Employment status varies widely between men and women: Eighty-six percent of the male immigrant workers and only 63 percent of the female workers are employed. This discrepancy is very likely the result of females being occupied with children, because about 82 percent, or 540 of the 662 workers who are out of the

An early morning line-up in Los Angeles finds Mexican men and women applying for their green cards, which would allow them to work legally in America. *(Carolina Kroon/Impact Visuals)*

workforce in the All Workers column, are females. Thus, the employment of immigrant workers differs along gender lines.

Turning to hourly wages, the constructed hourly wage is taken from several survey questions. This figure is called variable constructed hourly wage because for those who earn salaries rather than an hourly rate, their hourly pay is derived by dividing their weekly salary by the number of hours they worked that week. This allows the consideration of hourly pay for both salaried and nonsalaried workers.

From the constructed hourly pay, six wage categories represent the immigrant workers' hourly pay. About 5 percent of these immigrants were earning an hourly rate below the minimum wage, which at the time of the survey was $4.25 per hour. It should be noted that a majority of these low earners are women. About 25 percent of all workers earn between $4.25 and $6.00, which is also low. A disproportionate num-

ber of these low earners are also women: Seventeen percent of the men earn from $4.25 to $6.00 an hour, whereas 37 percent of the women earn this wage. Combining the low earnings categories shows that 56 percent of this sample earn $8.00 or less. Of all workers, 20 percent earn between $10.01 and $15.00 an hour. Of men, 25 percent earn between $10.01 and $15.00 an hour, while 12 percent of women's earnings are in this category. About 11 percent of the men and 5 percent of the women (8 percent of the sample) earn over $15.00 an hour. These data show that even after the immigrant workers obtained lawful permanent residence in the United States, which removed legal restrictions against working, most were still earning low wages, and female workers were earning significantly less than male workers.

Although hourly pay is an accurate measure of economic well-being, yearly income also has its benefits as a measure. Yearly income accounts for the labor market outcomes of immigrant workers through-

Table 1
Labor Market Outcomes from the 1992 Legalized Population Survey

	All Workers		Male Workers		Female Workers	
	%	*n*	%	*n*	%	*n*
Employment status						
Employed	76	2,989	86	1,854	63	1,135
Unemployed	8	298	8	172	7	126
Out of labor market	17	662	6	122	30	540
Total	100	3,949	100	2,148	100	1,801
Constructed hourly wage						
$1.00–$4.24	5	127	3	50	7	77
$4.25–$6.00	25	696	17	304	37	392
$6.01–$8.00	26	721	25	432	27	289
$8.01–$10.00	17	478	20	345	12	133
$10.01–$15.00	20	559	25	432	12	127
$15.01 and higher	8	238	11	185	5	53
Total	100	2,819	100	1,748	100	1,071
Individual yearly income in 1991						
$0–$2,999	7	196	3	56	13	140
$3,000–$8,999	18	529	12	216	29	313
$9,000–$14,999	30	868	28	501	34	367
$15,000–$24,999	28	807	35	626	17	181
$25,000 and higher	17	481	22	390	8	91
Total	100	2,881	100	1,789	100	1,092
Hours worked previous week						
Part time (1–34 hours)	15	451	9	169	25	282
Full time (35–40 hours)	61	1,811	61	1,127	60	684
Overtime (41+ hours)	24	713	30	547	15	166
Total	100	2,975	100	1,843	100	1,132
Formal labor market						
Payment by check	90	2,627	92	1,663	88	966
Total	100	2,907	100	1,808	100	1,099
Taxes deducted from pay	84	2,524	87	1,611	81	913
Total	100	2,987	100	1,854	100	1,133
Occupation						
Management	9	254	9	160	8	94
Technical	15	463	13	240	20	223
Laborers	29	876	32	595	25	281
Production	14	411	19	359	5	52
Service	29	855	21	386	41	469
Farm	4	129	6	114	1	15
Total	100	2,988	100	1,854	100	1,134

Source: Aguilera, Michael. "The Labor Market Outcomes of Undocumented and Documented Immigrants: A Social and Human Capital Comparison." Ph.D. diss., State University of New York, Stony Brook, 1999.

out a year, rather than solely the hourly earnings at one job in 1992. Because workers often have several jobs at the same time or may change jobs and employers, hourly earnings may vary from week to week. Yearly earnings, however, allows for the examination of an employee's entire income profile, which would overlook the highs and lows of hourly earnings at one particular point in time.

Examination of yearly income in 1991 illustrates that the immigrants' yearly earnings were low. Of all workers, 7 percent earn less than $3,000 annually. However, only 3 percent of the male immigrants but 13 percent of the female workers fall into this category. Of all workers, 18 percent earn from $3,000 to $8,999 annually. Of male workers, 12 percent earn $3,000 to $8,999 annually, but 29 percent of the female workers achieve this yearly income. Clearly, female immigrant workers are much more likely to earn low income: Forty-two percent of females earn less than $9,000 annually. On the upper part of the distribution, the story is quite the opposite. Of all workers, 28 percent are earning between $15,000 and $24,999 annually. Of the male workers, 35 percent fall into this range, while for females, it is only 17 percent. In the highest income category, 17 percent of all workers earn $25,000 or higher annually, with 22 percent of males but only 8 percent of females earning this yearly income. Male immigrant workers are more likely than female immigrant workers to be in the higher part of the income distribution. However, neither male nor female immigrant workers' annual income is very high.

An important component of income is the number of hours worked each week. Some workers preoccupied with other tasks outside of the labor market, such as educational attainment, raising children, and helping elderly parents may purposely choose to work part-time. For example, part of the difference between male and female immigrant workers' earnings may be explained by differences in the number of hours worked. We found that many women are excluded from the labor market altogether, and some women may work only part-time to supplement their husband's income while raising children. Hours worked addresses this issue. It also addresses the fact that those unable to obtain full-time employment are unlikely to earn high hourly wages and yearly incomes. Not only is part-time employment frequently low paying, but employers also often utilize part-time workers to avoid providing benefits.

Looking at the number of hours worked by all workers in the week prior to the 1992 survey, it is clear that most of these workers were able to acquire full-time employment. About 61 percent of all workers are working full-time and 24 percent are working overtime. In total (full-time plus overtime workers), 85 percent are working full-time. However, only 9 percent of the male workers are working part-time, while 25 percent of the female workers are working part-time. In total (full-time workers plus overtime workers), 91 percent of the males are working full-time that only 75 percent of the females. Males are twice as likely as females to be working overtime. These patterns seem to suggest that differences in gender roles lessen female immigrant workers' involvement in the labor force and that some employers may prefer to employ male workers.

Informal labor markets are defined as those where the government is unable to regulate the actions of employers. Such labor markets are inferior to formal labor markets for several reasons. Employers within the informal labor market are, by definition, breaking the law by avoiding taxation. Thus, they are also more likely to abuse minimum wage laws, labor laws, and safety concerns. These conditions provide immigrant workers employed within the informal labor market with employment that is unprotected, sporadic, and unregulated. Studies about informal labor market participation show that workers within these markets are workers with few alternatives. Immigrants are more likely than nonimmigrant workers to be employed within the informal labor market, because many are legally barred from working in the formal labor market. Further, many immigrants do not speak fluent English and do not possess high levels of education and skills applicable to formal labor markets within the United States.

Formal and informal labor market participation is often measured by the type of payment immigrant workers receive. Immigrants paid in cash are typically viewed as informal labor market participants because it is assumed that neither they nor their employers pay taxes on their earnings and the federal government is unable to regulate employment. Another measure of formal and informal labor market participation is whether taxes have been deducted from one's pay. In the LPS, immigrants could report that they were paid in cash, by check, or via a mixture of the two forms of payment. Also included in the survey are the few workers paid with a mixture of cash and check as formal labor market participants, as at least some of their pay is regulated. Immigrants who do not have taxes deducted from their pay are considered informal labor market participants.

Most employed immigrants work within the formal labor market. Of all workers in the LPS, 90 percent are paid with a check. Of male workers, 92 percent are paid with a check, and 88 percent of females are similarly paid. Thus, females are only slightly less likely to work within the formal labor market. Of all workers, 84 percent (87 percent of male and 81 percent of female workers) have taxes deducted from their pay. These data suggest that between 10 percent and 16 percent participate within the informal economy and that female workers are slightly more likely to participate in this economy than are male workers.

The final labor market outcome examined is occupation. The occupation within which immigrants work has a large impact on earnings, advancement opportunities, and overall employment conditions. Studies indicate that Hispanic immigrants do more poorly within the U.S. labor market than other workers in part because they are overrepresented in low-level and low-paying occupations. For example, the federal government specifically recruited Mexican immigrants into agricultural jobs through the Bracero Program between 1942 and 1964. Today, these workers are overrepresented in low-skill and low-paying jobs with deleterious consequences, because agricultural work is the lowest-paid occupation and exposes workers to dangerous pesticides.

Occupation is broken into six categories. In the LPS codebook, the category "Management" is titled "Managerial and Professional Specialty Occupations." Likewise, the category "Technical" is defined as "Technical, Sales, and Administrative Support Occupations." The category "Laborers" is defined as "Operators, Fabricators, and Laborers." "Production" is called "Precision Production, Craft, and Repair Occupations," and "Farm" is titled "Farming, Forestry, and Fishing Occupations." As these descriptions show, each occupational category includes many types of jobs.

Most immigrants work within occupations that are low paying and lack advancement opportunities. Only 9 percent of all workers are employed in management; women are very similar to men in terms of their representation in this occupational categorization. Of all workers, 15 percent work within technical occupations. Of female workers, 20 percent work in technical occupations, whereas only 13 percent of male workers are employed in this same occupation. Twenty-nine percent of individuals work in laborer occupations, with 32 percent of male and 25 percent of female workers being in this category. Of all workers, 14 percent are employed in production occupations. Men (19 percent) are much more likely than women (5 percent) to work in production. Twenty-nine percent of all workers are in service occupations. Of males, 21 percent work in service occupations; 41 percent of females work in service occupations. Only 4 percent of all workers are employed in farm occu-

pations, with 6 percent of male workers and only 1 percent of the females working in farm occupations. Many agricultural workers were accepted through IRCA as seasonal agricultural workers and may be less likely to be represented in this survey. The data show that few of these workers are employed in management occupations but are more likely to be employed in laborer and service occupations and, for male workers, production occupations. Thus occupational representation has negative consequences for the earnings, hourly pay, and advancement opportunities of immigrant workers.

Table 1 provides many important details about the employment lives of recently legalized immigrants and illustrates that these immigrants are doing very poorly within the labor market. However, it is necessary to look into theoretical explanations of why some immigrants fare better than others within the employment market. Many studies suggest that immigrants do not do as well as native workers within U.S. labor markets because they do not have as much human capital. "Human capital" refers to resources that employees possess, such as knowledge and skills. Sociologists Marta Tienda and Audrey Singer find that human capital is extremely important in determining wages.

EDUCATION AND EMPLOYMENT WELL-BEING

Most researchers that establish a connection between human capital and employment outcomes consider the number of years of education to be a key measure. Here, however, they examine education as a categorical variable, which means that several educational levels are grouped into distinct categories: those with less than a high school degree, those with a high school degree, and those with some college experience. The results of most studies show that immigrants who possess the least education do considerably worse within the U.S. labor market than do those with the most education. According to human capital theorists, immigrants who possess more education are able to obtain superior employment because they offer more skills that most employers desire.

Table 2 illustrates the relationship between human capital and labor market outcomes. To interpret this table, readers should compare the percentages in each educational category. For example, the employment of those with less than a high school degree should be

Table 2
Labor Market Outcomes and Educational Attainment of the 1992 LPS

	No high school degree		High school degree		Some college		Total
	%	n	%	n	%	n	N
Employment status							
Employed	74	1,866	80	803	87	319	
Unemployed	8	209	6	61	4	16	
Out of labor market	18	462	14	139	9	32	
Total	100	2,537	100	1,003	100	367	3,907
Constructed hourly wage							
$1.00–$4.24	6	101	3	21	2	5	
$4.25–$6.00	31	563	15	110	10	27	
$6.01–$8.00	28	505	23	171	17	48	
$8.01–$10.00	18	315	18	130	10	28	
$10.01–$15.00	14	243	29	214	33	93	
$15.01 and higher	4	64	12	86	28	77	
Total	100	1,791	100	732	100	278	2,801
Individual yearly income in 1991							
$0–$2,999	8	143	6	45	2	7	
$3,000–$8,999	23	422	12	88	6	18	
$9,000–$14,999	35	629	24	185	18	51	
$15,000–$24,999	26	459	33	249	31	91	
$25,000 and higher	8	144	25	192	43	124	
Total	100	1,797	100	759	100	291	2,847
Hours worked previous week							
Part time (1–34 hours)	17	307	14	109	10	30	
Full time (35–40 hours)	62	1,139	61	477	58	178	
Overtime (41+ hours)	22	399	26	202	32	98	
Total	100	1,845	100	788	100	306	2,939
Formal labor market							
Check payment	89	1,636	90	694	93	287	
Total	100	1,828	100	772	100	309	2,909
Taxes deducted from pay	83	1,545	86	691	86	273	
Total	100	1,866	100	804	100	319	2,989
Occupation							
Management	3	49	13	99	28	87	
Technical	8	152	27	210	31	98	
Laborers	35	641	24	194	12	38	
Production	16	288	11	90	9	27	
Service	33	605	23	186	19	59	
Farm	6	113	2	13	1	3	
Total	100	1,848	100	792	100	312	2,952

Source: Aguilera, Michael. "The Labor Market Outcomes of Undocumented and Documented Immigrants: A Social and Human Capital Comparison." Ph.D. diss., State University of New York, Stony Brook, 1999.

compared with that of those having a high school degree and those with some college training.

Regarding employment status, 74 percent of those immigrant workers who possess less than a high school degree, 80 percent of those workers with a high school degree, and 87 percent of those workers with some college are employed. Thus, immigrants who have some college experience are about 13 percent more likely to be employed than those with less than a high school degree. Similarly, education is negatively associated with being unemployed and out of the labor market. For example, those with less than a high school degree are twice as likely as those with some college education to be unemployed or out of the labor market. These data show that as education increases, the likelihood that an immigrant worker would be unemployed or out of the labor market decreases.

In terms of the constructed hourly wage, if we compare what immigrant workers earn per hour for each educational category, education is positively related with hourly wage. First, those with less than a high school degree are twice as likely as those with a high school degree to earn less than the $4.25 minimum wage. The proportion of this education category earning less than $4.25 is 6 percent, while it is 3 percent for those with a high school degree and only 2 percent for those with some college. In general, the earnings of immigrants with less than a high school degree are between $4.25 and $8.00 per hour, as 59 percent earn wages within this range, while only 4 percent earn over $15.00 an hour.

Those who obtained a high school degree and some college are earning considerably more than those with less than a high school degree. Some 70 percent of those with a high school degree earn $6.01 to $15.00 an hour. Those with some college education are much more inclined to earn the highest hourly pay; 61 percent earn more than $10.00 per hour, and 28 percent earn more than $15.00 an hour. These data show that as immigrants obtain more education, they also earn higher hourly wages.

Immigrant workers' annual earnings in 1991 are also positively related with the number of years of education obtained. Those with less than a high school degree earn the lowest yearly earnings and are the least likely to earn the highest income. Only 8 percent of the immigrants with less than a high school degree earn $25,000 or higher; for high school graduates, it is 25 percent, and for immigrants with some college, it is 43 percent. In general, those with a high school degree earn more than the immigrants who have less than a high school degree but less than those with some college. Those immigrants with some col-

lege earn the highest incomes and are the least likely to earn less than $9,000 annually. Thus, as with hourly earnings, yearly earnings are positively associated with the amount of education that immigrants possess.

A positive relationship exists between immigrants' educational attainment and the number of hours they work per week. Those with less than a high school degree are the most likely to work part-time and the least likely to work overtime. Those with some college are more likely than those without to work overtime and the least likely to work part-time. For example, 22 percent of those with less than a high school degree work overtime, while this percent for high school graduates is 26 percent. However, those with some college are more likely to work longer workweeks; 32 percent of those with some college work overtime. In general, there is a positive relationship between immigrants' level of education and hours worked, but those with some college are more likely to work overtime.

Formal labor market participation is positively related with immigrants' educational background, but this relationship is not strong. In terms of payment type, immigrant workers with less than a high school degree are the least likely to be paid with a check, while those with some college are the most likely. Eighty-nine percent of those with less than a high school degree are paid by check, 90 percent of those with a high school degree, and 93 percent of those with some college.

Having taxes deducted from immigrant workers' pay is positively related with education. Those with less than a high school degree are less likely to have taxes deducted from their pay than those with a high school degree and those with some college. Although the relationship between formal labor market participation and education of immigrant workers is not large, most evidence seems to support a positive relationship between years of education and formal labor market participation.

Occupational destination is related to the amount of education that immigrant workers possess. Those with less than a high school degree are more likely to be working in laborer, production, service, and agricultural occupations than are those with a high school degree and those with some college. Immigrant workers with a high school degree are more represented within management and technical occupations than individuals with less than a high school degree. Those with some college (59 percent) are the most likely to work in management and technical occupations.

ENGLISH FLUENCY AND EMPLOYMENT WELL-BEING

Although education is clearly important for economic adaptation in the United States, also significant is English language ability. Most U.S. employers require their employees to speak English. Most research suggests that for immigrants, the ability to speak English assists immigrant economic adaptation. The lack of an ability to speak English can have severe consequences for immigrant workers, leading to work in low-pay and low-skill occupations that offer few opportunities for advancement. A question from the LPS appeared in which immigrant workers were asked, "How well do you speak English?" Possible answers were "not at all," "not well," "well," and "very well." Researchers considered the relationship between English fluency and employment outcomes.

Table 3 illustrates the relationship between English fluency and the labor market outcomes of legalized immigrant workers. One may compare English ability categories for each labor market category. For example, those who do not speak English can be compared with those who do not speak English well and those who speak it well or very well.

English fluency is associated with the likelihood of being employed. Those who speak English well and very well do not differ much in terms of employment status, but those who speak English well and very well differ from those who do not speak English well or at all. Those who do not speak English well are much less likely to be employed than those who speak English well and very well. Those workers who do not speak English at all are 21 percent less likely to be employed as compared with those speaking English well and 19 percent less likely than those who speak English very well. Those who do not speak English at all are also the most likely to be unemployed and out of the labor market. Clearly, lacking an ability to speak English hinders employment options.

In terms of hourly wage, English ability also plays an important role. Those who speak English very well are the most likely to earn the highest hourly wages. Those who speak English well and very well are the least likely to earn the lowest hourly wages. The opposite is true of those who do not speak English at all—they are the most likely to earn the lowest hourly wages and the least likely to earn the highest hourly wages. The general pattern is that as the immigrant workers' fluency in English improves, their hourly wages increase dramatically.

The immigrant workers' English ability is also positively associated with yearly income. Those who do not speak English at all are twice as likely as those in any of the other English fluency categories to earn the lowest yearly earnings. They are also the least likely to earn the highest yearly incomes. The proportion of those who speak English very well who earn $25,000 or more is 36 percent, while it is 23 percent for those who speak English well, 9 percent for those who do not speak English well, and only 3 percent for those who do not speak English at all. The general pattern is that as immigrants' English fluency improves, they earn higher yearly incomes.

A positive relationship exists between hours worked and English ability. When the different fluency levels are compared for each hours worked category, those without the ability to speak English well or very well are the most likely to work part-time and the least likely to work overtime, whereas those who speak English very well are the most likely to work overtime. For example, those immigrants who speak English very well are 12 percent more likely than those who do not speak English at all to work overtime. Those who speak English very well are also the least likely to work part-time.

Formal labor market participation is positively related with English fluency. Those who speak English well or very well are the most likely to be paid with a check and to have taxes deducted from their pay. Those who do not speak English at all are the least likely to be paid with a check and to have taxes deducted from their pay. Again, this relationship is weak, but the general pattern is that a positive relationship exists between English ability and formal labor market participation, in which those with a superior ability to speak English are the most likely to participate in the formal labor market.

Regarding occupational representation, those who speak English very well are the most likely to work in management and technical occupations. Those who speak English very well are the least likely to work in production, service, and farm occupations. Those who do not speak English well or at all are the most likely to work in laborer, service, and farm occupations and the least likely to be represented in management and technical occupations. These data illustrate that the ability to speak English plays a role in occupational destination. Those who speak English well or very well are much more likely to work in occupations offering higher pay, benefits, and advancement opportunities. However, those not speaking English well or at all are overrepresented in jobs paying lower wages, without benefits, and with little opportunity for advancement.

Table 3
Labor Market Outcomes and English Fluency of the 1992 LPS

	Not at all		Not well		Well		Very well		Total
	%	n	%	n	%	n	%	n	N
Employment status									
Employed	63	448	76	1,207	84	771	82	593	
Unemployed	9	62	8	122	7	62	6	41	
Out of labor market	28	200	16	256	10	90	12	89	
Total	100	710	100	1,585	100	923	100	723	3,941
Constructed hourly wage									
$1.00–$4.24	8	36	5	58	3	20	3	13	
$4.25–$6.00	44	188	29	331	18	127	9	48	
$6.01–$8.00	30	126	28	326	24	169	19	99	
$8.01–$10.00	9	38	19	214	20	143	16	83	
$10.01–$15.00	7	29	15	171	26	189	32	168	
$15.01 and higher	2	10	5	52	10	69	21	107	
Total	100	427	100	1,152	100	717	100	518	2,814
Individual yearly income in 1991									
$0–$2,999	12	52	6	71	6	45	5	26	
$3,000–$8,999	32	138	22	260	12	86	8	44	
$9,000–$14,999	36	154	35	403	28	207	19	102	
$15,000–$24,999	17	75	28	327	31	228	32	177	
$25,000 and higher	3	14	9	99	23	170	36	197	
Total	100	433	100	1,160	100	736	100	546	2,875
Hours worked previous week									
Part time (1–34 hours)	17	74	17	199	14	106	12	72	
Full time (35–40 hours)	64	285	61	728	62	466	57	330	
Overtime (41+ hours)	19	86	22	263	24	184	31	177	
Total	100	445	100	1,190	100	756	100	579	2,970
Formal labor market									
Check payment	88	380	89	1,038	92	687	93	520	
Total	100	432	100	1,166	100	746	100	557	2,901
Taxes deducted from pay	82	363	83	986	87	665	87	505	
Total	100	444	100	1,193	100	764	100	580	2,981
Occupation									
Management	2	7	3	32	12	89	22	126	
Technical	5	23	8	91	20	150	34	198	
Laborers	41	184	35	420	26	195	12	72	
Production	14	61	15	177	15	117	10	56	
Service	29	129	34	410	25	192	21	124	
Farm	9	41	5	62	3	21	1	5	
Total	100	445	100	1,192	100	764	100	581	2,982

Source: Aguilera, Michael. "The Labor Market Outcomes of Undocumented and Documented Immigrants: A Social and Human Capital Comparison." Ph.D. diss., State University of New York, Stony Brook, 1999.

CONCLUSION

The examination of employment outcomes reveals that the immigrant workers legalized through IRCA have shown a commitment to employment, even if that employment is not in the highest-paying jobs. In general, their hourly pay and yearly earnings are quite low. This is expected given their overall low levels of human capital and their overall recent arrival relative to more established immigrants. Yet about 76 percent are employed and another 8 percent are looking for work in the U.S. labor force. About 17 percent are out of the labor market and not seeking employment, but about 82 percent of these individuals are females who are raising children or who choose not to work. Of those who found employment, 85 percent obtained full-time employment. In general, it is estimated that between 10 percent and 16 percent are working within the informal economy, as measured by their being paid in cash or not having taxes deducted from their pay. Many are working in low-paying occupations; however, a smaller percentage are making inroads to management and technical occupations.

In terms of the relationships between education and English fluency and the employment outcomes of the legalized population, the level of education that immigrants possess, as well as their English fluency, affect their employment opportunities. Education and fluency in English are positively related with employment, hourly wages, yearly earnings, the number of hours worked, formal labor market participation, and occupation.

The association between educational attainment and employment outcomes seems to support a human capital perspective. The human capital perspective would point toward immigrants obtaining education applicable to U.S. labor markets so that they can achieve economic success. This is especially pertinent because many immigrants come from countries whose educational systems are often considered by U.S. employers to be inferior to those in the United States. Additionally, foreign educational systems prepare their students for employment related more to the sending country's labor market, rather than that of the United States. In general, this group has not obtained the quality of education they need to compete in a postindustrial society—65 percent do not have high school degrees. Thus, policies addressing the immigrant population's need to obtain further education in trade schools or universities would increase their value to U.S. employers.

The finding that English fluency shapes employment opportunities suggests that immigrants who want to improve their employment can take steps to become more fluent in English. Because most employers and jobs require that employees speak English, those immigrants unable to speak English at a functional level are at a great disadvantage. Such workers can find employment, but it is in such occupations as private household cleaners and servants, cooks, maids and housemen, janitors and cleaners, farmworkers, dressmakers, textile cutting machine operators, laundering and dry-cleaning machine operators, slicing and cutting machine operators, welders and cutters, assemblers, construction laborers, and hand packers and packagers. These jobs share many negative similarities, including low pay, few benefits, physical danger to the worker, and few opportunities for advancement. To enter more desirable jobs, workers must assimilate linguistically.

Part of the process for immigrants receiving legal residence in the United States under IRCA required that they take English classes. Thus the federal government did recognize the importance of English attainment. But not all the immigrants became fluent in English after they took the required courses mandated by IRCA; by 1992, 40 percent could not speak English well, and 18 percent could not speak it at all. Research illustrates that such immigrants who lack English fluency are more likely to be unemployed or underemployed and generally to have poorer employment outcomes than their counterparts who speak English.

In general, encouraging immigrants to acquire fluency in English and higher educational levels would appear to be beneficial to both sides of the labor market arena. Immigrant workers would see improvement in their economic well-being, employers would gain valuable labor, and local and federal governments would reduce the indirect costs associated with underemployment and unemployment. Despite linguistic and educational barriers, these immigrants have been and continue to be an important aspect of the U.S. economy.

Michael B. Aguilera

See also: Economics and Labor (Part I, Sec. 3); Economics I: Pull Factors, Economics II: Push Factors (Part II, Sec. 1); Agriculture, Service Sector, Sweatshops and Factories, Underground Economy (Part II, Sec. 8); Global Economy and Immigration (Part II, Sec. 13); California's Farm Labor Law, 1975 (Part IV, Sec. 1); Report on the Shortage of Technology Workers, 1997 (Part IV, Sec. 2).

BIBLIOGRAPHY

Aguilera, Michael. "The Labor Market Outcomes of Undocumented and Documented Immigrants: A Social and Human Capital Comparison." Ph.D. diss., State University of New York, Stony Brook, 1999.

Hondagneu-Sotelo, Pierrette. *Gendered Transitions: Mexican Experiences of Immigration*. Los Angeles: University of California Press, 1994.

Mahler, Sara. *American Dreaming*. Princeton: Princeton University Press, 1995.

Powers, Mary, William Seltzer, and Jing Shi. "Gender Differences in the Occupational Status of Undocumented Immigrants in the United States: Experience before and after Legalization." *International Migration Review* 32 (Winter 1998): 1015–46.

Singer, Shirley, Roger Kramer, and Audrey Singer. *Characteristics and Labor Market Behavior of the Legalized Population Five Years following Legalization*. Washington, DC: Department of Labor, 1996.

Tam, Tony. "Sex Segregation and Occupational Gender Inequality in the United States: Devaluation or Specialized Training." *American Journal of Sociology* 96 (1997): 1652–92.

Tienda, Marta, and Audrey Singer. "Wage Mobility among Undocumented Workers in the United States." *International Migration Review* 29 (1996): 112–38.

PROFESSIONALS AND THE BRAIN DRAIN

The term "brain drain" in essence refers to emigration of the highly skilled from one country to another. Who is highly skilled varies across time and place. In early human societies and in the least developed countries today, the highly skilled include far fewer categories, such as doctors, scientists, researchers, teachers, and artists. In contemporary times and especially in developed countries today, the highly skilled encompass professionals (e.g., scientists, lawyers, judges, engineers, architects, doctors, nurses, pharmacists, dietitians, therapists, teachers, counselors, urban planners, librarians, writers, artists, entertainers, and athletes), technologists/technicians, managers, and their kindred workers. The highly skilled normally possess a high level of education, have extensive training and specialized skills, and work in a profession. In the literature, such terms as "professional migration," "migration of the highly skilled," "migration of talent and skills," and "migration of the highly trained" are often used interchangeably or in lieu of the term "brain drain," which reflects the perspective of sending countries. From the perspective of receiving countries, such a flow is really a "brain gain." A recent study by Professors Lucie Cheng and Philip Yang suggests that "brain flow" is a more accurate term, because migration of the highly skilled involves both losses and gains to societies and possibly a two-way movement, and this neutral term reflects both the sending and receiving country perspectives.

HISTORY OF BRAIN DRAINS

The brain drain is not a new phenomenon in human history. For example, until around 300 B.C., scholars, researchers, and teachers migrated from elsewhere to the great intellectual center of Athens. There, Plato founded the Academy in 388 B.C., and Aristotle established the Lyceum in 335 B.C., both of which were the first known institutions of learning and research. In about 300 B.C., the center of talented migration suddenly switched to Alexandria of ancient Egypt, which became a new world center of science, philosophy, scholarship, and art due to the government policy of the Ptolemaios dynasty to establish Hellenic culture and to surpass Athens as its center. Between 300 B.C. and 500 A.D., most of the best works in the world's science and philosophy were completed in Alexandria, and all the brains producing them appeared to come from elsewhere. Soon after 500 A.D., the intellectual center shifted to Gundi Sapur in East Persia, where the pro-Greek king Husraw Anushirvan built a university and attracted scholars, physicians, and scientists from around the world. In the eighth and ninth centuries, Jewish, Syrian, Persian, and Hindu scholars and artists moved to the great caliphs of the Abbasid dynasty in present-day Iraq. During the Middle Ages, scholars, scientists, teachers, and artists often migrated to European universities, especially those in Italy, France, Britain, and Spain. The economic, political, social, and intellectual demands for the development of knowledge in natural sciences and the humanities contributed to the migration. Interestingly, often the exodus of professors and students of a university from one nation-state to another led to the founding of a new university. For instance, the founding of Oxford was allegedly a result of such migration from Paris in the twelfth century. Cambridge was founded in 1209 as a result of a migration from Oxford.

The contemporary brain drain is largely a post–World War II phenomenon. The postwar brain drain differs from its historical counterpart in scope, intensity, and direction. The historical brain drain was limited to a few surrounding nation-states and was small in quantity; its flows were usually channeled toward

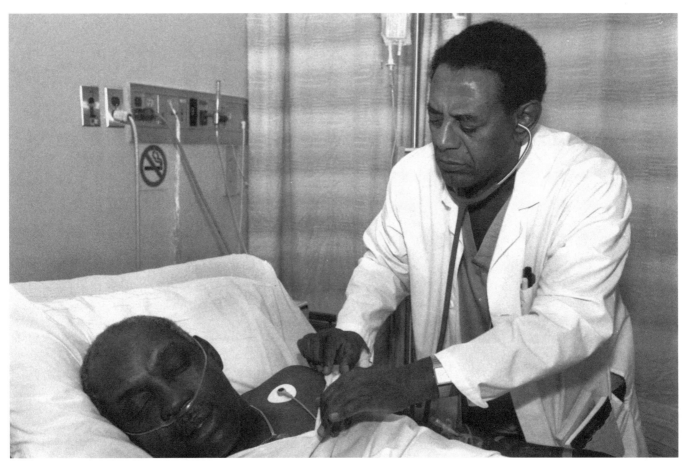

While the loss of medical professionals hurts many health systems in the developing world, it provides bilingual doctors—like this Ethiopian M.D.—for immigrants living in the United States. *(Mel Rosenthal)*

a new center of science and scholarship. However, the postwar brain drain has emerged as a global phenomenon involving many countries and professionals; the level has also risen tremendously. The direction has been primarily from less developed countries (LDCs) to more developed countries (MDCs).

Along with the rise in highly skilled migration came a heated debate over the brain drain. The debate began in the late 1960s and tapered off inconclusively by the mid-1970s. In the original discussion, the participants were sharply divided between "nationalists" and "internationalists." Guided by dependency theory, the nationalists believed that the brain drain was harmful to developing countries, which lose some of their brightest people, who are essential for national development, to advanced countries. They argued that the brain drain maintains and enlarges the gap between MDCs and LDCs and represents an exploitation of poor countries by rich ones. In contrast, focusing primarily on human capital theory, the internationalists viewed professional migration as a

symptom of an emerging world economy and as an action of individuals searching for jobs across national boundaries in order to gain high-yield returns to their education and training. Professional migration was seen as a beneficial process, since it reflects the free choices of individuals who choose to migrate. The internationalists generally denied that any damage was done to sending countries by the brain drain, on the grounds that the unemployment of professionals at home reduces their contribution to the home economy to zero and that remittances from highly skilled emigrants abroad more than compensate for their potential economic contribution had they stayed at home. Both the nationalist model and the internationalist model, however, failed to develop a broad explanatory framework that links professional migration to the larger global processes and global inequality, and neither can adequately assess the impacts of the brain drain. Recent studies of professional migration begin to address these deficiencies.

PROFESSIONAL MIGRATION TO THE UNITED STATES

The United States is currently the country that receives the largest number of highly skilled migrants in the world. However, notwithstanding the existence of a skilled component, early immigration to the United States was not professionally oriented. As proclaimed in the Statue of Liberty, the United States welcomed the tired, poor, homeless, tempest-tossed, "huddled masses."

There is some evidence that U.S. immigration policy had long attempted to facilitate the immigration of highly skilled people, but the effect was limited until the 1950s. For example, despite its exclusionary nature, the first Contract Labor Law of 1885 exempted from exclusion of entry actors, artists, lecturers, and "skilled aliens working in an industry not yet established in the United States." The Immigration Act of 1891 added ministers, "people of any recognized professions, and professors" to the list of people not subject to immigration restrictions. Although anti-Asian in nature, the Immigration Act of 1917 further added nursing to the exempted occupations. Despite these exemptions, only a small number of immigrant professionals managed to come in early waves of immigration. The Immigration Act of 1952 created a four-category preference system to allocate visas for quota immigrants. Half of the visas in the first preference category were given to workers with a level of "education, technical training, specialized experience, or exceptional ability." Nonetheless, the influx of the highly skilled did not materialize because they were fully absorbed by the post–World War II economic boom in Europe.

The Immigration and Nationality Act of 1965 downgraded immigrant professionals to the third preference and sixth preference categories and set aside only 20 percent of the available quotas to these workers. Despite this, the number of professional migrants has risen in aggregate and by region since 1965 because of the rising level of total immigration to the United States and because of the shifting sources of the highly skilled. As shown in the table, in 1965, highly skilled immigrants totaled 37,713, but the total number grew to 48,503 in 1975, 62,281 in 1985, and 89,027 in 1997. The growth rate from 1965 to 1997 was 136 percent.

The sources of highly skilled immigrants have also shifted. In 1965, Europe was one of the primary sources of the highly skilled (44.9 percent), but it dropped to the third place in 1985 and slightly rebounded to about 23 percent in 1997, largely due to the upsurge in the brain drain from the former Soviet Union and other former communist countries including Poland, Romania, Bulgaria, Albania, and former Yugoslavia. North and South America constituted another dominant source of professional immigrants in 1965 (45.3 percent), but its relative share has declined, with fluctuations, in the subsequent periods despite an increase in absolute number in 1997. In 1965, Asia supplied only about 8 percent of the highly trained; nevertheless, in 1975, it quickly jumped to the commanding position with a relative share of about 59 percent. It should be noted that this increase in the immigration of highly trained Asians was unplanned and unforeseen. Although its relative proportion slipped in 1985 (53.1 percent) and in 1997 (48 percent), the absolute numbers of Asian immigrant professionals have continued to grow. The number and proportion of the highly skilled from Africa have grown steadily over time from insignificance (1.6 percent) in 1965 to almost 9 percent in 1997. Albeit small, the absolute number of the highly trained from Oceania has also increased over time, but its proportion has remained quite stable.

As evidenced in the table, since 1965, several developing countries in Asia including the Philippines, India, China, Taiwan, and Korea have been consistently among the major donors of highly skilled immigrants. Several Latin American countries such as the Dominican Republic, Mexico, Cuba, and Jamaica have also sent large numbers of professional immigrants. None of these developing countries are among the poorest nations, however. Less well known is the fact that some highly developed countries such as Britain, Canada, and Germany also have been the top brain suppliers. Not shown in the table, Egypt and Nigeria have been among the largest donor countries of the highly skilled from Africa.

In 1966—the year immediately following the passage of the Immigration and Nationality Act of 1965—the 39,776 highly skilled immigrants admitted to the United States were concentrated in the occupational categories of managers (including farm managers), officials, and proprietors (24.5 percent); engineers (12.1 percent); teachers, except postsecondary (11.3 percent); nurses (9.0 percent); physicians and surgeons (6.4 percent); technicians (5.6 percent); accountants and auditors (3.6 percent); and professors and instructors (3.0 percent). In 1997, the leading occupational categories of the 89,027 highly skilled immigrants remained quite similar to those in 1966: executives, administrators, and managers (29.6 percent); engineers, surveyors, and mapping scientists (11.7 percent); technologists and technicians (9.2 percent); teachers, except postsecondary (8.9 percent); nurses (6.9 percent);

Number and Percentage of Highly Skilled Immigrants Admitted to the United States by Region and Selected Country of Birth, 1965, 1975, 1985, and 1997

Region and Country of Birth	1965		1975		1985		1997	
	Number	%	Number	%	Number	%	Number	%
Asia	2,854	7.5	28,489	58.7	33,074	53.1	42,866	48.0
China	615*	1.6	4,068*	8.4	3,376	5.4	9,082	10.2
India	222	0.6	6,637	13.7	5,323	8.5	8,841	9.9
Korea	112	0.3	3,977	8.2	2,782	4.5	2,037	2.3
Philippines	347	0.9	7,922	16.3	7,798	12.5	8,699	9.8
Taiwan	—	—	—	—	3,500	5.6	2,068	2.3
Other Asia	1,558	4.1	5,885	12.1	10,295	16.5	12,139	13.6
Europe	16,931	44.9	9,357	19.3	11,223	18.0	20,048	22.5
Britain	5,056	13.4	2,361	4.9	3,472	5.6	3,431	3.9
Germany	2,425	6.4	704	1.5	1,127	1.8	1,564	1.8
Poland	1,339	3.6	539	1.1	1,252	2.0	2,045	2.3
Romania	253	0.7	357	0.7	680	1.1	1,209	1.4
USSR	386	1.0	1,235	2.5	532	0.9	5,080	5.7
Other Europe	7,472	19.8	4,161	8.6	4,160	6.7	6,719	7.5
North & South America	17,070	45.3	8,357	17.2	14,387	23.1	17,498	19.7
Canada	5,656	15.0	1,256	2.6	2,685	4.3	3,502	3.9
Cuba	3,435	9.1	1,085	2.2	1,089	1.7	1,545	1.7
Dominican Republic	596	1.6	497	1.0	1,110	1.8	1,672	1.9
Jamaica	191	0.5	684	1.4	1,649	2.6	1,095	1.2
Mexico	873	2.3	1,141	2.4	1,757	2.8	1,569	1.8
Other Americas	6,319	16.8	3,694	7.6	6,097	9.8	8,115	9.1
Africa	610	1.6	1,742	3.6	2,864	4.6	7,620	8.6
Oceania	248	0.7	558	1.2	733	1.2	951	1.1
Unknown/Not Reported	0	0	0	0	0	0	44	0.1
Total	37,713	100.0	48,503	100.0	62,281	100.0	89,027	100.0

*Including Taiwan.
—Not available.
Sources: *Statistical Yearbook of the INS*, 1965, 1975, 1985, and 1997.

doctors (6.1 percent); writers, artists, entertainers, and athletes (5.9 percent); social, recreation, and religious workers (4.0); natural scientists (4.0); postsecondary teachers (3.9 percent); and mathematical and computer scientists (2.9 percent). There appears to be an occupational specialization among some sending countries. For instance, the Philippines is the largest donor of nurses and other health professionals, most of whom are females. India is the biggest supplier of engineers, scientists, and physicians, the majority of whom are males. China and Taiwan send a variety of professionals including engineers and scientists.

At times, the United States restricted certain categories of highly skilled immigrants from entering the country. For example, in the early 1970s, America entered a period of protracted economic stagnation. The

unemployment rate climbed to 8.5 percent in 1975 from 4.5 percent in 1965. At the same time, the number of foreign medical graduates increased dramatically, accounting for as much as 40 percent of the newly licensed doctors. Under pressure from the medical profession, Congress enacted the Health Professions Educational Assistance Act of 1976. This act restricted foreign medical graduates from entering the country either as immigrants or as exchange visitors and placed restrictions on foreign medical school graduates (both immigrants and nonimmigrants) in the United States for practice or training in the medical profession. Taking effect on January 10, 1977, the act contributed to a decrease in immigrant physicians. However, less than a year later, Congress passed the Act of 1977, which scaled back the restrictions by exempting those with national or international reputations in the field of medicine and certain foreign physicians already in the United States from the National Board of Medical Examiners examination requirement.

It should be noted that foreign students are not necessarily professional immigrants but are a major source of them. The United States receives the largest number of foreign students in the world. A significant proportion of them become immigrants after the completing of their degree programs and securing employment in this country. Asian countries are by far the largest suppliers of foreign students; currently, China tops the list. India, Korea, and Taiwan are also major suppliers of foreign students. It is no coincidence that these are also countries that experience high levels of brain drain to the United States.

DETERMINANTS OF THE BRAIN FLOW

There are several major explanations of highly skilled migration. Push-pull theory, often used in earlier analyses of the brain drain, contends that favorable conditions in the receiving country such as high salaries, high living standards, good research conditions, and career opportunities pull professional immigrants to the recipient country. On the other hand, unfavorable conditions in the sending country, such as unemployment or underemployment, low income, inadequate research facilities and equipment, monopolization of senior positions by old timers, excessive bureaucratic procedures, and political unrest and instability push the highly skilled to leave their homeland. A variant of the push-pull model emphasizes the important role of differentials between the home country and the host country in salary, logistic support, political and institutional stability, and opportunity for mobility in the professional immigration process. That is, the highly skilled decide to leave their homeland for another country because the differences between the home and host nations are large enough to warrant such a move. Critics have frequently pointed to the simplistic and ahistorical nature of the push-pull theory, which in the 1970s was challenged by dependency theory. This theory views the brain drain as an outcome of international imbalances between MDCs and LDCs and the dependency of the latter on the former. Integrating the push-pull theory with a world systems framework, more recent studies have attempted to link migration of the highly trained to broader global processes such as the global articula-

tion of higher education and unequal development on a global scale.

Following this latest trend and focusing on the United States, Cheng and Yang (1998), in our recent study, argued that professional migration to developed countries in general and to the United States in particular is a consequence of increasing global interaction and persistent global inequality across nations, both of which reflect a trend of intensified global integration. On the one hand, as the globalization process accelerates, interrelationships between countries, especially between the developing world and the developed world, are strengthened. Two important trends of global interaction are particularly relevant. One is the increasing economic interdependence among countries, especially between MDCs and LDCs. Modern technological advancement in MDCs has generated a rapid economic development and a transition from a manufacturing-based economy to a high-tech, information- and service-based economy, which together create a large demand for the highly trained that is unmet by MDCs. This high demand has led to the adoption of an immigration policy favoring the admission of highly skilled immigrants. Meanwhile, rapid technological progress and economic development in MDCs have resulted in the outflows of capital and technologies into LDCs in search of greater profits. The flows of capital and resources to LDCs have made the economies of MDCs and LDCs interdependent and inseparable and contributed to the formation of a pool of potential professional migrants and to the emergence of emigration as an option. This economic interdependence between LDCs and such MDCs as the United States heightens local professionals' awareness of international disparities, promotes their material and cultural aspirations, increases their level of Westernization, provides them with opportunities of networking, grants them easy access to information, prepares them for the international labor market, and thus increases their chance of migration to the United States. The other trend of global interaction is the growing articulation of higher education between MDCs and LDCs, which provides similar training of skills, shapes universal values, facilitates transnational ties, and therefore produces a large pool of internationally employable professionals. On the other hand, the globalization process continues to sustain and even enlarge national disparities in living standards, work and research conditions, professional employment opportunities, political and individual freedom, and children's educational opportunities. These disparities motivate the highly skilled to move to the United States. The larger the differences, the more likely they are to emigrate. Differences across nations in the degree of global interaction and global inequality together explain cross-national variations in professional migration to advanced countries and particularly to the United States.

Our empirical evidence clearly corroborates that economic and educational interactions between sending and receiving countries are important driving forces of professional migration. As the degrees of economic interaction and educational articulation between the sending country and the United States heighten, the level of highly trained migration to the United States rises. Consistent with evidence based on qualitative case studies, the gap in living conditions between the sending country and the United States is found to be an important determinant of professional migration to the United States. The difference in professional employment opportunities between the sending country and the United States also significantly increases the likelihood of professional migration. However, our cross-national data do not reveal significant effects on the level of professional migration of the disparities in research conditions, in children's educational opportunities, and in political conditions. The importance of these variables in the professional migration process needs to be empirically tested further.

IMPACT ON THE UNITED STATES

Migration of the highly skilled certainly has effects on both receiving and sending countries. As a recipient, the United States doubtlessly benefits from the brain drain, as it has gained much foreign talent. Among the most prominent is Albert Einstein, who emigrated to the United States from Germany in 1933. He was chosen the "man of the century" by *Time* magazine for its first issue of 2000. His $E=MC^2$ revolutionized the thinking of modern physics and had enormous implications for the development of science and technology in the last century. In addition to Einstein, talented immigrants make up high proportions of the renowned contributors to the sciences, humanities, and medicine in the United States. For instance, as of 1999, 33 percent of the total 251 U.S. Nobel Prize laureates (excluding the peace category) were foreign-born; the percent foreign-born was highest in physics (34 percent), followed by 33 percent in economics, 32 percent in physiology or medicine, and 26 percent in chemistry. In the United States, memberships in the National Academy of Sciences and the National Acad-

emy of Engineering are the highest honors for scientists and engineers. As of July 1996, 391, or 21 percent, of the 1,838 members of the National Academy of Sciences were foreign-born, and 245, or 14 percent, of the 1,953 members of the National Academy of Engineering were foreign-born.

Talented immigrants are also overrepresented in the field of performing arts. Immigrants receive a high proportion of the Kennedy Center honors given to persons who throughout their lifetimes have made significant contributions to American culture through the performing arts. From 1978—the first year the award was given—until 1999, 25 recipients, or 21 percent of the total of 117, were foreign-born.

The brain flow to the United States functions to supplement the domestic skilled-labor force. Immigrant professionals fill the labor shortage in selected industries. Their concentrations in the occupations of engineers, teachers, nurses, doctors, and technicians—a product of the U.S. Department of Labor policies and guidelines—evince their important roles in meeting the labor needs in these professions. Very often, immigrant professionals suffer downward occupational mobility, especially in the first few years of their arrival, which helps fill the less desirable positions in their professions that have been vacated by native workers. One case in point is the disproportionate concentration of foreign physicians in less prestigious hospitals, primarily those without a university affiliation.

In recent years, due to the rapid growth in high-tech industries, especially in the Internet, the supply of engineering and technical personnel has lagged far behind its demand. To resolve this labor scarcity problem, many high-tech companies have recruited foreign talent. As a result, in some corporations such as Intel, Motorola, and Mastech, over one-third of their high-tech staff are foreign-born, although many received advanced education in the United States. Similarly, in Silicon Valley, some one-third of the engineers are foreign-born. There was, however, a failed attempt in Congress to cut off these immigrants in order to prevent the loss of jobs to foreign workers and the lowering of wages of American high-tech workers. In response to this high-tech labor shortage, Congress finally enacted the American Competitiveness and Workforce Improvement Act, on October 21, 1998, which substantially increased the annual ceiling for the number of temporary foreign workers—H-1(b) visa holders—for the next three years. The ceiling was set at 115,000 in both fiscal years 1999 and 2000, 107,500 in 2001, and back to 65,000 in 2002. The act also required "H-1(b) dependent" firms (i.e., those with generally at least 15 percent of their workforce being H-1(b) workers) to add new attestation requirements for recruitment and layoff protection. It also required all firms to offer H-1(b) workers wages and benefits comparable to their U.S. workers. This act is likely to further stimulate the immigration of foreign professionals and technicians.

Additionally, highly skilled immigrants who are engaged in businesses or entrepreneurship often avail themselves of the connections with their home countries to boost U.S. exports to Asia and Latin America and to import products and services for American consumers. Highly skilled immigrants also consciously or unconsciously help bring in new ideas and new ways of doing business from their home countries to their professions in America.

IMPACT ON SENDING COUNTRIES

In the early brain-drain debate during the 1960s, the damage to the sending country was the gravest concern and its occurrence appeared to be a matter of consensus despite a dissension on the degree of its negative impact. Today, the atmosphere has changed. More often than not, we have heard talk about "brain exchange," "brain trust," and "brain gain." A more comprehensive and objective approach, however, is to recognize both gains and losses involved in the brain flow and to distinguish its micro and macro effects as well as its short-term and long-term effects.

From the perspective of individuals and families, immigrant professionals no doubt gain a higher salary, a more comfortable, modern lifestyle, a more desirable working environment, and more political and individual freedom. Their families in the home country also benefit from remittances, gifts, and information sent home. On the other hand, some professionals staying in the United States may relegate their role in society to a nonmanagerial or nonadministrative professional and limit their career mobility, especially in an environment of a "glass ceiling." Nonetheless, some do return to their homeland after establishing themselves in their professions in the United States and rise to prominence.

More importantly, the impact of brain flow has to be evaluated from the standpoint of society. In terms of national economy, the departure of highly skilled, able bodies can lower the productivity and efficiency of the home country in the short run, but this effect is probably more local than national and is difficult to measure quantitatively. In the long run, successful and affluent professional immigrants in the United States can bring back their skills, experiences, and funds to assist the homeland in its economic takeoff. A good example is that an increasing number of India's wealthy immigrant engineers who moved to the United States since the 1960s are returning home to start companies, make investments, and indulge in philanthropy.

Professional migration can affect the domestic market of skilled labor. For instance, the emigration of Filipino nurses to the United States in turn stimulated the expansion of nursing education in the Philippines. In 1950, there were only 17 nursing schools in the Philippines. By 1970, the number of schools had increased to 50, due to the chronic shortage of nurses in the United States. Hence, the production of nurses in the Philippines responded to the demand in the American market. In the years immediately after 1965, a shortage of nurses arose in the Philippines as a result of nurse emigration. However, by 1978, returned nurses and the increased local production of nurses left a large surplus, with 15,000 trained nurses in the country working in other professions.

In monetary terms, sending countries lose a large sum in educating and training the highly skilled. On the other hand, remittances sent home by highly skilled emigrants make up some of, or even exceed, the monetary losses. In addition, there are costs incurred by the United States in educating highly skilled immigrants who initially came as students. The existing evidence does not allow a uniform generalization about the net monetary impact of brain flow; some studies point to a net gain, while other studies indicate a net loss. A more reasonable conclusion is that the monetary impact in fact varies across countries and has to be determined on a case-by-case basis.

The impact of professional migration cannot be accurately assessed solely in economic and monetary terms. Its social and educational impact is tremendous. For example, feedback of information by highly skilled emigrants to their home countries through their families, relatives, friends, and former institutions helps spread new technology, new ideas, and new ways of doing business. Knowledge and skills learned and disseminated by professional immigrants as well as by students studying abroad facilitate the development of their home countries, which may eventually reduce their dependency on advanced countries. Immigrant professionals also help diffuse ideas of freedom, democracy, equality, and humanity, which in the long run can help transform their native societies.

In educational, research, and governmental institutions, the departure of a large number of highly qualified members has a disproportionate impact on the staffing and quality of these institutions. The brain drain can lead to the loss of actual or potential leaders, scholars, innovators, and artists. In some cases, this loss could have both short-term and long-term adverse impacts. Yet, some highly skilled migrants do return to their home countries after completing advanced education or working for a period in the United States. Very often, they take important positions in universities, colleges, research institutions, or government agencies. In universities and colleges, they influence teaching methodology, curriculum design, student quality, research activities and funding, and institutional management and administration. In other institutions, they influence the ways of planning, operation, and administration. Wherever they are, they often challenge traditional norms and values and consciously or unconsciously spread American values such as individualism, freedom, and democracy.

FUTURE OUTLOOK

As part of the globalization process, the internationalization of the professional labor market appears to be inevitable. As globalization accelerates, migration of the highly skilled worldwide and to the United States will continue to rise in the foreseeable future. The global economic restructuring creates a growing demand and ample employment opportunities for the highly trained, perpetuating global inequality provides incentives for the highly skilled to seek employment abroad, global articulation of higher education produces a pool of professionals with transferable values and skills for the global labor market, and burgeoning pan-citizenship offers a convenient avenue for immigrant professionals to move back and forth between their native and adopted countries. All of these together underlie a continuing upsurge in professional migration worldwide and to the United States. In the United States, Asian dominance in the supply of brains will likely continue, and we can also expect a rise in brain flow from the former Soviet Union and the former Eastern European communist bloc as well as from Africa.

Furthermore, the brain flow in the future is likely to become more dynamic and circular. Rather than remaining rooted in the host country, an increasing number of highly skilled migrants will move back and forth between the host and home countries on a regular basis and partake in economic, social, cultural, and political activities across national boundaries. They may have dual homes, dual lifestyles, dual careers, and dual identities. Transnationalism will emerge as a mode of adaptation for these transmigrants. As more and more immigrant professionals engage in transnational practices, the brain drain will metamorphose into a real brain gain for both the sending and receiving countries.

Philip Q. Yang

See also: Higher Education (Part II, Sec. 9); Report on the Shortage of Technology Workers, 1997 (Part IV, Sec. 2).

BIBLIOGRAPHY

Cheng, Lucie, and Philip Yang. "Global Interaction, Global Inequality, and Migration of the Highly Trained to the United States." *International Migration Review* 32:3 (1998): 626–53.

Das, M. S. "The 'Brain Drain' Controversy in a Comparative Perspective." *International Review of Sociology* 1:1 (1971): 55–65.

Greenwald, John, and Hannah Bloch. "Cutting off the Brains." *Time* 147:6 (February 5, 1996): 46, 1p, 1c.

Grubel, Herbert, and Anthony Scott. "International Flow of Human Capital." *American Economic Review* 56 (1966): 262–74.

Ong, Paul M., Lucie Cheng, and Leslie Evans. "Migration of Highly Educated Asians and Global Dynamics." *Asian and Pacific Migration Journal* 1: 3–4 (1992): 543–67.

Oteiza, Enrique. "A Differential Push-Pull Approach." In *The Brain Drain*, ed. by Walter Adams, pp. 120–34. New York: Macmillan, 1968.

———. "Emigracion de Profesionales, Tecnicosy Obreros Calificados Argentinos a Los Estados Unidos." *Desarrollo Economico* 10 (1971): 429–54.

SERVICE SECTOR

Immigration has increased at a time when the United States is becoming integrated into a global economic system in which national boundaries are increasingly irrelevant. Deindustrialization has occurred simultaneously with the expansion of a postindustrial service economy. Service jobs involve provision of an activity, often involving some social interaction, rather than the creation of an agricultural or industrial product. The service sector includes financial, health care, education, and business services provided to organizations and individuals. A portion of service sector work is advanced, requiring high education and skill, while other areas involve mainly unskilled labor.

During the last decade of the twentieth century, private-sector corporations experienced an increase in profits after they underwent economic restructuring. Major firms downsized operations, shifted to flexible production, and employed fewer workers. In manufacturing, the Fordist era of large firms with many workers operating machinery was increasingly replaced by flexible production, in which a majority of workers provide services, such as management or technical knowledge applications. Machine operation is subcontracted to small, less stable firms, or performed by capital-intensive machinery and industrial robots. This economic restructuring resulted in job displacement and unemployment in the nation's "Rustbelt" urban economies, while promoting growth in "Sunbelt" cities such as Los Angeles. The resultant economic vacuum provided opportunities for new immigrants in smaller firms paying low wages with reduced or no benefits. The service economy expanded concurrent to the decline in traditional manufacturing and provides many low wage jobs requiring few skills and reduced or no benefits.

EARLY ECONOMIC RESTRUCTURING AND GLOBAL CITY GROWTH

America's largest metropolitan complexes have become global cities from which the world's economy is managed and receives services. Global city economies are based on the production and export of specialized services and upper-tier managerial consulting. Highly specialized services, corporate headquarters, and high technology industries are the basis of new urban economies. For example, New York City has experienced a rapid expansion in FIRE (Finance, Insurance, and Real Estate), communications, business services, and legal services. Sociologist Saskia Sassen considers that the new urban economies are based on the growth of both limited but very-high-income jobs and extensive but very-low-income work. Because global cities are often the destination of new immigrants, they come to occupy the lower-wage tier. Directly, new immigrants are employed in low-level service jobs within the corporate structure. Indirectly, the new immigrants support the lifestyles of highly paid professional and technical workers. Additional jobs for immigrants are created in ancillary consumer services and in the downgraded manufacturing sector.

Low-wage semiskilled and unskilled service jobs do not require English-language proficiency. Indeed, the lifestyle consumption demands of higher income workers generates a direct need for low-wage service workers, and many of these jobs are in the informal sector. Sassen notes that many of these jobs are not captured in the official statistics because they are "off the books," and not necessarily because undocumented immigrants are employed.

Producer services for control and management of a global economy, including offshore manufacturing, is another major employment sector. New York and

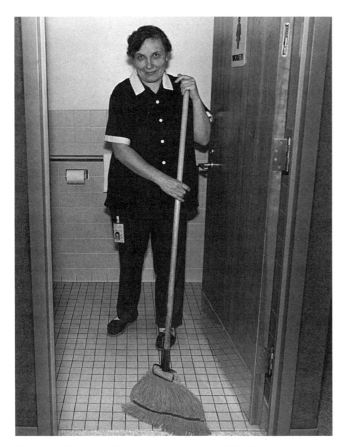

Many newly arrived immigrants, such as this Ukrainian woman janitor in Syracuse, New York, are forced to work in the lowest-paying jobs of the service sector. *(Mel Rosenthal)*

Los Angeles are examples of cities with expanding producer-service sectors. Corporate services, including banking, real estate, and telecommunications, employ a small, select group of highly educated, symbolic analysts at upper-income-tier salaries, while a majority of workers are increasingly relegated to marginal jobs. The result is income polarization between the haves and the have-nots. Economist Robert Reich classified the types of service jobs characteristic of the postindustrial economy into three types: (a) routine production services in which individuals perform repetitive tasks, whether word processing of business forms or wrapping locks for shipment; (b) in-person services involving repetitive jobs such as the provision of health care or fast food preparation; and (c) symbolic analyst services in which creative thinking and problem-solving skills requiring higher education are necessary. The late-twentieth-century economy was characterized by low-paid in-person service jobs with no benefits and similarly remunerated routine production services, both of which attracted new immigrants who replaced native-born workers. The small number of positions for highly compensated

symbolic analysts contributed to income polarization. In addition, jobs in routine production services were starting to be contracted to workers in developing nations, bringing jobs overseas to the potential immigrant, rather than vice versa.

SERVICE SECTOR GROWTH AND INTERNATIONAL DEVELOPMENT

The expansion of the service sector into the twenty-first century has had a major impact on both the United States and the developing world. At present, trade in services is expanding in immigrant-receiving countries, and is minimal or declining in underdeveloped, immigrant-sending countries such as Mexico. Concentration of service sector growth in countries such as the United States is tied to the phenomenon of "brain drain" and disruptive out-migration. Bimal Ghosh, an analyst with the International Labor Organization, has suggested that expansion of the routine services sector in developing countries such as Mexico through export of jobs from nations such as the United States would stabilize regional economies and control migration of persons across borders. Robert Reich, secretary of labor during the Clinton administration in the 1990s, has pointed out that these jobs comprised 25 percent of American employment in 1990, but paid low wages with minimal or nonexistent benefits.

Services are the largest sector of American employment and the biggest source of new jobs. In-person services cannot be exported, but wages and benefits vary widely, with a majority of workers receiving minimum wage or slightly higher and no benefits. Immigrant entrepreneurs and workers have been attracted to this expanding sector. It remains to be seen whether the value of these services will grow over time and regenerate the American middle class, which has been in numerical decline.

SERVICE SECTORS AND EARLY INCOME POLARIZATION

Scholars Harley Browning and Joachim Singleman distinguish between four sectors of the service industry: (a) producer services in which organizations provide services to other service organizations and individuals who own property, such as financial, advertising, and legal services; (b) distributive serv-

Although difficult to organize, the service sector and its many immigrant workers have seen a wave of strikes and union activity in recent years, as this picket line outside a New York City Chinatown restaurant makes clear. *(Impact Visuals)*

ices in which goods are transported or sold to consumers in transport, wholesale, and retail trade; (c) social services such as health and education; and (d) personal services, including restaurants, repair, entertainment, and lodging. In the popular imagination, personal services are most associated with the service sector.

According to the "polarization hypothesis," the service sector is divided into two tiers of workers. Early research evidence indicated that an elite group of highly educated and paid managers and professionals was counterpoised to a multitude of deskilled, low paid, often part-time clerical staff. Many lower paid service jobs involved catering to the needs of individuals and families, including fast food and other restaurants, retail sales, and dry cleaning. Public sector employees provided services such as policing, firefighting, social work, and sanitation, and receive better wages and benefits, but these services were subject to cutbacks during economic restructuring. The emergent postindustrial economy offered fewer well-paid jobs with benefits than did the manufacturing econ-

omy that preceded it. Employment in the lower tier of the service sector was associated with lower income, deterioration in benefits, and fewer opportunities for full-time employment.

ECONOMIC INFORMALIZATION

The early growth of the service sector was paralleled by increased informalization of the economy. Informalization refers to jobs that are subject to legal regulation of wage and working conditions but that operate in violation of these parameters. Immigrant workers, especially those who are undocumented and/or recent migrants are often employed in the informal sector. The early restructuring urban economies were characterized by an expanding upper tier of highly paid employment, a shrinking middle class tier, and a growing lower tier of services, including many informal sector jobs. Sassen indicates that the growth of a class of highly paid professional and technical workers encouraged "gentrification," a physical upgrading of residential building infrastructure and demand for ancillary consumer lifestyle services. These lower-tier jobs are labor-intensive. Examples include residential building attendants, dog walkers, and cleaners. Sassen points out that gentrification is a social force in informalization because of the need for renovation, alterations, woodworking, installations, and small-scale construction. Run-down low-income neighborhoods become sites of upper-tier residential and commercial areas. This work is short-term, labor-intensive, and necessitates high skill. Informalization of high-skill work, such as stonecutting and woodworking, is accomplished by hiring undocumented labor.

Sassen has hypothesized that social class and income polarization is a major condition for the growth of informalization in advanced economies, especially global cities. She believes that extensive immigration and the adaptive capacity of individuals from developing countries to survive under meager conditions are not a major cause of informalization and casualization of labor. Instead, advanced capitalism presents three trends that immigrant communities have been able to capitalize on. The first trend is the concentration of major growth sectors with highly polarized income distributions in major cities. For example, the business service sector has a highly paid managerial tier and a secondary tier of low-wage jobs such as janitorial work within its sector. Second, many small, low-cost service businesses have been established that cater to city residents, including the upper-income tier, nonresident workers who commute, and tourists. Intense competition among these businesses generates marginal returns and makes use of low-wage labor critical. Third, demand factors permit small, low-wage manufacturing firms serving local upper-tier income and immigrant markets to survive.

Although flexible work arrangements are considered a feature of advanced capitalism that generates a higher quality of life, Sassen considers that most informal work does not. It is low waged, without benefits and without seniority. Service sector growth is important in the casualization of labor. A business with a limited profit margin, such as catering, is forced to turn to low-wage, flexible labor. Nighttime, weekend, and holiday hours may be required. Not paying overtime is considered justified because the job is part-time. The forty-hour workweek lengthens into up to seventy hours. In this process, some business owners are tempted to "cook the books" and employ informal labor, a part of the underground economy. Informal labor takes place outside the arena of state regulations concerning the minimum wage,

health and safety, taxes, zoning, and other standards. The licensing fees, taxes, and restrictions that employers avoid help to maintain their profit margin.

Although immigration from underdeveloped countries is thought to be a cause of informalization, the structure of advanced capitalism may be creating opportunities that these immigrants utilize. Hence, backward sectors of the economy may be a result of a downgrading of work connected to the leading economic growth sectors. The informal sector in the United States may comprise more than a few individuals working off the books; it may be a well-organized set of relations of production, labor, and associated markets. Labor may be casualized, but the structure of the sector is not.

Three patterns characterized the informal economy in New York City during the early phase of economic restructuring: (a) a concentration of informal activities in immigrant communities for both local and external consumption; (b) increased informalization in city areas undergoing gentrification, which creates a neighborhood subeconomy; and (c) informality of labor in areas of industrial servicing and traditional manufacturing. These jobs may provide stability in immigrant communities by providing a diversity of jobs and opportunities to start businesses, which permits money spent on wages, goods, and services to recirculate within the community. The causes of immigrant informalization included foreign and regional competition in traditional manufacturing; gentrification; and inadequate provision of goods and services by the formal sector. The failure of the formal sector to capture this market may lie in high wages, inaccessible locations, or lack of participating businesses. The small economies of scale involved in such activity also contributed to informalization, while permitting a base for agglomeration in the future. Immigrant communities occupied a "favored" structural location for entrepeneurship and provided casual labor that could contribute to reexpansion of the urban middle class in later stages of globalization.

ETHNIC ENCLAVES AND TRIPARTITE URBAN DEVELOPMENT

Immigrant ethnic enclaves form around a concentration of ethnic business ownership. Contemporary immigrants' enclaves include Cubans in Miami, Koreans in Los Angeles, and the Chinese in New York. Initially, few post-1965 immigrant ethnic enclaves were established, and those that were established were characterized by low levels of investment and low wages. Due to the propensity of immigrants to select large metropolitan areas as their destinations, ethnic enclaves were found in a limited number of locations. In the late twentieth century, enclave economies greatly expanded in a few metropolitan areas and among certain immigrant ethnic groups. Simultaneously, other immigrant ethnic groups established occupational niches working for others. John Logan, Richard D. Alba, Michael Dill, and Min Zhou consider that the economic structure of larger cities has begun to change into a "tripartite" rather than a "dual city." The three sectors of the tripartite city are: (a) knowledge-intensive professional and producer services and capital-intensive manufacturing, which primarily involves non-Hispanic whites; (b) a semi-periphery of ethnic enclaves involving select immigrant groups in manufacturing sectors from which non-Hispanic whites have departed; and (c) a periphery in which other immigrant groups are employed. Entrepreneurial immigrant groups include Koreans, Chinese, Cubans, and Indians. Private-sector employment is concentrated among Mexican and Filipino immigrant groups. African Americans and Puerto Ricans had substantial employment in the public sector. South Asian Indians and the Japanese present a mixed case combining entrepreneurial activity in some metropolitan regions with private-sector work in others.

Immigrant entrepreneurial activity, especially among Koreans, Chinese, and South Asian Indians, has increased in the service businesses, and in traditional manufacturing that non-Hispanic whites have largely departed from. Chinese enclaves are more involved in FIRE (finance, insurance and real estate); South Asian Indians in hospitals; and Chinese, Indians, and Koreans in health services. Immigrant entrepreneurship has increased in wholesale trade, food stores, restaurants, other retail trade, and repair and other personal services.

While immigrant entrepreneurial activity in services has expanded, other immigrant and minority group job opportunities have weakened or stagnated. African Americans, Mexicans, Filipinos, and Puerto Ricans are largely dependent on other groups for employment. Aside from African American employment in public jobs, many still work in or own household service businesses, although their presence is declining in some metro regions. In addition, their employment has increased in transportation, hospitals, and social service organizations. African Americans are centered in a weak ethnic economy in contrast to what has developed among some immigrant groups. Mexicans, Filipinos, and Puerto Ricans are labor migrants whose employment resembles or is only slightly improved as compared to urban African Americans. The Japanese and South Asian Indians are an intermediate case in enclave development, while Cuban, Korean, and Chinese enclaves have expanded. Focusing on services, in Miami, Cubans have expanded their entrepreneurial involvement in traditional service-sector activities such as hospitals and business or professional services, while non-Hispanic whites continue to control the advanced service sector, especially finance, communications, business and professional services, education, and entertainment. Within the geographic boundaries of the ethnic enclave, however, Cubans are beginning to predominate in the advanced service sector. Chinese enclaves have increased their involvement in restaurants, food stores, and personal or social services with little expansion into other business sectors save in Los Angeles, where foreign capital has permitted expansion into banking and credit. The Korean economy has grown, with greater involvement in food, personal services, and other retail activities.

Recent research on ethnic enclave economies indicates that Cubans, Chinese, and Koreans have expanded their entrepreneurial activities in services. In contrast, Mexicans, Filipinos, and African Americans have low rates of business ownership, and South Asian Indians and the Japanese have intermediate rates. The expansion of immigrant business activity has played a role in the evolution of a tripartite economic structure. The tripartite economic structure is dependent on the strength of enclave economies but has potential for broadening immigrant mobility in the middle class.

The ability of immigrants to become self-employed in small- and medium-sized businesses is greater in cities with larger service sectors. Although Mexicans are primarily labor migrants, sociologists David Spener and Frank D. Bean have found that Mexican immigrant self-employment is higher in cities with greater concentrations of professional services and manufacturing employment. Self-employment occurs where there is weaker labor demand or an oversupply of workers. Self-employed Mexican immigrants are very likely to be employed in manual occupations, including service work. A study using 1990 census data of sixty metropolitan areas with high concentrations of Mexican immigrant workers found that approximately 25 percent of self-employed Mexican immigrants worked in manual services as compared to 12.8 percent of Asian immigrants/natives and 9.8 percent of non-Hispanic whites. Many are casual laborers who work on their own and sell their labor to employers or private households on an as-needed basis. Earnings of Mexican immigrants are impacted by inter-city variation in the size of the Mexican ethnic economy, or "enclave," as individuals are more likely to open businesses, including law, accounting, insurance, real estate, entertainment, public relations, marketing, and other services for a Spanish-speaking population.

Self-employed Mexican male immigrants earn more than immigrants with similar characteristics who have been in the United States ten years or less. Overall, women-owned and African American-owned businesses are more likely to be concentrated in the service sector than are Mexican self-employed, but San Diego, California, presents a different case.

SAN DIEGO SERVICE SECTOR

In San Diego, an immigrant enclave, or "co-ethnic" labor sector that is tied to Mexican immigrant networks has developed. A survey has indicated that 72 percent of services workers are foreign-born, as are 67 percent of hotel workers and 63 percent of restaurant workers. Wages were not subminimum. Service wages averaged $5.25 per hour; hotels, $5.10 per hour; and restaurants, $4.56 per hour. There was little differentiation in the average wage paid to legal ($6.50 per hour) and undocumented workers ($6.05 per hour). Small businesses are the primary employers of immigrants and employers operating immigrant-dependent firms are often Mexican or Mexican American in ethnicity. These businesses operate at a profit, but over one-third are just breaking even or had taken a loss.

San Diego immigrant-dependent enterprises use unskilled workers, with and without documents for lower-paying, dull, unclean, or hazardous work. Typical service sector positions for new immigrant workers are gardener, restaurant cook, household childcare, maid/houseman, and janitor. Employers prefer immigrants to native-born because they are reliable, punctual, and very flexible in their work hours. In California, increasing demand for private household service workers is a major force in immigrant employment. House cleaning, child- or eldercare and gardening are needed by dual career households, who consider such workers a necessity, not a luxury. These occupations are even recession proof.

LOS ANGELES SERVICE SECTOR

Los Angeles research indicated that the service occupations with the highest degree of informalization

were private household help; construction laborers; cleaning and building workers; food-related workers; freight, stock, and material handlers; and other handlers, cleaners, and laborers. Service occupations characterized by an intermediate level of informality included the construction trades; material-moving equipment operators; cashiers; motor vehicle operators; and health and personal workers. Los Angeles workers employed in occupations with higher levels of informalization worked privately, were less likely to be self-employed, received lower wages, and were more likely to be living in poverty. Latino immigrants, legal or unauthorized, were more often informally employed than any other ethnoracial group. When immigrants worked in informal-sector occupations, they received lower returns for their level of education than those employed in the formal sector. Immigrants arriving after 1970 received the lowest wages.

NEW YORK SERVICE SECTOR

There is a scholarly debate about the degree to which New York City's economic resurgence is based upon immigrant employment and the expansion of the service sector. One viewpoint, the "dual city," characterizes American cities as having grown in an hourglass pattern characterized by the aforementioned two-tier, high-income and low-income sectors. At the apex, a growth in producer services, including finance, insurance, management, law, and engineering, requires highly educated workers. The midpoint of middle-class professional occupations and highly paid, skilled, blue-collar work has shrunk. The apex is based on services, such as housekeepers, janitors, and fast food preparers, and immigrants are employed in these low-paid jobs that provide little chance of social mobility. This view of an hourglass job structure has been dubbed the "polarization hypothesis."

The economic restructuring of New York provided a substructure of low-wage support jobs in services. Sassen indicates that messengers, restaurant waiters, repairpersons, domestic servants, and many types of highly specialized service businesses, such as gourmet food stores, supply upper-tier professionals of the new city economy. Immigrants are often employed because they are seen as willing, cheap, flexible, and reliable. Economists Bennet Harrison and Barry Bluestone consider that the growth of a lower-tier service sector utilizing a supply of low-paid immigrant labor becomes the focal economic activity of the remaining city labor force. The cost of city living is so high that middle-class professional households must employ more than one earner. These dual-career households must turn to support services to do household tasks that they would have done in the past. Nannies, dog walkers, restaurant take-out, laundries, home improvement construction, and other family tasks are carried out by service laborers. The low wages paid to immigrant service workers help to subsidize the cost of professional employment for larger corporations and businesses. According to the "dual city" viewpoint, the advanced service sector is the major area of job expansion in New York. The polarization hypothesis, however, may only apply to the early stages of economic restructuring in global cities such as New York.

According to sociologist Roger Waldinger, growth of the service sector in New York City is only an early pattern in occupational growth and decline. Growth of low-skilled jobs in fast food and cleaning are only a portion of growth. Skilled blue-collar occupations in the United States have entered a decline in all sectors (craft, operative, labor, and service) except professional service. Occupational upgrading has occurred in professional, management, and sales jobs accounting for the vast majority of growth in the New York City job market. In New York, industries traditionally employing immigrants have absorbed many recent immigrants. New immigrants work overwhelmingly in the manufacturing and retail services. New immigrants are often employed in only one type of job in the service sector: personal services. In other expanding sectors—finance, insurance, real estate, business services, and professional services—immigrants are underrepresented. Waldinger has not found that advanced service industries exclusively rely on new immigrant workers. He disagrees with the viewpoint that urban economies rely on exploitation of immigrants. According to Waldinger, New York City's renewed economic success is based on occupational expansion rather than utilization of underpaid immigrant labor.

Services can be viewed as divided into an advanced sector that requires education and skills and a low-skilled sector. Because post-1965 immigration has contained both substreams of professionals and relatively less educated workers, Waldinger indicates that New York City has experienced significant expansion of the advanced service sector, which employs both native-born, including African Americans and other minorities, and new immigrant workers. Black immigrants in particular, but not Hispanics and Asians, are being absorbed into the advanced service sector. Hispanic and Asian immigrants have intensified their degree of overrepresentation in employment in the traditional manufacturing sector.

NEW YORK CITY HOTEL INDUSTRY AND ETHNIC SUCCESSION

The New York hotel industry provides an example of how ethnic succession has occurred in the twenty-first-century service sector. The New York hotel industry has provided increased employment over time, including many low-wage jobs often taken by newcomers. Because globalization of New York's economy involved development of the financial and business sectors, downtown firms needed hotel space for out-of-town and international clients. A boom in tourism provided additional economic stimulation for massive hotel building programs. The biggest hotel has more than 2,000 rooms and 1,400 employees.

The complex division of labor in these hotels involves a "front" with workers who interact with guests and a "back" sector. Waldinger describes a hotel as a large service factory with a back region in need of workers able to do heavy, unskilled work. In the mid-twentieth century, African Americans and Puerto Ricans had a substantial presence in the industry. African Americans employed in the hotel industry experienced discrimination in entering front region employment. White ethnic applicants were placed in front service positions such as desk clerk, waiters, waitresses, bar servers, banquet servers, and front elevator operator. African Americans tended to be hired for low-wage, dead-end jobs such as housekeeping, laundry, and maintenance. After the 1970s, European immigrants began to leave the industry and native minorities stayed while new immigrants began to enter. The recovery of the 1980s was marked by new immigrant advancement into positions previously held by white ethnics. As the hotel industry entered the twenty-first century, census statistics indicated that 60 percent of industry workers were foreign born. Asians were heavily represented, followed by Hispanics and immigrant blacks from the Caribbean. Dominicans and West Indians were especially likely to be employed. As the new immigrant presence increased, the process of ethnic succession initiated by the departure of white ethnics was complicated by the departure of African Americans. African Americans were still denied waiting and kitchen jobs, but front region clerical and some management positions were attained. The presence of African Americans in housekeeping drastically declined and they are underrepresented in the hotel industry workforce.

The New York hotel industry provides an example of how the U.S. service sector has been transformed. Rapid expansion of jobs, declining presence of native-born labor, and low productivity are characteristic. Because hotel jobs are not subject to automation and other capital-intensive replacement of human labor, productivity remains low and the expanding need for workers has created a labor crisis in many areas of the country, if not New York. Waldinger points out that New York's hotels now rely on a low-wage immigrant labor force. Immigrants have filled jobs held by departing white ethnics and African Americans, and have also acquired certain skilled positions. Hotels hire Thai, Chinese, Italian, and Greek immigrants with cooking skills such as preparation of hors d'ouevres. Immigrants have readily entered jobs as New York's ethnic population has become increasingly diversified as African Americans and Puerto Rican native-born workers have left.

Immigrants with some English-language ability are selected for employment, as even housekeepers need to communicate with hotel guests. Hotels that desire labor able to adjust to flexible staffing needs and changing hours find new immigrants to be desirable for back region positions. In the front region, hotels recruit non-Hispanic white students and actors. Although many African Americans are still employed in the New York hotel industry, hotels are preferentially hiring new immigrants. Even working in back region jobs is not necessarily a drawback, as a housekeeping or kitchen job will pay more than a front desk position. Waldinger found that the new immigrants employed in New York hotels are not a vulnerable labor group subject to wage exploitation. Similarly, pay rates do not greatly differ between union and nonunion hotels.

Although New York hotel employers have not actively recruited new immigrant labor, they express a preference for them. New immigrants have not been stigmatized by welfare participation and are perceived as harder working. New immigrants are viewed as proficient in the work, smiling and friendly, and as accepting of unskilled jobs. New immigrants are considered by managers as having a strong work ethic. In contrast, the structure of incentives in hotel work is less attractive for African Americans than in the past. African Americans view hotel service work as menial. It is a reminder of a past history of servitude, and not viewed as a job that demonstrates achievement. Because there is a legacy of discrimination in hiring of African Americans for front region jobs and the types of management positions now commonly offered—executive steward or executive housekeeper, which are low waged and out of the path for upward promotion—they are not attracted. In addition, an executive steward or housekeeper has

to fill in at times, performing menial work, a negative reminder of the past.

Past and contemporary discrimination operates against an African American presence in the hotel industry and works to present openings for new immigrants. In hotel kitchen employment, African Americans are greatly underrepresented. Kitchen working conditions, at temperatures up to 120 degrees Fahrenheit, are unpleasant. Entering kitchen work requires training as well, which immigrants are more likely to have. Lack of skills and lack of training opportunity are barriers to African Americans. In banquet waiting, no skill is required, but there is a long waiting period to move up into what can be a lucrative job. To become a banquet waiter, an individual needs to be employed in the front region for five years, have information about openings, and be willing to work a period of time on a roll call list. Contemporary banquet waiting is cliquish and said to be dominated by Greeks and Hispanics.

New immigrants predominate in New York hotel industry jobs rather than African Americans. This is not due to low wages or worker exploitation but to a series of barriers that are presented to African Americans. Past and present discrimination has served to channel African Americans into dead-end jobs, or into those jobs with limited advancement opportunity, reducing incentives to apply for front region jobs. New immigrants are connected to information networks that provide them with accurate information on getting better employment than African Americans get. African Americans with low skill, communication difficulties, or lack of computer training will also have difficulty getting front region management track jobs. An emphasis on middle-class presentation impedes hiring of native-born minority workers from inner-city backgrounds. Middle-class whites still compete for the better paid front region jobs, further reducing opportunity for native-born minorities.

Waldinger found that, in the New York hotel industry, real wages have actually risen over time. New immigrants are actually paid higher wages than African Americans. Immigrant competition does not appear to have driven down wages in the New York hotel industry. Immigrant workers found a supportive environment free of the barriers that were erected for native-born minorities. African Americans have exited from these unskilled service positions. Black rejection of stigmatized service work has combined with continued discrimination to restructure many types of hotel jobs as an immigrant niche. In addition, new immigrants did not push African Americans out of New York hotel work as their exodus began before an upsurge in immigration. The competition for African Americans is the flexible labor of actors and students who want temporary front region work, not immigrants. For low-skilled African Americans, the lack of access to job networks controlled by new immigrants has curtailed hotel employment. Insofar as hoteliers prefer new immigrants to African American workers, unless efforts are made to provide training, access to work information, and respite from discrimination, this sector of the native-born will lack opportunity in the hotel service sector in New York.

PHILADELPHIA SERVICE SECTOR

Philadelphia is another city that has emerged from a manufacturing past into a service-oriented future. Philadelphia's fastest growing employment occurs in business and law. Indian, Philippine, Korean, and Chinese immigrants are employed in health care and higher education. American retail industry has undergone a transition from small, individually owned businesses to the development of large, centralized chains. Chains often located in the suburbs, creating new opportunities in cities undergoing restructuring. Low profit margins have pushed both shop owners and chains to become more competitive by introducing flexibility into the labor force by hiring part-timers with no benefits. In Philadelphia, chain stores, Korean small shop owners, and non-Latino white owners compete for culturally diverse customers. Korean owners hired "buffer" workers to deal with multicultural diversity and gradually developed an orientation of "giving back to the community" similar to non-Latino whites. Increasingly, larger cities are offering opportunities for Korean entrepreneurs.

SUBURBAN IMMIGRANTS

El Salvadoran immigrants have found many jobs in household services on Long Island, New York. A shortage of native-born youth to fill positions created a niche for live-in housekeepers, nannies, house cleaners, landscapers, gardeners, car washers, painters, and pool cleaners. Low wages have attracted undocumented immigrants. Domestic workers tolerate often demeaning and confining work conditions in order to evade INS apprehension. In the early 1990s, live-in domestic workers earned from $150 to $200 a week, while house cleaners averaged $8 to $10 an hour.

DOMESTIC SERVICE

The growth of the traditional service sector has been accompanied by an ongoing casualization of new immigrant labor. Casualization refers to the increase in temporary employment and flexible hours. Whether serving as bus boys or cooks in restaurants, or gardening and cleaning houses, or doing other domestic work for private households, Latinos and other new immigrants are being paid a low wage with flexible hours that are highly dependent on consumer demand. Domestic service is a service-sector activity that has traditionally employed immigrant labor. This occupation demonstrates the engenderment of new immigrant incorporation. Paid household work is increasingly dramatically throughout the United States, but the extremity of increase is well documented only for California and the United States–Mexico border metropolitan areas, where close proximity to undocumented immigrant women has made utilization of unauthorized domestic workers a tradition that has depressed census statistics enumerating household workers.

Middle-class and upper-income dual-career couples, dual-earner working parents, and single mothers have come to seek the services of women caregivers and household workers. Domestic workers provide both live-in and part-time services. Mary Romero refers to part-time domestic labor as "job work." Job workers have several employers and clean different houses every one to two weeks for a specified wage. Job workers have greater independence and their jobs are less personalized, mitigating the potential for employee abuse. Job workers need to find multiple employers and negotiate their days and hours of work, which can be hectic. Because domestic work involves negotiation between two individuals, wage rates and terms of work can be highly variable, even within the work market of a single location. Immigrant women employed as live-in or day workers rely on employee or employer cooperative networks to locate jobs.

A single woman migrant has traditionally had limited job opportunities. By taking a live-in job, she is spared rent, transportation, food, and utility expenses, and may view her earnings as savings. In addition, an undocumented woman is protected from deportation and, usually, those who would take sexual advantage of her. There are definite drawbacks to this arrangement as the employer may take these expenses into account when determining the woman's wages. Her accommodations may range from having a "room" the size of a closet to eating old leftovers. The live-in's workday is fuzzy, and she may be called upon at any hour, without receiving a wage that accommodates the number of hours she works—a deceptive pay arrangement, but one that is traditionally accepted by casual labor. The duties of a live-in can also be extreme, from simultaneous housework and childcare to sitting up with a sick person all night. New immigrant women also experience isolation from kin and friends in the work environment.

The strength of a newly arrived immigrant woman's kinship network, its degree of penetration into the community, and establishment, determines whether she will be able to find work and its degree of marginality. Better positions are with a set employer who contracts for exclusive services. The relationship with these employer and/or network connections with other immigrant women can lead to additional referrals and work. Many immigrant women seek to maximize their earnings and take as many jobs as they can handle, working different jobs on the same day or on their "day off," and putting in long hours. Sociologist Pierette Hondagneu-Sotelo points out that constantly looking for jobs with better wages and working conditions is a constant feature of this work.

In a parallel to trends in the American economy, some immigrant women seeking their first job utilize a "subcontractor," another woman with a steady customer(s) who needs help. This provides an apprenticeship and can eventually lead to personal subcontracting. These initial subcontracted jobs can be extremely low paid with demanding working conditions that are exploitative and demeaning.

There is wide variation in wages within communities and between regions because of lack of a regulated system of payment. The strength of a labor market is not the only factor in wage rates because of the varying degree of isolation of the women who negotiate pay, especially undocumented women. Immigrant women exchange information about pay and working conditions in informal networks. An exceptionally low-paying or abusive employer becomes identified and may be avoided. Transportation is another factor that impacts wages as women without cars are forced to walk, use buses, or wait to be picked up to work in distant urban or suburban locations. Researchers have found that undocumented immigrant women earn less than women with papers.

Due to low wages and availability of work, many immigrant women do not earn enough to cover their expenses. Immigrant women may compensate by offering in-home day care, vending, or undertaking other jobs. Live-ins and job workers have little security. Because of the practice of having multiple em-

ployers and a movement toward more formalized employee-employer relations, employer loyalty to a given worker is limited. Similarly, if a domestic worker finds a better job, her employer may find heror himself short-handed.

UNIONIZATION

New immigrants are often stereotyped as unskilled workers who displace the native-born, especially African Americans. In 1980s Los Angeles, deindustrialization and economic restructuring resulted in greater service employment in such low-paying jobs as salespeople, waiters, cashiers, nurses aides, practical nurses, secretaries, and repair, typically nonunionized occupations. In economic desperation, some turned to street vending of produce, earning as little as $5 for six to eight hours.

A 1992 census study indicated that an income gap was emerging between Latino service professionals and manual service workers. Immigrant workers became involved in unionization campaigns and confrontations with restructuring firms, including hotel operations, which were cutting back on benefits and working conditions. Hotel employment was highly unionized, but Hyatt Regency, a major new immigrant and minority employer, broke with union custom, reducing medical benefits and demanding a ten-day work schedule to eliminate overtime, while introducing the right to terminate without appeal. The union local won a victory over Hyatt, which then sold its hotels to Koreana, which terminated all employees and slashed wages. The Hotel Employers council initiated a wage freeze, initiated greater worker payment for health benefits, and would not recognize job security. Systematic union opposition occurred in relation to changes in hotel ownership resulting in initiation of unfavorable labor practices.

Justice for Janitors was a major unionization effort in Los Angeles, initiated by the Service Employees International Union (SEIU). In the early 1980s, building owners experimented with hiring of small nonunion cleaning companies, which established their reputation. The larger nonunion companies were then bankrolled by the real estate industry, and Latino and Asian new immigrants were hired. Union membership plunged and a new core of Mexican and Central American nonunion janitors emerged. In a bilingual nonconfrontational unionization effort that avoided strikes, SEIU engaged subcontractors and unionized 90 percent of Los Angeles's downtown office building cleaners; SEIU later successfully extended its effort to the suburbs. Organizing and direct action paved the way for wage increases. Late-twentieth-century union actions, especially militant efforts, increasingly involved new immigrant workers.

Judith Warner

See also: Labor Markets for Recent Immigrants: A Statistical Portrait, Underground Economy, Unions and Union Organizing (Part II, Sec. 8).

BIBLIOGRAPHY

Acuna, Rodolfo F. *Anything But Mexican: Chicanos in Contemporary Los Angeles.* London: Verso, 1996.

Bonacich, Edna, and Ivan Light. *Immigrant Entrepreneurs: Koreans in Los Angeles, 1965–1982.* Berkeley, CA: University of California Press, 1988.

Browning, Harley, and Joachim Singlemann. "Industrial Transformation and Occupational Change in the U.S., 1960–1980." *Social Forces* 59 (1980): 246–64.

Cornelius, Wayne. "The Structural Embeddedness of Demand for Mexican Immigrant Labor." In *Crossings: Mexican Immigration in Interdisciplinary Perspectives,* ed. Marcelo M. Suarez-Orozco, pp. 113–44. Cambridge, MA: Harvard University Press, 1998.

DeFrietas, Gregory. *Inequality at Work: Hispanics in the U.S. Labor Force.* New York: Oxford University Press, 1991.

Feagin, Joe, and Michael P. Smith. "Cities and the New International Division of Labor: An Overview." In *The Capitalist City.* New York: Basil Blackwell, 1987.

Garcia, Jesus M. "The Hispanic Population in the United States." U.S. Census, P20–465RV. Washington, DC: Government Printing Office, 1992.

Ghosh, Bimal. *Gains from Global Linkages: Trade in Services and the Movement of People.* New York: St. Martin's, 1997.

Goode, Judith. "Encounters Over the Counter: Bosses, Workers, and Customers on a Changing Shopping Strip." In *Newcomers in the Workplace: Immigrants and the Restructuring of the U.S. Economy,* ed. Louise Lamphere, Alex Stepick, and Guillermo Grenier, pp. 251–80. Philadelphia: Temple University Press, 1994.

———. "Polishing the Rustbelt: Immigrants Enter a Restructuring Philadelphia." In *Newcomers in the Workplace: Immigrants and the Restructuring of the U.S. Economy,* ed. Louise Lamphere, Alex Stepick, and Guillermo Grenier, pp. 199–230. Philadelphia: Temple University Press, 1994.

Harrison, Bennet, and Barry Bluestone. *The Great U-Turn: Corporate Restructuring and the Polarizing of America.* New York: Basic Books, 1988.

Hertz, Rosanna. *More Equal Than Others.* Berkeley, CA: University of California Press, 1986.

Hondagneu-Sotelo, Pierette. *Gendered Transitions: Mexican Experiences of Immigration.* Berkeley, CA: University of California Press, 1994.

Logan, John R., Richard D. Alba, Michael Dill, and Min Zhou. "Ethnic Segmentation in the American Metropolis: Increasing Divergence in Economic Incorporation, 1980–1990." *International Migration Review* 34:1 (2000): 98–132.

———, and T. L. McNulty. "Ethnic Economies in Metropolitan Regions: Miami and Beyond." *Social Forces* 72 (1994): 691–724.

Mahler, Sarah J. *American Dreaming: Immigrant Life on the Margins.* Princeton, NJ: Princeton University Press, 1995.

Marcelli, Enrico A., Manuel Pastor Jr., and Pascale M. Joassart. "Estimating the Effects of Informal Economic Activity: Evidence from Los Angeles County." *Journal of Economic Issues* 33:3 (1999): 579–607.

Milkman, Ruth, Ellen Reese, and Benita Roth. "The Macrosociology of Paid Domestic Labor." *Work and Occupations* 25:4 (1998): 483–510.

Nelson, Joel I. "Work and Benefits: The Multiple Problems of Service Sector Employment." *Social Problems* 41:2 (1994): 240–56.

Negrey, Cynthia, and Mary Beth Zickel. "Industrial Shifts and Uneven Development: Patterns of Growth and Decline in U.S. Metropolitan Areas." *Urban Affairs Quarterly* 30:1 (1994): 27–47.

Reich, Robert. *The Work of Nations.* New York: Knopf, 1991.

Romero, Mary. "Domestic Service in the Transition from Urban to Rural Life: The Case of La Chicana." *Women's Studies* 13 (1987): 199–222.

———. "Chicanas Modernize Domestic Service." *Qualitative Sociology* 11 (1988): 319–34.

Saltzinger, Leslie. "A Maid by Any Other Name: The Transformation of 'Dirty Work' by Central American Immigrants." In *Ethnography Unbound: Power and Resistance in the Modern Metropolis,* ed. Michael Buroway et al., pp. 139–60. Berkeley, CA: University of California Press, 1991.

Sassen-Koob, Saskia. "The New Labor Demand in Global Cities." In *Cities in Transformation,* ed. M. P. Smith, pp. 139–71. Beverly Hills, CA: Sage, 1984.

———. *The Mobility of Labor and Capital: A Study in International Investment and Labor Flow.* New York: Cambridge University Press, 1988.

———. "New York City's Informal Economy." In *The Informal Economy: Studies in Advanced and Less Developed Countries,* ed. Alejandro Portes, Manuel Castells, and Lauren Benton. Baltimore, MD: The Johns Hopkins University Press, 1989.

———. *The Global City: New York, London, Tokyo.* Princeton, NJ: Princeton University Press, 1991.

———. *Guests and Aliens.* New York: The New Press, 1999.

Simon, Rita J., and Margo Corona DeLey. "The Work Experience of Undocumented Mexican Women Migrants in Los Angeles." *International Migration Review* 18:1 (1984): 212–29.

Spener, David, and Frank D. Bean. "Self-Employment Concentration and Earnings Among Mexican Immigrants in the U.S." *Social Forces* 77:3 (1999): 1021–47.

Stepick, Alex, Guillermo Grenier, Hafidh A. Hafidh, Sue Chafee, and Debbie Drazin. "The View from the Back of the House: Restaurants and Hotels in Miami." In *Newcomers in the Workplace: Immigrants and the Restructuring of the U.S. Economy,* ed. Louise Lamphere, Alex Stepick, and Guillermo Grenier, pp. 181–98. Philadelphia: Temple University Press, 1994.

Ruiz, Vicki L. "By the Day or the Week: Mexicana Domestic Workers in El Paso." In *Women on the U.S.–Mexico Border: Responses to Change*, ed. Vicki L. Ruiz and Susan Tiano, pp. 61–76. Boston: Allen and Unwin, 1987.

Waldinger, Roger. "From Ellis Island to LAX: Immigrant Prospects in the American City." *International Migration Review* 30:4 (1996): 1078–86.

———. *Still the Promised City? African Americans and New Immigrants in Postindustrial New York*. Cambridge, MA: Harvard University Press, 1996.

Wilson, K. L., and Alejandro Portes. "Immigrant Enclaves: An Analysis of the Labor Market Experiences of Cubans in Miami." *American Journal of Sociology* 86 (1980): 295–319.

Sweatshops and Factories

Prior to the Industrial Revolution of the late eighteenth and nineteenth centuries, manufacturing occurred on a small scale in small shops or homes. This is the origin of the term "cottage industry," which refers to workers involved in manufacturing in their home. "Factory" originates as an abbreviation of manufactory, which means existing in a separate building from the home. The location and form of the earliest factories were limited by their reliance on water sources. The long, narrow, multistory block building persisted through the late 1800s. The multistory buildings were soon replaced by single-story buildings. These newer factories were able to accommodate multiple industries. Developments in the 1890s revolutionized factory buildings. The newer factories were of various sizes and shapes, and made with steel-frame construction.

Throughout its history, the factory has reflected a utilitarian design. The open factory floor coincided with the development of scientific management, which dominated the philosophy of management from 1900 to 1930. The open floor allowed factory managers to arrange machinery for the most efficient production, using the straight-line flow of work, in which a product travels the shortest distance from one process to the next. This is more commonly referred to as work flow, because it is believed to increase productivity and speed the flow of work.

ORIGINS OF SWEATSHOPS IN AMERICA

The terms "sweating" and "sweating system" came into general use around 1850 to describe work that was contracted out of factories to be performed at home. Sweatshops were a less skilled, less regulated extension of factory work. There are three major features that all sweatshops had in common: unsanitary conditions, long hours, and low pay. These factors resulted in a low standard of living and exploitation of labor. The economic and social forces that gave rise to sweating were the general conditions of poverty that many immigrant populations faced upon arrival in the United States. The economic and social forces that led to sweatshop work were not confined to a particular industry or particular immigrant groups.

In America, sweatshops first became prominent during the Industrial Revolution, a period of dynamic transformation that drastically altered both the economy and how people worked. Industrialization brought to the workplace new technology and machinery as well as a division of labor. The division of labor in industry is a managerial strategy in which workers are divided by task. The division of labor was a means to organize workers and increase speed of production. The dramatic changes in industry resulted in mass production affecting workers as well as consumers. Sweatshops met the consumer demand for inexpensive goods, made by the cheapest labor force: new immigrants.

SWEATSHOPS AND IMMIGRANT WORKERS

Although sweating is generally considered as an industrial problem of exploited labor of immigrant populations, there were certainly cases of workers being upwardly displaced. In these cases, the unskilled immigrant workers were able to develop skills in the sweatshops that permitted them to move up to higher positions. The lower positions they previously filled were then taken up by new immigrant arrivals.

When immigration is due to political reasons, rather than to the draw of economic opportunity,

In recent decades, sweatshops, once considered a dark relic from the Industrial Revolution, have made a revival fueled by unskilled immigrants like these Chinese garment workers in New York City. *(Lina Pollotta/Impact Visuals)*

sweating becomes even more pronounced and the conditions making it possible are more persistent. This is due to the fact that many immigrants to America who are fleeing political persecution are illegal and arrive with little or no resources. Therefore, they are unable to work legally and must work immediately in order to survive. The immigrant easily becomes a victim of sweating because even if the immigrant enters the United States with skills, often the skills are not transferable to the American economy. In this case, the immigrant is forced to engage in an occupation that requires little skill and is inevitably low paid.

SWEATSHOPS IN THE NINETEENTH CENTURY

During the late nineteenth century, sweatshops began increasing at an unprecedented rate in the United

States. The influx of immigrants filled sweatshops in many industries—primarily in cities, because urban areas were the common immigrant destination. The immigrants usually migrated to neighborhoods that reflected their ethnicity and found work in the spreading sweatshops. Often, this sweatshop work involved taking work home to perform, because there was not enough room in the sweatshops to accommodate all of the workers. This only increased the difficulty of immigrant adjustment, as workers were often not paid for homework, or were given unbearable deadlines that prohibited both sleep and care of the family.

In addition to the difficulties that many new workers faced in the sweatshops, many seasoned workers in industry were antagonistic toward newer immigrants. Because these newer immigrant workers emigrated in large numbers and agreed to work for long hours at the lowest pay rates, it was feared that their employment would result in reduced wages and increased unemployment for all workers. Despite this antagonism from other workers, employers welcomed

Marchers in New York demonstrate against Immigration and Naturalization Service sweatshop raids, which result in deportations and limit immigrant workers' ability to protest poor working conditions. *(Maria Dumlao/Impact Visuals)*

immigrant workers, who consequently became the second enemy of the seasoned worker, following the employers.

SWEATSHOPS IN THE GARMENT INDUSTRY

Although there are and always have been sweatshops in various industries in the United States, perhaps the most notorious have been in the garment industry. In the early days of the clothing industry, in the nineteenth century, the volume of immigrants was at an all-time high. Many immigrants found work in the clothing industry, as a result of the massive expansion in the garment industry at the time. The garment industry made use of cheap labor. Its seasonal character resulted in work irregularity and long hours.

The garment industry had many types of workers and employers. In terms of sweating, the contractors were of great importance. Contractors were responsible for contracting work out. Contractors were called "outside" because they took work from the manufacturers and parceled it out to the workers. To recruit and mobilize labor for the job, the contractor worked to specifications set by the manufacturer. The manufacturers were said to maintain "inside shops" when they manufactured their work directly on their own premises.

THE GARMENT SWEATSHOP: PIECEWORK AND CONTRACTING

The sweating system in the garment industry was characteristic of Manhattan industry during the late nineteenth century. This was a direct consequence of the replacement of tailored goods by mass-produced ready-made goods. When a contractor would give material to "outsources" to be performed in homes,

Central America day laborers in Queens, New York, listen to a union organizer from the Center for Immigrant Rights. *(Impact Visuals)*

the workers were often the newest immigrants and often women. The least-skilled immigrants were most numerous in sweatshops. Sweating was also referred to as task work or piecework, as they were paid by the piece or the task, and the work was often performed in a "home" in a tenement building that had been converted to a workspace. The cutting room was where most of the clothing was distributed to task workers. A variety of piecework schemes existed. While most contractors were small masters unable to maintain their own shop, some higher-skilled garment workers and tailors also managed to subcontract a portion of their work outside.

Piecework was favored by contractors for their unskilled immigrant workers. They paid each worker per piece of work, rather than a wage or a salary. Piecework and hourly rates tended to yield roughly similar weekly earnings for immigrants, as well as place the full burden of efficiency on the worker. In the late 1800s, piecework grew among Jewish garment workers in manufacturing centers such as New York City. Piecework made garments available to the consumer at cheaper prices, greater speed, and greater

volume. This cheapness and efficiency displaced the value of the custom tailors.

The growth in piecework coincided with the growth of ready-made clothing, which refers to the manufacturing of clothing for all sizes, as opposed to custom clothing design. In the mid-nineteenth century, men's clothing production shifted from custom tailoring to ready-to-wear clothing. There were four situations in which ready-made clothing was manufactured in New York City: the small family shop, the transition shop, the outside shop, and the factory. The transition shop was also a workplace with sweatshop conditions; the outside shop involved sweatshop conditions at home; and the factory was generally the largest workplace, employing hundreds of immigrants.

In the 1880s, immigrant Jews from Russia began to significantly transform the garment industry. Production of both men's wear and women's wear changed to increased mechanization and the more specialized division of labor. This also increased the occurrence of sweating on a massive scale throughout the city. By the later 1880s, the older craft unions of skilled garment workers were overwhelmed by the new machinery and labor practices that undercut the wages and status of workers in the industry. Although the absolute number of male workers increased, it did not affect the relative proportions of male and female workers until about 1890. By the end of the 1890s, following a decade of major strikes that were sometimes supported by the community at large, only 10 to 15 percent of the garment workers belonged to unions.

In the garment industry sweatshops of the nineteenth century, there was no regularly stipulated number of hours, though many worked a minimum of twelve hours a day, six days a week. Lesser hours were possible in some of the better shops, but in all of them, busy times required work to the point of exhaustion. It was not uncommon for men and women to work sixteen to nineteen hours a day for weeks in succession.

By the end of the nineteenth century, in large garment centers such as New York City, Chicago, and Rochester, factories began to replace sweatshops. Men, women, and children, many recent immigrants to America, worked night and day sewing garments. In particular, women were becoming more prominent in the labor force. The factories had strict rules for their workers. Some resembled prisons. The doors were locked to ensure that no one would leave without permission. Workers were not allowed to speak to one another or sing. Disease was a constant danger in the shops, as the air was often filled with fumes from the machines and dust from the garments.

ORGANIZATION IN THE GARMENT SWEATSHOPS

In 1900, a small group of workers formed a union to speak for all workers in the industry. This group, the International Ladies' Garment Workers' Union (ILGWU), was to become the most influential group of organized garment workers fighting to improve their standard of living. Belonging to this national union with many locals increased the immigrant's power.

The garment industry historically gained its labor force from newer immigrants, as they are often poor, industrious, and lacking in marketable skills upon their arrival to cities. In the early 1900s, these immigrants were largely Jewish and Italian. Many Jews became leaders in the garment industry. Throughout the twentieth century, other immigrant groups, including

Puerto Ricans, Portuguese, and Slavs, found work in the clothing trade. However, more recently, the immigrant workers who predominate in garment sweatshops are arriving from Asia and Latin America.

WOMEN IMMIGRANTS IN SWEATSHOP WORK

The Triangle Shirtwaist Company tragedy of 1911 alerted many Americans to the atrocious working conditions of immigrant workers. However, a more particular concern that resonated after the tragedy was that the workers were women. Although by 1911 women had a strong presence in the industrial labor force, the Victorian ideal of genteel womanhood persisted. Therefore, the image of women jumping from the factory to their death stirred the nation. However, despite the shock and concern, little changed. Women were the majority in garment factories, and they continue to be the majority today.

Presently, women make up 90 percent of sweatshop laborers in the garment industry; they include legal and illegal immigrants who are unable to provide for themselves and their families by other means. The majority of these women are between the ages of fifteen and twenty-two years. Employment of those underage is in violation of child labor laws. However, many immigrant workers, particularly illegal immigrants, depend on the income of their older children to supplement the family income. The large number of young people in sweatshops is also a result of the many young and unmarried women who emigrate to the United States. For the most part, these young women are unable to continue their education when they come to America and must depend on sweatshop work for survival.

A particular difficulty that women immigrant workers are faced with in sweatshop work is sexual harassment, which is used by supervisors, along with corporal punishment and verbal abuse, to instill fear and ensure that employees comply in the sweatshops. Many women immigrants work in sweatshops that employ only women, a policy meant to ensure that the women are further controlled by the foreman and not in a position to be influenced or defended by male coworkers. Many sweatshops that engage in these practices forbid any form of organization or unionization even though it is illegal to do so. Therefore, there are still many women working in sweatshops who have no connection to any labor organizations that could aid in their conditions of employment.

Another particular problem that women immigrant workers face is the inability to learn English, because most of their time is spent in the sweatshop. Although many of these women have children who are being educated in the United States, they are unable to spend sufficient time with their children, who could teach them English. Without the mastery of English, there is little chance of immigrant women having the opportunity to leave sweatshop work for other employment.

SWEATSHOPS IN THE TWENTIETH CENTURY

By 1920, sweatshops and factories of the old type were eliminated largely as a result of legislation. These sweatshops included shops in which workers were locked in to work, received physical punishment for taking breaks, and received paltry wages. However, exploitative conditions still flourished under a more concealed setting, despite the tragedy at the Triangle Shirtwaist Company. Public knowledge of the travesties of sweatshops continued to grow, and, conversely, the covert nature of their operations grew as well.

Many different populations continued to endure the harsh conditions, as a rite of passage into the American workforce. For example, during the 1920s, Mexican immigrants moved into factory and sweatshop work with increasing frequency in the Southwest and Midwest. In 1925, a Labor Department official reported that every major corporation in California and Nevada that employed unskilled labor maintained a recruiter in Los Angeles who secured workers from the numerous agencies specializing in Mexican labor. Industries with the highest percentage of immigrant Mexican workers included stone, clay, glass products, textiles, metal machinery, food, and tobacco.

After this period, there was a decline in the arrival of newer immigrants, due to the Depression and World War II. As a result, sweatshop work continued, attracting immigrants who were unable to penetrate the more desirable positions in the workforce. Although the 1950s are commonly seen as a period of economic prosperity for America, sweatshop work persisted, and new immigrants continued to fill these positions, as competition for pricing was at an all-time high. This resulted in the need to cut costs on labor; hence, the continuation of sweatshop work.

In the 1970s, rather than the employers being the primary enemy of the sweatshop workers, the immigrants were faced with another evil: imports. Imports were flooding into the country in various industries, and thousands of workers were losing their jobs, because their product could be made more cheaply overseas. At the same time, sweatshops were being established in developing countries because of the lack of labor laws and the ability to pay workers even less, without having to invest in better working conditions.

The move to imports and the establishment of sweatshops in developing countries was a direct result of the increased worker legislation and protection in the United States that had been established by the 1970s. Therefore, rather than take the necessary precautions needed to verify that U.S. factories and former sweatshops were up to code, employers found it more economical to send the work to developing nations where sweatshop conditions existed openly without public or government intervention. These developing countries had no unions, no minimum wage, and no benefits.

Although large firms grew at an unprecedented rate in the United States, and the amount of work outsourced to sweatshops in developing countries increased, immigrants working in U.S. sweatshops continued. In the 1980s, although the work of ethnic associations, women's groups, and organized labor focused attention on sweatshop work, it continued. Sweatshop work became more common in industrial areas, often referred to as edge cities because they were situated on the edge between cities and suburbs in industrial centers that catered to work rather than residential growth. Therefore, out of the city centers, the sweatshops are less in the public eye than previously.

Throughout the twentieth century, jobs in sweatshops have been attained largely by social networks among immigrant groups. Earlier immigrants often act as liaisons between the contractor and the newer immigrant. The more established immigrant introduces the newer immigrant to the contractor and, in most cases, trains the newer immigrant in the work process, without additional pay. The incentive is to help members of the same nationality or ethnic group. Often multiple members of a single family will acquire work in a single sweatshop through this method; sweatshop work is often their only option.

Although today the most common access to sweatshop work for newer immigrants is through social ties to other sweatshop workers of the same nationality, another means of entrance is on the rise. This is used particularly by illegal immigrants, as they can only work in illegal positions, and it involves the connections to gangs. These gangs are often carrying on the smuggling of immigrants to America; then, for a high fee, they turn them over to sweatshop owners.

For example, many illegal immigrants coming from China have given as much as $48,000 to gangsters in order to get to America as part of a wave of immigration from China's coastal Fujian province. Police have estimated that there are 300 gang-run safe houses in the New York metropolitan area alone, where illegal immigrants live as they prepare to enter the workforce. New York City has become a magnet for these illegal Asian immigrants because of the decline of labor law enforcement in the city. In addition, in attempts to remain competitive with the Third World market, the New York City garment industry has continued to hire illegal immigrants in unlawfully operated sweatshops.

LEGAL ISSUES CONCERNING IMMIGRANTS WORKING IN SWEATSHOPS

The legal issues concerning immigrants working in sweatshops are many. However, because much sweatshop work has historically been illegal, it is difficult to gauge the magnitude of legality involved or to improve conditions for workers. Throughout history, many sweatshop workers have been illegal immigrants. Drawing attention to the unsanitary conditions, poor wages, and illegal treatment of them would only alert the authorities to their illegal status, so many of the greatest violations in sweatshop work continue to go unnoticed.

The first major attempt to regulate sweatshops was the Board of Health Act of 1892. This act provided that no room in any tenement used for eating or sleeping purposes should be used for the manufacture of clothing except by the immediate family living there, and then only after having secured a permit from the Board of Health. This law was supplemented by the amendments to the Factory Act in the same year. However, exceptions were permitted by the factory inspector. In addition, contractors and manufacturers made great efforts to ensure that the tenements they used were not residences. This legislation could not control the amount of work that individual workers took home to their residences to complete. There was no way to fully legislate the occurrence of sweatshop work, largely due to its decentralized nature. This first attack on the sweatshop in 1892 was rather weak; it merely prohibited the introduction, as workers, into the tenement workroom or workshop of persons who were not members of the family living in the apartment. The law thus merely attempted to limit the sweatshop to the family; but even in this, it was ineffective.

More progress in the elimination of the sweatshop was made after 1899, when a new law was passed requiring that a license should be applied for and obtained by anyone who intended to use a room in a tenement or dwelling, or in a building in the rear of tenements or dwellings for the purpose of work. This law led to a gradual decline of manufacturing in residential premises. It was one of the factors that resulted in the wholesale migration of the shops from the crowded tenement districts of urban residential neighborhoods to distinctly manufacturing districts within the city limits. This also resulted in changes in the composition of the workers.

As the number of immigrants rose dramatically in the early 1900s, the issue of sweatshop labor become entangled with debates over immigration policy. For example, after 1921, many advocates of permanent legislation to restrict immigration encouraged Congress to close the gates to foreigners, as a means to rid the country of sweatshop horrors.

Throughout the second half of the twentieth century there was continued attention to legal issues concerning sweatshops, focusing on compliance with child labor legislation as well as the conditions of the sweatshops themselves. There were great advances in awareness of illegality in sweatshops. However, as long as illegal immigrants will continue to work in these places, the illegal conditions will continue. Drawing attention to the illegal sweatshop conditions also draws attention to the illegal status of the immigrants. Legal immigrants have been drawn to unions to improve their working conditions. For the most part, unionization is most prevalent in factories where the working conditions have been deemed sanitary, the buildings have been inspected, and the employers are in compliance with legislation for hours worked and pay. Perhaps the greatest legal advancements in sweatshop work have been the continued attention of the public and the work of organized labor to improve the conditions of new immigrant workers.

THE FUTURE OF IMMIGRANT WORK IN SWEATSHOPS AND FACTORIES

Throughout the end of the twentieth and into the twenty-first century, the biggest change in factories and sweatshops has been automation, which has had a direct impact on immigrant workers. Primarily, the workers have less specialized work to perform, labeling them and keeping them at less skilled or unskilled positions. Therefore, movement out of sweatshop work into more regulated and high-paid factory work becomes less likely.

Another change, though for the benefit of workers, is the higher standard of comfort in factories. This has been particularly true for workers in the computer industry, where certain conditions are required to maintain the quality of the product, and the workplace must therefore accommodate that need. For example, for the assembly of computer chips, the environment must be dust-free, thereby indirectly ensuring that workers will work in a clean environment. Although the standards in factories increase due to advancement in technology, there are still hazards in factories and workshops.

The most recent attention to sweatshop work has been to be more actively involved in promoting legislation for better working conditions as well as calling attention to the plight of immigrant sweatshop workers. This has been most salient in the labor movement. For example, in 2000, the American Federation of Labor-Congress of Industrial Organizations (AFL-CIO) called for the restructuring of immigration policy to protect workplace rights and freedoms, in accord with holding employers accountable for exploitation of immigrant workers.

Teal Rothschild

See also: Impact of Immigration on the American Economy, Poverty (Part II, Sec. 7); Labor Markets for Recent Immigrants: A Statistical Portrait, Unions and Union Organizing (Part II, Sec. 8).

BIBLIOGRAPHY

Abrams, Fran. "Made in Saipan, If Only You Knew." *New Statesman* 129 (January 10, 2000): 4468.

Anner, John. "Sweatshop Workers Organize and Win." *The Progressive* 60 (June 1996): 15.

Barnes, Edward. "Slaves of New York." *Time,* November 2, 1998, 72–75.

Brown, Tom. "Sweatshops of the 1990s: Employees Who 'Survived' Downsizing Are Working Harder and Longer These Days." *Management Review* 85 (August 1996): 13–18.

Gonzalez, Rosalinda Mendez. "Capital Accumulation and Mexican Immigration to the United States: A Comparative Historical Study of the Political Economy of International Labor Migration." Ph.D. diss., University of California at Irvine, 1981.

Light, Ivan, and Carolyn Rosenstein. *Race, Ethnicity, and Entrepreneurship in Urban America.* New York: Aldine de Gruyter, 1995.

Min, Pyong Gap. *Caught in the Middle: Korean Communities in New York and Los Angeles.* Berkeley: University of California Press, 1996.

Mort, Jo-Ann. "Immigrant Dreams: Sweatshop Workers Speak." *Dissent* 43 (Fall 1996): 85–87.

Parmet, Robert. *Labor and Immigration in Industrial America.* Boston: Twayne Publishers, 1981.

Pope, Jesse Eliphalet. *The Clothing Industry in New York.* New York: Burt Franklin Press, 1970.

Reisler, Mark. *By the Sweat of Their Brow: Mexican Immigrant Labor in the United States.* Westport, CT: Greenwood Press, 1976.

Stein, Leon. *Out of the Sweatshop: The Struggle for Industrial Democracy.* New York: Quadrangle, 1977.

Sundstrom, Eric. *Work Places: The Psychology of the Physical Environment in Offices and Factories.* New York: Cambridge University Press, 1986.

Sweeney, Maria. "Sweating the Small Stuff: Mickey, Michael, and the Global Sweatshop." *Radical Teacher* 55 (1999): 11–14.

Waldinger, Roger D. *Through the Eye of the Needle: Immigrants and Enterprise in New York's Garment Trades.* New York: New York University Press, 1986.

———. *Still the Promised City: African Americans and New Immigrants in Postindustrial New York.* Cambridge, MA: Harvard University Press, 1996.

Waters, Mary C. "Immigrant Dreams and American Realities: The Causes and Consequences of the Ethnic Labor Market in American Cities." *Work and Occupations* 26:3 (August 1999): 352–64.

UNDERGROUND ECONOMY

The term "underground economy" refers to all income not measured by official figures, including income from work not reported for taxation, noncash transactions such as bartering, and criminal activities such as drug sales. Potentially, any person in the American economy can participate in the underground economy if he or she earns unreported income, but both legal and unauthorized immigrants are especially likely to be employed in this manner. Estimates of the extent of the underground economy are taken from reports on the overall circulation of money; it is extremely difficult to obtain a reliable figure on the amount of money changing hands in the underground economy.

An important part of the underground economy is referred to as the "informal sector." The informal sector produces and sells goods and services outside of the bureaucratic regulatory process that deals with maintaining the minimum wage, taxation, health and safety, zoning, and other legal requirements for work. The informal sector has traditionally been represented as a temporary feature of developing countries' economies, providing an alternative to unemployment and extreme poverty. It is anticipated that after development of an urban industrial base to absorb surplus labor, the informal sector would disappear from the Third World. However, the emergence of informal sectors in the immigrant ethnic enclaves of American metropolitan areas such as New York, Los Angeles, and Miami indicates that development does not preclude reversion to extralegal entrepreneurial and worker activity in the absence of effective labor law enforcement.

A major motive for acting as an employer and working in the informal economy is tax evasion. Undocumented domestic workers, gardeners, and handymen have become staples of the middle-class lifestyle despite government requirements that any earnings over $50 per quarter year be reported. The payment of such tax is the responsibility of the employer, and failure to withhold, enumerate, and pay tax carries a penalty. Further civil and criminal penalties can be invoked for deliberate tampering with an employee's tax-withholding statement.

National celebrity of a dubious nature resulted in 1993 during the Clinton administration when both Zoe Baird and Kimba Wood, candidates for attorney general, were discovered not to have paid such taxes for household workers, who also proved to be undocumented. It is striking that the failure to pay taxes for service labor within households extends into the upper classes. Yet the informalization of labor extends beyond household arrangements into the traditional service and manufacturing sectors of American society and profits native-born and immigrant entrepreneurs alike.

GLOBALIZATION, ECONOMIC RESTRUCTURING, AND INFORMALIZATION

The informal sector of the underground economy grew as a result of the globalization and restructuring of the American economy since the 1960s. In a global economy, the spatial mobility of financial capital, components, assembled goods, and human labor has made it possible for many manufacturing firms to pursue an eclectic strategy for relocation. In this process, the Frostbelt (consisting of industrial states in the North) was initially pitted against the Sunbelt (states in the South and Southwest), and, later, unskilled and skilled blue-collar workers have competed against labor in developing countries. In a worldwide economy, the outsourcing of production to subcontractors has encouraged some American contracting firms to adopt flexible production regimes, reduce wages, and cut corners on working conditions and safety. Post-1970 economic restructuring has been associated with increased employment of new immigrants, lowered

Many undocumented immigrant women, like this Caribbean nanny, find jobs taking care of native-born middle- and upper-class white children in private homes. *(Donna DeCesare/Impact Visuals)*

wages, and deunionization. In a changing economic climate, it has been speculated that without informal labor, vulnerable employment sectors such as manufacturing and construction would have suffered a more substantial decline.

Deindustrialization in the developed world has been accompanied by a general transition from a centralized assembly-line mode of production to a flexible, more decentralized system of production in which the private sector subcontracts routine service tasks. American manufacturing competes with low-wage labor in underdeveloped countries without enforcement of working conditions and safety standards similar to those in the United States. The loss of higher-paying, often unionized jobs with benefits has accompanied the rise of the informal sector, with participation by mainly immigrant and some native-born minority workers. The flexibility of subcontracting has

increased instability of employment for these workers, as it fluctuates with demand, and while it affords higher profits for the private sector, temporary employment creates informal workers.

The destabilization of manufacturing work and the growth of demand for services has attracted both immigrant and native-born entrepreneurs. Immigrant entrepreneurs may utilize family labor to reduce operating expenses, may act independently as street vendors, taxi drivers, and crafts producers, or may employ outside, often coethnic workers. Both immigrant and U.S.-born entrepreneurs operate small manufacturing or service concerns utilizing immigrant and minority labor. One example is the Los Angeles garment industry, in which immigrant and native-born entrepreneurs primarily employ Latino immigrants, many of whom work in the informal sector. Research done by Ivan Light, Richard B. Bernard, and Rebecca Kim indicates that the L.A. garment industry is about evenly divided between immigrant (often Asian) owners and non-Hispanic white owners. About 30 percent of immigrant-owned firm employees are coethnics. About one-half of all apparel firms employees are Latino immigrants. Native-born whites comprise about 22 percent of workers in the industry and tend to have employers of their own ethnicity. Informality is present in immigrant- and native-born-operated garment shops employing immigrants.

POPULATION DENSITY, RESTRUCTURING, AND INFORMALIZATION

Three structural trends are implicated in expansion of the informal sector in metropolitan areas. The first trend has been the growth of a legitimate advanced service sector of highly educated and paid workers who control and manage the global economy. The second trend has been a related increase in high-income workers whose lifestyle consumption demands provide for many low-wage traditional service jobs. These include many jobs taken by immigrants such as preparing special gourmet foods, making decorative objects and luxury apparel, cleaning, doing repairs and home improvement, running errands, and even walking dogs. The third trend has been the relocation of traditional manufacturing to lower-wage world regions, which has resulted in the downgrading of much remaining manufacturing. The garment, footwear, toy, and electronics industries have survived in the form of smaller firms that rely on subcontracted work. Many of these forms operate as sweatshops or send out industrial work to be carried out at home by immigrants.

Although research has concentrated on informalization of work in major cities, suburban areas are increasingly adopting this pattern. Suburban case study research indicates that undocumented Salvadoran immigrants have found a niche providing household services on Long Island, which is a residential suburb of New York City and a source of economic activity in its own right. Women work as live-in housekeepers, nannies, and live-out house cleaners, while men are active in landscaping, painting, and pool maintenance. Men gather at "shape-up" points where prospective employers come to hire. For Salvadoran males, work is seasonal and averages $8–$12 per hour, often with twelve-hour days, no access to sanitary facilities, and visual exposure to agents of the Immigration and Naturalization Service. Salvadoran women increasingly have access to home care jobs for seniors, providing companionship.

Suburban restaurants in Long Island often hire Salvadorans to work in the back of the restaurant in positions as dishwashers, bus boys, and cooks' assistants; the native-born work out front. Sarah Mahler indicates that workers are paid in cash and that many cases of exploitation are reported. In addition, South and Central Americans work in commercial and industrial cleaning on Long Island. Banquet halls, clubs, offices, and other enterprises hire cleaners. It can be projected that in the absence of extensive labor law surveillance and enforcement, informality will increase in the nation's suburban and exurban regions.

The use of native-born minority migrant laborers, foreign-born resident aliens, and immigrants and undocumented immigrants in agriculture is a forerunner of underground economic operations in business. The low wages, long hours, unpaid overtime, and poor working and safety conditions antedate the resurgence of these practices in urban and suburban areas. In addition, because of the use of undocumented labor, agribusiness and other farm owners have traditionally masked unlawful practices in their records. Intriguingly, since the passage of the Immigration Reform and Control Act (IRCA) of 1986 and implementation of employer sanctions for knowingly using undocumented workers, growers have turned to subcontracting as a way of displacing the risk.

UNDOCUMENTED IMMIGRANTS IN THE INFORMAL ECONOMY

Undocumented immigrants are a major source of workers in the underground economy. The passage of IRCA resulted in the implementation of civil and criminal sanctions for knowingly employing undocumented immigrants but did not provide for a national, difficult-to-forge identification card. The result has been thriving criminal enterprise in the production of forged documents. Immigrants who cannot afford to purchase fraudulent documentation for the purpose of working in the formal economy and newcomers with documentation can seek jobs "off the books." Employers of undocumented immigrants risk large fines and even the closing of their business. Yet off-the-record work benefits employers, who can reduce compensation, cut corners, and avoid payment of worker benefits and taxation, even as it is disadvantageous for immigrants. Sociologist Francisco Rivera-Batiz compared data on legal immigrants with the reported earnings of immigrants given amnesty in the 1980s. He indicates that with education, English-speaking ability, and time of residence held constant, legal immigrants earn more than undocumented workers. Illegal status facilitates recruitment into the informal sector, and Rivera-Batiz argues that attempts to strengthen sanctions against employers force immigrants further underground, depressing wages and working conditions rather than eliminating this practice.

The exact number of immigrants working in the informal economy is unknown, and academicians have often been skeptical of estimates of activity made by journalists and qualitative researchers. Yet case study research indicates that the informal economy began to expand in major American cities during the 1980s in the industrial and service sectors. Traditional manufacturing, which had often been unionized, began employing informal workers to sew clothes, stitch shoes, and assemble toys or electronic components. An example of skilled informalized work is photoengraving.

The informal sector makes it easier for undocumented workers to find employment in the United States. Sociologist Saskia Sassen's research on the economic utility of employing undocumented immigrant workers has raised questions about American immigration policy. Undocumented immigrant workers may be docile because they have a hard time finding employment and are easily intimidated by threat of deportation. Many immigrant entrepreneurs both take advantage of this problem and help coethnics when they hire undocumented members of their own community for subcontracted labor. Indeed, the size of the immigrant community is associated with the degree of participation in the informal economy. Immigrants, however, are not the explanation for the growth of the informal sector of the underground economy. It is integral to economic restructuring in both the developed and underdeveloped world. In the United States, however, immigrants are more likely to be informally employed than the native-born, whereas in developing economies, internal migrants take these jobs.

The purported unwillingness of the native-born to work in low-wage jobs with no opportunity for social mobility may create niches for immigrants. Lack of documentation and limited English fluency are factors associated with new immigrant attraction to the underground economy. Informal labor tends to be divided into two types: (1) unskilled, repetitive work, and (2) high-skilled work, such as stonecutting and woodworking. The level of informality in a given occupation can vary. In Los Angeles, economists estimate that the service occupations subject to the highest level of informality include private household positions, construction labor, cleaning, food-related jobs, and freight and warehouse work. In manufacturing, greater informality is found among nonprecision machine operators, fabricators, handlers, and inspectors. An intermediate level of informalization occurs in jobs that may require more skill or some form of licensing surveillance: precision production work, extractive or construction trade jobs, material-moving equipment operators, cashiers, motor vehicle operators, mechanics, repairers, and health or personal service providers. It is clear that informalization is associated with service work and manufacturing.

The combination of economic restructuring, high-volume immigration, and informalization results in a situation whereby all income earned by some households is unreported. Impoverished immigrant neighborhoods in metropolitan areas are sites where a majority participate in informal-sector activities. Demand by native consumers in the larger economy for informally produced goods, overseas competition, inadequate provision of goods and services by the formal sector, and access to inexpensive labor have fueled informalization.

Coethnic entrepreneurs have ready access to undocumented immigrants, who often seek them out for work. Immigrants from the developing world may find the low wages attractive, since wages paid in sweatshop employment in the United States are higher than in plants established in developing countries. Often immigrants are willing to accept low wages because they expect to return to their home country, where the wage differential will permit them

to achieve upward social mobility, or because it permits them to send remittances to better support family members in their country of origin. Undocumented workers may prefer to be paid in cash because if taxes and benefits are not taken out, it allows them to realize a higher rate of return in the short run.

NEW YORK CITY: THE GLOBAL CITY AND INFORMALIZATION

The new immigrants have been especially likely to settle in metropolitan destinations. During economic restructuring, New York City became a major destination for immigrants and experienced a dynamic expansion of goods and services produced in the informal economy. Regulations and laws covering the minimum wage, taxes, health and safety codes, and zoning were violated. Late in the twentieth century, increased economic polarization between a smaller, elite group of higher-paid professionals and a large, lower-paid, less skilled group promoted the rise of nonstandardized production and small-scale enterprise. The elite cadre of the work force became divorced from standard production tasks and everyday service labor even while their incomes expanded rapidly. Some capitalized on subcontracted industrial production, realizing extreme profits and salaries while simultaneously conserving income expended for private domestic service and other day-to-day aspects of an upper-income lifestyle through informalization.

In New York, construction provides an example of how increasing income polarization affects a trade. An elite group of high-rise contractors persists, although middle-income construction work has decreased due to displacement to subcontractors and their lower-paid workers. Small store construction and commercial and residential alterations and renovations are often done informally, without the required permits and in violation of city codes. Decreasing unionization is paralleled by an increase in unreported work by immigrants hired for subcontractors. Subcontractors work for the high-paid worker elite, which has supported commercial and residential gentrification of run-down properties. Urban areas undergoing commercial and residential gentrification create jobs in construction, woodworking, and furniture making.

Gentrified neighborhoods create informal service employment for immigrants. High-income gentrification is labor-intensive and increases the need for food preparation, cleaning, delivery, and other domestic services. In turn, gentrification has displaced both run-down residential neighborhoods and manufacturing sites. In addition, informal manufacturing shops that violate zoning regulations and other city codes may be located in New York's gentrifying districts, providing glasswork, auto repair, apparel, cabinets, and so on, while officials look the other way in order to keep these small businesses in operation.

New York City has maintained financial dominance and reemerged as a global city while experiencing the informalization of its traditional industry. Apparel, furniture, fixtures, shoes, toys, sporting goods, and electronic components have become increasingly involved in the underground economy. Even explosives manufacture has evaded full regulation. Informal manufacturing is concentrated in densely populated ethnic communities containing large populations of Hispanic, Chinese, Korean, and Eastern European immigrants. Saskia Sassen considers that the small size of these assembly sites and a disadvantageous tax status prompts a shift to the underground economy. The cultural and economic diversity of New York's ethnic communities is illustrated by the involvement of Chinatown in the garment industry and other ethnic diversification in establishing niches for informalization. In contrast, in Miami, Florida, the Cuban ethnic enclave has dominated the informal sector.

MIAMI'S INFORMAL SECTOR

Economic restructuring was one stimulus in the development of a Cuban enclave economy in Miami. Ethnic antagonism of native-born whites and African Americans toward Cubans and the nativistic rejection of immigrants encouraged informal business development and illegal labor practices. The Cuban enclave developed in connection to the national economy. Coethnic cooperation occurred in which immigrants voluntarily accepted substandard wages and conditions in return for later help in starting their own enterprises. This cooperation, however, was limited to coethnics, as Haitians have not been included.

In Miami, the later-arriving Haitian immigrants, who were racially stigmatized because of their darker color, were excluded from better positions and found a survival niche working for non-Hispanic whites alongside African Americans. Haitians in Miami have entered the informal sector as entrepreneurs and wage laborers, but their participation is isolated from the broader economy. Wage opportunities for Haitians exist in apparel, construction, hotels, restaurants, and

agriculture. Haitian businesses include dressmaking, shops, food vending, childcare, and transport. Haitian immigrants may be self-employed as semiskilled construction workers or in auto and electronics repair. In response to economic isolation, Haitians prefer wage labor to informal business operation, which is used to supplement regular earnings.

In contrast, the Cuban informal economy is integrated with the broader American economy, especially in construction, apparel, and the restaurant business. Despite or because of this interlinkage, U.S. Department of Labor records indicate that the most common type of labor violations in Miami are falsifying records to avoid overtime payment, homework, and the use of child labor. Falsification of records is not solely a practice of ethnic enterprise, as it is estimated that 40 percent of labor law violations occur in domestically owned firms.

CONSTRUCTION AND INFORMALIZATION IN MIAMI

Both economic restructuring and the new immigration contributed to the informalization of the ethnically segregated Miami construction industry. Until the late 1960s, unions controlled 90 percent of Miami's construction industry, but a nativistic policy of failing to accept Cuban workers prompted them to enter the informal sector. Cubans used pickup trucks and accepted cash payments for work at below-market rates. Cuban bankers supported Cuban entrepreneurs who started nonunion construction firms, which operated partly through informal means by taking off-the-record cash for completed work, paying workers in cash, and not deducting social security or taxes. The non-Latino white unions' failure to incorporate new immigrants produced a partial displacement of unionized non-Hispanic white workers and resulted in a division of construction into union, nonunion, and informal firms. Nonunion Cuban firms have formalized themselves and now control the new-housing market. Over time, Cuban construction wages have risen to two-thirds of the union wage scale and are far above the minimum wage. Cubans effectively undercut unionized construction through temporary labor law violations and then formalized their businesses and permitted a competitive upward expansion of wages. This suggests that informalization in an advanced economy may be a temporary practice that evolves into compliance with regulations and meets worker quality-of-life concerns.

MIAMI TOURISM AND HIDDEN INFORMAL LABOR

Although it is in decline, the Miami tourism industry supports a major nonunionized hotel and restaurant industry. Since the 1960s, non-Latino white workers have been displaced by new Latino and Haitian immigrants, while African-American employment has remained stable. Low labor costs are maintained through use of part-time labor and violation of labor laws. Illegal employment practices include subminimum-wage pay, failing to pay time and a half for overtime, violation of health and safety laws, and charging workers for uniforms and breakage.

Sociologist Alex Stepick considers that informality in the Miami restaurant industry resulted not from immigrant vulnerability, but from the absence of labor organization. Although larger hotels and restaurants are formalized, small ethnic restaurants have operated with some underground practices, gradually evolving toward formal practices as larger profit margins permitted. Later, economic informalization reoccurred when Central Americans and Haitians displaced Cubans who arrived in the Mariel boat lift. Cash payments with no social security or taxes deducted were so common that the U.S. Department of Labor organized a task force to educate Haitians about their rights.

Informalization in the Miami restaurant industry has resulted in investment in decor at the expense of health and safety standards in the kitchens, which ought to concern customers. Ethnic segregation characterizes this industry, as African Americans, who were not displaced by Latinos, and Haitians work primarily at jobs in the back of the restaurants, such as food preparer and dishwasher. Racialization has created a backstage whereby darker-skinned workers are out of public view and subject to informalization.

INFORMALIZATION IN THE MIAMI HAITIAN ENCLAVE

The Haitian ethnic enclave in Miami contains Haitian refugees who survive through casual self-employment. Casual labor occurs as a supplement to regular work in times of unemployment. Haitian small-business activities include dressmaking, tailoring, commerce, food preparation, child care, transportation, construction, and auto or electronic repair work purchased within the enclave. Haitian women may engage in street vending, door-to-door sales, and flea market sales. Small-scale female entrepreneurs may operate a meal service for single Haitian men out of their homes or offer day care at rock-bottom prices. Haitian men work as drivers using older American cars, vans, and school buses. Notably, the goods and services offered by these men and women are utilized by coethnics. The Haitian informal sector is not integrated into the broader economy and does not displace workers of other backgrounds. It is also by and large a poverty-level survival strategy. Miami's informal economy is segmented into Cuban and Haitian sectors, with the darker-skinned Haitians remaining marginalized.

INFORMAL MANUFACTURING IN MIAMI

The apparel industry, as in other globally connected metropolitan areas, illustrates how economic restructuring is connected to the devolution of worker wages and conditions. The unionized Frostbelt garment industry incurred substantial loss of jobs due to relocation to the Sunbelt and hiring of low-cost immigrant labor. Three types of firms and practices resulted: (1) labor-law-compliant firms, (2) labor-law-noncompliant firms, and (3) homework, a practice that is illegal in garment making.

In Miami, middle-aged Cuban women were able to combine household tasks with work. Some Cuban women entrepreneurs attained sufficient success to make their living rooms or garages into mini-sweatshops, employing other Cuban women. Through time, many Cuban women have become upwardly mobile and abandoned the garment industry, resulting in a labor shortage. Cubans prefer not to hire Haitian labor, and job openings have been only partially filled by Central and South American immigrants.

This loss of coethnic labor has resulted in increased informalization through homework. Homework substantially lowers overhead costs for firms, while making the process of worker hiring less contingent on Cuban ethnicity and even more indirect. Miami apparel industry practices represent one example of the devolution of a formal industry, due to overseas competition, into replicas of preunion nineteenth-century homework and sweatshops. Homework is also present in the form of home-operated business.

HOMEWORK

Homework is labor done in the home, whether through taking work home or operating a business. The underground economy is in operation when immigrant women entrepreneurs run unregistered day care centers, tailor shops, beauty salons, or other service businesses from their homes. In comparison to the low wages offered in many types of lower-tier service sector employment, their untaxed income is higher and there is no overhead for building space.

In the garment industry, homework is common. When mothers work at home, children are often co-opted into the labor force illegally. Homeworker hourly or piece-rate wages are very low. Women homeworkers, although illegal in New York City, provide labor but are pressured to declare themselves self-employed. Sociologists M. Patricia Fernández-Kelly and Anna M. Garcia have compared homework practices in the garment industry in Miami and Los Angeles. In Miami, Cuban housewives were able to work for coethnics to improve earnings while reconciling their role expectations as traditional housewives with paid work. In Los Angeles, the absence of coethnic enterprises increases undocumented Mexican women's labor market vulnerability, and apparel work outside or inside the home is considered a survival strategy of last resort. In synchronization with apparel homework, the garment sweatshop has re-emerged in America's major cities.

SWEATSHOPS

Traditional manufacturing is increasingly an activity of the underground economy. The twenty-first-century sweatshop has re-created the wages, long hours, and poor working conditions of nineteenth-century industrialization in the United States. Even child labor is reported, although both legal and undocumented adult immigrants predominate. Violations of labor law occur because formal-sector manufacturers and retailers subcontract production work due to lower costs and flexibility. Subcontractors, who operate on slim profit margins, "sweat" profit on the basis of lower wages, failure to pay overtime, and problematic working conditions. In New York City, Saskia Sassen found that six industries were especially likely to subcontract: (1) construction, especially interior projects being undertaken without building permits; (2) apparel; (3) footwear; (4) furniture making and woodworking; (5) in-home retail sales; and (6) electronics assembly. The immigrants taking these jobs work long hours, accept low pay, and often involve underage family members. Often, a piece rate is paid rather than an hourly wage, which can be a losing proposition for the less adept. In an urban environment where space is expensive, sweatshops, factory basements, and even homes become new sites of production. In cities such as New York, Miami, and Los Angeles, the availability of immigrant labor may attract these enterprises.

UNDERGROUND GARMENT INDUSTRY PRACTICES

The garment trade is the most widely recognized sweatshop industry in the United States. A recent U.S. Labor Department report on garment factories in Los Angeles and New York City found 60 percent in violation of wage and labor laws. From the nineteenth century to the present, the high proportion of cost of production attributed to labor, 27 percent as compared to 10 percent for other types of manufacturing, has encouraged subcontracting. Competition from garment manufacturers in developing countries has placed severe constraints on the ability of American garment manufacturers to produce competitively priced products. Designers and manufacturers have increasingly turned to subcontractors for cutting, sewing, and pressing—all of the basic operations that used to be coordinated in "hybrid" firms. Today, retailers and brand-name manufacturers find it easier to subcontract orders to firms employing women on sewing machines rather than to automate. The use of sweatshops, rather than automated retooling, which would require skilled labor, is due to seasonality and variability in consumer demand due to changes in fashion. Brand-name manufacturers and retailers take bids from American and overseas contractors, utilizing a global labor market. Competition forces bids so low that subcontractors "sweat" their profit from workers. This system of subcontracting ingeniously displaces the risk of sanctions for violation of labor laws and use of undocumented labor from the manufacturer to the subcontractor.

The contemporary garment industry structure has largely displaced unionized workers, although UNITE (Union of Needletrades, Industrial and Textile Employees, formerly the International Ladies' Garment Workers' Union [ILGWU] and the Amalgamated Clothing and Textile Workers' Union [ACTWU]) organizes a majority of New York City's Chinatown garment workers, and small-scale unionization efforts persist. Clothiers such as Macy's and Calvin Klein have utilized union workers, but newer producers, such as Gap, Inc., the Limited, JC Penney, Sears and Roebuck, Eddie Bauer, and private label designers such as Norma Kamali and Donna Karan have utilized nonunion subcontractors.

Coethnic entrepreneurs and undocumented labor have fueled sweatshop reemergence. In New York City, the *New York Times* estimated that almost two thousand sweatshops employing twenty to fifty immigrants each are in operation. Contractors are under extreme pressure to cut costs, and they use underground methods to cheapen work. Other workers are entirely in the gray area of the economy because their employment is kept off the books. The apparel industry is gendered, as immigrant women often remain without papers in undeclared jobs while male immigrants are able to move up and legalize. Immigrant women do not always see an advantage to maintaining regular employment because of loss of income when taxes and social security are deducted. Deepening gender inequality is the fact that garment entrepreneurs also tend to be male, although some immigrant women become highly skilled entrepreneurs. Women can have a hard time dealing with the traditional gender expectations of male coethnics and have difficulty in gaining their cooperation. Subcontractors are overwhelmingly male, defining an informal structure based on gender inequality.

Both high-priced and lower-priced clothing is produced in sweatshops or by homeworkers. Informalization is more prevalent in women's and children's wear than men's wear. Knitwear, furs, and embroidery are increasingly done under sweatshop or homework conditions. The nationality of immigrants involved in garment work varies with patterns of settlement and enclave development. In New York City, Dominicans, Colombians, Chinese, and Koreans tend to operate informal apparel enterprises, often employing coethnic immigrants. In California, Latinos predominate, although Vietnamese, Chinese, Koreans, and other Asians have high rates of ownership.

Scholar Edna Bonacich indicates that the California apparel industry routinely violates paying the minimum wage and overtime, hires illegal homeworkers, and tolerates child labor while failing to pay workers' compensation and unemployment insurance. Many of the workers in the Los Angeles garment industry are undocumented and work for piece rates. Piece rates can provide an optimal return for an experienced worker, but it is very difficult for a new worker to earn the minimum wage. The records needed to establish that the minimum wage is paid are sketchy or deliberately doctored. Benefits are almost nonexistent.

In California, ethnic antagonisms have developed between Asian contractors and Latino workers because of "sweated" labor. Edna Bonacich has pointed out that non-Latino white retailers and manufacturers are the primary beneficiaries of worker exploitation, but contractors are the focus of worker hostility. This process of ethnic scapegoating clouds public perception of why garment sweatshops are back in operation. Lack of unionization is also proffered as an explanation of why "sweated" labor has returned, but some traditional unions, such as UNITE in New York's Chinatown, have operated in the midst of pervasive informalization.

NEW YORK'S CHINATOWN GARMENT SWEATSHOPS AND IMMIGRATION POLICY

Garment factories comprise the majority of manufacturing in New York's Chinatown. In *Reconstructing Chinatown,* Jan Lin has estimated that the garment industry provides jobs for twenty-five thousand Chinese immigrant women. The garment industry has forward linkages to immigrant-owned wholesale and retail distribution and sales and has a dynamic impact upon the Chinatown economy. Garment production, along with tourism, is the primary source of new income input into the Chinese enclave economy. The evolution of New York's Chinatown garment industry demonstrates that U.S. immigration law—specifically IRCA—is connected to the downgrading of the traditional apparel industry.

The Chinatown apparel industry dominates New York garment making and is increasingly comprised of subcontracting firms employing both authorized and undocumented immigrants. The first impact of IRCA upon this industry was the legalization of a considerable number of undocumented Fuzhounese Chinese immigrants. Peter Kwong indicates that these immigrants now sponsor the entry of additional undocumented immigrants, but unauthorized workers face more-deprived working conditions because of another provision in IRCA for civil and criminal penalties against employers who knowingly hire workers without papers or process workers with fraudulent documents. The employer sanctions provision of IRCA lacks accountability, as employers do not need to verify the authenticity of fradulent documents and initially only receive a warning if found to be employing undocumented workers. In addition, independent contractors and the self-employed are exempt. Employer sanctions function as a "symbolic law" and have given employers more leverage over undocumented workers because labor law enforcement is poor. Below-minimum-wage pay and harsh working conditions are imposed because unauthorized workers are not likely to complain and risk being fired or exposed to the Immigration and Naturalization Service (INS).

In lieu of the INS, the New York State Apparel Industry Task Force has only five inspectors to monitor four thousand garment firms. The U.S. Department of Labor is charged with federal enforcement of labor laws, but the process of establishing industry accountability is complicated by the terms of the working relationship between the U.S. Department of Labor and the INS. Although a 1992 "Memorandum of Understanding" calls for cooperation between labor inspectors and the INS, the INS generally deports laborers rather than holding them to give evidence in cases against employers. This hinders investigations, and related media publicity further intimidates workers. Employer sanctions has further complicated issues of employee redress because undocumented workers cannot be reinstated at work, denying them any benefit from reporting violations. This practice also limits use of undocumented workers as informants, increasing the workload of overburdened labor inspectors. In addition, when cases are brought to court, the New York judiciary often sends employers found to have labor violations to educational seminars about labor law rather than imposing monetary penalties.

NEW YORK CHINATOWN GARMENT SWEATSHOPS AND UNIONIZATION

Of course, unions can also pursue worker grievances, but organized labor has been slow to respond to relocations, subcontracting, and the creation of a flexible labor force. All officially registered Chinese garment firms were organized by the ILGWU. Peter Kwong shows that the ILGWU and UNITE have organized over 90 percent of legal and undocumented workers in New York Chinatown apparel firms but are very ineffective in dealing with sweatshop violations. Chinese garment workers are organized from the top down because UNITE pledged retailer and manufacturer support to gain a steady supply of orders. Members are not included in union activities, and many

lack a shop representative to explain labor law to them. Union leaders and business agents assigned to shops are older, male, and of a different ethnicity, non-Latino whites, with a weak connection to workers. Nevertheless, Chinese immigrant workers participated in a very militant demonstration in 1982 because of the absence of a Chinese representative in negotiating the yearly contract. The union, however, has not tried mobilizing Chinese workers from below until recently, when new garment manufacturers have begun using nonunion contractors. Even nonunion contracting supports the union hierarchy, however, as the unions benefit from fines paid by manufacturers if the practice is discovered.

As garment outsourcing became internationalized and obtaining job orders more competitive, the ILGWU remained an owners union, arguing that strict adherence to labor laws would put firms out of business and blaming foreign subcontracting for workers problems. News media exposés of garment sweatshops have embarrassed the union, which is now calling for corporate responsibility and consumer boycotts of sweated goods. Nevertheless, Kwong argues that unless UNITE organizes the workers from below, it will be an ineffective union. Currently, he considers that the aging leadership discourages rank-and-file leadership, as it threatens their position in the union hierarchy. In New York City and nationwide, many steps need to be taken before sweatshop conditions can be stopped. Consumer boycotts of "sweated" clothes and purchase of "clean" clothes, whether subcontracted in the United States or abroad, are one step. Enforcement of labor law is another.

SWEATSHOP AND HOMEWORK LABOR LAW ENFORCEMENT

Although federal labor law prohibits the wage and working conditions prevalent in sweatshops, the use of subcontracting of production has made it difficult to prosecute corporations that initiate and profit from this practice. The passage of the 1999 California Sweatshop Reform Bill linked retailers that subcontract clothing production with manufacturing, identifying them as "guarantors" sharing a joint legal responsibility to provide a minimum wage and overtime pay with subcontractors.

Homework, a staple of the informalized sector of the garment industry, was explicitly made illegal by the Fair Labor Standards Act of 1938. It targeted garment production and associated activities, food preparation, toy assembly, use of flammable products, and "activities considered injurious to the health or well-being of individuals and neighborhoods." As a result of reinterpretation of the law, home electronics assembly is legal in Florida and California, but not New York. The 1938 law also provided an exemption for individuals who care for children, elderly, and disabled for pay. M. Patricia Fernández-Kelly and Anna M. Garcia have found that labor investigators may use creative interpretations of the law in order to avoid imposing hardship on individuals who are forced to perform assembly work at home.

Budgetary and staff limitations make it hard to thoroughly enforce U.S. labor laws. State agencies may further confuse the issue by telling homeworkers to obtain self-employment permits that the Labor Department Wage and Hour Division does not recognize. The Internal Revenue Service complicates the issue by recognizing a category of the self-employed as "statutory workers," which can include homeworkers, allowing employers and individuals to circumvent the ban on homework. Other examples of work that have been difficult to regulate include the use of domestic servants.

HOUSEHOLD SERVICE

The world of the family has been demarcated by a gender division of labor that is followed in informal employment. Undocumented immigrant women serve as live-ins or day workers. They clean houses, prepare food, and tend children or care for the elderly. Immigrant men of similar status and background are the gardeners, painters, carpenters, and workers who, if they can be located, will do housing maintenance at a lower cost for unreported cash income. Working middle- and upper-class women's need for assistance, a constant that has not been taken care of by husbands to any great extent, is increasingly filled by immigrant women from other cultural backgrounds.

The result is an underground labor market in which informal networks among women domestics and employers provide knowledge of work opportunities. Although the extremely personalized working condition can lead to employer abuse, the demand for labor is so great that poorly treated individuals do not have to stay in a bad job for long. Undocumented maids are a possible target of border patrol or INS enforcement, but little effort has been made to enforce civil penalties against private households, which include a $2,000 fine. The private atmosphere of the home protects individuals from detection at the same time that the informalization of employment permits spouses to offer varying, highly individualized wages and work expectations.

As in the nineteenth century, a live-in maid might be expected to be on call twenty-four hours a day. In regions with a surplus of undocumented labor, such as the U.S.-Mexico border, a novice might care for five children and do housework five days a week for $85. The underground activity of domestics is a marked form of casualization of labor because jobs can be easily moved and reestablished.

STREET VENDING

Unlicensed street vending, a form of casual labor, increased during American economic restructuring, and because it is so resonant with the needs of urban workers and tourists, it is likely to remain. Street vending is common in Mexico and Central America and has always been an informal feature of the economy of America's larger cities, although vendors are engaged in a contest for public space. Street vendors are highly mobile, putting up a booth and earning income until forced to move on before the police ticket them. As street vending increased in Los Angeles, the non-Hispanic white population negatively reacted to the increased visibility of Hispanic vendors and sought to oust them. In New York City, it is estimated that there are over ten thousand illegal street vendors selling everything from food to T-shirts at cut-rate prices.

In New York's Chinatown, sellers of produce, prepared food, clothing, and souvenirs predominate. A line of goods and a table or pushcart allow new immigrants to enter business with little capital. Vendors need to be licensed by the Department of Consumer Affairs and, if food is sold, the Health Department, but many vendors do not have business licenses. Confrontation with police and regulatory agencies has resulted, particularly in the term of Mayor Rudolph Giuliani. Stringent police clearance resulted in vendor demonstrations and an effort at relocation, which failed because street vendors prefer leeway to follow the foot traffic.

Self-employment as a street vendor can be viewed as a form of entrepreneurial innovation that benefits the larger society. Even immigrants at the bottom of the social ladder can become mobile by utilizing items and opportunities that would otherwise be wasted and unnoticed. Street vending is an urban activity that finds a ready market and eventually allows some individuals to invest in formal businesses in which all taxes are paid. Informal activities can grow into ethnic enterprises that expand the formal economy, and so represent a contrast to subcontracting industries or private businesses that permanently exist for the purpose of tax evasion and undercutting wages and benefits.

INFORMALIZATION, UNIONIZATION, AND URBAN ECONOMIC SURVIVAL AND CHANGE

In the wake of informalization and expansion of the underground economy, unionization has suffered. Unionizing efforts are undermined by distrust, the ease with which shops can close, and lack of enforcement of laws protecting unionized workers. The Chinatown restaurant industry provides an example of how informalization of labor practices has precipitated attempts to unionize with varying degrees of success. Unionization efforts in the 1980s resulted in victories for waiters at some larger, uptown Chinese restaurants. In the 1990s, restaurant owners attempted a rollback of benefits, including tip sharing with lower-paid women workers, longer work hours with no overtime, lower wages, and no benefits. Locked-out workers at the Silver Palace restaurant were mainly rehired, and a suit for $1 million in back wages and health benefits was launched. The restaurant filed for bankruptcy, reducing its liability to $160,000. This labor conflict serves to illuminate the attitude of the wider society toward immigrant workers. Originally, New Yorkers viewed Chinatown's workers as characterized by a strong work ethic and accepting of substandard conditions. After labor conflict and attempts to identify and ostracize Chinese workers in the larger community, television publicity and college student protest elicited a more realistic view of Chinatown's workers. Ending labor abuse is very much connected to publicity and overcoming stereotypes of immigrant workers.

Saskia Sassen suggests that integration into a global economy has resulted in economic and social polarization, increasing poverty, low-wage employment without fringe benefits, sweatshops, and homework. Entire localities, whether global cities or rural towns, are displaced by a production process oriented toward a world market. In the absence of a global infrastructure that facilitates the ability of local sites of production to participate in economic decision making, the ability to regulate wages and working conditions at a level supportive of a quality lifestyle has declined.

Instead of seeing immigrants as a negative force producing informalization in the economy, their presence provide a source of labor that permits the survival of the traditional manufacturing sector in large cities. Regarding the phenomenon of increasing income polarization in cities, however, it is important to understand the contribution of contracting to sweatshops and homeworkers in the creation of a wide divide between two income groups in American society. Contractors who exploit workers are minimally well-off, skimming enough profit to have decent housing and send their children to college. In manufacturing, retailing, and banking, nevertheless, six-digit salaries and benefits are dependent on a very high markup that rests on worker exploitation. Edna Bonacich views the situation in the Los Angeles garment industry as one in which a particular group of immigrants, Asians, as contractors are both victims of the system and exploiters of another immigrant group, Latinos or other Asians. The ultimate beneficiaries are the upper-tier, often native-born, professionals.

Economic data from Los Angeles indicate a relationship between informal employment, lower wages, reduced return on earnings for level of education, and increased poverty. Econometric research indicates that labor market segmentation into a lower-paid tier of immigrants working informally for others gives a boost to the wages of a complementary tier of native-born workers with formal employment. Such immigrant workers are not self-employed entrepreneurs putting in long hours, but possible victims of labor exploitation.

Recently, government has begun to recognize informal business entrepeneurship in the form of programs to support microenterprise. The relationship between informality and labor exploitation suggests that such policies should be developed in a selective manner. Informalization may contribute to labor exploitation and increasing income polarization in the United States.

Informalization, however, could contain the seeds of rebirth of a new American economy. Some immigration researchers consider that the degree of income polarization characteristic of early economic restructuring will ease as the advanced service sector and immigrant enclave economies expand. A possible scenario is that while non-Latino whites have had a high level of representation in the elite tier of owners and workers in restructuring urban economies, their at least partial departure from the businesses in the informal sector, such as the apparel industry, will pave the way for immigrant entrepreneurs. Immigrant enclaves may generate substantial economies that permit an improvement in wages and withdrawal from informalization, such as in the Cuban construction industry in Miami. Unfortunately, even this optimistic scenario depicts a remnant third sector of native-born minority members and working-class immigrant groups who remain in marginal employment. The temptation to engage in underground activities may remain as well, if labor law enforcement is not strengthened.

CRIMINAL UNDERGROUND ECONOMY

An important sector of the underground economy is dealing in illegal goods and services. Drug smuggling and sales, prostitution, stolen property resale, and many other criminal activities result in unreported income. The internationalization of American crime has occurred as globalization generates transnational organized crime involvement in drug smuggling, money laundering, and other corrupt activities.

Immigrants have often been linked to social ills such as violent crime and property crime in the popular imagination, but the opposite is more accurate. The vast majority of new immigrants are law-abiding, and immigration-related arrests rather than violent criminal activity predominate in their contact with the criminal justice system. The Bureau of Justice Statistics reports that arrests of noncitizens in U.S. courts from 1984 to 1994 increased 10 percent per year on average as compared to a 2 percent overall caseload increase. Forty-five percent were charged with a drug offense, while a majority of the remainder were charged with immigration offenses. In 1994, two-thirds of those charged with an immigration offense had reentered the United States after deportation, while 18.7 percent were convicted of smuggling immigrants and 12.4 percent of trafficking in fraudulent entry documents. Intriguingly, only 1.4 percent were charged with violent crimes, as compared to 8.5 percent of citizens in federal court, implying that the populist conception of immigrants as common criminals is misguided. Kristin Butcher and Anna Morrison Piehl have found that new immigrants are less likely to be institutionalized than the native-born, but that over time, in subsequent generations, crime rates increase, implying that criminal involvement is affected by assimilation to American society.

The view of immigrants as criminals is found along the United States–Mexico border, an area where organized criminal activity such as drug smuggling, human smuggling, and auto theft regularly occurs. Border residents harbor an unrealistic stereotype of all Mexicans and other Latinos, especially undocumented or new immigrants, as criminals. Pablo Villa's interviews with El Paso residents show that both European Americans and Mexican Americans viewed undocumented Mexicans as a cause of crime, including household burglary, robbery, and petty theft. Operation Blockade, which intensified border patrol control over crossing of the border, was hailed by El Paso residents as an answer to their crime problem. Crime statistics for the El Paso area, however, show that crime was decreasing before the reduction in undocumented entries and that the border patrol effort did not have an impact on the El Paso crime rate. It has previously been found that undocumented immigrants are blamed for crime but actually commit very little in the San Diego metropolitan region.

HUMAN SMUGGLING AND CONTRACT SLAVERY

Immigrants are a part of the global criminal underground economy because of human smuggling. It is estimated that the price of undocumented entry ranges from $25,000 up to $45,000 for those entering from distant destinations. In order to pay this cost, immigrants may be forced to labor in service jobs or at criminal activities. The Central Intelligence Agency has circulated within the federal government a report, "International Trafficking in Women to the United States: A Contemporary Manifestation of Slavery," estimating that up to fifty thousand women and children from Asia, Latin America, and Eastern Europe are being enticed to the United States under false pretenses each year. Forced criminal activities include prostitution, while other women and children may be obliged to work off the cost of their passage in indentured servitude as domestics or in sweatshops.

The economic restructuring of the American garment, shoemaking, and toy-making industries has been a factor in the informalization of work opportunities and utilization of a new immigrant workforce. In a few instances, the drive for profit has led to criminal enterprises in complete rather than partial violation of American labor laws and the human rights of immigrants. Karl Schoenberger has documented an illegal labor facility in El Monte, California, and the formation of substandard plants in the American territory of Northern Marianas in the Pacific, the location of the island of Saipan.

In the late 1990s, a garment sweatshop was discovered in an apartment complex in El Monte, California. Undocumented Thai immigrants were held in indentured servitude, a practice outlawed under federal civil rights laws. Workers were confined to the garment shop premises, which were ringed with barbed wire, unless accompanied by a guard. If they sought their freedom, threats against their persons and reprisals against their families were made. Although the clothing they sewed carried the "Made in the USA" label, workers had entered a situation of contract slavery, as they were told that they were simultaneously working off a smuggling fee and sending remittances to their families, but actually were being paid nothing while being held captive. El Monte sweatshop defendants received prison terms of two to seven years for conspiracy, harboring the undocumented, and practicing peonage. In a parallel lawsuit based on the concept of joint legal liability, the bonded Thai workers and additional unbonded Mexican workers received $2.5 million in compensation from the retailers who subcontracted work to the apparel shop owners. Prominent corporations that settled out of court included Montgomery Ward, Mervyn's, and Millers Outpost. No wrongdoing was admitted by the retailers.

Saipan is a South Pacific island outpost in the United States territory of the Marianas. Subcontractors such as Willy Tan have organized garment-stitching plants there that can use the "Made in the USA" label. Contract slavery was practiced through the bonding of Chinese and Filipino workers to pay off the cost of being brought to the American outpost. Legal wage rates were controlled by the Marianas government and were substantially below the American minimum. Workers toiled for twelve hours or more per day with unpaid overtime, in hazardous working conditions, under guard in compounds with barbed wire. Factories had locked fire exits and unhygienic toilets. Workers' freedom was constrained by confiscation of passports and return tickets. Workers who attempted to organize were penalized or fired. A U.S. Labor Department investigation led to payment of almost $10 million in back wages and substantial fines. Garment makers subcontracting to Saipan included Liz Claiborne, the Gap, Ralph Lauren, Levi Strauss and Co., and other major brands and designers.

Levi Strauss and Co., a privately held corporation, has developed a global outsourcing code of business ethics to protect its brand name. Although the extent to which the concern follows this code is obscured by a lack of independent monitoring, it provides a model for developing standards to control use of subcontractors resorting to illegal means of cost containment in the United States and abroad. By acknowledging that corporations providing a product and retailers have a joint moral and legal liability and pursuing this concept in the legal system, illegal profit taking based on violation of human rights can be curtailed.

ORGANIZED CRIME AND IMMIGRANTS

From the late nineteenth through the twenty-first centuries, organized crime has provided immigrants and native-born minorities with an alternative avenue to economic and social mobility. Although organized crime has been stable as an institution in American society since Prohibition, the groups that predominate in a given time period are subject to ethnic succession. In the twenty-first century, the Italian Mafia is being displaced by Hispanic, African-American, and new immigrant criminal organizations. Scholar Francis A. J. Ianni indicates that emergent organized crime groupings have not attained the level of organization of the Italian Mafia but speculates that they will evolve toward it. If new immigrant groupings develop bases of operation outside of their communities, become bonded by a principle such as kinship (which organized the originally immigrant Italian Mafia), and gain access to and are able to corrupt politicians, their power could increase to a level commensurate with organized Irish, Italian, and Jewish criminal groups of the past. Drug trafficking is the area in which demand may permit the greatest expansion of new immigrant criminal organization. The group known as the Cuban Connection has increasing involvement in cocaine distribution and illustrates this trend.

A few new immigrants are involved in organized crime groups that originated in their country of origin. Countries of origin of ethnic organized criminals include China, Colombia, Cuba, Jamaica, Haiti, Ghana, Japan, Nigeria, the Philippines, Venezuela, Vietnam, and the former Soviet Union. Ethnic crime organizations from East Asia are especially prevalent.

CHINESE IMMIGRANT ORGANIZED CRIME

Chinese gangs, tongs, and triads established in Los Angeles, New York, and other metropolitan areas have become involved in the illegal drug economy and are increasingly wealthy. Chinese, Vietnamese, and Taiwanese syndicates are predicted to be a major source of organized crime in the twenty-first century. By the 1970s, Chinese criminal organizations were involved in extortion and gambling. Today, Chinese organized crime is second in sophistication and scope only to the Italian Mafia and has international connections. For example, the U.S. Justice department believes that Chinese criminal organizations have displaced the New York Italian Mafia in the importation of heroin. The groups known as the Ghost Shadows, the Flying Dragons, and the Tung On are currently active in New York City. Chinese triads are involved in the international heroin trade and are allied with similar groups in cities across the United States.

Crime reporter William Kleinknecht suggests that members of Chinese criminal organizations are recruited from the new Chinese immigrant community rather than among those born in the United States. Kleinknecht predicts that these groups will remain immigrant-based and not become intergenerational in the way of the Italian Mafia in the past. Their chief operational sites are in Chinatowns and Chinese communities, and, with the exception of the heroin trade, their criminal acts are committed against other Chinese. In New York City, Chinese organized crime activities include massage parlors, protection rackets, prostitution, and gambling.

Organized Chinese criminals are involved in heroin smuggling, alien smuggling, money laundering, and high-tech property crime. Alien-smuggling syndicates charge from $25,000 to $35,000 a person, and estimates indicate that 400,000 to 600,000 undocumented Chinese immigrants were brought into the United States in the 1990s. Other organized Chinese criminal rackets include bookmaking, casino gambling, loan sharking, fronting through legal businesses, credit card fraud, and video poker fraud. Chinese organized crime is international because of the heroin trade, alien smuggling, and a multinational credit card fraud business. Credit card numbers surreptitiously copied in Hong Kong are placed on fraudulently manufactured cards circulated by Chinese organized criminals in Los Angeles and San Francisco.

A famous incident illustrating the operation of Chinese organized crime concerns the discovery of the *Golden Venture,* an old freighter that carried 282 undocumented Chinese immigrants under unspeakably inhumane crowded conditions. Males were packed into small rooms belowdecks, unable to leave, and given one small meal a day. Women were kept on deck and repeatedly raped by the crew. The Fuji-

anese gangs responsible for this incident and other human smuggling maintain an illegal system of indentured labor until passengers pay off the exorbitant price, $25,000 to $35,000, for the trip. Some undocumented Fujianese immigrants are kept captive in warehouses and basements and taken to provide slave labor in restaurants, garment factories, and massage parlors providing sex.

Because Chinese organized crime is an interethnic phenomenon dependent on immigration for recruits, later generations of the native-born are unlikely to continue the practice. Chinese Americans believe in education and the work ethic and will have many legitimate options. Chinese immigrants in gangs in their twenties may own restaurants by their thirties and do not recruit their children into crime.

VIETNAMESE IMMIGRANT ORGANIZED CRIME

Vietnamese organized criminals are unique because, as a refugee immigrant population, they are less rooted in particular communities. Their crimes tend to be intraethnic, as they are committed in Vietnamese ethnic communities located in various regions of the United States. In the late twentieth century, Vietnamese criminals initiated home-invasion robberies. Gang members penetrate the houses of Asian businesspeople and take undeclared cash and jewelry while terrorizing the family to the extent that they may not report the crime. Like other organized criminals, Vietnamese are increasingly involved in computer chip and auto theft, fraud, loan sharking, and bookmaking. Initially, they were employed in low-level jobs in Chinese gangs, but they are rising in the established Chinese organized crime hierarchy.

HISPANIC IMMIGRANT ORGANIZED CRIME

Colombian and Chinese drug suppliers work with Dominicans, Cubans, and Mexicans. Dominicans and Cubans are the most organized of the Hispanic crime groups, but success may bring upward mobility and their disappearance. Cuban organized criminals are no longer active in inner-city New York and New Jersey but still dominate organized crime in Miami. In Philadelphia and Detroit, Cubans are only able to be criminally active through alliances with other Hispanics. Similarly, Dominican organized criminal groups may decline over time. Currently, Dominicans are major importers and wholesalers of heroin and cocaine. Young Dominican immigrant males are recruited into the drug business, but this ethnic grouping is not moving toward developing a hierarchical criminal organization with diversified criminal activities. Much of the money earned from criminal activity is sent to the Dominican Republic. It is estimated that $100 million is wired to the Dominican Republic per year in remittances from the underground drug economy. Because of the differential cost of living in the Dominican Republic, Dominican criminals may seek to return and live off their invested earnings. The ephemeralness of Cuban and Dominican organized crime may pave the way for Mexican and Puerto Rican groups.

Hispanic organized crime has evolved in new immigrant communities. Currently, Cubans control cocaine distribution in the southeastern United States, while Dominican organized crime is concentrated in the Northeast. Mexican Americans have formed an organized crime association known as the Mexican Mafia in Texas, California, and the Southwest.

RUSSIAN IMMIGRANT ORGANIZED CRIME

Russian immigrants to the United States tend to be highly educated professionals, and few find their way to the inner-city living conditions that cultivate criminal connections. A few Russian immigrants, however, were able to organize a fuel-tax evasion scam, and it is possible, given the connection of Russian criminals with the Italian Mafia, that they may develop a long-term organized criminal organization. Currently, Russian mobs steal cars in the United States and Germany to ship to Eastern Europe. Russian immigrants also distribute Colombian cocaine.

IMMIGRANT ORGANIZED CRIME AND THE GLOBAL DRUG TRADE

The global drug trade is prompted by interdiction policies and criminalization of drug possession. It incorporates immigrants who cannot find other avenues to survival and social mobility. Transportation, wholesale and street peddling, and money launderering are just some of the criminal opportunities generated. William Kleinknecht predicts that, rather than one ethnic group, the formerly immigrant Italian Mafia, dominating organized crime and the drug trade, various immigrant and lower-class inner-city groups will combine to conduct organized criminal operations. For example, in the New York Blue Thunder heroin case, Italian gangsters bought heroin from Chinese suppliers, and it was partially distributed by a Puerto Rican gang. Similarly, Kleinknecht believes that panethnic Asian criminal organizations incorporating Chinese, Vietnamese, and Koreans will develop. In New York City, Korean gangs with names borrowed from the Chinese, such as Korean Fuk Ching, Korean Flying Dragons, and Korean Taiwanese Boys, are committing violent crimes, practicing extortion, and selling methamphetamine. In Los Angeles, the Mexican mafia, a Hispanic organized criminal organization, established a strong presence in heroin trafficking, gambling, and prostitution. In an ironic simulation of legal government practice, imprisoned members of the Mexican mafia have been collecting a "tax" on Hispanic street gang drug sales.

American law enforcement agencies such as the Federal Bureau of Investigation and the Bureau of Alcohol, Tobacco, and Firearms have brought many indictments against organized criminals of many ethnicities in the United States. American demand for narcotics, which is almost as strong as the demand for liquor was during Prohibition, makes it difficult to curb criminal entrepreneurs. Together with the lack of legitimate opportunity in the inner cities where low-income new immigrants tend to reside, a strong impetus is given for second-generation children of immigrants to turn to criminal gangs as a way of attaining social mobility in a world of limited prospects.

IMMIGRANT YOUTH CRIME

The rate of gang formation and serious juvenile criminal activity among new immigrant youth has varied by nationality and even by ethnic affiliation within country of origin. Sociologist Tony Water compiled statistics showing that from 1988 to 1996, after ten years in California, Laotians, Vietnamese, and Cambodian youth became involved in gang crime. Other sociologists have argued that ethnic Laotians in California had higher juvenile crime rates than the Hmong Laotians. Some Laotian youth gangs engaged in dealing of rock cocaine and methamphetamine. Among Latino immigrants, there has been a high rate of youth crime, especially in areas of first settlement. In contrast, Koreans have experienced a very low rate of youth crime in the same period. Tony Water theorizes that immigrant youth crime is primarily a problem of the second generation in groups with a high percentage of adolescent and youthful males, many of whom have problems in understanding the law. An exception is Laotians, where large numbers of foreign-born children entered American society and a youth crime wave occurred earlier. Scholars believe that for these groups, poverty is less important as a causal variable in youth crime than discrepancies between sending and host country culture and associated problems of youth adjustment.

If new immigrant delinquent gangs develop into organized crime groups, new policing challenges will develop. Both journalists and senior law enforcement personnel are concerned about expansion of ethnic street gangs into the drug trade and other criminal activities utilizing hierarchical networks. Research in San Diego and Chicago indicates that many juvenile gangs have ephemeral histories: highly active one year, largely disbanded the next. In San Diego, gangs that disband have aged out as individuals acquire adult responsibilities, have gone to other gangs, or have been subject to arrest, prosecution, and incarceration. In Chicago, Hispanic gangs that go on to organized criminal activity develop ties to other established organized criminal groups and use noncriminal relationships to advance illegal activities, such as the practice of offering protection to neighborhood stores. The Latin Kings and the Gangster Disciples have levels of leadership, role differentiation, regular meetings, and written rules. Drug sales permit extensive income to allow expansion of organized activities through such measures as establishing quotas for selling and role differentiation such as drug mixing and money pickups. The Gangster Disciples have evolved to the point that drug profits were reinvested in legitimate businesses, record and clothing shops, and apartments. They are involved in political campaigns, engaging in passing out leaflets, encouraging voter registration, and even soliciting contributions. This gang was organized to the point of having ties with gangs in other cities concerning drug and gun distribution.

Cities with established organized crime traditions, such as Chicago, Los Angeles, and New York, foster the development of new immigrant criminal gangs. In New York City, organized Chinese syndicates have recruited youth street gangs as "street soldiers." Vietnamese criminal gangs are present in New York City's Chinatown area and Orange County, California. The criminal activities of the Born to Kill gang include robberies, extortion, murder and other crimes. Members range from preteen to middle-aged and are connected

to organized Vietnamese crime. Similar to Laotians, a foreign-born population has turned to gangs as a means of status acquisition. The "lost generation" descends from the "boat people," impoverished peasants who fled communist Vietnam in homemade vessels. Exposed to war and subjected to poor living conditions in refugee camps in Hong Kong, Vietnamese and Eurasian youth received a bitter reception in the United States due to the perceived "loss" of the Vietnam War. Refugee youths were reunited with relatives and friends preoccupied with survival or were placed in foster homes. School dropout and runaway rates were high, and many joined youth gangs as a way of finding a surrogate family. Little Saigon in Westminster, California, is a site of drive-by shootings in imitation of Hispanic gangs and based on exposure to gang behavior of other ethnic groups in California correctional institutions. Home invasion or commercial robberies provide experience before recruitment into established Vietnamese organized crime.

The diversity of immigration has contributed to the complexity of both juvenile and organized crime in the United States. Despite the linkage of new immigrants and crime, it is likely that absorption into American society and social mobility will eventually end this involvement. In the meantime, immigrant organized crime groups and juvenile gangs provide a significant problem for law enforcement.

CONCLUSION

The underground economy is divided into two sectors: informal and criminal. The informal sector utilizes both documented and undocumented immigrant labor. It consists of both native-born and immigrant small firms or individual workers who violate labor or immigration laws. Informal operations are subject to primarily civil penalties, but they may also commit crimes, such as holding workers in contract slavery. The degree of regulation or prosecution of this sector is limited because of lack of civil and law enforcement personnel and funding. The criminal sector is an arena of operation for the native-born and both documented and undocumented immigrants. Immigrant organized crime and youth gangs conduct illegal activities, including human and drug smuggling. The government expends a great deal in resources to prevent undocumented immigration, a source of labor for the informal sector and a profitable activity for organized criminals, who systematically smuggle individuals and groups for astronomical fees. Law enforcement efforts to eliminate native-born and immigrant organized crime groups are intensive, but have never been highly successful because of the profitability of crime commission and demand for criminalized services that are provided. Thus, the underground economy creates a net loss for American society in two ways: (1) loss of social security and other payroll taxes and (2) the need to support extensive law enforcement organization and associated professional and judicial bureaucracies.

In the face of the social cost of the underground economy, it is difficult to perceive any social gain. Yet the extent and persistence of the informal sector has been instrumental in preventing loss of some traditional manufacturing and allows provision of extensive services that support immigrant communities and subsidizes the lifestyle of the native-born. Whether it is the need for cheap apparel or a reliance on undocumented domestics and caregivers, immigrants are providing labor that supports the framework of society and ensures the reproduction of the next generation. Megacorporations and the elite benefit from this immigrant subsidization of more favored professional and skilled workers because they do not have to pay a wage that supports the full cost of their lifestyles, even as they relocate low-waged labor abroad for even greater savings. Ultimately, new immigrants are footing much of the bill for America's twenty-first-century economic expansion. The informal sector, just like the criminal sector, supplies services in demand at an affordable price. The only cost is a lack of social justice and equal treatment for many new immigrants, documented and undocumented. The problems of exploitation that have become endemic to American society have international implications as well. The immigrant subsidization of the American economy through low wages and lack of benefits is paralleled by the condition of international workers employed by multinationals. In the twenty-first century, the treatment of immigrants employed in the informal sector and international workers is likely to generate international worker coalitions and a challenge to contemporary labor practices.

Judith Warner

See also: The Immigration and Naturalization Service, Legal and Illegal Immigration: A Statistical Overview (Part II, Sec. 2); Impact of Immigration on the American Economy (Part II, Sec. 7); Service Sector, Sweatshops and Factories (Part II, Sec. 8).

BIBLIOGRAPHY

Bonacich, Edna, and Richard P. Appelbaum. *Behind the Label: Inequality in the Los Angeles Apparel Industry.* Berkeley: University of California Press, 2000.

Butcher, Kristin F., and Ann Morrison Piehl. "Recent Immigrants: Unexpected Implications for Crime and Incarceration." *Industrial and Labor Relations Review* 51:4 (1998): 654–79.

Fernández-Kelly, M. Patricia, and Anna M. Garcia. "Informalization in the Core: Hispanic Women, Homework and the Advanced Capitalist State." In *The Informal Economy: Studies in Advanced and Less Developed Countries,* ed. Alejandro Portes, Manuel Castells, and Lauren Benton. Baltimore: Johns Hopkins University Press, 1989.

———. "Power Surrendered, Power Restored: The Politics of Work and Family Among Hispanic Garment Workers in California and Florida." In *Challenging Fronteras: Structuring Latina and Latino Lives in the U.S.,* ed. Mary Romero, Pierrette Hondagneu-Sotelo, and Vilma Ortiz. New York: Routledge, 1997.

Ianni, Francis A. J. *The Search for Structure: A Report on American Youth Today.* New York: Free Press, 1989.

Kleinknecht, William. *The New Ethnic Mobs: The Changing Face of Organized Crime in America.* New York: Free Press, 1996.

Kwong, Peter. *Forbidden Workers: Illegal Chinese Immigrants and American Labor.* New York: New Press, 1998.

Light, Ivan, Richard B. Bernard, and Rebecca Kim. "Immigrant Incorporation in the Garment Industry of Los Angeles." *International Migration Review* 33:1 (Spring 1999): 5–25.

Lin, Jan. *Reconstructing Chinatown: Ethnic Enclave, Global Change.* Minneapolis: University of Minnesota Press, 1998.

Mahler, Sarah J. *American Dreaming: Immigrant Life on the Margins.* Princeton, NJ: Princeton University Press, 1995.

Nash, June, and María Patricia Fernández-Kelly, eds. *Women, Men, and the International Division of Labor.* Albany: State University of New York Press, 1983.

Rivera-Batiz, Francisco, Selig L. Sechzer, and Ira N. Gang, eds. *U.S. Immigration Policy Reform in the 1980s: A Preliminary Assessment.* New York: Praeger, 1991.

Sassen, Saskia. *The Global City: New York, London, Tokyo.* Princeton, NJ: Princeton University Press, 1991.

———. *The Mobility of Labor and Capital: A Study in International Investment and Labor Flow.* New York: Cambridge University Press, 1988.

Schoenberger, Karl. *Levi's Children: Coming to Terms with Human Rights in the Global Marketplace.* New York: Atlantic Monthly Press, 2000.

Stepick, Alex, III, and Guillermo J. Grenier, eds. *Miami Now!: Immigration, Ethnicity, and Social Change.* Gainesville: University Press of Florida, 1992.

Villa, Pablo. *Crossing Borders: Reinforcing Borders: Social Categories, Metaphors, and Narrative Identities on the U.S.-Mexico Border.* Austin: University of Texas Press, 2000.

Water, Tony. *Crime and Immigrant Youth.* Thousand Oaks, CA: Sage, 1999.

UNIONS AND UNION ORGANIZING

In the late 1990s, leaders in government, business, and organized labor began to recognize the growing importance of immigrants. In a five-year period the Republican Party had gone from supporting California's Proposition 187 in 1994, denying public services to suspected illegal immigrants, to a national strategy to welcome new Latinos as potential voters into the party. The Immigration and Naturalization Service (INS), prodded by employers seeking to lower labor costs, has reduced raids on undocumented workers, and unions have embraced immigrants as a major source of membership growth. These changes are not so much ideological shifts in support for immigrants as pragmatic responses to the functioning of the political economy. Politicians want to win elections, employers want a cheap supply of labor, and unions want to grow.

BACKGROUND

For unions, the key issue in organizing immigrants is defending labor markets and workers from exploitation. New immigrant workers, many of whom perform jobs that once were unionized, are today an integral part of the American economy. There is growing evidence that the superexploitation of these workers exerts a widespread pernicious effect, depressing wage levels generally, undermining workplace safety provisions, and hindering union organizing efforts.

In recent decades, labor leaders have increasingly come to recognize the link between the growth of nonunion low-wage jobs held by immigrants and the deteriorating standard of living of the average American worker. Thus, from the union perspective, immigrant workers present two aspects. On one hand, they depress wages; on the other, they are ripe for organizing. Over the past twenty years, the estab-

lished labor movement, perhaps shortsightedly, has viewed undocumented workers primarily as competitors to unionized workers. The fall in organized labor's membership from about 35 percent of the workforce in 1955 to about 13 percent today reflects a long-standing neglect of low-wage industries, where in fact workers are relatively open to unionization. A large and growing share of new jobs in major U.S. cities are in low-wage manufacturing and service industries and are filled by documented and undocumented immigrants who until recently have been shunned by unions. Today, however, with efforts under way to revitalize organized labor, there is evidence that unions are beginning to take notice.

New immigrants are increasingly viewed by the American Federation of Labor-Congress of Industrial Organizations (AFL-CIO) and by international and local unions as vital to any upsurge in union membership. In a break with historical pattern, the labor movement has taken concrete action to be more welcoming to immigrants. An example of this shift is labor's reversal of position on a key element of the 1986 Immigration Reform and Control Act. The AFL-CIO originally lobbied for passage of the act, whose employer sanctions provision has been used by management to intimidate immigrant workers seeking union representation. Thus, in practice these sanctions fall more heavily on workers seeking to better their wages and living conditions than on employers. Although some unions have already negotiated clauses in collective bargaining agreements that protect undocumented workers from employer recriminations, the national leadership of the AFL-CIO has only more recently taken action. At its October 1999 national convention in Los Angeles, delegates voted for a resolution supporting repeal of the employer-sanctions provision, which had come to be viewed as a major constraint on the ability of immigrants to join unions. The AFL-CIO now views repeal as a necessary step in facilitating the organization of millions of immi-

Unions, which once saw foreigners as potential strikebreakers, have become increasingly aggressive in organizing immigrant workers in recent years. Here forty Chinese construction workers in New York protest after their company fired them for trying to organize a union. *(Donna Binder/Impact Visuals)*

grant workers into the labor movement. In February 2000, the AFL-CIO went a step further, calling for a comprehensive amnesty for the approximately 6 million undocumented immigrants living in the United States. The amnesty would greatly facilitate their organization and unionization.

THE INS CURTAILS ENFORCEMENT

In 1999, the INS significantly reduced the number of workplace raids. According to INS figures, arrests for the purpose of deportation declined from 22,000 in 1997 to 8,600 in 1999. Business leaders view undocumented immigrants as an indispensable source of labor during an economic boom. Because these typically low-wage workers offer the added benefit of lower labor costs, many employers in manufacturing and service industries welcome and even recruit them. The *New York Times* devoted substantive comment to

the subject, moving immigrants from a narrow labor issue to front-page news on the national and business pages. As *Times* journalist Louis Uchitelle observed in a March 9, 2000, article, "The new lenience helps explain why overall wage increases have been less than many economists and policy makers had expected, given an unemployment rate of only 4 percent and a strong demand for people to fill jobs that pay $8 an hour or less, which is 25 percent of all jobs. Immigrants—legal and illegal—have fed the pool of people available to take these lower paid jobs."

As the status of immigrant workers becomes a topic of greater institutional and public interest, the question of how to translate policy and macroeconomic changes into practical organizing activity takes on great importance. Unions have hardly begun to organize undocumented immigrants. Earlier organizing drives, sporadic for the most part, have occurred primarily in the Los Angeles and New York metro areas, which have concentrations of new immigrants significantly higher than most other cities. These pioneering efforts are important for understanding patterns of worker and employer responses to immigrant organizing drives, and in formulating strategies for future campaigns.

IMMIGRANTS IN THE NEW YORK CITY LABOR MARKET

Two key transformations in the United States labor market have occurred since 1985: industrial restructuring and informalization, and a historically unprecedented volatility in the market's ethnic character. Both factors have contributed to depressed wages and have threatened workers in previously unionized labor markets.

INDUSTRIAL RESTRUCTURING AND INFORMALIZATION

Industrial restructuring represents the most fundamental change in the economy. A profound shift has moved jobs from the manufacturing sector to retail trade and business and consumer services. A second, derivative change is informalization, a restructuring of work within these new sectors of the economy. While in the past, new immigrants were marginalized in the underground economy, today they are marginalized in the mainstream economy. Although informal activities are typically associated with third-world underground economies, there is growing recognition of the linkage of formal and informal sectors even in advanced industrial regions, where the formal sector depends increasingly on informal economic activities through subcontracting and outsourcing of production to firms employing low-wage immigrant labor. Informalization is characteristic not of industrial decline but of horizontal restructuring, often to meet the flexible needs of competitive global markets. To stimulate local economic competitiveness in regional, national, and global markets, federal and state regulatory bodies have ignored violations of rules governing wages, hours, and workplace safety.

Informalization in the United States encompasses the following features: (1) subcontracting to small-scale, horizontally dispersed industrial production that escapes formal labor market norms and regulations, (2) reduced government expenditures allocated to enforcement of wage and workday standards, the appearance of wages below the prevailing legal minimum, and declining enforcement of workplace health and safety standards, (3) reduction of government so-cial wage protections such as social security contributions and unemployment insurance, (4) the undermining of established relations between trade unions and workers, and (5) exclusion of organized labor as an arbiter of wages, benefits, and working conditions.

By the 1990s, a sizable and growing share of industrial production and services in New York was conducted by contractors and subcontractors employing new immigrants in small and medium-sized facilities dispersed throughout the city, separating workplaces from ethnic communities and weakening prospects for building the power of organized labor.

ETHNIC FLUX AND VOLATILITY

Whereas in earlier decades the ethnic character of immigrants in the United States exhibited a degree of stability, today the immigrant population is in a continual state of transformation. From 1921 to 1965, the ethnic character of immigrants held relatively steady, with most coming from Italy, Ireland, Eastern Europe, and other European regions that had sent earlier waves of immigrants to these shores. In unionized industries, recent immigrants from the same country typically replaced more established immigrants moving into higher-wage jobs. Though immigrant labor markets were never static, they were steady and predictable. The passage of the 1965 amendments to the 1952 Immigration and Nationality Act transformed immigration by eliminating country-of-origin quotas that had restricted immigration from non-European areas. The new legislation contributed to the expansion of immigration from Latin America, Asia, and the Caribbean, creating what Roger Waldinger calls "the new immigrants." The passage of the Immigration Control and Reform Act of 1986, intended to restrict the growth of unauthorized immigration, in fact did almost nothing to stem it. As the demand for labor increased, immigrants continued to come in large numbers. By the 1980s, globalization had made New York City a focal point of international labor migration, contributing to constant flux in the labor market as employers sought out less-secure workers who would accept lower wages. By the early 1990s, new immigrants were arriving from countries throughout the world, with new immigrant communities emerging in a few years that in the past would have taken generations. The growth of undocumented immigrants in traditionally unionized industries has obliged many unions to reassess long-standing practices of exclusion and has compelled a growing number to develop organizing strategies directed at these workers.

For example, in New York City, new undocumented immigrants from around the world have become major fixtures as bricklayers, demolition workers, and hazardous-waste workers on construction and building rehabilitation sites; as cooks, dishwashers, and busboys in restaurants; and as taxi drivers, domestic workers, and delivery people. They are increasingly the victims of exploitative employers who force them to accept bleak working conditions and wages below the federally mandated $5.15 an hour.

CHANGES IN THE WORKFORCE

A large majority of unions in America's leading cities consider the growth of immigrant workers in the workforce essential to the ability of their unions to survive, and consider ethnic changes to be somewhat important. Although a large majority of union organizers see changes in the demographics of their unions as very important, few appear to be targeting a specific immigrant population.

UNIONS AND IMMIGRANT ORGANIZING

Unions are divided on the question of whether immigrants are easier or harder than natives to organize. Recent interviews with union leaders in New York suggest that unions tend to organize immigrant groups familiar to them. Thus, unions that represent large numbers of Polish workers tend to see Polish workers as easier to organize and Latinos as harder; unions that represent Chinese workers see Chinese workers as easier to organize and Mexicans as harder to organize, and so on. The most common reasons given for immigrant receptiveness to union organizing include strong cultural ties, working-class traditions in home countries, and appeals to nationalism; the most common reasons given for immigrant opposition to union organizing include language barriers and traditional distrust of labor organizations and political institutions. Overall, recent studies show that most unions are driven not by overall policy and a considered approach, but by the immediate situations in which they find themselves.

Services to immigrant workers are an important means of promoting a favorable impression among target communities and eventually recruiting workers into unions. Although a growing number of unions provide services to unorganized immigrants, the large majority of unions do not.

APPROACHES TO BRINGING IMMIGRANTS INTO UNIONS

Unions use a variety of approaches to bring new members into their organizations, ranging from the organization of new shops to company hiring in unionized shops and union hiring halls. The rapidly growing undocumented population in the United States exerts a significant influence on the primary labor markets of unions and on their decisions to organize in these sectors. Union organizer respondents tend to have little experience in organizing undocumented workers. The field of organizing new immigrants is so new and the legal environment so volatile that union organizers have a limited amount of collective experience to draw on. Nonetheless, a surprisingly large number of unions have at least some experience with undocumented immigrants.

TYPES OF UNION ORGANIZING STRATEGIES

Unions engage in a range of strategies for organizing and recruiting immigrant workers into their unions. These strategies include (1) organizing immigrant workers outside the union's primary jurisdiction, (2) organizing immigrant workers within the primary jurisdiction to ensure survival, (3) organizing specific immigrant groups in industries not traditionally unionized, and (4) market/employer strategies that typically do not involve organizing. These four strategies are distinctive of unions that have actively decided to organize immigrants; the vast majority of unions either do nothing or are at the exploratory stage. It must be recognized, of course, that some union leaders may be diffident about revealing union organizing strategies or their lack. Four examples can be drawn from organizing immigrants in New York City.

ORGANIZING OUTSIDE THE JURISDICTION

One strategy unions employ to organize new immigrants is targeting an industry traditionally outside the union's jurisdiction. In the mid-1990s, the International Association of Machinists (IAM) District 15 launched a campaign to organize an entire workforce of limousine drivers, an industry outside its jurisdiction but never organized by another union. This burgeoning industry employs around twelve thousand drivers, most of them South Asians. These "black car" drivers are required to wear a suit and tie and pay their own car insurance, repairs, and other fees. Typically, drivers work over sixty hours a week and earn about $20,000 a year. Moreover, drivers are required to pay high franchise fees and all fines and legal fees, further reducing their wages. Indeed, most limousine companies maintain that the drivers are independent contractors and so have refused to recognize and bargain with unions seeking representation and contracts for these workers. In 1997, the union won an election at Elite Limousine Plus, one of New York City's largest "black car" companies, by a vote of 218–117, an election victory that Elite did not recognize. Even after the National Labor Relations Board ordered Elite to bargain with District 15, in November 1997, Elite steadfastly refused to bargain with the union, continuing to allege that the drivers were not employees but independent contractors. Finally, in January 1999, facing continued legal action, Elite Limousine negotiated a contract with the union that significantly improved the wages and working conditions of some seven hundred workers. District 15 anticipates that the contract will draw nonunion drivers to the company and push other drivers in the industry to fight for unionization.

ORGANIZE OR DIE

Unions faced with rapidly declining membership in their traditional jurisdictions are confronted with the decision to "organize or die." In New York City, new immigrants have entered the building trades industries in large numbers. Although immigrants still represent minorities in the more highly skilled segments of the industry (operating engineers, electricians, etc.), they have grown to majority status in lower-skilled segments (demolition, lead and asbestos abatement, carpentry). Union leaders in those areas have in consequence oriented their organizing strategies to appeal to immigrant workers.

The organization of immigrant asbestos workers from Eastern Europe and Latin America by the Laborers International Union of North America (LIUNA) Local 78 is an important case of a union that came back after all but disappearing because its old-line leadership, which represented an earlier immigrant group (here Italian), had failed to organize new immigrants in its industry. Between 1980 and 1995, as the asbestos removal industry expanded, undocumented immigrants from Latin America and Eastern Europe were recruited as laborers, eventually becoming a majority.

In 1996, LIUNA organizers initiated a campaign to organize two thousand immigrant workers in the industry, most of them undocumented. In 1996, the organizers successfully rebuilt a membership base, gained union recognition, and negotiated enforceable bargaining agreements with management. The union organized the workers by directly reaching out to new ethnic workers in their home neighborhoods in Queens and Brooklyn by identifying immigrant networks and by recruiting respected members of these networks as organizers. More than 95 percent of Local 78's members were born outside the United States. In 2000, Local 78 reported that 60 percent of twenty-four hundred new members are Polish, Russian, or Eastern European immigrants, while 40 percent are Ecuadorian or Colombian.

The union continues to maintain a staff of four organizers and up to ten volunteer organizers, a relatively large number for a small union. New members are recruited through organizing nonunion shops. Local 78 organizers say that the union continues to organize workers in the industry because Eastern European and Latino immigrants are a growing part of the workforce of asbestos removal workers. According to Pawel Kedzior, Local 78's business manager, the union has no experience organizing American-born workers.

FOLLOW THE ETHNIC GROUP

A third immigrant organizing strategy can be deployed by a union whose principal jurisdiction is an industry in decline. If such a union has experience with a particular ethnic group, it can target a growing industry with workers that the union has represented. The follow-the-ethnic-group strategy presupposes that a union with a culture of organizing and with strong connections to new immigrants in the labor force is in a better position to organize workers in an industry with which it has little or no experience than is an established union with jurisdiction but little connection to the workers. As the labor demographics of an industry change, the dominant union often fails to maintain an organizing culture and ties to the new community. As immigrants enter workplaces that are more recently established and frequently smaller (often subcontractors) and that have not been organized by the dominant union, a recomposition of the workforce occurs, along with a downward restructuring of wage scales. Such industrial restructuring frequently brings in new competitors who seek to slash costs by hiring minorities and new immigrants at wages substantially lower than those prevailing in the industry.

UNITE (Union of Needletrades, Industrial, and Textile Employees) Local 169, a union traditionally representing garment workers, has embarked on a campaign to organize immigrant workers from Latin America. Losing members in its core garment industry as a result of the relocation of industry to lower-wage areas in the U.S. South and overseas, the union has sought to organize workers in the service sector, a mainstay of the New York urban economy. Although the number of garment sweatshops has grown in New York City over the last decade, organizing these workers has proven increasingly difficult, as a result of the downward pressure on wages exerted by the continual flow of new immigrant workers into the labor market, and the ability of small subcontracting shops to close and relocate to evade unionization efforts. The large retail stores that control prices make it extremely difficult to organize and negotiate with the subcontractors, who have limited flexibility to raise wages.

About 80 percent of Local 169's three thousand members were born outside the United States, and 75 percent are immigrants from Central and South America. Although the union's demographic profile is relatively stable, its membership has declined considerably as garment production shops have closed and moved out of the area. As a result of these pressures, between 1985 and 2000 union membership in Local 169's core garment industry has been cut in half, to less than 20 percent of that workforce.

For a relatively small union, Local 169 maintains a relatively large staff of five organizers. The union has also recently initiated a volunteer organizing program. The union's organizing strategy focuses on the Mexican and Dominican immigrant communities as its primary targets because they are a growing part of the workforce and because the union has members in those groups. According to Jeffrey Eichler, the union is organizing immigrants from Latin America, irrespective of their documentation status, and these workers are the source of the union's power and political stability.

Local 169's primary organizing effort began in the summer of 1998, when the union began organizing workers employed in produce markets, primarily Korean-owned. Though most of the markets employ fewer than ten workers, there are an estimated fourteen thousand workers employed in New York City's two thousand or so greengrocers, the vast majority of whom are recent immigrants from Mexico. Their undocumented status is often used by employers to force them to accept illegally low wages and poor working conditions. Recent Mexican immigrants clean, prepare, and package fruit and vegetables and are frequently required to work twelve-hour days, six days per week, without overtime. They are paid below the federal minimum wage and have no medical insurance. A typical worker may earn $250 for a seventy-two-hour week ($3.47/hour), without benefits.

An initial effort to organize workers in Brighton Beach, Brooklyn, a Russian neighborhood with a high concentration of greengrocers, failed, due to fierce employer resistance. Korean storeowners in Brighton Beach threatened to fire Mexican workers and to report them to the INS if they voted for the union (some workers did so anyway). Against significant odds, an ongoing campaign on the Lower East Side of Manhattan has succeeded in obtaining union recognition agreements, collective bargaining agreements, and neutrality agreements throughout the neighborhood.

MARKET/EMPLOYER-BASED STRATEGIES

There is still a substantial part of the New York labor movement that receives workers rather than going out and organizing them. Their response to immigration is to provide services to workers when they become members. These unions tend to have larger market share, tend to have larger employers (educational institutions, telecommunications companies, government institutions), and are in industries where English is required. However, as employers in these industries flirt with informalization through privatization and contracting out of services, these unions, too, must grapple with the rise of new immigrants.

Most union organizing departments are unscientific and unsystematic in analyzing changing labor demographics and labor market economics. The majority of union leaders have no formal means of analyzing and transmitting information, so that new leaders often start from scratch.

As a result of the absence of clearly formulated organizing strategies, the targeting of immigrant labor market segments tends to be opportunistic and tactical. Frequently, union leaders organize on the basis of their previous experience and familiarity with workers and labor markets. Familiarity is a comfort factor. Unions interact with workers, employers, and labor markets that they know, which helps explain why immigrants are still not organized, though they constitute a large and growing segment of workers in previously unionized industries.

Union leaders frequently display a general reluctance to change organizational union cultures and make a radical rupture with the past. Ironically, although many unions are objectively radical economic institutions, their organizational cultures frequently prevent the mobilization of immigrants and other outsiders. However, to remain viable organizations, unions need to organize new groups of workers entering their labor markets. Thus, a central contradiction emerges: While unions are institutionally conservative organizations that seek stability, the political economy is in a wild state of flux. To survive, unions need to create industry strategies that are hard to conceive and even harder to implement.

For example, in south Florida, UNITE's garment organizing led to nursing home organizing, where it joined forces with the American Federation of State, County, and Municipal Employees (AFSCME). If unions are fortunate, all new immigrant workers will work in the same Standard Industrial Classification (SIC) code or industry, but this does not reflect the reality of the New York political economy. Nationalities tend not to be concentrated in one industry, and unions have many nationalities, not just one.

Immanuel Ness and Nick Unger

See also: Immigrant Politics I: Activism (Part II, Sec. 6); Agriculture, Labor Markets, Service Sector, Sweatshops and Factories (Part II, Sec. 8); California's Farm Labor Law, 1975 (Part IV, Sec. 1).

BIBLIOGRAPHY

Bacon, David. "Immigrant Workers Ask Labor 'Which Side Are You On?'" *Working USA: Journal of Labor and Society* 3:5 (2000).

Chishti, Muzaffar. "Unions, Immigrant Workers, and Employer Sanctions." *Working USA: Journal of Labor and Society* 4:1 (2000).

Delgado, Hector. *New Immigrants, Old Unions: Organizing Undocumented Workers in Los Angeles.* Philadelphia: Temple University Press, 1994.

Greenhouse, Steven. "Labor Urges Amnesty for Illegal Immigrants." *New York Times,* February 17, 2000.

Milkman, Ruth, ed. *Organizing Immigrants: The Challenge for Unions in Contemporary California.* Ithaca, NY: Cornell University Press, 2000.

Milkman, Ruth, and Kent Wong. *Voices from the Front Lines: Organizing Immigrant Workers in Los Angeles.* Los Angeles: Center for Labor Research and Education, University of California at Los Angeles, 2000.

Ness, Immanuel. "Trade Union Responses to Labor Market Deregulation and Informalization." Paper prepared for the International Political Science Association, August 1997.

Ness, Immanuel, and Nick Unger. "Union Approaches to Immigrant Organizing: A Review of New York City Locals." Paper prepared for the UCLEA Labor Education Conference, Milwaukee, Wisconsin, April 2000.

Portes, Alejandro, ed. *The Economic Sociology of Immigration.* New York: Russell Sage Foundation, 1995.

Portes, Alejandro, and Manuel Castels. "World Underneath: The Origins, Dynamics, and Effects of the Informal Economy," in *The Informal Economy: Studies in Advanced and Less Developed Countries,* ed. Alejandro Portes, Manuel Castels, and Lauren Benton. Baltimore: Johns Hopkins University Press, 1991.

Sassen, Saskia. *Globalization and Its Discontents.* New York: New Press, 1998.

Uchitelle, Louis. "I.N.S. Is Looking the Other Way as Illegal Immigrants Fill Jobs: Enforcement Changes in Face of Labor Shortage." *New York Times,* March 9, 2000.

Waldinger, Roger. *Still the Promised City? African Americans and New Immigrants in Postindustrial New York.* Cambridge, MA: Harvard University Press, 1996.

HEALTH, EDUCATION, AND WELFARE

Introduction

Health Care

Grace J. Yoo and Lisa Sun-Hee Park

Higher Education

I. Steven Krup, J.D., and Nathalie M. Krup

Immigrants and Health

Beth Merenstein

Mental Health

Gretchen S. Carnes

Public Schools

Sara Z. Poggio

Social Services

Héctor R. Cordero-Guzmán

Welfare and Public Benefits

Navid Ghani

INTRODUCTION

Part II, Section 9 of the *Encyclopedia of American Immigration* is concerned with immigrant health, education, and welfare, and includes entries devoted to all three of these aspects of immigrant life. The entries in this section include those on health, mental health, public schools, higher education, social services, and welfare.

Grace J. Yoo and Lisa Sun-Hee Park's essay on health care opens with a discussion of uninsured immigrants before examining changes in government policy concerning immigrants and health care. They then go on to the linguistic and cultural barriers that prevent immigrants from seeking health care.

The article on higher education and immigrants by I. Steven Krup, J.D., and Nathalie M. Krup begins with a discussion of enrollment of immigrants at U.S. institutions of higher learning and how universities compete for both immigrant and international students. Next, the authors examine the issue of international faculty and international higher education programs. In addition, the authors provide immigration rules for foreign faculty and students.

In her entry "Immigrants and Health," Beth Merenstein begins with general immigration health status before going on to discuss the subject as it pertains to various segments of the immigrant population, including Mexicans, Cubans, Haitians, Chinese, and Southeast Asians (both immigrants and refugees).

Gretchen S. Carnes begins her discussion on immigrants and mental health with the factors that aid immigrant acculturation, including churches and social organizations, pre-immigration preparedness, and self-help groups. The author then explores factors that contribute to depression among immigrants, including communications and language problems, racism and discrimination, and identity issues. In addition, Carnes examines mental health and gender, as well as the stages in adaptation and acculturation among immigrants of both sexes. Finally, she considers preventive measures for avoiding mental stress among immigrants and immigrant groups.

In her essay on public schools, Sara Z. Poggio begins with a history of immigrants and public schools from the early republic through 1965. In her discussion of public schools and recent immigration, the author examines how schools utilize assimilation mechanisms, and the various internal and external problems they entail.

Héctor R. Cordero-Guzmán's essay on social services opens with a discussion of the history of the subject, as well as an examination of the different kinds of services offered to immigrant populations today. Next, the author looks at the challenges to providing social services to immigrant communities.

In his entry on immigrants, immigration, and welfare, Navid Ghani begins with an examination of the rising immigration numbers of recent decades and how this has affected both welfare programs and the public's attitude toward immigrants' use of welfare. Next, Ghani looks into the question of whether welfare benefits in the United States spur immigrants to come here, before exploring how extensively immigrants make use of U.S. welfare benefits. Finally, he considers the question of welfare costs and income.

HEALTH CARE

*A*ccess to health care remains a concern for many immigrants today. Immigrants are repeatedly found to report no regular source and often delay seeking health care. Some of the most pressing impediments to accessing health care are the lack of health insurance and the changing federal and state policies on eligibility and citizenship status for Medicaid-funded health services. Even when immigrants are able to access health services, they might find it difficult to mediate their care because of their limited English proficiency. Their quality of care is often jeopardized because of the health care providers' inability to provide culturally and linguistically appropriate services.

UNINSURED IMMIGRANTS

Since 1965, the demographics of immigrants entering the United States have changed dramatically. Today, immigrants from Latin America make up 40 percent of the migration wave, and those from Asia contribute another 40 percent. Both these groups report high uninsured rates because of their limited access to job-based health insurance. Approximately 30 percent of Asian immigrants and 58 percent of Latino immigrants are uninsured. Households headed by immigrants from Mexico and Central and South America are the least likely to have health insurance, while those from Europe, Canada, and the Philippines are the most likely to be insured. Many immigrants, because of their limited English-language proficiency or low levels of education, hold jobs in the low-wage sector where employers do not provide health insurance. In certain states, access to insurance and health care for immigrants is limited. Immigrants are 2.5 times more likely to be uninsured than are U.S.-born citizens in the state. In California, 43 percent of the state's immigrant population are covered through

their job compared with 62 percent of native-born residents.

Several studies have documented the inability to access health care as a result of not having health insurance. Delays in seeking health care by immigrants due to lack of insurance may have serious health implications for immigrant communities. For example, Asian and Pacific Islander women have the lowest screening rates for pap smears and mammogram examinations among all Americans. Yet early detection for these cancers is crucial for women because detection at a later stage may mean higher mortality and lower survival rates. Although many barriers exist for women in the screening of breast and cervical cancers, poverty and lack of or insufficient health insurance remains a major barrier to cancer screenings in Asian and Pacific Islander women. The lack of access to preventive and health care services leads to higher rates of preventable diseases, injuries, and poorer health outcomes from illness and injury. Several studies looking at Asian immigrants and utilization of health services have documented that immigrants without insurance were more likely to forgo mainstream health care services and utilize traditional Asian medicine, whereas insured immigrants were more likely to use such preventive health care services as cancer screenings.

POLICY CHANGES

Medicaid is an important form of health coverage for many low-income immigrants. One-third of all Latino and Asian-American Medicaid recipients are immigrants. However, several federal and state policies have been enacted in recent years that have discouraged many immigrants from utilizing Medicaid-funded health services. The passage of California's Proposition 187 in November 1994 conveyed to immigrants the message that they were not welcome in the state's publicly funded schools, clinics, and hospitals, despite the fact that the initiative was never enacted. On August 22, 1996, President Clinton signed the federal welfare reform law known as the Personal Responsibility and Work/Reconciliation Opportunity Act (PL 104-193), which ended legal immigrants' eligibility for federal means-tested entitlements. Because of federal welfare reform, immigrants were no longer eligible for federal cash assistance, food stamps, and Medicaid.

In the final version of the 1996 welfare reform legislation, restrictions on immigrant benefits accounted for almost half of the total federal savings. Also, the 1996 welfare reform and the changes in immigration legislation enacted the same year—the Illegal Immigration Reform and Immigrant Responsibility Act (PL 104-208)—made the sharing of information between state Departments of Health Services (DHS) and the Immigration and Naturalization Service (INS) a requirement for Medicaid applicants. Therefore, for low-income immigrants to be eligible for Medicaid and for clinics and hospitals to be reimbursed for services rendered to Medicaid patients, the care facilities must report the patients' immigration status to the INS. Since the signing of this bill, there have been several restorations of benefits to immigrants, such as those contained in the Balanced Budget Act of 1997. States have been given the option to determine immigrants' eligibility for Medicaid and state cash assistance programs.

While undocumented immigrants are excluded from receiving most public welfare benefits, they are finding it even more difficult to obtain the limited health services they received prior to 1996. Moreover, states that wish to provide benefits to immigrants who entered the country without inspection or violated the terms of their visas must pass specific laws to do so. With respect to health care, undocumented immigrants are generally eligible for only emergency medical care and nonemergency pregnancy-related care in particular states. In a study of health care use among undocumented Latino immigrants, the sociologist Marc Berk and his colleagues found that undocumented immigrants obtain fewer ambulatory physician visits than other Latinos or the U.S. population as a whole. At the same time, however, their rates of hospital admission (except hospitalizations for childbirth) were comparable with documented immigrants. In addition, less than 1 percent of the 973 study respondents cited obtaining social services as their reason for emigrating. They concluded that excluding undocumented immigrants from receiving government-funded health care services is unlikely to

reduce the level of immigration. Rather, this exclusion—particularly of routine or preventive services—is likely to affect the well-being of children who are U.S. citizens living in immigrant households.

Changes in federal and state policies particularly affect California because it is home to one-third of all immigrants in the United States. One-fourth of the state's population was born outside the United States, making California the state with the highest concentration of immigrants. Despite California's decision to maintain eligibility for legal immigrants regardless of their date of entry into the United States, there has been growing confusion and fear among immigrant communities about the use of publicly funded benefits. Moreover, federal policy implementations of welfare reform have created a chilling effect that has discouraged use of Medi-Cal, a California health-care program for the poor, by immigrants who are legally eligible in California. The willingness of immigrants to trust the welfare system after the recent federal and state policy changes is a critical determinant of their willingness to enroll in Medi-Cal and seek services at publicly funded clinics and hospitals. Repeatedly, the health care providers serving low-income immigrants have cited the issue of "public charge" as a deterrent to Medi-Cal enrollment.

"Public charge" is a term the INS uses to describe immigrants who either have become or have the possibility of becoming dependent on federal or state government benefits. The INS can prevent an immigrant whom it judges likely to become a public charge from obtaining legal permanent residency. In addition, the INS can refuse readmission to the United States to immigrants who leave the country for more than 180 days and who, when they attempt to reenter, are judged likely to become a public charge. The INS can also deport a person found to be a public charge, though this is rarely done. Although neither the welfare nor the immigration legislation changed the definition of public charge, the current sharing of information between the INS and the U.S. Department of Health and Human Services raised fear and confusion about whether a noncitizen who is eligible to receive Medicaid may face adverse immigration consequences as a public charge for using those benefits.

After pressure from immigrant health advocates, the federal government announced that non-cash benefits, such as Medicaid, and special-purpose cash benefits that are not intended for income maintenance were not subject to public charge consideration. But the failure of the federal government to provide clarification of the potential impact of the use of non-cash benefits on future immigration status until May 1999, almost three years after the passage of the legislation, had a significant impact on immigrants.

CULTURAL AND LINGUISTIC COMPETENCY

Although lack of insurance is a major reason that many do not utilize health services, language has also been cited repeatedly as a reason that many immigrants do not access health care. Monolingual and limited-English-proficient immigrants face language and cultural barriers in health care settings, which makes linguistic and cultural competency a key issue facing the health care delivery system. Title VI of the Civil Rights Act of 1964 provides some legal protection for such populations because it prohibits discrimination based on race and national origin. This law requires health care and social service agencies that receive federal grants to provide competent language assistance. Because of the increasing racial and ethnic diversity of the United States, advocates and policymakers have continually pressed federal lawmakers for "linguistically and culturally competent [health] services" to improve utilization and effectiveness of treatment for different cultures. Culturally competent services incorporate respect for and understanding of ethnic and racial groups, as well as their histories, traditions, beliefs, and value systems.

As a result, a culturally competent facility ensures equitable services, appropriate services, and equitable outcomes. Cultural sensitivity is an important factor in determining the effectiveness of provider-client relations. In mental health services, an ethnic and language match between client and provider significantly decreases dropouts and predicts better outcomes for clients. Moreover, the lack of trained interpreters, bilingual staff, and translated materials in all types of health care settings and practices can impact the quality of care that immigrants receive. Language barriers can result in misdiagnoses of illnesses, unnecessary tests and procedures, patient dissatisfaction, or a physician obtaining inadequate consent from the patient. For example, Spanish-speaking patients have been found to be less likely than English-speaking patients to receive sufficient preventive information or referrals from their providers.

In August 2000, the U.S. Department of Health and Human Services reminded health care providers around the country of their legal obligation to provide translated materials and services to monolingual and limited-English-proficient immigrants. The new rules require hospitals, health maintenance organizations (HMOs), nursing homes, public clinics, senior centers, Head Start programs, and other health and social service providers that receive federal funds from the department to come up with a plan for providing translators or translated materials for monolingual and limited-English-proficient immigrants or risk losing federal funds. Although these are large gains in ensuring access and quality of care to monolingual and limited-English-proficient immigrants, the provision of linguistic and cultural competency in health services faces additional challenges as the nation's health care systems introduce managed care aimed at cutting health care costs by eliminating unnecessary procedures. Scholars J. Abe-Kim and D. Takeuchi suggest that health service delivery in managed care has been developed without a discussion of the needs of ethnic minorities. They write that access barriers already exist for ethnic minorities and that managed care only compounds these existing barriers. They suggest that cultural competence be used as a critical dimension of quality of care for ethnic minority populations. In addition, a 2000 study has noted that while Latinos and Asian Americans enrolled in managed care were more likely to report having a usual source of care and greater conformity of care, they also reported more difficulties obtaining care and less satisfaction with their care. In California, because of pressure from immigrant advocates, the state has required Medicaid-managed care plans to ensure twenty-four-hour access to interpreter services, translation of all written materials to non–English speakers, assessment of the linguistic capacity of employees, and a member-needs assessment. Although these plans are required to have these provisions, there have been no tools to assess the cultural and linguistic competency of managed care plans in their care of non-English-speaking patients.

As their numbers continue to grow, health care access and quality will continually be prime concerns for immigrants. Most immigrants come to this country to work. Yet even though there are more full-time workers in an immigrant family than a U.S.-citizen family, immigrants are twice as likely to be uninsured. Lack of insurance for immigrants, however, continues to be an issue of major concern. Moreover, this situation is only exacerbated by federal and state policies that have often changed and confused immigrants and health care providers as to whether it is safe to use publicly funded health care. The lack of language and cultural diversity found in health care settings and the increasing managed care penetration in the health care delivery system challenge immigrants and health care providers, immigrant advocates, policymakers, and others who are committed to equity and health care access.

Grace J. Yoo and Lisa Sun-Hee Park

See also: Immigrant Aid Societies and Organizations (Part II, Sec. 2); Children and Adolescent Immigrants, Elderly (Part II, Sec. 4); Legislation II: Immigrants in America (Part II, Sec. 5); Immigrants and Health, Mental Health, Social Services (Part II, Sec. 9); *LULAC et al. v. Wilson et al.*, 1995, California Proposition 187, 1994 (Part IV, Sec. 1); Title IV: Restricting Welfare and Public Benefits for Aliens, 1996, Recommendations for Prevention and Control of Tuberculosis Among Foreign-Born Persons, 1998 (Part IV, Sec. 2).

BIBLIOGRAPHY

Abe-Kim, Jennifer, and David Takeuchi. "Cultural Competence and Quality of Care: Issues for Mental Health Service Delivery in Managed Care." *American Psychologist* 3 (1996): 273–95.

Benjamin, A. E., Steven Wallace, Villa Villa, and Kathy McCarthy. *California Immigrants Have Mostly Lower Rates of Disability and Use of Disability Services Than State's US-Born Residents.* Los Angeles: UCLA Center for Health Policy Research, 2000.

Berk, Marc, Claudia Schur, Leo Chavez, and Martin Frankel. "Health Care Use Among Undocumented Latino Immigrants." *Health Affairs* 19:4 (2000): 51–64.

Brown, E. Richard, Victoria Ojeda, Roberta Wynn, and Rebecka Levan. *Racial and Ethnic Disparities in Access to Health Insurance and Health Care.* Los Angeles: UCLA Center for Health Policy Research, 2000.

Center for Mental Health Services. *Cultural Competence Standards in Managed Care Mental Health Services for Four Underserved/Underrepresented Racial/Ethnic Groups.* Rockville, MD: Center for Mental Health Services, 1998.

Coye, Molly, and Deborah Alvarez. *Medicaid, Managed Care, and Cultural Diversity in California.* New York: Commonwealth Fund, 1999.

Cross, T. L., B. M. Bazron, K. W. Dennis, and M. R. Issacs. *Towards a Culturally Competent System of Care.* Washington, DC: Georgetown University, 1989.

Ellwood, M. R., and Leighton Ku. "Welfare and Immigration Reforms: Unintended Side Effects for Medicaid" *Health Affairs* (May/June 1998): 137–43.

Fix, Michael, and Jeffrey Passel. *Trends in Noncitizens' and Citizens' Use of Public Benefits Following Welfare Reform: 1995–1997.* Washington, DC: Urban Institute, 1999.

Hernandez, Mario, and Mareasa Isaacs. *Promoting Cultural Competence in Children's Mental Health Services.* Baltimore: Paul Brookes Publishing, 1998.

Immigration and Naturalization Service. *Public Charge: Fact Sheet.* Washington, DC: Immigration and Naturalization Service, 1993.

———. *Statistical Yearbook of the Immigration and Naturalization Service.* Washington, DC: Government Printing Office, 1992.

Jenkins C. N., T. Lé, S. J. McPhee, S. Stewart, and N. T. Ha. "Health Care Access and Preventive Care Among Vietnamese Immigrants: Do Traditional Beliefs and Practices Pose Barriers?" *Social Science and Medicine* 43:7 (1996): 1049–56.

Latino Coalition for a Healthy California. *Fact Sheet: Latinos and Access to Health Care in California.* San Francisco: Latino Coalition for a Healthy California, 2000.

Kagawa-Singer, Marjorie, and Nadereh Pourat. "Asian American and Pacific Islander Breast and Cervical Carcinoma Screening Rates and Healthy People 2000 Objectives." *Cancer* 1:3 (2000): 696–705.

Kahn, James, Brian Haile, and Ellen Shaffer. *Health Insurance Expansion Strategies in California: Impact on Noncitizen Immigrants.* Berkeley: California Policy Research Center, 2000.

Kaiser Commission of Medicaid and the Uninsured. *Immigrants' Health Care: Coverage and Access.* Menlo Park, CA: Henry J. Kaiser Family Foundation, 2000.

Ku, Leighton, and Bethany Kessler. *Number and Cost of Immigrants on Medicaid: National and State Estimates.* Washington, DC: Urban Institute, 1997.

Lowell, B. L. "Immigrant Integration and Pending Legislation: Observations on Empirical Projections." In *Immigration and the Family,* ed. Alan Booth et al., pp. 271–80. Mahwah, NJ: Lawrence Erlbaum Associates, 1997.

Ma, G. X. "Between Two Worlds: The Use of Traditional and Western Health Services by Chinese Immigrants." *Journal of Community Health* 24:6 (1999): 421–37.

MaCurdy, Thomas, and Margaret O'Brien-Strain. *Reform Reversed? The Restoration of Welfare Benefits to Immigrants in California.* San Francisco, CA: Public Policy Institute of California, 1998.

Mayeno, Laurin, and Sherry Hiraota. "Access to Health Care." In *Confronting Critical Health Issues of Asian and Pacific Islander Americans,* ed. N. W. Zane et al., pp. 347–75. Newbury Park, CA: Sage Publications, 1994.

Morse, Ann, Jeremy Meadows, Kirsten Rasmussen, and Sheri Steisel. *America's Newcomers: Mending the Welfare Safety Net for Immigrants.* Washington, DC: National Conference of State Legislatures, 1998.

National Immigration Law Center. *Public Charge.* Los Angeles: National Immigration Law Center, 1997.

Park, Lisa, Rhonda Sarnoff, Catherine Bender, and C. C. Korenbrot. "Impact of Recent Welfare and Immigration Reforms on Use of Medicaid for Prenatal Care by Immigrants in California." *Journal of Immigrant Health* 2:1 (2000): 5–22.

Phillips, Kathryn, Michelle Mayer, and Lu Ann Aday. "Barriers to Care Among Racial/Ethnic Groups Under Managed Care." *Health Affairs* 19:4 (2000): 65–75.

Pourat, Nadereh, James Lubben, S. P. Wallace, and Alice Moon. "Predictors of Use of Traditional Korean Healers Among Elderly Koreans in Los Angeles." *Gerontologist* 39:6 (1999): 711–19.

Schlossberg, Claudia. *Not-Qualified Immigrants' Access to Public Health and Emergency Services After the Welfare Law.* Washington, DC: National Health and Law Program, 1998.

Schlossberg, Claudia, and Dinah Wiley. *The Impact of INS Public Charge Determination on Immigrant Access to Health Care*. Washington, DC: National Health and Law Program, 1998.

Sue, S., and N. W. Zane. "The Role of Culture and Cultural Techniques in Psychotherapy: A Critique and Reformulation." *American Psychologist* 42:1 (1987): 37–45.

Sue, S., D. Fujino, L. Hu, D. T. Takeuchi, and N. W. Zane. "Community Mental Health Services for Ethnic Minorities: A Test of the Cultural Responsiveness Hypothesis." *Journal of Consulting and Clinical Psychology* 59 (1991): 533–40.

Yoo, Grace. "Federal Welfare Reform and Asian Pacific Islander Communities in California: A View from the Grassroots." Paper presented at the Pacific Sociological Association Meetings, San Francisco, 1998.

Zimmermann, Wendy, and Michael Fix. *Declining Immigrant Applications for Medi-Cal and Welfare Benefits in Los Angeles County*. Washington, DC: Urban Institute, 1998.

HIGHER EDUCATION

The United States is the world's leader in higher education. As international travel, communications, and commerce have increased, higher education, like many other services, has expanded globally. Over 1.2 million students study abroad each academic year, and the United States hosts over a third of them. Almost 500,000 students study at over 2,700 institutions in the United States, while only about 70,000 U.S. students study abroad. Foreign student expenditures in the United States exceed $7 billion annually, approximately equal to total annual movie theater ticket sales, a major domestic industry. Nearly three-quarters of foreign student funding originates outside the United States, primarily from private or foreign government sources. Only 1 percent of foreign students receive direct financial support from the United States government, and only 16.5 percent are funded by American colleges and universities.

WHY FOREIGN STUDENTS COME TO THE UNITED STATES

International students are motivated to study in the United States for a variety of reasons. While these factors are listed individually below, it is apparent that the factors interact synergistically and have as their root America's success in providing an abundance of resources and freedoms in conjunction with previous higher educational successes.

1. American institutions maintain a reputation for academic excellence in virtually all fields, often offering the very best programs available anywhere in the world.

2. The faculty at American colleges and universities include the very best minds in their fields. For example, many Nobel laureates in the sciences ac-

tively teach and do research at American higher educational institutions.

3. American institutions offer students a wide variety of educational opportunities and freedoms in terms of specific courses, degree majors, time frames for course work completion, work-study programs, and extracurricular activities.

4. American institutions offer cutting-edge technology, often including state-of-the-art equipment, and offer programs that take advantage of formal and informal connections with leading commercial and technological firms.

5. American colleges' and universities' resources include leading laboratories, libraries, student newspapers, radio stations, and athletic facilities and sports teams.

6. American institutions provide students greater opportunities to acquire research and teaching assistant experience.

7. American institutions offer students great flexibility in designing their course of study, often having both fewer mandatory courses and more available electives.

8. American institutions provide international students with valuable support services, which include comprehensive orientation programs, tutoring in the English language and in course work, and assistance obtaining room and board and conforming to American culture.

9. The United States is the world's foremost travel destination, an inviting location for many people, including prospective students. The United States offers a wide variety of climate and living conditions—something for everyone, as well as political and religious freedom.

10. Many of the world's people have a goal or dream of immigrating to the United States and perceive

an American education as a step toward obtaining that goal. An American higher education degree can lead to an offer of employment in the United States.

11. Study in the United States is an excellent networking opportunity for future professional life. The Spanish word for this is *enchufe*, meaning "advantageous connections."

12. English is the language of international business, and while almost all international students are literate in English, having studied it at home, many come to the United States to perfect their English language skills and knowledge of American culture.

13. America, as the only superpower, is the economic and sociological model for globalization. According to Harvard University professor Stanley Hoffmann, "Americans are only dimly aware of the degree to which others consider globalization to be an American construct. It has an American script and carries with it American culture and American preferences and dislikes."

14. Prospective international students are able to view their predecessors as role models. Those who have been educated in the United States have achieved visible signs of success.

The leading sources of foreign students are China, Japan, Taiwan, India, Korea, Canada, Hong Kong, Malaysia, Indonesia, Thailand, and Germany. About two-thirds of the foreign students in the United States are from developing nations, the fewest coming from sub-Saharan Africa, Southeast Asia, and the island states of Oceania. Countries other than the United States have a higher percentage of students from developing nations. In Japan, 93 percent of foreign students are from developing nations; in France, 82 percent; Canada, 77 percent; Germany, 71 percent; and the United Kingdom, 68 percent.

International students in the United States are heavily represented in science, engineering, and mathematics. In 1994, foreign students earned 46,317 master's degrees, or 12 percent of all master's degrees awarded in the United States, and 11,538 doctorates, or 27 percent of all such degrees earned in the United States. Foreign students were more likely to earn science and engineering degrees than degrees in other disciplines. For example, in 1994, 31 percent of all science and engineering master's degrees and 41 percent of all science and engineering doctorates were earned by foreign students. Foreign students earned nearly half of all doctorates in mathematics. In the 1993–94 academic year, 37 percent of all foreign master's degree recipients and 61 percent of all foreign doctoral degree recipients earned degrees in science and engineering, as compared with 11 percent and 32 percent of all U.S. master and doctoral recipients, respectively. In 1995, students from China, Korea, Taiwan, India, and Canada made up 53 percent of international doctoral students at U.S. institutions. More than half of the Chinese students pursued natural science; about half the Taiwanese and Indian students worked in computer science and engineering.

International students are scattered throughout the United States but concentrated in the more populous states and urban areas. California has the most international students, followed by New York, Texas, Massachusetts, and Florida. Among urban areas, New York City has the most international students, about thirty thousand.

International students are typically well received on American campuses. Especially on larger campuses, social and religious affiliation organizations welcome a wide range of foreign students. Studies of student populations often target ethnicity but rarely isolate "foreign student" status. In numerous data collection efforts, higher education institutions collect little to no data on immigrant status. Similarly, in their direct dealings with students, faculty and staff report themselves rarely aware of immigrant status. Few in the education community believe that failure to distinguish this population is a shortcoming. If any valid criticism of international students exists, it is limited to language fluency and minor cultural differences. International students are fully integrated into American educational institutions. In fact, at least one college community, Amherst, Massachusetts, has considered giving its legal noncitizens, primarily international students, the right to vote in municipal elections.

About half the recipients of doctoral degrees intended to remain in the United States. More than 60 percent of the science and engineering doctors have definite commitments to remain in the United States before completing their education.

UNIVERSITIES

The United States benefits from international students and faculty. Foreign students increase diversity in the student body and teach U.S. students about other countries and cultures. Foreign faculty constitute a valuable resource in key areas of the country's university system. Over 59,000 foreign scholars, often senior researchers, come annually to higher education institutions in the United States.

Virtually every university boasts of its diversity, including the presence of international students. In the 1997–98 academic year, 491,000 international students attended United States universities and colleges. In the 1998–99 academic year, New York University (NYU) had the greatest number of international students at 4,749, or 12.9 percent of its population. The president of NYU states, "We literally recruit around the world."

At Harvard University, the International Office was established in 1944 to respond to the needs of Harvard's 250 foreign students. Ten years later, there were 800 foreign students and by 1961, there were over 1,000 foreign students and over 500 foreign scholars taught and conducted research. Now Harvard enrolls over 2,600 foreign students and sponsors over 2,000 foreign scholars, more foreign scholars than any other university in the United States.

Foreign student enrollment at Stanford University has also increased markedly. Over 3,200 noncitizen students from ninety-seven countries are enrolled; over 650 permanent residents; and over 2,500 non-immigrants. The foreign students represent 4 percent of undergraduates, 24 percent of graduate students, and 41 percent of postdoctoral students. Half of Stanford's international students are from Asia, a quarter from Europe, 16 percent from the Americas, 6 percent from Middle East, 2 percent from the Pacific Basin, and 1 percent from sub-Saharan Africa. China is the leading country of origin, followed by Canada, Japan, India, Taiwan, South Korea, Germany, and the United Kingdom. Engineering is the most popular field for international students, nearly one thousand students representing almost 30 percent of all engineering students. Other popular specialty fields for Stanford's international students are earth science (36 percent) and business (21 percent). Majors with the highest percentage of international students are physiology (67 percent), petroleum engineering (66 percent), and food research (55 percent). Males outnumber female international students by four to one. About 30 percent of Stanford's international students are married.

Yale University has a need-blind admissions policy designed to guarantee that all qualified applicants are considered regardless of their financial situation. However, Yale caps the amount of aid it grants to international students. In 1996, the cap was $250,000 per year and scheduled to increase to $380,000 by 2002, only enough to fund about sixteen international students per year. In contrast, Yale spends about $32 million per year for American and Canadian students. Thus, Yale is able to admit only 2 percent need-

blind international students as compared with 20 percent need-blind American students. Nevertheless, the number of international students at Yale has been growing, tripling in just three years from 2.5 percent of the student body to about 7.5 percent.

Columbia University's international student population reached about 4.5 percent of the student body by the late 1990s. Countries most heavily represented are Korea, Japan, Thailand, Taiwan, and Canada. In addition to its location in a major world city, Columbia endeavors to increase international student presence by making them feel welcome.

The University of Iowa employs about two hundred international faculty members and researchers, most in H-1B, or temporary worker, status. The university promotes its chances of H-1B temporary professionals by indicating its willingness to sponsor employment-based immigration petitions in appropriate circumstances.

COMPETITION FOR INTERNATIONAL STUDENTS

Intense competition for international students exists between domestic universities and between United States and foreign universities. While foreign student enrollment in the U.S. is growing, the rate of growth has slowed to 2 percent per year. Enrollment from Asia, the largest source of foreign students, suffered because of that continent's severe economic crisis. Enrollment from Malaysia, Indonesia, South Korea, and Thailand, now at just over 75,000 students, is down by more than 10,000 from the previous year. America's percentage of the world's international students has declined over the past fifteen years from approximately 40 to 33 percent.

The most intense foreign competition for international students is from universities in Australia, Canada, Britain, and Germany. Generally, tuition is lower at these schools, and governments of these countries are more actively promoting educational opportunities. For international students, United States universities often charge more than $20,000 tuition, double that of most overseas universities. Japan has a goal of enrolling 100,000 foreign students in 2000. Australia also aggressively recruits students, especially in Asia.

Nearly five hundred U.S. educational advising centers around the world specialize in providing information and assistance to prospective international students. Promoting education in the United States, these centers are located in the U.S. embassy or consulate, the United States Information Service, or such other venues as libraries, binational centers, Fulbright Commission offices, or private organizations like World Learning, the Council on International Educational Exchange, the American Council of Teachers of Russian, the Institute for International Education, and the Council for International Exchange of Scholars.

Critics of U.S. policy assert that the United States does not do enough to actively recruit foreign students, charges too much, fails to facilitate the issuance of F visas, and does not address the needs of foreign students. Many of the regulations governing the behavior of designated school officials—school promoters officially sanctioned by the government to recruit students in foreign countries—are designed to limit overt competition for foreign students. Recently, an additional $95 visa fee for foreign students has been proposed. Critics perceive this fee as an additional impediment to the successful recruitment of foreign students.

Studies describing the factors affecting international student mobility have developed the "push-pull" model. The "push" factors are conditions in the home country that create a general interest in overseas education. Two important push factors are the wealth and development status of the home country and the extent to which the home country devotes its resources to human development—the Human Development Index (HDI). The "pull" factors are the reasons a specific host country is selected.

INTERNATIONAL FACULTY

Both advantages and disadvantages of employing foreign faculty exist. Students benefit from different points of view and exposure to various cultures. Generally, the numbers of visiting professors have been increasing.

Foreign faculty fill an essential role in the university community, especially in science, engineering, mathematics, business, and information technology fields where American employees are in short supply. One significant criticism, especially of lower-ranked instructors in science, engineering, and mathematics programs, is language difficulty. The Missouri legislature has considered bills to require English language proficiency for state university instructors.

As noted above, foreign-born Nobel laureates in the sciences now benefit educational institutions in the United States. Other fields have profited from international faculty in many ways. For example, Peter Singer, a philosopher, is now a professor at Princeton University. He was born in Australia, educated at the University of Melbourne and Oxford University, and is an example of a very prominent but controversial faculty member who, as a bioethicist, leads a school of thought promoting animal rights and redefining views of our own human rights.

INTERNATIONAL HIGHER EDUCATION PROGRAMS

There are for-profit and not-for-profit private institutions and public programs to promote international education. Begun in 1946, the flagship international educational program sponsored by the United States, the fiercely competitive Fulbright Program, brings foreign students and scholars to the United States and sponsors American citizens abroad. The program has provided more than 230,000 participants (86,000 from the United States and 144,000 from other countries)—chosen for their leadership potential—the opportunity to observe and experience the political, economic, educational, and cultural institutions of 140 countries. Fulbright alumni include Nobel and Pulitzer Prize winners, political leaders, judges, and top corporate executives. Since its founding in 1964, the privately owned American Institute for Foreign Study (AIFS) has been a leader in organizing cultural and educational exchange programs throughout the world for about one million students, faculty, and au pairs.

IMMIGRATION RULES FOR FOREIGN FACULTY

IMMIGRANT AS FACULTY MEMBER

A person who is a lawful permanent resident has, with few exceptions, the same rights as a United States citizen, including the right to almost any type of lawful employment. Therefore, a lawful permanent resident, regardless of how he or she immigrated, can be employed in higher education. The few exceptions include citizenship requirements that may be applicable to government employment. Examples are teaching or researching at government institutions or private organizations, under government contract, in a field that is classified or secret for national security purposes.

IMMIGRANT AS PROSPECTIVE FACULTY MEMBER

A person who is not a lawful permanent resident can use a job offer as a prospective faculty member to obtain an employment-based preference and immigrate in accordance with a hierarchy of requirements such that the most highly qualified alien receives the greatest preference (first preference) and less outstandingly qualified aliens receive lesser preferences (second and third preference).

First-Preference Prospective Faculty Member

Under Title 8, United States Code section 1153(b)(1), three categories of aliens are eligible for first preference. One of these categories, "Outstanding Professors and Researchers," is specifically targeted toward faculty.

To be classified under this category, an alien must have at least three years' experience in teaching or research in the academic area, be internationally recognized as outstanding in a specific academic area, and must be obtaining a tenured or tenure track teaching position at a higher education institution or a research position at a private company with at least three researchers. Further, this applicant must satisfy the Immigration and Naturalization Service (INS) that at least two of the following six criteria are met:

1. Has received major prizes or awards

2. Is a member of associations requiring outstanding achievement

3. Has had his work be the subject of professional journal articles

4. Has participated as a reviewer of the work of others

5. Has contributed original research to the field

6. Has authored scholarly books or international journal articles in the field

While the first two items above are difficult to achieve, items 3 through 6 put this category of immigration within the reach of many experienced professors.

The other two categories of first-preference aliens, "Aliens of Extraordinary Ability" and "Multinational Managers and Executives," are not specifically designed for higher education but can be used if the qualifications are met. "Aliens of extraordinary ability" in sciences, art, business, athletics, or, most relevant here, education are the "small percentage to have

risen to the very top of the field of endeavor" and must either have received a major, internationally acclaimed award (for example, the Nobel Prize) or meet three of the following eleven criteria:

1. Have received a national or international award

2. Be a member of an association requiring outstanding achievement

3. Have been the subject of published material

4. Have been a judge of the work of others

5. Have made significant original contributions to the field

6. Have authored scholarly articles

7. Have had artistic work displayed at exhibitions

8. Have had a critical role in organizations with distinguished reputations

9. Be paid more than most in the field

10. Be a commercial success in performing arts

11. Submit other comparable evidence of extraordinary ability

Faculty within the higher education institution community can meet three of these criteria.

Certain "multinational managers and executives" are eligible for first preference. Although this preference was intended for the corporate world, nothing prevents an administrator in higher education from benefiting from it under the proper circumstances, which could occur if a higher education institution were to transfer its administrators from one campus to another across international boundaries. The immigration law does take into account privately owned educational institutions, for example, by making rules concerning change of ownership in connection with the issuance of Form I-20, discussed below.

Second-Preference Prospective Faculty Member

Pursuant to Title 8, United States Code section 1153(b)(2), two categories of aliens, "Members of the Professions" and "Aliens of Exceptional Ability," are entitled to second preference.

"Members of the professions" are required to have a degree beyond the baccalaureate and, unless their immigration is "in the public interest," must be immigrating to a job requiring such a degree. These requirements are often met in the higher education community.

"Aliens of exceptional ability" in the arts, sciences,

or business must have expertise significantly above the ordinary and must meet three of the following seven criteria:

1. An academic record showing a degree, diploma, certificate, or similar award

2. A license or certification to practice in the field

3. At least ten years' documented experience

4. A high salary

5. Professional association membership

6. Recognition for significant achievement

7. Other comparable evidence

Third-Preference Prospective Faculty Member

Pursuant to Title 8, United States Code section 1153(b)(3), third-preference immigration is available to "skilled workers" with at least two years' experience; "professionals" who have at least a baccalaureate degree and a labor certification for a job that requires at least a baccalaureate degree; or certain "other workers." While higher education institutions rely on these workers for staff and support positions, most faculty positions are likely to be filled through first and second preference.

LABOR CERTIFICATION FOR SECOND- AND THIRD-PREFERENCE FACULTY

Second-preference immigrants, unless their immigration is considered in the "national interest," and third-preference immigrants must obtain either a labor certification or a waiver of a labor certification. A labor certification is given by the U.S. Department of Labor after it is shown that immigration will not displace a citizen worker. Historically, colleges and universities retain a tremendous advantage in the labor certification process. Most prospective employers who apply for a labor certification must initially establish minimum requirements for the job, and those requirements must be acceptable to the Department of Labor. The employer will not receive the labor certificate if any citizen who meets the minimum requirements is ready, willing, and able to take the job, even if the alien is more qualified. This requirement differs for college and university faculty. Unlike other employers, higher education institutions are permitted to establish committees of their staff to evaluate applicants and may select the candidate of their choice even if numerous citizens meet the minimum requirements.

Title 20, Code of Federal Regulations section 656.21, enables colleges and universities to use a "competitive" selection process in which the hiring authority documents the recruitment procedure and sets forth their reasons for the selection. This permits the institution to select the most qualified applicant, not the minimally qualified citizen. Furthermore, it gives discretion to the institution to determine the qualifications.

NONIMMMIGRANT STATUS OF FACULTY

Faculty may be considered for several types of non-immigrant status in the United States, including H-1B, "Temporary Worker"; J-1, "Exchange Visitor"; Q, "Cultural Exchange Visitor"; O, "Outstanding" Non-immigrant; and B-1, "Visitor for Business."

Nonimmigrant H-1B "Temporary Worker" as Faculty Member

For a maximum of six years, an alien may be admitted to the United States to be employed in a "specialty occupation." The definition of "specialty occupation" is "an occupation that requires: (a) theoretical and practical application of a body of highly specialized knowledge, and (b) attainment of a bachelor's or higher degree in the specific specialty (or its equivalent) as a minimum for entry into the occupation," and can include faculty. Also required is approval of a "labor condition application" through which the Department of Labor certifies that prevailing working and wage conditions are met. Unlike the other non-immigrant categories, there is a numerical limitation on the number of H-1B visas which can be issued, and especially because of the explosive growth of alien employment in information technology, there is keen competition for the available visas. According to the INS, colleges and universities use about 5 percent of the available H-1B visas.

A typical progression for a nonimmigrant professional desiring to remain in the United States permanently and lawfully often includes a stint as an H-1B while steps to immigrate are taken.

Nonimmigrant J-1 "Exchange Visitor" as Faculty Member

As defined in Title 8, United States Code section 1101(a)(15)(j), a J-1 exchange visitor may be a professor, teacher, student, or other scholar coming temporarily to the United States "as a participant in a program designated by the Director of the United States Information Agency, for the purpose of teaching, instructing or lecturing, studying, observing, conducting research, consulting, demonstrating special skills, or receiving training." Professors who are teaching or conducting research in an institution of higher education are typically limited to a stay of three years and thirty days.

As a general rule, nonimmigrants may apply to change status to other categories or adjust status to permanent resident. However, many J-1 exchange visitors are prohibited from doing so without first leaving the United States for two years. This two-year foreign residence requirement applies to J-1 aliens whose skill is included in a list of skills the Department of State maintains are needed in the home country, whose program was funded by the government, or who came to the United States for graduate medical education. A complex and seemingly harsh body of law has been developed to cover applications for waiver of this two-year foreign residence requirement. Court challenges to these rules have failed based on the reasoning that the J-1 "Exchange Visitor" program is part of the foreign policy of the United States in which the executive branch has plenary powers.

Nonimmigrant O-1 "Extraordinary Alien" as Faculty Member

Title 8, Code of Federal Regulations section 214.2(o), defines an O-1 "Extraordinary Ability" alien as one with a "level of expertise indicating that the person is one of the small percentage who have arisen to the very top of the field of endeavor."

Nonimmigrant Q "Cultural Exchange Visitor" as Faculty Member

Title 8, United States Code section 1101(a)(15)(q), defines a Q "Cultural Exchange Alien" as a person coming to the United States for a period not to exceed fifteen months and "a participant in an international cultural exchange program designated by the Attorney General for the purpose of providing practical training, employment, and the sharing of the history, culture, and traditions of the country of the alien's nationality and who will be employed under the same wages and working conditions as domestic workers."

Nonimmigrant B-1 "Visitor for Business" as a Guest Lecturer

A foreign faculty member coming intermittently to a conference or to make a presentation would likely arrive under the B-1 "Visitor for Business" category.

Current policy limits honoraria to no more than six in six months.

IMMIGRATION RULES FOR FOREIGN STUDENTS

IMMIGRANT STUDENTS

A lawful permanent resident alien is able to attend higher education institutions. There is no way an alien can obtain immigrant status through being a student; however, the degree and profession acquired often becomes the basis for an employment-based immigration petition.

NONIMMIGRANT STUDENTS

Many categories of nonimmigrants are eligible to attend school in the United States. Dependents of almost every nonimmigrant are able to attend school, and a primary nonimmigrant may attend school provided it does not interfere with the duties imposed by his or her status. For example, an H-1B "Temporary Worker" nonimmigrant and his or her dependents can attend school, the only limitation being that the H-1B "Temporary Worker" must remain employed as required by his or her visa status.

There are three categories of nonimmigrants who may be admitted to the United States for the primary purpose of their education: F "Academic Student"; M "Nonacademic Student"; and J-1 "Exchange Visitor."

Nonimmigrant F "Academic Student"

Title 8, United States Code section 1101(a)(15)(f), defines an F-1 student as an alien "having a residence abroad in a foreign country which he has no intention of abandoning, who is a bona fide student qualified to pursue a full course of study and who seeks to enter the United States temporarily and solely for the purpose of pursuing such a course of study at an established college, university, seminary, conservatory, academic high school, elementary school, or other academic institution or in a language training program in the United States . . . approved by the Attorney General." Any accompanying spouse or children are designated F-2.

To enroll foreign students, a school must obtain permission from the Immigration and Naturalization Service and must name a "designated school official" (DSO) who commits to obey INS regulations. An approved school is authorized to issue Form I-20AB, a key to obtaining an F visa (Form I-20MN for an M visa). To issue the I-20 (AB or MN), the DSO must confirm that the student has submitted an application for admission and the required supporting documentation and that the school determined the applicant meets the standards for admission. If a school or its DSO fails to abide by the applicable rules, the INS will withdraw its approval. Some of the specific reasons to withdraw approval follow:

1. Failure to properly maintain and report information about foreign F and M students

2. False statements

3. Issuance of Form I-20 to persons who will not be enrolled in the school

4. Failure to operate as a bona fide educational institution

5. Promotion of the school's authorization to enroll foreign students except by using the following statement: "This school is authorized under Federal law to enroll nonimmigrant alien student"

6. Using the DSO primarily as a student recruiter

Most prospective students will apply abroad for an F visa at a consulate in their home country after having been accepted at and receiving a Form I-20 from a United States educational institution. The consular officer will review the I-20 and will need to be convinced that the prospective student has sufficient funds available and the language ability to study in the United States. Further, as with most other nonimmigrant visas, the consular officer will need to be convinced that the student will leave the United States at the required time.

The Department of State does not permit visa issuance more than ninety days before the start of school, and occasionally, a prospective student will want to come to the United States before selecting a school. In these instances, a prospective student will be given a B-2 Visitor Visa, which is annotated "prospective student," to facilitate his or her change of status to student in the United States by the INS. A B-2 visitor without the annotation will have difficulty persuading the INS that he or she did not intentionally evade overseas processing of the student visa application.

Until 1996, F student visas could be given to public elementary school students. Now ninth grade is the earliest public school grade that an F student may attend, and she or he is limited to only one year of public school between grades nine and twelve. Such students must reimburse public schools for the cost of their education. These limitations do not apply to private schools.

F-1 students are admitted to the United States for "duration of status," the time needed to complete the academic program covered by the I-20, plus any authorized practical training, plus sixty days. To remain in status, the F student must maintain a full-time course load. Unless the DSO determines otherwise, undergraduates must take at least twelve credit hours. For graduate students, the school's definition of full time is used.

For much of the twentieth century, student employment was permitted only if there was an unanticipated adverse change in the student's financial situation. In the 1990s, employment became permitted automatically under certain conditions. "On-campus" employment of up to twenty hours per week while school is in session and full-time during breaks is allowed. Recently, the INS has permitted additional employment if necessary because of Asian currency devaluation. Curricular practical training—employment that is an integral part of the F student's curriculum—is permitted, as is practical training, after completion of studies, for up to a year. The practical training must be logically connected to the F student's curriculum and appropriate for the degree level.

The F student can transfer schools or change degree programs with a new I-20AB and permission of the INS, within fifteen days of starting the new program. The F-2 dependent spouse or children can remain lawfully in the United States and can attend school, but they may not work. On the other hand, J-2, that is, spouses and dependent children of J-1 exchange visitors are permitted to work.

Nonimmigrant J "Exchange Visitors"

J "exchange visitors" can be students or faculty. Their program must be organized by sponsors approved by the United States Information Agency. The sponsor selects a "responsible officer" whose duties are similar to those of the DSO described above and who issues Form IAP-66, which parallels Form I-20.

Nonimmigrant M "Nonacademic Students"

Title 8, United States Code section 1101(a)(15)(m), defines an M-1 student as an alien "having a residence in a foreign country which he has no intention of abandoning (seeking) to enter the United States temporarily and solely for the purpose of pursuing a full course of study at an established vocational or other recognized nonacademic institution (other than a language training program) . . . approved by the Attorney General." An M-1 student is admitted to the United States for the thirty days beyond the time set forth on her or his Form I-20MN, not to exceed one year. The M student must take at least twelve hours of classes or twenty-two hours of shop or lab per week. Except with INS permission for a maximum of six months after completion of studies for practical training, an M student may not be employed. Unlike an F student, an M student may not change her or his educational objective and may not receive H-1B "Temporary Worker" status based on her or his M student education. The spouse and children (designated M-2) may not be employed.

I. Steven Krup, J.D., and Nathalie M. Krup

See also: Economics I: Pull Factors (Part II, Sec. 1); Professionals and the Brain Drain (Part II, Sec. 8); Public Schools (Part II, Sec. 9); Science, Sports (Part II, Sec. 10); Report on the Shortage of Technology Workers, 1997 (Part IV, Sec. 2).

BIBLIOGRAPHY

Goodman, Allan. "American Colleges Keep Opening Gates Wider to Foreigners." *USA Today*, December 6, 1999, 6D.

Hoffmann, Stanley. "America—Is It Too Proud for Its Own Good?" *Miami Herald*, January 23, 2000, L1.

Choi, Hyaeweol. *An International Scientific Community—Asian Scholars in the United States.* New York: Praeger, 1995.

Itano, Nicole. "Yale to Raise Foreign Student Aid." *Yale Daily News*, November 21, 1997.

Lester, Will. "Foreign Students in U.S. Up 5.1 Percent." Associated Press wireservice, December 7, 1998.

National Center for Education Statistics. *Digest of Education Statistics.* Washington, DC: National Center for Education Statistics, 1996.

———. *Issue Brief: Degrees Earned by Foreign Graduate Students: Fields of Study and Plans after Graduation.* Washington, DC: National Center for Education Statistics, November 1997.

Sullivan, Jake. "More Foreign Students but No More Foreign Aid." *Yale Daily News*, September 12, 1996.

IMMIGRANTS AND HEALTH

Between 1892 and 1954, officials at Ellis Island in New York Harbor inspected over 12 million immigrants. During the peak immigration years of 1890 and the 1920s, the number of those turned away never exceeded 3 percent; however, of those rejected, an increasing percentage were excluded for medical reasons. The chief ground for exclusion was physical unfitness, with trachoma (a contagious form of conjunctivitis that can lead to blindness) being the most frequently cited contagious disease. During the period of peak immigration in the early 1900s, most of the immigrants were from southern and eastern European countries. Much has changed since then, and since the late 1900s a majority of immigrants have come from Latin American and Asian countries.

In 1875, Congress first exercised the power to ban immigrants based on various categories, including such contagious diseases as tuberculosis, cholera, smallpox, and yellow fever. Over the years, other health-related exclusions have been added. For example, in 1987, HIV infection was added to the list of contagious diseases. A medical examination is required for all immigrants requesting permanent status in the United States, and any communicable diseases found are grounds for exclusion.

Both immigrants and refugees can be excluded based on the following communicable diseases: tuberculosis, HIV infection, syphilis, chancroid, gonorrhea, granuloma inguinale, lymphogranuloma venereum, and Hansen's disease (leprosy). By federal law, refugees are also required to undergo medical examination, both in their host country and once they reach the United States. Of recent refugee groups, Southeast Asians are the most numerous. Among this group, studies have concluded that the two most frequent medical conditions are parasitic infections and tuberculosis. Among the Southeast Asian refugee children, there have been high incidences of intestinal parasites, positive tuberculosis, and hepatitis B.

The health issues and concerns are not necessarily the same for immigrants and refugees. Between 1981 and 1996, the four countries sending the largest number of immigrants into the United States were Mexico, the Philippines, Vietnam, and China. In contrast, between the same time period, the top four countries for refugees were Vietnam, Russia, Laos, and Cambodia.

There are a variety of problems in attempting to understand and address immigrant and refugee health concerns. One of the main issues arises from the lack of comprehensive studies done after the initial period of entrance into the United States and the health screening tests have been completed. Additionally, most of the health statistics collected make few distinctions among immigrant groups based on race or ethnicity. For example, it is difficult to extrapolate the specifics of health concerns for Mexican Americans, because the literature makes little separation of those born in Mexico versus those born in the United States. Finally, the very definition of an immigrant has not been used consistently in various studies, making cross-reference difficult. One new resource attempting to bridge this gap in immigrant health information is the *Journal of Immigrant Health*, an international, interdisciplinary publication devoted to original research with contributors in various fields, such as public health and policy, medicine and nursing, immigration law, and sociology and anthropology.

GENERAL IMMIGRATION HEALTH STATUS

Regardless of the deficiency in comprehensive immigrant health studies, the conclusions drawn from published sources indicate that foreign-born persons have better overall health status than the U.S.-born. The most recent immigrants were found to be even healthier than the foreign-born who have lived in the United States for ten years or more. It is possible that earlier

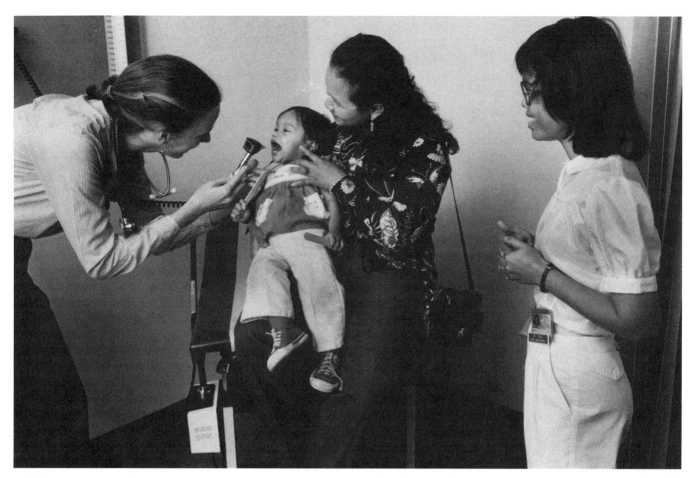

A Bronx, New York, doctor examines a Cambodian refugee baby who is suffering from lead poisoning. Overcrowded living conditions in substandard housing have produced outbreaks of environmentally caused diseases among urban immigrant populations. *(Kathleen Foster/Impact Visuals)*

cohorts of immigrants were as healthy as more recent immigrants at the time of their arrival, but that as their duration of residence increases, their health deteriorates. Possible explanations for this include lower socioeconomic status that may put immigrants at risk for certain acquired physical conditions, limited access to medical care, or lack of comprehensive immunization shots. For example, many Latino groups have a health advantage characterized by cultural behaviors such as the tendency to drink and smoke less, as well as to eat a more nutritious diet. As they become increasingly assimilated and acculturated to the United States, they often lose this health benefit and increase their risks for heart disease, cancer, and stroke. In order to account for the acculturation effects, various communities have adopted the Centers for Disease Control's (CDC) *Behavioral Risk Factor Surveillance System*, which includes questions on such sociodemographic traits as nutrition practices, exercise, and tobacco use.

Before examining the two major sources of U.S.

immigration—Latin America and Asia—and thus the primary sources for health information, it is useful to mention that few studies have been done that examine certain health factors for immigrants from Eastern Europe, the Middle East, and Africa. Of the information that is available, it is possible to determine tuberculosis rates for these various groups. One study done to examine tuberculosis cases found that, between 1986 and 1994, sub-Saharan African immigrants had a rate of 58.5 per 100,000 reported tuberculosis cases; Middle Eastern immigrants a rate of 20.4, and those from the former Soviet Union and Eastern Bloc nations in Europe had a rate of 11.9. Studies of hepatitis B indicate that between 1979 and 1991, Iraqis, Ethiopians, and Bulgarians presented relatively high rates of hepatitis B surface antigen: Iraq, 13 percent positive; Ethiopia, 9.4 percent; Bulgaria, 5.3 percent. Other than these specific cases, very few studies have been undertaken that look exclusively at any one of these groups.

LATINO POPULATION

As mentioned previously, it is difficult to distinguish between U.S.-born Latino groups and foreign-born Latino groups. Nevertheless, some initial conclusions can be drawn from the research with regard to the Latino population. Included in the examination of Latino immigrants are those coming from South and Central American countries, as well as the Caribbean and West Indian Islands. As a group, Latinos in the United States have a significant proportion of their population living in lower socioeconomic conditions, which can foster inadequate living arrangements and hygiene. This population also travels to or emigrates from countries with higher rates of infectious diseases. This can lead to increased morbidity from bacterial gastrointestinal diseases, parasitic infections, and hepatitis A infections.

With regard to both socioeconomic status and frequent travel, seasonal migrant workers—mostly Latinos and members of various Asian groups—suffer a high rate of work-related health issues. Poor health status because of hazardous substances, poor nutrition, and negligible health care leads to the most common ailments of nausea and dizziness, eye problems, hearing loss, and skin rashes.

A major source of morbidity among Latino populations is diabetes mellitus. Diabetes, which can be related to limited resources, accounts for the fact that approximately 14 percent of all Latinos in the United States suffer from type 2 diabetes. Latinos also have a mortality rate from the disease that is twice that of white Americans. Within Latino groups, Mexican-born Latinos have higher prevalence rates of diabetes than Cuban-born and Central and South Americans. Additionally, failure by many immigrant women to receive prenatal care means that diabetes that emerges during pregnancy often goes undetected.

Another source of high rates of morbidity and mortality among various Latino populations is AIDS. Although, as mentioned previously, all immigrant groups are tested for HIV before they can enter the United States, various studies have noted the increases in HIV rates among Latinos in both the United States and Mexico. In 1999, Latinos made up 18 percent of the total U.S. AIDS population. Most of the Latin American male and female immigrants who contract HIV do so through sexual transmission.

Studies of tuberculosis in 1994 found 42 percent of the 24 million cases in the United States to be of Latin American origin. With regard to cancer, studies conducted in California on immigrants from various parts of Latin America found that the most extreme risks for certain cancers were among those born in Central American countries versus those born in Mexico. For immigrant women, there were relatively high risks of gallbladder and cervix cancer, while immigrant males had low risks of colon and prostate cancer.

MEXICAN IMMIGRANTS

Between 1960 and 1980, the Mexican-born population in the United States more than tripled; and between 1981 and 1996, Mexicans were the largest group of immigrants in the United States, contributing 3,304,682 legal immigrants as well as several million more illegal immigrants. Mexican immigrants have incomes substantially lower than those of other foreign-born immigrants or U.S.-born residents, yet health status for first-generation immigrants remains relatively good. However, later generations exhibit higher rates of alcoholism and cirrhosis. Mexican immigrants living in poor neighborhoods often lack access to health care or immunization services and are more vulnerable to sexually transmitted and communicable diseases.

Mexico is also the country of origin for the largest number of foreign-born tuberculosis cases. Of Latin American tuberculosis patients, Mexicans constitute 56.8 percent. In 1997, Mexico was the country of origin for 22 percent of the tuberculosis cases for the foreign born.

There is a general pattern of lower cancer mortality among Mexican-born than among white Americans. However, there is a substantially higher mortality rate for Mexican-born males and females from stomach and liver cancer. Additionally, for Mexican-born females, there is a mortality rate from cancer of the cervix that is twice that of white American females. Yet Mexican-born females have lower rates for breast, lung, and colon cancer, about half the rate for white American females. Mortality rates from cancer of the lung, prostate, colon, pancreas, and leukemia for Mexican-born males is lower than those for white American males.

The unique situation of Mexican Americans living on the border between the United States and Mexico has led to the creation of *colonias*—densely populated housing developments in rural areas along the borders in Texas, New Mexico, Arizona, and California. Although two-thirds of the residents are U.S. citizens, most heads of households are Mexican born. Colonias are physically isolated from major cities, and residents live in conditions akin to third-world environments, characterized by poverty, substandard housing, and overcrowding. For example, 70 percent of the residents have no access to fresh water, sewage hookups, gas, or electric power. Because of these conditions, communicable illnesses such as measles, mumps, and rubella have much higher rates of occurrence in colonias than in the rest of the United States. Specifically, residents in the colonias have a rate of 40 measles cases per 100,000 versus the rest of the country's rate of 11 per 100,000. Late or no prenatal care is common in the border counties, and the colonias have twice the fertility rates of the national average.

CUBAN IMMIGRANTS

The 1990 census counted 736,971 Cuban-born immigrants living in the United States. The high socioeconomic status of the pre-1980 Cuban immigrants reflects the relatively good health of the older Cuban immigrants. While more recent Cuban immigrants have had lower socioeconomic status than the earlier immigrants, few health studies focus on Cuban immigrants as a whole. One of the few diseases that has been examined is rates of cancer among the Cuban immigrant population.

Although Latinos in general have lower cancer rates than U.S.-born persons, Cuban immigrants have the highest mortality rate among Latino subgroups for all cancers. However, compared to U.S.-born whites, Cuban-born immigrants have relatively low mortality rates for stomach, lung, rectal, and cervical cancer. Liver cancer is the one area in which Cuban-born immigrants have higher death rates than Cubans in Cuba or U.S.-born whites.

HAITIAN IMMIGRANTS

When President François Duvalier was first elected in 1957, large numbers of Haitians began emigrating. After his son Jean Claude Duvalier succeeded him in 1971, economic deprivation continued to push immigrants to come to the United States, many illegally, often risking their lives in small boats. A vast majority of Haitian immigrants and refugees are concentrated in southeast Florida and New York City. Many, while maintaining strong ethnic enclaves, tend to live in low socioeconomic conditions that produce health problems related to poverty.

The underdevelopment of Haiti is reflected in the lower status of Haitian health. Within Haiti, prevent-

able childhood diseases are prevalent, indicating lower levels of immunization. The recorded infant mortality rate in Haiti is 129.9 per 1,000 live births, and the average life expectancy is 48 years.

Among rural Haitians migrating to the United States, there is a high prevalence of dietary deficiencies and anemia. For example, Vitamin A-related corneal scars have been found, especially among the poorest children. The most commonly reported chronic conditions for Haitians are serious eye trouble, skin problems, allergies, and arthritis or rheumatism. Additionally, untreated conditions, such as cancer, are high because Haitians are unlikely to be treated by a doctor until they feel pain. Although cases of tuberculosis are declining in the United States overall, cases among the foreign born continue to account for an increasing amount. Of reported cases of active tuberculosis, between 1986 and 1994, Haitians accounted for 2,650 cases, or a rate of 133 per 100,000 reported cases.

In 1992 in Guantánamo Bay, Cuba, 140 Haitian refugees were gathered together by United States officials and told they were HIV positive and would be denied entrance into the United States based on health exclusion policies. It was not until a year and a half later that a federal judge ordered the U.S. government to allow the Haitian refugees to enter the country. Even before this situation, Haitians were already being stigmatized by association with the disease, and tens of thousands faced discrimination and ostracization. Although it took two years for the CDC to drop Haitians from their list of high-risk carriers, the relationship between Haitian immigrants and AIDS has proved to be spurious, as readily acknowledged in 1985 by the Center for Infectious Diseases director, Dr. Walter Dowdle.

ASIAN IMMIGRANTS

As mentioned with regard to Latino immigrant groups, Asian immigrant studies also conflate immigrant Asian ethnic groups with U.S.-born Asian ethnic groups. Additionally, the term "Asian and Pacific Islander" is often used as a pan-ethnic classification, encompassing more than fifty different ethnic, cultural, national, and regional groups. For example, this broad category includes Asians from diverse areas such as China, Korea, Vietnam, Cambodia, and the Philippines. In 1997, Asian and Pacific Islanders numbered approximately 10 million persons and made up 3.7 percent of the U.S. population. Estimates have suggested an increase of five times this number by 2050, with the growth due largely to immigration. As of 1997, six of ten Asians were foreign born; and among Filipinos in the United States, 64 percent are foreign born.

It is difficult to extrapolate data specifically about the various Asian immigrant groups because many studies integrate information on both the foreign-born and the U.S.-born Asian groups. Nevertheless, several studies have been done that focus research on immigrant Asian groups. The following sections will look at overall health status for Asians and Pacific Islanders, and two specific subsections will explore information particular to Chinese immigrants and Southeast Asian immigrants (and refugees).

As Asian and Pacific Islanders emigrate to the United States, increased acculturation often means a change in healthy dietary practices and decreased exercise levels. These factors contribute to the high risks for obesity and non-insulin-dependent diabetes mellitus. All Asian and Pacific Islanders have higher rates of this type of diabetes than white Americans.

Another disease that occurs more frequently in Asian and Pacific Islanders than in white Americans is a carrier rate for hepatitis B of 5 to 15 percent. Tuberculosis rates in Asia are five to twenty times higher than in the United States. A study conducted from 1986 to 1993 found 2,262 cases of diagnosed tuberculosis for South Koreans. In 1997, immigrants from the Philippines constituted 14 percent of the foreign-born tuberculosis cases. However, younger persons, as well as those who emigrate at a younger age, are at lower risk for infection with tuberculosis. The cases of foreign-born Asian groups with high numbers of tuberculosis cases, though, do not include those of immigrants from Japan, India, or mainland China.

Incidence of cancer in the Asian and Pacific Islander group is, as a whole, lower than it is for white Americans. One study examining Chinese, Japanese, and Filipinos in Hawaii and California found that for all groups, there was a morbidity rate of at least a hundred cases less than the rates for white Americans. Nevertheless, Asian and Pacific Islanders have a relatively high rate of some cancers. For example, the incidence of stomach cancer is three to six times higher among Japanese than among U.S.-born whites.

While Asian and Pacific Islander women have lower rates of breast cancer than other ethnic groups, this fact is misleading in that breast cancer is still the main site of cancer for all subgroups of the Asian and Pacific Islander female population. Additionally, cancer of the cervix is another common site of cancer among Asian and Pacific Islanders. Finally, although perceived not to be a problem among Asian groups, Asian and Pacific Islanders constitute 1 percent of the

U.S. AIDS population. However, of the total world HIV-positive population of 23 million, Asian countries combined have approximately 6.6 million persons infected.

CHINESE IMMIGRANTS

Between 1981 and 1996, China had the fourth highest rate of immigration to the United States, totaling 539,267. As mentioned previously, Asian and Pacific Islanders have high rates among the foreign-born population for tuberculosis. However, Chinese immigrants, taken together with Indian, Haitian, and Korean immigrants, constitute 3 to 6 percent of the total foreign-born tuberculosis cases. According to a study examining the tuberculosis cases for the foreign born relative to their length of U.S. residence, between 1986 to 1993, immigrants from mainland China accounted for 1.5 percent of the tuberculosis cases. Compared to Filipino, Japanese, and Koreans, within Asian and Pacific Islander groups, Chinese also have lower rates of adult male smokers.

Liver cancer, although not included in the top five cancer mortality rates for black or white Americans, is the second most prevalent cause of death among Chinese Americans. Other common sites of cancer among Chinese include the oral cavity and nasopharynx, esophagus, and stomach.

SOUTHEAST ASIAN IMMIGRANTS AND REFUGEES

Included in the Southeast Asian immigrant category are persons immigrating from Laos, Cambodia, Thailand, and Vietnam. These include both immigrants and refugees. Between 1981 and 1996, Vietnam, Laos, and Cambodia accounted for three of the largest refugee numbers, comprising a total of 677,622. In discussing the health status of Southeast Asian refugees, it is important to recognize the often deteriorating circumstances in their home country that forced the refugee to leave, as well as the difficult conditions refugees often face on the journey to the United States. For example, a study on self-reported health and psychological distress noted that two of five Vietnamese and three of five Cambodians rated their health as less than good. Additionally, there is the added problem that many Southeast Asians do not speak English, a situation that contributes to a lower rate of acquiring the right attention for medical needs. For example, a study conducted in San Diego found that 60 percent of Southeast Asians cited language as a major problem in obtaining health care, with Cambodians and Laotians having the most difficulty.

The two most frequent problems cited among Southeast Asian refugees are parasitic infections (e.g., hookworm) and tuberculosis, as well as high levels of dental problems. Anemia, hepatitis B antigenemia, hematological disorders, and dermatological problems all occur among Southeast Asians at a greater than 10 percent incidence rate. For the Hmong from Laos, cases of Sudden Unexpected Nocturnal Death Syndrome have been studied extensively, but as yet remain unexplained. Southeast Asians also have high levels of smoking; for Laotians 92 percent, Cambodians 71 percent, and 55 to 65 percent for Vietnamese.

As already mentioned, tuberculosis is a problem for Southeast Asian immigrants and refugees. A study examining tuberculosis cases among the foreign born from 1986 to 1993 found that the Asian region—other than Japan, India, and mainland China—accounted for 16,643 cases of diagnosed tuberculosis. Vietnam accounted for 4,941 cases, Cambodia for 977 cases, and Laos for 878 cases.

The other common problem for Southeast Asian groups, as mentioned above, are parasitic infections, one in particular being the occurrence of malaria. In 1980, in the United States, 1,864 cases of malaria were reported. This represented an increase of 500 percent since 1975. Of the reported cases, 99 percent were imported and 82 percent were from the foreign born. Among the foreign born, 55 percent or 1,034 occurred in Southeast Asian refugees. Hepatitis B surface antigen rates are also high among refugees from Southeast Asia, with a range between 11.7 percent and 15.5 percent.

Over the years, the U.S. government has altered the medical definitions and descriptions for terms of immigrant exclusion. A medical examination is required for all legal immigrants and refugees, with grounds for exclusion based on communicable disease. While studies of immigrants at this stage can provide some information about immigrants' health status, much more is needed to explore the health problems immigrants face once they have become more permanent residents. Additionally, health studies must begin to distinguish between *immigrant* racial and ethnic groups and *U.S.-born* racial and ethnic groups.

It is also important to recognize that the health concerns are not the same for all immigrant groups or refugees. For example, cases of tuberculosis are far more prevalent in some areas than others, such as Southeast Asia. Most specifically, immigrants entering from countries that are more underdeveloped tend not to have had immunization shots, which can lead to disease or infection once they arrive in the United States. Immigrants also tend to be in better health overall, yet the more they become acculturated to the American lifestyle, the more their health deteriorates. Thus, in order to fully understand immigrant health problems and status, we must examine various factors including socioeconomic status, rates of disease and infection upon entrance versus over time of residence in the United States, and cultural practices, such as dietary habits and rates of exercise.

Beth Merenstein

See also: Fertility (Part II, Sec. 3); Elderly (Part II, Sec. 4) Poverty (Part II, Sec. 7); Mental Health (Part II, Sec. 9); Recommendation for Prevention and Control of Tuberculosis Among Foreign-Born Persons, 1998 (Part IV, Sec. 2).

BIBLIOGRAPHY

Centers for Disease Control and Prevention. "Screening for Hepatitis B Virus Infection among Refugees Arriving in the United States, 1979–1991." *Morbidity Mortality Weekly Report* 40: 45 (1991): 784–86.

———. "Report of the Working Group on TB among Foreign-Born Persons." *Morbidity Mortality Weekly Report* 47: RR-16 (1998).

Davidhizar, Ruth, and Gregory A. Bechtel. "Health and Quality of Life within Colonias Settlements along the United States and Mexico Border." *Public Health Nursing* 16:4 (1999): 301–6.

DeSantis, Lydia. "Health Care Orientations of Cuban and Haitian Immigrant Mothers: Implications for Health Care Professionals." *Medical Anthropology* 12 (1989): 69–89.

Flaskerud, Jacquelyn H., and Sue Kim. "Health Problems of Asian and Latino Immigrants." *Nursing Clinics of North America* 34:2 (1999): 359–80.

Hann, Richard. "Parasitic Infestations." In *Confronting Critical Health Issues of Asian and Pacific Islander Americans*, ed. Nolan W. S. Zane, David T. Takeuchi, and Kathleen N. J. Young, 302–15. Thousand Oaks, CA: Sage, 1994.

Jenkins, Christopher N. H., and Marjorie Kagawa-Singer. "Cancer." In *Confronting Critical Health Issues of Asian and Pacific Islander Americans*, ed. Nolan W. S. Zane, David T. Takeuchi, and Kathleen N. J. Young, 105–47. Thousand Oaks, CA: Sage, 1994.

Kamineni, A., M. A. Williams, S. M. Schwartz, L. S. Cook, and N. S. Weiss. "The Incidence of Gastric Carcinoma in Asian Migrants to the U.S. and their Descendants." *Cancer Causes Control* 10:1 (1999): 77–83.

Kennedy, James, Deborah J. Seymour, and Barbara J. Hummel. "A Comprehensive Refugee Health Screening Program." *Public Health Report* 114 (1999): 469–77.

Kraut, Alan M. *Silent Travelers: Germs, Genes, and the "Immigrant Menace."* New York: Basic Books, 1994.

Kuo, JoAnn, and Kathryn Porter. "Health Status of Asian Americans: United States, 1992–1994." *Advance Data* 298 (1998): 1–16.

Kuo, W. H., and Tsai Y. "Social Networking, Hardiness and Immigrant's Mental Health." *Journal of Health Social Behavior* 27 (1986): 133–49.

Laguerre, Michel S. "Haitian Americans." In *Ethnicity and Medical Care*, ed. Alan Harwood, 172–210. Cambridge, MA: Harvard University Press, 1981.

Loue, Sana, and Arwen Bunce. "The Assessment of Immigration Status in Health Research." *Vital and Health Statistics* Series 2, Number 127 (1999).

Mack, Thomas, Ann Walker, Wendy Mack, and Leslie Bernstein. "Cancer in Hispanics in Los Angeles County." *National Cancer Institute Monograph* 69 (1985): 99–104.

Mayeno, Laurin, and Sherry Hirota. "Access to Health Care." In *Confronting Critical Health Issues of Asian and Pacific Islander Americans*, ed. Nolan W. S. Zane, David T. Takeuchi, and Kathleen N. J. Young, 347–75. Thousand Oaks, CA: Sage, 1994.

McKenna, Matthew T., Eugene McCray, and Ida Onorato. "The Epidemiology of Tuberculosis among the Foreign-Born Persons in the United States, 1986 to 1993." *New England Journal of Medicine* 332:16 (1995): 1071–6.

Meinhardt, Kenneth, Soleng Tom, Philip Tse, and Connie Young Yu. "Southeast Asian Refugees in the 'Silicon Valley': The Asian Health Assessment Project." *Amerasia* 12:2 (1985–1986): 43–65.

Rosenwaike, Ira. "Cancer Mortality among Mexican Immigrants to the United States." *Public Health Reports* 103:2 (1988): 195–201.

Sakala, Carol. "Migrant and Seasonal Farmworkers in the United States: A Review of Health Hazards, Status, and Policy." *International Migration Review, Special Issue: Migration and Health* 21:3 (1987): 659–71.

Saphir, Ann. "Asian Americans and Cancer: Discarding the Myth of the 'Model Minority.'" *Journal of the National Cancer Institute* 89 (1997): 1572–4.

Shai, Donna. "Cancer Mortality in Cuba and among the Cuban-Born in the United States: 1979–1981." *Public Health Report* 106 (1991): 68–73.

Shoop, Lyn G. "Health Based Exclusion Grounds in United States Immigration Policy: Homosexuals, HIV Infection and the Medical Examination of Aliens." *Catholic University Journal of Contemporary Health, Law and Policy* 9 (1993): 521–44.

Sumaya, Ciro V. "Major Infectious Diseases Causing Excess Morbidity in the Hispanic Population." In *Health Policy and the Hispanic*, ed. Antonio Furino, 76–96. Boulder, CO: Westview Press, 1992.

Tabora, B., and Flaskerud, J. H. "Depression among Chinese Americans: A Review of the Literature." *Issues in Mental Health Nursing* 15 (1994): 569–84.

Torres-Gil, Fernando. "Immigration's Impact on Health and Human Services." In *The California-Mexico Connection*, ed. Abraham F. Lowenthal and Katrina Burgess, 164–75. Stanford, CA: Stanford University Press, 1993.

Torrez, Adriana. "Immigrant Health is Paradox." *Fort Worth Star-Telegram*, October 15, 1999, 1–3.

Young, Rosalie F., Allen Bukoff, John B. Waller, Jr., and Stephen B. Blount. "Health Status, Health Problems and Practices among Refugees from the Middle East, Eastern Europe and Southeast Asia." *International Migration Review*. 21:3 (1987): 760–82.

Zuber, Patrick L., Matthew T. McKenna, Nancy J. Binkin, Ida M. Onorato, and Kenneth G. Castro. "Long-Term Risks of Tuberculosis among Foreign-Born Persons in the United States." *Journal of the American Medical Association* 278:4 (1997): 304–7.

MENTAL HEALTH

In the consideration of mental health and immigration, several topics are typically discussed. Naturally, the causes of depression among immigrants are important to examine in order to determine ways to alleviate it. Factors that aid in the adaptation process are also important. Likewise, factors that hinder the acculturation process are a significant element of immigrants' mental health. Females have substantially different and higher rates of depressive episodes than do males. Additionally, psychologists have developed general adaptation stages to immigration which appear to pertain to a great number of immigrants' experiences. Another topic within the discussion of mental health and immigration is "hardiness," or how mentally healthy an individual was before emigrating. Finally, one's culture contributes to adjustment after immigration, because different cultures have different concepts of self.

FACTORS THAT AID ACCULTURATION

There are a great number of social stresses involved in leaving one's homeland and resettling and adapting to a new environment in a host country. Social networking is one of the most important elements in encouraging a smooth acculturation process. Much stress results from isolation. Linguistic and cultural barriers increase the likelihood of isolation, and many immigrants do not have family or friends in the United States before they arrive. Although having contacts here before arrival is assumed to aid in adaptation, this is not *always* the case. Studies have shown that the mere existence of family living in the United States does not necessarily mean that immigrants will experience less mental strain than those who do not have family here. Rather, what

appears to help immigrants alleviate mental and social stresses is contact with and support from their U.S. relatives, and not merely their presence.

In addition to feeling socially isolated in the United States, most immigrants miss family and friends back home. According to Rim Shin Kyung, thinking about loved ones in their home country often exaggerates feelings of social isolation in the United States. Another contribution to feelings of social isolation is some immigrants' fear that they will lose contact with their homeland. Many immigrants do not have a lot of money to spend on plane tickets to visit or regular telephone calls with family members back home; those who have access to e-mail or fax machines have more opportunity to stay in contact. The most important factor in visiting one's home country is finances.

CHURCHES AND SOCIAL ORGANIZATIONS

Churches and social organizations have provided an important means for immigrants from the same country or region to meet once in the United States and to give support to one another. Especially for nonwhite or non-English-speaking immigrants, churches are a way for individuals to establish social networks. These immigrants would otherwise have few, if any, means for association.

Today, for example, Korean churches play a vital role in bringing together Korean Americans in a social setting and providing support to members. Different generations of immigrants attend church for different reasons. Generally, first-generation immigrants attend ethnic churches both for social and spiritual reasons, whereas second-generation immigrants attend more for spiritual reasons alone. For

In Chicago, drama therapist Keith Whipple, in tie, works with Cambodian refugees who are suffering from torture-induced posttraumatic stress disorder. *(Loren Santow/Impact Visuals)*

first-generation immigrants, ethnic churches are a place where they can speak their native language and meet others who share the same values and customs. "Much of their unique cultural behavior is mutually reinforced in social contacts provided by the church," according to sociologist Hyung-chan Kim. Among the Hmong refugees in Minnesota, however, less contact with other Hmong is associated with fewer emotional problems.

Another contributing factor to the mental health of immigrants is how much contact they have with fellow church members from the host country. Research indicates that the more contact with the population in the host country, the greater likelihood that depression can be avoided. Also, immigrants who maintain a lot of contact with friends and family back home tend to reduce their efforts at establishing social networks in the host country and thus are more susceptible to depression after immigration.

PREPAREDNESS BEFORE LEAVING THE HOME COUNTRY

Another factor that aids in the acculturation process is that of preparedness before leaving the home country. In general, the more preparation by individuals before immigrating, the smoother their transition into American society. One of the key things that immigrants can do to reduce the risk of experiencing depressive symptoms before leaving their home country is to learn about living in the United States. Studies have shown that immigrants who have friends or family already living in the United States that have informed them about life in America have fewer episodes of depression than other immigrants.

Another important factor that can help reduce the risk of immigrants' experiencing depression is career or job preparation before leaving the home country. Additionally, studies indicate that immigrants who are able to find jobs in the United States similar to the job they had in their home country are less likely to experience depressive symptoms.

SELF-HELP GROUPS

Many psychologists and others who work in the mental health field have suggested that self-help groups can aid immigrants (especially females) who experience difficulty adapting to life in the United States. It is not uncommon for immigrants in the United States to avoid seeking psychological help until a crisis point has been reached. Before seeking counseling, immigrants have normally exhausted all other alternatives, including "prayer meetings, pastors, acupuncture, herbal medicine, and internist doctors," according to the sociologist Luke Kim. This is most likely the case owing to feelings of shame and embarrassment. Often, immigrants do not voluntarily seek help and instead are referred by courts, community agencies, schools, law enforcement agencies, or family members. Psychological stress frequently exhibits itself through somatic symptoms rather than through feelings of sadness or depression. Numerous immigrants initially go to medical doctors complaining of insomnia, upset stomach, headaches, and a variety of other symptoms, only to be referred to psychiatrists. Many immigrant psychiatric patients seek medication and have no interest in psychotherapy. This is often attributed to feelings of shame among patients.

Many women from Asian countries do not express anger or aggression because it is considered confrontational, ugly behavior. Such lack of assertiveness can, however, contribute to low self-esteem and depression. Asian-American women need to learn to be more assertive in order to improve their mental health. Psychologists often recommend that immigrant women seek information and help through books, courses, or, even better, self-help groups so that they can share their experiences with others who are experiencing similar difficulties.

In Asian societies, Confucian and Taoist ideology are part of the social makeup. Talking positively about oneself is considered immature and even repugnant to others. As a general rule, others are put above the self. American society is structured in an opposite manner, with an emphasis on the individual and independence. Therefore, adjusting and adapting to American society is often difficult for immigrants and sometimes can be the cause of depressive symptoms.

FACTORS THAT CONTRIBUTE TO DEPRESSION AMONG IMMIGRANTS IN AMERICA

COMMUNICATION AND LANGUAGE PROBLEMS

Virtually all immigrants from non-English-speaking countries report that once they became fluent in English, they face less stress in their daily lives. Both language and communication are important to the concept of self. "Communication is a self-reflective process at subconscious and conscious levels that constructs the individual self in his environment," says Won H. Chang. Thus, it comes as no surprise that once immigrants learn English they experience fewer episodes of depression. Acculturation can occur directly through language because it is "the process by which two groups of individuals with different cultural backgrounds bring about change in the original culture patterns as a result of contact," says Chang. Assuming that language is a part of culture, then immigrants learning, speaking, and using English can be considered a part of the acculturation process. According to Chang, "Communication is an underlying power in acculturation by which an individual accumulates control over change in order to cope with a new environment." Learning English is probably the most powerful combatant against depression that immigrants have available to them.

RACISM AND DISCRIMINATION

Perhaps the most detrimental area in which immigrants experience racial discrimination is in the workplace. It is difficult for immigrants to secure employment in American firms because of racial discrimination, lack of training and skill, and language barriers. Underemployment, unemployment, and difficulties attaining top jobs in one's field are common among immigrants. Generally, unemployed immigrants almost always report higher levels of anxiety and depressive symptoms than do employed immigrants. This, however, is not always the case. Among the Hmong refugees in Minnesota, for example, employment tends to be related to higher levels of depression. In addition, many immigrants experience hardship getting licensed in their fields owing to language difficulties associated with licensing exams. Employment is generally more significant for men's mental health than for that of women because traditionally the male's concept of self comes primarily from his career. Likewise, the family is generally more significant for women's mental health than for men's, because the female's sense of self traditionally comes from her family. These observations are generalizations but are useful in understanding the causes of depression, especially when considering immigrants from patriarchal societies.

Racism does not occur only from whites toward immigrants of color. It is not uncommon for one ethnic group to have racist feelings toward another—for African Americans, for example, to exhibit racist behavior toward first-generation immigrants from Asia or Latin America. Furthermore, individuals with mixed racial backgrounds may experience an even higher frequency of racism than other immigrant groups. Individuals of Vietnamese and American parents who immigrate to the United States report especially high rates of racism, probably on account of the Vietnam War.

Immigrants who experience discrimination are more likely to experience depressive symptoms. Many immigrants who feel that they are underemployed or underpaid in their employment experience great levels of anxiety and depression. Many feel that they are exploited by their employers and discriminated against by their fellow workers. At least in part, immigrants are discriminated against because of some native-born or naturalized Americans' perceptions that they are taking the jobs of American workers.

IDENTITY PROBLEMS

It is not uncommon for immigrants to experience problems concerning self-identity. This is especially true for immigrants who come from smaller countries and therefore have few friends from their own country. Bilingual education is not offered for every language for which its needed. Again, immigrants who come from a smaller country speaking a language not spoken by many people in the United States will have difficulties gaining access to bilingual education for their children. Sometimes immigrant children from Korea, for example, are simply put in Chinese bilingual education, which is detrimental to their self-identity. Additionally, many states have laws that prohibit classes with enrollments of less than thirty students, so if not enough students need instruction in a certain language, then bilingual classes in that language are not offered.

As individuals take on American culture and customs, they frequently shed their own. Some immigrants who are learning English, for example, attempt to abandon their native language in hopes of learning English more quickly. When the native language is abandoned by first-generation immigrants, second-generation immigrants often never learn their parents'

native language and lose a part of their identity. Additionally, immigrants should not be discouraged from speaking their native languages, because doing so may "perpetuate the notion of cultural or language inferiority, especially in view of their already fragile and threatened identity," say the sociologists Emeka Nwadiora and Harriette McAdoo.

It has been shown that rejecting American culture altogether and maintaining the culture of the home country tends to increase the likelihood that an immigrant will experience depression or anxiety. Abandoning one's native culture is linked to depression owing to identity issues as well as peer treatment from fellow immigrants. Fellow immigrants tend to view abandoning one's native culture as an insult. Taking on a bicultural perspective has been demonstrated to be the best way to cope with acculturation for immigrants in the United States. The more different the native culture is, the more important bicultural behavior becomes. Thus, the most mentally healthy immigrants are those who maintain some customs and traditions from their home country, at the same time as they take on some American customs.

GENDER ROLES AND DIFFERENCES

Many countries function in a patriarchal manner. Traditionally, the man/father/husband takes on an authoritative role in which he makes most of the decisions. Many immigrants experience marital problems after immigrating to the United States due to gender role conflicts. According to Confucian teaching, for example, women are obedient to their husbands, in-laws, and sons, and there exist four virtues that a woman should possess: chastity, reticence, a pleasing manner, and domestic skills. Although many aspects of such a traditional society as China have been modified in the past two decades as a result of Western influence, there is still a strong presence of many traditional customs and attitudes. After immigration to the United States, many women feel more freedom and realize increased employment opportunities. This does, however, often result in marital conflict and a questioning of one's own identity. In Korea, for example, the male is served first at a restaurant, walks through doors first, and so forth, while in the United States, the opposite is the cultural norm. Many Asian couples find adapting to such differences to be a difficult process.

Many studies have shown that regardless of their native country, female immigrants tend to experience higher rates of depression than do men. This is the case because women from patriarchal societies (such as Korea, Iraq, and Iran, for example) must alter their gender roles more so than their male counterparts in the acculturation process. In general, women are more likely to resist taking on American customs than men are, which also adds to mental stress. Likewise, men are more likely to take on the behavioral customs of the United States, which accounts, at least partially, for their higher levels of mental health.

STAGES IN ADAPTATION AND ACCULTURATION

Studies concerning various stages in adaptation and acculturation of immigrants have found varying results. Most studies indicate that the initial stage of immigration (the first six months) is a period of euphoria for most immigrants. This, however, is not the case among most refugees. Thus, the circumstances from which the individual comes have a profound effect on his or her mental state during the first six months after immigration. Some scholars believe there to be four main phases of immigrant adaptation. First, immigrants experience a "honeymoon" phase in which they are simply happy to be in the United States. Second, they experience disappointment as a result of being in the United States, dealing with problems such as unemployment, racial discrimination, or financial problems. Third, immigrants begin to adapt to American society and take on cultural norms of behavior, thus feeling less alienated. They place less emphasis on the negative aspects of living in American society and achieve a degree of contentment. Fourth, immigrants begin to function effectively as members of American society and are no longer constantly aware of being different.

Changes in climate, food, social status, and economic status also affect an individual's adaptation to the United States. Moreover, demographics such as age, marital status, sex, and education have varying degrees of statistical significance in their relationship with depressive symptoms among immigrants in America. Sociologists have shown, for example, that the older immigrants are when they immigrate to the United States, the less likely they are to take on American customs, which leads to higher levels of depressive symptoms.

It is not uncommon for immigrants to experience a crisis period following the first six months after immigration, a period that can last from six months to six years. There is a consensus among psychologists that the longer the amount of time spent in the United States, the fewer depressive symptoms an immigrant will exhibit. This is most likely due to adaptation and acculturation. As immigrants establish interpersonal and intrapersonal relations in the United States, not only do they benefit from the social contact involved but they also undergo some psychological and behavioral changes that aid in their acculturation process.

Immigrants who come from countries whose cultures differ drastically from that of the United States have a higher potential for experiencing depressive symptoms after their arrival because they face more adaptation than do immigrants who come from cultures similar to that of the United States. Additionally, immigrants who come from countries with political and/or economic strife will most likely have already faced many hardships, and depending on the individual, such past experiences can either help or hinder adaptation in the United States.

Not all factors affecting depression among immigrants are endogenous. Some people are simply better at adapting to new situations than others. Individuals with higher levels of self-esteem, for example, are more likely to adapt smoothly to a new environment, because those with higher self-esteem are more likely to view their life as self-directed and to believe that they are responsible for their life situation. The less "hardy" person is one who believes his or her life is not controlled by the individual but that one's environment is responsible for fatalistically directing life. A more "hardy" person would possess assertiveness in attaining goals and display initiative and a willingness to take risks, with an ability to face uncertainty without experiencing any substantial depressive symptoms.

PREVENTATIVE MEASURES FOR AVOIDING MENTAL STRESS

One of the most important actions that immigrants can take to prevent experiencing depressive symptoms is to prepare for their lives in the United States. Learning about life in the United States from friends or family before departure can help prepare immigrants for what to expect on arrival. Another key factor in avoiding anxiety and depression after immigration is employment. Most employed immigrants experience lower rates of depressive episodes. Therefore, if an immigrant can attain employment before arrival in the United States, he or she will have a greater likelihood of avoiding depression. Knowledge of English is an additional factor that helps immigrants avoid mental health problems. Finally, taking on some American customs while maintaining their home country culture provides a better opportunity for immigrants to achieve mental health in the United States.

Gretchen S. Carnes

See also: Health Care, Immigrants and Health, Social Services (Part II, Sec. 9).

BIBLIOGRAPHY

Chang, Won H. "Communication and Acculturation." In *The Korean Diaspora*, ed. Hyung-chan Kim.

Choy, Bong-Youn. *Koreans in America*. Chicago: Nelson-Hall, 1979.

Ghaffarian, Shireen. "The Acculturation of Iranian Immigrants in the United States and the Implications for Mental Health." *Journal of Social Psychology* 138 (October 1998): 645–54.

Kim, Hyung-chan, ed. *The Korean Diaspora*. Santa Barbara, CA: ABC-Clio Press, 1977.

Kim, Luke I. "The Mental Health of Korean American Women." In *Korean American Women—from Tradition to Modern Feminism*, ed. Young I. Song and Ailee Moon. Westport, CT: Praeger, 1998.

Kuo, Wen H., and Yung-Mei Tsai. "Social Networking, Hardiness, and Immigrants' Mental Health." *Health and Social Behavior* 27 (June 1986): 133–49.

Kyung, Rim Shin, ed. "Psychological Predictors of Depressive Symptoms in Korean-American Women in New York City." *Women and Health* 2 (1994): 73–82.

Nwadiora, Emeka, and Harriette McAdoo. "Acculturative Stress Among Amerasian Refugees: Gender and Racial Differences." *Adolescence* 31 (Summer 1996): 477–87.

Pernice, Regina, and Judith Brook. "Refugees' and Immigrants' Mental Health: Association of Demographic and Post-Immigration Factors." *Journal of Social Psychology* 136 (August 1996): 511–19.

Ritsner, Michael, and Alexander Ponizovsky. "Psychological Distress Through Immigration: The Two-Phase Temporal Pattern?" *International Journal of Social Psychiatry* 45 (Summer 1999): 125–39.

ℙUBLIC SCHOOLS

Immigration to this country has continued since the first settlements by English immigrants to the Atlantic coastal regions and over the decades has included people from throughout the world. During the hundred years following 1815, more than 35 million people arrived in America from many parts of the world, and all of them had to go through a transformative process to turn them into Americans. Arguably, public schools represent the most important institution in that process. In short, there is no other institution in American society that has played the role of public schools in the process of adjustment of immigrants to its values and norms. Public schools have been and continue to be socialization agents of immigrant populations, both children and their parents.

The role of public schools in the adaptation of the immigrants to their new society was recognized early in America's development. It was the task of the public schools to transform these millions of newcomers, from many cultures and speaking many languages, into Americans.

America has evolved over time from a country in which immigrants and native-born Americans shared many cultural traits to a country in which later waves of immigrants were from cultures that differed in many ways from native-born Americans and previous immigrants. As would be expected, this evolution had an impact on the public school system and how, and how well, it integrated the newcomers into American society.

Historically, on the whole, public schools have been successful in integrating immigrants into American society, but this has not been without difficulties. Now, though the process of integrating migrants into American society continues, the nature of the difficulties is changing.

HISTORY OF EARLY IMMIGRATION TO AMERICA

In 1790, the American population was predominantly of British origin and received approximately ten thousand persons every year. Up to 1830, immigration was mainly from the British Isles. From 1830 to 1882, immigration increased, particularly from Germany, Scandinavia, and Ireland. Though immigrants from these parts of Europe shared many cultural traits with Americans, some immigrants were viewed negatively. Even though the rapid industrialization in America required cheap labor, some employers started to object to paupers, criminals, and other undesirables among the aliens, and they viewed Catholics negatively. Partly because of their Catholic faith, Irish immigrants, in particular, faced discrimination.

The year 1882 represents a turning point in the history of American immigration. It was the climax of the movement of immigrants from western and northern Europe to the United States and the beginning of the massive arrival of immigrants from southern and eastern Europe. It was also the beginning of federal control of immigration and the passage of the Chinese Exclusion Act, followed by legislation prohibiting the entry of lunatics, criminals, beggars, and anarchists. The post-1882 immigration, in contrast to the previous immigration from Germany, England, Scandinavia, France, Holland, and other western European countries, included Italians, Poles, Greeks, Portuguese, Russians, and other Slavs. Within about twenty years, 80 percent of the immigration stream was of eastern and southern European origin. Enormous cultural differences between the new eastern European immigrants and the American population with its recent western European migrants made the latest group seem less desirable. Furthermore, the new immigrants

Traditionally, public schools have been one of the main institutions for integrating immigrants into American life. In this Philadelphia school, a Cambodian student learns the rudiments of English. *(Harvey Finkle/Impact Visuals)*

were mostly Catholics and Jews, which deepened the cultural differences with native-born Americans and the recent western European immigrants, who were predominantly Protestant. These new immigrants created and settled heavily in ethnic islands in major cities across the United States.

Following World War I, there was a period of xenophobia and sentiment against immigrants. In this context, Congress passed the Quota Act of 1921 with two purposes, to restrict the total volume of immigration and to encourage immigration from western Europe. Three years later Congress passed the Quota Act of 1924, which reinforced discrimination against eastern European immigrants and barred Asian immigrants. Both acts established quota systems based on the number of people of a particular nationality residing in the United States in 1890.

Some of these restrictions were removed after

World War II, and in 1952 legislation gave a token quota to Asians. The system of quotas changed with the Immigration and Nationality Act of 1952 and when presidential actions established new quotas in 1953. Since then, the quotas were often revised, allowing an enormous number of refugees and displaced persons to enter the United States.

RECENT IMMIGRATION

Since 1965, three broad groups of new immigrants have entered the United States: legal immigrants, illegal immigrants, and refugees. Legal immigrants are the largest of these three groups. Of the almost 10 million entrants into the United States in the 1980s, nine hundred thousand were refugees, roughly 3 million were illegal (over 2 million of the illegal immigrants became legal during the decade), and the remaining millions were legal. These groups are very different in many aspects, such as their nationality, socioeconomic status, and adjustment to the United States.

In 1965 new legislation gave preferences to applicants who had relatives in the United States or to applicants who have special occupational skills needed in the United States. At the same time, Congress also terminated the Bracero Program, which had funneled temporary Mexican immigration into agriculture in the southwestern United States for more than two decades. The consequence of these two changes in legislation and of changes in the economy, American foreign policy, and world politics was that the character of immigration in the subsequent decades changed. Economic motivation for Mexican workers in agriculture continued and resulted in increased illegal immigration, while there was an increase in legal Asian and Latin American immigration.

While the decline of European and Canadian immigration since 1965 is remarkable, the number of people from developing countries has steadily grown. In 1990, legal immigration from Asia, Latin America, the Caribbean, and Africa constituted 82 percent of all legal immigration. Asians have shown the largest increase, from 7 percent in 1965 to 46 percent in 1990. The composition of the Asian immigrants includes: Chinese (Hong Kong, Taiwan, China, and Singapore), 17 percent; Filipinos, 18 percent; Indians, Bangladeshis, Sri Lankans, and Pakistanis, 13 percent; Koreans, 10 percent; and Vietnamese, Cambodians, Laotians, and Thais, 24 percent. Latin Americans are second in terms of legal migrants. They represented approximately 20 percent of all immigrants in 1990. Of Latin Americans, 42 percent were Mexican; Caribbean immigrants represented 13 percent of total legal immigration in 1990. Other Latin Americans come from Central America, particularly from El Salvador and Guatemala, and South America. Immigrants from Haiti, the Dominican Republic, and Jamaica are increasing the black population in the United States. Africa contributes only 3 percent of the legal migrants.

PUBLIC SCHOOLS AND IMMIGRATION: AN ESSENTIALLY HOMOGENEOUS AMERICA

The American population has evolved over time from a relatively culturally homogeneous population to a culturally heterogeneous population, and the role of public schools in the lives of immigrants evolved in parallel with the changing nature of the American population. Early America was perceived as essentially homogeneous. The free population was perceived as primarily white, English-speaking, and of western European origin and remained so until the waves of immigrants from eastern and southern Europe began to change the nature of the population. In this context of a homogeneous America, assimilation into American society was simply Americanization, and the term was used as a synonym for assimilation.

A representative perception of public schools and their role in the integration of the immigrant population into American society was captured by Ohio reformer Calvin Stowe, who in 1835 warned teachers, "It is altogether essential to our national strength and peace, if not even to our national existence, that the foreigners who settle on our soil, should cease to be Europeans and become Americans." Stowe, the husband of author Harriet Beecher Stowe, added that the schools should create a national feeling and unity of thought and action. He believed that the role of public schools was to create a nationalist feeling that would reduce the risk of social disintegration. In the nineteenth-century educational establishment, linguistic assimilation was the ultimate goal for immigrant students. William Torrey Harris, St. Louis public school superintendent and later U.S. commissioner of education, believed that the schools must "Americanize" children from different cultural and linguistic backgrounds.

The same perspective is found in the early years of the twentieth century. In 1919, Frank Thompson

realized that public schools had an important role in preparing Americans for citizenship, defended the need for a common language for native-born and immigrants, and believed that public schools could be under public control and be mandated to conform to specified curricula. He also thought that private schools would conform to some extent to the mandates for public schools. In Thompson's conception, *Americanization* and *nationalization* were synonymous with *assimilation,* and the process included learning English and participating in America democracy. Americanization implied that immigrants would forget or reject the set of norms and values of their native culture and replace them with American norms and values. He was concerned with the methods used to teach immigrants, especially adult immigrants, and was concerned with the total effectiveness of America's methods of educating immigrants in both American language and in participating as citizens in American democracy.

Thompson indicated many of the problems arising in the Americanization process experienced by immigrants, child and adult. Adult immigrants could not be expected to be integrated into American society or be taught English through regular classes in the public school system. The issue of compulsory attendance of evening classes was discussed throughout the country, but a consensus was never achieved. The challenge was to make adult immigrants attend evening school and, once they voluntarily attended, to make the classes efficient and meaningful. Some of the problems faced by adult immigrants were related to the fact that learning is based on reading, and many adult immigrants, particularly immigrants from southern Europe, had lower rates of literacy than immigrants from western Europe. Adult immigrants who needed basic communication skills to improve their working conditions were sometimes annoyed by interminable drills to improve their accent, trying to satisfy their teacher's obsession with proper pronunciation. These and other methodological problems in the teaching of the English language to adult immigrants were critically evaluated by Thompson.

Adult immigrants got much help in their adaptation to the new culture and the English language from private organizations such as the Young Men's Christian Association (YMCA), which instructed immigrants in "free-enterprise values." Industrialists started an Americanization campaign with the intention of countering the influence of the growing labor movement. In 1915, the National Americanization Committee launched the "English First" project in Detroit. Employers such as Henry Ford made after-work-hours attendance mandatory for all foreign workers.

The idea of Americanizing immigrant children was challenging for Americans themselves, and in defining their own values more self-consciously in the process of teaching the newcomers, they realized that Americanization implied more than teaching the English language and civics lessons. It included erasing the past and history of the family of the immigrant children. It implied new personal habits—clean hands, use of the toothbrush, neat dress—and belonging to an idealized middle-class family and ultimately believing in the American dream. It also implied glorifying American history and heroes, and implied English was the only language through which to realize the America presented to the immigrants.

There were many critics of this model of Americanization for integrating the newcomer to American society. From the academic point of view, the model was less than perfect. It disoriented and frustrated children, who had to abandon their own language and adopt English. This was not an entirely benign process. Immigrant children who abandoned their native tongues were more likely to flounder in English-language classrooms. In 1908, 13 percent of immigrant children in New York City went to high school, compared with 32 percent of nonimmigrant whites.

Processes in the public school created some problems for the psychological well-being of the students. As early as 1908, Jane Addams, the founder of modern social work, voiced concern about the consequences that the process of assimilation would have on immigrant families. She suggested that the Americanization process would create problems within the family because it created a conflict of values and loyalties for children. Children were told that everything that constituted their parents' world, history, values, language, and culture needed to be forgotten and replaced by America and its history, values, language, and culture. This message undermined the authority of the family and contradicted one of the most important values taught by American public schools, which was respect and love for family. It was difficult for a child to conform to both sets of expectations. Growing up in an immigrant family is often marked by wide linguistic and other acculturative gaps between parents and children that can exacerbate intergenerational conflicts and cause the children to feel embarrassed rather than proud of their parents as they try to fit in with native peers.

PUBLIC SCHOOLS AND IMMIGRATION: AN ESSENTIALLY HETEROGENEOUS AMERICA

As the more diverse waves of immigrants settled in the United States, America started to look at itself as a diverse and pluralistic society. As this happened, assimilation implied something more complex and sometimes more difficult to achieve, as it involved, of necessity, respecting differences and valuing them, looking at them not as a problem but as a blessing. This changed perception of America affected the approach of public schools to the education of immigrants.

If, in the nineteenth century, the ideal was to erase from immigrant children's conception of the world the cultural values of their country of origin, at the beginning of the new millennium the situation is different. At this time, because of the nature of the more recent immigrants, the country has undergone a change from a relatively culturally homogeneous population to one of considerable cultural heterogeneity. At least in theory, public schools look at themselves as part of the adjustment process of the child and the family, trying in many cases to help students not only to adapt and succeed in American society, but also to keep and value their own culture.

Over time, public schools went from a position of absolute confidence in their ability to change both the culture and language of immigrant children to American culture and English to a more modest approach of being able to teach them English to facilitate their social adjustment. The failure of public schools to change both culture and language gave birth to speculations about "genetic deficiencies" of different races or "deficient" cultures, the latter illustrated by the so-called familism of the Hispanic population. These speculations were not scientifically tested and were used to explain the failure of the Americanization of certain ethnic groups and used as a justification to keep these groups economically subordinated. In the 1940s some educators started to realize the futility of coercive assimilation while opposing the idea of a genetic origin for underachievement by minority and immigrant students. It is in this context that cultural-deprivation theory pointed to environmental factors instead of genetic origins. Among others, these factors included parents' failure to stress academic attainment, so-called lower-class values (such as favoring living in the present instead of planning for the future), and inadequate English-language skills.

English as a Second Language (ESL) methodology,

developed in the 1930s to meet the needs of foreign diplomats and foreign university students, was prescribed for language-minority children and simply provides training in English for non-English speakers. ESL has an advantage over remedial reading because it takes into account the child's lack of oral English proficiency. Some authors consider ESL an improvement over sink-or-swim language instruction where no additional training in English is given, but others believe that by considering the student only as a non-English-speaker, ESL fails to use all the cultural background that minority or immigrant children retain from their own background and culture.

Bilingual education is another approach used to solve the problem of lack of English proficiency in minority and immigrant children. This method was used in educating Cubans who fled the Castro revolution of 1959 and resettled in Miami. The principle is to teach non-English-speaking children in their own language the curricula that English-speaking students get in English. There are many advantages in this method, including the higher quality of the knowledge that the students get when they are not constrained by struggling with a new oral and written language, but the opponents of bilingual programs claim, among other arguments, that given the number of nationalities and languages now present in classrooms in the United States, bilingual education is not a viable solution. As a result, many states have adopted ESL methods as the most efficient solution to the problem of English proficiency. Bilingual education was introduced by Title VII of the Elementary and Secondary Education Act, but the law did not require the school to use a language other than English to receive financial support, and as a consequence results of the application of the law were contradictory.

PUBLIC SCHOOL SYSTEM INTEGRATION OF IMMIGRANTS: INTERNAL PROBLEMS

At the beginning of the twenty-first century, the United States public school system faces several problems in accomplishing its task of integrating the children of the diverse immigrant population into American society. We can distinguish two main sources of problems faced by public schools in their goal to help the minority and immigrant students to become a part of American society: problems originating in the school environment, and those that are caused by fac-

tors related to students' individual, familial, or cultural backgrounds.

Problems that originate in the school environment include failure of the curricula and teaching methods to reach the multicultural audience (students from many different countries and cultures and speaking a variety of languages); teachers poorly trained in dealing with different cultural backgrounds present in the classrooms; budget problems (providing adequate resources in areas with an inadequate tax base, a common problem in the poor areas in which immigrants settle); lack of counselors, aides, and other staff with knowledge of the languages that are present in the classrooms; and problems associated with a backlash against immigrants.

In *Central American Refugees and U.S. High Schools*, a 1989 study of public schools with a significant immigrant population, sociologist Marcelo Suárez-Orozco examined Central American immigrant children in a major urban center in the western United States. His description of the schools in which he had observed Central American immigrant children in their first years of life in the United States reveals some of the problems that the public school system has to overcome in order to face the difficult task of integrating new immigrants into American society. The composition of the student body was representative of the majority, migrant and minority population of the country: Hispanic (33 percent), Chinese (20 percent), black (14 percent), Filipino (12 percent). To solve the problem of lack of English proficiency, ESL classes were taught, and some basic topics were taught in Spanish (for Central American students) rather than English. Even though the school had a large number of Hispanic, Chinese, and Filipino students, there were no bilingual counselors in any language. This was an important constraint for the students, who, because of their poor English ability, were additionally frustrated when they were placed in a mathematics or a science class of lower level than the one they needed and were capable of completing because of courses completed in their country of origin.

Not only did the curricula not include topics related in some way to the students' nationalities, but some teachers were not very informed about the cultural differences among students from different countries. For example, teachers were not always able to recognize differences between Hispanic students from the different Spanish-speaking countries. They were also not aware of the history of, or current events in, the students' countries of origin. In general, teachers did not pay much attention to cultural factors the students saw as important to their own self-image.

In general, the culture of the American classroom

is very different from the culture of the classroom immigrant students experienced in their native countries. Instead of a great deal of structure—dress codes, formal relations with teachers—American classrooms are far looser, often providing less discipline. For Salvadoran and Guatemalan students, the way in which students treat teachers in American schools is disrespectful and out of place. This situation can both embarrass and disorient students.

The factors mentioned by the students in Suárez-Orozco's study are common to most schools that have a significant population of immigrants and minorities and illustrate some of the inadequacies of public school systems in the way they deal with typical problems facing them as a result of having a diverse student population. Another reality faced by public schools in areas in which the students are predominantly minorities and immigrants is the increasing level of violence among students, the presence of gangs, and the sale and use of drugs within school facilities. For immigrant students who came to this country to escape the violence and the turmoil of civil war, as in the case of many Central American immigrants, this reality is more than uncomfortable. Students simply do not want to continue attending classes if they fear violence.

PUBLIC SCHOOL SYSTEM INTEGRATION OF IMMIGRANTS: EXTERNAL PROBLEMS

The second type of problem faced by the public school system is related to aspects of the personal, familial, and cultural background of the students. Immigrant children do not arrive in a vacuum. They bring with them their past, and they and the families in which they live bring with them their culture and their experiences in it. Some children have experienced trauma, stemming from having encountered violence in their native country. The immigrants' cultures have expectations of children's roles in the home, school, and community, expectations that are frequently gender-specific. When these expectations as conveyed within the family conflict with expectations conveyed by the school and community, the discord can be a source of trauma. Culture, the past, and the present situation all affect a child's day-to-day performance and are reflected in academic and social achievement.

Studies have demonstrated that the process of immigrating, particularly from regions of internal conflict, produces trauma in the child through various

mechanisms. One is simply the separation from loved ones necessitated by the move to a new country. Another is the witnessing of acts of violence, either in the home or as a consequence of civil war. A third is the shock of having to deal with a new and different culture. These traumatic events have been shown to result in family disruption and a variety of disorders, including mild to serious behavioral problems that would interfere with academic achievement and social integration of the immigrant children. Additionally, intergenerational discrepancies in the pace of adjustment between parent or guardian and children (children adjust faster than their parents) create family disruption. Other studies have demonstrated that learning difficulties and school failure were associated with behavioral disorders among immigrant children.

In his study of Central American refugees in American high schools, Suárez-Orozco found that the youngest children "seemed to succumb to the effects of the legacy of terror of Central America, the bad and overcrowded schools, the need to work, poor living conditions, lack of proper parental/community supervisors, or peer group pressure." Another problem is a lack of motivation, which led a number of students to lose interest in school. In some cases, older children are aware of the hardships that their parents have endured and feel that these sacrifices have been made so that the children could live in a more affluent society. Parents and other relatives wanted the students to stay in school and do well because the students had an opportunity they never had. The awareness of parental desires and sacrifices becomes a real psychological burden, interfering with academic achievement.

Another important problem originates in the perceptions that students, parents, and teachers have of each other based in their cultures; a related issue is the miscommunication that results in part from these perceptions and sometimes is further complicated by the lack of a common language. A recent study of Central American parents and Maryland public school teachers indicates some of the ways cultural differences and the lack of a common language affect perceptions and communication. Teachers believed that parents were uninterested in their children's education because the parents did not attend parent-teacher meetings or answer communications to them in English. The problem here was that the parents did not understand English and simply didn't understand the expectations that teachers have of the extent of parent involvement. Additionally, these parents felt that their major obligation to their children was to work and provide the resources for the children to attend school. From the parents' perspective, they feel that academic problems are the teacher's responsibility, because they are unable to do anything about academic matters such as their children having difficulties with English or helping their children with homework. A communication problem exists between the parents and teachers because of the "rule" that negative information about children is to be conveyed by the teachers in a positive context; because of cultural differences, the parents focused on the positive part of the message and did not get the negative part of the message.

Thus there are many individual, family, and cultural characteristics immigrants bring with them that can affect the effectiveness of the public school.

Throughout America's history, public schools have played a major role in integrating immigrants into American society. An important part of the integration process was the public school's insistence that the immigrant children learn English, and to a somewhat lesser extent that they learn the norms and values of American society. Adult immigrants learned much the same material as children, some of it through their children and less of it through the public schools and at different rates than the children. Because the characteristics of the immigrants changed over time from relative cultural homogeneity to cultural heterogeneity, different mechanisms had to be employed by the public school systems to produce an English-speaking populace with a common core culture, yet with a tolerance for some diversity.

Sara Z. Poggio

See also: Economics I: Pull Factors (Part II, Sec. 1); The Economic Debate Over Immigration (Part II, Sec. 7); Higher Education (Part II, Sec. 9); *Lau v. Nichols*, 1974, *Plyler v. Doe*, 1982, California Proposition 63, 1986, California Proposition 187, 1994, California Proposition 227, 1998 (Part IV, Sec. 1); New York State Report on Multicultural Textbooks, 1991 (Part IV, Sec. 2).

BIBLIOGRAPHY

Aronowitz, S. "The Social and Emotional Adjustment of Immigrant Children: A Review of the Literature." *International Migration Review* 23:2 (1988): 237–57.

Barrera, Mario. *Race and Class in the Southwest: A Theory of Racial Inequality.* Notre Dame, IN: University of Notre Dame Press, 1979.

Bernard, William. *The Acculturation of Immigrant Groups into American Society.* Montclair, NJ: Patterson Smith, 1971.

Crawford, James. *Bilingual Education: History, Politics, Theory, and Practice.* 4th ed. Los Angeles: Bilingual Educational Services, 1999.

Edmonston, Barry, and Jeffrey Passel. "Ethnic Demography: U.S. Immigration and Ethnic Variations." In *Immigration and Ethnicity: The Integration of America's Newest Arrivals,* ed. B. Edmonston and J. Passel. Washington, DC: The Urban Institute Press, 1994.

Hurwist, Judi, and Mary Sadler Tesconi, eds. *Challenges to Education: Readings for Analysis of Major Issues.* New York: Dodd, Mead, 1972.

Poggio, Sara. "Parental Perceptions of Problems Educating their Children: Central American Migrants to the Washington-Baltimore Area." Paper presented at the Midwest Sociological Society, Chicago, April 19–22, 2000.

Rumbaut, Ruben G. "Passages to Adulthood: The Adaptation of Children of Immigrants in Southern California." In *Children of Immigrants: Health, Adjustment, and Public Assistance,* ed. Donald J. Hernandez. Washington, DC: National Academy Press, 1999.

Suárez-Orozco, Marcelo. *Central American Refugees and U.S. High Schools: A Psychosocial Study of Motivation and Achievement.* Stanford: Stanford University Press, 1989.

Taft, R., and D. Cahill. *Initial Adjustment to Schooling of Immigrant Families.* Canberra: Australian Government Publishing Services, 1978.

Tyack, David. *Turning Points in American Educational History.* Waltham, MA: Blaisdell Publishing, 1967.

Vander Zander, James. "Sources of American Minorities." In *Challenges to Education: Readings for Analysis of Major Issues,* ed. Judi Hurwist and Mary Sadler Tesconi. New York: Dodd, Mead, 1972.

SOCIAL SERVICES

Social services, which are often provided by community-based organizations, are central to the management of the migration experience; to the reconstitution, formation, and management of immigrant networks and social capital; and to the socioeconomic adaptation and incorporation of immigrants to the new social structure. In the United States, there is a long history of immigrant groups, organizations, and aid societies that have provided a range of social services to immigrant populations. Social services to immigrant populations can be grouped into five main categories. First, there are general social services that involve a range of economic, social, and health services and programs. Second, there are immigration-related services. Third, organizations provide a range of community services that involve activities that lead to the development of networks among residents (or members of the ethnic/national origin group) and other organizations in the community with the purpose of developing the physical, social, cultural, and human resources of the population. Fourth, there are services for persons undergoing special circumstances. The fifth area of services includes services for specific subgroups of the population, which services are often based on age, gender, or sexual orientation.

HISTORY OF SOCIAL SERVICES TO IMMIGRANTS

In response to increased industrialization, urbanization, and migration there were significant efforts at the start of the twentieth century to develop social services to immigrant and other low-income populations. In her work, social activist Jane Addams and her collaborators explore the social history and provide the intellectual underpinnings of the settlement house movement, based mostly on the experiences of the Hull House in Chicago. Sociologist Albert Kennedy and his collaborators discuss and provide materials on the history of settlements in New York City and their social services. Historian Allen Davis also documents the history of settlement houses and their efforts to provide social and educational services to immigrants at the start of the twentieth century. He states that "the settlement house, at its best, became a social center, school, homemaking class, kindergarten, play and recreation center, and an informal housing and employment bureau." Most of the reform efforts involved the development of services and strategies to address the negative impacts of the convergence between advanced industrialization, concentrated urban poverty, and increasing immigration. Unlike many assimilationists and nativists, however, Jane Addams found social work compatible with respect for the culture and origin of immigrants. Historian Shpak Rivka Lissak says that Jane Addams "viewed with deep sympathy the cultural heritage of immigrants and encouraged them to preserve their national holidays and customs, their dress, their crafts and folklore."

SOCIAL SERVICES PROVIDED TO IMMIGRANT POPULATIONS

During the last few decades, community-based organizations (CBOs) have developed a range of social services for immigrant and nonimmigrant (often low income) populations. A survey conducted with a large sample of immigrant groups, organizations, and service providers in New York City revealed that community-based organizations render thirty-two different kinds of services to immigrant populations (see Table 1). Community-based social services can be grouped into five main categories. The first category is general social services, which involve a

Latino demonstrators hold up signs protesting California Proposition 187, a 1994 initiative that would have cut off social services to most undocumented immigrants. *(Jerome Friar/Impact Visuals)*

range of economic, educational, social, and health services and programs. The second category is specific immigration-related services that are provided exclusively to immigrant populations. The third category is organizations that are engaged in a number of activities, services, and programs that are not individual or family centered but instead involve the development of networks between residents and other organizations in the community with the purpose of developing the physical, social, cultural, and human resources of the neighborhood. The fourth category area of services includes services for persons with special circumstances or conditions. The fifth category of services includes services and programs for particular subgroups of the population, which are often based on age, gender, or sexual orientation.

Table 1
Social Services Provided by Immigrant Groups, Organizations, and Service Providers

Social services
  Benefits counseling
  Business counseling
  Educational services
  Employment & training services
  Family counseling/Case management services
  Food/Nutrition services
  General health services
  General legal services
  General social services
  Housing services
  Mental health services
  Substance abuse treatment
  Transportation assistance
Immigration-related services
  Citizenship services
  Immigration legal services
  Interpretation & translation services
Community services
  Community relations/Organizing/Advocacy
  Conflict resolution
  Cultural heritage
  Economic issues
  Labor rights & laws
Services for individuals and families in special circumstances
  Crime-victim services
  Disability services
  Domestic-violence services
  Emergency services
  HIV/AIDS services
Services for specific subgroups of the population
  Children's services
  Day-care services
  Gay/Lesbian issues
  Senior-citizen services
  Women's services
  Youth services

Source: Hector Cordero-Guzmán. "Assessing the Role of Community Based Organizations in the Socio-Economic Adaptation and Incorporation of Immigrants." Paper presented at the panel on *The Impact of Immigration on New York City* at the Annual Meetings of the Population Association of America, March 1999; Shirley Jenkins, ed. *Ethnic Associations and the Welfare State: Services to Immigrants in Five Countries.* New York: Columbia University Press, 1988; Nicholas A. Vace, Susan B. De Vaney, and Joe Wittmer, eds. *Experiencing and Counseling Multicultural and Diverse Populations.* New York: Taylor & Francis, 1995.

GENERAL SOCIAL SERVICES

General social services involves a wide array of economic, social, and health services and programs that are designed to improve the socioeconomic status of the population. Specific social services include (a) benefits counseling—advising individuals and families on what types of benefits, entitlements, and other programs they are eligible for and helps them to prepare an individual and family service strategy, assists in the preparation of forms, and advocates with other organizations and agencies on behalf of families and children; (b) business counseling—programs designed to help individuals who have small businesses, or entrepreneurs, with technical assistance and support in all aspects of managing their business including business plans, raising capital, accounting, inventory, and other aspects of management; (c) educational services—educational activities and programs such as Adult Basic Literacy (ABL), English as a Second Language (ESL), and General Equivalency Degree (GED) classes. Many organizations provide Adult Basic Education (ABE), ESL, and GED classes to their populations. Some organizations provide ABE or ESL programs from beginners to intermediate to more advanced classes, native language literacy services, and GED classes coordinated with other CBOs, or with nearby community colleges, with immigrants benefiting particularly from these kinds of services and programs; (d) employment and training (or workforce development) services—programs designed to prepare individuals for work and place them in employment. These programs range from short-term one- to three-week job-readiness programs where résumés, interview skills, and career expectations are emphasized, to six-month skills training in specific crafts and occupations; (e) family counseling/case management services—providing general advice, support, and counseling to families on personal issues, mental health, relations between family members, family problems, and related types of social work and case management; (f) food/nutrition services—food pantries, meal programs for children and the elderly, counseling on access to food stamps, nutrition programs, and access to child and infant nutrition programs; (g) general health services—access to primary care and family doctors for the prevention, diagnosis, and treatment of all health-related matters; (h) general legal services—free legal advice on matters related to program access and participation, personal issues, family issues, criminal matters, and other legal issues; (j) housing services—programs that increase access to home ownership, assessment of rental housing, weathering and renovation of apartments, tenant management, property management, and related housing services; (k) mental health services—mostly prevention and treatment programs and some emergency services; (l) substance abuse treatment—programs designed to prevent individuals from using controlled substances and for the treatment of substance abusers; and (m) transportation assistance—programs and services that provide transportation to schools, jobs, shopping, and other activities.

IMMIGRATION-RELATED SERVICES

Immigration services are a second type of social service provided to immigrant populations. Many organizations provide citizenship classes and immigration support services that help immigrants with the naturalization exam and many other aspects of the immigration process. These services include (a) citizenship services—the citizenship classes and support services necessary for the naturalization exam; civics classes and other services, programs, activities, and workshops designed to facilitate the adaptation and incorporation of immigrants into their communities and into the country; (b) immigration legal services—preparation of all of the legal paperwork involved in the immigration and naturalization process. Some of the services include legal advice and counsel; help with INS forms and procedures; certified fingerprinting; adjustment of status; alien relative petitions; visa extensions and advanced parole; work authorization; affidavits of support (I-864 and I-134); diversity lottery visas; replacement of green cards; and related services; and (c) interpretation and translation services—translation and interpretation of documents and other materials to and from English into and from other languages.

COMMUNITY SERVICES

A primary function of community-based organizations is to engage in a coordinated and sustained effort of "community building." Immigrant groups, organizations, and service providers are often engaged in activities, services, and programs that are not individual or family centered, but which involve the development of networks between residents and other organizations in the community with the purpose of developing the physical, social, cultural, and human resources of the community. There are several types of these kinds of community services and programs: (a) community relations/organizing/advocacy—advocating on behalf of the community and its members, or their ethnic national origin group; organizing residents and group members around issues of relevance and importance to the community; and advocating to elected officials, government bureaucrats, and others on issues of central importance to the community; (b) conflict resolution—programs aimed at teaching conflict resolution techniques and/or improving levels of information and knowledge between various groups that reside in a community in order to monitor and minimize tensions; (c) cultural heritage—art exhibits, theatrical productions, television, video, films, music, radio, and other kinds of festivals, productions, and activities of an artistic or cultural nature; (d) economic issues—programs related to community economic development and to the development of the economic and physical infrastructure of immigrant communities; and (e) labor rights and laws—programs designed to teach workers about labor rights and laws; advocate and negotiate with employers on behalf of workers; and, in some instances, issue claims for back wages, complaints for poor working conditions, and bring public attention to unscrupulous employers and unfair labor practices.

SERVICES FOR INDIVIDUALS AND FAMILIES IN SPECIAL CIRCUMSTANCES

Another set of services provided by community-based organizations involves programs for individuals undergoing special circumstances. These services include (a) crime victim services—support, guidance, and advice; (b) disability services programs related to access, awareness, and activities for persons with disabilities; (c) domestic violence services—programs related to prevention and counseling for victims; (d) emergency services—services for persons and families that have undergone or are undergoing traumatic events and other kinds of food, shelter, and health emergencies; and (e) HIV/AIDS services—programs related to prevention programs and support for individuals living with HIV/AIDS. This also includes programs that provide contact to countries of origin and arrangements for continuity of care, visits to relatives, and other related health and social services.

SERVICES FOR SPECIFIC SUBGROUPS OF THE POPULATION

The fifth main area of services involves services and programs for particular subgroups of the population, which programs are often based on age, gender, or sexual orientation. Included in this category are (a) children's services—programs for children from the ages of six to thirteen years of age; (b) day care services—activities and programs for children less than five years of age; (c) gay/lesbian issues—programs aimed at increasing awareness, information, services, and other supports; (d) senior citizen services—health, social and other services for seniors; (e) women's services—programs targeting women; and (f) youth services—programs for teenagers and young adults. Many organizations provide school system supports in order to help immigrant and non-immigrant parents to "navigate" the intricacies of the school system in the United States and to be more effective at helping their children achieve their potential in school. Youth services also include interventions and development programs for children and youth in school and after school, and interventions designed to ensure that children are receiving an adequate mix and level of in-school and after-school supports.

The immigrant social service delivery system varies by community depending on the history of the neighborhood's organizational structure, immigrant political networks, the involvement of the group with the existing service delivery system, the priorities of funders, and the characteristics and needs of the population. An analysis of service provision and language capacity among eight organizations in a high immigration area of Queens, New York, for example, found that most organizations provided benefits counseling, citizenship services, educational services, general social services, immigration legal services, and interpretation and translation services. On the other hand, very few organizations had programs dealing with conflict resolution, crime victim services, disability services, food/nutrition services, general health services, housing services, and substance abuse treatment. None of the agencies indicated that they provided business counseling, day care services, economic issues, emergency services, family counseling/case management services, gay and lesbian issues, general legal services, transportation assistance, and women's services, but there were other organizations in New York City that provided these types of social services, and many expressed an interest and need to develop these types of programs. Of the eight organizations, six indicated that they had licensed legal staff on-site, one indicated that it had licensed medical staff on-site, and three agencies indicated that they had licensed mental health staff on-site. In terms of coverage of languages spoken by staff of the various agencies, seven of the eight agencies indicated that there was someone on staff that spoke Spanish, three had staff that spoke Chinese (Mandarin), two had staff that spoke Korean, Hindu, and Italian, and at least one agency had staff that spoke Portuguese, Romanian, Arabic, Greek, Croatian, Japanese, French, Polish, Russian, Urdu, Haitian Creole, Pardo, Hebrew, and Turkish.

THE CHALLENGES OF SOCIAL SERVICE PROVISION TO IMMIGRANT POPULATIONS

Most of the discussed social services are provided both to immigrant and nonimmigrant populations, but the literature suggests that there are specific challenges associated with providing social services to immigrant populations. Some of these difficulties include language differences and barriers, differences in knowledge about social services, cultural sensitivity, awareness of the most appropriate method to deliver services, and recognition of some groups' particular needs. A review of the recent experiences of immigrant service providers indicates that there are three broad sets of challenges to immigrant service provision. The first set of challenges is related to the particular needs of immigrant populations. The second set of challenges relates to the role of organizations in providing services to immigrants. A third set of challenges emanates from complex changes in the social structure and in the policy environment.

CHALLENGES RELATED TO THE PARTICULAR NEEDS OF IMMIGRANT POPULATIONS

The first set of challenges faced by immigrant service providers has to do with culture and ethnic/national origin–specific practices. Ethnic/national origin groups differ in their social class background and in their socioeconomic characteristics, and these influence the amount and types of services that particular groups will need and seek. Second, groups differ in terms of their migration experience. Refugee populations, particularly those coming from countries where there are civil wars or famine, have often gone through traumatic experiences that need to be taken into account when assessing needs and providing services. Language is a third important factor that has to be considered by service providers. Service providers need to have staff that is capable of communicating with the clients, or potential clients, in order to competently assess needs and deliver services efficiently. Awareness of cultural differences in communi-

nication styles and manners is also central to effective service delivery.

Another set of factors that impact service delivery to immigrant populations involves differences in levels of experience with nongovernmental organizations (NGOs), the role of organizational services, and differences in the role of the civil society and the welfare state in the country of origin. Group differences in the premigration experience are also related to knowledge about social services, differences in what is considered a need or a problem, and differences in ways of dealing with needs and problems in the country of origin and in the new country. Lastly, organizations need to take into account a number of chilling effects that mitigate against immigrant access to social services and their main dimensions. Chilling effects have five main components: lack of knowledge about programs; lack of legal access to programs; loss of access due to changes in rules and regulations; denial of access (with or without cause); and fear of repercussions in the present or in the future for having received services or for having participated in particular programs. These factors make it more difficult for immigrants to access and receive needed social services.

ORGANIZATIONAL-LEVEL CHALLENGES

A second set of challenges that community-based organizations and other agencies face in providing services to immigrants is related to the characteristics, functioning, and capacities of service providers. First, in many organizations there is a need for more staff that has both professional and cultural competence. Culturally sensitive staff is central to the recruitment, monitoring, and effective delivery of services to immigrant populations. The second challenge faced by organizations relates to the lack of resources and funding for dedicated services to immigrant populations. Many organizations, particularly those servicing low-income populations, have a very high demand for services from individuals and families, but have very limited resources, and often lack general operating funds. Organizations also find it difficult to convince funders to undertake new (often more risky) initiatives. The limited funding that exists for particular programs for immigrants tends to come with many guidelines and extensive requirements for eligibility and reporting. And, while there are pressures from funding sources to specialize in particular services and populations, at the same time there is pressure from clients for organizations to provide more comprehensive social services. A third challenge faced by organizations in providing services to immigrants is the lack of knowledge about specific needs of certain immigrant groups, and lack of information about effective, culturally sensitive, and relevant ways to deliver services to particular populations. Many immigrant organizations suggest that there is a lack of appreciation among some mainstream providers of the particular needs of certain groups, and that it takes education, communication, and research to have certain needs and services recognized and addressed in immigrant communities.

CHALLENGES RELATED TO CHANGES IN THE SOCIAL STRUCTURE AND IN THE POLICY ENVIRONMENT

In addition to challenges related to culture and ethnic/national origin–specific practices (or the characteristics of clients), and organization-related challenges to service provision, there are elements of the social structure and the policy environment that impact social service delivery to immigrants. First is the sheer diversity of groups and the variety of needs that exist among immigrant groups. Organizations in many North American cities deal with a variety of populations coming from many parts of the world, some of whom are not familiar with American society and customs. Their challenge is to serve a multicultural population while being both inclusive of others and sensitive to the particular needs of specific groups. A second structural challenge relates to the lack of coordination that currently exists between social services in sending and receiving areas. The continuity of education experiences, health care, and other services is often interrupted by migration events and is compromised by the lack of contact between providers in sending and receiving areas. A third main challenge involves the interaction between immigrant organizations, service providers, and the political system. A social service is a valuable public good and organizations need political contacts to exert influence and to ensure that they are included in service contracts. Elected officials and government bureaucrats, on the other hand, have an interest in controlling aspects of the service delivery system. This can lead to a range of relations from patronage, to compromise, to hostility and difference in agendas, vision, and practice between elected officials and service providers. Lastly, recent changes in immigration and welfare policy have had a significant impact on social services to immigrant populations. The immigrant service delivery system suffered a shock in 1996 with the passage and implementation of the most sweeping changes in immigration and welfare policy in a generation. Immigrant community-based organizations, and the thousands of immigrant families and children that depend on various programs for their well-being, have had to adjust to the changes brought about by a more restrictive and punitive policy environment. As the demand for social services increased, many immigrants lost access to services in areas such as children's services, day care, education, food and nutrition, legal services, health services, mental health services, senior citizen services, substance abuse treatment, and youth services.

As immigrant communities emerge and grow immigrant families and children receive services from established social service agencies. However, as these communities develop better knowledge of the local service delivery system, a professional base of social workers and related social service personnel, and an ability to raise operating and program funds, they begin to form new organizations to provide a range of particularly needed services for their specific communities. The survival of immigrant organizations depends on the ability of social service providers to provide cost-effective services to their clients, their capacity to manage complicated changes in immigration and welfare policy, and their ability to establish a balance between services and advocacy, fundraising and self-sufficiency, and service to all constituencies versus targeted services.

Héctor R. Cordero-Guzmán

See also: Immigrant Aid Societies and Organizations (Part II, Sec. 2); Legislation II: Immigrants in America (Part II, Sec. 5); Poverty (Part II, Sec. 7); Health Care, Welfare and Public Benefits (Part II, Sec. 9); Personal Responsibility and Work Opportunity Reconciliation Act, 1996, *LULAC et al. v. Wilson et al.*, 1995, California Proposition 187, 1994 (Part IV, Sec. 1); Title IV: Restricting Welfare and Public Benefits for Aliens, 1996 (Part IV, Sec. 2).

BIBLIOGRAPHY

Addams, Jane, et al. *Philanthropy and Social Progress.* New York: Books for Libraries, 1893.

Archdeacon, Thomas. *Becoming American: An Ethnic History.* New York: Free Press, 1983.

Cardenas, Gilberto, and Antonio Ugalde, eds. *Health and Social Services Among International Labor Migrants.* Austin, TX: University of Texas Press, 1998.

Cordero-Guzmán, Héctor. "Assessing the Role of Community-Based Organizations in the Socio-Economic Adaptation and Incorporation of Immigrants." Paper presented at the panel on *The Impact of Immigration on New York City* at the Annual Meetings of the Population Association of America, March 1999.

———. "An Analysis of Socio-Economic, Demographic, and Community Characteristics, Immigration Services, and Social Services in Sunnyside and Surrounding Areas of Queens." Report prepared for Sunnyside Community Services, Queens, NY, November 1999.

Davis, Allen F. *Spearheads for Reform: The Social Settlements and the Progressive Movements, 1890–1914.* New York: Oxford University Press, 1967.

Davis, Allen, and Mary Bryant. *Eighty Years at Hull House.* Chicago: Quadrangle Books, 1969.

Jenkins, Shirley. *The Ethnic Dilemma in Social Services.* New York: The Free Press, 1981.

———, ed. *Ethnic Associations and the Welfare State: Services to Immigrants in Five Countries.* New York: Columbia University Press, 1988.

Kennedy, Albert, et al., eds. *Social Settlements in New York City.* New York: Columbia University Press, 1935.

Lissak, Shpak Rivka. *Pluralism and Progressives: Hull House and the New Immigrants, 1890–1919.* Chicago: University of Chicago Press, 1989.

Padilla, Yolanda. "Social Services to Mexican American Populations in the United States." In *Health and Social Services Among International Labor Migrants,* ed. Gilberto Cardenas and Antonio Ugalde. Austin, TX: University of Texas Press, 1998.

Vace, Nicholas A., Susan B. DeVaney, and Joe Wittmer, eds. *Experiencing and Counseling Multicultural and Diverse Populations.* New York: Taylor & Francis, 1995.

Woods, Robert A., and Albert J. Kennedy. *The Settlement Horizon.* New Brunswick, NJ: Transaction Books, 1990.

WELFARE AND PUBLIC BENEFITS

The question about the use of welfare services by immigrants and its negative impact on the economy has become a major social issue in the United States. Perhaps the most controversial issues in the debate revolve around the hypothesis that immigrants are more likely to participate in social services and have a higher probability of participating in the welfare programs than natives. Ultimately the key question becomes: Do immigrants contribute to or detract from the American economy? In 1996 the United States passed a law limiting the access of immigrants to welfare, Supplemental Security Income (SSI), Medicaid, and food stamps. This law represented a significant change in American attitudes toward immigration.

Professor Donald Huddle of Rice University has stated that these limitations also tightened the obligation of sponsors of immigrants to provide them with the basic essentials in case of illness or unemployment, and that immigrants continue to have access to expensive public services programs, such as health care and public education. Huddle further stated that in terms of fiscal implications, the annual net costs of public services to immigrants entering the United States rose from $42.5 billion in 1992 to an estimated $64 billion in 1996. The net costs were computed after accounting for local, state, and federal taxes paid by these immigrants. In testimony before the Ways and Means Committee of the House of Representatives, researchers Michael Fix, Jeffrey S. Passel, and Wendy Zimmermann argued that since Huddle estimated a net cost for immigration in 1992 of $42.5 billion, his underestimation of revenue by $50 billion offset the net cost from immigrants. According to them, immigrants show a net *surplus* across all levels of government, not a net *cost*. In his article "Immigration, the Issue-in-Waiting," George J. Borjas, a professor of public policy at Harvard University, examined one of the most contentious topics of debate in the United States. While analyzing the current immigration issue, he pointed out that immigrants were more likely to rely on public welfare and social services than natives.

In discussing the impact of immigrants on taxes and welfare, it is essential to distinguish the federal sphere from the state and local spheres, and first-generation immigrants from second-generation immigrants. In *Immigrants in New York: Their Legal Status, Incomes, and Taxes,* Rebecca L. Clark and Jeffrey S. Passel have argued that the bulk of tax contributions from immigrants goes to the federal government, while large costs, especially those associated with primary and secondary education, have fallen to the states. In New York, for example, of the $19.3 billion in taxes paid by immigrants in 1994, $13.3 billion (69 percent) went to the federal government. The remaining $6 billion (31 percent) went to state and local governments. Their study showed that most undocumented immigrants pay Social Security and income taxes. This suggests that the present economic system exploits undocumented immigrants, rather than the opposite. They also highlighted a problem in classification. Although native-born children of immigrants raise the cost of education, when these children become adults and begin working and paying taxes they are counted as natives. "The fiscal impacts of second-generation Americans, whether they are children or adult, should be attributed to the same group—to immigrants or to natives," Clark and Passel argued. "Counting second-generation Americans as immigrants when they are young and costly, but as natives when they start contributing taxes, biases analyses toward finding that immigrants are a fiscal burden." Professors George J. Borjas and Lynette Hilton, on the contrary, argued that the immigrant-native differences in the probability of receiving cash benefits is small, but the gap widens once other programs are included. Their argument led to the conclusion that immigrants are most likely to participate in social services and

Demanding extensions for families without jobs, Anglos and Asian Americans in Boston protest the new two-year limits on welfare payments. *(Marilyn Humphries/Impact Visuals)*

that they have a higher probability of participating in the welfare system than natives.

IMMIGRANTS TO THE UNITED STATES: A BRIEF BACKGROUND

Over the years, the flow of immigration into the United States has varied greatly (see Table 1). Immigration reached record levels in the decades before and after the turn of the twentieth century. Laws passed in the 1920s, however, lowered immigration by setting quotas on the number of immigrants each nation could send. Since the 1960s, when new immigration laws went into effect, large-scale immigration resumed. These laws, specifically the Immigration and Nationality Act of 1965, abolished the system of national origin that favored immigration from northern and western Europe and introduced numerical quotas

on immigration from the Western Hemisphere. The Refugee Act of 1980 made it possible for many refugees to enter the United States, and also made them eligible for federal social services. In addition, the Immigration Reform and Control Act of 1986 offered legal immigrant status to persons living illegally in the United States. These changes made family reunification and occupational skills the determining factors concerning who was allowed to immigrate.

Immigration since 1965 has come mainly from Asia, Mexico, and the Caribbean Islands. Table 1 shows that the number of legal immigrants coming to the United States during the 1980s—7.3 million—was surpassed previously only in the decade of 1901 to 1910, when 8.8 million immigrants arrived. Recent studies on immigration estimate that if refugees, special agricultural workers, and people granted political asylum are also added, then the number of immigrants in the 1980s was actually 10 million. The pace of immigration remained high in the 1990s. The Im-

Table 1
Immigrants to the United States, 1881–1990

Period	Immigrants admitted (000,000s)	Rate[1]	Percentage of population foreign-born[2]
1881–1890	5.25	NA	NA
1891–1900	3.7	NA	NA
1901–1910	8.8	10.4	NA
1911–1920	5.7	5.7	13.2
1921–1930	4.1	3.5	11.6
1931–1940	0.5	0.4	8.8
1941–1950	1.0	0.7	6.9
1951–1960	2.5	1.5	5.4
1961–1970	3.3	1.7	4.7
1971–1980	4.5	2.1	6.7
1981–1990	7.3	3.0	8.6

Source: U.S. Immigration and Naturalization Service, U.S. Bureau of the Census. *Statistical Abstract of the United States.* Washington, DC, 1991.
[1] Annual rate per 1,000 U.S. population.
[2] Includes both undocumented and documented foreign-born residents.

migration and Naturalization Service reported that the number of legal immigrants admitted in 1996 totaled 912,900—27 percent above the 720,461 immigrants admitted in 1995 and 14 percent higher than the 804,416 immigrants admitted in 1994. Most immigrants admitted as legal permanent residents were relatives of U.S. citizens (native-born or naturalized) or people granted admission based on their occupational skills. Some were allowed entry if they possessed advanced degrees or were wealthy investors.

In the 1980s and 1990s, immigration became increasingly controversial as Americans began debating whether immigrants were burdening taxpayers as a result of their use of public assistance. This controversy led to California's Proposition 187 in 1994. In this statewide referendum, California voters overwhelmingly approved restrictions on undocumented immigrants' access to public education, health care (except emergency medical services), and other social services. The ongoing controversy prompted Congress to pass the Personal Responsibility and Work Opportunity Reconciliation Act and the Illegal Immigration Reform and Immigrant Responsibility Act in 1996. This legislation made it easier to deport immigrants without documents, extended the list of crimes that led to deportation, and made it harder for long-standing residents to avoid deportation.

MOTIVATION FOR MIGRATION AND CONSEQUENCES

In the last few decades, a large increase of population movements from poor and politically unstable parts of the world toward the industrial countries of North America and Europe has taken place. Ideological and cultural links have drawn many immigrants to Europe from the continent's former colonies. For example, Vietnamese and Algerian emigration to France and Indian and Pakistani emigration to Britain were partly the result of their colonial past. In other European countries without much of a colonial history, such as Germany, immigrants arrived as guest workers, which meant that they were supposed to return to their home country when their labor was no longer required. Scandinavia, which consists of Norway, Sweden, and Denmark, recognized that many immigrants were unlikely to return home, and these countries made an official policy to accommodate them on the basis of equality. This meant that immigrants should have the same rights and obligations as natives. Norway went even further, allowing immigrants the right to vote in local and regional elections, thus making itself the first country to give noncitizen immigrants political rights. The Scandinavian countries have generally seen immigrants as permanent settlers who were to be assimilated or incorporated.

In the European economic climate of the last two decades, however, acceptance of immigrants has been less forthcoming. Immigrants have been seen as competitors for jobs and housing and often blamed for wider social problems. Calls for restriction on immigration and even repatriation for those who have already settled have also been voiced. The immigration problem in Europe is connected closely with the issue of how to deal with the escalating cost of the social welfare state and the effects of growing ethnic diversity on the societies of immigration countries. The people in these countries have demanded a restrictive immigration policy to control the influx of immigrants into their countries. In a national election in Austria in 2000, a radical right-wing party formed a coalition government by gaining considerable support for its anti-immigration views. In France, the government tightened citizenship requirements by removing automatic citizenship for children born on French soil to immigrant parents. In Germany, citizenship goes with the bloodline, making it almost impossible for a child born in Germany of a Turkish guest worker to become a German citizen. Controlling immigration has thus become a top domestic issue in Europe.

PUBLIC ASSISTANCE, EDUCATION, AND INCORPORATION

Both in Europe and the United States, public assistance and the expenditures made to assist immigrants remain a key factor in the immigration debate. Table 2 includes all immigrants to the United States from Asia, Africa, and the Western Hemisphere, including European immigrants. The table does not break down state expenditures into different categories or classify immigrants into different generations or groups. Immigrant and native rates of public assistance are compared by using two variables, individuals and households. Table 2 indicates that there is only a marginal difference between immigrants and their native-born counterparts in terms of receiving public assistance. This marginal difference could be explained by the initial hardship after immigration and other problems related to settling down in a new country. One recent New York study found that with their integration into American society, the welfare dependency of these immigrants would diminish. The study also concluded that immigrants pay roughly the same percentage of taxes and revenues as natives do. Economist John W. Isbister notes that "immigrants . . . occasion government expenditures in health, education, and welfare, but they also generate taxes. The immigrant/native difference in the probability of receiving welfare benefits is relatively small."

COSTS AND INCOME

Several post-1990 studies about the net costs of immigration to the United States indicate that immigrants, both legal and undocumented, do not come to the United States to use public benefits. These findings indicate that the level of public assistance received by immigrants is not much higher than that received by natives, and in some cases it is lower. These immigrants are in the workforce, and they pay taxes and Social Security contributions. Moreover, the American economy does not have to subsidize them during the "unproductive" period of childhood, as it does with natives. Therefore, these immigrants are likely to contribute more to society than they receive in benefits. Over time, many immigrants learn necessary skills, generate income, and rise economically. They thus help to finance such social services as housing, education, and old-age pensions for natives. Further, many jobs held by immigrants are created by immigrants to provide goods and services to other im-

migrants. Those jobs would not exist if immigrants were not here. Also, immigrants are consumers of goods and services provided by natives, and their presence creates jobs for other Americans. This holds for undocumented immigrants and refugees as well as for legal immigrants. If welfare use among refugees presents a problem, then it is a specific problem of refugee policy, rather than a general problem of immigration policy.

Little evidence supports the hypothesis that immigrants come to the United States to use public welfare. Existing federal and state laws prohibit undocumented immigrants from receiving public benefits. Legal immigrants are also denied food stamps, Medicaid, and Supplemental Security Income (SSI) for five years after their arrival. Asylum seekers whose appeal is pending have no claims to social services. Table 3 reflects the variation of public assistance at the state level, which ranges from 5.1 percent in New Jersey to 11.8 percent in California. In Florida and New York, 8.0 percent and 9.7 percent of immigrant households, respectively, receive public benefits. The welfare usage among native-born population was 5.4 in the case of New Jersey and 8.7 percent in California. For Florida and New York, the percentage of native-born receiving public benefits was 5.6 percent and 7.9 percent, respectively. For immigrants residing in New Jersey, levels of public benefits were slightly lower than those received by the native-born population. A study by Thomas J. Espenshade and Vanessa E. King in 1994 on New Jersey (see Table 2) shows the average amount of social welfare assistance received by native-born households was $1,838, while the average amount received by immigrant households was $1,780. Other studies have also found that the native-born receive more assistance than immigrants.

The data presented in this section were based on a few states and do not necessarily mean that the rate of public assistance for immigrants is much higher in the country as a whole. Table 2, however, provides a more general picture of the fiscal cost of immigration to the United States. In Table 2 it can be seen that the percentage and number of immigrants receiving public benefits on the national level are not much higher than those of the native-born. The 1990 census found that in 1989, 9.1 percent of the entire immigrant population and 7.5 percent of native-born households received benefits from social welfare programs. Fix, Passel, and Zimmermann found that in 1994, 6.6 percent of immigrants and 4.9 percent of the native-born received public assistance. Borjas and Hilton, however, compared the average welfare benefits received on a monthly basis in 1990–91 (Table 2) by native and immigrant households and found striking differences.

Table 2
The Net Fiscal Cost of Immigration to the United States: Legal Immigrants and Illegal Immigrants

Author(s)	Year	Legal immigrants (in billions)	Illegal immigrants (in billions)	Natives receiving welfare	Immigrants receiving welfare	Legal pop. (in millions)	Illegal pop. (in millions)	Area studied	Comments
Huddle	1993	$27	$19	—	—	—	3	National level	Assistance to refugees is included in this study.
Huddle	1994	$36	$19	—	—	—	4	National level	Immigrants constituted 7.5% of the U.S. population in 1993. They increased to 9.3% in 1996. This resulted in expanding costs of immigration. Assistance to refugees is included.
Huddle	1996	$40	$24	—	$2668 per immigrant	18	6	National level	The Huddle studies (1993, 1994, 1996) have estimated the net fiscal costs of immigration from a national perspective. Assistance to refugees is included.
Borjas	1994	—	—	8.6% (1990)	12% (1990)	—	—	California	The high percentage of the welfare rate is attributed to the number of undocumented aliens and their children born in the United States.
Espenshade/King	1994	—	—	$1,836 per HH* (1994)	$1,788 per HH* (1994)	3.3	—	New Jersey	Welfare benefits are not lower for natives.
Clark	1994	—	—	15%	12%	22	3.4	New Jersey	Cost of education for immigrants 11.8% (70% to legal immigrants and 30% to children of undocumented immigrants).
Espenshade/Rothman	1992	—	—	7.9% (1980)	8.8% in (1980)	—	—	National level	The difference is very slight.
Nancy Collins	1991	—	—	$1,310 per HH (1979)	$1,289 per HH (1979)	—	—	New Jersey	In this study native use of welfare is higher.
Fix, Passel, Zimmermann	1994	—	—	4.9% (1994)	6.6% (1994)	—	—	National level	Welfare benefits are higher for natives.
Borjas, Hilton	1995	—	—	6.5% (1990/91)	9.2% (1990/91)	—	—	National level	Welfare assistance to refugees is included in this table.
U.S. Census	1990	—	—	7.5% per HH (1989)	9.1% per HH (1989)	—	—	National level	On the national level the difference is marginal.

Sources: Donald Huddle. *The Net National Cost of Immigrants.* Washington, DC: Immigration and Naturalization Service, 1996; George Borjas. "Immigration and Welfare 1970–1990." Working Paper. San Diego: University of California, 1994; L. Rebecca Clark. *The Costs of Providing Public Assistance and Education to Immigrants.* Washington, DC: Urban Institute Library, 1994.
*HH = household

Table 3
Public Welfare—Percentage of Households Receiving Public Assistance in 1989

States	Native-born (%)	Immigrants (%)
New Jersey	5.4	5.1
Florida	5.6	8.0
New York	7.9	9.7
California	8.7	11.8

Source: U.S. Census, 1990.

For immigrants, 9.2 percent received food stamps, compared to 6.5 percent of natives. For SSI, Medicaid, and other assistance, 26.1 percent of immigrants and 16.3 percent of natives received aid. However, if SSI is measured separately, 0.8 percent of immigrants and 0.6 percent of natives received aid. This reveals that the gap between immigrants and natives is wider on some assistance programs than others. In a similar study of California in 1994, Borjas found that undocumented immigrants and their children and the most recent of immigrants are more dependent on welfare than others. The figures from researcher Rebecca L. Clark in Table 2 show that in 1994, immigrants nationally—excluding refugees, asylum seekers, and undocumented immigrants—received lower average welfare payments than did natives. If these categories are divided into different assistance programs, it can be seen that the average SSI payments to immigrants are 1.7 percent higher than those to natives. According to this study, the cost of educating immigrants and their children is $11.8 billion per year, 30 percent of which goes to educating the children of undocumented immigrants. Many critics of immigration point out that taxpayers' money spent on educating immigrant children could be utilized for some other public purpose.

Others, however, argue that the expenditure on education benefits society as well as immigrant children. The money spent on immigrant education goes to school administration, teachers, and others involved in the school system. Education is a form of human capital, and therefore the money spent on immigrants, refugees, and their children produces literacy and skills, which will ultimately benefit the American economy and society. Restricting access to public education will harm these children and likely cause greater problems to society in the future.

Incorporation, the process by which immigrants become integrated into American society, requires access to information and knowledge of the nation's laws, customs, and history. To incorporate successfully, immigrants must possess or develop skills and learn the English language. They also must become aware of their civil obligations and responsibilities. Such knowledge will raise their productivity and make them less likely to depend on the social welfare system. As sociologist Herman Kurthen points out, "Any measure that helps immigrants become fully integrated into the labor market and education system will decrease the fiscal burden of the welfare state." With immigration at peak levels, this burden will remain constant, and Americans will likely continue to debate the merits of the present-day cost of welfare and public benefits versus the long-range return of immigrant contributions to the economy.

Navid Ghani

See also: Immigrant Aid Societies and Organizations (Part II, Sec. 2); Children and Adolescent Immigrants, Elderly (Part II, Sec. 4); Legislation II: Immigrants in America (Part II, Sec. 5); Public Opinion and Immigration (Part II, Sec. 6); The Economic Debate Over Immigration, Poverty (Part II, Sec. 7); Health Care, Social Services (Part II, Sec. 9); Illegal Immigration Reform and Immigrant Responsibility Act, 1996, Personal Responsibility and Work Opportunity Reconciliation Act, 1996, California Proposition 187, 1994 (Part IV, Sec. 1); Title IV: Restricting Welfare and Public Benefits for Aliens, 1996 (Part IV, Sec. 2).

BIBLIOGRAPHY

Borjas, George. *Friends or Strangers: The Impact of Immigrants on the U.S. Economy.* New York: Basic Books, 1990.

———. "Immigration, the Issue-in-Waiting." *New York Times,* April 2, 1999.

———. "Immigration and Welfare, 1970–1990." Working paper. University of California, San Diego, 1994.

Borjas, George, and Lynette Hilton. "Immigration and the Welfare State: Immigrant Participation in Means-Tested Entitlement Programs." *Quarterly Journal of Economics* 111:2 (1996): 575–604.

Clark, L. Rebecca. *The Costs of Providing Public Assistance and Education to Immigrants.* Washington, DC: Urban Institute, 1994.

Clark, L. Rebecca, and Jeffrey S. Passel. *Immigrants in New York: Their Legal Status, Incomes, and Taxes.* Washington, DC: Urban Institute, 1998.

Espenshade, Thomas J., and Vanessa E. King. "State and Local Fiscal Impacts of U.S. Immigrants: Evidence from New Jersey." *Population Research and Policy Review* 13:3 (1984): 225–56.

Fix, Michael, and Jeffery S. Passel. *Immigration and Immigrants: Setting the Record Straight.* Washington, DC: Urban Institute, 1994.

Fix, Michael, Jeffrey S. Passel, and Wendy Zimmermann. "The Use of SSI and Other Welfare Program for Immigrants." Testimony before the House of Representatives Ways and Means Committee, May 23, 1996.

Habermas, Jürgen. "Citizenship and National Identity: Some Reflections on the Future of Europe." *Praxis International* 12 (1992): 1–9.

Huddle, Donald. *The Net National Cost of Immigrants.* Washington, DC: Immigration and Nationalization Service, 1996.

Isbister, J. *The Immigration Debate: Remaking America.* Bloomfield, CT: Kumarian Press, 1996.

Immigration and Naturalization Service. *Characteristics of Immigrants: Statistical Year Book of the Immigration and Naturalization Service.* Washington, DC, 1998.

Kurthen, H. "Germany at the Crossroads: National Identity and the Challenges of Immigration." *International Migration Review* 29:4 (1995): 914–38.

———. "Immigration and the Welfare State in Comparison: Differences in the Incorporation of Immigrant Minorities in Germany and the United States." *International Migration Review* 31:3 (1997): 721–31.

Ministry of Labor and Local Affairs. *Migration and Multicultural Norway.* White Paper no. 17. Oslo, 1996–97.

Portes, A., and Rubén G. Rumbaut. *Immigrant America.* Berkeley: University of California Press, 1996.

Report to Congressional Requester. *Illegal Aliens.* Washington, DC: Government Printing Office, 1995.

Senate Subcommittee on Human Resources. "The Impact of Immigration on Public Welfare Programs." Washington, DC, November 1993.

CULTURE AND SOCIETY

INTRODUCTION

The entries in Part II, Section 10 of the *Encyclopedia of American Immigration* are devoted to culture and society. Most of the entries concern immigrant contributions to media, arts, and popular culture. They include three separate articles on the arts: literature, performing, and visual. In addition, there are entries on the immigrant press, as well as television, film, and radio. Other entries discuss immigrant participation in the sciences and sports. There are also entries on language, both foreign and English as a Second Language. The article on genealogy looks at the fascination Americans have in tracing their immigrant roots. Finally, there is an entry on the way in which immigrants are portrayed in the media.

In "Arts I: Literature," Kanta Kochhar-Lindgren explores the rich tradition of immigrant writings in America. The author provides a rundown of the many immigrant groups in America, highlighting some of the better-known authors and works in each. In a second entry, Kochhar-Lindgren does the same for the immigrant performing arts tradition.

In the next entry, Akel Kahera looks at a specific type of visual art within recent immigrant communities: the religious structure. The author examines the various styles of mosques, synagogues, and Eastern religion temples created within these neighborhoods.

In the entry on English as a Second Language, Pamela Boehm examines the various programs that have been developed to teach the subject from the elementary level through adults. Boehm also discusses the various theories that linguists have developed concerning the learning of English and other languages. In addition, she considers the various teaching techniques employed by English instructors.

In "Film, Radio, and Television," James Castonguay explores the various roles played by immigrants in these media, including as producers, directors, actors, writers, and other personnel. The author examines the subject both in its historical context and

today, looking at the ways in which immigrants have fit into and altered the various media in the United States.

In her article on genealogy, Jennifer Harrison begins by discussing how genealogical research is conducted, as well as the various places genealogical records exist. In addition, the author examines the obstacles to such research.

The entry on language by Benjamin Bailey begins with an exploration of language shifts across immigrant generations before moving on to a discussion of second-generation bilingualism. Next, Bailey delves into history, examining why English became the dominant language in the United States. The author also discusses how immigrants adapt to American English and looks into the language rights of ethnic minorities in this country. In addition, Bailey explores the question of linguistic nativism, both in its contemporary and historical contexts. Finally, the author considers the relationship between language and identity among immigrants, as well as how language adaptation affects acculturation and economic mobility.

In "Media Portrayal of Immigrants," Paul Magro explores how the various media in America have looked at and presented immigrants and immigrant life to their audiences. Beginning with a historical overview of immigrants on the American stage and in American literature, the author also discusses the portrayal of immigrants in movies and television.

In the entry on immigration's impact on popular culture, Michael Lloyd Gruver provides a decade-by-decade discussion of how immigrants have gradually introduced America to cultural influences from around the world.

The entry on the press by Bénédicte Deschamps examines the history of the immigrant press in America, as well as its contemporary situation. The author begins by considering the problems of defining what an immigrant press actually is before examining the functions of the ethnic press. Deschamps also covers the numbers and different types of immigrant publications, as well as offering a brief history of the immigrant press from colonial times to the present.

In his entry on science, I. Steven Krup, J.D., starts off by looking into immigration law and scientists be-fore offering a detailed rundown of the contributions that immigrants have made to American science.

Matt Clavin's entry on sports also provides a de-tailed rundown of the many contributions made by immigrants to both amateur and professional sports in America, historically and today.

ARTS I: LITERATURE

Since the 1960s there has been increasing attention to immigrant literature in the United States. In addition to the civil rights and women's movement, the increased number of immigrants who came to the United States as a result of the Immigration and Nationality Act of 1965 has precipitated this interest in multiple perspectives and diverse voices. Along with the growing recognition of the rights of African Americans, Hispanic, Native Americans, and Asian Americans also demanded acknowledgment of their rights, and with their increasing inclusion in the public sphere, there has been a proliferation of immigrant voices and immigrant literature. As various ethnic groups, including white ethnicities, have examined their disparate histories, the organizing metaphor for marking this new cultural moment has shifted from the "melting pot" to the mosaic, a model for heterogeneous exchange.

Early in this developing discussion, the immigrant literature tended to be viewed as that coming from European immigrants or their American-born children, and it typically included such texts as O. E. Rölvaag's *Giants in the Earth* (1927), Upton Sinclair's *The Jungle* (1906), Anzia Yezierska's novels and short stories, and the novels of Michael Gold and Henry Roth. Other immigrants—such as Asian, Hispanic, and West Indian—were viewed as minorities, not as immigrants. However, the work of writers from these immigrant groups and particularly women such as Maxine Hong Kingston and Sandra Cisneros, who were born in the United States, and Bharati Mukherjee, eventually came to be included in the discussion.

Each of the historical, political, and social circumstances surrounding the immigrant's frame of reference has differed, but, as a genre, immigrant literature tends to deal with the complexities of negotiating becoming American. Immigrants have come to the United States for a variety of reasons, and these rationales, ranging from economic issues to religion, adventure, political persecution, or wives who often had no choice, influenced the process of becoming American. Immigrants had a variety of factors to deal with—the ties one felt to the homeland, the ensuing sense of dislocation, and the political and social frames affecting life in the United States.

As immigrant literature has developed within a particular group, the thematic focus and development has tended to fall into three stages. The first generation often deals with maintenance of loyalty to the homeland. The second generation of writers tends to address issues related to the tensions between their parents' values and those of the American mainstream. The questions of assimilation are, of course, vastly complex, and it is worth noting that European immigrants could choose to become U.S. citizens but this was not an option for Asian immigrants until after World War II, although the children born here were considered legal citizens. The third generation of writers often focuses on a multiple identity that recognizes and grapples with the complexities of one's background and the American cultural landscape.

ARAB-AMERICAN LITERATURE

Though early generations of Arab Americans worked to present their foreignness in respectable ways, subsequent generations became more invested in passing as "regular" Americans. As a result, they generated less literature. Since World War II there has been a renewal in ethnic consciousness. Arab-American writers continue to examine their cross-cultural positions, and, within that arena, concern and guilt about the Middle East Arab-Israeli conflict has been prevalent.

Ameen Rihani is considered the first great Arab American writer, the founder of "Adab Al-Mahjar" (immigrant literature). His best work, *The Book of Khalid* (1911), is a satire about a young Arab man who is exiled from home and goes to America, but who eventually returns to Lebanon. Thematically, the work deals with reconciling issues surrounding matter and spirit and East and West. A prolific writer, Rihani's work included essays, poetry, short stories, art critiques, and twenty-nine volumes in English. Rahini also did a considerable amount of writing in Arabic, and having been influenced by Walt Whitman, he introduced the notion of free verse into Arab poetry. Rahini was a mentor to another well-known Arab-American writer, Kahlil Gibran, who wrote *The Prophet* (1923).

Later works turn from interest in, and attachment to, the homeland to issues related to immigration and to questions related to identity in a society often suspicious of Arabs and Asians. *Which Way to Mecca, Jack?* is an autobiography by William Peter Blatty (who also wrote *The Exorcist*), tracing the author's life as a young Arab American during his two-year stint at the U.S. Information Agency, and his impersonation in Hollywood as an Arabian prince, Prince Khairallah el Aswad el Xeer. Eugene Paul Nassar's *Wind of the Land* is an autobiography in poem form that centers on his interest in maintaining his ethnic roots. Leading Arab-American poetry has been collected in two anthologies, *Wrapping the Grape Leaves: A Sheaf of Contemporary Arab-American Poets* (1982), and *Grape Leaves: A Century of Arab-American Poetry* (1988), as well as work by Naomi Shihab Nye.

More current Arab-American novels attempt to deromanticize the Arab in the United States and look more objectively at the complexities of leading bicultural lives. Elmaz Abinader's *Children of Roojme, A Family's Journey from Lebanon* (1991), for example, tells Abinader's family story of the fight for survival for three generations during the first half of the century. Diana Abu-Jaber's *Arabian Jazz* (1993) deals with the Ramouf family, which lives in upstate New York, and the issues that develop around the efforts to get one of the daughters married. Joseph Geha's *Through and Through: Toledo Stories* (1990) is a set of stories that range from the 1930s to the present about an extended Arab family in an Arab neighborhood in Toledo, Ohio.

ARMENIAN-AMERICAN LITERATURE

Significant Armenian immigration first took place during the nineteenth century, and much Armenian writing was circulated through the Armenian newspapers. Armenian Americans who came to the United States from 1880 to 1925 faced considerable prejudice. Additionally, the genocide of the Armenians in Tur-

key in 1915 forms a central backdrop for much of Armenian letters, though not all Armenian diasporas are linked to this event.

William Saroyan (1908–1981) is the most well known Armenian-American writer. Early works by Saroyan deal with the "crazy" Armenian. *Rock Wagram* (1951) features Arak Vagranian, who is raised in the Armenian community of Fresno, California, by immigrant parents and his grandmother. Arak, who has trouble accepting his parents' culture, eventually leaves home and pursues a career in film, taking on the stage name of Rock Wagram. Saroyan's *My Name Is Aram* (1940) focuses on Aram's telling of his stories about growing up in an Armenian immigrant family.

Peter Sourian's *The Gate* (1965) deals with the unresolved tensions among three generations of men in the Stepanyan family: Paul, a writer; his father Sarkis, an MIT-trained engineer; and his grandfather Vahan, who survived the Turkish massacres. In *Voyages* (1971), by Peter Najarian, the main character, Aram (after Saroyan's *My Name Is Aram*), lives in a New Jersey tenement and later a Lower Manhattan apartment. He seeks to come to terms with his Armenian past; however, his father has been paralyzed by a stroke, and like Aram, has no memories. Among other Armenian-American works, *Daughters of Memory* (1986) by Peter Najarian, deals with an Armenian-American artist's search for the "elusive essence of eternal woman." *Passage to Ararat (Hungry Mind Finds)* (1975), by Michael Arlen, is about his quest to find out why his father keeps his Armenian identity a secret. Carol Edgarian's *Rise the Euphrates* (1994) revolves around three generations of women who live in the Connecticut town of Memorial and the ways in which the granddaughter is caught between the world of her grandmother—who survived the Armenian massacres—and her mother.

Armenian-American poets include Michael Akillian (*The Eating of Names: Poems*, 1983), Peter Balakian (*Bloody News from My Friends: Poems*, 1996), and Diana Der Hovanessian (*Any Day Now*, 1999; *Circle Dancers*, 1997).

CHINESE-AMERICAN LITERATURE

Chinese immigrants to the United States faced considerable racism. The confluence of Chinese and American culture, as exhibited in the literature, reflects an examination of questions about different cultural traditions and an investment in the warrior tradition, as well as geographic and cultural differences.

Songs of Gold Mountain (in two volumes, 1911,

Maxine Hong Kingston is one of the country's best-selling Chinese-American authors. *(Jane Scherr)*

1915) is a collection of poems on racist experiences faced by Chinese immigrant laborers at the turn of the century. Sui Sin Far (Edith Maud Eaton) (1867–1914), the daughter of a Chinese mother and an English father, wrote extensively about the Chinese-American experience, particularly for newspapers. A number of her stories were collected into a book, *Mrs. Spring Fragrance* (1912).

The next series of Chinese-American works deal with the pull between the demands of the parents to remain true to their cultural background and that of the American mainstream. Some examples include Pardee Lowe's *Father and Glorious Descendent* (1943) and Jade Snow Wong's *Fifth Chinese Daughter* (1950). Wong tells the largely autobiographical story of a girl growing up in a traditional Chinese family in San Francisco in pre–World War II Chinatown and who wants to go to college and have more freedom than was typically accorded Chinese women. Louis Chu's *Eat a Bowl of Tea* (1961) deals with the bachelor society

in Chinatown, pushed toward change by the presence of a Chinese girl brought in by an impotent bachelor.

The next group of works strives to articulate the Chinese-American identity. In 1969, Jeffrey Chan, Frank Chin, and Shawn Wong formed a writers' collective and edited the first major anthology of Asian-American literature, called *Aiiieeeee! An Anthology of Asian American Writers* (1974). Frank Chin's works include *The Chinaman Pacific and Frisco R. R. Co.* (1988) and *Donald Duk* (1991). The latter is about an eleven-year-old boy named Donald who hates his Chinese heritage, but with the aid of his uncle, who is a Peking Opera performer, and the exchange of a variety of stories with his father and a white friend his age, Donald comes to terms with his background.

Maxine Hong Kingston's *The Woman Warrior: Memoirs of a Girlhood Among Ghosts* (1976) revolves around the experience of a Chinese girl growing up in the Chinese-American community and attending both public and Chinese schools. It includes the stories she hears about her aunt who disgraced the family, her mother while in medical school, and a legendary woman warrior and hero. Kingston's *China Men* (1980) focuses on historical stories from the mid-nineteenth century to the present, and *Tripmaster Monkey* (1990) centers on issues related to the presence of Asian Americans and the arts.

Jeffrey Paul Chan's stories include "Jackrabbit" (1974), "Auntie Tsia Lays Dying" (1972), and "The Chinese in Haifa" (1974). Shawn Wong's *Homebase: A Novel* (1979) is about a fourth-generation Chinese American and how he comes to terms with his Chinese-American identity through stories about some of his relatives, such as his great-grandfather, who came to the United States in the 1860s to work on the railroad.

Other works include Nieh Hua-ling's *Mulberry and Peach: Two Women of China* (1988) and Yu Li-Hua's *See the Palm Trees Again* (1966). Amy Tan's *Joy Luck Club* (1989) consists of sixteen interlocking stories about mothers growing up in China and daughters growing up in Chinatown in San Francisco. *The Kitchen God's Wife* (1991) is the story of a woman's experiences in China during World War II and her marriage to a corrupt military officer.

Gish Jen's *Typical American* (1991) deals with Ralph Chang, who comes to the United States for a university education but quits school in order to run a take-out business. *Mona in the Promised Land* (1996) centers on Mona Chang, who, after deciding to switch to Judaism and becoming known as Changowitz, must negotiate among multiple ethnicities.

CARIBBEAN-AMERICAN LITERATURE

Caribbean-American literature reflects grappling with a 500-year reign of violence, due to domination first by Spain and then the United States. Lots of attention has been paid to recovering or imagining a past in the absence of records, and these efforts reflect the concern with image of the diaspora as well as raise questions about identity. The first wave of writers comes from the first three decades of the twentieth century, and they emerged from the working and landless classes who then became landlords, professionals, and businesspeople. Claude McKay, who dealt with issues of class and ethnicity as well as the oral culture and the poetry of the underclass, was a central presence in the Harlem Renaissance of the 1920s. McKay's *Home to Harlem* (1928) traces the parallel lives of two very different young men. Ray, the son of a prominent Haitian official, goes to Howard University, quits, and takes a job as a railroad porter. During that process, Ray meets Jake, an American black, looking for a good time in the Harlem jazz clubs. Other works by McKay include *Banjo: A Story Without a Plot* (1929) and *Banana Bottom* (1933).

The second wave of writers deals with the concepts of Empire and Englishness and includes Wilson Harris from Guyana and Edward Kamau Braithwaite and George Lamming from Barbados. Lamming's *In the Castle of My Skin* (1953) deals with his story about growing up in Barbados. When the unrest in Trinidad spills over to Barbados, Lamming goes to America; there he is struck by a sense of lost racial heritage. Other works include Derek Walcott's *The Arkansas Testament* (1987) and V. S. Naipul's *A Turn in the South*.

The third wave of Caribbean-American writers dates from 1960s to the present, many of whom are artists, writers, and academics. This group reflects the influence of Caribbean oral culture on their writing; additionally, the role of women is much more visible. Paule Marshall's *Brown Girl Brownstones* (1959) is a story about Selina Boyce, who lives in Brooklyn with her husband and daughter. Her husband is a womanizer, and he wants to go back to the Caribbean. He eventually joins a religious society. Audre Lorde's *Zami: A New Spelling of My Name: Biomythography* (1982) is an autobiography about Lorde's early years as a writer and as a black lesbian in New York City. Jamaica Kincaid has written the critically acclaimed *Lucy* (1991) and *My Brother* (1997).

Cuban-American author Oscar Hijuelos won the Pulitzer Prize for literature in 1990 for his novel *The Mambo Kings Play Songs of Love*. (Sigrid Estrada)

CUBAN-AMERICAN LITERATURE

Cuban-American literature reflects a strong interest in testing the limits of language and writing. These authors focus on metaphor, music, and the island's tangled history with the United States. Cuban-American writers are divided into several groups: those who left Cuba before the revolution, such as Alejo Carpentier; those who left as children of immigrants, such as Gustavo Perez-Firmat and Pablo Medina; and those who grew up in the United States, such as Oscar Hijuelos, Christina García, and Elías Miguel Muñoz. There are also those Cuban-American writers who grew up during the revolution but who left much later, such as Reinaldo Arenas. Cuban-American writers often have to deal with two issues once they leave—the stance they take among themselves regarding their relationship to their home island as well as the way that they do not easily fit into the Latino populations in the United States.

Alejo Carpentier's *Our House in the Last World* (1987) is the story of Alejo Santini, who helps get money together for the freedom fighters, an act that his sister and family resent. In contrast, his son remains tied to the old Cuban community.

Christina García's *Dreaming in Cuban* (1992) is about three generations of women in the del Pino family: Celia, the matriarch, who grew up in pre-Castro Cuba and stayed after the revolution, a loyal supporter of Castro until the 1980s, and her two daughters, Felicia and Lourdes. The first practices santería magic; the other leaves her husband and goes to New York.

Oscar Hijuelos's *Mambo Kings Play Songs of Love* (1990) revolves around two musician brothers who leave Cuba, and whose career highlight is to meet Desi Arnaz. *Empress of the Splendid Season* (1999) is the story of Lydia Espera, who grew up in pre-Castro Cuba. After defying her father she is banished to New York, where she marries, raises a family, and spends her life as a cleaning lady.

Ricardo Pau-Llosa's *Bread of the Imagined* (1992) is a collection of poems. *Exiled Memories* (1990) by Pablo Medina deals with issues related to linguistic invasion in the way that the United States came to the Cuba.

DOMINICAN-AMERICAN LITERATURE

Often neglected by critics and reviewers, Dominican-American literature is not written in or translated into English. Most immigration to the United States began with the 1961 assassination of General Rafael Trujillo and the April revolution of 1965 when U.S. Marines invaded. Much Dominican-American literature focuses on creating a home through the use of language, and it also deals with the fears and anxieties of living under the Trujillo regime.

In *Labyrinth* (1959), Enrique Laguerre tracks the murders of journalist Andre Requena in 1952 and the 1956 disappearance of Columbia University professor Jesús de Galíndez as he was entering a New York subway station. Viriato Sención's 1992 *They Forged the Signature of God* is a story that takes place during the final years of the "Tirano" or tyrannous regime, and it centers on a seminary student, Antonio Bell, who is imprisoned at the school for his protest against the dictatorship. Julia Alvarez's *How the García Girls Lost Their Accent* (1992) centers on the lives of four Dominican-American daughters of the Garcia family and how they embrace American culture.

FILIPINO-AMERICAN LITERATURE

Filipino-American literature reflects a particular set of issues in immigrant literary discourse, and how the tensions between postcolonial discourse and the immigrant experience converge. During the first wave of immigration from 1906 to 1946, the Philippines were a colony of the United States, and citizenship remained elusive for Filipino immigrants. The Philippines gained independence in 1946, and the second large wave of immigration occurred from 1965 to 1984, a period influenced by the instability of the Ferdinand Marcos regime.

Carlos Bulosan's *America Is in the Heart* (1946), a semiautobiography, deals with the experiences of Filipino men coming to the United States in the 1920s and 1930s. After terrible travel experiences across the sea, the men still arrived with hope, but this sense shifts after they end up in a cannery in Alaska where they must fend for themselves in a hostile environment. Bulosan also deals with the tales of young men who emigrate from the Philippines in *If You Want to Know What We Are* (1983).

Jessica Hagedorn is one of the more well known contemporary Filipino-American writers. Some of her books include *Dangerous Music: The Poetry and Prose of Jessica Hagedorn* (1975) and *Pet Food and Tropical Apparitions* (1981), a narrative about gender switching and a young woman who wants to be a writer. *Dogeaters* (1990) tells the story of a Filipino girl, already involved in American culture, who comes to the United States. At first she does not experience any alienation, but learns later that she does not really feel at home in either culture.

Linda Ty-Casper's *Dread Empire* (1980), *Fortress in the Plaza* (1985), *Awaiting Trespass: A Passion* (1985), *Wings of Stone* (1986), and *Ten Thousand Seeds* (1987) chronicle the stories of resistance to colonization from the 1896 rebellion against Spain to the turmoil of the Marcos era. Other works inlcude Michelle Cruz Skinner's *Balikbayan, A Filipino Homecoming* (1988), Ninotchka Rosca's *State of War* (1988) and *Twice Blessed* (1992), Marianne Villanueva's *Ginseng and Other Tales from Manila* (1991), and Peter Bacho's *Cebu* (1991), a story about a Filipino-American priest and his need to bury his late mother in the Philippines. New poets include Vince Gotera, Eugene Gloria, and Alfred Encarnacion.

GREEK-AMERICAN LITERATURE

Greek-American literature dates from the nineteenth century, beginning with personal narratives that mediate between America as an exotic locale and America as a modern nation. Some of these works include John Stephanini's *Personal Narrative* (1827), Christophorus Castanis's *The Greek Exile* (1851), Demetra Vaka Brown's *Haremlik* (1909), and George Demetrios's *When I Was a Boy in Greece* (1913).

Theano Papzoglou Margaris (1909–1991) was the first Greek American to explore the immigrant motif and the tensions between the old and new worlds. Since World War II, the writing has become more experimental and the immigration story not as common. Other works that question the concept of "Greekness" include Kimon Lolos's *Respite* (1961), Stratis Haviaras's *When the Tree Sings* (1979), Nicholas Gage's *Eleni* (1983), Irina Spanidou's *God's Snake* (1986), and Olga Broumas's *Beginning with O* (1977).

INDIAN-AMERICAN LITERATURE

Indian-American literature is very young—in part because "Asian Indian" was not viewed as a separate ethnic category until the 1986 census. Additionally, large numbers of Indians did not begin to come to the United States until the 1960s. Indian-American literature often centers on how to balance a dual affiliation between the homeland and the present. Because of the educational and economic level of current Indian-American writers, they tend to chronicle the hopes and conflicts of the middle class.

Bharati Mukherjee is one of the most well known Indian-American writers, and, in general, her work tracks the transition from expatriate/exile to immigrant/citizen. Her works include *The Tiger's Daughter* (1971), *Wife* (1975), *The Middleman and Other Stories* (1988), and *Jasmine* (1989), about an illegal alien and the pressure on her to assimilate. *The Holder of the Word* (1994) reverses the trajectory and looks at how an American woman could survive in India in the seventeenth century.

Meena Alexander, who grew up in India and Sudan, has written *Fault Lines* (1993), which focuses on the disorientation of a woman without a history, and *House of a Thousand Doors* (1988). Other works include Indira Ganesan's *The Journey* (1990) and Abraham Verghese's *My Own Country: A Doctor's Story* (1994), which concerns his work as a doctor in eastern Tennessee. Agha Shahid Ali's poetry includes *The Half-Inch Himalayas* (1987) and *A Nostalgist's Map of America* (1991).

IRANIAN-AMERICAN LITERATURE

For Iranian writers there is already a long history of displacement and exile of Persian literati having to work outside their country. Nevertheless, many writers have felt attached to the native language and maintaining ties to the Persian culture from a distance. In the last two decades that attitude has changed somewhat, and more Iranian Americans are writing in English.

Works by Iranian-American writers include Taghi Modarressi's *The Book of Absent People* (1986) and *The Pilgrim's Rules of Etiquette* (1989). Though he writes in Farsi, his works are translated into English, and he is particularly interested in the power of the accented voice that carries a hidden message. Nahid Rachlin's *Foreigner* (1978) deals with the culture shock that Feri experiences when first coming to the United States and also when she returns to Iran some years later for a visit. Rachlin's other works include *Married to a Stranger* (1983) and *The Heart's Desire: A Novel* (1995). Gina Barkhordar Nahai's *Cry of the Peacock* (1991) deals with Iranian Jews from 1796 to 1982, and her *Moonlight on the Avenue of Faith* (1999), written in the style of magic realism, is the story of Roxana, who is born in Tehran and ends up in Los Angeles. Bahman Sholevar's two collections of poetry, *Rooted in Volcanic Ashes: Collection of Poems* (1987) and *Making Connections: Poems of Exile (1979)*, depict his wanderlust.

IRISH-AMERICAN LITERATURE

Early Irish-American writing cast the prefamine Irish situation as a kind of burlesque. The next group of immigrants were the famine refugees (1845–1870)—cheap laborers often depicted as violent and shiftless and considered an economic burden on others. Some of these early works include Mary Anne Madden Sadlier's *Bessy Conway: Or, the Irish Girl in America* (1861), *Con O'Regan: Or, Emigrant Life in the New World* (1885), and *Willy Burke: Or the Irish Orphan in America* (1850). Other writers include Fitz James O'Brien and John Boyle O'Reilly.

The group of immigrants that arrived between 1870 and 1900 tended to be ambitious and more literate than their predecessors. By 1920, immigration had begun to decrease. Eugene O'Neill, following in the tradition of John Synge and Sean O'Casey, wrote numerous plays, including *The Long Voyage Home* (1917), *The Emperor Jones* (1920), and *Strange Interlude* (1928).

James T. Farrell's *Studs T. Lonigan* (1935) is the story of a second-generation Irish American whose grandfather was an immigrant laborer and whose father was a businessman who moved his family to a middle-class neighborhood. Studs rebels against his father's success, joins a gang, and eventually dies at twenty-nine. Betty Smith's *A Tree Grows in Brooklyn* (1943) is about Irish-American life at the turn of the twentieth century in Brooklyn. *The Other Side* (1989), by Mary Gordon, revolves around the story of Ellen Costello, who steals money from her father's shop in order to go to America, the "other side." She eventually marries Vincent McNamara, a skilled mechanic, and lives in the suburbs, but she never overcomes her sense of guilt. Other well-known Irish-American writers include Elizabeth Cullinan, James Carroll, F. Scott Fitzgerald, Mary McCarthy, John O'Hara, Flannery O'Connor, and Edwin O'Connor.

ITALIAN-AMERICAN LITERATURE

From 1880 to 1920, immigration from Italy to the United States included primarily agricultural laborers. These immigrants resisted literacy because it had often been used against them by people in power. Once settled in the United States, the Italian Americans became more interested in literacy as a way of exerting control. In the 1930s and 1940s, though, immigration declined and more Italian intellectuals, such as Arturo Vivante, P. M. Pasinetti, and Niccolo Tucci, relocated in the United States. Their literary interests focused on esthetic concerns rather than ethnic issues. By the end of World War II, there was another resurgence in immigration. More recently, there has been an upsurge of writers, such as Paolo Valesio, who write in Italian and are published in both Italy and the United States.

Pietro Di Donato's *Christ in Concrete* (1939) is the story of Geronimo, an immigrant from Abruzzi who works in the building trade and is crushed by a construction accident. His son, twelve-year-old Paulie, goes to work in his father's place, but also goes to night school to improve his situation. Tina De Rosa's *Paper Fish* (1980) deals with three generations of the Bellasca family; Carmolina hears stories from her grandmother about how her parents adapted to the United States. In Joseph Arleo's *The Grand Street Collector* (1970), Natale Sbagliato assassinates a radical

editor of an Italian newspaper in New York City and flees to Italy, and it is not until much later that his son finds out why he left America so precipitously.

Umbertina: A Novel (1979), by Helen Barolini, is a fourth-generation novel in which Umbertina comes to the United States with her husband and three children. She develops her simple sandwich stand into a successful import business. Dorothy Calvetti Bryant's *Miss Giordano* (1978) deals with a family's moves from Vermont to Illinois to Colorado and finally to Montana, the father's lung disease that developed from mining, and the daughter's growing up to become a high school English teacher. Other Italian-American works include Arturo Vivante's *The French Girls of Killini* (1967), *A Goodly Babe* (1966); P. M. Pasinetti's *Venetian Red* (1960), *The Smile on the Face of the Lion* (1965), and *From the Academy Bridge* (1970); and Niccolo Tucci's *Before My Time*.

JAPANESE-AMERICAN LITERATURE

Early Japanese-American writers continued to focus on an Oriental perspective. Later writers explored the Japanese-American identity and wartime issues. Most early Japanese-American writing was published in Japanese-American newspapers and journals. Early Japanese-American literature includes the poetry of Yone Noguchi's *From the Eastern Shore* (1910) and Sadakichi Hartmann's *My Rubaiyat* (1913), *Tanka and Haikai: Fourteen Japanese Rhythms* (1915), as well as Etsu Inagakî Sugimoto's novel, *A Daughter of the Samurai* (1925).

The first major Japanese-American writer, Toshio Mori, tells about the Japanese community in *Yokohama, California* (1949). In *The Chauvinist and Other Stories* (1979), Mori writes about the Japanese colony in Oakland, California, during the 1930s and 1940s. The stories include "The Travelers," about *nisei*, or second-generation Japanese, who leave the Utah internment camp and move everywhere. Their jobs include working at a chicken hatchery in Arkansas and maintaining candy machines. In Mori's works, he creates a migrant language that provided resistance to the cultural mainstream.

Monica Itoi Sone's *Nisei Daughter* (1953) chronicles the release of Japanese Americans from internment after World War II. In Margaret Harada's *The Sun Shines on the Immigrant* (1960), Yoshio Mori comes to Hawaii to work as a contract laborer, then as a chauffeur. His son eventually runs a taxi business; his daughter becomes a school teacher. Though he praises Hawaii, he longs to go back to Japan for a visit. John Okada's *No-*

No Boy (1957) investigates the sense of being neither Japanese nor American and the ways in which identity is mobile. Hisaye Yamamoto's *Seventeen Syllables and Other Stories* (1988) is written from within the immigrant experience and deals with women's issues. Yoshiko Uchida's *Picture Bride* (1987) deals with Hana, who first comes to the United States to be married as a picture bride, a woman whose picture is sent ahead for the groom's consideration.

Japanese-American literature is also strongly developed in Hawaii. Kazuo Miyamoto's *Hawaii: End of the Rainbow* (1964) concerns the Arata, Mayeda, and Murayama families and their lives on a sugar plantation. Other works include *Sachio: A Daughter of Hawaii* (1977) by Patsy Saiki, and *All I Asking for Is My Body* (1988) and *Plantation Boy* (1998) by Milton Murayama. Cynthia Kadohata's *The Floating World* (1989) and *In the Heart of the Valley of Love* (1992) deal with Olivia, who spends her childhood in a "ukiyo" or "floating world" as her father travels in search of jobs. Eventually, traveling becomes a type of home.

JEWISH-AMERICAN LITERATURE

In the English version of Abraham Cahan's *Yekl, A Tale of the New York Ghetto* (1896), Yekl comes to the United States, changes his name to Jake, and meets Mamie. Later, Jake's wife, Gitl, and his son come to join him, but he refuses to give up his mistress, so his marriage ends in divorce. Abraham Cahan's *The Imported Bridegroom and Other Stories of the New York Ghetto* (1898) is a collection of stories about New York in the 1890s. The main story is about Dr. Stroom, who goes home to eastern Europe to find his daughter a husband. He brings back a Talmudic scholar, who at first the daughter rejects, but then accepts when the new husband becomes Americanized. In Cahan's *The Rise of David Levinsky* (1917), David's mother wants him to become a Talmudic scholar, but instead he emigrates to New York, gets a job in a garment shop, and rises in business.

Anzia Yezierska wrote a number of stories about the Jewish-American woman's experience in the United States. For example, in Yezierska's *Bread Givers* (1925)—subtitled "A Struggle between a Father of the Old World and a Daughter of the New" (1925)—Sara Smolensky leaves home, goes to night school while she works, gets a scholarship to college, and becomes a teacher. Yezierska's works also include *Children of Loneliness* (1923) and *Hungry Hearts* (1920).

Leo Rosten's *The Education of H*Y*M*A*N K*A*P*L*A*N* (1937) tells a story of immigration in the early part of the century, is centered on the characters of Mr. Parkhill and his adult immigrant students in New York in the 1930s. This humorous book recounts the foibles and pitfalls of learning English and becoming American.

In Henry Roth's *Call It Sleep* (1934), David Schearl and his mother, Geryl, meet Albert, his father, at Ellis Island. The father thinks that David is not his son and terrorizes him. David works to adjust to the tough street life, attends Hebrew school, and has an accident in which he almost dies.

The Adventures of Mottel, the Cantor's Son (1953), by Shalom Aleichem (pseudonym of Solomon Rabinowitz), deals with Mottel's travels from Russia to the United States (again to Ellis Island) and of how he takes on American names and finds a variety of jobs. Late-twentieth-century writers include Isaac Bashevis Singer, Bernard Malamud, Saul Bellow, Philip Roth, and Cynthia Ozick.

KOREAN-AMERICAN LITERATURE

Driven by economic and political necessity, many Koreans fled to the United States from 1910 to 1945, during the Japanese occupation of their country. The next group came after World War II and the Korean War (1950–53), and the third group as a result of the Immigration and Nationality Act of 1965. Central to the work of many Korean-American writers is the issue of living on adopted soil.

Such works include Alice Choi's memoir, *A Picture Bride from Korea: The Life History of a Korean American Woman in Hawaii* (1978), Kumi Kilburn's *No Dogs and Chinese Allowed* (1978)—dealing with mixed ethnic identity—and Ronyoung's Kim's *Clay Walls* (1986), about Chun and Haseu, who come to the United States after Korea is taken over by Japan. They are from the nobility class (*yangban*), but in the United States they have to take jobs such as cleaning toilets. The mother, Haseu, eventually has a chance to take the children back to Korea, but she realizes that she was not any better off there.

Other works include Mary Paik Lee's *Quiet Odyssey: A Pioneer Korean Woman in America* (1990), about a woman who came to the United States in 1905 at the age of five and how she encounters racial prejudice; Richard Kim's *The Martyred* (1964), about twelve Christian ministers who were killed by the North Korean Communists; Sook Nyul Choi's *Year of Impossible Goodbyes* (1991); and Induk Pahk's *September Monkey*

(1954), *Hour of the Tiger* (1965), and *The Cock Still Crows* (1977).

Yong-Ik Kim's *The Diving Gourd* (1962) and *Blue in the Seed* (1964) deal with longing for the old world. Willyce Kim, in *Eating Artichokes* (1972), rejects the submissive role of women and explores lesbianism and women's rights. Her other books include *Under the Rolling Sky* (1976), *Dancer Dawkins and the California Kid* (1985), and *Dead Heat* (1988).

Chang-rae Lee's *Native Speaker* (1995) revolves around Henry Park, a Korean American, who works as an industrial spy and helps bring about the downfall of an up-and-coming politician. His *A Gesture Life* (1999) explores Franklin Hata's problems of fitting in, first as a medical officer in Japan's Imperial Army and then in the New York suburb of Bedley Run as the owner of a medical supply store.

MEXICAN-AMERICAN LITERATURE

In much Mexican-American writing there is a sense of dual identity. This is seen, for example, in José Antonio Villarreal's *Pocho* (1959)—its focus emerges from crossing the borders between the United States and Mexico, which has led to a strong sense of binationalism. As writers strive to overcome and transform those tensions, they often write about issues related to assimilation and resistance to assimilation. In this process, the Chicano identity is talked of as *chicanismo* and often reflects a fluid, nonlinear sense of time. In recent years, there has been a particular interest in challenging the "normative" view of American history.

Sandra Cisnero's *The House on Mango Street* (1983) is told by Esperanza Cordero, who lives in a poor Hispanic neighborhood in the Chicago of the 1970s. Ernesto Galarza's *Barrio Boy* (1971) is an autobiographical novel that tracks the author's journey from a mountain village in central Mexico to a *barrio* in California, his introduction to American culture through the schools, and his later unsuccessful efforts to organize laborers.

Bless Me, Ultima (1972) is Rudolfo A. Anaya's story about Antonio Marez, who lives in a remote area in northern New Mexico. Anaya has also written *Other Heart of Aztlán* (1976) and *The Silence of Llano* (1982). In *A Shroud in the Family*, by Lionel G. García (1987), a Chicano family confronts the Anglo culture in Houston and challenges the historical accounts of Texas heros.

PAKISTANI-AMERICAN LITERATURE

Pakistani-American writers are a very new group of writers dealing with alienation, the memory of colonialism, the partition from India, and other problems of nationalism. There are not yet any second-generation writers.

Zulfikar Ghose's work ranges from *The Loss of India* (poetry) (1964) to *Confessions of a Native Alien* (1965) to his novel *The Triple Mirror of the Self* (1992). Bapsi Sidhwa's *The Crow Eaters: A Novel (Alive Again Series)* (1978) is an ironic look at the life of the Parsi. *Cracking India: A Novel* (1985) deals with the partition of India from the point of view of a child and its effects on women, and *American Brat* (1993) is a social comedy on America from the point of view of a sixteen-year-old Parsi girl. Sara Suleri's *Meatless Days* (1989) describes growing up in Pakistan as the daughter of a Pakistani father and a Welsh mother and then moving to the United States. Aurangzeb Alamgir Hashmi has written *The Oath and the Omen* (1976), *America Is a Punjabi Word* (1979), and *My Second in Kentucky* (1981).

PUERTO RICAN LITERATURE

Puerto Rican literature poses a problem of classification because Puerto Ricans are "immigrant-citizens" of the United States. Still, it provides an important opportunity to look at the notion of migration within the nation. The early period of Puerto Rican writing spans from 1900 to 1945. Jesús Colón's (1901–1974) *A Puerto Rican in New York, and Other Sketches* (1959) tracks the different experiences of labor from the point of view of a black Latino. Bernado Vega's *Memorias de Bernado de Vega* (1984) focuses on the cultural history of the burgeoning barrio. Arturo Alfonso Schomberg (1874–1938), a bibliophile, wrote on Caribbean and Latin American issues, while Pedro Juan Labarthe (1906–) wrote the more personal *Son of Two Nations: The Private Life of a Columbia Student.*

During the post–World War II "Great Migration," Puerto Rican writers criticized imperialism, mass migration, and the "bicultural, bilingual quality of *puertorriqueñidad,* (literally, "Puerto Rican-ness") and writers included Pedro Juan Soto, Jaime Carrero, René Marques, and Enrique Laguerre.

By the 1960s interest grew in exploring a new language for the Puerto Rican writer and audience and this interest resulted in the *Nuyorican* renaissance

(1965–1970). The Nuyoricans or neoricans wanted to create a temporal and spatial break from the island, and Miguel Algarín's Nuyorican Poet's Café was a key site for the performance of this new poetry. Well-known Nuyorican poets include Miguel Algarín, Pedro Pietri, and Piri Thomas.

VIETNAMESE-AMERICAN LITERATURE

Blue Dragon, White Tiger: A Tet Story (1983), by Tran Van Dinh, deals with how the author escapes from the Communists on a boat with twenty other intellectuals. They are robbed and raped before they reach Thailand, but finally manage to get some assistance to go to the United States.

In *When Heaven and Earth Changed Places: A Vietnamese Woman's Journey from War to Peace* (1989), Le Ly Hayslip chronicles her return to Vietnam ten years after she left, and she notes the changes amidst her recollections. Her *Child of War, Woman of Peace* (1993) deals with the narrator's difficulties after being widowed twice and having to work as a domestic in order to make ends meet. Things finally stabilize and she becomes a social activist, eventually founding the East Meets West Foundation.

America possesses an extraordinarily rich store of immigrant literature. The reasons for this are both historical and literary. America, of course, is a land of immigrants, so the potential pool of authors is great.

At the same time, there is something inherently compelling in the immigrant story. An initial motivation, obstacles facing the protagonist, and ultimate resolution are basic elements in narrative fiction, as well as the stages in a real-life immigrant's journey. Indeed, it can be argued that the very idea of journey—so much a part of America's literary heritage—is a product of our collective immigrant background.

Kanta Kochhar-Lindgren

See also: Film, Radio, and Television, Language, Press (Part II, Sec. 10).

BIBLIOGRAPHY

Kanellos, Nicolas, and Claudio Esteva-Fabregat. *Handbook of Hispanic Cultures in the United States: Literature and Art.* Vols. 1 and 2. Houston: Arte Publico Press, 1993.

Knippling, Alpana Sharma. *New Immigrant Literature in the United States: A Sourcebook to Our Multicultural Literary Heritage.* Westport, CT: Greenwood Press, 1996.

Lowe, Lisa. *Immigrant Acts.* Durham, NC: Duke University Press, 1996.

Muller, Gilbert. *New Strangers in Paradise: The Immigrant Experience and Contemporary American Fiction.* Lexington: University of Kentucky Press, 1999.

Simone, Roberta. *The Immigrant Experience in American Fiction: An Annotated Bibliography.* Lanham, MD: Scarecrow Press, 1995.

Wong, Sau-ling Cynthia. *Reading Asian American Literature: From Necessity to Extravagance.* Princeton, NJ: Princeton University Press, 1993.

ARTS II: PERFORMING ARTS

Within a number of early immigrant communities in the United States, various theatrical and musical groups emerged as sites for building social cohesion or providing entertainment. Several of the early musical groups performed works from both the home and the new country. Theatrical groups often performed in their members' native language, and plays included classics as well as vaudeville numbers. Examples of early immigrant performance groups range from Corporación Musical Mexícana Hidalgo, Lars Anders och Jan Anders, the Men's Singing Group, and the Belgian Drama Group. As the community theater venues developed and after the immigrant groups became more settled, the communities and respective playwrights began to explore issues of ethnic identity and social problems like poverty and assimilation. Such performance numbers might showcase the "greenhorn" or the new immigrant who could not quite get things right. Some communities also developed works that addressed social inequality and political concerns.

From 1925 to 1950, a decline occurred in the production of immigrant theater, a shift which resulted from the new immigration laws of 1924 that restricted the number of immigrants allowed into the United States at any one time. Other factors included an improvement in income levels, Americanization, and shifting geographic locations. The influx of movies, radio, and television also influenced the decline in community commitment to theater.

Nevertheless, the civil rights movement of the 1960s led to a renewed interest and investment in ethnic identity and cultural change. Refugees from Eastern Europe and immigrants from Puerto Rico, Asia, and Latin America fueled the new theaters, as did aging immigrants who became involved in a resurgence of their theaters. The Puerto Rican Traveling Theater, for example, began performing in the 1960s; by 1977 there were four Asian-American theater companies in New York City. In the ethnic theaters, classic plays—in Armenian, Baltic, Polish, and Yiddish—were also performed.

As the "new ethnicity" of the 1960s and 1970s revived interest in immigrant performing arts, these immigrant performing art troupes also became more skilled (active) in staging theaters that reached beyond the parameters of the immediate ethnic community. In some cases, this change led to greater visibility within the cultural mainstream. For example, the Theater for Asian American Performing Artists in New York City had staged skits on anti-Asian discrimination for the U.S. Commission on Civil Rights. Members later transformed this work into *Asian American Blues* and performed it at Lincoln Center during the July 4, 1976, bicentennial celebration. In other cases, performances were staged as a countersite to the mainstream production, such as El Teatro Campesino, which used a theatrical format in order to address many of the social problems facing the Chicano population.

ARMENIAN-AMERICAN THEATER

A record exists of some early Armenian theater performance groups, such as Raffi (1903) and Adamian (1908), and Arshak II (1898), which was produced in Carnegie Hall, is the earliest known Armenian-American performance. As a result of the diaspora created from the Armenian genocide in Turkey during World War I, the Armenian-American theater had a strong growth period following the war. After the Armenians reached a point where they could make a living in the new country, they became interested in depicting and exploring the issues regarding their status in the new country. Much Armenian-American theater was produced by amateurs and semiprofessionals. In the 1920s and 1930s, the Armenian Art Theatre, managed by Hovhannes Zarifian, produced a

A Russian-American dance troupe poses in native costume on the boardwalk in Brighton Beach, New York. *(Mel Rosenthal)*

number of both Armenian and non-Armenian plays, including *The Robber, The Devil, Trilby, Bride and the Mother-in-Law, The Vartanantz War,* and *Typhon.* Outside New York City, there was also significant activity in Fresno, Boston, and Detroit.

In New York City, the Kimatian Theater Lovers Group, run by Elia Kimatian, produced plays from a classical repertoire. For example, in 1942, the group performed *Ascension Day,* made up of excerpts from

the Armenian opera *Anoush.* Other works include Vahan Krikor's *Swan Song* (1946) about a man who falls in love with a much younger woman, as well as Alexandre Shirvanzade's *For the Sake of Honor* (1948) and Levon Shant's *The Princess of the Fallen Castle.*

There were also a number of plays written or adapted by Kimatian on Armenian issues. *Victims of War* (1946), for example, addresses the immigrant situation regarding intermarriage, through the story of an Armenian girl who marries an American during World War II due to a shortage of Armenian men. Raffi's *Samuel* is about the conflict between Christianity and Zoroastrianism, and *Dagh* (1948), an adaptation of Franz Werfel's novel *Forty Days of Musa* about a group of Armenians surrounded in battle by the Turks during WWI. A 1953 play based on a short story about the biblical Feast of the Transfiguration concerns Armenian gypsies, and *The Fired Upon* (1958), about the flight of Armenian soldiers from Turkey who arrive on Russian soil only to be fired on and have to retreat back into Turkey. The theater group was comprised of native-born Americans whose Armenian was not as skillful as that of the members of the Zarifian group. The Sevan Theatrical Group formed by Angel Havagimian produced Yervunt Odian's *Merchant Artin Agha* (1970); Shirvanzade's *For the Sake of Honor*, which dealt with the greed of an industrialist and with his daughter who commits suicide to save the integrity of the family; and *Did She Have the Right?* (1978) by Shirvanzade, which revolves around the story of a woman who leaves her husband.

There was a rebirth of interest in Armenian culture from in the 1960s to the 1990s. Ethnic awareness was reinforced, among other things, by political strife in Armenia. Leslie Ayvazian's play *Nine Armenians* (1998), for example, revolves around the story of teenager Ani, who after the death of her immigrant grandfather insists on returning to Armenia to recover her heritage. This continuing interest also led to the support for and development of a huge cultural complex, the St. Vartan Armenian Cathedral complex and the Armenian General Benevolent Union, which has housed a variety of Armenian performances.

ASIAN-AMERICAN THEATER

In the 1800s in the San Francisco area, there was considerable traditional performance: Cantonese operas as well as musical concerts and puppet shows. Some examples of groups that staged these performances include the Tung Hook Tong Troupe (1852) and the Shanghai Theater Company (1855). These Chinese performances drew considerable attention and support and eventually led to more performances based more on Asian-American cultural issues.

Gladys Li's play *The Submission of Rosie Moy* (1928), apparently the first Asian-American play, centered on the story of a Chinese-American girl who refused to go through with an arranged marriage. Additional works by Li include *The White Serpent* (1924) and *The*

Law of Wu Wei (1925). Other early examples of Asian-American plays include Wai Wee Chun's *For You a Lei* (1936) and *A Marginal Woman* (1936); Bessie Toishigawa's *Nisei* (1947) and *Reunion* (1947); and Patsy Saiki's *The Return* (1959), *The Return of Sam Patch* (1966), and *Second Choice* (1959).

The Asian-American actor's interest in developing a theatrical milieu freed of Asian-American stereotypes fueled writing in the late 1960s and 1970s. In 1968, for example, the East West Players sponsored a national play writing contest for Asian Americans. As a result of these efforts, such well-known Asian American playwrights as Frank Chin, Momoko Iko, Wakako Yamauchi, and Ed Sakamoto launched their careers. Momoko Iko, for example, reworked a novel about the internment during World War II into the play *Gold Watch* (1972).

Rising numbers of middle-class Asian immigrants in recent years has increased interest in Asian-American theater. During this time, the subject matter of the plays began to shift from a concern with family matters, issues of cultural difference, and assimilation to questions regarding intermarriage. A second generation of Asian-American playwrights includes Genny Lim, Jeannie Barroga, Elizabeth Wong, Velina Houston, Philip Kan Gotanda, Jessica Hagedorn, David Hwang, and R. A. Shiomi. Ping Chong, who has a long track record of experimental theater works dating back to the 1960s, has developed a number of works in the 1990s that deal explicitly with cross-cultural issues, including *Undesirable Elements* and the *East/West Trilogy*.

Some Asian-American theater companies include East West Players, Asian American Theater Company, Pan Asian Repertory, Seattle's Northwest Asian American Theater Company, Teatro Ng Tanan (Filipino), and Silk Road Playhouse (Korean). Two Asian-American theaters, Angel Island Theatre Co. and Mina-sama-no, are based in Chicago. Other playwrights include Amy Hill, Jude Narita, Brenda Aoki, Chungmi Kim, Mari Sunaide, Marilyn Tokuda, Patty Toy, Szu Wang, and David Henry Hwang.

DANISH-AMERICAN THEATER

Danish-American theater spanned the 1870s to the 1950s. During the second half of the nineteenth century, major Danish-American theaters were established in Chicago, Minneapolis, and Seattle. Theater from 1870–1908 in Minneapolis tended to focus on Danish comedy and could be seen in such clubs as Norsk Dramatisk, Skandinaviske Forening, Den

Danske Dramatiske Klub, and Den Dansk-Dramatiske Forening. In the 1920s, the Young People's Society produced one of the first examples of an immigrant story, *Den Som Gaar Køkkenvej*, about an immigrant who goes to live on a prairie farm.

Seattle's Danish dramatic society, Harmonien, was run by Elfrida Pedersen. One of the society's favorite performance pieces was the popular song "Seattle Reyven" (1924) about an eighteen-year-old immigrant from Denmark who travels across the ocean and the United States to settle in Seattle. Other productions included dramatized versions of Hans Christian Andersen fairy tales.

FINNISH-AMERICAN THEATER

In the 1880s significant Finnish immigration to the United States occurred as a result of poor living conditions, including overpopulation and starvation. Other Finns left for the States seeking adventure or escape from political repression. Many Finns settled in Michigan, Minnesota, Massachusetts, Washington, and Oregon. A primary organizational focus for Finnish communities was the local socialist chapter, often also serving as a temperance society. Temperance stages in Massachusetts included the Alku (Beginning) Society of Maynard; the Sovittaja, (Conciliator) Society of Worcester; and the more famous Uljas Koitto (Heroic Sunrise) in Quincy.

Labor clubs tended to invest in local theaters in order to build the community at large as well as to accumulate sufficient funds to run drama schools. Despite the fact that more popular entertainment plays tended to be the moneymakers, many people thought the theaters should focus on the teachings of Karl Marx.

Moses Hahl saw the theater as a vehicle for passing on the ideology. He thought acting classes should be eliminated and courses on dialectical materialism should be taught to the actors and actresses. The Finnish Cooperative Wholesale focused on plays that addressed some of these issues: *A Gala Day in a Cooperative Store*; *A Woman's Way*, about unfair trade practices; and *The Potato War Coop*, about the best way to market potatoes.

Lauri Lemberg, who wrote for the socialist stage and Industrial Workers of the World (IWW) theater in the 1920s is known for such works as *Shakaalit* (Shekels), *Salaliitto* (The Plot), and *Phoenix*. These works were responses to the corruption of "factory owners and law officers." Lemberg, however, also wrote comedies and musical folk plays.

World War II marks the end of this cycle in Finnish-American theater as a result of the shift in interest away from the Finnish ethnic community.

HISPANIC THEATER IN THE UNITED STATES

Early Hispanic theater in the United States was influenced by the dance-drama of Native Americans and the religious theaters of the early Spanish missionaries. Central to this theatrical practice was the use of *pastorela*, or the shepherd's play, which in addition to the biblical figures of the Nativity story included commedia-dell'arte-like figures such as a "lecherous hermit and a comic bumbling shepherd named Bato." This genre influenced subsequent theater with its zeal, grassroots focus, the use of masks, comedy, and slapstick. One of the earliest reported Hispanic performances in this country took place in what is now New Mexico under the influence of Juan de Oñate. It featured an improvisational storytelling style at night by the campfire as well as productions of the *Moros y cristianos*, the story of the fight between the Christians and the Moors in northern Spain during the Crusades.

Although performances such as *Astucias por heerdar un sobrino a su tío*, a cloak-and-dagger play, are recorded as early as 1789, what is known as the first of modern Hispanic theater in the States began in the mid-nineteenth century in California, as a result of the ease of steamship travel along the West Coast. By the 1860s, theater was becoming so popular that companies that once traveled were beginning to settle down; for example, the Campanía Española e la Familia Estrella settled in San Francisco. The evening's program included a three- or four-act drama as well as shorter pieces such as songs and dances. Nevertheless, most of the dramatic pieces were melodramas by peninsular Spanish authors, such as José Zorilla or Mariano José de Larra.

In the last decade of the nineteenth century, as theatrical venues expanded because of the availability of rail and the car, theater activity increased in the border states, including such forms as the mobile tent theaters (*carpas*), circus theaters, and smaller, makeshift companies. By this time, theaters in Los Angeles also had fostered enough interest in the Hispanic theater to support five major theater companies, which had shows that changed daily. San Antonio's "most important" house was Teatro Nacional. There, production included Spanish drama, *zarzuelas*, or Spanish operettas, and, also by 1923, works by Mexican playwrights.

At the same time, Los Angeles had become a major center for developing new Hispanic theatrical works and talent. Many of the plays addressed the Mexican situation in California: Eduard Carillio's *El Proceso de Aurelio Pompo* (The Trial of Aurelio Pompa) about the unfair sentencing of a Mexican immigrant; and Gabriel Navarro's *Los emigrados* and *El sacrificio* (The Sacrifice) about Mexican-American expatriate life in Los Angeles during the revolution.

The most prolific playwright was Adalberto Elías González, and one of his most well known works, *Los amores de ramona* (The Loves of Ramona), based on a novel, was a box office success. Other works included *Los misioneros* (The Missionaries) and *Los expatriados* (The Expatriates), which addressed the needs of the audience to connect with their history on both sides of the border.

Nevertheless, the rise of vaudeville began to challenge the ongoing success of the earlier theaters. The development of the *revista* (theatrical review) examined the Mexican character, music, dialects, and folklore. Under the revolution it emphasized the concerns of the working class. A number of the Los Angeles revistas satirized the Mexican Revolution. In the *revistas*, we see the experiences of the new immigrants addressed. In the 1920s the shift occurs from cultural shock to cultural conflict, especially as racism in the States becomes more pronounced. During this time, the character of the *pelado* (forerunner to the sad-sack characters developed by Mexican comedian Cantiflas) originated in the tent theaters of the Southwest and stayed in existence until the 1950s, a genre that had roots in the circus clown tradition. One of the most famous performers of the pelado character was Romulado Tirado.

Playwright Antonio Guzmán Aguilera was originally based in Mexico City as a journalist, though he still toured with his theatrical company. In 1924, however, he had a "falling out" with President Obregón and subsequently shifted to Los Angeles. Some of his most well known revistas include *Alma Tricolor* (Three-Colored Soul); *La huerta de Don Adolfo* (Don Adolfo's Garden; a reference to President Adolfo de Huerta); and *Exploración presidencial* (A Presidential Exploration). New revistas were based on Los Angeles life: *Los Angeles vacilador* (Swinging Los Angeles); *Evite peligro* (Avoid Danger); and *El eco de México* (The Echo from Mexico).

In San Antonio, after being pushed out of the theaters by vaudeville, the Hispanic theater kept going in community halls and churches. The *carpas* (tent performances) became even more important in the Southwest and in popular culture Mexican-American tradition and served as a vehicle for airing cultural conflict. Immigrants had particular concerns with language and lifestyle issues, and they addressed *pocho*, or the Americanized status, in their performances. From this work there developed the stereotype of the *pachucho*, a typically Mexican-American figure. The most famous *carpas* were Carpa García and Carpa Cubana, and they included trapeze artists, rope walkers, jugglers, and clowns.

By the 1890s, the Hispanic theater began to develop in New York City. Cuban plays ranged from *De lo vivo a pintado* (From Life to the Painted Version) by Tomás Mendoza about a deceased hero of the revolutionary war, to *La fuga de Evangelina* (The Escape of Evangelina), a story about the escape from prison of a heroine of the independence movement.

The popular musical revue in New York City was the *Obra bufa cubana*, or Cuban blackface farce. This genre included stock character types of the negrito (blackface), *mulatto*, and *gallego* (Galician) and relied heavily on Afro-Cuban song and dance. In 1932, Mt. Morris Theater opened and was eventually named El Teatro Hispano. The theater ran until the 1950s and included a number of productions by both Cuban and Puerto Rican playwrights.

In 1953, the production at the Church of San Sebastian of *La carreta* (The Oxcart) by René Marqués, which deals with the dislocation of a Puerto Rican family from their mountain village to New York City, catapulted this playwright's work into the international limelight. This event also helped paved the way for more contemporary work in Hispanic theater.

In the 1960s, Luis Valdez's work on the West Coast with El Teatro Campesino helped facilitate a rebirth of interest and concern regarding Hispanic theater. Other groups included El Nuevo Teatro Pobre de las Américas (The New Poor People's Theater of the Americas), Teatro Orilla (Marginal Theater), Teatro Guazamara (Whatsamara Theater), the Puerto Rican Traveling Theater, and the Nuyorican poets and playwrights.

GERMAN-AMERICAN THEATER

German-American theater spanned from 1830 to 1930. In the 1800s in a number of cities, German Americans were quick to put up theater halls and share their use with English-speaking theater groups. Much of the interest in German-American theaters revolved around the emphasis on ethnic theater as a vehicle for connecting the old and the new life. As a result, the first productions were heavily influenced by German theater, particularly three types: *volksstück* (folk-drama), *schicksalsdrama* (fate tragedy), and *schwank* (farce). These types of theater were used to reinforce Germanness.

The first immigration wave was from the 1830s to the 1840s. The German Amateur Theatrical Society of Philadelphia ran from 1830 to 1860. In 1854, the Alte Stadttheater opened in New York and brought the theories and directing practices of Karl Menniger to the States. The longest-standing German-American theater was Milwaukee's Pabsttheater, where German classical and modern theater was produced. Germans supported theater through attendance and money.

The decline of German-American theater occurred after the turn of the century. It was influenced by the events of the two world wars as well as the assimilation of German immigrants into the cultural mainstream and the loss of German as a living language for immigrants and their descendants in the United States.

IRISH-AMERICAN THEATER

There were five stages in the development of the Irish-American theater: before 1830, 1830–1860, 1860–1890, 1890–1918, and 1918 to the present. Early Irish immigrants had some education and finances and were subsequently willing to support the theater. The staged Irishman appeared as early as 1820 and can be seen in the plays of John Brougham, such as *His Last Legs* (1840), *The Irish Yankee, or the Birthday of Freedom* (1840), and *Temptation, or the Irish Emigrant* (1849). The stage Irishman, often called "Pat," "Paddy," or "Teague," had an Irish brogue, told perpetual jokes, and made many blunders in speech and behavior. The immigrant Irishman was the stage Irishman in an American setting, and this character emerged as one that embodied the contrast between the speech and culture of immigrant Irish and those of the native-born American. Over time, the caricatures faded, as the Irish became more assimilated.

From 1830 to 1860, a central Irish character emerged called Mose the Bowery B'hoy, "boaster and brawler, heroic fire fighter, and guardian angel of the greenhorns and of Linda the Cigar Girl." There are a number of Mose adventures: *A Glance at Philadelphia* (1848), *The Mysteries and Miseries of New York* (1850), *New York as It Is* (1851), *Linda the Cigar Girl, or Mose Among the Conspirators* (1856), and *Mose in California*

(1857). This character reflects a strong interest in fire departments that initially were volunteer units. As they became municipal, this character type also faded from the literature.

From 1860 to 1890, plays tended to emphasize the romanticism of Irish exile: Dion Boucicault's comic plays included *The Colleen Bawn* (1860), *Arrah-na-Pogue* (1864), and *The Shaugraun* (1874). *The Octoroon* (1859) is a play about slavery written just after John Brown's raid.

Edward Harrigan developed the Mulligan cycle, a series of realistic plays about an Irish immigrant grocer who achieved some political status. The titles include *The Mulligan Guard* (1873), *The Mulligan Guard and Skidmores* (1875), *The Mulligan Picnic* (1878; revised 1880), *The Mulligan Guard Ball* (1879), *The Mulligan Guard Chowder* (1879), *The Mulligan Guard Christmas* (1879), *The Mulligan Guard Surprise* (1880), *The Mulligan Guard Nominee* (1880), and *The Mulligan's Silver Wedding* (1891).

Other Harrigan plays addressed the social problems facing the immigrants: *Squatter Sovereignty* (1882) questions the legal rights to the shantytown on *East 72nd Street* (1886) and *The Leather Patch* (1886) dealt with lower-class New York life. As the Irish Americans gained entry into the middle class, the Irish-American audience became less interested in the stage Irish, stage immigrant characters, and other culturally peripheral characters.

The next time period in Irish-American theater history, 1890–1918, addresses the issues relating to the growth of political power. *A Tammany Tiger* (1896) by Gratton Donnelley concerns two politicians running for the same office. Other plays of the period include George Broadhurst's *The Man of the Hour* (1906) and James Barcus's *The Governor's Boss* (1914) and *The Boss* (1911). These works explored local elections and political leadership.

Eugene O'Neill (1888–1953), arguably the most famous Irish-American playwright, began his career when his play *Bound East for Cardiff* was produced by the Provincetown Players in 1916. His autobiographical play *Long Day's Journey into Night* (1957) reflects the conflict between family and larger social structures. Other Irish-American plays explore the individual versus the family, church, and politics, including Annie Nichols's *Abbie's Irish Rose* (1922), Philip Barry's *The Joyous Season* (1934), and Frank Gilroy's *The Subject Was Roses* (1965). Other works include Emmet Lavery's *The First Legion* (1934) and William Alfred's *Hogan's Goat* (1965), about the Irish Americans in Brooklyn in the 1890s.

Irish-American drama societies also helped to further Irish-American performing arts, such as the Thomas Davis Irish Players (TDIP) based in New York and begun in 1933. Particularly popular works were John Murphy's *The Country Boy* (1960) and John B. Keane's *Many Young Men of Twenty* (1961). Other groups include the Irish Rebel Theatre at the Irish Arts Center, founded in 1972 and the Committee on Irish Ethnicity's Traveling Theatre, established in 1974.

ITALIAN-AMERICAN THEATER

Prior to 1870, the fist recorded Italian-American playwright is Lorenzo da Ponte, who wrote plays in Italian to be performed by his students. An Italian-American theater began to develop during the last thirty years of the nineteenth century. From 1871 to 1900 in New York City, a number of plays were produced as special benefit performances for needy people in Italy.

Health and economic factors in Italy drove immigration up; a number of immigrants ended up in the ghettos, where the chief places to socialize were the church, social clubs, and coffeehouses. Il Circolo Filodrammatico Italo-Americano produced a number of plays from both Europe and New York City, and the productions also included extra acts, such as magic tricks and acts, dancing skits, and grand marches. A prime playwright whose works were staged by Il Circolo was Bernadino Ciambello; some of his works were *Figlia Maledetta* (Cursed Daughter) (1892), *Ramo d'Ulivio* (Olive Branch), *Cuore di Fanciulli* (Heart of Children) (1893), and *I Misteri di Mulberry* (The Mysteries of Mulberry) (1893).

Among other groups, La Compagnia Comico-Drammatica Italiana produced Neopolitan plays, particularly Pulcinello-style comedy skits, and is the first example of a working professional theater. La Compagnia Comico-Drammatica-Italiana A. Mairi e P. Rapone produced the works of Shakespeare. Additional performance venues included the marionette theaters, such as Il Teatro delle Marionette, and the coffeehouses, such as Il Caffè-Concerto.

In San Francisco's Societe Filodrammatiche, Antonietta Pisanelli both performed and spearheaded considerable theatrical business ventures. One such effort involved the opening up of nickelodeons, or show places that offered performance fare for a nickel. Also, Pisanelli was instrumental in the Italian immigrant figure, Fafariello.

MEXICAN-AMERICAN THEATER

Because the Spanish originally occupied certain areas in the States and then later the Mexicans, in tracing Mexican-American theater we have to note that from 1598 to 1823, inhabitants of those areas were called Spanish, and from 1823 to 1845, they were called Mexicans, and not until after 1845, Mexican Americans. Early Mexican-American theater primarily consisted of visits from Mexican theater troupes. From the 1870s to 1929, several professional theater groups from Mexico performed in the States, for example, the Hernández-Villalongín troupe. In 1900, they were invited to perform in the San Antonio Opera House. By 1910, the troupe was performing more in the States than in Mexico. Two works that the troupe often performed were *El Cinco de Mayo* and *Los Heroes de Tacubaya*.

In 1910, with the revolution in Mexico, tens of thousands of Mexicans fled across the border, and this shift in demographics further fueled the interest in theater. Performances consisted of plays and *corridos* (ballads)—songs about various regions of Mexico and the borderlands. These works often emphasized Western civilization in the nineteenth century, Hispanic community in the Southwest, strong family ties, and loyalty to relatives over friends.

During the Depression, the entertainment shifted to the movies and vaudeville shows, and as a result, there were fewer professional theater performances. Some community theater continued, for example, such plays as *Las Pastoreles*.

Nevertheless, theater activity was at a low until the emergence of the work of El Teatro Campesino in the 1960s. In 1965, Cesar Chavez organized a farm workers' strike in northern California. Luis Valdez, who had been working with the San Francisco Mime Troupe, quit and took up Chavez's work by supporting the workers' strike with guerrilla theater. This theater had similarities with the agitprop radical or avant-garde theaters of the 1920s–30s. Eventually, Valdez organized a group of workers in a theater, called El Teatro Campesino. Valdez and his fellow performers developed a community-based theatrical approach that revolved around the use of *actos*. In this format, issues were performed in outline form, and strikers urged to join the action and come up with solutions.

Valdez eventually broke off from the United Farm Workers in order to address a number of injustices that the Chicano population had to face, such as inadequate schools and discrimination in jobs, housing, and other benefits. In his work he emphasized *La*

Raza, that is, Mexican-American racial dignity, creating a theatrical format for social protest rather than aesthetics. Other theaters sprang up in California and the Southwest.

By 1972, Valdez had begun probing poetic rather than rhetorical methods of theater. *Zoot Suit,* one of his most well known plays, works to raise Mexican-American self-consciousness, to nurture Mexican-Americans' cultural tradition, and to develop a lively social movement dedicated to improving the lot of La Raza.

POLISH-AMERICAN THEATER

Polish drama societies were founded in Chicago (1873); New York (1876); Winona, Minnesota (1885); Brooklyn, Pittsburgh, Philadelphia, Grand Rapids, and Milwaukee (1886); and Buffalo and Detroit (1889). These theaters were part of a growing and extensive network of Polish-American theaters across the country.

In Chicago, Theofila Samolinska, the "Nightingale of Polonia," was a central figure in the development of Polish-American theater. She sang in musicals and was also a fighter for women's rights, speaker, writer, poet, actress, and political activist leader. She wrote *Three Floras* and *Emancipation of Women.*

The demise of Polish-American theater was due to the restriction of immigration from Poland after 1920, the introduction of radio and television, and the Anglicization of all ethnic groups.

PUERTO RICAN–AMERICAN THEATER

Puerto Rican–American theater was influenced by the early Hispanic theater tradition that had emerged in New York City and by the rapid increase in Puerto Rican immigrants in the 1940s and 1950s. Nearly 70 percent of the Puerto Rican immigrants to the States ended up in New York City. The rise of the radical Puerto Rican–American theater is related to the black arts movement, the work of El Teatro Campesino, and the work of alternative groups such as the San Francisco Mime Troupe and the Bread and Puppet Theater. Theaters such as the Puerto Rican Traveling Group, Teatro de Orilla, and Nuyorican groups were committed to *puertorriqueñidad,* of the essence of being Puerto Rican.

La emancipación del obrero (The Emancipation of the Workers, 1903) is one of the earliest known works of the Puerto Rican theater, and it reflects the concern of the time with political and social conditions brought on by the United States occupation. In this allegorical play, Juan represents the worker's cause; Pedro, economic slavery; the Priest, worries; the Politician, oppression; the Magistrate, injustice; and the Master, the capitalist system. This focus opened up the possibility for theater to grow away from its aristocratic orientation and to begin to become more of a theater for the populace. Other examples of theatrical works on the island from this time period include *Futuro* (Future, 1911) and *El poder del obrero o la mejor venganza* (The Workers' Power, or the Best Revenge, 1915).

Esta noche juega el joker (Tonight the Joker Is Wild, 1937) by Fernando Sierra Berdecia is the first Puerto Rican play to deal with immigrant life on the mainland. The pivotal point in Puerto Rican–American theater history is *La Carreta* (1952) by René Marqués, which addresses the experiences of a Puerto Rican family who moves to New York.

Other important works include Pedro Juan Soto's adaptations of the short stories "The Guest," "Scribbles," and "The Innocents"; Manuel Méndez Ballester's *Encrucijada* (Crossroads, 1958) and *Pipo Subway no sabe reir* (Pipo Subway Can't Laugh, 1972); and Jaime Carrero's *Noo Yall.* Playwrights sought to create works that relate to the collective experience of Puerto Ricans, and the Puerto Rican audience was often more familiar with popular and native music and dance than with theater. As a result, performances may include the popular forms. The language of choice fluctuates between Spanish, English, or "Spanglish"; it reflects the political directives of the theater company. For example, the Nuyorican Poets' Café works mostly in English and Spanglish, and this group is most interested in addressing issues that face the Lower East Side community as well as survival strategies.

The Puerto Rican Traveling Troupe (PRTT) was founded in 1965. This bilingual theater company was interested in the relevance of what they do to the street audience as well as in the reflections of the Hispanic tradition and artistic quality. In 1969, PRTT produced *Encrucijada* by Ballester, a play that looks at the breakdown of a family once they come to New York. Other works include *The Golden Streets* by Piri Thomas and *La pasión segun Antígone Pérez* by Luis Rafael Sánchez.

Nuyorican Poets' Café emerged on the Lower East Side of Manhattan and reflected the contemporary scene, life on the Lower East Side, and survival strategies for Puerto Ricans born on the mainland. These writers emphasized the importance of combining performance and the reading of poetry. As a result, new forms of theater have been explored, such as Miguel Piñero's *Short Eyes* (1975) and *Leaf People* (1976).

Other theater groups include the Latin Insomniacs and the Puerto Rican Bilingual Workshop.

Kanta Kochhar-Lindgren

See also: Film, Radio, and Television, Foreign and Immigrant Influence on American Popular Culture, Language (Part II, Sec. 10).

BIBLIOGRAPHY

Antush, John, ed. *Recent Puerto Rican Theater: Five Plays from New York.* Houston: Arte Público, 1991.

Cortino, Rudolfo, ed. *Cuban American Theater.* Houston: Arte Público, 1991.

Houston, Velina, ed. *The Politics of Life: Four Plays by Asian American Women.* Philadelphia: Temple University Press, 1993.

Huerta, Jorge. *Chicano Theater: Themes and Forms.* Tempe, AZ: Bilingual, 1982.

———. *Necessary Theater: Six Plays About the Chicano Experience.* Houston: Arte Público, 1989.

Kanellos, Nicolás. *Hispanic Theater in the United States.* Houston: Arte Público, 1984.

———. *A History of Hispanic Theatre in the United States: Origins to 1940.* Austin: University of Texas Press, 1990.

———. *Mexican American Theatre: Then and Now.* Houston: Arte Público, 1983.

Lomelí, Francisco, ed. *Handbook of Hispanic Cultures in the United States: Literature and Art.* Houston: Arte Público, 1993.

Seller, Maxine Schwartz, ed. *Ethnic Theatre in the United States.* Westport, CT: Greenwood Press, 1983.

ARTS III: VISUAL AND RELIGIOUS ARTS

The principles that underlie sacred art and architecture are fundamentally linked to religious communities in the East and the West. Space, form, and aesthetic expression may be affected by varying geographical or regional conditions, but the operative tenets of dogma remain constant. Dogma transcends aesthetic considerations, although aesthetic considerations are recognized as being inseparable from belief. Sacred aesthetics are inextricably linked to sacred symbols and forms and are thus reflected in the laying out of sacred space. Within the character of sacred space, we often find principles of traditional form. That is, religious practice invariably influences the principles and the process of art and architecture.

Even the dynamics that involve change of habitat clearly maintain various cultural anachronisms of time and place. For example, in America the status given to religious aesthetics involves a whole range of "migrating styles," which are perpetuated in various types of motifs, form, and space without regard for time and place. Therefore, hybrid renditions of traditional styles have emerged due to the presence of diaspora religious communities from Europe, Africa, and the Far East. Undoubtedly, the primary importance of an aesthetic image lies in how it facilitates religious identity; however, the idea of an American character may be viewed as an alternative response to the regional context. This American character is articulated in different ways. Sometimes it follows an emotional interpretation of an extant example from an alien context. Often it is characterized by one or more of the dominant features of an older model, copied and broken down into a more easily perceptible visual expression; sometimes it is heavily embellished with symbolic architectural elements that are key to the overall composition and function.

Of further interest in trying to articulate the relationship between diaspora and the aesthetics of migrating styles is the need to make drastic architectural modifications in order to comply with American building codes. This allows for the conversion of a traditional image into a new image that is decidedly American.

Within the last fifty years a new generation of religious clients have emerged in America, including Muslims, Hindus, and Buddhists, and as the form of each group's type of edifice—such as mosque or temple—becomes fully established in the American landscape, our perception of the aesthetic expression of these new American religious edifices will need greater attention.

THE AMERICAN MOSQUE (MASJID)

The practice of Islam in America takes its religious precedents and aesthetic traditions quite seriously, drawing heavily from doctrinal understanding of iconography and architectural knowledge largely derived from extant styles in the Muslim world. The aesthetic traditions of Muslim religious edifices, specifically the decorative and spatial styles of mosque architecture that have evolved since the first mosque was built by the Prophet Muhammad in the seventh century C.E. in Arabia, share aesthetic values with similar structures recently built in North America. Five aesthetic principles have shaped the formative principles of a mosque since the seventh century: structure of belief, order, space, materials, and symbols. These formative principles can be found in mosques built in the United States since the 1950s; in America, these principles are largely responsive to the religious and cultural needs of the immigrant community.

Today there are an estimated fifteen hundred to three thousand mosques serving 6 to 8 million adherents of the Islamic faith in North America. Forty-five percent of the American Muslim community are native-born African Americans, and 55 percent are

This mural by an immigrant artist depicts residents of a Latino neighborhood in El Paso, Texas. (Jack Kurtz/Impact Visuals)

immigrants from Asia, sub-Saharan Africa, North Africa, and the Indian subcontinent. Most of the mosques were built in the last forty years; no known Muslim religious buildings survive from the antebellum period, when the first African Muslims from West Africa were brought to the United States.

There are no formal design standards for an American mosque. It was only recently that mosque standards were included in the religious building section of the American Architectural Graphic Standards, which is consulted by professional architects and architectural students. In the absence of design standards, American architects who have been commissioned to design mosques over the past four decades have exercised absolute freedom in interpreting planning prerequisites to meet American code requirements. In some instances they have exercised free interpretation of extant aesthetic themes—for example, in trying to grasp the client's own preferences for regional religious images from his or her native land, or in trying to solve the more practical problem of determining the *qiblah* axis (the Mecca orientation). The forces that shape the American mosque are therefore

challenging, complex, and unique when seen in terms of aesthetics and the ethnic diversity that exists in the Muslim community. Many types of design issues related to ethnicity have resulted in a modest but growing architectural discourse about cultural interpretation, anachronism, and ideas of identity facing the Muslim diaspora community.

Four American mosques present an interesting overview of the problem of aesthetics, and the interpretation of belief, order, space, materials, and symbols. In the first example, the Islamic Center in Washington, D.C. (1957), the architect chose to replicate a spatial image and various types of visual motifs from the past. A New Mexico mosque, Dar al-Islam Foundation Islamic Center Village (1980), invokes traditional building techniques and materials from ancient Nubia. The use of geometric order is reflected in the design of the Islamic Society of North America (ISNA) headquarters in Plainfield, Indiana (1982). A final approach redefines the vocabulary of belief, order, space, materials, and symbols; this can be seen in the Manhattan mosque, and the New York Islamic Cultural

Center designed by Skidmore Owings and Merill (1990).

THE ISLAMIC CENTER IN WASHINGTON, D.C.

The cornerstone of the Islamic Center in Washington, D.C., was laid in 1949, and the center was formally inaugurated by President Dwight Eisenhower in 1957. It was built primarily for the transient Muslim diplomatic community and Muslim immigrants who began to arrive in America after World War II. Although it was not the first mosque or the oldest established in America, it was the first to be built in a major American city. Like other American mosques and Islamic centers, the edifice employs a unique aesthetic vocabulary.

The architect Abdur Rahman Rossi, an Italian Muslim, was employed by the Egyptian Ministry of Endowment to design the building. He applied medieval Cairene aesthetic references internally and externally, selecting fifteenth-century Mamluk motifs for the building. The history of Muslim architecture is a key consideration for an architect who aims to gratify an immigrant Muslim client. There are problems with the indiscriminate use of a well-known convention or an influencing custom, however; in attempting to replicate extant features from the past, aesthetics may be severely compromised.

By reanimating an image from the past, the first generation of Muslim immigrants from the Middle East and the Indian subcontinent have held firmly to the production of a recognizable religious image. The utilization of a religious image gives outward expression and meaning to the presence of an Islamic practice in North America. Beyond the aspect of a place for communal worship, a recognizable image imparts identity and also produces an emotional charge. Emotions and sentiments are evoked through the agency of memory; despite geographical, historical, and chronological nuances, the features of an extant image, when reanimated, become a common aesthetic ethos and are happily embraced by the community. By recalling an image from the past, one no longer remains in an alien environment, but becomes part of an environment where belief and emotions are nourished by familiar aesthetic themes.

While the symbolic meaning of the inscriptions would satisfy one with a quiet, devotional disposition, the mosque's form evokes the image of a religious prototype that has been reanimated from the fifteenth century.

THE MOSQUE AT ABIQUIU, NEW MEXICO

The late Egyptian architect Hassan Fathy was commissioned to design and build a mosque and prepare the master plan for the Dar al-Islam Foundation Islamic Center Village, a "traditional" Muslim village at Abiquiu, New Mexico. The mesa site is framed by surrounding arid hills and several snow-capped mountains visible in the distance. Abiquiu, the Charma Valley, and its immediate surroundings have a long history. The area was populated before the arrival of the Spanish by several native Indian peoples, and Spanish settlers arrived in 1598. The harsh environmental conditions at Abiquiu provided an ideal setting for Los Hermanos de la Luz, the Penitente Brotherhood, which was widely embraced by the Spanish settlers.

Fathy's mosque and its ancillary buildings undoubtedly belong to the site, which proposes a clean, demarcated space for worship facing Mecca. The reflective aura of the mosque and the *madrassah* become apparent upon entering the contemplative silence of the sanctuary. Traditional adobe technique worked well for the choice of site and the project itself. By using adobe construction, Fathy remained faithful to his tectonic tradition, using a natural material that implicitly endorses the notion of "small is beautiful."

The original idea was to establish an American Muslim village, the largest and most comprehensive of its kind. The Abiquiu site shares an empathic relationship with Fathy's theory of creativity: human orientation, inward and outward correlation of intimate spaces, and above all a natural form that blends with the landscape. Fathy's balanced spiritual awareness of a sense of unity between building, landscape, and user imposes an intangible order on the building and the site. Fathy's reasoning for the mosque and the Abiquiu site is a reaffirmation of Nubian building traditions. The New Mexico mosque architecture depicts an association with *fitrah*: natural tendency, innate character, temperament, natural disposition, truth, and order. These terms confer a definition of existence that are entirely apart from the maxims virtue, commodity, and delight espoused by the second-century C.E. Roman architect Vitruvius. Fathy's architecture is anticlassical; his tectonic rules decide surface treatment and delineate spaces for rest, prayer, and contemplation.

The plan for the New Mexico site is therefore a concept that appeals to the human spirit. Not only is there a tendency to consider the character of the site in terms of its psychological impulse, but it is in a manner of speaking a spiritual place: a container that naturally embodies physical space. In this sense Fathy's building tradition can be thought of as a leit-motif, giving value and meaning to the sense of human existence.

ISLAMIC SOCIETY OF NORTH AMERICA, PLAINFIELD, INDIANA

Professor Gulzar Haider employs geometry as an ordering theme in the design of the Islamic Society of North America at Plainfield, Indiana. This analytical approach to the problem of space and form is a problem common to both East and West. When geometric elements of the square are juxtaposed, a set of very interesting additive and repetitive spatial cores is created. In this scheme, the multiunit geometric themes employed have to do with a two-tiered order: first, their essence and esoteric structure, and second, their external appearance. There is no attempt to defuse the hierarchies of spaces that emerge as a result of juxtaposition. Geometry is central to the design of the building, to the extent that Koranic inscriptions have been deemphasized. Unlike the Manhattan mosque, where the inscriptions can be considered as simply a decorative agent, in Haider's scheme, decoration is disassociated in order to allow the essence and primacy of geometry to dominate. By emphasizing the elements of a cosmological geometric form and deemphasizing text, the architect has achieved a desired balance that considers both American construction methods and the spirit of the extant tradition of using geometry as an ordering principle.

Haider's appeal to reason and experience in terms of what he calls the guiding principles for architecture in a non-Islamic environment is seriously challenging: Geometry promotes the organization of a spatial pattern, the hierarchy of symbolic elements that are in equilibrium. Haider discourages the use of imitational forms and encourages a design program that emphasizes a cognition of the mosque in the American environment. Haider's theory stands as an example of what we have discussed earlier with regard to the use of the historical past as a kind of aesthetic continuum. What makes his theory important is the fact that Haider understands the problem of architecture for Muslim communities in those parts of the world that are ideologically, culturally, and historically non-Islamic. The architect manages to capture the spirit of a geometric theme, a morphology that is so prevalent in the Islamic cosmology. Haider has achieved a balance between the use of technology suited to the construction industry in America and the spirit of a tradition.

ISLAMIC CULTURAL CENTER, NEW YORK CITY, NEW YORK

The New York Islamic Cultural Center mosque confronts the issue of tradition and modernity by seeking to reinterpret various aesthetic themes associated with an extant model found in the Muslim world. There are several observations to be made in this regard. First, the surface motifs reflect geometric themes, which are employed as a unifying element throughout the mosque's interior and exterior. The geometric motifs bear a close resemblance to Piet Mondrian's paintings, particularly his work entitled *Broadway Boogie Woogie*. These motifs can be seen primarily on the carpet where worshipers assemble for prayer in horizontal and parallel rows facing the *qiblah*. They also appear in the surface treatment of the *minbar*, the exterior façade, and in several other interior elements as well. Geometry is a fundamental theme in Muslim cosmology, but in this case it comes closer to a modernist, secular interpretation rather than to a traditional, cosmological one. The corollary of this argument is that a building tradition should be modified only if the needs of the community make it necessary or essential. This view prevails in some sectors of the community today; and is always a source of discontent. Third, there are convincing reasons to endorse the innovative approach taken by the architect, since form and space can be adapted to novel uses that serve the purpose of the community. Nevertheless, the problem of defining what aspect of form and space is traditional or modern—while including the legal aspect of religious practice—has led to dissenting opinions. Dissenting opinions would seem not to have any legal footing, since architectural judgment has little effect on religious practice because the physical requirements of a mosque is largely the outcome of community consensus. Evidence of dissent can be found in the case of the Manhattan mosque in spite of the cosmopolitan makeup of the New York City community.

THE AMERICAN SYNAGOGUE

There have been a number of recent studies that focus on the evolution of the American synagogue. Several of these have considered the relationship between architectural design and environment, which stresses the relations between the upward social mobility of the American Jewish community and its traditional patterns of congregational life. In *The Americanization of the Synagogue, 1820–1870*, Leon A. Jick noted that "what was true of immigrants generally was even more evident among Jews. Their ties to the old country had always been more tenuous than those of other ethnic minorities; their desire for acculturation had always been strong." Paralleling Jick's work is that of Gerard R. Wolfe, *The Synagogues of New York's Lower East Side,* and Charlton W. Tebeau, *Synagogue in the Central City.* These studies as well as others discuss the development of the American synagogue, its psychological value, and the evolving aesthetic conditions that embody a diaspora community. Many of the synagogues under discussion here were built by non-Jewish architects, and to what extent their designs were determined by the wishes of the congregation they served is not easy to tell. American architects have wrestled with the need to provide a building in keeping with Jewish philosophy of life and with Jewish rituals, since there is no specific "Jewish" style. For example, in medieval Spain synagogues were built in the Arab-Islamic (Moorish) style.

Between 1650 and 1880 there were two major waves of Jewish immigration to America; thus the American synagogue has a history of more than three hundred years. The Mill Street Synagogue built in lower Manhattan in 1730—measuring thirty-five feet square—but no longer standing is widely acknowledged as the oldest synagogue in America. The oldest extant religious edifice, the Touro Sephardic Synagogue, dates to 1763 and is located in Newport, Rhode Island. Whereas the eighteenth-century Touro Synagogue was built in the Georgian style, the twentieth-century (Reform) Temple Emanu-El on Fifth Avenue in New York City, built in 1929, adopted the Romanesque style. These two examples suggest a type of architectural evolution whereby the environment has a direct grounding and determinate effect on religious or cultural sentiment, taste, financial conditions, as well as the way people decide upon a style, even if the process is not necessarily a predictable one.

Several examples of the stylistic features of the synagogues built across America from the eighteenth century to the present day reveal both experimentation as well as alien influences. In Philadelphia the second Cherry Street Synagogue—measuring thirty feet by sixty feet and known as the Mikveh Israel Synagogue—was built by the architect William Strickland in 1826 and was demolished in 1860. The building was described in the *Philadelphia Guide Book* as having a dome supported by Egyptian columns copied from the temple of Dendera. This style, belonging to the early period of the Egyptian revival in the United States, was the first of two American synagogues built in that style, which had a stylistic precedent in Europe. Strickland also used Egyptian motifs in the First

Presbyterian Church (also known as the Downtown Presbyterian Church) at Nashville, Tennessee (1851). Plates of the Napoleonic expedition were widely used in Europe and later in America; one example in Europe was the Great Synagogue of London (1790), which served an Ashkenazic congregation. Another Philadelphia synagogue, the Crown Street Synagogue (1849), was conspicuously Egyptian. The two columns at the entrance of the building had papyrus motifs obviously copied from the plates of the Napoleonic expedition. By the middle of the 1850s, the Egyptian style had exhausted itself, and the exterior features that had captured the imagination of architects such as Strickland were no longer in vogue.

In the late nineteenth century, attitudes toward the Moorish style suggest that it had assumed new emphasis, although the criterion for aesthetic accuracy in copying the style had declined. While American architects and builders found the Moorish style profoundly enlightening, it was put to use in outright contradiction to conventional building practices, meaning, and description. The New York Crystal Palace's bazaars, markets, and exhibition halls, all built in 1851 were often decorated with Moorish arches and Islamic tracery, and the interior of the buildings, although an oddity, preserved certain decorative elements of the thirteenth-century Al-Hambra Palace.

Exactly how the Moorish style became an accepted architectural treatment of the Jewish synagogue in America is a subject of debate. One explanation is derived from the fact that Jews and Muslims shared a common architectural legacy in medieval Spain prior to being expelled. In the design of the Moorish-style synagogue, Jewish and non-Jewish architects borrowed heavily from the influence of medieval Spain, which had already spread to the rest of Europe in buildings by architects such as Gottfried Semper, Otto Simonson, and Ernst Zwirner. Jewish immigrants from Europe who traveled to America in the nineteenth century apparently brought the style along with them; for example, the B'nai Yeshurun synagogue, designed by James Keys Wilson in Cincinnati in 1864, is principally composed of Moorish elements. The Plum Street Temple, as it was also called, was described as an "Alhambra temple with slender pillars and thirteen domes."

The influx of Jewish intellectuals to the United States in the 1930s and 1940s included the Jewish architect Eric Mendelson, who had been affiliated with the Expressionist movement in Germany and later the Bauhaus movement. Between 1946 and 1952 Mendelson participated in several large-scale design projects for synagogues and community centers in the United States. Among these is the Park Synagogue Anashe

Emeth Beth Tefilo congregation in Cleveland, which was completed in 1952. The circular assembly hall of the synagogue is enclosed by a huge, monumental dome measuring one hundred feet in diameter. Arnold Whittick explains Mendelson's use of the dome—a symbolic form—as intrinsically related to Mendelson's belief that in Judaism, God is not remote or mysterious but near, and the heavens and earth are united in the Spirit of God. In his synagogue, which is essentially all dome, there are no walls that would support the dome and thereby divide the heavens from the earth.

Recent trends in the design of the American synagogue suggest that quiet elegance has replaced the eclectic styles of the eighteenth and late nineteenth century, which is achieved mostly with the introduction of modern elements and the omission of unnecessary, sluggish details.

THE AMERICAN HINDU TEMPLE

Only recently has Hinduism been acknowledged as having a strong religious presence in America. As the Hindu population grows, the emergence of Hindu religious architecture serves to unite the diaspora community. Hindu temples are often part of a larger complex known as an ashram, an establishment comprised of the main temple, guest housing, various support buildings, gardens, and orchards. Both temples and ashrams provide a place of worship and retreat, as well as a center for traditional Indian celebrations. Today, there are temples in at least twenty-five states, serving a diverse community of immigrant and converted Hindus. Though there are no formal standards for the design of a Hindu temple in America, identifiable features and stylistic traditions prevail, drawing heavily from extant styles and religious precedent. Religious structures constructed in America no longer adhere to the strict boundaries of form, style, and proportion found in the Shastras, the ancient Indian texts on architecture. Architects rely on a doctrinal understanding of cultural and religious symbolism and have more freedom to interpret and adapt these to the differing circumstances found in America.

Significant collaboration between Indian and American architects during the design of a temple is often pursued. In most cases, *shilpi,* artisans from India trained in the tradition of temple architecture, are brought to America to embellish architectural elements found throughout the structure. *Shilpi* help to preserve a rich history of decorative embellishment steeped in religious symbolism. The resulting character is central to the overall experience of the Hindu temple. Architects face unique considerations when designing Hindu temples and ashrams in America. The questions of identity, religious and aesthetic symbolism, and construction approach are of utmost concern. Two Hindu temples built in the United States have dealt with these questions in varying ways: the Sri Lakshmi Temple in Ashland, Massachusetts, and the Shree Raseshwari Radha Rani Temple at Barsana Dham, located in Austin, Texas.

The Sri Lakshmi Temple draws heavily from extant styles and recognizable religious precedent. Building upon the emotions and sentiments of an informed aesthetic language, the Sri Lakshmi Temple nourishes the familiar within an unfamiliar setting. Built in the 1980s, the temple serves as a focal point for the immigrant Hindu community in New England. Features similar to those found in temples of southern India shape the identity of the temple. For example, formative principles of massing and tectonics can be seen in the plan. The four key features are the *rajagopuram, dwajasthambam, mahamandapam,* and *sikhara.* The *rajagopuram,* or gateway, serves as the grand entrance to the temple. This striking fifty-foot-tall feature, like that of south Indian architecture, is highly ornate and is the most prominent feature on the temple grounds. A flagpole, or *dwajasthambam,* is used to announce special occasions and Hindu activities and is placed between the *rajagopuram* and the *mahamandapam,* the main body of the temple. The foremost significance of the sanctum is expressed in a tower or spire form known as the *sikhara.* The altar and image of the deity can be found in the most sacred chamber, the *garbha griha,* nested within the *sikhara.* Like traditional temples in India, Sri Lakshmi Temple adheres to the models derived from religious considerations and is responsive to the needs of the community.

The Shree Raseshwari Radha Rani Temple, the largest Hindu temple complex in America, also draws from extant styles. However, the architecture is a conglomeration of many aesthetic styles connected to both north and south India, as well as modern and traditional forms and materials. The temple serves as focal point for the ashram complex and is open to visitors. Like Barsana Dham, the ashram facilities are conducive to Western culture and hold great appeal for many Americans, both for religious services and celebrations and for relaxation and participation in weekend seminars. The structures at Barsana Dham, built in the 1990s, are consistent in function with ashrams built in India hundreds of years ago. The complex houses both sacred and secular buildings ranging from the ornate to ordinary, from the symbolically expressive to the quietly simple. Buildings include the Shree Raseshwari Radha Rani Temple and main office, resident and guest housing, detached pavilions, and ancillary structures. Each plays a role in the collective identity of Barsana Dham.

One first enters the complex of Barsana Dham through a gateway and tree-lined road. Together, these act as an important transition from public to private domain and serve as a threshold to clear one's mind of outside influences. From the parking lot, one's attention is focused on the temple and the celebrated tower form, while allowing for a glimpse of the temple grounds. The outward expression of the *garbha griha* takes on the traditional aesthetic vocabulary of the *sikhara*. This allows the visitor or devotee to locate the sacred center from any point on the temple grounds. Like temple architecture in northern India, the *sikhara* is the most prominent architectural element of the building and can be broken down into distinct elements: the base or platform *(pista)*, lower shaft *(bada)*, tapering upper shaft *(chhapra)*, and finial *(kalasa)*.

Guests walk to the entrance of the temple through a covered loggia. Here, the identity and aesthetic symbolism of the temple is brought to the fingertips of the visitor as they pass by a multitude of columns. The carved column details of the loggia display the decorative exuberance of *shilpi* artisans. Altogether, eighty-four columns line the edge of the loggia and *mandapa,* an open hall or pavilion, which connects the temple with the guest lodging and other ancillary buildings. The Prayer Hall continues the theme of decorative exuberance found in other portions of the temple. This room displays the *garbha griha,* which contains the altar and image of the god to whom the temple is dedicated. To further the spiritual effect, a painting of the sky was executed on the ceiling, and the Upanisads, Hindu scripture, were quoted in a band around the room, creating a peaceful and serene setting.

Architects must have had the visitor and user of the space in mind when designing the Prayer Hall. On either side of the *garbha griha* are floor-to-ceiling windows that allow for natural daylight as well as a view of the temple grounds. This juxtaposition is accentuated by the nature of the materials used. From the exterior of the building, one sees the reflective surface of the golden-colored glass, picking up on the golden accents of the *sikhara*. Not only is the façade of the temple affected, but climatic issues of the building enclosure must also be handled carefully so that the visitor in the Prayer Hall is not uncomfortable. This combination of traditional tectonics with modern

desires for light and view creates an interesting aesthetic that modifies the overall appearance of the structure. The most unique feature of Barsana Dham and Shree Raseshwari Radha Rani Temple lies in its depiction of the holy district of Braj, India. On the temple grounds are representations of important places in Braj, such as Prem Sarovar Lake, Govardhan Hill, and a stream representing the Yamuna River of Vrindaban. It is customary for Hindus to travel to places of holy designation for religious fulfillment. While many devotees in the United States cannot participate in such pilgrimages, they can find relief at Barsana Dham. The design of Barsana Dham and Shree Raseshwari Radha Rani Temple relies heavily on symbolism, calling to mind the cultural heritage and atmosphere of India. This symbolism defines the architecture, yet the construction methodology and codes in America work to modify and perhaps thereby redefine the symbolism.

THE AMERICAN BUDDHIST TEMPLE

The practice of Buddhism in America has grown enormously in the last twenty-five years, bolstered largely by revisions in U.S. immigration laws, which have led to an increase in Asian-American Buddhist communities *(sanghas),* and by a growing interest in Buddhism on the part of Anglo-Americans as well. Today there are established Buddhist *sanghas* in several North American cities: Boston, San Francisco, Berkeley, Washington, D.C., Austin, Texas, Toronto, Montreal, and Halifax. Many of these communities are of South and Southeast Asian origin—China, Korea, Japan, Tibet, and Vietnam. An exhaustive list of Buddhist community centers and places of retreat can be found in Don Morreale's *Buddhist America: Centers, Retreats, Practices.*

When Buddhism went from India to China, it underwent many centuries of integration with indigenous Chinese culture already rich with Confucian and Taoist values. Historically Buddhism has evolved and changed in its expression of the Dharma that is its core. While the Japanese Buddhist tradition is of the Zen lineages, the Vajrayāna tradition, also known as Shingon, exists as well. These subtleties and the distinction of each particular teaching have been discussed at length by Charles S. Prebish in *Luminous Passage: The Practice and Study of Buddhism in America.* For example, Chinese Buddhism includes five traditional schools (Tantric, Ch'an, T'ien-t'ai, Vinaya, and Chin-t'u). Prebish notes that Chinese Buddhism in the United States is dominated by four groups with various branches: the Dharma Realm Buddhist Association, the Buddhist Association of the United States, the Institute of Chung-Hwa Buddhist Culture, and Hsi Lai Temple.

Buddhist practices in the United States are as diverse as the groups mentioned earlier, moving from very traditional to an integrated adaptation of each teaching—an example is the practice of insight meditation or *vipassanâ*. The dynamics of immigration, distinctions between monks and laity, and ritual have played a part in the development of American Buddhism. Many of these nuances have been discussed at length by Charles Prebish and Kenneth Tanka in *The Faces of Buddhism in America*. At one particular American Zen monastery, the membership consists of monks, students, and converts to Buddhism, who can choose to participate in either of two ninety-day practice periods a year, one in summer and one in winter. They can also participate in up to fifteen major *sesshin* a year. The *sesshin* is the quintessential Zen practice, combining long hours of *zazen* a day (*zazen* or *dokusan* is a one-to-one meeting with the *roshi* in which the practitioner offers a response to a *kōan*) with *sûtras* (worship, chantings, teachings) said in Japanese. Chanting is central to religious life of the temple. Virtually every rite begins with a chant.

Traditionally, there are two types of Buddhist temples. The first combines a tall, symbolic feature (a stupa or pagoda—a devotional reliquary mound) with a temple hall; the second and later type consisted of buildings around a courtyard. Both examples can be found in the United States. While many temples are located in houses, old school buildings, or store fronts, the Wat Thai temple in Los Angeles is one of the many temples built across the United States since the 1980s. In Austin, Texas, a courtyard-type temple affiliated with the Venerable Master Hsing Yun—founder of the Taiwan-based Guang Shan International Buddhist Order—was recently constructed. This order emphasizes education and service and maintains universities, Buddhist colleges, libraries, and publishing houses. It has the largest number of female monastics of any Buddhist order today. The Hsi Lai Temple in Austin, Texas, has in residence a fully ordained female precept-holding nun or *sramanerika*. A similar example of the courtyard type of temple exists in Los Angeles. A model of the Great Stupa of Dharmakya can be found at Rocky Mountain Shambala Center at Red Feather Lakes, Colorado. It represents both a high regard for the Buddhist architectural tradition noted earlier and the willingness to innovate that is encountered in much of Tibetan Buddhism in America. This temple, which was built over many years, has merged Tibetan precedents with American concrete construction technology. In contrast, the BCA (Buddhist Churches of America) San Francisco headquaters has a prominent stupa located on the roof of the building; it is reputed to be the oldest stupa found in the United States.

One of the defining elements in what we have described as diaspora aesthetics may well be the simulation of two modes of aesthetic reasoning, one universal and the other particular. First, the aesthetic image of the universal embraces convention and origin; it expresses its own mimetic essence as well by asserting meaning and truth. It is self-evident in its relationship to the world, and therefore it maintains the right to exist. Second, the particular mode of expression seeks to find its own American identity in the face of obvious social and cultural realities; it is an innovative gesture that represents innovation and change.

The temple, the mosque, and the synagogue are candid examples of diaspora aesthetics. The visual possibilities that these edifices have introduced to the American landscape admit of the affirmative elements of America immigration—ethnicity, religion, and cultural identity. Each edifice in its essence and appearance has a valued origin, which is characteristic of a particular place and time. Each example is a spiritual paradigm with references to a historical type, but in its evolution and presence in America it also confronts what that type should look like. In so doing, each edifice establishes its own categorical reference through spatial repetition, cultural representation, and visual affinity.

Akel Kahera

See also: Film, Radio, and Television, Foreign and Immigrant Influence on American Popular Culture (Part II, Sec. 10).

BIBLIOGRAPHY

Ebersole, Robert. *Black Pagoda.* Gainesville: University of Florida Press, 1957.

Fletcher, Sir Banister. *A History of Architecture on the Comparative Method.* New York: Charles Scribner's Sons, 1961.

Haider, Gulzar. "Brother in Islam, Please Draw Us a Mosque: Muslims in the West: A Personal Account." In *Expressions of Islam in Buildings,* proceedings of an international seminar held in Jakarta and Yogyakarta, 15–19 October 1990, pp. 155–66. Jakarta, Indonesia: Aga Khan Trust for Cultures.

Jick, Leon A. *The Americanization of the Synagogue, 1820–1870.* Hanover, NH: University Press of New England, 1976.

Kahera, Akel Ismail. "Image, Text and Form: Complexities of Aesthetics in an American Mosque." *Studies in Contemporary Islam* 1:2 (1999): 73–85.

Kahera, Akel, and Latif Abdul-Malik. "Designing the American Mosque." *Islamic Horizons* (September–October 1996): 40–41.

Khalidi, Omar. "Approaches to Mosque Design in North America." In *Muslims on the Americanization Path?*, ed. Yvonne Haddad and John Esposito, pp. 399–424. Atlanta: Scholars Press, 1998.

Metcaff, Barbara Daly. *Making Muslim Space in North America and Europe.* Berkeley: University of California Press, 1996.

Morreale, Don, ed. *Buddhist America: Centers, Retreats, Practices.* Santa Fe, NM: John Muir Publications, 1988.

Orlinsky, Harry, ed. *The Synagogue: Studies in Origins, Archeology, and Architecture.* New York: KTAV Publishing House, 1975.

Prebish, Charles S. *Luminous Passage: The Practice and Study of Buddhism in America.* Berkeley: University of California Press, 1999.

Prebish, Charles S., and Kenneth K. Tanka. *The Faces of Buddhism in America.* Berkeley: University of California Press, 1998.

Raz, Ram. *Essay on the Architecture of the Hindus.* Delhi: Indological Book House, 1972.

Seager, Richard H. *Buddhism in America.* New York: Columbia University Press, 1999.

Tebeau, Charlton. *Synagogue in the Central City: Temple Israel of Greater Miami, 1922–1972.* Oxford, OH: Miami University Press, 1972.

Thomas, Wendell. *Hinduism Invades America.* New York: Beacon Press, 1930.

Wischitzer, Rachel. *Synagogue Architecture in the United States: History and Interpretation.* Philadelphia: Jewish Publication Society of America, 1955.

———. *The Architecture of the European Synagogue.* Philadelphia: Jewish Publication Society of America, 1964.

Wolfe, Gerard R. *The Synagogues of New York's Lower East Side.* New York: New York University Press, 1978.

ENGLISH AS A SECOND LANGUAGE

English as a Second Language (ESL) is concerned with the development and acquisition of English communication skills (reading, speaking, writing, and listening) among individuals whose native language is not English. English as a Second Language courses for limited-English-proficient (LEP) children and youth have been incorporated into local educational institutions and college and university (including community and tribal) curricula since the 1960s. Additionally, ESL programs have long been an important component of community-based organizations and government programs that work with LEP adults. The 1990 census reports that 25.5 million adults in the United States speak a language other than English. Of those, over 5 million indicate that they do not speak English well or do not speak it at all. While English is not the official language of the United States, studies show that it is necessary to have a working knowledge of the English language if only to obtain the basic necessities (housing, food, education, education, and health care).

ENGLISH AS A SECOND LANGUAGE

Generally speaking, ESL programs are English-only instructional programs that seek to develop English language proficiency to the extent that students are able to communicate socially, academically, and professionally. English as a Second Language programs typically fall into two broad categories, content or traditional, both of which, unless part of a bilingual education program, typically remove the students from mainstream classes for part or all of a day. Once removed from the classroom, students with LEP are then given special instruction in the English language (traditional) and other subjects (content).

Likewise, adults in traditional ESL classes learn English without use of the native language, and the instruction usually focuses on those words and phrases which the adults need to know to survive in English-speaking environments. Traditional ESL courses are not designed to teach English while utilizing a student's native language. While traditional and content ESL programs may have been moderately successful, studies suggest that students who learn ESL while simultaneously maintaining and affirming their native language realize higher grades and score higher on standardized test scores than do students who study only English.

As the demand for ESL instruction has increased, so have the pedagogical approaches for teaching ESL changed. English as a Second Language combines the ideas from applied linguistics, anthropology, and cognitive science and reflects many of the recent shifts that have occurred in second-language learning and adult literacy education. Additionally, the changing theoretical and practical approaches to teaching ESL are in response to the widely varying groups of students for whom English is a second language: international students, immigrants, second-generation immigrants, refugees, and native-born North Americans. Students of ESL, like students of any discipline, have very different levels of proficiency and bring to the classroom a variety of cultural experiences, values, and needs. According to recent studies, the more effective ESL classrooms are those which promote second-language acquisition as a learning process that links the unique experiences of the learner to culture, language, and learning as opposed to teaching literacy as a set of skills, isolated from personal experience. Recent trends in ESL instruction for adults and kindergarten through twelfth grade (K–12) reflect this change from teacher-centered to learner-centered instruction.

A cottage industry of English-language schools has been created in many American cities to serve the wave of recent immigrants. (Anne Burns)

K–12 ESL

English as a Second Language for K–12 has experienced many pedagogical developments in the past decade. Perhaps the greatest impetus for change in K–12 ESL methodology, curriculum, and practice has been the changing demographics of the United States and the national education standards movement that has been implemented in most states. The standards movement came about in an effort to ensure that all students in a state were learning the same basic information in several content areas regardless of where they attended school. All students are required to test their knowledge on state-mandated standardized tests at various levels in their education (i.e., an exam in fourth, eighth, and twelfth grades, and so forth). The content curriculum standards requirements have had an enormous impact on ESL teaching professionals as well as mainstream professionals who are challenged to find ways to adapt their content-area curriculum to the needs of the ESL students.

PROGRAMS

ESL programs use only English for teaching. Some ESL programs are used with bilingual education programs, but most are incorporated in schools where no other second-language acquisition program exists. The following are English-only program types:

1. *Sheltered English.* Students remain in the mainstream classroom and are taught subject matter in English. Instruction is in a particular content area and is carefully created and organized to promote English-language acquisition. The teacher organizes appropriate instruction around the content (math, reading, science); modifies language during instruction (speaks slowly and clearly, repeats words); supports verbal explanations with nonverbal actions (pictures, graphs, facial expressions).

2. *ESL Pullout.* Students remain in the mainstream classroom for most of the day and are pulled out

Catholic Sister Yamile Saleh teaches English to Haitian immigrants at a Catholic Community Center in the Little Haiti section of Miami. *(Jack Kurtz/Impact Visuals)*

of the class on a regular basis to receive instruction in English-language development. The purpose of the pullout class is to help the students become proficient in English.

3. *English-Language Development.* Limited-English-proficient students are taught all their subject matter in a classroom separate from native English-speaking students. The teacher in English language development is a second-language professional.

THEORY

There are several theoretical perspectives that shape ESL programs in K–12 programs. The purpose of all ESL programs is to create a learning environment that will foster the acquisition of language proficiency in English equal to, or surpassing, that of students' native language. In most instances, this means acquiring English phonology, syntax, and semantics so that they

can use them in a range of social contexts—in academics, with friends and employers, and so on. Adherents of the following theoretical perspectives differ in the ways that they believe ESL students learn and in what they believe to be the fundamental goal of second-language acquisition.

FUNCTIONAL/NOTIONAL

Functional/notional theory combines the function of language (what purpose language is used for) with the instances in which language is used (e.g., a person may ask [function] for a pen [notion]. Language is seen as a skill that is needed to get things done. The things that "get done" with language are the "functions," and "notions" are the spatial, temporal or existential things. The focus is on what language does as opposed to how it works grammatically. According to Anna Uhl Chamot, "a functional ESL curriculum must go beyond the threshold level of social communicative skills and provide instruction and development in the cognitive and academic language skills needed in the classroom," and a functional/notional curriculum meets these needs. In functional/notional classrooms, the students' objectives are focused on what the learner will actually do with the language, not the language description or structure. The needs of the student are determined by completing an assessment, and instruction is typically individualized.

SYSTEMS BEHAVIORAL DESIGN

Systems behavioral design (SBD) is based on the theoretical perspective of psychologist B. F. Skinner, who is considered the father of behaviorism. Adherents to the philosophy of behaviorism believe that learning occurs within the context of a teacher-directed, stimulus-response methodology. The acquisition of knowledge is determined by measurable behavioral changes. At the crux of this philosophy are two important concepts: incremental learning ultimately leading to mastery learning. Systems behavioral design is based on the premise that, given an appropriate amount of time, students can learn anything so long as it is learned in the proper sequence (i.e., one must learn to walk before running, or in the case of ESL, one must learn a simple sentence before a complex sentence). Therefore, successful implementation of SBD necessitates that the teacher set objectives, create activities that will enable students to master the objectives, and develop a system of measurements to evaluate the students' progress. Ideally, students are evaluated before entering the classroom so that teachers are effectively able to define the curriculum content for the learner. The main goal of SBD is the acquisition of knowledge in a systematic, teacher-directed manner.

PROBLEM POSING APPROACH

The problem posing approach (PPA) is based on the belief that the curriculum comes from the students' real-life experiences and concerns. Proponents of PPA believe that students learn best when they are actively involved in the process of defining and creating the content and that language cannot be separated from the culture. In other words, language must be learned in a cultural context. What is important to the students will motivate them to learn the language because they see an immediate purpose to the acquisition of the second language. Therefore, the organization of the course is related to cultural themes rather than the structural analysis of the language. Unlike SBD, the PPA does not follow a particular sequence; rather, the approach is process oriented and seeks to develop critical thinking skills and the ability to synthesize.

The problem posing approach uses two important concepts—praxis and dialogue. Praxis involves reflection and action; dialogue is the point where praxis occurs (the discussion of vocabulary, ideas, thoughts, and opinions). Dialogue occurs throughout the process and is where the education of language (reading, writing, speaking) takes place. For example, during class a student shares her parents' concern about their lack of transportation. Her family's car broke down and the estimates for repairs are very high. Because they live in a rural community, finding public transportation has been difficult for them. With the teacher's guidance, the class decides to explore transportation and car repair options in the community. The initial reflection may require students to use English to gather information (action) from local resources. When the students come together, they share (dialogue) their information with one another, again using English. They may also discuss solutions that are used in their individual cultures (reflection) and compare them (action) with those which are available in the host culture in an effort to come up with a new option (dialogue). Throughout the process, the students are engaged in all levels of second-language acquisition and are simultaneously learning the fundamentals of the English language (vocabulary, sentence structure, and so on).

WHOLE LANGUAGE/NATURAL APPROACH

The whole language approach (WLA) is a theoretical perspective on teaching ESL that is based on the premise that children learn language as naturally as they learn to walk and talk. This approach requires that language be kept "whole," which means that the instructional approaches should promote the integration of speaking, reading, listening, and writing in ways that reflect natural language use. For example, teachers may read a story aloud, asking the children to join in either reciting the story verbally or drawing a picture; children hear stories told at storytime; children engage in holistic writing when they draw pictures or write their own symbols.

PRACTICE: INSTRUCTIONAL TECHNIQUES

Instructional techniques are strategies for presenting the curriculum to students. Although the application of the techniques depends on the ESL program model that a school adheres to and the theoretical approach of the teacher, many of the techniques represent variations of common themes.

TOTAL PHYSICAL RESPONSE

Total physical response (TPR) was developed by James Asher and has been used in introductory ESL classes extensively for the past thirty years. Total physical response is based on the notion that students learn more when they are active participants in the learning process. In this case, "active" means actually physically doing something beyond sitting in a chair at a desk and listening to the teacher. Asher believes that "there is an intimate relationship between language and the child's body." Therefore, the task of the teacher is to engage the student on both an intellectual and physiological level. Total physical response lessons are most effective when they are organized around simple, sequential concepts that the students can act out. For example, a teacher might have a lesson titled "Getting Ready for School," which could include the following actions accompanied by simple sentences: waking up, yawning, walking through one's room, brushing teeth, taking a bath, and so on. The goal is to teach the students the meaning of words, sentences, and concepts through action.

COUNSELING-LEARNING

Counseling-learning (CL), developed by psychologist Charles Curran, is a technique that aims to create a safe, secure, and stress-free learning environment for students. Curan believes that students will learn a second language if they are in a secure environment. The key to the creation of a secure environment has to do with the teacher's ability to possess a genuine understanding for the students in the classroom. According to Curran, this understanding includes (1) the teacher's nonjudgmental acceptance of the students; (2) the teacher's belief that the students can get along peacefully, and (3) the sharing of personal experiences when appropriate. Curran summarizes these ideas in an acronym, SARD (security, aggressiveness/attention, reflection/retention, and discrimination).

The student's sense of security is the foundation to the CL approach. The more secure that students feel, the more willing they are to take risks and try new learning experiences. Additionally, students will learn more because they will not be preoccupied with conscious or unconscious fears and anxieties. The teacher creates a secure environment in a number of ways including behaving in a nonjudgmental manner and gradually introducing the students to new concepts. Eventually the students will rely less on the teacher and more on themselves, thereby resulting in a more balanced relationship with the teacher.

As the students become more secure, they also become more confident and aggressive in their efforts to acquire new information (i.e., asking questions, developing new vocabulary). This process also reinforces their sense of security, as they are more willing to receive the attention that comes with speaking out. Throughout the learning process, the teacher reflects back to the student his/her thoughts about the lesson, questions, and so forth. Regardless of the teacher's opinion (the lesson was good or poor), the teacher communicates to the student in a very supportive manner. The students then reflect on what the teacher has said and may discuss the material for clarification, or the teacher may present the lesson in a different format (e.g., film, drawing) until the students understand the lesson. The students and teacher continue to interact until it is clear that the students have retained the new information. The teacher then encourages the students to discriminate between the newly acquired knowledge and the former knowledge. The goal is to have the students understand what they have learned and how it has been integrated into what they knew previously.

SUGGESTOPEDIA

Suggestopedia was created by Georgi Lozanov and can be equated to performance learning as practiced by Augusto Boal. The philosophical underpinning to suggestopedia is that students learn when they are not inhibited on either a conscious or unconscious level (hampered by fear, insecurity, self-consciousness). This is an important concern for ESL students, especially for those who remain in a mainstream classroom and are constantly conscious of their limited English proficiency. Suggestopedia is a several-day process that involves role-playing/acting, rhythmic breathing, music, and a degree of meditation. Students are given "new" identities (i.e., new name, history) in the belief that the new identity will lessen students' fears and inhibitions as all the students become excited about their "new self." The teacher then proceeds to review prior course material while introducing new material. The next part of the process involves teaching the students a rhythmic breathing technique similar to that which is used when one practices yoga. While the students are in their yoga positions and performing the rhythmic breathing, the teacher reads the lesson they just reviewed. The teacher repeats the lesson at least three times, each time in a more assertive tone. After the third time, the teacher asks the students to repeat the lesson. Following the students' response, the teacher plays classical music in an effort to draw the students out of their relaxed state. It is thought that by tapping into the students' unconscious, they learn and retain the language better. While all teachers may not have the time to investigate and acquire the teaching technique of suggestopedia, what can clearly be taken from this technique and applied in any classroom is the awareness that students may learn more when they are in stress- and anxiety-free environments and that role-playing (new identities) is a good tool to achieve that end.

COOPERATIVE/GROUP LEARNING

Cooperative/group learning is based on the belief that learning occurs more frequently in peer interaction as opposed to adult-youth (teacher-student) interaction. At the crux of this learning technique is the formation of a group and the assignment of group goals so that the group works collaboratively to achieve the goal. Oftentimes, cooperative/group learning also necessitates the physical restructuring of the classroom (chairs in a circle as opposed to lines), assigning group responsibilities, and group grading to reinforce the process of group learning. Ultimately, groups can be assigned certain classroom responsibilities, which helps to foster a sense of group autonomy so that the group becomes responsible for part of the learning process. In such instances, the teacher is on the periphery, assuming the role of observer and facilitator as needed.

THEMATIC INSTRUCTION

Thematic instruction uses topics or themes as the focal point for organizing the curriculum and has long been used in primary as well as secondary education. Thematic instruction is useful for students in ESL classes because it provides a conceptual framework wherein the students are able to use their writing, reading, and speaking skills as they learn the content of a particular subject area. Thematic instruction tends to be most effective when the students are involved in the selection of a theme and the creation of activities related to the theme. During the selection process, students use all their English skills to brainstorm and communicate ideas and to process information as they become active learners. Additionally, they begin to see themselves as integral to the learning process when their ideas are accepted, discussed, and used in classroom instruction.

SCAFFOLDING

The goal of scaffolding it is to make language clear enough to stand on its own without the teacher using gestures or other visual cues, which is a necessary cognitive academic skill. Some examples are a stable physical environment (i.e., workstations) and a daily schedule that remains constant throughout the school year. In both examples, the students come to know the routine and are able to associate certain physical objects with particular functions, thereby learning the meaning of English words, phrases, and so forth, which culminates in cognitive development.

CONTENT-AREA ACTIVITIES

Statistics indicate that the majority of students who learn ESL do so by being immersed into English-speaking classrooms for the majority of the school day. The expectation is that LEP students will learn the curriculum in the content area in the same manner that the native English speakers do. One of the challenges of teaching ESL students in English-speaking classrooms is how to ensure that LEP students learn the content. Several scholars posit that children learning ESL in an English-speaking classroom would benefit from the content-area material becoming a vehicle for language development. For example, the teachers could put the children in groups so that the children ask one another questions about their personal experiences, thoughts, and knowledge pertaining to the

specific subject matter. They are thus able to practice speaking in a culturally relevant context as opposed to plugging through the material, not incorporating the students' experiences in the course.

SUSTAINED CONTENT STUDY

Sustained content study offers students the ability to develop text analysis and writing skills by reading and writing extensively in one subject area over a period of time. The benefits are that they become familiar with the writing conventions of a particular discipline and they write over a long period of time, which affords them the opportunity to write, revise, and rewrite. According to Marcia Pally, sustained content study is not a standard strategy of ESL courses. However, recent studies have demonstrated that sustained content study can benefit ESL students by having them practice the skills that will be required of them in mainstream academic and professional settings.

ADULT ESL

Although many of the theoretical perspectives used in K–12 ESL instruction can be applied or modified to adult ESL courses, adult ESL has grown tremendously in the United States and has fast become a separate area of instruction. The main theoretical approaches/techniques fall into the following categories for adult ESL: learner centered, Freirean or participatory instruction; whole language instruction; language experience instruction; learner reading, writing, and publishing; and competency-based instruction. The aforementioned ESL programs may include the following types of instruction: basic literacy, general ESL, family literacy, workplace literacy, or community-based literacy.

THEORY AND PRACTICE: LEARNER CENTERED

Learner-centered instruction provides opportunities for classroom (teacher and student) negotiation of form, content, and classroom rules of behavior which creates a favorable environment for ESL students. Also called Freirean (after the educator Paulo Freire) or participatory instruction, the learner-centered approach bases the content of the curriculum on issues drawn from the students' real-life experiences. This approach contrasts with teacher-centered instruction, where the teacher is the center of classroom instruction, predetermining what is most important for the students to learn and how they will be taught. The focus is switched to the learner, and the curriculum and activities and methods of teaching are guided by the students' experiences. The foundation of the learner-centered classroom is the process of problem posing and dialogue. During the problem-posing component, the teacher introduces the students to culturally relevant pictures, stories, and songs and then asks the students a series of open-ended questions about the materials in an effort to lead the students into meaningful discussion (dialogue) about the significance of the materials to their lives. For introductory ESL students, this process can be fostered by focusing early instruction on students' descriptive vocabulary and teaching them to ask questions, thereby exchanging information in English. Another useful technique in fostering the process is having students share their oral histories and draw pictures about their life experiences as a basis for discussion.

The learner-centered approach is grounded in the belief that when students actively contribute to the development of the curriculum, they come to see a concrete purpose for the literacy they acquire. As opposed to the teacher developing a detailed curriculum that is concerned with the fundamental elements of reading and writing English, a teacher using the learner-centered approach will become part of the circle of students', guiding the discussion, but not defining what is important for the students learn.

LANGUAGE EXPERIENCE APPROACH AND LEARNER WRITING AND PUBLISHING APPROACH

Both the language experience approach (LEA) and the learner writing and publishing approach (LWPA) have reading and writing as the key components to the learning process. In LEA, the students orally share a particular experience (problem, story, personal history). The teacher or another student writes what the student is saying and then dictates it back to the students. The students write the dictation, which then becomes reading material and ultimately an exercise in English semantics, syntax, and phonology. Depending on the teaching strategy, students might break into small groups or remain in one group and practice reading, speaking, and writing.

The learner writing and publishing approach is similar to LEA in that the students generate the ideas for writing material. However, in LWPA, the students discuss a particular topic (current event, group concern, problem) orally and then leave the group to compose their own narrative about the topic. After the students have written the narratives, they are collected and dispersed for peer evaluation and critique. The process is repeated until the students are content with a final draft. The goal is to develop strong writing skills, ultimately publishing articles in local newspapers, magazines, and the like.

COMPETENCY-BASED EDUCATION

Competency-based education (CBE) has been widely used in adult ESL since the 1970s. A competency is an objective for students to achieve. Common competencies for adult ESL range from learning how to communicate one's basic survival skills (filling out an application, asking directions, taking notes, following directions) to studying for an exam or employment training. Competency-based education has four components: assessment of learner needs, selection of competencies, instruction for those competencies, and evaluation of the learner's progress.

CHILDREN'S LITERATURE

Since as early as 1981, studies have increasingly demonstrated that one of the strategies for teaching ESL in secondary and postsecondary education as well as in adult education programs is through instruction based on children's literature. Children's literature, particularly picture books, is very useful for students with diverse English-language proficiencies and reading levels because exciting pictures accompany the text. Additionally, children's literature typically has universal themes and is culturally diverse. The use of children's literature and picture books can stimulate the students' minds, thereby encouraging the development of their reading, speaking, and even writing skills.

According to scholar Betty Smallwood, the use of children's literature in the adult ESL classroom is most effective when the teacher divides the lesson into three parts: before, during, and after. During the first section, the teacher should clearly and sensitively explain the purpose for using children's literature and then introduce the story. During the story introduction, the teacher should take care to point out any new vocabulary and identify goals for the students to attain during the lesson. The second part, "during," is the actual reading of the story. The teacher should read the story aloud with enthusiasm and be sure to reference the accompanying pictures. After the reading, the teacher may then ask for questions, reactions, and responses to the goal that was identified at the beginning of the lesson.

Pamela Boehm

See also: Segmented Assimilation (Part II, Sec. 4); Public Opinion and Immigration (Part II, Sec. 6); Public Schools (Part II, Sec. 9); Arts I: Literature, Film, Radio, and Television, Language, Press (Part II, Sec. 10); *Lau v. Nichols*, 1974, California Proposition 227, 1998 (Part IV, Sec. 1).

BIBLIOGRAPHY

Allen, V. G. "Literature as a Support to Language Acquisition." In *When They Don't All Speak English: Integrating the ESL Students into the Regular Classroom*, ed. Pat Rigg and Virginia G. Allen, pp. 55–64. Urbana, IL: National Council of Teachers of English, 1989.

———. "Selecting Materials for the Reading Instruction of ESL Children." In *Kids Come in All Languages: Reading Instruction for ESL Students*, ed. K. Spangenberg-Urbschat and R. Pritchard, pp. 108–31. Newark: International Reading Association, 1994.

Anton, Marta. "The Discourse of the Learner-Centered Classroom: Sociocultural Perspectives on Teacher-Learner Interaction in the Second-Language Classroom." *Modern Language Journal* 83 (1999): 303–17.

Asher, James J. *Learning Another Language Through Actions: The Complete Teacher's Guidebook*. Los Gatos, CA: Sky Oaks Productions, 1977.

Auerbach, E. R., and D. Burgess. "The Hidden Curriculum of Survival ESL." *TESOL Quarterly* 10 (1985): 475–95.

Bancroft, Jane W. "The Lozanov Method and Its American Adaptations." *Modern Language Journal* 62 (1977): 167–75.

Boal, Augusto. *The Rainbow of Desire: The Boal Method of Theatre and Therapy*. New York: Routledge, 1995.

Chamot, Anna Uhl. "Toward a Functional ESL Curriculum in the Elementary School." In *Methodology in TESOL: A Book of Readings*, ed. Michael H. Long and Jack Richards. Boston: Heinle and Heinle Publishers, 1985.

Chamot, Anna Uhl, and Pamela Beard El-Dinary. "Children's Learning Strategies in Language Immersion Classrooms." *Modern Language Journal* 83 (1999): 319–35.

Cullinan, B. E. "Whole Language and Children's Literature." *Language Arts* 69 (1992): 426–30.

Curran, Charles A. *Counseling-Learning in Second Languages*. Apple River, IL: Apple River Press, 1976.

Edwards, John, ed. *Linguistic Minorities, Policies, and Pluralism*. London: Academic Press, 1984.

Enright, D. S., and M. L. McCloskey. *Integrating English: Developing English Language and Literacy in the Multilingual Classroom*. Reading, MA: Addison-Wesley, 1985.

Faltis, Christian J., and Paula Wolfe, eds. *So Much to Say: Adolescents, Bilingualism, and ESL in the Secondary School*. New York: Teachers College, Columbia University, 1999.

Freire, Paulo. *Pedagogy of the Oppressed*. New York: Continuum Publishing Corporation, 1970.

Fu, Danling. *"My Trouble Is My English": Asian Students and the American Dream*. Portsmouth: Boynton/Cook Publishers, 1994.

Goodman, K. *What's Whole in Whole Language*. Concord, NH: Heinemann Publishing, 1986.

Green, Jay. "A Meta-Analysis of the Effectiveness of Bilingual Education." Paper presented at the University of Texas at Austin, March 1998.

Gunderson, Barbara. "Cooperative Structures in the Foreign Language Classroom." In *Teaching for Tomorrow in the Foreign Language Classroom*, ed. Reid E. Baker. Skokie, IL: National Textbook Company, 1977.

Hadaway, Nancy L., and JaNae Mundy. "Children's Informational Picture Books Visit a Secondary ESL Classroom." *Journal of Adolescent and Adult Literacy* 42 (1998): 464–75.

Hill, Clifford, and Kate Parry, eds. *From Testing to Assessment: English as an International Language*. New York: Longman Publishers, 1994.

Hudelson, Sarah. "Teaching English Through Content-Area Activities." In *When They Don't All Speak English: Integrating the ESL Student into the Regular Classroom*, ed. Pat Rigg and Virginia G. Allen. Urbana, IL: National Council of Teachers of English, 1989.

Johnson, D. W., R. T. Johnson, and E. J. Holubec. *Circles of Learning: Cooperation in the Classroom*. Edina, MN: Interaction Book Company, 1986.

Johnson, Keith. "Introduction: Some Background, Some Key Terms, and Some Definitions." In *Communication in the Classroom*, ed. Keith Johnson and Keith Morrow, pp. 1–12. Essex, England: Longman Group, 1981.

Judd, Elliot L. "Language Policy, Curriculum Development, and TESOL Instruction: A Search for Compatibility." *TESOL Quarterly* 15:1 (1981): 59–66.

Krashen, Stephen D. "The Theoretical and Practical Relevance of Simple Codes in Second Language Acquisition." In *Research in Second Language Acquisition*, ed. Robin Scarcella and Stephen Krashen, pp. 7–18. Rowley, MA: Newbury House Publishers, 1999.

Lanteigne, Betty, and David Schwarzer. "The Progress of Rafael in English and Family Reading: A Case Study." *Journal of Adolescent and Adult Literacy* 41 (1997): 36–45.

Long, Michael, and Jack Richards, eds. *Methodology in TESOL: A Book of Readings*. Boston: Heinle and Heinle Publishers, 1986.

Lozanov, Georgi. *Suggestology and Outlines of Suggestopedy*. New York: Gordon and Breach, 1978.

Pally, Marcia. "Film Studies Drive Literacy Development for ESL University Students." *Journal of Adolescent and Adult Literacy* 41 (1997): 620–29.

Raimes, A. *Techniques in Teaching Writing*. Oxford: Oxford University Press, 1983.

Ramirez, David. "Performance of Redesignated Fluent-English Proficient Students." In *San Francisco Unified School District Language Academy: 1998 Annual Evaluation*. San Francisco: Language Academy, 1997.

Reid, Joy M., ed. *Understanding Learning Styles in the Second Language Classroom.* Englewood Cliffs, NJ: Prentice Hall, 1998.

Skinner, B. F. *Beyond Freedom and Dignity.* New York: Knopf, 1971.

———. "The Science of Learning and the Art of Teaching." *Harvard Educational Review* (1954): 86–97.

Smallwood, Betty Ansin. *Using Multicultural Children's Literature in Adult ESL Classes.* Washington, DC: National Clearinghouse on Literacy Education, 1998.

Taylor, Barry. "Teaching ESL: Incorporating a Communicative, Student-Centered Component." *TESOL Quarterly* 17:1 (1983): 69–89.

Thomas, Wayne, and Virginia Collier. *School Effectiveness for Language Minority Students.* Washington, DC: National Clearinghouse for Bilingual Education, April 1997.

Trueba, Henry T., ed. *Success or Failure: Learning and the Language Minority Student.* Cambridge: Newbury House Publishers, 1986.

Wallerstein, Nina. *Language and Culture in Conflict: Problem-Posing in the ESL Classroom.* Reading, MA: Addison-Wesley Publishers, 1981.

ESL WEB SITES

While a number of Web sites focus on ESL, the following have a solid reputation for providing a variety of useful information ranging from ESL teaching techniques to academic articles on ESL pedagogy:

The Center for Applied Linguistics	www.cal.org
TESOL Publications	www.tesol.org
Everything ESL	www.everythingesl.net

GENERAL INDEX

Country of origin, **2**:560
  brain drain. *See* Brain drain
  communication with. *See*
    Transnational communication
  economies, **2**:597–599
  immigrant politics, **2**:553–559
  immigrants admitted by
    (1951–1990), **1**:196*t*
  organized crime groups, **2**:681
  preparedness before leaving,
    2:718–719
County government, **2**:521
Court Interpreters Act (1978),
  3:815; **4**:1507*g*
Covenant on Civil and Political
  Rights (CCPR), **3**:995, 996–997,
  999
Covenant on Economic, Social and
  Cultural Rights, **3**:997
CPA. *See* Comprehensive Plan of
  Action
CPS. *See* Current Population
  Survey
Creel, George, **1**:144
Crèvecoeur, Michel, **4**:1495
Crime
  aggravated felonies, **2**:514
  causation theories, **2**:493
  immigrant youth, **2**:683–684
  against immigrants, **2**:496,
    497–498
  institutional, **2**:496–497
  justice system discrimination,
    2:497
  organized, **2**:681–683
  prisoner transfer treaties, **4**:1326
  rate of immigrant *vs.* native,
    2:574
  transnational, **1**:326
  underground economy, **2**:680
  victim services, **2**:733
  See also specific ethnic group
Criminal alien tracking, **4**:1325
Criminals, foreign
  1875 legislation, **2**:501–502
  antebellum legislation,
    2:500–501
Cristero Revolt, **3**:1141
Croatian immigrants, **1**:301; **4**:1239,
  1243*t*
Cuba
  Coast Guard and, **1**:316

Cuba *(continued)*
  González, Elián. *See* González,
    Elián
  relations with United States,
    1:173–174; **3**:1005–1006
  Spain's loss of, **1**:14
Cuban Adjustment Act, **3**:1115
Cuban American National
  Foundation (CANF), **1**:289;
  2:550, 556; **3**:1117; **4**:1507*g*
Cuban Connection, **2**:681
Cuban immigrants
  character loans, **2**:580
  crime, **2**:682–683
  culture and cultural identity,
    3:1116–1117
  demographics, **3**:1109
  drug trafficking, **2**:681, 683
  entrepreneurship, **1**:207, 326;
    2:582; **3**:1113
  family relations, **2**:444–445
  health, **2**:713
  history of, **1**:173–174; **3**:1109–1116
  immigration policy, **1**:212–213
  literature, **2**:752–753
  Mariel boatlift. *See* Mariel
    boatlift
  number of, **1**:196
  politics
    homeland, **2**:553, 555, 556
    partisan identification, **2**:550;
      3:1116–1117
  refugees, **1**:160, 167, 191, 204,
    289, 300; **3**:1005–1006,
    1115–1116
  remittances, **2**:598
  repatriation, **1**:319
  resettlement grants, **4**:1349–1350
  settlement patterns, **2**:416
    Miami, **2**:416; **3**:931–933,
    1112–1116
  social capital, **2**:465–466
  voter turnout, **2**:549
Cuban Missile Crisis, **3**:931, 1112
Cuban Relocation Program, **3**:933
Cuban Revolutionary Junta, **2**:553
Cuban-Haitian Special Entrant,
  3:934, 1006
Cubic air law (1870), **1**:80
Cultural affinity hypothesis, **2**:565,
  566
Cultural difference, **2**:450–451

Cultural division of labor theory,
  1:226, 227
Cultural Exchange Alien. *See* Q
  Cultural Exchange Alien
Cultural Exchange Visitor. *See* Q
  Cultural Exchange Alien
Cultural expansionism, **1**:198–199
Cultural institutions, **1**:112
Cultural theory of
  entrepreneurship, **2**:579–580
Culture and cultural identity
  film, radio, and television,
    3:786–798
  folkways, **1**:130
  heritage programs, **2**:733; **3**:904
  influence on American popular
    culture, **3**:800–805
  literature, **1**:129–130; **2**:749–758
  music and dance, **1**:128–129;
    3:802–803, 804
  retaining, **2**:462
  social mobility and, **2**:465
  theater, **2**:759–767
  visual and religious arts,
    2:768–775
  See also specific ethnic group
Current Population Survey (CPS),
  2:390–392, 400; **4**:1508*g*
Czech immigrants, **1**:92, 93;
  4:1238–1243 *passim*
Czolgosz, Leon, **1**:145; **4**:1288

D

Dale, Thomas, **1**:32
Dance, **1**:128–129, 130–131
Danish immigrants, **1**:94;
  2:761–762
Dar al-Islam Foundation Islamic
  Center Village (New Mexico),
  2:770–771
Daughter communities, **1**:252–253
Daughters of the American
  Revolution (DAR), **1**:287, 288
Davis, Gray, **2**:507, 541
De Bright, Josefina Fierro, **1**:171
De León, Juan Ponce, **1**:14, 15
De Narváez, Pánfilo, **1**:15
De Soto, Hernando, **1**:15
Debs, Eugene V., **1**:144, 145
Debt, government (international),
  1:272–273

Haitian Refugee Immigration Fairness Act (HRIFA), 1:282; 4:1509*g*

Haitian refugees, 1:204–205, 282, 289–290
Bush's order on return of, 4:1356–1366
interdiction at sea, 1:316–319; 3:1006
refused asylum, 1:289, 291; 3:935, 1005–1006
See also Haitian immigrants

Haitians, District Court on Admission of (1993), 4:1381–1386

Hamilton, Alexander, 1:71

Harding, Warren G., 1:152; 2:504

Harrison, Benjamin, 2:502

Hart, Philip, 1:184; 2:506

Hart-Cellar Act, 1:167–168, 172, 184–185, 199–200; 3:865
definition of, 4:1509*g*

Harvard University, 2:703

Hate Crime Statistics Act, 2:497

Hate crimes, 1:226; 2:497–498; 4:1509*g*

Hawaii
Chinese immigrants, 1:78; 3:1160
Filipino immigrants, 4:1200
Japanese immigrants, 1:111, 162
Oceania immigrants, 4:1193, 1195–1196

Hayakawa, Samuel Ichiye, 1:230; 2:542

Hayes, Rutherford B., 1:69, 81; 2:502; 3:1002

Head tax. *See* Taxes

Health, 1:116–117
of elderly immigrants, 2:433–434
food/nutrition services, 2:732
general status of immigrant, 2:710–711
and passenger ship legislation, 2:500, 501, 502–503
and poverty, 2:427–428
See also Disease; Health care; Mental health; specific ethnic group

Health care, 2:486–487, 696–698

Health Professions Educational Assistance Act (1976), 2:644

Hebrew Immigrant Aid Society, 1:287; 4:1245

Hegemony, 4:1509*g*

Helms, Jesse A., 4:1417–1418

Helms-Burton law, 2:556

Hennessey, David, 2:491–492

Hepatitis B, 2:711

Herzegovina, 1:301

Herzl, Theodore, 3:1023–1024

Hesburgh, Theodore M., 1:255

Hess, Moses, 3:1023

Hindu temples, 2:773–774

Hinduism, 3:881–885

Hippies, 3:803

Hirabayashi, Gordon, 1:165

Hirabayashi v. United States (1943), 1:165; 4:1369–1370

Hispanic immigrants. *See* Latin American immigrants

History of the English Settlement in Edwards County, Illinois (1818), 4:1466–1469

Hitler, Adolf, 1:140, 156, 157, 158, 287

HIV. *See* AIDS/HIV

Hmong, 1:191, 198, 291, 300; 4:1226, 1509*g*

Ho Ah Kow v. Matthew Noonan, 1:80

Holocaust, 1:158–159; 4:1242, 1248

Home Teacher Act (1915), 1:170

Homeland. *See* Country of origin

Homeownership, 2:586–587

Homestead Act (1862), 1:92; 2:619

Homestead strike, 1:145

Homosexuals. *See* Gay and lesbians

Hong Kong immigrants, 4:1228–1229

Hoover, Herbert, 1:69, 153, 156; 2:505

Hoover, J. Edgar, 1:146

Horticulture. *See* Agriculture

Host polities, integration into, 3:998–999

Host societies, international law, 3:997–998

Hotel industry, New York, 2:655–657

Hounds, 3:966

House and Senate immigration committees, 2:527

Household services. *See* Domestic services

Housing
architectural style, 2:589
conditions, 1:114–116; 2:588–589, 590; 3:960
effect of jobs on, 1:119
homeownership, 2:586–587
restrictive laws, 2:589
social service programs, 2:732
urban, 2:586–587, 588–589

Houston
Asian immigrants, 3:906–908
Central American immigrants, 3:905–906
Chinese immigrants, 3:1160
contemporary immigration, 3:901–903
Indian immigrants, 3:908
Japanese immigrants, 3:907–908
Mexican immigrants, 3:903–905
settlement patterns, 2:411

How an Emigrant May Succeed in the United States, 4:1502–1503

Howitt, E., 4:1472

Hsia, Maria, 2:551

Huang, John, 2:551

Hudson, Henry, 1:21, 30

Huerta, Dolores, 2:626; 3:962

Huguenots, 1:23, 35, 90; 4:1265, 1509*g*

Hui. *See* Kye

Hull House, 1:115; 2:730, 117

Human capital, 2:577, 581, 634

Human ingenuity, 2:531–532

Human rights
integration, 3:997–999
violations, 1:347; 2:497

Human Rights Committee, 3:997

Human Rights Watch, 3:1115–1116

Human smuggling. *See* Smuggling, human

Hungarian immigrants, 4:1238–1243 *passim*
refugees, 1:160, 191, 288, 300–301; 3:1004

I

Idaho, 1:77; 4:1265

Identity
cultural. *See* Culture and cultural identity
ethnic, 1:126–127

Office of Special Council for Immigrant Related Unfair Employment Practices, **2:**487–488

Office of the Superintendent of Immigration, **1:**344

Official English movement. *See* English Only

Old immigrants, **1:**112, 115

Olmecs, **1:**12

Omega 7, **3:**1117

One Nation Party (Australia), **3:**1016

One-and-a-half generation, **2:**424, 425

Operation Able Manner, **1:**319

Operation Able Response, **1:**319

Operation Able Vigil, **1:**319

Operation Blockade. *See* Operation Hold the Line

Operation Bootstrap, **1:**173, 268

Operation Boulder, **4:**1512*g*

Operation Eagle Pull, **1:**186; **4:**1512*g*

Operation Exodus, **4:**1249

Operation Ezra, **3:**1028

Operation Gatekeeper, **1:**352; **3:**927, 1006, 1143; **4:**1512*g*

Operation Guardian, **3:**927

Operation Hold the Line, **1:**352; **3:**927, 1143; **4:**1404, 1512*g*

Operation Joshua, **3:**1029

Operation Magic Carpet, **3:**1028

Operation Moshe, **3:**1029

Operation Nehemiah, **3:**1028

Operation Pedro Pan, **3:**932

Operation Safeguard, **1:**352; **3:**1143; **4:**1512*g*

Operation Solomon, **3:**1029

Operation Vanguard, **1:**347

Operation Wetback, **1:**154, 172, 215, 346; **2:**622, 625; **3:**1142; **4:**1513*g*

Opinion polls. *See* Public opinion polls

Opium War, **1:**77

Order of the Sons of America, **2:**535

Order of the Star Spangled Banner, **1:**72

Orderly Departure Program (ODP), **1:**190, 193, 212, 213; **4:**1513*g*

Oregon, **1:**78, 111

Organized crime. *See* Crime

Organized immigrant groups, **1:**326–327

Organized recruitment. *See* Employment

Oriental Exclusion Act (1924), **3:**863

Orphans. *See* Adoption

Ottoman Empire immigrants, **3:**1186–1187

Outmigration, **3:**991

Overman, Lee, **1:**145

Overpopulation
  natural disasters/environmental crises and, **1:**277–280
  See also Population

Overseas Pakistani Foundation, **2:**599

Overstays, **1:**354–355

Oyama v. California (1948), **2:**515

P

Pacific Mail Steamship Company, **1:**75

Pacific Railroad Act, **1:**94

Paddy stereotype, **1:**60

Page, Horace F., **4:**1281

Page Act (1875), **3:**1157; **4:**1281

Paine, Thomas, **1:**43, 45, 244–245

Pakistani immigrants, **3:**891; **4:**1209–1210
  literature, **2:**757
  remittances, **2:**597, 599

Pale, **1:**286; **4:**1513*g*

Palestine. *See* Israel

Palmer, A. Mitchell, **1:**140, 146, 147, 148, 151; **2:**485

Palmer raids, **1:**140, 146, 147–148; **4:**1513*g*

Parachute kids, **4:**1231–1232, 1513*g*

Paris peace agreement (1991), **1:**190–191

Parochial schools, **1:**60, 72, 113; **4:**1513*g*

Parole, **4:**1327

Partisan identification, **2:**550

Passenger ships
  1882 legislation, **2:**502
  antebellum legislation, **2:**449, 500, 501

Passenger ships *(continued)*
  British Passenger Act (1803), **4:**1253, 1258
  passenger lists, **4:**1279
  quarantined, **2:**502–503
  See also Boats

Passfield White Paper (1930), **3:**1025

Paternalistic engagements, **2:**556–557

Pauper immigrants. *See* Poor immigrants

Pax Americana, **1:**267

Pearl Harbor, **1:**141, 163, 346; **2:**538

Penn, William, **1:**22, 31, 33

Pennsylvania
  Amish, **1:**22, **3:**858–859; **4:**1505*g*
  diversity, **1:**45
  Germantown, **1:**33–34, 67, 90
  Philadelphia. *See* Philadelphia
  Quakers, **1:**21–22
  slave trade, **1:**41

People v. George W. Hall, **1:**80

People's Party. *See* Populist Party

Perestroika, **3:**1030; **4:**1513*g*

Peripheral nations, **4:**1513*g*

Permanent migrants, **2:**404

Permanent Resident Card. *See* Green card

Permanent residents, **2:**509, 510–511; **4:**1513*g*
  campaign contributions, **2:**550, 551
  sponsorship for, **2:**516

Perot, Ross, **2:**567

Persian Gulf War, **1:**231, 351

Personal Responsibility and Work Opportunity Reconciliation Act (1996), **1:**218–219; **2:**486, 518, 522, 591, 697, 739; **4:**1439
  text, **4:**1328–1329

Peruvian immigrants, **3:**941–942, 1083, 1085

Petition for Alien Fiancée, **1:**364–365

Petition for Alien Relative, **1:**364, 369–370

Philadelphia
  collective conflict, **1:**225
  immigration station, **1:**110
  service sector, **2:**657
  settlement patterns, **2:**411

V

Value of an Immigrant (1871),
4:1414–1415
Verity, *Ridge v.*, 2:399
Veterans of Foreign War (VFW),
1:288
Viceroyalty, 1:16–17
Vietnam, 1:186, 188–189, 247
Vietnam War, 1:300; 3:803
protests, 2:540
See also Amerasian Children Act
(1977)
Vietnamese immigrants
crime, 2:682
discrimination/violence against,
1:290–291
family relations, 2:466
gender roles and work, 2:455
literature, 2:758
model minority, 4:1224
refugees, 1:186–194, 212,
290–291, 300; 4:1219,
1219–1222
repatriation, 1:190, 213
settlement patterns, 2:414–415;
4:1224
Houston, 3:906
Los Angeles, 3:916
Washington, D.C., 3:980–981
Violence Against Women Act
(VAWA), 1:367
Virginia
Jamestown, 1:23, 26, 27–28,
31–32, 67
restrictive legislation, 2:521
slave trade, 1:40, 41
Virginia Company, 1:23, 26, 27, 31;
4:1515g
Virginia House of Burgesses, 1:28
Visas
definition of, 4:1515g
overstaying, 1:204
policy on, 4:1303
refugee, 3:1004–1005
See also specific visa
Visitor for Business. *See* B-1 Visitor
for Business
Visual and religious arts,
2:768–775
VOLAGS, 1:187
Volstead Act, 2:492

Voluntary departure status, 2:478
Voluntary international
immigration, 1:312
Voluntary return migrants, 2:404
Volunteerism, 2:455–457
Voter registration and turnout,
2:549
Voting rights, 1:71; 2:515, 519,
544–545
in homeland, 2:548
Voting Rights Act (1965),
2:540–541, 545; 3:815

W

Wages. *See* Earnings
Wagner, Robert F., 1:157–158, 287
Wagner-Rogers bill, 1:157–158
Walker, Francis A., 2:398–399, 505
Wall Street bombing (1920), 1:148
Walloons, 1:31
Walter, Francis E., 1:182
War brides, definition of, 4:1515g
War Brides Act (1945), 1:154, 288,
297, 346, 364; 2:442, 505;
3:1173–1174; 4:1255–1256
definition of, 4:1516g
War of 1812, 1:51
War on Poverty, 2:609
War Refugee Board (WRB), 1:159;
4:1516g
War refugees. *See* Refugees
War Relocation Authority (WRA),
1:142; 4:1516g
Wartime Civil Control
Administration Assembly,
1:142
Wartime Relocation and
Internment of Civilians,
Commission for (CWRIC),
2:542
Washington, D.C.
African Americans, 3:974
collective conflict, 1:225
contemporary immigration,
3:978–981
early immigrants, 3:976–977,
978
settlement patterns, 1:206; 2:411
urban growth and change,
3:974–976
Washington, George, 1:43; 4:1494

Washington, Seattle immigration
station, 1:111
Watson, Thomas J., 1:140
Welfare benefits, 2:516
cost of, 2:573
under IIRIRA, 4:1326–1327
immigrant compared with
native, 2:601, 740–742
Title IV: Restricting Welfare and
Public Benefits from Aliens
(1996), 4:1439–1451
Welfare reform, 2:549, 591,
696–697, 737
impact of, 2:575
public opinion on, 2:563–564, 566
Welfare Reform Act (1996). *See*
Personal Responsibility and
Work Opportunity
Reconciliation Act
Welsh immigrants, 1:35
Wendish immigrants, 4:1243t
West Africa, 3:1070–1074
slave trade, 1:37–40
West India Company, 1:21, 31
West Indian immigrants, 1:175;
2:416–417; 4:1254
West Indian Reform Association,
1:175
Western Association Contracting
Company (WACC), 2:626
Western Europe, 4:1262–1269
migration in, 3:1039–1045
Westward expansion, 1:89–94;
2:501–502
Wet feet, dry feet, 1:319; 3:935;
4:1516g
"What Does America Offer to the
German Immigrant?" (1853),
4:1480–1482
Whig Party, 1:72, 73
White Australia Policy, 3:1008
White Slave Traffic Act (1910),
2:503; 4:1289
White supremacy, 1:140; 3:968–969
Whom We Shall Welcome (1953),
3:1002; 4:1336–1344
Wicca, 3:861
Wife-import. *See* Mail-order brides
Wilson, Woodrow, 1:63, 140, 150,
247; 2:503, 504, 554; 3:1002
Wilson et al., *LULAC et al. v.*, 4:1387
Wisconsin, 1:92, 93, 96

Numbers in bold indicate volume; g indicates glossary.

GEOGRAPHICAL INDEX

LEGAL AND JUDICIAL INDEX

Numbers in bold indicate volume; g indicates glossary.

Numbers in bold indicate volume; g indicates glossary.